나혼자 끝내는 新 토익

기출모의
1200제

나혼자 끝내는 新토익
기출모의 1200제 LC+RC

지은이 김랑 · 박자은 · 넥서스토익연구소
펴낸이 임상진
펴낸곳 (주)넥서스

초판 1쇄 발행 2019년 1월 5일
초판 6쇄 발행 2024년 4월 1일

출판신고 1992년 4월 3일 제311-2002-2호
10880 경기도 파주시 지목로 5
Tel (02)330-5500 Fax (02)330-5555

ISBN 979-11-6165-552-9 13740

www.nexusbook.com

토익 최신 유형을 반영한 최종 마무리 문제집 + 해설집

나혼자 끝내는 新토익

기출모의 1200제

김랑·박자은·넥서스토익연구소 지음

넥서스

PREFACE

취업, 승진, 이직을 위한 다양한 스펙들이 점점 늘어나는 요즘, 토익 점수는 이중 단연 1순위로 갖춰야 할 필수 스펙입니다. 개정된 토익 시험에서 짧은 기간에 고득점을 받기 위해서는 보다 내실 있는 영어 실력이 필요하기 때문에 전문적인 강의나 공신력 있는 교재의 도움을 받는 것이 어느 때보다 중요해졌습니다.

토익은 본인의 목표 점수대에 맞게 전략적으로 공부해야 효율적으로 끝낼 수 있습니다. 800점 대의 점수가 필요한 수험생이라면 전체 유형의 약 10% 정도를 차지하는 고난이도 문제를 맞히기 위해서 너무 스트레스를 받기보다는 매달 반복적으로 출제되는 문제 유형을 확실하게 정복하는 것이 효과적입니다. 900점 이상의 고득점을 노린다면 PART 3, 4의 '시각 정보 연계 문제'와 PART 6의 '알맞은 문장 고르기 문제', PART 7의 '삼중 지문 유형'에서 다른 수험생들보다 상대적으로 우위를 점해야 합니다.

본 책은 최신 토익 트렌드에 맞는 실전 문제들과 각 문제 유형에 대한 완벽한 솔루션을 제시함으로써 수험생들이 단기간에 목표 점수에 도달하는 데 큰 도움이 될 수 있도록 만들었습니다. 토익의 방대한 이론보다는 시험장에서 바로 적용할 수 있는 포인트를 다룸으로써 실전 감각을 다질 수 있도록 하였습니다. 정기토익 난이도 및 그 유형과 유사한 문제로 엄선했으며, 다년간의 강의와 연구를 통한 필자만의 노하우를 해설에 담아 마치 현장 강의를 듣는 듯한 상세하고 정확한 설명을 제공합니다. YBM 대표 토익강사로서 독자들의 빠른 토익 목표 달성을 위해 사명감을 가지고 만든 교재입니다.

이 책을 집필하는 데 많은 도움을 주신 넥서스에 깊이 감사드리며, 필자의 강의와 연구에 아낌없이 도움을 주시는 김선화 원장님, 박우천 국장님, 김영철 회장님, 신옥화 선생님, 강명희 선생님에게도 감사의 말을 전합니다.

저자 김랑, 박자은, 넥서스토익연구소

▌▌ CONTENTS

- 머리말
- 구성과 특징
- 신토익 핵심 정보
- 나혼토 학습 스케줄
- 나혼토 실력 점검

Actual Test **1**   14

Actual Test **2**   58

Actual Test **3**   100

Actual Test **4**   144

Actual Test **5**   188

Actual Test **6**   230

- 토익 점수 환산표   270
- OMR Sheets   271

⊕ 별책 부록   정답+스크립트+해석+해설

FEATURES

신토익
최신 경향의
실전 모의고사 6회

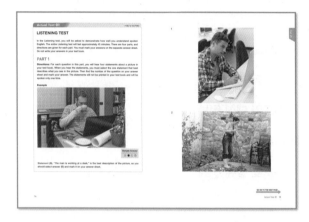

신토익 최신 출제 경향을 반영한 모의고사로 실전을 완벽 대비할 수 있습니다. LC와 RC를 한 권으로 구성한 실전 6회분으로 정기 토익 시험을 대비해서 실제 시험 환경과 같이 최종 마무리를 할 수 있습니다.

저자의 노하우가 담긴
쉽고 자세한
정답 및 해설

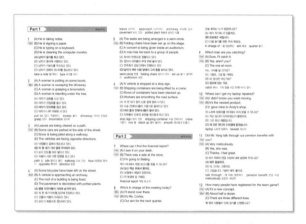

해설집을 따로 구매할 필요 없이 한 권에 담아 정답 및 해설을 확인하며 바로 복습할 수 있습니다. 정답 키워드가 되는 부분을 표시하여 쉽게 정답을 찾고 이해할 수 있도록 구성하였습니다.

혼자서도
토익을 끝낼 수 있는
막강 무료 부가자료

(1) 실전용·복습용·고사장 버전 MP3
실전용, 복습용 MP3 외에 실제 고사장 소음이 들어간
버전까지 제공하므로 실제 시험 환경과 가장 유사하게
대비할 수 있습니다.

(2) 모바일 단어장
본 도서에 수록된 어휘 중에서 중요한 어휘를 언제
어디서든 복습할 수 있도록 모바일 단어장을 제공합니다.

(3) 온라인 받아쓰기
Listening 받아쓰기 프로그램을 통해 청취력뿐만 아니라
영어 실력을 향상시킬 수 있습니다.

(4) 어휘 리스트 & 테스트
본문에 수록된 어휘 중에서도 특히 중요한 빈출 어휘 리스
트와 이를 학습할 수 있는 온라인 테스트지를 제공합니다.
www.nexusbook.com

MP3 바로 듣기
정답 자동 채점
모바일 단어장
받아쓰기 테스트

혼공족들을 위한 막강 무료 부가자료
www.nexusbook.com

3가지 버전
MP3

모바일
단어장

받아쓰기
정답 자동 채점

어휘 리스트
& 테스트

쉽고 빠른
MP3 이용법

콜롬북스 APP

(1) 구글 플레이, 앱스토어에서 "콜롬북스" 어플 설치
(아래 QR코드 이용 또는 "콜롬북스"라고 검색해서
설치 가능)

(2) 넥서스 또는 도서명으로 검색

(3) 실전용, 복습용, 고사장 버전의 3종 MP3 다운로드

신토익 핵심 정보

2016년 5월 29일 정기시험부터 현재의 영어 사용 환경을 반영한 신(新)토익이 시행되었습니다. 전체 문항 수와 시험 시간은 동일하지만 각 파트별로 문항 수는 변화가 있으며 그동안 출제되지 않았던 그래프와 문자 메시지, 채팅, 삼중 지문 등 새로운 지문 유형과 문제가 출제됩니다.

신토익 시험의 구성

구성	Part	Part별 내용	문항수	시간	배점
Listening Comprehension	1	사진 묘사	6	45분	495점
	2	질의 응답	25		
	3	짧은 대화	39		
	4	설명문	30		
Reading Comprehension	5	단문 공란 채우기	30	75분	495점
	6	장문 공란 채우기	16		
	7	단일 지문	29		
		이중 지문	10		
		삼중 지문	15		
Total	7 Parts		200문제	120분	990점

신토익 이후 달라진 부분

Part 1   문항 10개에서 6개로 감소
Part 2   문항 30개에서 25개로 감소
Part 3   문항 30개에서 39개로 증가, 〈3인 대화〉, 〈5턴 이상의 대화〉, 〈의도 파악, 시각 정보 연계 문제〉 추가
Part 4   문항 30개로 기존과 동일, 〈의도 파악 문제〉, 〈시각 정보 연계 문제〉 추가
Part 5   문항 40개에서 30개로 감소
Part 6   문항 12개에서 16개로 증가, 〈알맞은 문장 고르기〉 추가
Part 7   문항 48개에서 54개로 증가, 〈문자 메시지 · 온라인 채팅 지문〉, 〈의도 파악, 문장삽입 문제〉, 〈삼중 지문〉 추가

🔍 신토익 핵심 정보

Part 3	화자의 의도 파악 문제	2~3문항	대화문에서 화자가 한 말의 의도를 묻는 유형
	시각 정보 연계 문제	2~3문항	대화문과 시각 정보(도표, 그래픽 등)간 연관 관계를 파악하는 유형
	3인 대화	대화 지문 1~2개	일부 대화문에서 세 명 이상의 화자가 등장함
	5턴 이상의 대화		주고 받는 대화가 5턴 이상으로 늘어난 대화 유형
Part 4	화자의 의도 파악 문제	2~3문항	담화문에서 화자가 한 말의 의도를 묻는 유형
	시각 정보 연계 문제	2~3문항	담화문과 시각 정보(도표, 그래픽 등)간 연관 관계를 파악하는 유형
Part 6	알맞은 문장 고르기	4문항 (지문당 1문항)	• 지문의 흐름상 빈칸에 들어갈 알맞은 문장 고르기 • 선택지가 모두 문장으로 제시되며 문맥 파악이 필수
Part 7	문장 삽입 문제	2문항 (지문당 1문항)	주어진 문장을 삽입할 수 있는 적절한 위치 고르기
	문자 메시지 · 온라인 채팅	각각 지문 1개	2명이 대화하는 문자 메시지, 다수가 참여하는 온라인 채팅
	의도 파악 문제	2문항 (지문당 1문항)	• 화자가 말한 말의 의도를 묻는 문제 • 문자 메시지, 온라인 채팅 지문에서 출제
	삼중 지문	지문 3개	세 개의 연계 지문에 대한 이해도를 묻는 문제

나혼토 학습 스케줄

초급 수험자   기본서로 공부는 했지만 아직 700점 넘기가 힘들어요.

기본서로 공부를 했다고는 하지만 아직 실전 연습이 부족할 수도 있습니다. 실제 토익 시험을 보면서 시간이 부족한 경우가 많은데 이는 평소에 실전처럼 시간을 기록하며 연습을 하는 것이 중요합니다. 또한 어휘 실력이 부족한 시기이므로 온라인으로 제공되는 어휘테스트도 활용해 보세요. (www.nexusbook.com에서 어휘리스트/테스트 제공)

1일차	2일차	3일차	4일차	5일차	6일차
Actual Test 1 문제 풀이 & 정답 확인	Actual Test 1 LC 해설 확인 & 받아쓰기	Actual Test 1 RC 해설 확인 & 어휘 복습	Actual Test 2 문제 풀이 & 정답 확인	Actual Test 2 LC 해설 확인 & 받아쓰기	Actual Test 2 RC 해설 확인 & 어휘 복습
7일차	8일차	9일차	10일차	11일차	12일차
Actual Test 3 문제 풀이 & 정답 확인	Actual Test 3 LC 해설 확인 & 받아쓰기	Actual Test 3 RC 해설 확인 & 어휘 복습	Actual Test 4 문제 풀이 & 정답 확인	Actual Test 4 LC 해설 확인 & 받아쓰기	Actual Test 4 RC 해설 확인 & 어휘 복습
13일차	14일차	15일차	16일차	17일차	18일차
Actual Test 5 문제 풀이 & 정답 확인	Actual Test 5 LC 해설 확인 & 받아쓰기	Actual Test 5 RC 해설 확인 & 어휘 복습	Actual Test 6 문제 풀이 & 정답 확인	Actual Test 6 LC 해설 확인 & 받아쓰기	Actual Test 6 RC 해설 확인 & 어휘 복습

중급 수험자   감을 잡은 거 같은데 800점 전후로 왔다갔다 해요.

토익 공부도 좀 해보고 토익 시험도 2~3번 봤지만 여전히 점수가 잘 오르지 않는 경우입니다. LC는 실전 연습도 중요하지만 받아쓰기를 통해 다시 한번 복습해 보는 것이 좋습니다. RC는 각 파트별로 권장 풀이 시간에 맞춰 풀어보면서 취약한 부분이 어디인지 점검해 보세요.

1일차	2일차	3일차	4일차	5일차	6일차
Actual Test 1 문제 풀이	Actual Test 1 정답 및 해설 확인	Actual Test 2 문제 풀이	Actual Test 2 정답 및 해설 확인	Actual Test 3 문제 풀이	Actual Test 3 정답 및 해설 확인
7일차	8일차	9일차	10일차	11일차	12일차
Actual Test 4 문제 풀이	Actual Test 4 정답 및 해설 확인	Actual Test 5 문제 풀이	Actual Test 5 정답 및 해설 확인	Actual Test 6 문제 풀이	Actual Test 6 정답 및 해설 확인

고급 수험자   900점 이상을 목표로 하고 있지만 쉽지 않아요.

가끔은 정말 시험을 잘 봤다고 생각하지만 예상치 못한 곳에서 틀리는 문제가 있는 경우입니다. 한 번 틀렸던 문제들은 다시 틀리는 경우가 많으므로 꼭 다시 점검해 보세요.

1일차	2일차	3일차	4일차	5일차	6일차
Actual Test 1 & 해설	Actual Test 2 & 해설	Actual Test 3 & 해설	Actual Test 4 & 해설	Actual Test 5 & 해설	Actual Test 6 & 해설

나혼토 실력 점검

테스트가 끝난 후 각 테스트별로 점검해 보세요. 테스트별로 맞은 개수를 확인하며 실력이 향상됨을 체크해 보세요.

정답 확인 전

	테스트 날짜	시험 소요 시간	체감 난이도
Actual Test 01			상 중 하
Actual Test 02			상 중 하
Actual Test 03			상 중 하
Actual Test 04			상 중 하
Actual Test 05			상 중 하
Actual Test 06			상 중 하

정답 확인 후

	맞힌 개수		환산 점수	총점
Actual Test 01	LC:			점
	RC:			
Actual Test 02	LC:			점
	RC:			
Actual Test 03	LC:			점
	RC:			
Actual Test 04	LC:			점
	RC:			
Actual Test 05	LC:			점
	RC:			
Actual Test 06	LC:			점
	RC:			

* 환산 점수는 270페이지에 있는 환산 점수표를 이용해 주세요.

Actual Test

01

시작 시간	:
종료 시간	:

LISTENING TEST

In the Listening test, you will be asked to demonstrate how well you understand spoken English. The entire Listening test will last approximately 45 minutes. There are four parts, and directions are given for each part. You must mark your answers on the separate answer sheet. Do not write your answers in your test book.

PART 1

Directions: For each question in this part, you will hear four statements about a picture in your test book. When you hear the statements, you must select the one statement that best describes what you see in the picture. Then find the number of the question on your answer sheet and mark your answer. The statements will not be printed in your test book and will be spoken only one time.

Example

Statement (B), "The man is working at a desk," is the best description of the picture, so you should select answer (B) and mark it on your answer sheet.

1

2

GO ON TO THE NEXT PAGE

3

4

5

6

GO ON TO THE NEXT PAGE

PART 2

Directions: You will hear a question or statement and three responses spoken in English. They will not be printed in your test book and will be spoken only one time. Select the best response to the question or statement and mark the letter (A), (B), or (C) on your answer sheet.

7   Mark your answer on your answer sheet.

8   Mark your answer on your answer sheet.

9   Mark your answer on your answer sheet.

10 Mark your answer on your answer sheet.

11 Mark your answer on your answer sheet.

12 Mark your answer on your answer sheet.

13 Mark your answer on your answer sheet.

14 Mark your answer on your answer sheet.

15 Mark your answer on your answer sheet.

16 Mark your answer on your answer sheet.

17 Mark your answer on your answer sheet.

18 Mark your answer on your answer sheet.

19 Mark your answer on your answer sheet.

20 Mark your answer on your answer sheet.

21 Mark your answer on your answer sheet.

22 Mark your answer on your answer sheet.

23 Mark your answer on your answer sheet.

24 Mark your answer on your answer sheet.

25 Mark your answer on your answer sheet.

26 Mark your answer on your answer sheet.

27 Mark your answer on your answer sheet.

28 Mark your answer on your answer sheet.

29 Mark your answer on your answer sheet.

30 Mark your answer on your answer sheet.

31 Mark your answer on your answer sheet.

PART 3

Directions: You will hear some conversations between two or more people. You will be asked to answer three questions about what the speakers say in each conversation. Select the best response to each question and mark the letter (A), (B), (C), or (D) on your answer sheet. The conversations will not be printed in your test book and will be spoken only one time.

32 What does the man want to do?

(A) Recruit an assistant
(B) Get a degree
(C) Have a facial
(D) Visit a Web site

33 Why did the woman contact the college?

(A) To locate a suitable salon
(B) To sign up for a college course
(C) To rent some equipment
(D) To find trained job applicants

34 Why does the woman recommend the Health and Beauty Web site?

(A) It features useful advice.
(B) It is only for professionals.
(C) It has a lot of users.
(D) It is simple to navigate.

35 What does the man ask about?

(A) The woman's availability
(B) The amount of tax to be returned
(C) The return from a vacation
(D) The call to a client

36 What does the woman plan to do this week?

(A) Finalize a seminar
(B) Visit the tax office
(C) Attend a ceremony
(D) Provide some paperwork

37 What does the man suggest doing?

(A) Setting up a conference call
(B) Filling out a registration form
(C) Submitting the required documentation
(D) Making a phone call

38 What event does the woman want to attend?

(A) A movie premiere
(B) A sporting event
(C) A book launch
(D) A theater performance

39 What is the problem?

(A) A phone system is not working.
(B) A representative reserved the wrong tickets.
(C) A credit card was stolen.
(D) A game is sold out.

40 What information does the man request?

(A) A reference number
(B) A business address
(C) The name of an event
(D) Credit card details

41 Who most likely is the woman?

(A) A technical director
(B) A human resources manager
(C) A temporary worker
(D) A factory worker

42 Why is the man calling?

(A) To request a reference
(B) To submit his portfolio
(C) To ask about employment
(D) To explain a forthcoming training session

43 What does the man offer to send?

(A) An extended contract
(B) A draft design
(C) An upgraded portfolio
(D) An updated résumé

GO ON TO THE NEXT PAGE

44 Where does the conversation most likely take place?

(A) At a hotel
(B) At a rental agency
(C) At a weekend retreat
(D) At a conference hall

45 What does the woman mention about the problem?

(A) A free bus service
(B) Details of a special offer
(C) The date of a new hotel opening
(D) Discounts at the restaurant

46 What does the man explain to the woman?

(A) The discount applies only on certain days.
(B) There will be a two-hour delay.
(C) The hotel is closed to the public.
(D) The promotion has false information.

47 What problem are the speakers discussing?

(A) Changing a menu
(B) Rescheduling an event
(C) Being understaffed
(D) Hiring employees

48 What does the woman offer to do?

(A) Wash dishes
(B) Meet a client
(C) Move tables
(D) Serve food

49 What does the woman mean when she says, "I don't think you have to worry about that"?

(A) She believes she can handle the task.
(B) She is able to help cooking.
(C) She is having some trouble with the customer.
(D) She thinks the men can't solve the problem.

50 What does the woman plan to write about?

(A) Professional landscaping
(B) Farming
(C) Public transportation
(D) Fashion trends

51 What did the man receive from the woman?

(A) A billing statement
(B) Samples of her work
(C) A rental contract
(D) References

52 What does the woman mean when she says, "Absolutely"?

(A) She will answer some questions.
(B) She can't call at the moment.
(C) She will not be able to complete the draft by the deadline.
(D) She agrees to the man's suggestion.

53 Why will Amanda be late for the meeting?

(A) She is still on site.
(B) She has to make a phone call.
(C) She is caught in traffic congestion.
(D) She has lost the keys to the office.

54 What did Amanda ask the man to do?

(A) Fetch a hard hat
(B) Drive straight to the office
(C) Take notes at a meeting
(D) Get some keys from her desk

55 What does the man say he will do next?

(A) Pick up some work supplies
(B) Contact a supervisor
(C) Link up his computer
(D) Call the site manager

56 Where does the woman work?

(A) At an educational institute
(B) At a convention center
(C) At a stationery store
(D) At a staffing agency

57 What does the man ask about the job?

(A) The starting date
(B) The salary
(C) The duration
(D) The location

58 Why does the man say, "Not a problem"?

(A) He doesn't have any questions at the moment.
(B) He wants to start on a different date.
(C) He can start working on Monday.
(D) He can take the job right away.

59 What does the woman want to do?

(A) Request a collection service
(B) Hold a new dance class
(C) Alter a previous order
(D) Have an area specially designed

60 What does the man say he can do?

(A) Comment on her work
(B) Design a dance stage
(C) Check a building guarantee
(D) Obtain an approximate estimate

61 What does the woman request?

(A) Contact information
(B) Design samples
(C) Blueprint drawings
(D) A stock catalog

62 What are the speakers mainly discussing?

(A) Factory installations
(B) Security systems
(C) A new brand launch
(D) A fashion magazine

63 What does the woman ask for?

(A) A list of security cameras
(B) An Internet address
(C) A purchase order number
(D) Details of a magazine

64 What does the man offer to do?

(A) Give the woman his magazine
(B) Install a security device
(C) Review a feature
(D) Purchase products online

GO ON TO THE NEXT PAGE

Manager's Office | Staff Room | Copy Room

A102 | A103 | A104 | A105

Inventory	
Item	Quantity
Dining table	6
Stool	5
Table cloth	2
Small-sized rug	7

65 Why is the man calling?

(A) To cancel an appointment
(B) To place an order
(C) To arrange a delivery
(D) To obtain contact information

66 Look at the graphic. Where is the LCD computer monitor supposed to go?

(A) A102
(B) A103
(C) A104
(D) A105

67 When will the speakers most likely meet?

(A) At 2:00 P.M.
(B) At 3:00 P.M.
(C) At 4:00 P.M.
(D) At 5:30 P.M.

68 What are the speakers discussing?

(A) The duration of a promotional event
(B) The recent inventory
(C) Sales figures of a new product
(D) Strategies for promoting the business

69 Look at the graphic. Which item will the man order right away?

(A) Dining table
(B) Stool
(C) Table cloth
(D) Small-sized rug

70 What does the woman say she will do in a few weeks?

(A) Make a list of items
(B) Repair a broken display
(C) Invite customers to the shop
(D) Promote an event

PART 4

Directions: You will hear some talks given by a single speaker. You will be asked to answer three questions about what the speaker says in each talk. Select the best response to each question and mark the letter (A), (B), (C), or (D) on your answer sheet. The talks will not be printed in your test book and will be spoken only one time.

71 Where does the speaker work?

(A) At an accounting firm
(B) At a construction materials supplier
(C) At an office supply store
(D) At a window replacement company

72 Why is the speaker calling?

(A) To query an order
(B) To offer a discount
(C) To explain shipment costs
(D) To cancel a delivery

73 What is the listener asked to do?

(A) Email a reply
(B) Return a phone call
(C) Check an estimate
(D) Provide a credit card

74 Who most likely is the speaker?

(A) A ship employee
(B) A local singer
(C) A park attendant
(D) An entertainer

75 According to the speaker, where will dinner be served?

(A) On the beach
(B) In the lobby
(C) In the cafeteria
(D) On the deck

76 What will the listeners attend after dinner?

(A) A play
(B) A welcome speech
(C) A film
(D) A concert

77 What have listeners been learning?

(A) New employee orientation
(B) Technology training
(C) First aid in the office
(D) Improving production techniques

78 What does the speaker ask listeners to complete?

(A) A questionnaire
(B) A timetable
(C) A consent form
(D) A test

79 Why would listeners provide an e-mail address?

(A) To receive a list of advanced classes
(B) To apply for employment opportunities
(C) To cancel a reservation
(D) To get details of trainer's notes

80 What is being advertised?

(A) Retail opportunities
(B) Offices for hire
(C) Sports training
(D) Sales consulting

81 What new service did the company recently add?

(A) Internet selling
(B) Web page design
(C) Facility management
(D) Mail handling

82 What will happen next month?

(A) Prices will increase.
(B) More staff will be recruited.
(C) A new location will open.
(D) An online seminar will be offered.

GO ON TO THE NEXT PAGE

83 What kind of company does the speaker work for?

(A) A retail store
(B) A packaging company
(C) A fitness corporation
(D) An illustration company

84 What has the company recently done?

(A) Moved to Germany
(B) Opened a new branch
(C) Signed a contract
(D) Launched a new product range

85 According to the speaker, what will listeners do over the next few weeks?

(A) Recruit new employees
(B) Design a building
(C) Prepare work samples
(D) Join a health club

---

86 What products are being discussed?

(A) Solar cells
(B) Heating systems
(C) Computer programs
(D) Home insulation

87 According to the speaker, what might surprise listeners about these products?

(A) They are cheap to install.
(B) They are selling very well.
(C) They cost little to maintain.
(D) They teach directions to use.

88 What does the speaker mean when he says, "This is as good as it gets"?

(A) The system is in good condition.
(B) He can't make the system better.
(C) His staff is very knowledgeable.
(D) He thinks he is offering a good deal.

89 Who is the speaker?

(A) A building manager
(B) A contractor
(C) A mover
(D) An inspector

90 What does the woman mean when she says, "that's not an option anymore"?

(A) A service is no longer available.
(B) A lease has been terminated.
(C) A building failed to pass inspection.
(D) A date needs to be changed.

91 What does the woman offer to do?

(A) Arrange a moving service
(B) Contact the listener under certain condition
(C) Supervise an installation
(D) Give a discount

Receipt	
Doughnut	$1.75
Chocolate cake	$2.50
Apple pie	$3.00
Pastry	$4.25
Total	$11.50

92 Why is the speaker calling?

(A) To cancel an order
(B) To report a missing item
(C) To arrange a delivery
(D) To request a refund

93 Look at the graphic. What is the price of the item the speaker refers to?

(A) $1.75
(B) $2.50
(C) $3.00
(D) $4.25

94 What does the speaker want the listener to do?

(A) Get in touch with him
(B) Give him a refund
(C) Email the list
(D) Upgrade the shipping method

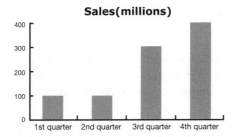

Sales(millions)

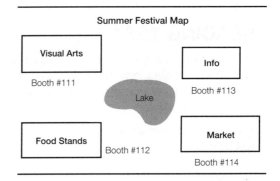

Summer Festival Map

95 Where most likely does the speaker work?

(A) At a phone company
(B) At an accounting firm
(C) At a lighting maker
(D) At an appliance manufacturer

96 Look at the graphic. When did the company release the new products?

(A) 1st quarter
(B) 2nd quarter
(C) 3rd quarter
(D) 4th quarter

97 What does the speaker say she will do for the listeners?

(A) Treat them to dinner
(B) Give them a financial incentive
(C) Present an award
(D) Let them take a vacation

98 What does the speaker say about the Summer Festival?

(A) He plans to attend it.
(B) There is not much room to park cars.
(C) He will perform there.
(D) He is one of the sponsors.

99 Look at the graphic. Where will the radio station be broadcasting from?

(A) Booth #111
(B) Booth #112
(C) Booth #113
(D) Booth #114

100 According to the speaker, what can listeners do at the Summer Festival's Web site?

(A) Buy tickets
(B) Reserve seats
(C) Get a certificate
(D) Obtain maps

This is the end of the Listening test. Turn to Part 5 in your test book.

GO ON TO THE NEXT PAGE

READING TEST

In the Reading test, you will read a variety of texts and answer several different types of reading comprehension questions. The entire Reading test will last 75 minutes. There are three parts, and directions are given for each part. You are encouraged to answer as many questions as possible within the time allowed.

You must mark your answers on the separate answer sheet. Do not write your answers in your test book.

PART 5

Directions: A word or phrase is missing in each of the sentences below. Four answer choices are given below each sentence. Select the best answer to complete the sentence. Then mark the letter (A), (B), (C), or (D) on your answer sheet.

101 The Amoti Management executives have decided to uphold the funding ------- of the research department team.

(A) deciding
(B) decisions
(C) decide
(D) decides

102 To conserve energy, please switch off electrical appliances before ------- the workplace.

(A) to leave
(B) leaves
(C) leaving
(D) left

103 The National Painting and Decorating Show features chances to listen to specific ------- from experienced craftsmen.

(A) case
(B) advice
(C) songs
(D) house

104 The KKL Group has a vacancy ------- an experienced management accountant.

(A) across
(B) for
(C) through
(D) off

105 Salaries are ------- to remain the same this quarter due to the plunge in domestic consumption.

(A) liked
(B) likely
(C) likened
(D) likeable

106 Ms. Lucas forecasts that the entire regeneration program should be completed ------- the end of the month.

(A) by
(B) until
(C) of
(D) on

107 A recent questionnaire revealed that over 50 percent of online customers plan to renew ------- broadband connection with the same company.

(A) them
(B) theirs
(C) they
(D) their

108 To ------- to a customer service representative, please dial the number located at the bottom of this form.

(A) tell
(B) mention
(C) speak
(D) inform

109 Even though Ms. Onaissis will be unable to attend this week's seminar, -------, along with all the department managers, will be at the one next week.

(A) she
(B) her
(C) hers
(D) herself

110 The acquisition of Titan Industries should help Pacific Holdings ------- its business strategies.

(A) diversity
(B) diverse
(C) diversify
(D) diversely

111 Without updated security software, computer systems are ------- to numerous viruses.

(A) superior
(B) exemplary
(C) vulnerable
(D) cautious

112 Elias Store's security department reacted ------- to employees' concerns over a suspicious package.

(A) prompt
(B) promptly
(C) prompting
(D) promptness

113 Travelers must show appropriate identification ------- boarding any domestic flight.

(A) in addition
(B) such as
(C) although
(D) when

114 Long-distance lorry drivers are forbidden from entering Park Avenue because the road is too -------.

(A) narrow
(B) narrowly
(C) narrows
(D) narrower

115 The headquarters for Acoho International are located ------- the post office in Springhill.

(A) near
(B) besides
(C) close
(D) next

116 Since a winner has not yet been -------, the judges will have to further assess the competing entries.

(A) decided
(B) decisive
(C) deciding
(D) decision

117 If the university you have applied for is full, your name will ------- be placed on a waiting list in case someone drops out.

(A) intermittently
(B) automatically
(C) progressively
(D) considerably

118 By ------- old buses with new, more fuel-efficient models, Kennewick was able to save on maintenance and repairs.

(A) replacement
(B) replacing
(C) replace
(D) replaced

119 ------- for Artist of the Year must be received by the judging committee before 3:00 P.M. on Monday.

(A) Authorities
(B) Performances
(C) Occurrences
(D) Nominations

120 Thanks to our excellent sales records, our sales executives can ------- look forward to bonuses this month.

(A) which
(B) all
(C) another
(D) any

GO ON TO THE NEXT PAGE

121 Richard K. Norse's mystery story *House In The Mist* has been ------- as the best novel of the decade.

(A) totaled
(B) alleviated
(C) billed
(D) consisted

122 Most consumers, ------- given a choice between a cheap and a high-quality appliance, put product quality first.

(A) who
(B) which
(C) when
(D) what

123 Howard Financial is pleased to ------- its loyal customers with the best consulting services available in the region.

(A) provide
(B) providing
(C) provided
(D) provider

124 If Voks Tech had agreed to make a contract, the necessary funds -------.

(A) send
(B) would have sent
(C) were sent
(D) would have been sent

125 By the time the fire on Birdseed Lane was reported, it ------- to the neighborhood.

(A) spreading
(B) spreads
(C) were spread
(D) had spread

126 In August, the Connors Gallery will display a number of works by the ------- artist James McNeil.

(A) distinguished
(B) founded
(C) estimated
(D) allocated

127 The training, ------- was scheduled to begin on June 20, was put off for three weeks.

(A) which
(B) this
(C) what
(D) that

128 The planners of the music festival tomorrow at Jenkins Park are considering postponing the event ------- the weather clears up tonight.

(A) even if
(B) nevertheless
(C) regardless of
(D) so that

129 Although the Clearfit water purifier was a success this summer, it has been ------- unreliable by the Quality Guidelines Association.

(A) inspected
(B) conducted
(C) deemed
(D) allowed

130 Several tenants of the Sandrine Building reported that they frequently had to ------- a lot of noise.

(A) participate in
(B) put forth
(C) contend with
(D) aspire to

PART 6

Directions: Read the texts that follow. A word, phrase, or sentence is missing in parts of each text. Four answer choices for each question are given below the text. Select the best answer to complete the text. Then mark the letter (A), (B), (C), or (D) on your answer sheet.

Questions 131-134 refer to the following e-mail.

To: service@blueoceanair.com
From: james.gimbel@cmail.com
Re: Reservation Error

Hi there. My name's James Gimbel. I made a reservation on a flight from Sydney to Washington on Tuesday, July 12. I was planning to return to Washington to celebrate my 10th anniversary with my wife. My ------- number is 5774001. On the day of my departure, which was July 15,
                    131.
I arrived at the airport an hour early. I ------- went to one of Blueocean Air's check-in kiosks.
                                     132.
When I entered my reservation information to the kiosk, it said that my check-in status was invalid. I rushed to one of your representatives and let her know what happened to me, presenting the printed confirmation e-mail. -------. She said I had to wait until a seat was available. I stood
                                   133.
nervously next to the counter for two hours before boarding the plane at the last minute.

I was so upset and really disappointed with your system. I would like your explanation ------- this
                                                              134.
issue. Please call my cell phone number as soon as possible.

Thank you,

James Gimbel

131 (A) book
    (B) booking
    (C) booked
    (D) bookable

132 (A) gradually
    (B) substantially
    (C) comprehensively
    (D) immediately

133 (A) Therefore, I had to make an additional payment.
    (B) Then, she put me on the waiting list.
    (C) Unfortunately, the printer was not working.
    (D) Afterward, she required me to open my luggage.

134 (A) beyond
    (B) concerning
    (C) along
    (D) up to

GO ON TO THE NEXT PAGE

Questions 135-138 refer to the following letter.

Anna Ruben
80-5 Winston Flats
2917 Woody Avenue
Riverside, CA 89723

Dear Ms. Ruben:

Thank you for your request for information regarding your bank account. The $20 fee was included in your latest statement because your August payment was received late. -------.
                                                               135.
Because of this, we are ------- the normal charge. Your account has been revised accordingly.
                      136.
To guarantee that your monthly payments are ------- on time, we advise that you sign up for our
                                       137.
automatic debit option. With this service, you can pay the minimum amount due on a -------
                                                       138.
amount on a regular basis. Visit www.chvasbankingservice.com/payments for details.

Should you have questions or concerns, I can be contacted at d.adelaide@chvasbankinservice.com.

Thank you for your business.

Dana Adelaide

Account Specialist

---

135 (A) You can pay this late fee either electronically or in person.
(B) We encourage you to open a new savings account.
(C) However, we understand that you are a longtime client of good standing.
(D) You should complete necessary forms to be reimbursed by the end of the month.

136 (A) expecting
(B) imposing
(C) waiving
(D) honoring

137 (A) already
(B) always
(C) evenly
(D) shortly

138 (A) specified
(B) specifying
(C) specifically
(D) specification

Questions 139-142 refer to the following notice.

Fitness Center Closing

Most of the Acebody fitness centers will be closed starting on Monday, August 14, for an -------
139.
renovation. Major upgrades include the newest exercise equipment, a new coat of interior paint,

and new flooring and fixtures. After considering opinions from our center -------, we will add
140.
more GX rooms and sauna facilities. As we will have more GX rooms on the second floor, some

of equipment such as bench presses and treadmills will be moved to the first floor.

The closure may last several months. -------.
141.
You'll still be able to use the following branches:

- Wellers location (25 Main Blvd.)

- Paradise location (8 Brea Dr.)

- Aquatic location (110 East St.)

------- a location near you, visit www.acebodyfit.com and speak to a gym staff member through
142.
online chatting service.

---

139 (A) extend
(B) extensively
(C) extensive
(D) extending

140 (A) candidates
(B) patrons
(C) pedestrians
(D) passengers

141 (A) We expect to reopen our doors on December 1.
(B) You can register for a dance class at www.acebodyfit.com.
(C) Regular exercise is considered necessary for your health.
(D) The gym is scheduled to open at 10 A.M. tomorrow.

142 (A) Find
(B) Having found
(C) To be found
(D) To find

GO ON TO THE NEXT PAGE

To: All employees
From: Director, HR Department
Re: Personnel Changes

After a ------- passed at a board meeting on February 10, Melrose System is delighted to
143.
announce the following personnel changes. We believe Melrose System will continue growing

steadily under the new management.

Angela Lansbury, the senior accounting director, has been appointed as chief financial officer.

She will be ------- responsible for supervising all budget management and investment strategies.
144.

------- we are expanding our international business, the company has established a new position:
145.
international business director. Andy Griffith, the domestic sales manager, has been assigned to

this position, and he will oversee all of the company's global operations.

John Walton, the senior marketing manager, has been promoted to the domestic sales manager

position. -------. He will be in charge of developing the sales strategies designed to achieve
146.
short-term and long-term growth for our business in the domestic market.

143 (A) resolves
(B) resolved
(C) resolving
(D) resolution

144 (A) regularly
(B) primarily
(C) relatively
(D) positively

145 (A) Now that
(B) Rather than
(C) During
(D) Whether

146 (A) As of next month, he will be working
overseas.
(B) He will take over Andy Griffith's duties.
(C) This will be an addition to his
responsibilities as CFO.
(D) He will take care of all of the company's
budget estimates.

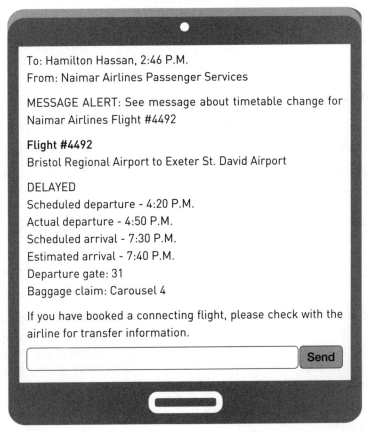

PART 7

Directions: In this part you will read a selection of texts, such as magazine and newspaper articles, e-mails, and instant messages. Each text or set of texts is followed by several questions. Select the best answer for each question and mark the letter (A), (B), (C), or (D) on your answer sheet.

Questions 147-148 refer to the following text message.

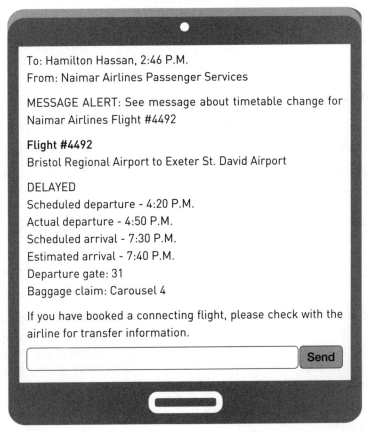

To: Hamilton Hassan, 2:46 P.M.
From: Naimar Airlines Passenger Services

MESSAGE ALERT: See message about timetable change for Naimar Airlines Flight #4492

Flight #4492
Bristol Regional Airport to Exeter St. David Airport

DELAYED
Scheduled departure - 4:20 P.M.
Actual departure - 4:50 P.M.
Scheduled arrival - 7:30 P.M.
Estimated arrival - 7:40 P.M.
Departure gate: 31
Baggage claim: Carousel 4

If you have booked a connecting flight, please check with the airline for transfer information.

Send

147 Why was the text message sent?
(A) To confirm a flight booking
(B) To announce a change in flight status
(C) To inform a passenger of the departure gate
(D) To provide an update about connecting flights

148 What is indicated about Mr. Hassan?
(A) He will depart from Bristol.
(B) He paid for his flight in Exeter.
(C) He checked two bags onto a flight.
(D) He lost his ticket information.

GO ON TO THE NEXT PAGE

Join us for the

Grand Opening of Jackson's on April 18!

To celebrate the opening of our new store, Jackson's is offering "Buy One, Get One Half Price" over the first week of trading. So come and see our handbags and shoes. Make a choice from more than 20 brand names including:

- Yanto
- Siegried
- La Manche
- Indigo
- Peach Mama

Jackson's is located between Helton Clothing and Food For All in the Cherish Vale Shopping Center. We are open seven days a week during regular shopping hours.

Take a look at the March 30 issue of the *Cherish Vale Herald* for a profile of the new Jackson's store manager, Ellie Juno.

Offer is limited to five items per customer.

---

149 What is sold at Jackson's?

(A) Food
(B) Clothing
(C) Fashion accessories
(D) Sports equipment

150 According to the flyer, what can customers do on April 18-24?

(A) Receive a free copy of the *Cherish Vale Herald*
(B) Attend a press reception for the opening of a new store
(C) Purchase one item and receive another half price
(D) Present the flyer for a further discount

151 What is mentioned about Jackson's?

(A) It is advertising for employees.
(B) It is situated in a shopping mall.
(C) Its owner will be interviewed by Ellie Juno.
(D) Its opening will be on March 30.

Questions 152-153 refer to the following notice.

Namaski

The Namaski Group is dedicated to protecting the environment and ensures that every attempt is made to prevent our waste from being sent to a landfill. We have a policy of encouraging our customers to dispose of our products responsibly at the end of the product's lifecycle. If you buy a product from one of our Namaski stores, we will gladly deliver the appliance to you. At the same time, we will happily collect your old appliance and take it to our disposal facility. Alternatively, you can make arrangements to have your old appliance delivered to our disposal plant. Your local Namaski store can also give you a list of other disposal facilities near to you that offer similar environmentally friendly disposal methods for any-sized electrical appliance.

152 What is the purpose of the notice?

(A) To promote a new line of electrical goods
(B) To indicate that a delivery has been postponed
(C) To alert customers to a discount offer
(D) To describe available services

153 According to the notice, what information does Namaski offer?

(A) The names of nearby disposal centers
(B) Published client reviews of products
(C) Recent research on environmental disposal methods
(D) Descriptions of the company's production depots

GO ON TO THE NEXT PAGE

Clearview Film Studios

686 Whale Avenue, Surrey, UK

March 30
Ms. Imogen Cranford
34 Thames Street, Clarendon Apt. 121
Surrey, UK

Dear Ms. Cranford,

Thank you for your interest in Clearview Film Studios. Our client Ian Blaine has mentioned you as a suitable candidate for the position of catering manager, and we have now received your application form.

I'd like to arrange an interview with you on Wednesday April 17, at 1:00 P.M. Please contact my assistant, Shimla Shem, as soon as possible to confirm that this is an acceptable time. She can be reached at 010-555-9234.

Also, I would be grateful if you would resend your résumé to me via e-mail. The résumé you submitted online through our Web site was corrupted and we could not view the last page of the document.

Finally, please find enclosed several mandatory forms you must complete and bring with you to the interview. We look forward to hearing from you.

Sincerely,

Edward Trent
Human Resource Manager

Enclosures

154 Why does Mr. Trent write to Ms. Cranford?

(A) To arrange an appointment
(B) To ask for a recommendation
(C) To inquire about a job opening
(D) To request alterations to an online form

155 Whom is Ms. Cranford asked to contact?

(A) Mr. Blaine
(B) The production manager
(C) The studio executive
(D) Ms. Shem

156 What problem does Mr. Trent mention?

(A) He was unable to check some part of an electrical document.
(B) The vacancy Ms. Cranford applied for has already been filled.
(C) The person Ms. Cranford mentioned as a reference could not be contacted.
(D) The application Ms. Cranford sent was received after the deadline.

Questions 157-158 refer to the following text message chain.

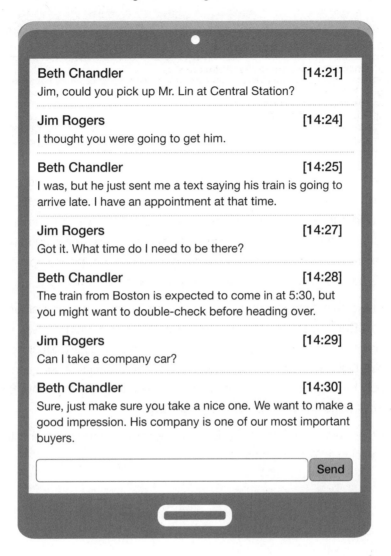

Beth Chandler [14:21]
Jim, could you pick up Mr. Lin at Central Station?

Jim Rogers [14:24]
I thought you were going to get him.

Beth Chandler [14:25]
I was, but he just sent me a text saying his train is going to arrive late. I have an appointment at that time.

Jim Rogers [14:27]
Got it. What time do I need to be there?

Beth Chandler [14:28]
The train from Boston is expected to come in at 5:30, but you might want to double-check before heading over.

Jim Rogers [14:29]
Can I take a company car?

Beth Chandler [14:30]
Sure, just make sure you take a nice one. We want to make a good impression. His company is one of our most important buyers.

Send

157 What is most likely true about Mr. Lin?

(A) He rescheduled a meeting.
(B) He boarded the train late.
(C) He is Ms. Chandler's boss.
(D) He is traveling from Boston.

158 At 14:27, what does Mr. Rogers most likely mean when he writes, "Got it"?

(A) He knows where Central Station is located.
(B) He is going to get in touch with Mr. Lin.
(C) He understands the reason for the request.
(D) He realizes that trains are sometimes late.

GO ON TO THE NEXT PAGE

Questions 159-161 refer to the following e-mail.

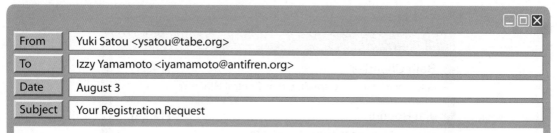

From	Yuki Satou <ysatou@tabe.org>
To	Izzy Yamamoto <iyamamoto@antifren.org>
Date	August 3
Subject	Your Registration Request

Dear Mr. Yamamoto,

Thank you for your interest in our Construction Industry Update Convention planned for September 15. Regrettably, we are no longer receiving attendance requests, as the event has already sold out. Please let me know if you would like to be put on our waiting list. Should anyone already registered be unable to attend, we will offer spots to those on the list. If we are unable to offer you a place on this occasion, please note that the CIU Convention is held every quarter, with our next event planned for January.

May I also take this opportunity to invite you to become a member of the Tokyo Association of Building Engineers (TABE)? Membership is $300 per year and you will receive a number of benefits. These include inclusion in an industry directory, a discount card for a local building supply firm, and the opportunity to join us at our quarterly cocktail party. To apply for membership, please call our membership office at (440) 555-9943 or visit the relevant page on our Web site, www.tabe.org.

I hope that there will be a place for you at our upcoming convention and that you will consider becoming a TABE member.

Best regards,

Yuki Satou
Tokyo Association of Building Engineers
www.tabe.org
Tel: (440) 555-9943
Fax: (440) 555-4631

159 What is indicated about the Construction Industry Update Convention?

(A) It is held four times a year.
(B) It is chaired by Ms. Satou.
(C) It is a new initiative.
(D) It is relocating to a larger venue.

160 What does Ms. Satou suggest that Mr. Yamamoto do?

(A) Request a refund
(B) Send his contact information to her
(C) Make an appointment with her
(D) Join an organization

161 What is mentioned as a benefit offered to TABE members?

(A) A list of recommended lawyers
(B) Advance registration for seminars
(C) Reserved seating at seminars
(D) An invitation to a social event

GO ON TO THE NEXT PAGE

Questions 162-164 refer to the following memo.

To: S&L Manufacturing Group
From: Financial Forecast Committee
Date: April 14
Re: Analysis report

S&L has a well-established reputation for producing the highest quality packaged meals, having been involved in the mass catering industry for many years. However, we are now facing a crisis. As you may be aware, packaging costs have increased significantly by 12 percent over the last three years. We have discussed numerous options to allow us to cover these costs. The general consensus is that we increase the prices of our product lines, but a rise in prices involves the risk of losing customers.

Please bear in mind we have extremely effective business strategies. Our social media promotions are widely viewed and we receive a good response from our customers. We suggest that we keep advertising costs the same. However, we have to seek to find new and more cost-effective packaging designs. This way, we can maintain our pricing strategy without discouraging potential customers and this will help us recoup any losses.

Jane Cox

162 What is stated about S&L Manufacturing Group?

(A) They manufacture packaging for the catering industry.
(B) They are well regarded in their field.
(C) They are a global company.
(D) They have invested in new product research.

163 Why does S&L Manufacturing Group have a problem?

(A) Production has become more expensive.
(B) Few of their business strategies have been successful.
(C) The quality of their products has decreased.
(D) Their advertisements are not popular.

164 What does the committee recommend S&L Manufacturing Group do?

(A) Increase prices universally
(B) Invest in more economical packaging
(C) Shut down production
(D) Increase new product development

Questions **165-168** refer to the following article.

Spotlight on Alexandria Businesses

The Main Square Business Association and the Supporting Alexandria Organization have amalgamated to host the first Alexandria Business Platform. –[1]–. Organized for Saturday, August 24, from 11:30 A.M. to 8:30 P.M., it will be held in the Main Square and will offer local businesses the opportunity to display their goods and services. For any business that wants to raise its profile in the community, this will be the ideal showcase.

The goal is to provide a platform for a variety of local businesses and performers in Alexandria to highlight their talents. Local shops and boutiques will be displaying their goods, and local restaurants and cafés will offer samples, some even cooking in the open air. –[2]–.

The event will be free and open to the public. Booths for interested parties are available for a rental fee of €100 for the day. As there are a limited number of booths available, vendors are encouraged to reserve theirs as soon as possible. –[3]–. Applicants should fill out an event application form and send it with a €50 non-refundable deposit to Husama Al Enani at henani@alex.org by July 3. –[4]–.

165 For whom is the article most likely intended?

(A) Husama Al Enani
(B) Local business owners
(C) Cookery professionals
(D) Employees of the Main Square Business Association

166 What is NOT mentioned as an action that interested vendors should take?

(A) Paying a sum of money up front
(B) Filling out a form
(C) Submitting a product sample
(D) Emailing details

167 What is indicated about the showcase?

(A) Two organizations are sponsoring the event.
(B) Visitors will be expected to pay to attend.
(C) There will be a surplus of stands available to rent.
(D) The event was well attended in the past.

168 In which of the positions marked [1], [2], [3], and [4] does the following sentence best belong?

"In addition, Amateur performers and artists will be performing throughout the event."

(A) [1]
(B) [2]
(C) [3]
(D) [4]

GO ON TO THE NEXT PAGE

Questions 169-171 refer to the following online chat discussion.

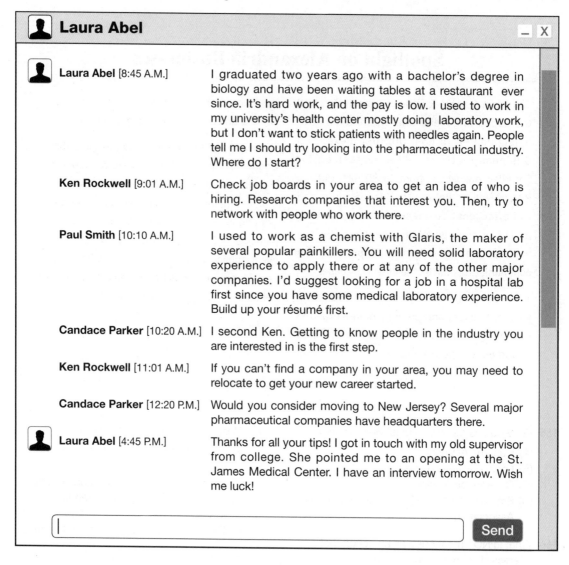

Laura Abel   − X

Laura Abel [8:45 A.M.]   I graduated two years ago with a bachelor's degree in biology and have been waiting tables at a restaurant ever since. It's hard work, and the pay is low. I used to work in my university's health center mostly doing laboratory work, but I don't want to stick patients with needles again. People tell me I should try looking into the pharmaceutical industry. Where do I start?

Ken Rockwell [9:01 A.M.]   Check job boards in your area to get an idea of who is hiring. Research companies that interest you. Then, try to network with people who work there.

Paul Smith [10:10 A.M.]   I used to work as a chemist with Glaris, the maker of several popular painkillers. You will need solid laboratory experience to apply there or at any of the other major companies. I'd suggest looking for a job in a hospital lab first since you have some medical laboratory experience. Build up your résumé first.

Candace Parker [10:20 A.M.]   I second Ken. Getting to know people in the industry you are interested in is the first step.

Ken Rockwell [11:01 A.M.]   If you can't find a company in your area, you may need to relocate to get your new career started.

Candace Parker [12:20 P.M.]   Would you consider moving to New Jersey? Several major pharmaceutical companies have headquarters there.

Laura Abel [4:45 P.M.]   Thanks for all your tips! I got in touch with my old supervisor from college. She pointed me to an opening at the St. James Medical Center. I have an interview tomorrow. Wish me luck!

Send

169 What is suggested about Mr. Smith?

    (A) He worked in the pharmaceutical industry.

    (B) He used to manage a laboratory.

    (C) He currently lives in New Jersey.

    (D) His company is accepting applications.

170 At 10:20 A.M, what does Ms. Parker most likely mean when she writes, "I second Ken"?

    (A) She followed Mr. Rockwell's advice before.

    (B) She thinks it is important to make connections.

    (C) She currently works for a drug maker.

    (D) She wants to meet new people.

171 What is most likely true about Ms. Abel?

    (A) She will return to her former employer.

    (B) She recently revised her résumé.

    (C) She plans to go back to school.

    (D) She applied for a job at a hospital.

GO ON TO THE NEXT PAGE

	E-Mail Message	

From: hamish@dunfair.com
To: lmckenzie@hotline.com
Subject: Dunfair Island Food Festival
Date: June 2

Dear Ms. McKenzie,

Thank you for inquiring about the Dunfair Island Food Festival. –[1]–. For more than five years, we have been hosting this festival held exclusively by the residents of Dunfair Island. Cakes, savories, candy, special occasion menus and main courses are some of the foodstuffs on offer, all made by local chefs. We only allow food that is freshly cooked on the day of the festival using local ingredients, and we send inspectors to check the foods; we do not allow any pre-packaged food. Prices range from £1 cookies to wedding cakes priced at £100 and upwards. –[2]–.

On the first Saturday of every month, we also hold the Dunfair Craft Evening, which features goods made by local residents and businesses, and we offer free refreshments between 4 and 6 P.M. –[3]–. This event is always very well attended and typically attracts more than 50 tourists and residents. Sales tend to be brisk, especially throughout the summer months which are the height of the tourist season.

If you would like to join the Dunfair Island Food Festival family, please email visual images of your specialized food and include a list of ingredients used. –[4]–. Also please mention any catering qualifications you have. We will contact you within seven days with further instructions.

Best Regards,

Hamish Green

Administrator, Dunfair Island Food Festival

172 What is the purpose of the e-mail?

(A) To explain how an event operates
(B) To publicize Dunfair Craft Evening
(C) To order some items to be handmade
(D) To promote a cookery competition

173 Who most likely is Ms. McKenzie?

(A) A craftsperson
(B) A tourist
(C) A restaurant employee
(D) A chef

174 What is indicated about all the items for sale at Dunfair Island Food Festival?

(A) Nothing is priced higher than £100.
(B) Their prices are reduced by 30% in June, July and August.
(C) They are made by Dunfair Island residents.
(D) They use ingredients from around the world.

175 In which of the positions marked [1], [2], [3], and [4] does the following sentence best belong?

"Vendors must pay a 10% commission on the food they sell."

(A) [1]
(B) [2]
(C) [3]
(D) [4]

Wotamba Real Estate Company

Serving businesses in Brisbane, Cairns and the Gold Coast for more than a decade

Featured Listings

395 Lyons Place: 170 square meters. Office space in excellent condition in purpose-built complex. Main reception area, multiple offices, and three medium conference rooms. Parking area shared with rest of complex. Great Gold Coast location.

229 Bayland View: 280 square meters. Entire ground floor of Georgian building in Brisbane. Fully equipped for catering purposes. In good condition. Electrical appliances also included.

12 Watama Avenue: 320 square meters. Upmarket double-tiered commercial premises in the center of Brisbane's tourist district. Brand new fixtures and fittings, including a 20-meter-long marble floor with ivory inset.

7 Adelaide Street: 320 square meters. Fitted for restaurant or catering purposes but can be used for retail purposes. Busy location on a main street. Close to Cairns.

We have many more office and retail spaces for sale or lease!
For full listings, visit our Web site at www.wotambarealty.com or contact us by telephone at (330) 555-3593 or by e-mail at properties@wotambarealty.com.

Restaurant Announces New Home

December 1 — Jasmine Palace, the popular Thai restaurant, reopened at a new venue yesterday at 211 Matin Boulevard. Local folk group, Skippy Beat, supplied musical entertainment, and owners Chai and Lan Yong provided guests with a sumptuous banquet featuring dishes typically served on special occasions in their home town of Bangkok. Guests came in hundreds, with loyal customers first on the guest list. Chai Yong gave a short speech in which he thanked the generosity and support of the local community. "Thank you to the residents of Brisbane who took us into their community when we came from Thailand and who have continued to support our restaurant ever since."

Jasmine Palace was opened seven years ago, and since then, the restaurant has become so popular that the existing premises simply could not accommodate the number of customers. "Our previous restaurant had less than 300 square meters of floor space and parking was a problem, as customers had to park in the adjacent car park," said Mr. Yong. "The sales representative at Wotamba Real Estate, who arranged for our old place to be one of his company's featured properties, was invaluable in helping us find this place with its excellent dining and catering facilities, as well as its central location in the heart of the Brisbane community."

One of the restaurant's most fervent supporting customers is Councilor James Taylor, who has struck up a close relationship with the family. He gave a short address to the guests. Replying to a question about the reopening, Councilor Taylor said, "Jasmine Palace has secured its place in the Brisbane local community. I am sure that this new location will only enhance its popularity."

176 What is suggested about Wotamba Real Estate Company?

    (A) It sells properties in multiple cities.

    (B) It concentrates on the rental market.

    (C) It currently has only four properties for sale.

    (D) It prefers to deal with vendors face to face.

177 What is the main purpose of the article?

    (A) To teach traditional Thai cookery

    (B) To announce the sale of a local restaurant

    (C) To profile a Brisbane city official

    (D) To report on an event at a business

178 According to the article, why did Jasmine Palace relocate?

    (A) A new lease was refused.

    (B) Its owners decided to move to Brisbane.

    (C) The previous location was too small.

    (D) The new premises have more modern facilities.

179 Where most likely was Jasmine Palace previously located?

    (A) On Bayland View

    (B) On Adelaide Street

    (C) On Watama Avenue

    (D) On Lyons Place

180 What is indicated about the Yongs?

    (A) They are friends of Councillor Taylor.

    (B) They are musical performers.

    (C) They are regular customers of Jasmine Palace.

    (D) They are originally from the Gold Coast.

GO ON TO THE NEXT PAGE

E-Mail Message

To: Gita Litovic <glitovic@voicedesign.com>
From: Sasha Timovis <stimovis@manatidesign.com>
Subject: Design Delite
Date: December 12

Dear Ms. Gita Litovic,

As a regular client of Manatidesign, you will be interested in the launch of our newly updated version Design Delite. The most advanced and efficient package of design solutions software on the market now has even more options!

Design Delite still has all of the standard features included in previous versions, such as drawing tools to create technical drawings, shapes, logos and animations. However, the latest version includes advanced options for intricate vector filter effects, colours and 3D effects. Additionally, you will be able to upgrade and add-on new features to Design Delite as the software is constantly being updated.

We are inviting you to participate in an online training session, free of charge, where the trainer will provide expert advice and demonstrations on how to use the software. Furthermore, just by taking part in this workshop, you will receive a 10% discount and free installation on any future Manatidesign product. To register, you must go to our Web site and follow the link for online registration; you can also see a list of our entire product portfolio.

Sincerely,

Sasha Timovis
Technical Services Manager

INVOICE

From:	Manatidesign	To:	Gita Litovic
	11 Yassa Road		Voice Design studio
	Dubrovnic 34963		992 Mayfair Street
	Bulgaria		London W11
			United Kingdom

Order Date: January 6
Shipping date: January 7
Expected delivery date: January 11

Item	Quantity	Description	Cost
AC41	1	Design Delite (business edition)	$525.00
	1	10 percent discount	$ -52.50
	1	Shipping	$ 0.00

All sales are final. No refunds or exchanges.
For technical support, visit our Web site at www.manatidesign.com/support.

181 Why did Ms. Timovis email Ms. Litovic?

(A) To recommend a new product
(B) To offer installation advice
(C) To request feedback on a workshop
(D) To remind her to attend a meeting

182 What is true about Design Delite?

(A) It is capable of creating accounting databases.
(B) It is an updated version of a previously released product.
(C) It can only be purchased online.
(D) It is twice as efficient as similar products from competitors.

183 When did Ms. Litovic make a purchase?

(A) On January 6
(B) On January 7
(C) On January 11
(D) On January 14

184 What is indicated about Ms. Litovic?

(A) She paid for overnight delivery.
(B) She purchased the software for residential purposes.
(C) She ordered more than one copy of the same software.
(D) She participated in a training session.

185 What is mentioned about Manatidesign?

(A) It offers one-to-one training sessions.
(B) It provides refunds and exchanges for software.
(C) It provides online customer assistance.
(D) It accepts registration by mail.

GO ON TO THE NEXT PAGE

CIELO IMAGES

A premier wedding photography and videography company

Whether it is traditional, modern, or something in between, your wedding is very special. Cielo Images can work with you to make sure it is documented in your own special way. For the past ten years, we have worked with hundreds of couples to create memorable photographs and videos. Based in Rohaton, our team of talented professionals can travel to locations within 200 kilometers. In addition to wedding ceremonies and receptions, we do bridal showers, bachelor/bachelorette parties, and post-wedding brunches. Contact us at info@cieloimages.com.

To: mjones@jmail.com
From: info@cieloimages.com
Date: January 28
Re: Availability
Attachment: Reservation Form

Dear Ms. Jones:

Thank you for expressing interest in Cielo Images. We are available on the day of your wedding. The location you mentioned works for us. If you would like to make a reservation, please complete the attached form and email it back to us to tentatively save the date. We will then contact you to set up a preliminary meeting. At the meeting, we will discuss your needs and budget. To hold the reservation, we ask that you make a $200 nonrefundable deposit at that time. About two weeks before your actual wedding date, we will set up a final appointment with you to review your plans. If you have any questions, feel free to contact me at this e-mail address or call 555-9090.

Sincerely,
Lorna Taylor

Cielo Images   <u>Reservation Form</u>

Name: <u>Marion Jones</u>
Phone number: <u>(412) 555-6736</u>
Date(s) needed: <u>Saturday, May 1</u>
Time(s) needed: <u>2:00 P.M. – 7:00 P.M.</u>
Location(s): <u>Bickford Park, Sudbury Court Reception Center</u>

Description of your needs: My fiancé and I would like you to shoot our wedding ceremony and reception. We are still discussing the possibility of having a video made as well, but we would like to discuss the costs with you first. If possible, could we see some samples of your work?

---

186 What is indicated about Cielo Images?

(A) It charges an initial consultation fee.
(B) It can staff an event on May 1.
(C) It can send ten employees.
(D) It will make a video for Ms. Jones.

187 What is most likely true about Ms. Jones?

(A) She plans to be married indoors.
(B) She is having a large wedding reception.
(C) She initially called Ms. Taylor.
(D) She will meet with Cielo in April.

188 According to the e-mail, what must Ms. Jones do to ensure that Cielo will photograph her event?

(A) Make an initial payment
(B) Submit proper identification
(C) Contact a wedding planner
(D) Visit Ms. Taylor's office

189 What is suggested about Bickford Park?

(A) It is an inexpensive place to rent.
(B) It hosts many weddings a year.
(C) It is capable of hosting many guests.
(D) It is within 200 km of Rohaton.

190 In the form, the word "shoot" in line 6 is closest in meaning to

(A) attend
(B) document
(C) photograph
(D) service

GO ON TO THE NEXT PAGE

Questions 191-195 refer to the following notice, form, and e-mail.

● ● ●

To	ALL TENANTS
Subject	CHILDCARE CENTER OPENING SOON

Precious Wishes has signed a contract to open a childcare center in the Burton Building. The facility will be located on the third floor. Licensed childcare professionals will provide basic daycare services with a strong educational component for children ages three months to five years.

Hours: Monday through Friday, 7:00 A.M. to 6:30 P.M.

Applications are now being accepted for children of employees or tenants in the building. Space is limited. The deadline to apply is January 31.

For monthly rates, meal schedules, application forms, and more, visit www.preciouswishes.com.

Precious Wishes

Application Form

Name: *Laurie Waters*

Employer: *Jackson Consulting*

Phone (work): *(505) 555-0334*

Phone (personal): *(505) 555-2217*

E-mail: *lwaters@jacksonconsulting.com*

Number of children to be enrolled: *2*

Age(s) of children to be enrolled: *14 months, 4 years*

Days needed: [√] *Monday* [√] *Tuesday* [√] *Wednesday* [√] *Thursday* [√] *Friday*

Hours needed: [ ] *half day (5 hours or less)* [√] *full day (5 + hours)*

Additional information: *My daughter is allergic to peanuts.*

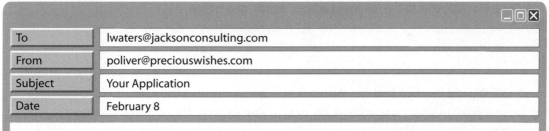

To	lwaters@jacksonconsulting.com
From	poliver@preciouswishes.com
Subject	Your Application
Date	February 8

Dear Ms. Waters:

Thank you for applying for a space at our newest location. Interest in the facility has far exceeded our capacity. Therefore, we have been placing children in the order in which applications were received.

Although we are not able to offer you a space at this time, you have been placed on the waiting list. You are currently number seven out of forty-two. When a position opens up, you will be notified. You will then have 48 hours to decide whether to accept or reject the position.

If, at any time, you would like to be removed from the list, kindly let us know. However, we are unable to refund the $50 per child application fee submitted along with your application.

Sincerely,

Patricia Oliver

191 What is NOT indicated about Precious Wishes?

(A) It will expand its new facility.
(B) It has multiple locations.
(C) It employs trained staff.
(D) It offers care for infants.

192 In the notice, the word "rates" in paragraph 3, line 1, is closest in meaning to

(A) costs
(B) numbers
(C) ranks
(D) speeds

193 What is suggested about Jackson Consulting?

(A) It is located on the third floor.
(B) It rents space in the Burton Building.
(C) Many of its employees have kids.
(D) It is Precious Wishes' landlord.

194 Why did Ms. Oliver write to Ms. Waters?

(A) To offer her a space at a new location
(B) To request a payment for childcare
(C) To move her forward on a list
(D) To inform her of the status of her request

195 What is most likely true about Ms. Waters?

(A) She will find another childcare provider.
(B) She works four days a week.
(C) She will cancel her application.
(D) She gave $100 to Precious Wishes.

GO ON TO THE NEXT PAGE

DANTON (July 1) – Last weekend, thousands of Linwood residents came out to celebrate the grand opening of Sunshine Market. Occupying 5,000 square meters in the ground floor of the recently renovated six-story Lancing Building, the new grocery store offers a wide variety of fresh produce, meats, bread, and more.

While the Linwood neighborhood has seen significant growth over the past decade, one thing it has lacked is a grocery store. In fact, residents have had to travel a minimum of 5 kilometers to shop for food. The new store, located in the heart of Linwood, has 15,000 residents living within 1 kilometer.

The city purchased the Lancing Building last year as part of Mayor Justin Bendix's Downtown and Beyond plan. Since taking office two years ago, the mayor has made economic development of the downtown area and its surrounding neighborhoods his top priority.

To	Kaley Chase <kchase@sunshinemarket.com>
From	Justin Bendix <jbendix@cityofdanton.gov>
Subject	Parking Issues
Date	August 28

Dear Ms. Chase:

Thank you for contacting me with your concerns about parking on Main Street. I understand the frustration that you and your customers must be experiencing. Rest assured that the city is dedicated to remedying this situation. We are currently moving forward with the second phase of our development plan. It includes the construction of a new parking garage on the corner of 10th Avenue and Main Street, approximately 500 meters from your store. Parking will be free for your customers.

Regards,

Justin Bendix

NOTICE

To: All Customers

We have received numerous complaints about the parking situation in front of the store. Please avoid parking there. Instead, use Coleman Street behind the store or any of the nearby side streets. If you are unable to carry your groceries to your vehicle, our staff will be more than happy to assist you.

The city has assured us that it is working hard to find a solution to this pressing issue. In the meantime, your patience and cooperation are greatly appreciated.

Sincerely,

The Management
Sunshine Market

---

196 What is suggested about Linwood?

(A) City buses do not serve the area.
(B) Many of its residents work downtown.
(C) There used to be no proper grocery store before Sunshine Market.
(D) Economic growth has been limited there.

197 What is most likely true about the Downtown and Beyond plan?

(A) It proposes to add more housing.
(B) It will be completed in two years.
(C) It was started by the former mayor.
(D) It will expand available parking.

198 What is the purpose of the notice?

(A) To explain a situation
(B) To voice a complaint
(C) To criticize customers
(D) To propose a new service

199 In the notice, the word "hard" in paragraph 2, line 1, is closest in meaning to

(A) strongly
(B) diligently
(C) firmly
(D) mostly

200 What is suggested about Sunshine Market?

(A) It is located on Main Street.
(B) It has about 5,000 customers.
(C) Few customers have their own cars.
(D) It will build a new parking lot.

GO ON TO THE NEXT PAGE

잠깐!! 시작 전 **꼭** 확인하세요!

- 실제 시험과 같이 책상을 정리하고 마음의 준비를 하세요.
- 핸드폰은 잠깐 끄고 대신 아날로그 시계를 활용해 보세요.
- 제한 시간은 120분입니다. 제한 시간을 꼭 지켜주세요.
- 어렵다고 넘어가지 마세요. 가능하면 차례대로 풀어 보세요.

Actual Test

02

시작 시간   :

종료 시간   :

LISTENING TEST

In the Listening test, you will be asked to demonstrate how well you understand spoken English. The entire Listening test will last approximately 45 minutes. There are four parts, and directions are given for each part. You must mark your answers on the separate answer sheet. Do not write your answers in your test book.

PART 1

Directions: For each question in this part, you will hear four statements about a picture in your test book. When you hear the statements, you must select the one statement that best describes what you see in the picture. Then find the number of the question on your answer sheet and mark your answer. The statements will not be printed in your test book and will be spoken only one time.

Example

Sample Answer

Ⓐ ● Ⓒ Ⓓ

Statement (B), "The man is working at a desk," is the best description of the picture, so you should select answer (B) and mark it on your answer sheet.

1

2

GO ON TO THE NEXT PAGE

3

4

5

6

GO ON TO THE NEXT PAGE ▶

PART 2

Directions: You will hear a question or statement and three responses spoken in English. They will not be printed in your test book and will be spoken only one time. Select the best response to the question or statement and mark the letter (A), (B), or (C) on your answer sheet.

7	Mark your answer on your answer sheet.	20	Mark your answer on your answer sheet.
8	Mark your answer on your answer sheet.	21	Mark your answer on your answer sheet.
9	Mark your answer on your answer sheet.	22	Mark your answer on your answer sheet.
10	Mark your answer on your answer sheet.	23	Mark your answer on your answer sheet.
11	Mark your answer on your answer sheet.	24	Mark your answer on your answer sheet.
12	Mark your answer on your answer sheet.	25	Mark your answer on your answer sheet.
13	Mark your answer on your answer sheet.	26	Mark your answer on your answer sheet.
14	Mark your answer on your answer sheet.	27	Mark your answer on your answer sheet.
15	Mark your answer on your answer sheet.	28	Mark your answer on your answer sheet.
16	Mark your answer on your answer sheet.	29	Mark your answer on your answer sheet.
17	Mark your answer on your answer sheet.	30	Mark your answer on your answer sheet.
18	Mark your answer on your answer sheet.	31	Mark your answer on your answer sheet.
19	Mark your answer on your answer sheet.		

PART 3

Directions: You will hear some conversations between two or more people. You will be asked to answer three questions about what the speakers say in each conversation. Select the best response to each question and mark the letter (A), (B), (C), or (D) on your answer sheet. The conversations will not be printed in your test book and will be spoken only one time.

32 Where are the speakers going?
  (A) To an exhibition
  (B) To a museum
  (C) To a taxi stand
  (D) To a friend's house

33 What will happen in 20 minutes?
  (A) A meeting
  (B) A bus ride
  (C) A talk
  (D) A display

34 Why does the woman suggest that she and the man walk?
  (A) There are no available taxis.
  (B) The walk would do them good.
  (C) They are close to the venue.
  (D) Buses are expensive.

35 What are the speakers mainly discussing?
  (A) Returning an item
  (B) Repairing an item of clothing
  (C) Hiring a furniture maker
  (D) Arranging a delivery

36 What day will the man be available?
  (A) Monday
  (B) Thursday
  (C) Friday
  (D) Sunday

37 According to the woman, what requires an extra fee?
  (A) An extended guarantee
  (B) Overnight shipping
  (C) A bespoke design
  (D) Removal of the existing item

38 What event does the man plan to attend?
  (A) A sports event
  (B) A concert
  (C) A theater performance
  (D) A school play

39 Why is the woman surprised?
  (A) A performance has been relocated.
  (B) An event has been cancelled.
  (C) Space is available.
  (D) Parking is charged.

40 What should the woman do by the end of the day?
  (A) Contact the booking desk
  (B) Change a schedule
  (C) Confirm her intention to attend
  (D) Issue an invitation

41 What has the woman decided to do?
  (A) Sell a building
  (B) Extend the lease
  (C) Increase the rent
  (D) Renovate a house

42 According to the woman, who will come to the unit on Saturday?
  (A) A contracting team
  (B) A vendor
  (C) A few of friends
  (D) A work crew

43 What request does the man make?
  (A) That a contract be renewed
  (B) That the dates be rearranged
  (C) That the rent be reduced
  (D) That the exterior be painted

GO ON TO THE NEXT PAGE ▶

44 Where does the woman work?

(A) At a travel agency
(B) At an employment agency
(C) At a fast food chain
(D) At a clothing store

45 What does the woman offer the man?

(A) An apprenticeship
(B) Some food samples
(C) Travel opportunities
(D) A franchise

46 What was the woman particularly interested in?

(A) A résumé
(B) A reference letter
(C) A portfolio
(D) A travel schedule

47 Where do the speakers most likely work?

(A) At a pharmacy
(B) At a fitness center
(C) At a copy center
(D) At a doctor's office

48 What does the man say he needs to see?

(A) A bill
(B) Medical information
(C) A billing statement
(D) A label

49 Why does the man say, "No harm done"?

(A) He is glad the bills are found.
(B) He has an idea to organize files.
(C) He is not concerned about the issue.
(D) He is satisfied with the women's performance.

50 Why is the woman calling?

(A) To return a key
(B) To change a reservation
(C) To dispute a charge
(D) To inform the man of the payday

51 What does the man say happened?

(A) A door was damaged.
(B) A reservation was canceled.
(C) A key was lost.
(D) All pensions were already rented out.

52 What does the woman mean when she says, "I don't get it"?

(A) She was lost in the area.
(B) She never received an inspection report.
(C) She thinks the door is too expensive.
(D) She doesn't understand the reason for the fee.

53 What are the speakers mainly discussing?

(A) A construction material
(B) A bid for a contract
(C) An affected deadline
(D) A completed task

54 Why does the man say, "that's a shame"?

(A) He is not proud of what the woman did.
(B) He is expressing sympathy.
(C) He expected the result.
(D) He is excited to hear the news.

55 What does the man remind the woman about?

(A) She has gained experience.
(B) She will need his help soon.
(C) She has to put in a higher bid.
(D) She was recently hired.

56 What position is the man applying for?

(A) Second in command
(B) Company engineer
(C) Colonel in chief
(D) Chief lieutenant

57 What does the man say he was in charge of?

(A) Planning a campaign
(B) Training army personnel
(C) Teaching at a school
(D) Constructing a building

58 Why did the man leave his last post?

(A) He was employed on a temporary basis.
(B) He was offered a better position.
(C) He wanted to diversify.
(D) He moved to a different city.

---

59 Where do the speakers most likely work?

(A) In a doctor's office
(B) In a decorating shop
(C) In an employment agency
(D) At a music store

60 What does the man ask the woman about?

(A) The location of some information
(B) The time of an interview
(C) The contact details of a painter
(D) The cost of an item

61 What does the woman say is happening today?

(A) A business is relocating.
(B) New equipment is being installed.
(C) An office is being refurbished.
(D) A filing system is being updated.

62 What type of work does the man most likely do?

(A) He designs products.
(B) He coordinates training sessions.
(C) He provides landscape services.
(D) He heads advertising campaigns.

63 What are the speakers mainly discussing?

(A) Sports equipment
(B) Gardening clothing
(C) A cleaning product
(D) A wireless computer

64 According to the man, what will happen this week?

(A) A marketing campaign will be launched.
(B) A manufacturing process will start.
(C) A product will be ready for sale.
(D) A research study will take place.

GO ON TO THE NEXT PAGE

Staff	Extension
Paul Smith	234
Ronny Hanks	235
Ginger Harrison	236
Kelly Shaffer	237

Lunch Menu	
Fresh Salad	$8
Hearty Soup	$9
Personal Pizza	$12
Salmon Sandwich	$7

65 According to the woman, what does the man have 45 days to do?

(A) Apply for a promotion
(B) Register his driving license
(C) Enroll in an insurance plan
(D) Hire a full-time employee

66 What does the man want to obtain?

(A) An insurance card
(B) A list of entire staff
(C) A new phone number
(D) Information about specific benefits

67 Look at the graphic. What number will the man call?

(A) 234
(B) 235
(C) 236
(D) 237

68 What does the man say he needs to do at noon?

(A) Have a business meeting
(B) Take a bus
(C) See a friend
(D) Return to the office

69 Look at the graphic. How much will the man pay for his food?

(A) $8
(B) $9
(C) $12
(D) $7

70 What does the woman say she will do next?

(A) Set the man's table with dishes
(B) Return with a part of the man's order
(C) Bring the check
(D) Buy a bottle of wine

PART 4

Directions: You will hear some talks given by a single speaker. You will be asked to answer three questions about what the speaker says in each talk. Select the best response to each question and mark the letter (A), (B), (C), or (D) on your answer sheet. The talks will not be printed in your test book and will be spoken only one time.

71 What happened today at the municipal library?

(A) An extension was opened.
(B) A new curator was appointed.
(C) An exhibit space closed.
(D) Some media were invited.

72 Who is Richard Blaine?

(A) A teacher
(B) A librarian
(C) A curator
(D) An architect

73 According to the speaker, what will the library offer on Sunday?

(A) Free food and drink
(B) Free computer access
(C) Instructional videos
(D) Library vouchers

74 What kind of business did the caller reach?

(A) A department store
(B) A solicitor's firm
(C) A royal residence
(D) A governmental department

75 Why is the business closed?

(A) A national holiday is observed.
(B) Some departments have merged.
(C) A ceremony is taking place.
(D) The office has shut down.

76 When will the business reopen?

(A) After a few hours
(B) Tomorrow
(C) In two days
(D) Next week

77 What is being advertised?

(A) Appliance maintenance
(B) Residential repairs
(C) Technician training
(D) Cooking classes

78 Why are listeners asked to call?

(A) To reach an agreement
(B) To arrange an inspection
(C) To receive a new oven
(D) To sign up for discounts

79 What will happen at the beginning of the month?

(A) Payments will be collected.
(B) A program will start.
(C) A discount scheme comes into force.
(D) A report will be issued.

80 What type of event is being held?

(A) An art gallery opening
(B) An awards ceremony
(C) A conservative meeting
(D) A play preview

81 What field does Ms. Jukkin work in?

(A) Writing
(B) Teaching
(C) Catering
(D) Publishing

82 What will listeners most likely do next?

(A) Watch a video
(B) Hear a speech
(C) Eat a meal
(D) Pick up a brochure

GO ON TO THE NEXT PAGE

83 Where most likely does the speaker work?

(A) At a used car lot
(B) At a gas station
(C) At a supermarket
(D) At a vehicle repair outlet

84 What does Mr. Ubamo want to do?

(A) Ask for a job
(B) Repair his truck
(C) Advertise a business
(D) Sell a vehicle

85 What should Mr. Ubamo do when he returns the call?

(A) Speak to a manager
(B) Ask for an estimate
(C) Negotiate the price
(D) Provide credit card details

86 Who most likely is the speaker?

(A) A guide
(B) An animal activist
(C) A fitness trainer
(D) A logger

87 What does the man mean when he says, "No one can guarantee anything, though"?

(A) He is uncertain if they are going in the right direction.
(B) He is uncertain if the weather will be good.
(C) He cannot be sure this hike is not hard.
(D) He cannot be sure they will see any animals.

88 What does the speaker suggest the listeners do?

(A) Wear warm cloths
(B) Bring a map
(C) Carry water
(D) Stay with a group

89 What most likely was the topic of the seminar?

(A) Organizing a task force
(B) Cooperating with colleagues
(C) Coordinating a hiring process
(D) Arranging assignments effectively

90 What did the speaker pass out to the listeners?

(A) A recent article
(B) A list of resources
(C) An enrollment form
(D) A list of attendees

91 Why does the speaker say, "Make sure to go over all of these"?

(A) To celebrate a product launch
(B) To give an assignment
(C) To promote other seminars
(D) To recommend Web sites

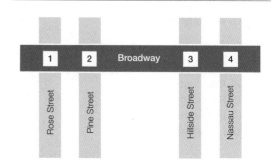

92 What is causing traffic delays at exit number 4?

(A) A car accident
(B) A slippery road
(C) Road repair work
(D) A scheduled town event

93 What does the Transportation Department recommend?

(A) Using detours
(B) Commuting by public transportation
(C) Not passing through downtown
(D) Avoiding a certain bridge

94 Look at the graphic. What traffic light is not working?

(A) 1
(B) 2
(C) 3
(D) 4

The amount of negative feedback

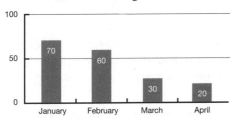

INVOICE	
Product Number	Description
P365	Soccer ball (# 3)
P345	Basketball (# 2)
P443	Running shoes (# 2 pairs)
P334	Track Jacket (# 1)

95 What does the speaker say about the customer service team?

(A) It was recently transferred.
(B) It received a pay increase.
(C) Its workforce has been expanded.
(D) It still needs to improve.

96 What was the cause of negative comments?

(A) An ambiguous policy
(B) An expensive service price
(C) Untrained staff
(D) A defective product

97 Look at the graphic. When was the training session held?

(A) In January
(B) In February
(C) In March
(D) In April

98 Why is the speaker calling?

(A) To cancel an order
(B) To ask a preference
(C) To ask for a payment
(D) To sell a product

99 Look at the graphic. Which item is currently out of stock?

(A) P365
(B) P345
(C) P443
(D) P334

100 What does the speaker offer to do?

(A) Refund some money
(B) Waive a shipping fee
(C) Upgrade a shipping method
(D) Cancel an order

This is the end of the Listening test. Turn to Part 5 in your test book.

GO ON TO THE NEXT PAGE

READING TEST

In the Reading test, you will read a variety of texts and answer several different types of reading comprehension questions. The entire Reading test will last 75 minutes. There are three parts, and directions are given for each part. You are encouraged to answer as many questions as possible within the time allowed.

You must mark your answers on the separate answer sheet. Do not write your answers in your test book.

PART 5

Directions: A word or phrase is missing in each of the sentences below. Four answer choices are given below each sentence. Select the best answer to complete the sentence. Then mark the letter (A), (B), (C), or (D) on your answer sheet.

101 Mr. Lin has handed in his expense claim, but Ms. Anker has not yet finished -------.

    (A) hers
    (B) her
    (C) herself
    (D) she

102 HTR Company offers ------- wireless service at affordable yearly rates.

    (A) reliable
    (B) reliant
    (C) reliably
    (D) reliability

103 Fun & Turn ------- an online newsletter that is emailed to customers.

    (A) publisher
    (B) publishes
    (C) publish
    (D) publishable

104 ------- the Internet is an excellent place to exchange ideas, many people now join online forums.

    (A) Because
    (B) So
    (C) Owing to
    (D) After

105 When ------- a moving company, you should ask for an accurate estimate.

    (A) choice
    (B) choosing
    (C) chosen
    (D) choose

106 Mr. Dorson is considered a welcome ------- to the financial team because of his extensive knowledge in the area.

    (A) output
    (B) addition
    (C) response
    (D) reception

107 Creating an impressive résumé of ------- can be easy and simple with the help of the Job-hunt program.

    (A) you
    (B) your own
    (C) your
    (D) yourself

108 The battery life of your laptop can ------- by shutting it down when not in use.

    (A) extends
    (B) have extended
    (C) be extended
    (D) extending

109 Employees who want to access the office ------- the holiday must request permission in advance.

(A) since
(B) among
(C) during
(D) next

110 In an effort ------- compliance, auditors have to check all areas of the factory.

(A) ensures
(B) to be ensured
(C) to ensure
(D) were ensured

111 You should become thoroughly ------- with the software program before you take an on-line class.

(A) familiarization
(B) familiarize
(C) familiarity
(D) familiar

112 JPR Mortgage Company makes it easy to get a housing loan ------- your present financial status.

(A) depending
(B) regardless of
(C) even if
(D) as long as

113 Following a long discussion, the proposal to update the lobby furnishings was ------- accepted.

(A) finally
(B) rarely
(C) exactly
(D) immensely

114 Reservations ------- through the hotel Web site must be confirmed 12 hours before check-in.

(A) make
(B) are made
(C) made
(D) will make

115 Earlier this year, Bashir Khan interviewed several celebrities ------- have appeared on the cover of the *Star on Stage* magazine.

(A) since
(B) recently
(C) where
(D) who

116 Representatives of several local shops reported remarkable sales this year ------- the region's weak economy.

(A) even though
(B) in case
(C) provided that
(D) notwithstanding

117 Marston Breweries recruited extra staff members to ------- unprecedented demand throughout the holiday period.

(A) estimate
(B) advertise
(C) propose
(D) accommodate

118 Your questions will be given ------- attention and you will receive a phone call within three business days.

(A) prompt
(B) promptly
(C) promptness
(D) more promptly

119 Clive and Dunn's Fitness Center has ------- in boxing and martial arts for over 5 years.

(A) offered
(B) specialized
(C) maintained
(D) consisted

120 All events planned for the Three Corners Hotel ------- until damage to the main hall has been fixed.

(A) are postponing
(B) will be postponed
(C) should postpone
(D) postponing

GO ON TO THE NEXT PAGE

121 Cinquento Limited has become more ------- focused on social media advertising over the past twelve months.

(A) narrowly
(B) narrowing
(C) narrower
(D) narrows

122 The event venue is ------- enough to accommodate more than 1,000 people from all around the city.

(A) included
(B) overall
(C) insufficient
(D) spacious

123 ------- Yingtan Motors begins trading in Japan is dependent on the feasibility report being undertaken by its financial consultants.

(A) Whether
(B) Although
(C) While
(D) Despite

124 The Gourmet Best restaurant is seeking an apprentice with a strong interest in ------- the culinary art.

(A) to learn
(B) will learn
(C) learning
(D) learns

125 Market research reports show that a hotel's level of ------- can directly affect customer satisfaction.

(A) clean
(B) cleanly
(C) cleanlier
(D) cleanliness

126 Cough medication manufactured by Procten Limited is formulated ------- for adults and should not be given to young children.

(A) alternatively
(B) partially
(C) mutually
(D) exclusively

127 The development of containers in specific sizes and shapes helped boost ------- across the entire shipping industry.

(A) standardize
(B) standardized
(C) more standardized
(D) standardization

128 ------- using our online bill payment system, you must first fill in the registration form.

(A) Before
(B) So that
(C) In order
(D) According to

129 It has been increasingly difficult to ------- authentic antique furniture from imitations.

(A) integrate
(B) suppose
(C) distinguish
(D) modify

130 Daley Incorporated intends to hold a company picnic to ------- cooperation and teamwork among all employees.

(A) proceed
(B) facilitate
(C) retrieve
(D) convince

PART 6

Directions: Read the texts that follow. A word, phrase, or sentence is missing in parts of each text. Four answer choices for each question are given below the text. Select the best answer to complete the text. Then mark the letter (A), (B), (C), or (D) on your answer sheet.

Questions 131-134 refer to the following memo.

MEMO

To: All Technical Support Staff Members
From: Fiona Norton
Subject: Training Courses

Over the next two weeks, we will be offering several ------- training courses to employees in our
                                               131.

department. The objective of these programs is to provide technical support staff members with

an opportunity to enhance their expertise and knowledge. The six-hour workshops will deal with

an array of topics, including addressing frequent technical issues, satisfying particular customer

needs, and improving productivity. ------- the courses are not mandatory, employees are strongly
                                      132.

advised to participate. All training-related expenses ------- by the company.
                                            133.

The courses are being organized by Joice Training (www.joicetraining.com). -------.
                                                      134.

---

131 (A) compulsory
    (B) constant
    (C) lengthy
    (D) optional

132 (A) Due to
    (B) Even though
    (C) So that
    (D) While

133 (A) were covered
    (B) will have covered
    (C) will be covered
    (D) have covered

134 (A) We apologize for any inconvenience this
        may cause.
    (B) Those interested can find a schedule on
        the company's Web site.
    (C) Only those supervisors who have
        completed a course can obtain
        certificates.
    (D) Thank you for your help in resolving this
        challenging situation.

GO ON TO THE NEXT PAGE

Questions 135-138 refer to the following press release.

Los Angeles — Tocom Financial has announced that it will ------- a new investment advisory
                                                             135.
service for retail clients by the end of the month. This new service will combine the expertise of a

------- advisor with the convenience of a mobile application.
  136.

Here's how it works. -------. After answering a series of questions and entering personal financial
                     137.
information, users will be contacted by a financial advisor who will provide guidance customized

to each unique situation. Users can chat with their assigned advisors around the clock if they

have further questions.

The cost for this service ------- to be about 0.5% of managed assets per year. Users' assets
                          138.
must be held in a Tocom Financial account, where several hundred investment options are

available.

135 (A) waive
(B) imitate
(C) unveil
(D) cancel

136 (A) profession
(B) professional
(C) professionally
(D) professionalism

137 (A) Users should first download an
application on their smartphones.
(B) Customers are worried about personal
information leakage.
(C) Please browse our Web site to view
additional products.
(D) Computer software has advanced
considerably recently.

138 (A) expects
(B) expected
(C) is expected
(D) has expected

Questions 139-142 refer to the following e-mail.

To: Canberra Finance Department
From: Brett Ling
Date: August 12
Subject: Legal Filing

Dear all:

I am writing with news and updates from the Government finance department. -------, there is a
139.
new law that requires all tax invoices and corporation documents to be submitted electronically.

I know some of us are already familiar with the online system at www.canberracorp/govfiling and

have found it quite complex. -------. Then enter the password, ensuring that you enter the correct
140.
reference number so that ------- individual details can be entered in the correct place.
141.

Please contact me via e-mail with any questions about this -------.
142.

Yours,

Brett Ling

139 (A) Additionally
(B) Initially
(C) Conversely
(D) Apparently

140 (A) You first need to find the relevant page
for inputting information.
(B) You should print out the registration form.
(C) You can take online courses to get used
to it.
(D) A fine may be imposed unless you follow
the tax regulation.

141 (A) their
(B) your
(C) his
(D) my

142 (A) procedure
(B) research
(C) report
(D) problem

GO ON TO THE NEXT PAGE

To: Cecilia Feridino <cferidino@hmail.net>
From: Darcey Kerr <dkerr@homedecor.com>
Subject: Your submission
Date: June 10

Dear Ms. Feridino:

Thank you for your submission to our -------. Your article, "How to make your home look better,"
143.
------- in the July issue of *Home Decor* with only small changes. Both of the photographs that
144.
you sent us will accompany the text. As indicated in your contract, you will be given $300 for the

work. I believe you said you would now like it deposited directly into your checking account. -------.
145.

It is always a pleasure to work with you. Should you have ------- ideas for future publication,
146.
please let me know.

Sincerely,

Darcey Kerr
Editor-in-chief
Home Decor

143 (A) publication
(B) photographer
(C) council
(D) exhibition

144 (A) appeared
(B) will appear
(C) to appear
(D) has appeared

145 (A) The terms of the contract can be
renegotiated in two years.
(B) If so, please verify your account
information with our payroll department.
(C) This is a great chance to increase your
salary.
(D) Therefore, we are unable to process your
payment now.

146 (A) adding
(B) additional
(C) addition
(D) additionally

PART 7

Directions: In this part you will read a selection of texts, such as magazine and newspaper articles, e-mails, and instant messages. Each text or set of texts is followed by several questions. Select the best answer for each question and mark the letter (A), (B), (C), or (D) on your answer sheet.

Questions 147-148 refer to the following information.

The following pages illustrate how to work your new Tanvak printer and how to connect it to electronic devices in your home. If any of the instructions confuse you, please call a Tanvak customer service team member during working hours. Service centers and all contact details are listed alphabetically on Page 4.

147 Where would the information most likely appear?

(A) In an owner's manual
(B) In a product catalog
(C) In a telephone directory
(D) In an employee manual

148 According to the information, how can a Tanvak representative help?

(A) By explaining a return policy
(B) By processing invoices
(C) By scheduling a service call
(D) By clarifying instructions

GO ON TO THE NEXT PAGE

Lamas Heritage Center

The Lamas Heritage Center holds more than one million books, photographs, and artifacts related to the cultural history of our local areas. The center provides information and resources on historic and significant events that have shaped our traditions. Together with a comprehensive historical collection of books and letters, the center contains a selection of photographs and images from other communities and countries that have influenced our heritage. Our extensive collection of published works and archives can be accessed by local residents as well as tourists and visitors. The center's history section contains a number of ancient artifacts with a photographic display that contains thousands of images, some taken by local people. We can provide copies of any of the photographs for a small charge. Appointments and reference assistance to those wishing to use our archives are available upon request.

149 What is the information about?

(A) A community event
(B) A research library
(C) A local photography course
(D) A tourist information center

150 What is available for purchase?

(A) Traditional gifts
(B) Replica documents
(C) Copies of magazine articles
(D) Reprints of photographs

Questions 151-152 refer to the following text message chain.

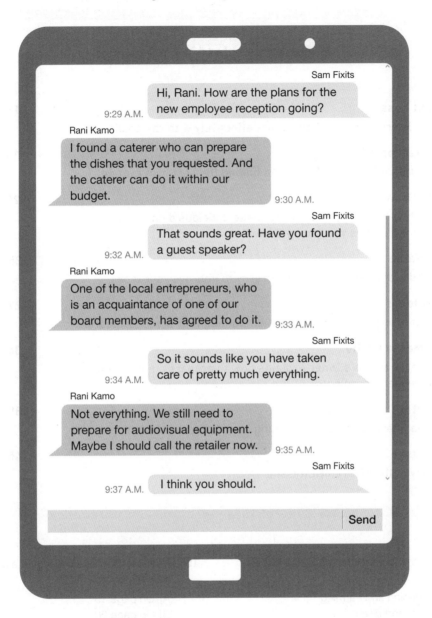

Sam Fixits

Hi, Rani. How are the plans for the new employee reception going?

9:29 A.M.

Rani Kamo

I found a caterer who can prepare the dishes that you requested. And the caterer can do it within our budget.

9:30 A.M.

Sam Fixits

That sounds great. Have you found a guest speaker?

9:32 A.M.

Rani Kamo

One of the local entrepreneurs, who is an acquaintance of one of our board members, has agreed to do it.

9:33 A.M.

Sam Fixits

So it sounds like you have taken care of pretty much everything.

9:34 A.M.

Rani Kamo

Not everything. We still need to prepare for audiovisual equipment. Maybe I should call the retailer now.

9:35 A.M.

Sam Fixits

I think you should.

9:37 A.M.

Send

151 What is indicated about the reception?

(A) A board member will be the speaker.
(B) The food will not cost more than expected.
(C) The equipment has already been set up.
(D) Ms. Kamo is a new employee.

152 At 9:37 A.M., what does Mr. Fixits mean when he writes, "I think you should"?

(A) He wants Ms. Kamo to pick up the equipment.
(B) He agrees that the reception is a good idea.
(C) He wants Ms. Kamo to contact the store.
(D) He has to end the conversation immediately.

GO ON TO THE NEXT PAGE

Questions 153-155 refer to the following table of contents in a magazine.

CONTENTS

Issue 613

Weight Loss   **11**
Amelia Sparks explains how to diet effectively with raw foods.

Exercise for All   **15**
Our editors offer essential tips on finding the best gym routine.

Home Grown   **20**
Cate Kitova demonstrates how to make delicious dishes with healthy vegetables you grow yourself.

Face Value   **25**
Lea Cedra discusses cosmetic surgery to improve your looks.

Great Ideas   **29**
Paloma Gregg shares images of her walking tour across Bulgaria.

Chef Massa Frulio   **34**
The chef at Massa's Diner explains how to prepare a perfect meal using low fat ingredients.

Walk It Off   **39**
Rowena Shaw explains why walking and hiking are the best exercise.

Next Issue   **45**
Preview of the SEPTEMBER issue

153 What is the focus of the magazine?

(A) Exercise and Sports
(B) Gardening and Farming
(C) Health and Beauty
(D) Food and Cooking

154 According to the table of contents, who recently traveled abroad?

(A) Ms. Gregg
(B) Mr. Kitova
(C) Mr. Massa
(D) Ms. Shaw

155 Where in the magazine would a recipe most likely be found?

(A) On page 15
(B) On page 20
(C) On page 25
(D) On page 45

Questions 156-158 refer to the following notice.

Blenratha Talent Contest

Do you have a talent other people would like to see? Then apply for a place in the Blenratha Talent Contest.

What is the Blenratha Talent Contest?

The contest was started by Alex Balden, a resident of Blenratha, who also owns the Red Lion Public House on the High Street and was looking for an actor to perform at his venue. -[1]-. The winner of the competition will be rewarded with 100 pounds to launch their performance career. Last year's winner, for example, went on to play at sold out venues around the UK. The winner will be judged by local residents and a representative from St. Andrew's School of Musical Theater at the Blenratha Community Center on August 21. -[2]-.

Am I eligible?

The contest is open to every Scottish national, regardless of age, status or ability. Amateur and semi-professional artists are welcome to enter. -[3]-.

How can I apply?

Entries must be submitted either by mail or by e-mail by July 2. Application forms and entry details can be found on our Web site: www.blenratha/sc/entry_form. If you have any questions, Hamish Roscoe is your main contact at (050) 555-0258. -[4]-. If you want to put forward your name as a member of the judging panel, please contact Brenda Rhys, our evaluation coordinator, at (050) 555-0259.

156 What is stated about the Red Lion?

(A) It hosts talent shows weekly.
(B) It is located outside of Blenratha.
(C) It is owned by Alex Balden.
(D) It is next to St. Andrew's School of Musical Theater.

157 According to the notice, why would an individual contact Ms. Rhys?

(A) To request a deadline extension
(B) To volunteer to help determine the contest winner
(C) To confirm attendance
(D) To inquire about official rules

158 In which of the positions marked [1], [2], [3], and [4] does the following sentence best belong?

"Entries are also welcomed from those who have entered the competition in previous years."

(A) [1]
(B) [2]
(C) [3]
(D) [4]

GO ON TO THE NEXT PAGE

No more anti-social behavior in the city

By Grace Galento

In an effort to ease anti-social behavior in the streets of Entebbe, the city council is planning changes to the legal drinking hours. –[1]–. "Our city is at its loudest and rowdiest at nighttime," said Aruba Challis, spokesperson for the Entebbe City Council. "That's because local people and tourists alike head to the downtown region to enjoy the entertainment available, including bars, nightclubs and casinos. When visitors come into town, they generally come by free public buses so they don't have to worry about drinking and driving. This leads to increased disruptions on the street." –[2]–.

Currently, certain bars are offering half-price drinks from 6 P.M. to 8 P.M., and some bars offer cheap drinks all through the night. "This needs to change." Ms. Challis said. "We'd like to introduce a common pricing structure as other cities do, where prices are the same in every venue." –[3]–.

If the proposed change goes into effect, it will be one of many introduced recently. In May, a new card system limits the number of drinks purchased per person from 6 P.M. to 8 P.M. –[4]–.

159 What is suggested about Entebbe?

(A) It has too many entertainment venues.
(B) It must pay a surcharge on alcohol.
(C) It has trouble with disorderly behavior.
(D) It has a problem with drunk driving.

160 What is the city council considering?

(A) Raising the prices of drinks
(B) Creating new parking areas
(C) Lowering the amount of people allowed in a bar
(D) Introducing security staff

161 What has recently happened in Entebbe?

(A) Some downtown stores were damaged.
(B) It became harder to get a license to open a bar.
(C) Many more bars and clubs were opened.
(D) New monitoring measures for drinkers were introduced.

162 In which of the positions marked [1], [2], [3], and [4] does the following sentence best belong?

"The card is given at the door and stamped upon each purchase."

(A) [1]
(B) [2]
(C) [3]
(D) [4]

Questions **163-165** refer to the following online chat discussion.

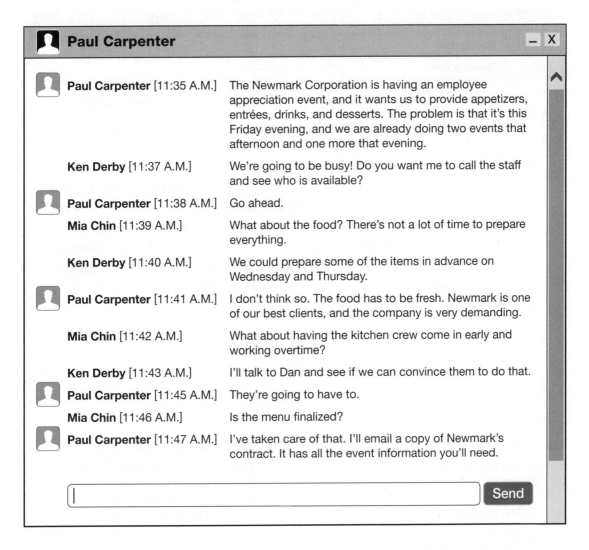

Paul Carpenter — X

Paul Carpenter [11:35 A.M.]   The Newmark Corporation is having an employee appreciation event, and it wants us to provide appetizers, entrées, drinks, and desserts. The problem is that it's this Friday evening, and we are already doing two events that afternoon and one more that evening.

Ken Derby [11:37 A.M.]   We're going to be busy! Do you want me to call the staff and see who is available?

Paul Carpenter [11:38 A.M.]   Go ahead.

Mia Chin [11:39 A.M.]   What about the food? There's not a lot of time to prepare everything.

Ken Derby [11:40 A.M.]   We could prepare some of the items in advance on Wednesday and Thursday.

Paul Carpenter [11:41 A.M.]   I don't think so. The food has to be fresh. Newmark is one of our best clients, and the company is very demanding.

Mia Chin [11:42 A.M.]   What about having the kitchen crew come in early and working overtime?

Ken Derby [11:43 A.M.]   I'll talk to Dan and see if we can convince them to do that.

Paul Carpenter [11:45 A.M.]   They're going to have to.

Mia Chin [11:46 A.M.]   Is the menu finalized?

Paul Carpenter [11:47 A.M.]   I've taken care of that. I'll email a copy of Newmark's contract. It has all the event information you'll need.

Send

163 At what kind of company do the writers' most likely work?

(A) A restaurant
(B) A catering company
(C) A grocery store
(D) A hotel

164 Why do the writers need additional staff?

(A) A client demanded additional services.
(B) An order was not completed on time.
(C) An event was added to their schedule.
(D) A mistake was made with the scheduling.

165 At 11:45 A.M., what does Mr. Carpenter mean when he writes, "They're going to have to"?

(A) He is requiring the kitchen crew to work extra.
(B) He wants the clients to be treated with extra care.
(C) He doesn't have time to explain the situation to Dan.
(D) He needs the serving staff to come into work early.

GO ON TO THE NEXT PAGE

Questions 166-167 refer to the following e-mail.

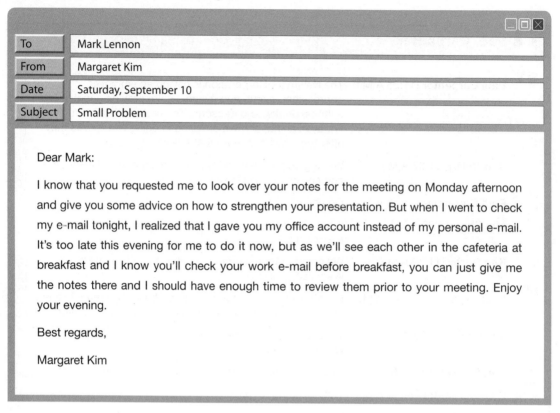

To   Mark Lennon

From   Margaret Kim

Date   Saturday, September 10

Subject   Small Problem

Dear Mark:

I know that you requested me to look over your notes for the meeting on Monday afternoon and give you some advice on how to strengthen your presentation. But when I went to check my e-mail tonight, I realized that I gave you my office account instead of my personal e-mail. It's too late this evening for me to do it now, but as we'll see each other in the cafeteria at breakfast and I know you'll check your work e-mail before breakfast, you can just give me the notes there and I should have enough time to review them prior to your meeting. Enjoy your evening.

Best regards,

Margaret Kim

166 What problem did Ms. Kim experience?

(A) She lost Mr. Lennon's notes.
(B) She did not have time to meet Mr. Lennon.
(C) She provided the wrong contact information.
(D) She forgot to check her e-mail account.

167 What does Ms. Kim ask Mr. Lennon to do?

(A) Give her the material in person
(B) Ask another employee for help
(C) Send the documents via fax
(D) Stop by her office in the morning

Questions168-171 refer to the following flyer.

Have you recently relocated to Miami?
Join our orientation: Getting Around Miami.

Presentation Schedule

10:00 A.M. Hitting the City - options for public transport (Room 212)	

11:00 A.M. Renting a condominium or house in Miami (Room 212)	**11:00 A.M.** Dealing with finance and banking (Room 206)

12:00 P.M. Getting to know your neighbors (Room 208)	**12:00 P.M.** Finding employment in Miami (Room 206)

1:00 P.M. Out and about in Miami — a round-up of local events and attractions (Room 204)	

Please note that some of the presentations clash time-wise, so you need to decide which one to attend that will be of most value to you. The talk about public transportation and finding suitable accommodation are very popular, so in order to guarantee your seat, please arrive early.

These talks are all conducted in English, but there are translated transcripts in French, Spanish and Arabic. Food and drinks are available for purchase.

After the last presentation, you are invited to take a guided tour of the main areas of attraction. A long-term resident of Miami Beach and a member of the Orientation Committee will be leading the tour. For more details, visit www.miamiwelcoming.com.

168 For whom is the flyer likely intended?

(A) Miami town officials
(B) Tourists visiting America
(C) Miami tourist board members
(D) Residents who are new to the area

169 Where are the most popular presentations held?

(A) In Room 212
(B) In Room 208
(C) In Room 206
(D) In Room 204

170 What is indicated about the Miami Orientation Committee?

(A) It provides free transport to visitors.
(B) It will soon offer a wider variety of services.
(C) It has offices in multiple locations.
(D) It provides materials in several languages.

171 According to the flyer, what can attendees do after the presentations?

(A) Go on a tour of the city
(B) Request membership details
(C) Reserve seats to public events
(D) Enjoy a free lunch

GO ON TO THE NEXT PAGE

July 15 — Axis 24, the company that provided photographic images for the acclaimed KeepActive TV campaign, has been nominated for the international Schiffer Prize, which has been rewarding excellence in published photography and graphic illustrations for more than 20 years. Chosen from more than 3,000 entrants, Axis 24 is the only Karachi-based photographic studio to ever be nominated. On the 20 August, a ceremony will be held in Cologne, Germany, where the winners of this year's Schiffer Prize will be announced.

"We are extremely proud of this nomination, which is a tribute to the high level of professionalism, expertise, and creativity within the company," said Aslam Minish, founder and CEO of the company.

The Schiffer Prize judges comprise a group of six top executives from advertising agencies around the world. They commented that Axis 24 was chosen for its quality and innovation within its photographic portfolio.

"We photograph everything from wildlife to sporting activities, people and nature," continued Mr. Minish, "and we liaise with our clients to ensure the end product is better than they could possibly have imagined."

Aside from the prestige of the nomination, business has increased for Axis 24, as has its public profile. When the names of the nominees were announced, the studio was inundated with requests from interested parties wanting to commission work from them. "The only way we can meet this increased demand is to hire more professional photographers and technical staff, which is precisely what our next move will be," said Mr. Minish.

More information about Axis 24 can be found at www.axis24.co.pk. Details about the Schiffer Prize are at www.schifferprize.org.

172 What is the purpose of the article?

(A) To highlight a company's accomplishments

(B) To describe the work of a famous artist

(C) To invite entrants to a photographic contest

(D) To nominate an executive for an award

173 What is suggested about the Schiffer Prize?

(A) It is a prestigious award with worldwide influence.

(B) It has been won by a Karachi-based company before.

(C) It was established by a single individual.

(D) It was first awarded to a photographic company.

174 What is NOT mentioned as an area of Axis 24 photographs?

(A) Sporting events

(B) Billboards

(C) Nature

(D) People

175 According to the article, what does Mr. Minish plan to do?

(A) Increase his public relations budget

(B) Open another photographic studio

(C) Hire additional employees

(D) Attend a ceremony in Karachi

GO ON TO THE NEXT PAGE

Questions 176-180 refer to the following Web page and e-mail.

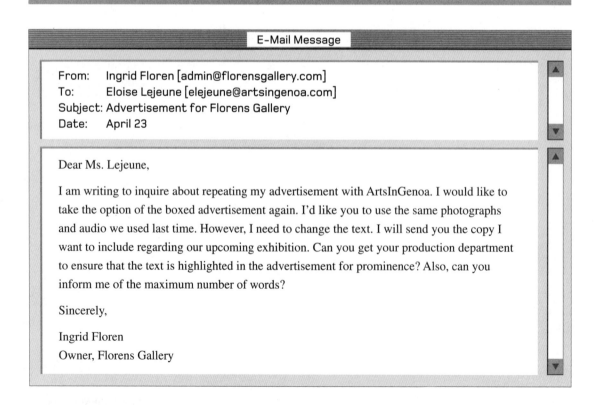

HOME | Contact us | Place an order | Customer reviews

Advertising with ArtsInGenoa: ArtsInGenoa is a long-established Web site with nearly 20,000 followers who visit us for reliable, detailed information about entertainment and attractions in the Genoa region.

Advertisements on our Web page can be displayed in the following format types:

Format 1	Format 2
A vertical banner will appear at the side of a page, either to the right or left. Audio effects and visuals cannot be displayed.	Medium-sized advertisement will appear centered at the beginning of a page. One image and one video can be included along with text.
Format 3	**Format 4**
A horizontal header banner that scrolls across the top of the page. Audio can be included.	Our largest advertisement, a boxed advertisement with up to ten photographs, video, audio and text.

To purchase advertising, please contact Eloise Lejeune at elejeune@artsingenoa.com.

E-Mail Message

From: Ingrid Floren [admin@florensgallery.com]
To: Eloise Lejeune [elejeune@artsingenoa.com]
Subject: Advertisement for Florens Gallery
Date: April 23

Dear Ms. Lejeune,

I am writing to inquire about repeating my advertisement with ArtsInGenoa. I would like to take the option of the boxed advertisement again. I'd like you to use the same photographs and audio we used last time. However, I need to change the text. I will send you the copy I want to include regarding our upcoming exhibition. Can you get your production department to ensure that the text is highlighted in the advertisement for prominence? Also, can you inform me of the maximum number of words?

Sincerely,

Ingrid Floren
Owner, Florens Gallery

176 Where does Ms. Lejeune work?

    (A) At an advertising agency
    (B) At a marketing research firm
    (C) At a gallery in Genoa
    (D) At an arts-related Web site

177 What is stated about Format 1?

    (A) It does not allow visuals.
    (B) It is the most expensive.
    (C) It can include the most text.
    (D) It can be prepared quickly.

178 In what advertisement format, is Ms. Florens most likely interested?

    (A) Format 1
    (B) Format 2
    (C) Format 3
    (D) Format 4

179 What is suggested about Florens Gallery?

    (A) It is being renovated.
    (B) It recently displayed a new exhibition.
    (C) It will be closed until further notice.
    (D) It has advertised in ArtsInGenoa before.

180 What does Ms. Floren ask about the text?

    (A) What font size it should be
    (B) What length it should be
    (C) Which format is the best
    (D) How much it costs to publish it

GO ON TO THE NEXT PAGE

ANISTON FRUIT GROWERS

Fruits and Vegetables
87 Wisteria Road, Somerset YL3
(013) 90 72 65 58
www.aniston.co.uk

If you want to grow your own fruits and vegetables, come to Aniston Fruit Growers. We offer a huge selection of plants and seeds from all over the world. Take a tour across our 6 acre working farm and decide which fruits and vegetables you'd like to grow. We offer four categories of products:

Section 1: Ground-growing fruits and vegetables

Section 2: Tree-growing fruits

Section 3: Root vegetables

Section 4: Exotic fruits and vegetables from around the world

Our gardeners speak many different languages and will be happy to answer any queries about the best practices for growing, nurturing and picking fruits and vegetables.

Looking for something exotic and different? At the entrance, ask for our master gardener, who will show you our international produce.

After you make your selection, Aniston Fruit Growers can ship your order anywhere in the UK.

Aniston Fruit Growers Order Form

Type	Quantity
1. Red peppers	100
2. Green chilies	100
3. Fruit tree: apples	1
4. Raspberry plants	300
5. Strawberry plants	200

Customer Name: Angela Stallard
Delivery Date: March 12
Address: 26 Hill Rise, Yeovil, Somerset
Phone: (01398) 319553

When you have completed your order form, please hand it in at the service desk. The assistant will check your order, answer questions, and confirm if the items are in stock. Customers should receive their order within a week of the original order. Damaged plants or trees must be reported within one day of their delivery to your location.

181 What is suggested about Aniston Fruit Growers?

(A) It allows customers to explore its gardens.

(B) It often ships exotic vegetables internationally.

(C) It sells most of its produce to local farms and orchards.

(D) It will replace any fruit trees that fail to flourish.

182 According to the advertisement, what information can employees give customers?

(A) Selecting the best recipes for exotic produce

(B) Geographical origins of each fruit and vegetable

(C) Pricing for discounts on large orders

(D) Advice on how to grow fruits and vegetables

183 How can customers ask for unusual plants?

(A) By speaking to a master gardener

(B) By mailing a separate application to the company

(C) By visiting the Fruit Growers' Web site

(D) By handing an order form to a gardening expert

184 Where will the Fruit Growers employees find most of Ms. Stallard's order?

(A) In section 1

(B) In section 2

(C) In section 3

(D) In section 4

185 According to the form, what must Ms. Stallard do by March 13?

(A) Inform the company of any problems with her purchase

(B) Pay for her fruit tree order plus the delivery charge

(C) Return any extra plants that were delivered in error

(D) Plant the items that she has purchased

GO ON TO THE NEXT PAGE

Questions 186-190 refer to the following Web page, list and article.

---

http://www.sandeventcontest.com

Event Name: Summer Sand Sculpture Contest

Location: Marquise Beach, Nova Scotia

Dates: August 15-18

Contact: Jeremy Chan

About: This annual event, now in its fifth year, brings in over 80 professional and amateur contestants from around the world and includes both solo and team categories with about 12,000 visitors in attendance in the preceding year. The contest has become one of the most popular beach events in Nova Scotia. Marquise Beach, one of the largest sandy beaches in this part of Canada, is located about 40 minutes from Halifax. In addition to sculpting, the four-day festival boasts music performances, an array of food vendors, and sand-sculpting classes for visitors. Admission is free, but there is a $10 charge for parking.

The Winners of the Fifth Annual Summer Sand Sculpture Contest

* Solo Category

Placement	Name	Country	The title
First Prize	Rachel Murtagh	Australia	Green Mermaid
Second Prize	Melinda Graham	New Zealand	Pod of Dolphin
Third Prize	Jamari Yoneda	U.S.	Hearst Castle
Fourth Prize	John Peters	Brazil	Pirate Ship
Fifth Prize	Jimar Guimond	Canada	Sea Creatures

What's new in Halifax?

By Eileen Tao

The annual Summer Sand Sculpture Contest took place last week and it was the perfect way to say farewell to the summer season. Thanks to the especially beautiful weather, the number of visitors was double that of the previous year.

The contest drew sculptures for both the solo and team categories. Shells, seaweeds, driftwood, and other natural materials were incorporated in some of the larger-than-life sculptures that depicted everything from sea life to free-form designs.

Rachel Murtagh from Australia beat two-time champion Melinda Graham from New Zealand with her Green Mermaid sculpture which was richly ornamented with sea glasses. All the sculptures were great but my personal favorite was Pirate Ship. The use of driftwood for a base for the sculpture was something I have never seen before.

Spectators could join the fun, too. Sculpting experts who were not competing led a free class in which everyone could participate. This, as well as entertainment and foods, provided the perfect way to enjoy the end of the summer.

186 What is indicated about contestants?

(A) They are all amateurs.
(B) They are asked to sign up in advance.
(C) They personally know Mr. Chan.
(D) They are from a variety of countries.

187 In the article, the word "drew" in the paragraph 2, line 1, is closest in meaning to

(A) withdrew
(B) attracted
(C) transferred
(D) pictured

188 What is indicated about this year's event?

(A) It had more than 20,000 visitors.
(B) It cost $10 per person to attend.
(C) It was longer than last year's event.
(D) It was held in Marquise Beach for the first time.

189 What is stated about Ms. Graham?

(A) She used seashells in her sculpture.
(B) She has given sand sculpting classes.
(C) She has won the competition previously.
(D) She recently moved to New Zealand.

190 Whose sculpture did Ms. Tao like the most?

(A) Ms. Murtagh's
(B) Mr. Yoneda's
(C) Mr. Peters'
(D) Ms. Guimond's

GO ON TO THE NEXT PAGE

Refer acquaintances to PineTop Financial, and everyone benefits!*

We appreciate the trust that you place in PineTop Financial. As a Loyal Member, you have access to our complete line of financial products and get our best rates.

To express our sincere thanks, we would like to give you $20 for each friend or family member you refer to us who opens an account. We will also give them $20 immediately after making an initial deposit of over $200 into a PineTop Online Savings Account or PineTop Investment Brokerage Account. All they need to do is register at www.PineTop.com and use special code PP880.

*This offer is only available to Loyal Members in good standing. Referrals must be new customers. Existing and former PineTop Financial employees are ineligible to participate.

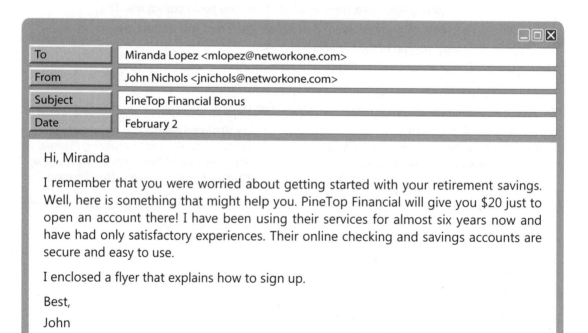

To	Miranda Lopez <mlopez@networkone.com>
From	John Nichols <jnichols@networkone.com>
Subject	PineTop Financial Bonus
Date	February 2

Hi, Miranda

I remember that you were worried about getting started with your retirement savings. Well, here is something that might help you. PineTop Financial will give you $20 just to open an account there! I have been using their services for almost six years now and have had only satisfactory experiences. Their online checking and savings accounts are secure and easy to use.

I enclosed a flyer that explains how to sign up.

Best,

John

Miranda Lopez
201 Newport Road
Salem, MA 50084

April 25

Dear Ms. Lopez:

Welcome to PineTop Financial. We opened a PineTop Online Savings Account in your name on April 15. Please check the attached Terms & Conditions and Fee Schedule.

To thank you for your new membership, we will deposit $20 into your account. The deposit should be made within 30 days of your opening date.

You can access your account by visiting www.PineTop.com. Please enter your account number and the temporary password below. Once you log in, you should reset your username and password.

Account Number: 78082210
Temporary Password: jj99-0dff-8822-ss

Should you have any inquiries, don't hesitate to call us at 1-600-555-6690.

Sincerely,

Lynn Cardona
New Accounts Representative

191 For whom is the announcement intended?

(A) PineTop Financial employees
(B) Potential investors
(C) Stockholders
(D) Existing account holders

192 Why did Mr. Nichols write to Ms. Lopez?

(A) To give some tips on investment
(B) To extend a special offer to her
(C) To confirm a recent account deposit
(D) To introduce a financial consultant

193 What is most likely true about Mr. Nichols?

(A) He is a PineTop Financial Loyal Member.
(B) He barely knows Ms. Lopez.
(C) He is employed by PineTop Financial.
(D) He recently opened a new account.

194 In the e-mail, the word "flyer" in paragraph 2, line 1, is closest in meaning to

(A) application
(B) newspaper
(C) handout
(D) receipt

195 What is suggested about Ms. Lopez?

(A) She is an existing PineTop Financial customer.
(B) She works at the same place as Lynn Cardona.
(C) She deposited more than $200 in her account.
(D) She is planning to retire in the near future.

GO ON TO THE NEXT PAGE

Questions 196-200 refer to the following announcement, schedule, and e-mail.

Management Training Seminars

New Seminar This Spring!
Basic Supervision

Congratulations on your promotion to a supervisory position. You are now the one who is in charge.

Learn the skills necessary for success in this new and challenging job. Our Basic Supervision Seminar will teach you what you need to get started. You will learn how to...

- delegate tasks effectively
- motivate employees
- deliver criticism
- plan and meet deadlines
- train new employees

This one-day seminar introduces you to many of the skills you will need to be an effective supervisor. The skills you learn will not only benefit you but will also enhance your effectiveness within your organization. To download a brochure, visit www.abc.com.

Management Training Seminars
Dover, DE   April 7-10

Basic Supervision	Tuesday, April 7 9:00 A.M. – 5:00 P.M.
	Learn the skills needed to become an effective supervisor.
Leadership and Team Building	Wednesday, April 8 8:30 A.M. – 4:30 P.M.
	Develop a set of strategies for building and leading a winning team.
Constructive Criticism	Thursday, April 9 9:00 A.M. – 5:00 P.M.
	Learn ways to bring about positive change in employees. This seminar covers effective techniques for delivering constructive criticism without making enemies.
Mastering Management	Friday, April 10 8:30 A.M. – 4:30 P.M.
	Become the best manager you can be. Learn how to implement proven techniques in today's professional workplace. Prerequisite: Advanced Management Course.

Seminars include instructional materials. In addition, participants will receive access to our online resource library.

From: vincent.baca@valenza.com
To: mpoplar@abc.com
Subject: Dover Management Seminars
Date: April 15

Dear Mr. Poplar:

I want to thank you again for the generous discount you provided to Valenza Designs that enabled nine of our employees to attend your seminars in our city last week. All of the participants, including me, have been talking about how much we learned in last week's training sessions. As in past seminars, I learned a lot from Reginald Carter. Not only is he a knowledgeable instructor, but he also models the leadership skills he teaches. I thought I had learned everything I could in his advanced management course. But I was wrong!

Sincerely,
Vincent Baca

196 In the announcement, the word "enhance" in paragraph 4, line 2, is closest in meaning to

(A) complement
(B) desire
(C) improve
(D) lead

197 What is indicated about the Dover seminars?

(A) They will be repeated at a later date.
(B) They are being offered at a discount.
(C) They require advanced registration.
(D) They give learning materials to participants.

198 What skills will probably NOT be taught at the April 7 seminar?

(A) How to instruct new staff members
(B) How to ask for promotions
(C) How to manage one's time
(D) How to correct others

199 What seminar did Mr. Carter most likely lead in Dover?

(A) Basic Supervision
(B) Leadership and Team Building
(C) Constructive Criticism
(D) Mastering Management

200 What is suggested about Mr. Baca?

(A) He supervises other employees.
(B) He attended a seminar for no charge.
(C) He is the owner of Valenza Designs.
(D) He used to work with Mr. Carter.

GO ON TO THE NEXT PAGE

잠깐!! 시작 전 **꼭** 확인하세요!

- 실제 시험과 같이 책상을 정리하고 마음의 준비를 하세요.
- 핸드폰은 잠깐 끄고 대신 아날로그 시계를 활용해 보세요.
- 제한 시간은 120분입니다. 제한 시간을 꼭 지켜주세요.
- 어렵다고 넘어가지 마세요. 가능하면 차례대로 풀어 보세요.

Actual Test

03

시작 시간	:	
종료 시간	:	

LISTENING TEST

In the Listening test, you will be asked to demonstrate how well you understand spoken English. The entire Listening test will last approximately 45 minutes. There are four parts, and directions are given for each part. You must mark your answers on the separate answer sheet. Do not write your answers in your test book.

PART 1

Directions: For each question in this part, you will hear four statements about a picture in your test book. When you hear the statements, you must select the one statement that best describes what you see in the picture. Then find the number of the question on your answer sheet and mark your answer. The statements will not be printed in your test book and will be spoken only one time.

Example

Sample Answer

Ⓐ ● Ⓒ Ⓓ

Statement (B), "The man is working at a desk," is the best description of the picture, so you should select answer (B) and mark it on your answer sheet.

1

2

GO ON TO THE NEXT PAGE

3

4

5

6

GO ON TO THE NEXT PAGE

PART 2

Directions: You will hear a question or statement and three responses spoken in English. They will not be printed in your test book and will be spoken only one time. Select the best response to the question or statement and mark the letter (A), (B), or (C) on your answer sheet.

7   Mark your answer on your answer sheet.

8   Mark your answer on your answer sheet.

9   Mark your answer on your answer sheet.

10 Mark your answer on your answer sheet.

11 Mark your answer on your answer sheet.

12 Mark your answer on your answer sheet.

13 Mark your answer on your answer sheet.

14 Mark your answer on your answer sheet.

15 Mark your answer on your answer sheet.

16 Mark your answer on your answer sheet.

17 Mark your answer on your answer sheet.

18 Mark your answer on your answer sheet.

19 Mark your answer on your answer sheet.

20 Mark your answer on your answer sheet.

21 Mark your answer on your answer sheet.

22 Mark your answer on your answer sheet.

23 Mark your answer on your answer sheet.

24 Mark your answer on your answer sheet.

25 Mark your answer on your answer sheet.

26 Mark your answer on your answer sheet.

27 Mark your answer on your answer sheet.

28 Mark your answer on your answer sheet.

29 Mark your answer on your answer sheet.

30 Mark your answer on your answer sheet.

31 Mark your answer on your answer sheet.

PART 3

Directions: You will hear some conversations between two or more people. You will be asked to answer three questions about what the speakers say in each conversation. Select the best response to each question and mark the letter (A), (B), (C), or (D) on your answer sheet. The conversations will not be printed in your test book and will be spoken only one time.

32 What is the man's complaint?

(A) His heating system does not work.
(B) His booking was cancelled.
(C) His taxi was late.
(D) His luggage is missing.

33 What does the woman offer the man?

(A) A free lift to the concert
(B) A complimentary meal
(C) An upgraded accommodation
(D) Early check-in options

34 What does the man request?

(A) An apology
(B) A partial refund
(C) Free taxi rides
(D) Assistance with his bags

---

35 What does the woman want to do?

(A) Volunteer at a gallery
(B) Register for health care
(C) Get some legal advice
(D) Undergo surgery

36 What does the man say the woman has to do?

(A) Provide her date of birth
(B) Make a contribution
(C) Attend a medical test
(D) Present her health card

37 What does the man give the woman?

(A) A list of staff
(B) A policy document
(C) A disclaimer
(D) A replacement card

38 What are the speakers discussing?

(A) Ordering supplies
(B) Installing software
(C) Scheduling an event
(D) Buying devices

39 What does the woman say she will do next?

(A) Meet with a superior
(B) Finish her work
(C) Speak with a coworker
(D) Check her schedule

40 What does the man mean when he says, "I'd say that's not anytime soon"?

(A) They are too busy to meet with the manager.
(B) They have other projects to focus on now.
(C) They are unable to purchase keyboards now.
(D) They have not received the keyboards yet.

GO ON TO THE NEXT PAGE

41 Where is the conversation taking place?

(A) At a warehouse
(B) At a delivery office
(C) At a florist shop
(D) At a hospital

42 According to the woman, why is the room number wrong?

(A) The room is occupied by a male.
(B) The patients are not allowed packages.
(C) The building only has a small number of rooms.
(D) The street name is incorrect.

43 What does the woman say she will do next?

(A) Arrange for a delivery
(B) Order some food
(C) Call for a porter
(D) Contact Ms. Callard

44 Why is the woman calling?

(A) To report to a customer
(B) To propose a project
(C) To request some changes
(D) To ask for information

45 What does the woman ask the man to do?

(A) Go over her work
(B) Add color to visual aids
(C) Contact a client
(D) Remove some colors on the graphs

46 Why does the man say, "That's not an issue"?

(A) He currently has been assigned a lot of projects.
(B) He is worried about a deadline being affected.
(C) He is almost finished writing a report.
(D) He has no problem meeting the woman's request.

47 What does the woman ask the man to do?

(A) Bring an item from stock
(B) Contact some students
(C) Turn out the lights
(D) Rearrange a cupboard

48 Why is the man unable to help?

(A) A delivery has been delayed.
(B) Some equipment has been damaged.
(C) A student requires his assistance.
(D) A lab has been closed down.

49 What will happen at 12:00?

(A) A replacement tutor will be sent.
(B) The man will buy some light bulbs.
(C) The woman's students will arrive.
(D) Different equipment will be used.

50 What does Carstairs Inc. want to advertise?

(A) A job opportunity
(B) A product
(C) An event
(D) A warehouse

51 What does the woman suggest?

(A) Offering online discounts
(B) Hiring a marketing expert
(C) Advertising in specialist media
(D) Advertising on the radio

52 What does the man say about the woman's suggestion?

(A) It was unsuccessful in the past.
(B) It will take too long.
(C) It was not possible for the company.
(D) It was too expensive to run.

53 According to the woman, what is the problem with the dress?

(A) The dress didn't fit.
(B) The fastener was faulty.
(C) The size is too small.
(D) The price is too high.

54 What will the man send to the woman?

(A) A document
(B) A new dress
(C) A discount voucher
(D) A full refund

55 What does the woman say she would prefer?

(A) To change the color of the dress
(B) To choose a different item
(C) To receive a refund
(D) To wait for a replacement

56 What problem has the woman identified?

(A) A training session has not been finished.
(B) Some documents are out of date.
(C) Some registration forms have not been collected.
(D) Some employees have given false information.

57 What does the woman say about workers who were certified more than a year ago?

(A) They need to resubmit their details.
(B) They need to undergo a written test.
(C) They have to pay for extra tuition.
(D) They must contact their supervisors.

58 What does the man ask the woman to do?

(A) Archive some documents
(B) Send some warnings
(C) Organize a workshop
(D) Provide names of workers

59 What are the speakers discussing?

(A) A growing population in certain areas
(B) An industry's hiring trend
(C) Business expansion
(D) A popular city for sales people

60 What is implied about professionals in their 30s?

(A) They are willing to relocate for work.
(B) They want to live in cities.
(C) They are a new market.
(D) They are paid well.

61 What does the woman offer to do?

(A) Collect market data
(B) Speak with building designers
(C) Put together a report
(D) Tour some buildings

GO ON TO THE NEXT PAGE

62 Where do the speakers work?

(A) At a fitness club
(B) At a doctor's surgery
(C) At a theater
(D) At a police station

63 Why will the man miss work today?

(A) He is not feeling well.
(B) He has lost his voice.
(C) He does not have a car.
(D) He has a crisis at home.

64 What do the speakers say about Miguel?

(A) He needs to be fitted for a costume.
(B) He is always reliable.
(C) He needs some additional training.
(D) He is not happy about the role.

Room	Day of reservation
4A	Monday
7B	Tuesday
4C	Wednesday
2D	Thursday

65 What most likely will the man do tomorrow?

(A) Pick up some materials
(B) Meet a client
(C) Test some devices
(D) Finish a presentation

66 What problem does the man mention?

(A) A screen is malfunctioning.
(B) An event needs to be put off.
(C) A room is not available.
(D) Some equipment is not working.

67 Look at the graphic. What room did the man reserve?

(A) Room 4A
(B) Room 7B
(C) Room 4C
(D) Room 2D

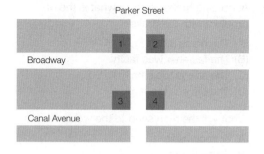

68 What does the man want to do?

(A) Visit an exhibit
(B) Book a room
(C) Park his car
(D) Take a bus

69 Look at the graphic. Where is the national museum?

(A) 1
(B) 2
(C) 3
(D) 4

70 What does the woman offer to do?

(A) Write down directions
(B) Walk the man to his destination
(C) Give the man a map
(D) Call a taxi

PART 4

Directions: You will hear some talks given by a single speaker. You will be asked to answer three questions about what the speaker says in each talk. Select the best response to each question and mark the letter (A), (B), (C), or (D) on your answer sheet. The talks will not be printed in your test book and will be spoken only one time.

71 Where does the announcement most likely take place?

(A) On a train
(B) On a boat
(C) On a plane
(D) On a bus

72 What does the speaker point out as unusual?

(A) An animal at the castle
(B) A ruined tower structure
(C) A treat for the local community
(D) An unusual weather pattern

73 What does the speaker recommend the listeners do?

(A) Book a meal
(B) Watch the birds
(C) Listen to music
(D) Take pictures

74 What type of product is being discussed?

(A) Electronic devices
(B) Clothing
(C) Athletic equipment
(D) Office supplies

75 What does the speaker say she will give the listeners?

(A) A product sample
(B) Completed questionnaires
(C) Sales updates
(D) A revised budget

76 What are listeners asked to think about?

(A) Ideas for cutting costs
(B) Strategies for attracting customers
(C) Locations for a new shopping center
(D) Names for new products

77 What is the speaker planning to do this weekend?

(A) Go on a sporting trip
(B) Purchase some ice skates
(C) Visit a sporting event
(D) Attend a convention

78 According to the speaker, what must people do to receive a discount?

(A) Arrive by bus
(B) Show a membership card
(C) Present a discount voucher
(D) Make a group booking

79 What does the speaker say he wants to do on Monday morning?

(A) Make a booking
(B) Reserve a hotel room
(C) Deliver some items
(D) Go on a trip

80 According to the speaker, what is taking place tomorrow?

(A) A major delivery
(B) A factory tour
(C) A management meeting
(D) A safety audit

81 Who will visit the plant?

(A) Suppliers
(B) Paramedics
(C) Inspectors
(D) Management

82 What are listeners asked to do later today?

(A) Check compulsory instructions
(B) Upload guidelines
(C) Submit a purchase order
(D) Evacuate the building

GO ON TO THE NEXT PAGE

83 What is being discussed?

(A) A press conference
(B) A client seminar
(C) A product launch
(D) A company anniversary

84 According to the speaker, what is surprising?

(A) Rapid decrease of competitors
(B) The growth of the business
(C) The success of the advertising
(D) A change in a work schedule

85 Why are listeners asked to email Mel Cushing?

(A) To take part in a survey
(B) To assist with preparations
(C) To distribute leaflets
(D) To book a conference room

86 What topic will the woman talk about?

(A) Hiring team leaders
(B) Raising productivity
(C) Improving sales
(D) Transferring employees

87 Why does the woman say, "Now, here's my understanding"?

(A) She recently presented some findings.
(B) She wants to write a summary.
(C) She trained her staff.
(D) She is going to tell her opinion.

88 What are listeners asked to do?

(A) Write down some thoughts
(B) Talk with their coworkers
(C) Read some information
(D) Change their work station

89 Where does the speaker most likely work?

(A) At a cleaning product manufacturer
(B) At a commercial airline
(C) At a car dealership
(D) At a food market

90 When can listeners get the information packets?

(A) Today
(B) Tomorrow
(C) Next week
(D) In two weeks

91 What does the man mean when he says, "So this is it then"?

(A) He will demonstrate how the product works.
(B) He is ready to end the meeting.
(C) He will go over the packets next time.
(D) He wants listeners to design some ideas.

Train	From	Arriving At
121	JFK	Platform 2
141	Newark	Platform 7
161	Union	Platform 1
171	Jay	Platform 10

92 What are the listeners asked to do?

(A) Store their belongings properly
(B) Not get off the train before an announcement
(C) Check their belongings before disembarking
(D) Move to a different platform

93 Look at the graphic. Where did the train leave from?

(A) JFK
(B) Newark
(C) Union
(D) Jay

94 Why can't passengers use the main entrance?

(A) Improvement work is being done.
(B) The place is too crowded at the moment.
(C) It has been shut down for a routine inspection.
(D) Cleaning work is taking place.

New Work Schedule	
Area	Day
Cafeteria	Monday
Breakroom	Tuesday Thursday
Storage space	Wednesday Friday
Lobby	Saturday

95 What is the broadcast about?

(A) Building maintenance
(B) Traffic congestion
(C) A road closure
(D) A new bus schedule

96 What are commuters advised to do?

(A) Leave earlier
(B) Take a detour
(C) Avoid using public transportation in the area
(D) Drive slowly

97 Look at the graphic. What number shows where the construction will take place?

(A) 1
(B) 2
(C) 3
(D) 4

98 What is the purpose of the announcement?

(A) To get feedback
(B) To assign a task
(C) To promote a product
(D) To change a plan

99 What is mentioned about the new material?

(A) It takes longer to settle in.
(B) It is less expensive.
(C) It is more durable.
(D) It is easier to use.

100 Look at the graphic. What day was the lobby originally scheduled to be worked on?

(A) Monday
(B) Tuesday
(C) Wednesday
(D) Saturday

This is the end of the Listening test. Turn to Part 5 in your test book.

GO ON TO THE NEXT PAGE

READING TEST

In the Reading test, you will read a variety of texts and answer several different types of reading comprehension questions. The entire Reading test will last 75 minutes. There are three parts, and directions are given for each part. You are encouraged to answer as many questions as possible within the time allowed.

You must mark your answers on the separate answer sheet. Do not write your answers in your test book.

PART 5

Directions: A word or phrase is missing in each of the sentences below. Four answer choices are given below each sentence. Select the best answer to complete the sentence. Then mark the letter (A), (B), (C), or (D) on your answer sheet.

101 Mr. Kim ------- his thesis on the financial state of the automobile industry next Wednesday.

(A) finished
(B) finishing
(C) to finish
(D) will finish

102 Sales representatives should be as ------- as possible when negotiating prices with customers.

(A) flexible
(B) flexed
(C) flexing
(D) flexibility

103 Please allow at least two to three weeks for ------- of your order.

(A) method
(B) quantity
(C) delivery
(D) model

104 Clarks offers the region's widest ------- of winter footwear for both adults and young people.

(A) selection
(B) selected
(C) selects
(D) selecting

105 All guests to the Solnova Solar Power Plant must report to the reception desk ------- upon arrival.

(A) partially
(B) timely
(C) closely
(D) immediately

106 When taking a holiday, leave your co-workers ------- instructions regarding how to deal with client requests in your absence.

(A) whole
(B) blank
(C) repetitive
(D) clear

107 The deadline for ------- of business proposals is Wednesday, June 6th, at 5:00 P.M.

(A) submit
(B) submission
(C) submits
(D) submitted

108 The American Equestrian Association's Web site provides members ------- easy access to the latest news about horses.

(A) with
(B) into
(C) beside
(D) up

109 Yamaha ------- requires groups of five or above to sign up in advance for factory tours.
(A) normal
(B) normality
(C) norm
(D) normally

110 Zrinka Milioti ------- assumed the role of chief information officer at Hansard Electricals on October 9th.
(A) namely
(B) collectively
(C) officially
(D) densely

111 Before activating the projector, firmly connect ------- cable to your device.
(A) there
(B) which
(C) its
(D) those

112 All part-time and full-time employees of Mantello's Snacks and Drinks are ------- to attend the president's annual information gatherings.
(A) contributed
(B) expected
(C) noticed
(D) conducted

113 The recording of the public hearing will be available on the city council Web site ------- the meeting.
(A) since
(B) between
(C) within
(D) throughout

114 While the building is being repaired, some staff members may be temporarily relocated ------- different workspaces.
(A) at
(B) on
(C) to
(D) as

115 Visit the Jarrah Placement Project Web site and ------- today for the computer programming seminar.
(A) registering
(B) registered
(C) registration
(D) register

116 Congressman Robert Smith is going to ------- his bid for reelection during a broadcast news conference at 7:00 P.M. tomorrow.
(A) announce
(B) notify
(C) interfere
(D) level

117 *The Devizes Weekly* has been ------- ranked among the most popular publications in Woodland Hills.
(A) consistency
(B) consistencies
(C) consistently
(D) consistent

118 Please confirm that all packages are packed properly ------- they are shipped to the warehouse.
(A) as much as
(B) such as
(C) whether
(D) before

119 Renovations to the lobby are not ------- to be finished before the beginning of next month.
(A) typical
(B) probably
(C) likely
(D) usual

120 *Operating System Magazine* forecasts that the ------- for iron and steel used in electronic parts will peak during the next ten years.
(A) materials
(B) demand
(C) appliances
(D) resource

GO ON TO THE NEXT PAGE

121 Neo Country Club may require customers to show identification for ------- their personal belongings.

(A) retrieve
(B) retrieved
(C) retrieval
(D) retrieving

122 ------- wishes to visit this year's marketing seminar must contact Mr. Qureshi by August 1.

(A) Nobody
(B) Whoever
(C) Whatever
(D) Somebody

123 CFO Rowan Winsvold expressed her ------- to everyone who posted ideas for reducing operating costs.

(A) imitation
(B) exposure
(C) gratitude
(D) abundance

124 The air-conditioning machine will not operate without a valve ------- the flow of liquid.

(A) regulated
(B) will regulate
(C) regulates
(D) to regulate

125 The training representative sent a memo to all employees ------- the upcoming training seminar.

(A) resulting
(B) following
(C) usually
(D) concerning

126 Resch Community Airport displays artworks painted by Matthew Benton, a local aviation -------.

(A) enthusiast
(B) enthused
(C) enthusiastically
(D) enthusiasm

127 The recent trend ------- investing in precious stones is expected to continue.

(A) near
(B) toward
(C) though
(D) along

128 With Blueocean Financial Services, new clients must install antivirus software ------- they can access their account information online.

(A) unless
(B) so that
(C) as though
(D) whereas

129 Because of higher-than-predicted profits in the last nine months, Giampanidou Designs is understandably ------- about its expansion.

(A) devoted
(B) optimistic
(C) impressive
(D) ample

130 Had Starship Entertainment not given the actor a chance, another company --------- so.

(A) should do
(B) has done
(C) would have done
(D) was done

PART 6

Directions: Read the texts that follow. A word, phrase, or sentence is missing in parts of each text. Four answer choices for each question are given below the text. Select the best answer to complete the text. Then mark the letter (A), (B), (C), or (D) on your answer sheet.

Questions 131-134 refer to the following article.

Nature Park Coming Soon

The opening ------- for the city's new Nature Park will be held on Sunday, April 2. The mayor, city
      131.
council members, reporters, and several local celebrities will be in attendance. The official ribbon

cutting is scheduled for 10:30 A.M., ------- by the mayor's welcoming speech. Light snacks
      132.
and beverages will be served by a local restaurant. There will also be entertainment events,

including a dance performance and magic show. ------- admission is free and open to the public,
      133.
registration should be made online in advance. Interested individuals can view the details at

www.natureparkopening.com. -------. So arrive early.
      134.

---

131 (A) remark
(B) ceremony
(C) demonstration
(D) presentation

132 (A) following
(B) follows
(C) will follow
(D) followed

133 (A) Now that
(B) Although
(C) Besides
(D) As though

134 (A) It is important to preserve nature.
(B) There will be food available for purchase.
(C) The number of seats is limited.
(D) The event has been postponed due to inclement weather.

GO ON TO THE NEXT PAGE

Explore the village of Bourton via one of our regularly arranged bicycle tours. Sponsored by the Bourton Tourism Academy, ------- tour is headed by an expert cyclist and features a different
135.
perspective of the village.

The most popular route encompasses Downvale Valley, the village's industrial -------. In addition
136.
to three working mills and one factory, Downvale Valley is home to a working tin mine and several craft shops that represent the history of the region. -------. It ------- with a refreshing meal at the
137.   **138.**
Green Man pub, one of Bourton's oldest public houses.

To register for the Downvale Valley tour or to find out more about the other tours, call the Bourton Tourism Academy at 050-555-6939.

135 (A) each
(B) whose
(C) either
(D) this

136 (A) factories
(B) programs
(C) district
(D) revolution

137 (A) Visitors should wear safety gear.
(B) The tour lasts approximately three hours.
(C) Riding a bike is good for health.
(D) This guide will explain the history of the town.

138 (A) concludes
(B) exits
(C) orders
(D) reserves

Questions **139-142** refer to the following e-mail.

To: muamba@nigermail.com
From: subscriptions@befitmagazine.com
Subject: Subscription renewal
Date: September 20

Dear Mr. Muamba:

Your subscription to *Be Fit Magazine* ------- on September 30. To ensure you don't miss any of
139.
our award-winning articles on general health and fitness, don't forget to renew your subscription

for another twelve months at the specially low rate of $30.00. -------, renewing your subscription
140.
before the end of the month entitles you to receive other publications from George Dent

Publishing at a discounted rate. -------.
141.

Just complete the online renewal form at www.befitmagazine.com/subscription -------.
142.
September 23.

Regards,

Subscription Services

139 (A) having expired
(B) will expire
(C) expired
(D) expiring

140 (A) Consequently
(B) However
(C) Instead
(D) Additionally

141 (A) This offer is valid only for first-time
subscribers.
(B) We received your submission for our
November issue.
(C) This includes *Exercise Routine* and *Dress
to Impress*.
(D) You are cordially invited to the award
ceremony.

142 (A) into
(B) by
(C) at
(D) until

GO ON TO THE NEXT PAGE

Questions 143-146 refer to the following notice.

NOTICE

TO: Museum Staff

As of March 5, the east wing of the main museum building will be closed owing to -------.
143.

The elevators and light switches in the building are old and need to be replaced.

Signs will be posted alerting patrons that the area is off-limits. Staff members needing to enter

that part of the building can do so on a limited basis. -------.
144.

Finally, shipments normally delivered to the east wing's loading dock will ------- be rerouted to
145.

the north wing mailroom. We will return to normal delivery protocols ------- work is completed.
146.

Thank you for your patience in advance.

Ail Yasof

Director of the Goldsun Museum

---

143 (A) construct
(B) constructor
(C) construction
(D) constructively

144 (A) Employees are advised to take time off during construction.
(B) Permission must be obtained from a supervisor.
(C) Some events will still be held in the east wing.
(D) Confidential documents will be stored in protective boxes.

145 (A) hardly
(B) temporarily
(C) formally
(D) permanently

146 (A) following
(B) promptly
(C) later
(D) once

PART 7

Directions: In this part you will read a selection of texts, such as magazine and newspaper articles, e-mails, and instant messages. Each text or set of texts is followed by several questions. Select the best answer for each question and mark the letter (A), (B), (C), or (D) on your answer sheet.

Questions 147-148 refer to the following text message.

To: Joshua Ismail

From: Blue Hill Surgery Center

This is a message from Dr. Kazanis. We have made an appointment for you for Wednesday, January 13, at 9:00 A.M. If you wish to accept this appointment, please press 1 to confirm.

If you cannot make it at the time specified, please call our office at 143-555-1856 to reschedule.

Thank you.

[....] [**Send**]

147 Why was the message sent?

(A) To ask about a procedure
(B) To announce a cancellation
(C) To change an appointment
(D) To ask for confirmation

148 What is Mr. Ismail instructed to do to change an appointment?

(A) Call the office
(B) Visit the office
(C) Send a text message
(D) Send a fax

GO ON TO THE NEXT PAGE

Questions 149-150 refer to the following e-mail.

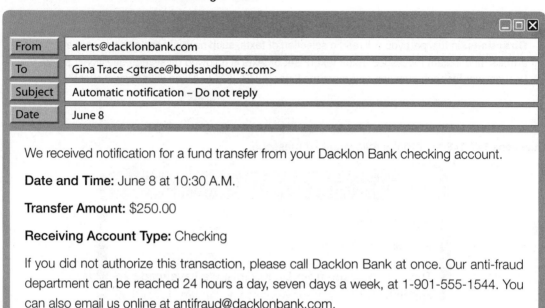

From	alerts@dacklonbank.com
To	Gina Trace <gtrace@budsandbows.com>
Subject	Automatic notification – Do not reply
Date	June 8

We received notification for a fund transfer from your Dacklon Bank checking account.

Date and Time: June 8 at 10:30 A.M.

Transfer Amount: $250.00

Receiving Account Type: Checking

If you did not authorize this transaction, please call Dacklon Bank at once. Our anti-fraud department can be reached 24 hours a day, seven days a week, at 1-901-555-1544. You can also email us online at antifraud@dacklonbank.com.

149 What is the purpose of the e-mail?
(A) To invite Ms. Trace to make a deposit
(B) To inform Ms. Trace about a financial transaction
(C) To request payment of an outstanding amount
(D) To explain a new anti-fraud initiative

150 What is indicated about Dacklon Bank's anti-fraud department?
(A) It is accessible at all times.
(B) Its opening hours have altered.
(C) It can be contacted by post.
(D) Its Web site has a new address.

Questions 151-152 refer to the following text message chain.

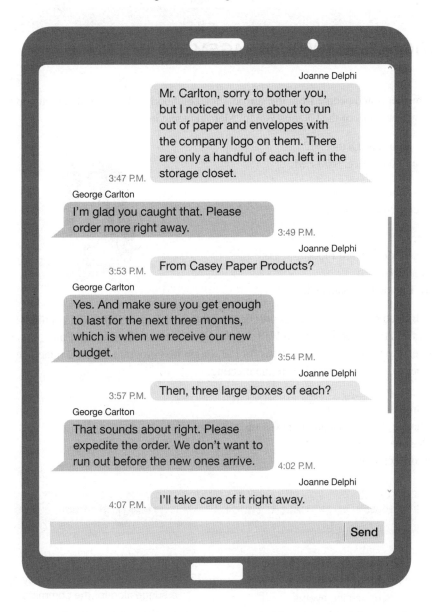

Joanne Delphi

Mr. Carlton, sorry to bother you, but I noticed we are about to run out of paper and envelopes with the company logo on them. There are only a handful of each left in the storage closet.
3:47 P.M.

George Carlton

I'm glad you caught that. Please order more right away.
3:49 P.M.

Joanne Delphi

3:53 P.M. From Casey Paper Products?

George Carlton

Yes. And make sure you get enough to last for the next three months, which is when we receive our new budget.
3:54 P.M.

Joanne Delphi

3:57 P.M. Then, three large boxes of each?

George Carlton

That sounds about right. Please expedite the order. We don't want to run out before the new ones arrive.
4:02 P.M.

Joanne Delphi

4:07 P.M. I'll take care of it right away.

Send

151 At 4:02 P.M., what does Mr. Carlton most likely mean when he writes, "That sounds about right"?

(A) He appreciates Ms. Delphi's reporting the problem to him.
(B) He thinks Ms. Delphi estimated the correct amount.
(C) He is about to tell Ms. Delphi some additional information.
(D) He wants Ms. Delphi to pay attention to the instructions.

152 What will Ms. Delphi most likely do next?

(A) Reschedule a shipment
(B) Mail some letters
(C) Place an order for stationery
(D) Prepare a budget

GO ON TO THE NEXT PAGE

NOTICE OF WEIGHT MANAGEMENT MEETINGS

October 3

Local residents and people from the surrounding neighborhoods are invited to attend the following meetings of the Chamis Weight Management Group:

- Date: Saturday, October 22
  Dietary committee, 6:00 P.M.

- Date: Saturday, October 29
  Exercise committee, 6:30 P.M.

- Venue
  The Sea View, Third Floor
  Seeman Hall
  2018 Rue de la Grande, Chamis

Timetables and training schedules will be available on Tuesday, October 4 at public libraries and the foyer of Seeman Hall and the Chamis Public Swimming Pool.
Local residents who have suggestions for the weight loss program should contact the organizer at least three days before the meeting.

Send requests to:
Janis Grousson, Organizer
The Chamis Weight Management Group
2018 Rue de la Grande, Chamis
jgrousson@chamis.fr

153 What is the purpose of the notice?

(A) To publicize upcoming events
(B) To inaugurate a weight gain regimen
(C) To advertise a new venue
(D) To announce a recruitment drive

154 When will a discussion about exercise take place?

(A) On October 3
(B) On October 4
(C) On October 22
(D) On October 29

155 What should people do if they have a suggestion for the committee?

(A) Email Ms. Grousson
(B) Call the committee
(C) Attend the first meeting
(D) Sign up at Seeman Hall

Questions 156-157 refer to the following receipt.

JB Sports
El Marina
Spain 1139

YOUR ONLINE VENDOR OF SPORT AND LEISURE GEAR

Customer: *Samira Lahon*
Shipping Address: *301 Lumago Street, Seville, SP 1295*
Order Number: *99842 (placed on November 11, 10:32 A.M.)*

Quantity	Item	Amount
1	Blue Designer Sneakers (Manufacturer: Corrilo)	Subtotal: 58.00 Tax: 5.80
1	Green Slingback Sandals (Manufacturer: Grandissimo)	Expedited Shipping: 11.00 Order Total: 74.80 Amount paid via Credit Card: 74.80 Balance Due: 0.00

Order Shipped on November 11, 3:05 P.M.

*Thank you for your purchase. If you are not happy with the items, please return them within 14 days unworn or accompanied with the original packaging. For more details on returning or exchanging a purchase, see www.jbsports/sp/returns.

156 What kind of product does JB Sports sell?

(A) Literary material
(B) Footwear
(C) Musical instruments
(D) DVDs

157 What is indicated about Ms. Lahon?

(A) She received a parcel on November 11.
(B) She regularly buys from JB Sports.
(C) She plans to buy more shoes.
(D) She paid for quick delivery.

GO ON TO THE NEXT PAGE

☐☐☒

http://www.raphaelcomputers.com

Raphael Computer Repairs

| HOME | SERVICES | TESTIMONIALS | REQUEST APPOINTMENT | CONTACT US |

What our customers are saying...

Rating: ★ ★ ★ ★ ★

Date of service: August 7

Type of service: Installation of RZ 33 Home Automation System

Last week, I realized the computer terminal for my home automation system was faulty. -[1]-. I recalled a leaflet for Raphael Computer Repairs was posted on my front door, so I called the number. -[2]-. Even though it was late afternoon and the business was about to close, the owner, Ziggy Raphael, agreed to come round to my house straight after he closed the shop. He took a look at the computer terminal and told me I could either upgrade it or have it repaired. Since it was a few years old, I choose to have it upgraded. Mr. Raphael demonstrated a number of different models and I decided upon one with a much larger memory capacity.

I thought it would take a while for it to be ordered and delivered, but Mr. Raphael had one in his van and installed it that same day. -[3]-. His secretary called the following day to ensure that the system was working correctly. The entire experience demonstrates the excellent customer service presented by Raphael Computer Repairs and I will definitely recommend his services again. -[4]-.

Carla Lamos

158 Why has the information most likely been included on the Web site?

(A) To explain a company policy
(B) To describe an installation process
(C) To attract potential customers
(D) To advertise a new product

159 What is indicated about Mr. Raphael?

(A) He shares a mailbox with Ms. Lamos.
(B) He completed work for Ms. Lamos on the same day she requested it.
(C) He charges an extra fee for installing larger computer terminals.
(D) His secretary contacted Ms. Lamos on August 7.

160 In which of the positions marked [1], [2], [3], and [4] does the following sentence best belong?

"He didn't even charge me extra for working during off hours."

(A) [1]
(B) [2]
(C) [3]
(D) [4]

GO ON TO THE NEXT PAGE

Questions 161-164 refer to the following flyer.

◐◑ Janssen's DVD is moving!

Janssen's DVD, recognized as the town's biggest collection of videos and DVDs for sale, is expanding. We began at our location on in Farrier Street six years ago, and it is now time to move to 331 Sadlers Row, former home of the Flickson Bakery. We will continue to sell DVDs, videos and CDs as well as comic books, but the extra space will enable us to grow into the electronic games market.

Our Farrier Street store will close on Friday, May 18, and Janssen's DVD will host a grand opening party for the new store on Saturday, May 19, from 9 A.M. to 5 P.M. We are inviting all of our customers to join us at the event, which will be catered by Cuisine Café, our new neighbor.

Come and see our new merchandise and taste Cuisine Café's delicious sandwiches and beverages. Also present will be Randy Cloche, star of the new indie film, *Tracing James*, and he will be around to sign autographs and meet people.

To prepare for our relocation, we will be getting rid of some of our old stock. During April, the price of some DVDs and videos will be reduced by up to 50 percent, so seize the opportunity to pick up some of your favorite films at a bargain.

161 What is indicated about Janssen's DVD?

(A) It is increasing its staffing levels.
(B) It will be moving next to Flickson Bakery.
(C) It is amalgamating with Cuisine Café.
(D) It has been in business for six years.

162 What does Janssen's DVD currently NOT offer?

(A) Video games
(B) Comic books
(C) CDs
(D) DVDs

163 Who is Mr. Cloche?

(A) An actor
(B) A manager of a café
(C) A store owner
(D) A photographer

164 According to the flier, what will happen in April?

(A) A grand opening will be held.
(B) A discount will be offered.
(C) Free DVDs will be given out.
(D) A new inventory will be delivered.

Benzema Motor Care — Internal Job Posting

This position is open to internal candidates until the end of the month. Subsequently, the position will be advertised to external candidates.

Title: Chief Mechanic

Description:
- Support Benzema Motor Care by servicing more vehicles in the company's three main areas of maintenance, repair and servicing.
- Perform MOTs, body work repair and vehicle analytics on all vehicle models.
- Maintain customer service with key clientele.

Principal Duties:
- Check cars and other vehicles and diagnose problem areas
- Perform computer analytics on selected company cars
- Prepare detailed servicing using multiple repair systems
- Serve as a liaison between car manufacturers and garage staff

Requirements:
- A minimum of three years' experience in our Vehicle Maintenance Department
- A detailed understanding of car maintenance

To apply for this position, please submit your résumé, cover letter and contact information of two references by February 11 to Kemar Nahn, Garage Manager, at knahn@benzema.org.

---

165 What is mentioned as a requirement of the position?

(A) A business degree
(B) In-depth knowledge of car maintenance
(C) Experience working with customers
(D) A valid driving license

166 What should a candidate do to apply?

(A) Send the requested documents to Ms. Nahn
(B) Have a supervisor refer a candidate
(C) Fill out an application form
(D) Schedule an interview by February 11

167 Where would the notice most likely appear?

(A) In a public database of automobile jobs
(B) In a memo to staff at Benzema Motor Care
(C) In the recruitment section of a newspaper
(D) In a letter to chief mechanics

168 What is NOT included in the responsibilities of the chief mechanic?

(A) Liaise with car manufacturers
(B) Diagnose vehicular faults
(C) Undertake car servicing
(D) Update the company's client list

GO ON TO THE NEXT PAGE

Questions 169-171 refer to the following online chat discussion.

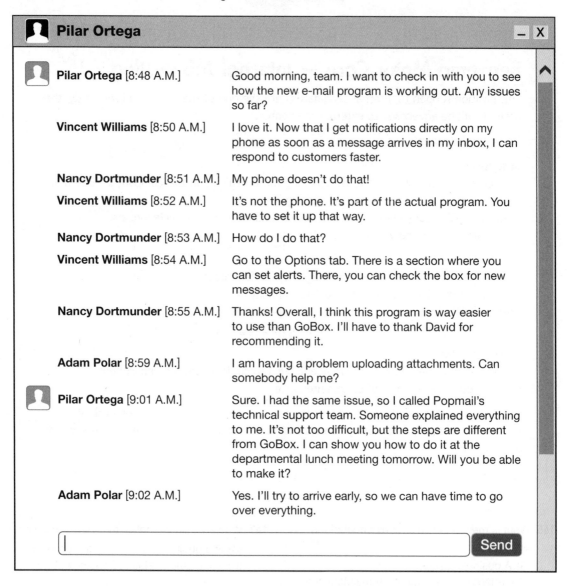

Pilar Ortega   _ X

Pilar Ortega [8:48 A.M.]   Good morning, team. I want to check in with you to see how the new e-mail program is working out. Any issues so far?

Vincent Williams [8:50 A.M.]   I love it. Now that I get notifications directly on my phone as soon as a message arrives in my inbox, I can respond to customers faster.

Nancy Dortmunder [8:51 A.M.]   My phone doesn't do that!

Vincent Williams [8:52 A.M.]   It's not the phone. It's part of the actual program. You have to set it up that way.

Nancy Dortmunder [8:53 A.M.]   How do I do that?

Vincent Williams [8:54 A.M.]   Go to the Options tab. There is a section where you can set alerts. There, you can check the box for new messages.

Nancy Dortmunder [8:55 A.M.]   Thanks! Overall, I think this program is way easier to use than GoBox. I'll have to thank David for recommending it.

Adam Polar [8:59 A.M.]   I am having a problem uploading attachments. Can somebody help me?

Pilar Ortega [9:01 A.M.]   Sure. I had the same issue, so I called Popmail's technical support team. Someone explained everything to me. It's not too difficult, but the steps are different from GoBox. I can show you how to do it at the departmental lunch meeting tomorrow. Will you be able to make it?

Adam Polar [9:02 A.M.]   Yes. I'll try to arrive early, so we can have time to go over everything.

[   ] Send

169 At 8:51 A.M., why does Ms. Dortmunder write, "My phone doesn't do that"?

(A) She wants to adjust her phone's settings.
(B) She is unable to check e-mail on her phone.
(C) She is surprised that Mr. Williams gets alerts.
(D) She wants to respond to customer e-mails faster.

170 Why did Ms. Ortega contact technical support?

(A) To set up alerts on her phone
(B) To install a new e-mail program
(C) To learn how to attach files
(D) To upgrade GoBox software

171 What is suggested about Mr. Polar?

(A) He recommended Popmail to the team.
(B) He will give a presentation at the meeting.
(C) He has a lunch appointment today.
(D) He will get assistance from Ms. Ortega tomorrow.

GO ON TO THE NEXT PAGE

March 30

Duncan Kamal, CEO
Erin Call Center
1000 Sprint Road
Birmingham, Alabama USA

Dear Mr. Kamal,

I'm writing to tell you that Temps Today has been taken over by WRE Employment, one of the biggest names in the supply of temporary staff. Temps Today will continue to operate under the same name, but some of our prices will be affected. –[1]–. As one of our most valued customers, I would like to personally inform you of the changes so you can make appropriate decisions.

While the cost of supplying temporary agency staff largely remains the same, the hourly rate for our call center operatives has been revised. –[2]–. Our new hourly rates are as follows:

Up to 4 operatives, $15 per person per hour
5-9 operatives, $11 per person per hour
10-24 operatives, $10 per person per hour
25-49 operatives, $9 per person per hour
50 or more operatives, $8 per person per hour

Under the new pricing system, we calculate the charges for supplying call center staff based on the number of people you require per month. –[3]–. Therefore, if on your next request you ask for the same number of operatives as you did in February, you will be charged the lowest monthly fee ($8 per person per hour), only fifty cents more than under the old system.

As a WRE Employment company, we will also supply additional skilled temporary staff. –[4]–. In addition, our Web site now offers numerous convenient extra features, including account history and personnel skills requirements.

If you have any questions regarding the changes, please do not hesitate to contact us. We will continue to provide you with the same excellent and upmarket service that you have been enjoying for a number of years. Thank you for your continued business.

Sincerely,

Alexis Chan

Alexis Chan
Temps Today
Vice President, Customer Service

172 What is a purpose of the letter?

    (A) To report a staffing shortage

    (B) To announce a new training scheme

    (C) To advertise the opening of a new Web site

    (D) To explain a change in the fee structure

173 According to the letter, what did WRE Employment recently do?

    (A) Acquire another company

    (B) Change its location

    (C) Hire a new vice president

    (D) Relocate to Alabama

174 Who is Mr. Kamal?

    (A) A temporary call center worker

    (B) An owner of WRE Employment

    (C) A personal financial advisor

    (D) A customer of Temps Today

175 In which of the positions marked [1], [2], [3], and [4] does the following sentence best belong?

"For example, we can supply caterers for any event at a moment's notice."

    (A) [1]

    (B) [2]

    (C) [3]

    (D) [4]

GO ON TO THE NEXT PAGE

Spanish Vacation Home

⌂ Property: 2619 Madrid Exclusive 3-bedroom town-house Minimum stay: 4 nights For more information, click *here*.	⌂ Property: 9110 Aragon Stay three consecutive nights and enjoy 4th night free. Suitable for those wanting to escape from the busy pace of life to a peaceful haven. Sea view. For more information, click *here*.
⌂ Property: 4716 Castile 2-bedroom apartments Close to the city and excellent base for modern city life Vibrant environment For more information, click *here*.	⌂ Property: 6130 Andalusia With private jetty $1400 per week For more information, click *here*.

E-Mail Message

To: Alberto Uemura <auemura@spholidayrentals.co.esp>
From: Gayle Ince <gince@ckalltd.co.esp>
Date: September 21
Re: Property 4716

Hello, Mr. Uemura:

I dealt with you last summer when I went on holiday with my fiancé to Andalusia and I was very happy with both our accommodations and the level of service you provided. However, the destination was not to my taste. It was too quiet and remote. This year, I would prefer something in the city, preferably with more than two bedrooms and access to the nightlife. I am also reluctant to spend more than $900–1,000 for a week. I'm interested in property 4716. Could you provide me with availability and details for this? It seems to meet my needs.

I look forward to your reply.

Regards,
Gayle Ince

176 What property offers a free night's stay?

(A) Property 2619
(B) Property 9110
(C) Property 4716
(D) Property 6130

177 Why did Ms. Ince send the e-mail?

(A) To cancel a deposit
(B) To pay for a booking
(C) To request information
(D) To ask for travel advice

178 What aspect of her previous vacation did Ms. Ince find unsatisfactory?

(A) Cleanliness in the rented apartment
(B) Service provided by the booking agent
(C) Slow pace of life in the region nearby
(D) Distance to her rented property

179 Why is the property 6130 probably unsuitable for Ms. Ince?

(A) She wants accommodation with more than two bedrooms.
(B) She is looking for something cheaper.
(C) She wants to stay in a town house.
(D) She doesn't want to travel to the coast.

180 What location is Ms. Ince interested in?

(A) Madrid
(B) Aragon
(C) Castile
(D) Andalusia

GO ON TO THE NEXT PAGE

Questions 181–185 refer to the following memo and e-mail.

To: All employees
From: Angharad Reece, Director of HR
Subject: Survey Feedback
Date: December 30

In November, our human resources department carried out a comprehensive customer questionnaire that covered several areas of our business. The results showed that the majority of our customers are generally pleased with our services, particularly when compared to other loan approval firms. However, some areas for improvement were identified.

A general complaint was that it takes an unacceptably long time to process new accounts. Currently, when we are approached by a customer, the initial loan procedure requires three signatures from our loans department and financial checking office. Thus, it often takes as long as three weeks for money to be transferred into bank accounts.

Therefore, beginning next month, new loan approvals of less than $1,000 require only one signature from the senior loan officer. This policy will reduce the processing time and help us better serve our customers.

If you have any questions, please don't hesitate to contact me.

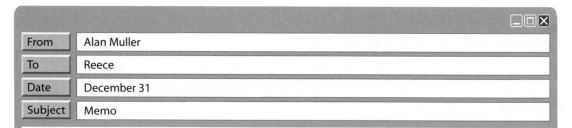

From	Alan Muller
To	Reece
Date	December 31
Subject	Memo

Hello Angharad,

I saw the memo you issued yesterday, and I think the new proposal is an excellent idea. When my department compiled the results of the survey, a number of customers revealed they had waited weeks for an approval to be processed. In addition to your idea, I believe we could speed up the process even more by allowing approval to be signed electronically. One of our suppliers, Ashton & Jones, has recently installed software that enables them to handle most of their transactions online. I think we should consider a similar system. I would be willing to look into it.

Alan

181 What does Ms. Reece announce in the memo?

(A) A merger with another firm
(B) More surveys for senior sales staff
(C) Hiring of extra financial staff
(D) A new procedure for approving contracts

182 According to the memo, what is the purpose of the change?

(A) To reduce loan officers' workload
(B) To eliminate unnecessary delays
(C) To improve communication within the organization
(D) To expand the size of the workforce

183 When will the change go into effect?

(A) In January
(B) In February
(C) In November
(D) In December

184 What department does Mr. Muller work?

(A) Financial
(B) Sales
(C) Human Resources
(D) Client Relations

185 What does Mr. Muller recommend?

(A) Participating in a survey
(B) Trying a computer software program
(C) Reducing client fees
(D) Increasing the loan approval limit

Test 03

GO ON TO THE NEXT PAGE

Questions 186-190 refer to the following schedule, e-mail, and notice.

Key Building
Schedule for Janitors
Weeks of September 1 – October 4

Employee	Days (Hours)
Tom Jackson	Monday-Friday (9:30 A.M. – 1:30 P.M.)
Alan Chin	Monday-Friday (6:30 P.M. – 10:30 P.M.)
James Kumar	Monday, Wednesday, Friday (2:30 P.M. – 8:30 P.M)
Rodney Reinhardt	Tuesday, Thursday (2:30 P.M. – 8:30 P.M.) Saturday (8:00 A.M. – 2:00 P.M.)

If you are unable to work an assigned shift, please contact your supervisor as soon as possible.

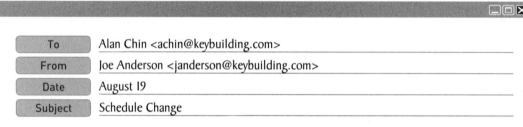

To	Alan Chin <achin@keybuilding.com>
From	Joe Anderson <janderson@keybuilding.com>
Date	August 19
Subject	Schedule Change

Dear Alan:

Thanks for letting me know that you are expecting your family to visit you during the week of September 1-7. Tom has agreed to switch schedules with you for that one week. That week after that, both you and Tom will return to your assigned shifts for the remainder of the month.

Since the requested shift is not your regular one, please talk with Tom about what specific tasks need to be completed. You might also need to contact Security so that they can let you in to clean locked rooms.

Let me know if you have any questions.

Thanks,
Joe

NEW TIME ENTRY SYSTEM

All Key Building employees will be required to use a new Web-based time entry system, called Synergy, starting the week of September 29 – October 4. Because Synergy can be accessed from any mobile device, employees will no longer have to come in to the Personnel Office to submit paper timesheets. Instead, they need to log on with a username and password and enter their hours worked.

To show employees how to use Synergy, David Harrison will be offering training sessions on the following dates:

Security	Monday, September 22 (10:00 A.M. – 11:30 A.M.)
Accounting	Tuesday, September 23 (3:00 P.M. – 4:30 P.M.)
Maintenance	Wednesday, September 24 (2:00 P.M. – 3:30 P.M.)
Administration	Thursday, September 25 (8:30 A.M. – 10:00 A.M.)

Employees should attend the training session on the date their department is scheduled. If that is not possible, please contact Mr. Harrison at extension 1212 to arrange to attend another session.

186 What is indicated about Mr. Jackson?

(A) He normally works on Saturdays.
(B) His family lives in the Key Building.
(C) He will change his schedule for one month.
(D) He will work five evenings in September.

187 What is suggested about Mr. Anderson?

(A) He will lead the Synergy training sessions.
(B) He is Mr. Chin's manager.
(C) He will take one week off.
(D) He owns the Key Building.

188 In the e-mail, the word "regular" in paragraph 2, line 1, is closest in meaning to

(A) assigned
(B) lengthy
(C) trained
(D) usual

189 Why are employees asked to attend a training session?

(A) To obtain their usernames and passwords
(B) To learn a new program
(C) To meet their personnel officer
(D) To update their timesheets

190 On what day will Mr. Reinhardt most likely be trained to use Synergy?

(A) September 22
(B) September 23
(C) September 24
(D) September 25

GO ON TO THE NEXT PAGE

People Mover Is Expanding

People Mover, the nation's fastest growing city-to-city bus service, is planning to begin offering services to nineteen new destinations, including Bolton, Newport, Westville, Allentown, and Grover City. People Mover will start serving Bolton and Newport on April 15. Service to smaller cities will be rolled out in May and June.

To celebrate the expansion, we are giving away 100 round-trip tickets to/from any of the new destinations. No purchase is necessary to enter. Simply fill out the form on our Web site at www.peoplemover.com. Entries must be received by March 31.

Charlestown (June 3)

Charlestown residents have waited nearly three years for the restoration of direct intercity bus service. That all changed on Saturday when the first People Mover bus picked up 28 passengers in front of the now shuttered Union Street Terminal.

"I'm looking forward to seeing my relatives in Richmond," said Danica Baker, who eagerly boarded the bus. Since National Bus Lines shut down, Ms. Baker has taken local buses and taxies all the way to the city. "I'm so happy that People Mover is here now," she added.

Representatives from the mayor's office say they plan to renovate and reopen the city's only intercity bus terminal later this year. In the meantime, People Mover will stop on Eldritch Street directly in front of the building. Current schedules can be found at www.peoplemover.com or by calling 1-888-555-8399.

Elizabeth Lewis
873 Harper Road
Charlestown
June 28

Dear Ms. Lewis:

Congratulations! You have been selected to receive a trip on People Mover to any destination of your choice. You can claim your ticket by bringing this letter to any bus terminal served by People Mover or by calling 1-888-555-8789. The ticket will remain valid for up to twelve months from the date it is issued.

We look forward to serving you.

Karen Coleman
Vice President of Client Services
People Mover

191 What is suggested about Charlestown?

(A) It is less populous than Newport.
(B) It received new bus service before Bolton.
(C) It used to be served by People Mover.
(D) It no longer has public transportation.

192 What is indicated about National Bus Lines?

(A) It used to offer service to Bolton.
(B) It was recently acquired by People Mover.
(C) It currently operates out of Richmond.
(D) It went out of business three years ago.

193 What is suggested about Charlestown's local government?

(A) It currently employs Ms. Lewis.
(B) It plans to fix up Union Street Terminal.
(C) It operates a taxi service.
(D) It signed a contract with People Mover.

194 What is most likely true about Ms. Lewis?

(A) She entered the People Mover contest online.
(B) She received her ticket in the mail.
(C) She occasionally travels to Richmond.
(D) She will travel before the end of the year.

195 In the letter, the word "claim" in paragraph 1, line 2, is closest in meaning to

(A) assert
(B) obtain
(C) purchase
(D) reserve

GO ON TO THE NEXT PAGE

Questions 196-200 refer to the following e-mail, Web page, and article.

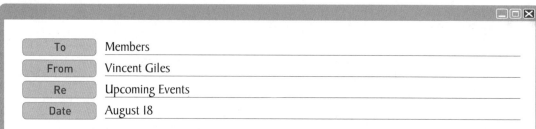

To	Members
From	Vincent Giles
Re	Upcoming Events
Date	August 18

Thanks to all of you who came out to the opening of "Wild at Heart" earlier this month. For those who were unable to attend, this traveling exhibit features over one hundred photographs by Alejandro Saragossa. His work will remain on display at the Newberry Museum until February of next year. "Wild at Heart" features stunning black and white portraits and landscapes from Brazil.

In addition to a special lecture by Mr. Saragossa, the Newberry Museum has some exciting events planned for the month of September. Visit our Web site for an up-to-date schedule. Members do not have to pay admission for Third Thursday events.

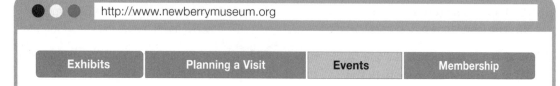

http://www.newberrymuseum.org

| Exhibits | Planning a Visit | Events | Membership |

September 3 Family Day: 10:00 A.M. – 5:00 P.M.

Free admission for parents and their children. Arts and crafts activities for the kids in the atrium.

September 10 Book Signing: Noon – 2:00 P.M.

Local historian Daniel Colton will be signing copies of his newest work, *Chase Ford: Past and Present*, available for sale in the museum's gift shop. (Members get 10% off.)

September 22 Third Thursday: 6:00 P.M. – 9:00 P.M.

Socialize, stroll through the galleries, and enjoy live jazz by Earth Sounds. Food and beverages available for purchase from the museum café.

September 25 Special Event: 2:00 P.M. – 4:00 P.M.

Join Alejandro Saragossa for a lecture. Mr. Saragossa will talk about his life and work, currently on display at the museum.

Soulful Photos Come to the Newberry

by Richard Dean

Painter Manuel Solares once said that great art can touch the soul. Perhaps he was thinking of the photography of Alejandro Saragossa. His photographs are remarkably beautiful. When I visited the Newberry Museum last weekend, Mr. Saragossa talked about the inspiration for his art, his love of travel, and the challenges faced by artistic photographers in today's media-saturated world. Even if you missed the talk, you still have time to view an exhibit of his favorite photos of the past decade, many in his native country. Details available at www.newberrymuseum.com.

196 What is NOT indicated about "Wild at Heart"?

(A) It features pictures of people.
(B) It includes a lecture by the artist.
(C) It opened in August.
(D) It will stay at the Newberry Museum permanently.

197 What is suggested about Newberry Museum members?

(A) They receive special invitations.
(B) They can see Earth Sounds for free.
(C) They get discounts on all gift shop purchases.
(D) They pay a monthly membership fee.

198 When did Mr. Dean most likely visit the Newberry Museum?

(A) On September 3
(B) On September 10
(C) On September 22
(D) On September 25

199 What is indicated about Mr. Saragossa?

(A) He is traveling for five months.
(B) His career started ten years ago.
(C) He was born in Brazil.
(D) His work is displayed online.

200 In the article, the word "missed" in paragraph 1, line 8, is closest in meaning to

(A) arrived late to
(B) avoided seeing
(C) failed to attend
(D) felt sad about

GO ON TO THE NEXT PAGE

Actual Test

04

시작 시간   :

종료 시간   :

LISTENING TEST

In the Listening test, you will be asked to demonstrate how well you understand spoken English. The entire Listening test will last approximately 45 minutes. There are four parts, and directions are given for each part. You must mark your answers on the separate answer sheet. Do not write your answers in your test book.

PART 1

Directions: For each question in this part, you will hear four statements about a picture in your test book. When you hear the statements, you must select the one statement that best describes what you see in the picture. Then find the number of the question on your answer sheet and mark your answer. The statements will not be printed in your test book and will be spoken only one time.

Example

Sample Answer
Ⓐ ● Ⓒ Ⓓ

Statement (B), "The man is working at a desk," is the best description of the picture, so you should select answer (B) and mark it on your answer sheet.

1

2

GO ON TO THE NEXT PAGE ➡

3

4

5

6

GO ON TO THE NEXT PAGE

PART 2

Directions: You will hear a question or statement and three responses spoken in English. They will not be printed in your test book and will be spoken only one time. Select the best response to the question or statement and mark the letter (A), (B), or (C) on your answer sheet.

7   Mark your answer on your answer sheet.

8   Mark your answer on your answer sheet.

9   Mark your answer on your answer sheet.

10   Mark your answer on your answer sheet.

11   Mark your answer on your answer sheet.

12   Mark your answer on your answer sheet.

13   Mark your answer on your answer sheet.

14   Mark your answer on your answer sheet.

15   Mark your answer on your answer sheet.

16   Mark your answer on your answer sheet.

17   Mark your answer on your answer sheet.

18   Mark your answer on your answer sheet.

19   Mark your answer on your answer sheet.

20   Mark your answer on your answer sheet.

21   Mark your answer on your answer sheet.

22   Mark your answer on your answer sheet.

23   Mark your answer on your answer sheet.

24   Mark your answer on your answer sheet.

25   Mark your answer on your answer sheet.

26   Mark your answer on your answer sheet.

27   Mark your answer on your answer sheet.

28   Mark your answer on your answer sheet.

29   Mark your answer on your answer sheet.

30   Mark your answer on your answer sheet.

31   Mark your answer on your answer sheet.

PART 3

Directions: You will hear some conversations between two or more people. You will be asked to answer three questions about what the speakers say in each conversation. Select the best response to each question and mark the letter (A), (B), (C), or (D) on your answer sheet. The conversations will not be printed in your test book and will be spoken only one time.

32 Where is the conversation most likely taking place?

(A) At an outdoor concert
(B) At a tourist information office
(C) At a riverside
(D) At a general store

33 What does the woman recommend?

(A) Walking along the hillside
(B) Swimming in the local pool
(C) Exploring the environment
(D) Experiencing water sport activities

34 What does the woman give the man?

(A) An invoice
(B) A map
(C) A booklet
(D) A ticket

35 What did the man write about?

(A) His unique tours
(B) Working with Alaskans
(C) His favorite TV film
(D) Writing for television

36 Why is the man pleased?

(A) He was offered a job in Alaska.
(B) His idea will be published.
(C) His television will be replaced.
(D) His script has been accepted.

37 Why does the woman want to meet with the man?

(A) To talk about some programs
(B) To perform an audition
(C) To take part in a documentary
(D) To discuss film rights

38 What does the man offer to do?

(A) Replace an old machine
(B) Call a coworker
(C) Email an acquaintance
(D) Look up the schedule

39 Why is Jorge needed?

(A) To install a program
(B) To make photocopies
(C) To call technical support
(D) To make some repairs

40 Why does the man say, "Haley in our office is pretty good at office equipment"?

(A) To revise some schedule
(B) To recommend Haley for a promotion
(C) To suggest that Haley help with some machines
(D) To propose using another piece of equipment

41 What event has the woman recently attended?

(A) A computer seminar
(B) A fund-raising lunch
(C) A presentation
(D) A writing conference

42 What alternative does the woman suggest?

(A) Hiring an external consultant
(B) Producing an updated memo
(C) Adjusting the layout of a brochure
(D) Getting someone else to prepare a presentation

43 What do the speakers agree to do?

(A) Meet today
(B) Talk with a manager
(C) Arrange a date
(D) Present a paper

GO ON TO THE NEXT PAGE

44 Who most likely is the woman contacting?

(A) A paint supplier
(B) A clothing designer
(C) A garden expert
(D) A furniture manufacturer

45 What does the woman want to do?

(A) Select a decorator
(B) See a product sample
(C) Speak to a designer
(D) Receive an estimate

46 According to the man, how can the woman place a future order?

(A) By completing an online form
(B) By calling directly
(C) By sending an e-mail
(D) By mailing a request

---

47 What did the man do recently?

(A) He set up a new establishment.
(B) He developed new software.
(C) He signed up for a course.
(D) He demonstrated a new product.

48 What does the man mean when he says, "It's now progressing quite fast"?

(A) He has become busy recently.
(B) The class is picking up speed.
(C) He thinks the course is easy.
(D) The class is very difficult to follow.

49 What is the man going to participate in?

(A) An upcoming lecture
(B) His favorite show
(C) A project
(D) A professional workshop

50 Who are the speakers expecting?

(A) Business customers
(B) Job applicants
(C) Health enthusiasts
(D) Luncheon guests

51 What will the man do later this evening?

(A) Present some merchandise
(B) Give a tour of the hotel
(C) Organize a party
(D) Change a schedule

52 What does the woman say she needs to do?

(A) Contact a supplier
(B) Meet the guests
(C) Prepare a menu
(D) Call a colleague

---

53 What are the speakers discussing?

(A) A commercial property sale
(B) A building program
(C) Travel schedules
(D) Financial matters

54 What does the woman mention about Mr. Graston?

(A) He is reluctant to sell.
(B) His debts are mounting.
(C) His lease has expired.
(D) He is moving abroad.

55 What does the man say he will suggest to Mr. Graston?

(A) Performing an inspection
(B) Reducing the price
(C) Purchasing an automobile
(D) Taking out a loan

56 According to the man, what has changed?

(A) A travel plan
(B) The availability of a client
(C) The terms of a contract
(D) A meeting time

57 What problem does the woman mention?

(A) She has booked the wrong flight.
(B) She is going on a vacation.
(C) Her computer keeps breaking down.
(D) She has an appointment in the morning.

58 What does the man say the woman will have time to do?

(A) Send over a document
(B) Drive around
(C) Reserve a lunch
(D) Return to the office

59 What does the woman want to know?

(A) The period of the promotion
(B) The price of a product
(C) Information about a specific item
(D) Directions to the store

60 What does the man say about the promotion?

(A) It will last until the end of the week.
(B) It is only available online.
(C) It is only for a specific product.
(D) It hasn't started yet.

61 Why does the man say, "Let me walk you through our Web site now"?

(A) To make an online order
(B) To negotiate a price
(C) To show some information
(D) To explain some download methods

62 What does the woman say she needs?

(A) A booking form
(B) An entertainment room
(C) A price breakdown
(D) Rented accommodation

63 What does the man ask the woman about?

(A) Her date of birth
(B) Her passport number
(C) The size of her party
(D) The location of her venue

64 What will the man most likely do next?

(A) Check prior bookings
(B) Speak to a colleague
(C) Provide an estimate
(D) Source alternative arrangements

GO ON TO THE NEXT PAGE

Discount code (Available only from 10/3 to 10/13)	
Items	**Discount Rates**
Table	50%
Chair	40%
Sofa	30%
Bed frame (Cherrywood)	25%
Bed mattress (Memory form)	20%
Bed frame (Cherrywood) & Bed mattress (Memory form) as a set	30%

Product Number	Descriptions	Price
CM1350	High speed with 13-inch monitor	$125
CM1550	High speed with 15-inch monitor	$150
CM1750	High speed with 17-inch monitor	$185
CM1950	High speed with 19-inch monitor	$230

65 What is the man planning to do?

(A) Use a discount coupon
(B) Move out of a current apartment
(C) Purchase some furniture
(D) Find more information about the promotion

66 What does the man indicate about the business?

(A) It offers only a few kinds of products.
(B) It is popular.
(C) This is his first time to purchase from the business.
(D) All kinds of items are on sale.

67 Look at the graphic. Which discount will the man receive?

(A) 40%
(B) 30%
(C) 25%
(D) 20%

68 What are the speakers mainly discussing?

(A) Preparing for a new staff member
(B) Replacing computers
(C) Transferring important files
(D) Furnishing a lobby

69 What does the woman say she did?

(A) Rescheduled a date
(B) Contacted another department
(C) Replaced some furniture
(D) Located missing files

70 Look at the graphic. What product will the woman most likely purchase?

(A) CM1350
(B) CM1550
(C) CM1750
(D) CM1950

PART 4

Directions: You will hear some talks given by a single speaker. You will be asked to answer three questions about what the speaker says in each talk. Select the best response to each question and mark the letter (A), (B), (C), or (D) on your answer sheet. The talks will not be printed in your test book and will be spoken only one time.

71 Why is the speaker calling?

(A) To approve a design
(B) To arrange a meeting
(C) To extend a deadline
(D) To place an order

72 What event is the speaker planning?

(A) A global gathering
(B) An advertising presentation
(C) A construction project
(D) A store renovation

73 What information does the speaker request?

(A) Expected time
(B) A printing deadline
(C) A cost estimate
(D) A meeting agenda

74 What type of business is Hannaford's?

(A) A travel agency
(B) A beauty shop
(C) A dental clinic
(D) A café

75 What day is the business open late?

(A) On Tuesday
(B) On Wednesday
(C) On Thursday
(D) On Saturday

76 What does the speaker recommend?

(A) Asking for a discount
(B) Visiting another salon
(C) Changing an appointment
(D) Leaving a message

77 Where most likely is the announcement being heard?

(A) In a train station
(B) At the airport
(C) In a plane
(D) In a bus

78 What should people traveling to Switzerland do?

(A) Take transport to the customs hall
(B) Go to another terminal
(C) Wait for luggage removal
(D) Exit via the main hall

79 According to the announcement, what is offered to some passengers?

(A) Car park payment
(B) Ticket machines
(C) Refreshment stands
(D) Transportation

80 What event is ending?

(A) A company picnic
(B) A computer demonstration
(C) A sporting event
(D) A nature tour

81 What must participants in the competition do?

(A) Translate names correctly
(B) Identify wild flowers
(C) Map out a route
(D) Draw a diagram

82 What are the listeners cautioned about?

(A) Feeding the animals
(B) Getting out of the designated paths
(C) Leaving trash
(D) Walking through the enclosures

GO ON TO THE NEXT PAGE

83 Where is the announcement being made?

(A) At a harbor
(B) At a theme park
(C) At a lake
(D) At a museum

84 Why are listeners told they will need to wait?

(A) A tour guide is delayed.
(B) A dinner has not been delivered.
(C) The transport has not arrived.
(D) The weather is inclement.

85 What are listeners asked to do?

(A) Form two separate groups
(B) Return at another time
(C) Find a viewpoint as quickly as possible
(D) Board the boat in an orderly manner

---

86 Where does the listener most likely work?

(A) At a gallery
(B) At a stationary store
(C) At a paint manufacturer
(D) At a graphic design firm

87 What does the man imply when he says, "it's not what we were expecting"?

(A) He was surprised with a quick response.
(B) He wants a better result.
(C) He doesn't like the color scheme.
(D) He wants to cancel the order.

88 What does the speaker want to do?

(A) Reschedule the appointment
(B) Order more products
(C) Arrange a meeting
(D) Change the colors

89 What is available in the reception hall?

(A) Brochures
(B) Maps
(C) Food and drinks
(D) A gift shop

90 What does the speaker imply when she says, "Please remember the Modern Precious collection is not expected to last very long"?

(A) The product sale has ended recently.
(B) Many people are waiting to buy items.
(C) People need to purchase the items quickly.
(D) There is only a small selection of artwork.

91 What will the listeners do next?

(A) Buy some souvenirs
(B) Look over a special collection
(C) Introduce themselves to each other
(D) Leave the building

Agenda	
Welcoming speech	Paul Baker
Financial report	Yohey Ogawa
New product	Beda Hari
Team restructuring	Lisa Whang

92 Where does the speaker most likely work?

(A) At a stock trading company
(B) At a computer manufacturer
(C) At an Internet service provider
(D) At an electronics retailer

93 Look at the graphic. Who is most likely speaking?

(A) Paul Baker
(B) Yohey Ogawa
(C) Beda Hari
(D) Lisa Whang

94 According to the speaker, what will the business do in two weeks?

(A) Sign an exclusive deal
(B) Open a new branch
(C) Release new software
(D) Begin selling new items online

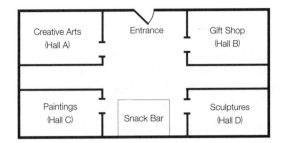

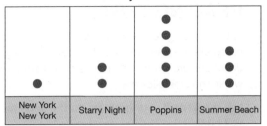

Survey Result

95 Look at the graphic. Which area is unavailable to the public?

(A) Hall A
(B) Hall B
(C) Hall C
(D) Hall D

96 What does the speaker recommend the listeners do?

(A) Visit another museum
(B) Meet a painter
(C) See a live demonstration
(D) Purchase some gifts

97 Who is John Grisham?

(A) A collector
(B) A local potter
(C) A museum curator
(D) The tour guide

98 Look at the graphic. Which production will be selected?

(A) New York New York
(B) Starry Night
(C) Poppins
(D) Summer Beach

99 Why does the speaker praise Sophia?

(A) She wrote scripts well.
(B) She performed her role well.
(C) She made social media updates.
(D) She sold lots of tickets.

100 What does the speaker remind the listeners to do?

(A) Cast actors for roles
(B) Call Sophia
(C) Inform people of updates
(D) Buy many tickets

This is the end of the Listening test. Turn to Part 5 in your test book.

GO ON TO THE NEXT PAGE

READING TEST

In the Reading test, you will read a variety of texts and answer several different types of reading comprehension questions. The entire Reading test will last 75 minutes. There are three parts, and directions are given for each part. You are encouraged to answer as many questions as possible within the time allowed.

You must mark your answers on the separate answer sheet. Do not write your answers in your test book.

PART 5

Directions: A word or phrase is missing in each of the sentences below. Four answer choices are given below each sentence. Select the best answer to complete the sentence. Then mark the letter (A), (B), (C), or (D) on your answer sheet.

101 Jonas Pet Supplies will soon open factories in ------- Holland and Spain.

(A) yet
(B) but
(C) either
(D) both

102 Please donate money to the Moonlight Gallery and show ------- support for the visual arts.

(A) your
(B) yourselves
(C) yours
(D) yourself

103 New Age Eye customers will be delighted to find out about our new ------- rates on plastic lenses.

(A) easier
(B) lower
(C) thicker
(D) louder

104 Bachman Machinery professionals can ------- design custom-tailored solutions to suit your production needs.

(A) skillful
(B) skills
(C) skill
(D) skillfully

105 ------- the workshop is over, all participants are welcome to enjoy free refreshments next door.

(A) When
(B) Still
(C) Though
(D) Soon

106 Ms. Rosy ------- her business associates that the merger should be completed by August 30.

(A) stated
(B) informed
(C) confirmed
(D) agreed

107 Professor Franco is planning a general meeting to obtain feedback ------- senior tax professionals.

(A) from
(B) as
(C) past
(D) at

108 Mr. Han ------- offered to help his co-workers learn to use the network software.

(A) variably
(B) accurately
(C) generously
(D) entirely

109 Our computer store has secured a 30 percent discount on the ------- cost of new software.

(A) totaling
(B) totals
(C) total
(D) totally

110 Merrick Financial Consultants can help retailers ------- their newly launched businesses into more lucrative enterprises.

(A) develops
(B) developed
(C) develop
(D) development

111 The Urban Committee confirmed the sale of the historic Winchester House ------- concerns raised by the Barton Legacy Committee.

(A) except
(B) within
(C) onto
(D) despite

112 With more than 5 million copies sold, *June Daily's Financial Guide* offers ------- information to business marketers.

(A) valuable
(B) eager
(C) aware
(D) numerous

113 At Fabulous Drapes, all weekly salaries are deposited ------- into workers' bank accounts.

(A) directed
(B) directly
(C) direction
(D) directs

114 In her farewell speech, Ms. Juno described her ------- path to becoming a well-known journalist.

(A) challenging
(B) challenges
(C) challenger
(D) challenge

115 James Computers will be closed tomorrow in ------- of the public holiday.

(A) observance
(B) observant
(C) observe
(D) observer

116 The City of Reedville owns and maintains 20 public parks, six of ------- have swimming facilities.

(A) all
(B) them
(C) which
(D) that

117 Ms. Reynolds told her staff that overtime hours ------- to guarantee that the wind turbines can be completed in time for tomorrow's shipment.

(A) have approved
(B) approved
(C) having been approved
(D) have been approved

118 Despite an overwhelmingly positive public ------- to the idea, raising funds to build a new park was difficult.

(A) approval
(B) response
(C) display
(D) creation

119 Insoft Technologies has aggressively recruited ------- of the best software developers in the region.

(A) some
(B) every
(C) other
(D) much

120 Sevenstar Shoe, which began as a small local shop, is now an internationally ------- brand.

(A) recognize
(B) recognized
(C) recognizer
(D) recognizing

GO ON TO THE NEXT PAGE

121 All employees are ------- to sign out at the end of the day so that the cleaning staff knows when the office is empty.

(A) inquired
(B) reminded
(C) denied
(D) committed

122 Renovations in the Gallery showrooms will be completed gradually ------- a six-week time period.

(A) above
(B) down
(C) over
(D) into

123 According to the long-term weather forecast report, heavy rain is expected to last for the ------- of the month.

(A) exception
(B) remainder
(C) boundary
(D) anticipation

124 In his address, Vice Chancellor Dale Clark compared the recent performance of Collins & Tuft ------- HG Consulting Group.

(A) rather
(B) indeed
(C) to that of
(D) what is more

125 It is ------- that Murray Almon will be reelected as chairman of the Civil Defense League.

(A) probable
(B) qualified
(C) constant
(D) endless

126 ------- completing the entrance test for the accounting course, please ensure you fill in your current employer and a contact number.

(A) While
(B) During
(C) In addition
(D) Assuming that

127 Following a meticulous inspection of the building, we found out that the storm damage was more ------- than first estimated.

(A) effective
(B) accurate
(C) apparent
(D) severe

128 By the time the acquisition was announced, Alpha Carriers -------- developing new business strategies.

(A) begins
(B) will begin
(C) had begun
(D) having begun

129 Shine Media will promote its new online music service, Jelly Music, ------- an extensive social media marketing campaign.

(A) under
(B) among
(C) below
(D) through

130 Animal Welfare's promotional campaign has resulted in a ------- 50 percent rise in donations over the last 3 months.

(A) receptive
(B) remarkable
(C) tedious
(D) perpetual

PART 6

Directions: Read the texts that follow. A word, phrase, or sentence is missing in parts of each text. Four answer choices for each question are given below the text. Select the best answer to complete the text. Then mark the letter (A), (B), (C), or (D) on your answer sheet.

Questions 131-134 refer to the following notice.

Increasing expenses have made us review the contracts with our suppliers. -------, we have
131.
decided to change ink suppliers.

As of August 1, all future purchases of ink will come from Dory Ink. The existing stock of ink
should still be used until it runs out. However, workers must familiarize themselves with any
instructions and procedures before using the new ink. It is essential that the ------- procedures
132.
be used with their respective product lines.

-------. These will be distributed to all workers as soon as the first shipment of new ink arrives.
133.
Please review the instructions thoroughly. Any inquiries about use of the new products can be
directed to me (555-2250) or our Dory Ink sales -------, Mary Henry (1-200-555-0444).
134.

131 (A) Otherwise
(B) Nevertheless
(C) Namely
(D) Consequently

132 (A) obsolete
(B) appropriate
(C) manual
(D) obvious

133 (A) Dory Ink is among the bestselling brands
of ink for industrial applications.
(B) Employees should undergo special
training on how to properly use a printer.
(C) Dory Ink has instructional brochures
explaining how to use their products.
(D) We can reduce costs by using less ink
and making two-sided copies.

134 (A) representative
(B) represented
(C) representation
(D) represent

GO ON TO THE NEXT PAGE

Questions 135-138 refer to the following letter.

Mickey Orden, Director
Clear Water Fishing Supplies
89 Hennz Road
Dayton, Ohio 45377

Dear Mr. Orden:

My supervisor, Judy Petrie, recently spoke to me about a job opportunity for a production designer in our Los Angeles office. She thought that I would be an excellent person for the job. -------.
   135.

This transfer ------- me the chance to associate again with Jessica Antz, the interior design
                    136.
manager in Los Angeles. Ms. Antz and I collaborated on the National Fly Fishing project when she was working here in Dayton.

Ms. Petrie has ------- full support for the move and she has offered to put her approval in writing
                 137.
for you. I have included my résumé and thank you in advance for your -------.
                                                                        138.

Sincerely,

Jason Tate
Production Design Specialist
Enclosures

135 (A) In addition, she has already completed the internship in a design firm.
(B) Therefore, I would like you to consider my application for a transfer to the Los Angeles office.
(C) However, my experience working overseas makes me a perfect fit for the job.
(D) Otherwise, I will decide to relocate to another country.

136 (A) did allow
(B) would allow
(C) has allowed
(D) was allowing

137 (A) relied
(B) questioned
(C) expressed
(D) wanted

138 (A) ideas
(B) progress
(C) consideration
(D) patience

Questions 139-142 refer to the following memo.

From: Cody Allen
To: All KPN employees

As you are aware, KPN has undergone some major renovations over the past six months. During that time, our Human Resources Department has made many adjustments ------- still trying to
139.
provide outstanding service. Since our employees are our most valuable assets, we would like to hear about your experiences with the changes.

------- is a single-page survey. This confidential survey is being conducted by Superb Research,
140.
a company that has provided KPN with marketing research and analysis for almost a decade.

Your straightforward and timely feedback will help determine goals for the department. All responses will be kept -------. Please submit the completed form to HR by Monday, June 10.
141.

-------. We always appreciate your dedication to KPN.
142.

139 (A) after
(B) without
(C) unlike
(D) while

140 (A) Enclosure
(B) To enclose
(C) Enclosed
(D) Enclosing

141 (A) anonymous
(B) unattended
(C) sustainable
(D) dependent

142 (A) We have made a considerable effort to improve employee satisfaction.
(B) It has been an honor to serve all employees at KPN.
(C) Thank you in advance for your time and opinions.
(D) Please upload your suggestions to our Web site.

Questions 143-146 refer to the following e-mail.

To: Catering Department Staff
From: Novek Ivanovic
Date: April 22
Subject: New Coffee Machine

Dear Colleagues:

Today, a new coffee machine was installed in the common room as a replacement for the old one

that constantly broke down. We hope that this model will be more -------.
143.

It is a large-capacity reputable coffee maker. -------. To ensure effective maintenance for the
144.
coffee machine, only use the accessories that are supplied ------- paper cups and milk sachets
145.
rather than using any others.

You may experience problems initially when using the machine. If so, you can ------- the
146.
instructions that we will put on the notice board next to the machine.

Regards,

Novek

---

143 (A) reliable
(B) achievable
(C) portable
(D) detectable

144 (A) We need to buy the newest line of
machinery.
(B) The following is how to make a decent
cup of coffee.
(C) All employees are required to attend the
cooking class.
(D) We also have a warranty that it will last
for at least ten years.

145 (A) of these
(B) as well
(C) such as
(D) sort of

146 (A) revise
(B) discard
(C) approve
(D) consult

PART 7

Directions: In this part you will read a selection of texts, such as magazine and newspaper articles, e-mails, and instant messages. Each text or set of texts is followed by several questions. Select the best answer for each question and mark the letter (A), (B), (C), or (D) on your answer sheet.

Questions 147-48 refer to the following schedule.

Reservations for Room 8, November 5-9

	MONDAY Nov. 5	TUESDAY Nov. 6	WEDNESDAY Nov. 7	THURSDAY Nov. 8	FRIDAY Nov. 9
10:00 A.M.	Stories for Children		Stories for Children		Youth Writing Society
11:00 A.M.		Lecture by Author Darryl Doolage		Science Fiction Reading	
Noon			Summer Book Program Party		Friends of Literature Meeting
1:00 P.M.	Stories for Children			Poetry Club Meeting	
2:00 P.M.			Board Meeting		
3:00 P.M.		Job Application and Interviewing Skills Lesson			

147 Where is Room 8 most likely located?

(A) In a department store
(B) In a public library
(C) In an art gallery
(D) In an employment agency

148 What event is scheduled on the same day as the Youth Writing Society?

(A) Stories for Children
(B) Friends of Literature Meeting
(C) Science Fiction Reading
(D) Poetry Club Meeting

GO ON TO THE NEXT PAGE

Questions 149-151 refer to the following text message chain.

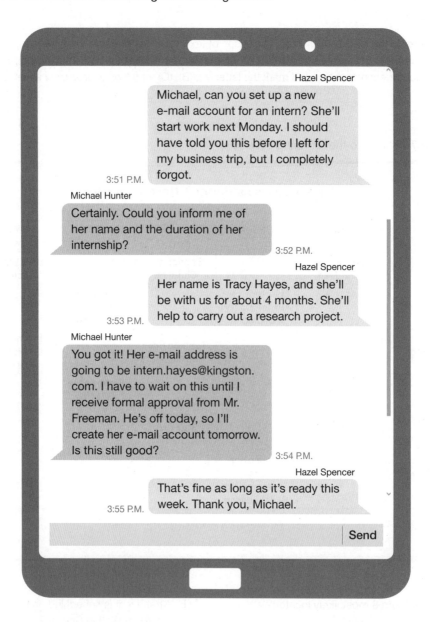

Hazel Spencer

Michael, can you set up a new e-mail account for an intern? She'll start work next Monday. I should have told you this before I left for my business trip, but I completely forgot.

3:51 P.M.

Michael Hunter

Certainly. Could you inform me of her name and the duration of her internship?

3:52 P.M.

Hazel Spencer

Her name is Tracy Hayes, and she'll be with us for about 4 months. She'll help to carry out a research project.

3:53 P.M.

Michael Hunter

You got it! Her e-mail address is going to be intern.hayes@kingston.com. I have to wait on this until I receive formal approval from Mr. Freeman. He's off today, so I'll create her e-mail account tomorrow. Is this still good?

3:54 P.M.

Hazel Spencer

That's fine as long as it's ready this week. Thank you, Michael.

3:55 P.M.

Send

149 What is implied about Tracy Hayes?

(A) She is on a business trip.
(B) She needs to send an e-mail now.
(C) She will start her internship soon.
(D) She will work full-time after her internship.

150 At 3:54 P.M., what does Mr. Hunter mean when he writes, "You got it"?

(A) He will make a new e-mail account.
(B) He will forward an e-mail to someone.
(C) He will lead a research project.
(D) He will give an orientation to interns.

151 What does Mr. Hunter have to wait for?

(A) A network engineer
(B) A person's approval
(C) A formal document
(D) A job interview

Questions 152-154 refer to the following e-mail.

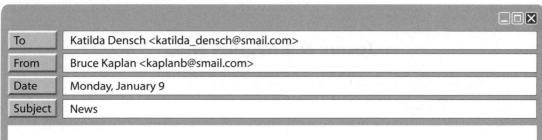

Dear Katilda,

Thank you again for arranging my visit to the Memphis offices last month. It was very fruitful and enjoyable, and I look forward to visiting again soon. While I was there, you noted that you would be interested in relocating to France to be near your mother. I wanted to let you know that our Paris office currently has a position available in the accounting department. We are looking for a tax expert, a job for which I think you would be highly qualified. The job responsibilities are much like those of your management accountant position in Memphis. The opening will be publicly advertised at the end of next month, but we will begin soliciting applications from within the organization this week. If you are interested in submitting an application, please let me know, and I'll email the job details and application right away.

Best regards,
Bruce Kaplan

152 What is the purpose of the e-mail?

(A) To discuss travel arrangements
(B) To encourage Ms. Densch to apply for a job
(C) To inform Ms. Densch of an upcoming business meeting
(D) To explain the company's recent restructuring

153 According to the e-mail, why is Ms. Densch interested in moving to Paris?

(A) To tour the area with Mr. Kaplan
(B) To work in a position with more responsibility
(C) To live closer to a family member
(D) To collaborate with Mr. Kaplan on a project

154 What does Mr. Kaplan offer to do for Ms. Densch?

(A) Arrange for her to meet the project manager
(B) Find a place for her to stay
(C) Send her additional information
(D) Answer her questions

GO ON TO THE NEXT PAGE

Jones & Vargoes Inc.

Positions are for the night shift (5:00 P.M. – 10:00 P.M.), unless otherwise indicated.

Warehouse Manager

Must have a high school diploma, strong awareness of stock control procedures, and experience in a busy production environment. Must also have a basic knowledge of technology and finance. Previous management work is desirable but not essential.

Factory Technician

Must have relevant qualifications, at least two years of experience working in a factory environment. Must also be capable of operating heavy equipment. Night work is a necessity.

Personal Assistant

Must have a high school diploma, excellent typing skills and experience in a retail establishment. Some night work is necessary.

Distribution Manager and Stock Assistants

Must be diligent and reliable. Some night work is required in the case of the stock assistant positions.

Please send résumés to: Human resources
Jones & Vargoes Inc.
Distribution center
1415 Cambridge Rd.
Boston, MA, 02109

No phone calls or e-mails, please.

---

155 What is a requirement for the warehouse manager position?

(A) A degree in marketing
(B) Some knowledge of finance
(C) Previous management experience
(D) A willingness to work the night shift

156 What position does NOT involve night shifts?

(A) Distribution manager
(B) Personal assistant
(C) Factory technician
(D) Stock assistant

157 How will candidates apply for the positions?

(A) Online
(B) In person
(C) By mail
(D) By telephone

James Institute for Marketing

Are you looking for a marketing-degree program? –[1]–.

This is a twelve-month program — with entry dates in February, June, and October and a wide variety of courses in cross-cultural marketing and international advertising. Classes are led by distinguished personnel, most of whom hold senior positions in reputable advertising and trading companies and bring real-work information to the classroom. –[2]–. This, plus overseas internship options in leading international businesses, has led to the National Association of Marketers to consistently rate our program among the top three in the country.

The application fee is $100 for residents and $120 for overseas applicants. –[3]–. Mention this advertisement and you will not have to pay the application fee, provided the documents are submitted on or before October 30. The regular application deadline is November 30. Applicants are encouraged to seek scholarships and sponsorship. –[4]–. If you have questions and need more information, visit our Web site at www.jamesmarketing.edu.

158 What is suggested about the Excellence Marketing Program?

(A) It takes two years to finish.
(B) It has an excellent reputation.
(C) It has two enrollment times.
(D) It recently added faculty employees.

159 According to the advertisement, what is NOT available to students?

(A) Access to professors with professional expertise
(B) An opportunity to gain experience abroad
(C) The chance to take courses online
(D) The opportunity of getting financial assistance

160 In which of the positions marked [1], [2], [3], and [4] does the following sentence best belong?

"Then look no further than the Excellence Marketing Program at the James Institute for Marketing."

(A) [1]
(B) [2]
(C) [3]
(D) [4]

GO ON TO THE NEXT PAGE

Judy Jones
20 Hessa Street
Jefferson, Maine 04348

September 20

Paul Duveshnie, Manager
All Fashions Magazine
Dennis Road
Jefferson, Maine 04348

Dear. Mr. Duveshnie,

I'm writing to inform you that I intend to resign as photographer at *All Fashions Magazine*, to take effect on October 30. I am notifying you one month in advance, as outlined in our contract.

For some time, I have been thinking about starting my own full-time photography venture. One month ago, I won a prize from the Organization of Master Photographers as an individual photographer. The winnings included a financial prize that will allow me to start my own venture.

During my time at the magazine, I learned so much about this field. My colleagues at the photography department helped me develop not only as an artist, but also as a business professional. Even though I will build my new career as a professional photographer, I will genuinely miss my time here and all of you. It is my hope that we will stay in touch as I begin this new adventure in my life. I wish you and the company future success.

Sincerely,
Judy Jones
Judy Jones

161 Why did Ms. Jones write to Mr. Duveshnie?

(A) To ask for a transfer
(B) To ask for a promotion
(C) To apply for a funding program
(D) To advise him of a decision

162 What did Ms. Jones recently receive?

(A) Opportunity to be trained by a well-known visual artist
(B) Recognition for her outstanding work
(C) A letter of appreciation from an independent photographer for special assistance
(D) A three-year contract as supervisor for the photography department

163 What did the Organization of Master Photographers help Ms. Jones to do?

(A) Make the decision to work part-time instead of full-time
(B) Leave her position as head of the photography department
(C) Choose to focus on a personal goal
(D) Apply for a small-business loan

GO ON TO THE NEXT PAGE

Questions 164-166 refer to the following online chat discussion.

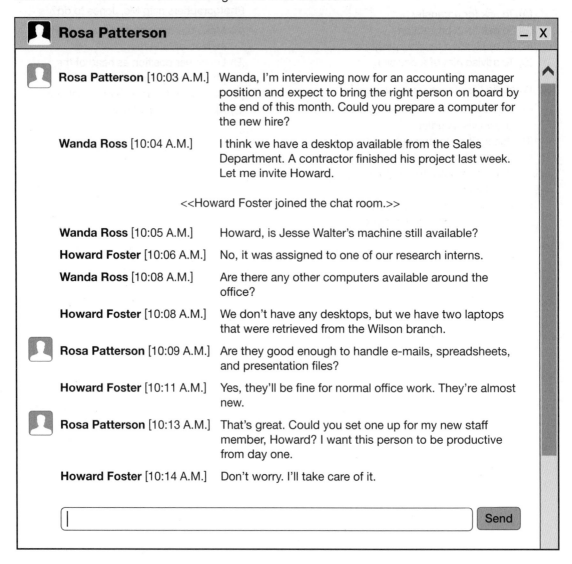

Rosa Patterson   − X

Rosa Patterson [10:03 A.M.]   Wanda, I'm interviewing now for an accounting manager position and expect to bring the right person on board by the end of this month. Could you prepare a computer for the new hire?

Wanda Ross [10:04 A.M.]   I think we have a desktop available from the Sales Department. A contractor finished his project last week. Let me invite Howard.

<<Howard Foster joined the chat room.>>

Wanda Ross [10:05 A.M.]   Howard, is Jesse Walter's machine still available?

Howard Foster [10:06 A.M.]   No, it was assigned to one of our research interns.

Wanda Ross [10:08 A.M.]   Are there any other computers available around the office?

Howard Foster [10:08 A.M.]   We don't have any desktops, but we have two laptops that were retrieved from the Wilson branch.

Rosa Patterson [10:09 A.M.]   Are they good enough to handle e-mails, spreadsheets, and presentation files?

Howard Foster [10:11 A.M.]   Yes, they'll be fine for normal office work. They're almost new.

Rosa Patterson [10:13 A.M.]   That's great. Could you set one up for my new staff member, Howard? I want this person to be productive from day one.

Howard Foster [10:14 A.M.]   Don't worry. I'll take care of it.

Send

164 Why did Ms. Ross invite Mr. Foster?

(A) To explain what she wanted to order

(B) To ask questions about a new hire

(C) To request that he retrieve some computers

(D) To ask about the availability of office equipment

165 What is suggested about Ms. Patterson?

(A) She plans to hire some interns.

(B) She wants to upgrade some computers for her staff.

(C) She wants her new staff member to work without delay.

(D) She used to work at the Wilson branch.

166 At 10:14 A.M., what does Mr. Foster mean when he writes, "I'll take care of it"?

(A) He will review a financial report.

(B) He will reserve a conference room.

(C) He will order a computer online.

(D) He will set up a computer.

GO ON TO THE NEXT PAGE

Dear Local Residents,

Beginning next week, La Marler will be known as Evonia Road Bistro. The restaurant will also undergo several modifications, including an enlargement of its outside patio area and refurbishing of the main dining room to provide more space. Please be assured that under its new manager, Paul Gant, the restaurant will offer the same delicious French food at the low prices you have come to expect. Please enjoy our continued service.

167 According to the advertisement, what is being changed about the restaurant?

(A) The type of food served
(B) The pricing of the food
(C) Its location
(D) Its name

168 What is suggested about Mr. Gant?

(A) He owns other businesses in the neighborhood.
(B) He plans to develop the restaurant's seating capacity.
(C) He has lived on Evonia Road for several years.
(D) He used to work at La Marler.

Questions 169-171 refer to the following notice.

Corporate Library Cards

The state university library system extends borrowing privileges to the business community. Employees of any company with offices in our city are eligible for the privilege of a corporate card.

The yearly fee for each card issued to a worker at an organization is $40. Government and nonprofit entities are exempt from these payments.

Corporate library cards are meant for employees who conduct research for their organizations. These individuals must take responsibility for all the materials they borrow. Fines imposed by the library for overdue or missing materials are the liability of the card-holder.

To obtain a corporate card, employees must apply in person at the university library. Applicants are required to provide photo identification and a letter from their employer as proof of their employment. The fee is due with the application. A receipt can be provided for reimbursement purposes.

If you have any queries about the corporate card, please contact the circulation desk at 855-555-3001.

169 What is the purpose of the notice?

(A) To correct a mistake
(B) To explain a service
(C) To put forward an idea
(D) To announce an event

170 What is stated about annual fees?

(A) They can be paid by credit card.
(B) They are unlikely to increase.
(C) They are not applicable to some types of organizations.
(D) They are higher for non-local businesses.

171 What is NOT required at the time of application?

(A) A signed contract
(B) Proof of identity
(C) A payment
(D) Employment details

GO ON TO THE NEXT PAGE

June 5 – Botanist Reeva Dubchec announced yesterday that she is donating one million dollars over a period of two years to Tunney Natural Heritage project. The contribution comes at a crucial time, as the project's funding has been strained for the past three years. –[1]–.

"We're thrilled to receive Ms. Dubchec's generous gift." said Tunney Natural Heritage president James McNulty. "It will go a long way toward conserving the natural cornerstone of our community."

Natural Heritage was launched a decade ago by the Nature Reserve Society (NRS) to restore and preserve natural resorts from the town's early years. It was originally funded by tax revenue; however, three years ago the town council decided to move much of that income away from the NRS and into a new land development project. –[2]–.

Five months ago, NRS began soliciting private gifts from larger businesses in the community. "Along with a letter asking for donations, we sent photographs of several natural sites in need of maintenance," Mr. McNulty recalled. One such site was the Orchid Heritage Site where former resident Reeva Dubchec was a frequent visitor. "I didn't know about Reeva's personal connection to the site until she called me and asked how she could help." Mr. McNulty said.

Tunney residents and leadership have responded with great delight to the news of the donation. Mayor Jim Connor and members of the town council have considered putting honorary plaques in several natural landmarks to make the town appealing to new residents, visitors, and businesses. –[3]–.

"When I was a child, I was inspired by the natural sites in Tunney. They were instrumental in helping me choose my career studying plant life. This donation is not just about preserving the town's resources. –[4]–. It's about investing in its future," Ms. Dubchec said.

Richard Dobbs
Local Contributor

172 According to the article, why was the project losing funding?

(A) Because building costs increased
(B) Because the local government decreased its financial support
(C) Because the renovation work was complete
(D) Because Tunney's population had decreased

173 Who is currently NOT a resident of Tunney?

(A) James McNulty
(B) Reeva Dubchek
(C) Jim Connor
(D) Richard Dobbs

174 What does Ms. Dubchec say about the nature reserves in Tunney?

(A) They made her decide to become a botanist.
(B) They are too costly to maintain.
(C) Each one should bear a plaque indicating the year it was built.
(D) Local organizations should pay to restore them.

175 In which of the positions marked [1], [2], [3], and [4] does the following sentence best belong?

"Since then, financial support for natural resource maintenance has remained limited."

(A) [1]
(B) [2]
(C) [3]
(D) [4]

GO ON TO THE NEXT PAGE

Questions 176-180 refer to the following e-mails.

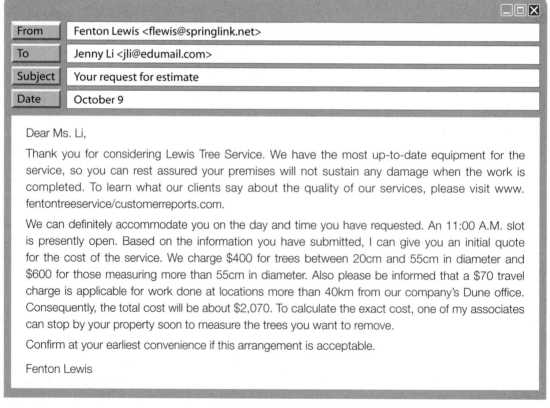

E-Mail Message

From: Jenny Li <jli@edumail.com>
To: Fenton Lewis <flewis@springlink.net>
Re: Estimate
Date: October 8

Dear Mr. Lewis,

I was referred to you by Lee-Anne Fuentes, a neighbor in the town of Ithaca. I would like to obtain an estimate for removing four Leyland cypresses from my garden, which have become a safety issue.

They are about 13 meters high: two are approximately 45 centimeters in diameter while the others have a diameter of about 75 centimeters. They are standing within 4 meters of my house and two meters of the hedge.

Would a team be available around 11 o'clock in the morning on Friday, 15 October? October, November and December are the busiest times for people like us who work in the tourist industry. The only day that I can afford is next Friday.

I look forward to hearing from you soon.

Sincerely,
Jenny Li

From: Fenton Lewis <flewis@springlink.net>
To: Jenny Li <jli@edumail.com>
Subject: Your request for estimate
Date: October 9

Dear Ms. Li,

Thank you for considering Lewis Tree Service. We have the most up-to-date equipment for the service, so you can rest assured your premises will not sustain any damage when the work is completed. To learn what our clients say about the quality of our services, please visit www.fentontreeservice/customerreports.com.

We can definitely accommodate you on the day and time you have requested. An 11:00 A.M. slot is presently open. Based on the information you have submitted, I can give you an initial quote for the cost of the service. We charge $400 for trees between 20cm and 55cm in diameter and $600 for those measuring more than 55cm in diameter. Also please be informed that a $70 travel charge is applicable for work done at locations more than 40km from our company's Dune office. Consequently, the total cost will be about $2,070. To calculate the exact cost, one of my associates can stop by your property soon to measure the trees you want to remove.

Confirm at your earliest convenience if this arrangement is acceptable.

Fenton Lewis

176 What information does Ms. Li NOT provide in the e-mail to Mr. Lewis?

(A) The height of some plants in her garden
(B) The type of employment she has
(C) The street she lives on
(D) The day she can take off from work

177 What is suggested about Ms. Li?

(A) She previously had work done in her garden by Lewis Tree Service.
(B) She plans to go on vacation in March.
(C) She lives more than 40km from Lewis Tree Service's office.
(D) She will receive a discount from Lewis Tree Service.

178 In the second e-mail, the word "sustain" in paragraph 1, line 2, is closest in meaning to

(A) assess
(B) suffer
(C) support
(D) cause

179 What does Mr. Lewis recommend that Ms. Li do?

(A) Buy new equipment for her garden
(B) Telephone him at 11 A.M.
(C) Visit his office to provide him with exact measurement of the trees
(D) Read on-line customer reviews about his service

180 When does Mr. Lewis agree to do the work?

(A) On November 10
(B) On October 15
(C) On October 3
(D) On October 2

Test 04

GO ON TO THE NEXT PAGE

Hayworth House
in the heart of Downtown Lanshow

New Mixed-Use Property Opening February 1
Residential, Business, and Commercial Spaces for Rent

Modern, state-of-the-art construction flanked by shops and cafés. Close to bus stop.
Across the street from Hayworth Lake and Hiking. Spring-fed lake and hiking trails nearby.

Apartments (Floor 4-8): one-, two-, and three-bedroom apartments, each with kitchen, full bathroom, living/ dining room, and spacious closets. Storage facilities in basement available for a minor monthly fee. Free underground parking for tenants and visitors. Shared laundry facilities on floor 6 and 8. Roof garden to be added.

Offices (Floor 2-3): Flexible office spaces can be divided as needed while space is available. Suitable for single offices and complete company office suites. Several layout options to choose from.

Retail Stores (Street level): Two storefronts offered. Both 500 square meters. Retail use only.

Prices and leasing information provided on request:
Please direct residential inquiries to Leonora Dean (080) 555-6705 or ldean@hayworth.com.
Direct commercial inquiries to Gina Fitzgerald (080) 555-6707 or gfitz@hayworth.com.

From	Michael Peck<mpeck@plaw.com>
To	Gina Fitzgerald <gfitz@hayworth.com>
Title	Hayworth House
Date	14:23, November 21

Dear Ms. Fitzgerald,

If it would be possible to organize the office space at Hayworth House to accommodate a total of 50 employees, both lawyers and support workers, I would be interested in visiting the property at your earliest convenience.

Our current premises, just a few blocks from Hayworth House, is too small to accommodate any additional people. My firm's business has been growing rapidly, and we will be employing several new staff members in the near future to handle our growing caseload.

Sincerely,
Peck

181 What is indicated about Hayworth House?

(A) It's on a bus route.
(B) It was designed by a local professional.
(C) Its opening has been delayed.
(D) It's on the edge of the city.

182 According to the advertisement, what is available to residential tenants for an additional cost?

(A) Underground parking
(B) Basement storage
(C) Use of a shared garden
(D) Shared laundry facilities

183 What type of tenant is NOT allowed to occupy the building?

(A) A wholesaler
(B) A clothing store
(C) An advertising agency
(D) A family of three people

184 What is suggested about Mr. Peck's firm?

(A) It recently increased its fees.
(B) It is relocating to Lanshow.
(C) It has enjoyed increasing success.
(D) It buys and renovates commercial properties.

185 What part of Hayworth House would most likely interest Mr. Peck?

(A) Floors 4-8
(B) Floors 2-3
(C) Street level spaces
(D) The basement

GO ON TO THE NEXT PAGE

Questions 186-190 refer to the following e-mail, announcement, and letter.

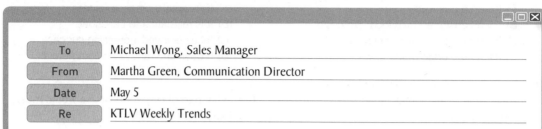

To	Michael Wong, Sales Manager
From	Martha Green, Communication Director
Date	May 5
Re	KTLV Weekly Trends

Dear Michael:

Thank you for informing me that you have been contacted by a TV broadcasting station. I have reviewed the program summary you submitted, and it looks like they want you because of your professional expertise. I discussed this issue with Vice President Lauren Parker, and she gave permission for you to appear on the show. Jeremy Diaz from the General Administration Department will help you to prepare for the show. Please give him a list of products that you need for the show.

Before the show, please keep in mind the following rules that you should follow when communicating with the media.

• Do not talk about personnel issues at the company.
• Do not discuss any future business plans that have not been mentioned in press releases.
• Do not disclose sensitive information that is related to the company's clients and customers.
• Please avoid discussing any emergencies or crises at the company.

I hope you can positively portray our brand and products. Good luck.

Best Wishes,
Martha Green

Our Employee on KTLV Weekly Trends

On Saturday, May 24, Michael Wong from the Marketing Department will be a guest on the TV show Weekly Trends. The senior sales manager will talk about recent trends in the camping market. On the show, he will talk about our tents, sleeping bags, and cookware as he gives some tips on camping. Weekly Trends is one of the top-rated shows and has a 12.3 rating with adults ages 18-49. We hope his appearance on the show helps promote our brand and products. The show will air from 8 to 9 P.M. on Channel 15. It will also be streamed at www.KTLV.com. If you don't make it on time or want to watch the show again, please visit the KTLV Web site.

May 28

Michael Wong
Orleans Sports, Inc.
1610 Wisconsin Ave,
Milwaukee, WI 53233

Dear Mr. Wong:

We are so happy that we had you as a guest on our show. The show on May 24 was quite successful, and the ratings were higher than we had expected. We have received a lot of positive feedback from our viewers. They said your tips on outdoor camping were very useful and informative. Thank you for your efforts and contributions.

In spite of your request, we didn't edit out what you said about the new product launch in a few months. Despite your concerns, the new camping equipment was officially mentioned in a press release by your company. We double-checked with Martha Green at your company.

I would like to ask if you could appear on our show one more time in July. We are planning to air a summer special show about outdoor activities on July 19. The show will start airing at 8 P.M. and will last for 2 hours. We really hope we can have you back on our show then. We look forward to hearing from you as soon as possible.

Sincerely,
Brian Duff
Senior Producer, KTLV

186 According to the e-mail, who will assist Mr. Wong with his TV appearance?

(A) Martha Green
(B) Lauren Parker
(C) Jeremy Diaz
(D) Brian Duff

187 In the e-mail, the word "expertise" in paragraph 1, line 3, is closest in meaning to

(A) knowledge
(B) impression
(C) look
(D) opinion

188 What is the purpose of the announcement?

(A) To promote new camping equipment
(B) To provide camping tips for people
(C) To tell the ratings of a TV show
(D) To encourage people to watch a TV program

189 Why did Mr. Wong ask that what he said on the show be edited?

(A) He disclosed sensitive information about his client.
(B) He talked about a personnel issue regarding a coworker.
(C) He mentioned a future business plan of his company.
(D) He indicated that his company was having financial difficulties.

190 How will the special show differ from the regular show?

(A) It will start at 9 P.M.
(B) It will air one hour longer.
(C) It will be broadcast on Sunday.
(D) It will be on Channel 16.

GO ON TO THE NEXT PAGE

Questions 191-195 refer to the following advertisement and e-mails.

Ottawa Online Business Conference

October is the biggest month for the staff members at the Ottawa Online Business Conference because our annual conference takes place then. However, the biggest month for attendees is June. That is the early-bird registration month for the upcoming 27th OOBC. It means that rates go up on July 1. Now is the best time to save on registration fees, especially for companies sending a group of people. If you register this month, you can save $100 per person. In addition to giving you an early-bird discount, we will present you with a $50 gift card which can be used at the Royal Hotel, Ace Hotel, or Next Hotel. The best news for all registrants in June is that one lucky participant will receive a free 3-night hotel stay during the conference. You must be registered by June 30 to have a chance to be the winner.

We can't wait to see you at the Ottawa Online Business Conference. The best chance to learn about sustainable online business practices is waiting for you. Register today for the best rates.

E-Mail Message

To: reservations@royalhotel.com
From: richard.morris@estrada.com
Date: June 28
Re: Reservation

Hello. My name is Richard Morris, and I work at Estrada, Inc. My company plans to dispatch some employees to attend the 27th Ottawa Online Business Conference in October. We talked with some OOBC people, and they recommended your hotel because of the location and service provided by your hotel staff. I would like to know if you have any rooms available for them. I tried to make a reservation at your Web site but could not find an option for a group reservation.

Eleven of them will stay from October 12 to 14, and they need three single rooms and four double rooms. If it is possible, they would prefer to stay on the same floor. I want to make sure that they can use their OOBC gift cards, too.

If the rooms are available, please contact me and tell me what to do to reserve the rooms at your hotel.

Sincerely,
Richard Morris
General Department
Estrada, Inc.

To: olga.carter@estrada.com
From: james.stanley@royalhotel.com
Date: October 22
Re: Reservation

Dear Ms. Carter,

Thank you for contacting the Royal Hotel, Ottawa. I am writing to respond to your e-mail on October 20. As you requested, we checked your account immediately and discovered that we overcharged you. A staff member didn't apply the OOBC gift card you presented. We recently hired a new payment service company, and some of our staff members have not gotten accustomed to using the new system. We sincerely apologize for the mistake. Since you stayed in a single room at a rate of $100 for three nights, we were supposed to charge you $250 after applying the gift card.

We want to reassure you that we are doing our best to correct this error. The overcharged amount will be refunded to your credit card account in two business days. As a token of our apology, we would also like to give you a free night pass, which you can use to stay for one night for free at any Royal Hotel around the world.

Once again, we apologize for any inconvenience this may have caused you. We look forward to serving you again.

James Stanley
General Manager
Royal Hotel, Ottawa

---

191 What is implied about the Ottawa Online Business Conference?

(A) The staff members are busiest in June.
(B) It will last for five days in June.
(C) The registration fee is the lowest in June.
(D) All attendees will have a chance to win a lottery.

192 In the advertisement, the word "sustainable" in paragraph 2, line 2, is closest in meaning to

(A) likely to occur
(B) existing in reality
(C) able to be moved easily
(D) capable of being continued

193 What is NOT mentioned about employees at Estrada, Inc.?

(A) Eleven of them will attend a conference.
(B) They need seven rooms at a hotel.
(C) They would like to stay on the same floor.
(D) They want to have rooms with a good view.

194 What did Mr. Stanley say about the cause of the problem?

(A) The payment system was temporarily broken.
(B) An employee was unfamiliar with a new system.
(C) The gift card expired in October.
(D) The guest's name was changed at the last minute.

195 How much did the hotel charge Ms. Carter?

(A) $300
(B) $350
(C) $400
(D) $500

GO ON TO THE NEXT PAGE

Questions 196-200 refer to the following notice, article, and Web page.

NOTICE OF PUBLIC HEARING

This notice is to inform you of a public hearing. After the hearing, the Richmond Department of City Planning will decide whether to adopt the proposed plan. All interested people are invited to attend. You may listen and will have a chance to speak regarding the proposed project.

TOPIC OF HEARING: Pamela Boulevard Project
Proposal for roadway improvements including restoring the sewage system, pavement construction, and traffic signal upgrades on Pamela Boulevard.

PLACE: Richmond City Hall
523 West 8th Street
Richmond City, GA 30003

HEARING DATE: Thursday, September 9
TIME: 6:00 P.M. – 8:00 P.M.
FOR ADDITIONAL INFORMATION CONTACT: Richmond Department of City Planning at 555-3217

Pamela Boulevard Project Approved

Richmond City, Georgia - Richmond City has approved a $1.2 million restoration of Pamela Boulevard, which is a critical roadway for residents. City officials say construction is scheduled to start early next year. The construction comes after the roadway was severely flooded and shut down during heavy rainfall last summer. The sewage system was also damaged as Richmond City's aging sewers were not designed for heavy rain. The project also includes pavement reconstruction and traffic signal upgrades.

"When the roadway becomes impassable due to heavy rain, those living in the southern part of the city cannot gain access to the major roads," Mayor James Norris said. "The road upgrade project will enhance access to the main highway entrance during the rainy season."

The city held a public hearing on September 9, and more than 200 citizens participated by raising their voices. They said that the money should be put directly into replacing the old sewage system.

"We listened to the citizens, and their biggest concern was the reconstruction of Pamela Boulevard. It was a big deal, so that's where we put most of the city's budget," the mayor said.

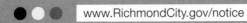

www.RichmondCity.gov/notice

During the weeks from February 1 to October 31, the following road repairs may cause a reduction in lanes or lane closures. The Department of City Planning will make every effort to complete the necessary work as quickly as possible. We hope the citizens of Richmond City will enjoy the improvements once they are complete.

Pamela Boulevard Project
- When: February – June
- Description: Sewage system improvements and upgrading of traffic signals on Pamela Boulevard

Hayman Road Project
- When: March – September
- Description: Addition of a bike trail and updating of the pedestrian crossings on Hayman Road

Westfield Bridge Project
- When: May – October
- Description: Repairs on the bridge and bridge railing

Annapolis Street Project
- When: June – October
- Description: Reconstruction of the intersection

Information on expected traffic disruptions and detours will be posted on the city's Web page. To receive automatic alerts of all the updates, please sign up for our e-mail and text alerts HERE.

196 What is NOT proposed for the Pamela Boulevard Project?

(A) Roadway pavement
(B) Traffic light installation
(C) Sewage pipe replacement
(D) Repairs of sidewalks

197 What is true about the hearing?

(A) It was about a bridge repair project.
(B) The mayor didn't attend it because of heavy rain.
(C) It was held at City Hall with a few hundred people present.
(D) Citizens disapproved of the project.

198 According to the article, what problem was mentioned about Pamela Boulevard?

(A) It was too dark to drive on.
(B) It was flooded in the summer.
(C) It was too narrow for traffic to pass through.
(D) It was slippery in winter.

199 In the article, the word "impassable" in paragraph 2, line 1, is closest in meaning to

(A) renovated
(B) blocked
(C) dirty
(D) lifted

200 What is the purpose of the Web page?

(A) To announce community events
(B) To give alerts of upcoming storms
(C) To provide information on traffic disruptions
(D) To hire construction companies

GO ON TO THE NEXT PAGE

Actual Test

05

🕐	시작 시간	:	
	종료 시간	:	

LISTENING TEST

In the Listening test, you will be asked to demonstrate how well you understand spoken English. The entire Listening test will last approximately 45 minutes. There are four parts, and directions are given for each part. You must mark your answers on the separate answer sheet. Do not write your answers in your test book.

PART 1

Directions: For each question in this part, you will hear four statements about a picture in your test book. When you hear the statements, you must select the one statement that best describes what you see in the picture. Then find the number of the question on your answer sheet and mark your answer. The statements will not be printed in your test book and will be spoken only one time.

Example

Sample Answer
Ⓐ ● Ⓒ Ⓓ

Statement (B), "The man is working at a desk," is the best description of the picture, so you should select answer (B) and mark it on your answer sheet.

1

2

GO ON TO THE NEXT PAGE

3

4

5

6

GO ON TO THE NEXT PAGE ▶

PART 2

Directions: You will hear a question or statement and three responses spoken in English. They will not be printed in your test book and will be spoken only one time. Select the best response to the question or statement and mark the letter (A), (B), or (C) on your answer sheet.

7 Mark your answer on your answer sheet.

8 Mark your answer on your answer sheet.

9 Mark your answer on your answer sheet.

10 Mark your answer on your answer sheet.

11 Mark your answer on your answer sheet.

12 Mark your answer on your answer sheet.

13 Mark your answer on your answer sheet.

14 Mark your answer on your answer sheet.

15 Mark your answer on your answer sheet.

16 Mark your answer on your answer sheet.

17 Mark your answer on your answer sheet.

18 Mark your answer on your answer sheet.

19 Mark your answer on your answer sheet.

20 Mark your answer on your answer sheet.

21 Mark your answer on your answer sheet.

22 Mark your answer on your answer sheet.

23 Mark your answer on your answer sheet.

24 Mark your answer on your answer sheet.

25 Mark your answer on your answer sheet.

26 Mark your answer on your answer sheet.

27 Mark your answer on your answer sheet.

28 Mark your answer on your answer sheet.

29 Mark your answer on your answer sheet.

30 Mark your answer on your answer sheet.

31 Mark your answer on your answer sheet.

PART 3

Directions: You will hear some conversations between two or more people. You will be asked to answer three questions about what the speakers say in each conversation. Select the best response to each question and mark the letter (A), (B), (C), or (D) on your answer sheet. The conversations will not be printed in your test book and will be spoken only one time.

32 Who most likely is the woman?

(A) A supplier
(B) A restaurant worker
(C) A chef
(D) An office employee

33 Why does the woman apologize?

(A) She provided the wrong meal.
(B) There is a mistake in the order.
(C) A business is closing late.
(D) An order was not completed on time.

34 What will the man do next?

(A) Go to a neighbor
(B) Pay for an order
(C) Send an e-mail
(D) Do some shopping

35 What did the woman have to do this week?

(A) Go on a vacation
(B) Cancel her account
(C) Join a different department
(D) Work extra hours

36 Where will the woman go on Monday?

(A) To a mountainous area
(B) To a station
(C) To a park
(D) To a concert

37 What does the man suggest the woman do?

(A) Work from home
(B) Negotiate a pay raise
(C) Ride in a cable car
(D) Go to watch a sports event

38 What are the speakers mainly discussing?

(A) A computer system
(B) A delivery charge
(C) A work agenda
(D) A piece of item

39 What does the man plan to do?

(A) Talk to a customer
(B) Write up an order
(C) Make an appointment
(D) Send an invoice

40 According to the woman, what will happen in two weeks?

(A) An order will be cancelled.
(B) A catalog will be released.
(C) Some products will be back in stock.
(D) A computer brand will become obsolete.

41 What type of position has been advertised?

(A) Architect
(B) Designer
(C) Legal clerk
(D) Lab Technician

42 Where did the woman work most recently?

(A) In Ireland
(B) In Scotland
(C) In England
(D) In Wales

43 What does the man ask the woman to do?

(A) Send in further information
(B) Fill out an online form
(C) Check for more details
(D) Submit a portfolio

GO ON TO THE NEXT PAGE

44 What does the man ask about the office?

(A) Where it is located
(B) When it is available
(C) How many other businesses are there
(D) How much is the rent

45 What is unique about the unit?

(A) Its scenic view
(B) Its storage space
(C) Its historic site
(D) Its reduced price

46 When will the woman meet the man?

(A) At 10:00 A.M.
(B) At 11:00 A.M.
(C) At 1:00 P.M.
(D) At 11:00 P.M.

47 What will the man probably do this afternoon?

(A) Have a meeting with coworkers
(B) Attend an appointment with a client
(C) Pick up a friend
(D) Go to a show downtown

48 What was the man supposed to do at 3:00 P.M.?

(A) Attend a workshop
(B) Visit a branch office
(C) Meet with new employees
(D) Discuss issues with the marketing team

49 What does the man mean when he says, "Come to think of it, I'd better do it myself"?

(A) He will cancel a reservation.
(B) He will contact a coworker.
(C) He will attend a meeting.
(D) He will email some reports.

50 What does the woman ask the man to help her with?

(A) Serving drinks
(B) Moving some tables
(C) Preparing meals
(D) Changing his shifts

51 Why is the man concerned?

(A) They might be short staffed.
(B) The party might get out of hand.
(C) The kitchen will not be open.
(D) The ingredients may not be available.

52 What did some customers request?

(A) More floor space
(B) A vegetarian menu
(C) A beachfront view
(D) An event calendar

53 What is the conversation mainly about?

(A) A sales result
(B) A retiring employee
(C) Candidates for a position
(D) A company's anniversary

54 What does the woman mean when she says, "I couldn't agree more"?

(A) Now is the time for recruiting.
(B) 10 years' working experience is a requirement.
(C) An internal promotion is a fast way to fill a position.
(D) The company needs to contact a staffing agency.

55 According to the woman, what do the board members want?

(A) Increased sales
(B) Relocation of one of their branches
(C) Adding new delivery locations
(D) Restructuring of the sales team

56 According to the woman, why did Mr. Bloomberg call her?

(A) To inquire about the status of the project
(B) To discuss costs
(C) To reschedule a deadline
(D) To change a flooring material

57 What does the man mention about Mr. Bloomberg?

(A) He doesn't like changing plans.
(B) He asked for an additional discount.
(C) He is unpredictable.
(D) He is a frequent client.

58 What does the woman mean when she says, "That is what I was going to propose, actually"?

(A) A new floor plan is needed for the client.
(B) Mr. Bloomberg is a demanding client.
(C) Hiring workers will help meet the deadline.
(D) Mr. Ferrell is a popular contractor.

59 Why is the man calling?

(A) To ask about a special deal
(B) To reply to a consumer survey
(C) To track a delivery
(D) To inquire about his savings

60 What products are the speakers discussing?

(A) Electronic products
(B) Gardening equipment
(C) Cooking appliances
(D) Vehicle accessories

61 What information is the woman told to submit on the Web site?

(A) A delivery schedule
(B) A shipping number
(C) A promotional code
(D) A credit card billing address

62 Who is the woman?

(A) A florist
(B) A shop owner
(C) A customer
(D) A sales representative

63 What concern does the man mention about the display?

(A) The cost involved in the process
(B) The time consumption for his employees
(C) The amount of space required
(D) The timespan of delivery

64 What information does the brochure contain?

(A) A timetable
(B) Cost information
(C) A list of other stores
(D) A flower sample

GO ON TO THE NEXT PAGE

Hubert Research Center - 3rd Floor	
Laboratory	Room 301
Incubation Room	Room 302
Low-Pressure Chamber	Room 303
High-Pressure Chamber	Room 304

Mr. Brooks' schedule	
Tuesday	Urban Kitchen
Wednesday	Polly's Restaurant
Thursday	Top Cloud (in Hotel Dublin)
Friday	New York Diner

65 Look at the graphic. Where did the man stay last night?

(A) Room 301
(B) Room 302
(C) Room 303
(D) Room 304

66 What happened to the man?

(A) He lost a garage key.
(B) He left his house door open.
(C) He was locked inside a space.
(D) He was under pressure with his task.

67 According to the man, why didn't he sleep well?

(A) The space was cold.
(B) The space was scary.
(C) The space was stuffy.
(D) The space was too noisy.

68 What are the speakers preparing for?

(A) An appreciation event
(B) A retirement party
(C) A grand opening
(D) An employee workshop

69 What does the woman say she did last night?

(A) Searched for a location
(B) Sampled some food
(C) Paid a deposit
(D) Picked up supplies

70 Look at the graphic. What is the name of the catering service that the woman contacted?

(A) Urban Kitchen
(B) Polly's Restaurant
(C) Top Cloud
(D) New York Diner

PART 4

Directions: You will hear some talks given by a single speaker. You will be asked to answer three questions about what the speaker says in each talk. Select the best response to each question and mark the letter (A), (B), (C), or (D) on your answer sheet. The talks will not be printed in your test book and will be spoken only one time.

71 What is being advertised?

(A) A beverage
(B) A store
(C) A food bar
(D) A dessert

72 According to the speaker, what can be found at the Plusto Web site?

(A) Details of ingredients
(B) A list of vegetable growers
(C) A map of store locations
(D) Discount coupons

73 What will happen next month?

(A) A new flavor will be launched.
(B) Different-colored packaging will be offered.
(C) Prices will be reduced.
(D) A company name will change.

74 What type of business created the message?

(A) A delivery service
(B) A bus company
(C) A telephone exchange
(D) A travel agency

75 What new service does the business offer?

(A) A web-based payment option
(B) Mobile message alerts
(C) Priority delivery options
(D) An online tracking system

76 Why would a listener press star?

(A) To speak to an operator
(B) To return to the main menu
(C) To have this message repeated
(D) To hear the message again

77 Who most likely is the speaker?

(A) A fitness trainer
(B) An army doctor
(C) A sports journalist
(D) A medical expert

78 What are the listeners preparing to do in two months?

(A) Run a race
(B) Take part in an endurance test
(C) Travel overseas
(D) Participate in a fitness program

79 What does the speaker encourage the listeners to do?

(A) Take weekly breaks
(B) Purchase appropriate weapons
(C) Consult a medical professional daily
(D) Keep a personal log

80 Where does the talk most likely take place?

(A) At a factory
(B) At a restaurant
(C) At a photographic studio
(D) At a museum

81 What does the speaker say listeners will receive?

(A) Food samples
(B) A choice of desserts
(C) A photograph
(D) A cookery opportunity

82 What does the speaker ask the listeners to do in the reception?

(A) Check out a picture
(B) Leave their possessions
(C) Form a line
(D) Listen to an audio message

GO ON TO THE NEXT PAGE ▶

83 What is the main topic of the report?

(A) A concert opening
(B) A community
(C) A sports competition
(D) A municipal fair

84 What problem does the speaker mention?

(A) Bad weather is forecast.
(B) Traffic is expected to be heavy.
(C) Parking is limited.
(D) Some events have been cancelled.

85 What does the speaker suggest listeners do?

(A) Bring a packed lunch
(B) Use public transport
(C) Run in the park
(D) Wear suitable clothing

---

86 Who most likely are the listeners?

(A) Library users
(B) Librarians
(C) Shoppers
(D) Seminar participants

87 What is being announced?

(A) An art exhibition
(B) A community fair
(C) An art class
(D) A painting action

88 What does the speaker imply when she says, "This is to avoid interruptions"?

(A) The listeners should register for the event.
(B) The listeners should be punctual for the event.
(C) The listeners should wait in a line.
(D) The listeners should hold their questions for a while.

89 What is the purpose of the advertisement?

(A) To publicize a grand opening
(B) To advertise job openings
(C) To inform the customers of the origin of the produce
(D) To promote a sale

90 What is Fresh Groceries mainly selling?

(A) Meat
(B) Dairy products
(C) Bakery
(D) Fruits and vegetables

91 What does the speaker mean when he says, "That's our trick of the trade"?

(A) Their products are cheap.
(B) Their products are grown locally.
(C) They import products.
(D) The products are all organic.

Received	Vendor	Item	Quantity
12/14	Ralph	Blazer	25
12/15	Dash	Sweater	30
12/16	Custom	Trousers	40
12/17	Hiller	Accessory	120

92 What most likely is the speaker's job?

(A) Clothing designer
(B) Store manager
(C) Delivery person
(D) Inspector

93 Look at the graphic. What quantity will the speaker add to the inventory?

(A) 25
(B) 30
(C) 40
(D) 120

94 What does the speaker say he will do when he returns?

(A) Change the price tags
(B) Send back arrivals
(C) Inspect the displays
(D) Alter some pants

Lincoln Blvd.

Rocky Building

Y-Mall

Press Center

Floral Ave.

11th St.

Victoria Plaza

12th St.

Winner	Trumpet Shell Weight (Pound)
Brian	5
Jim	4.5
John	3
Jason	4

95 What will visitors receive?

(A) A complimentary gift
(B) A voucher for a meal
(C) A discount coupon
(D) A gift certificate

96 What does the speaker mention about Tom & Stephany's products?

(A) They are shipped at no charge.
(B) They are custom made.
(C) They are popular.
(D) They are made by top designers.

97 Look at the graphic. Where is Tom & Stephany most likely located?

(A) At the Press Center
(B) At Y-Mall
(C) At Victoria Plaza
(D) At the Rocky Building

98 According to the speaker, what is the purpose of the event?

(A) To raise trumpet shells
(B) To revitalize local business
(C) To honor a person
(D) To celebrate the opening of a season

99 Look at the graphic. Who won the special prize?

(A) Brian
(B) Jim
(C) John
(D) Jason

100 What will listeners probably hear next?

(A) Music
(B) Local news
(C) Advertisements
(D) A traffic report

This is the end of the Listening test. Turn to Part 5 in your test book.

GO ON TO THE NEXT PAGE

READING TEST

In the Reading test, you will read a variety of texts and answer several different types of reading comprehension questions. The entire Reading test will last 75 minutes. There are three parts, and directions are given for each part. You are encouraged to answer as many questions as possible within the time allowed.

You must mark your answers on the separate answer sheet. Do not write your answers in your test book.

PART 5

Directions: A word or phrase is missing in each of the sentences below. Four answer choices are given below each sentence. Select the best answer to complete the sentence. Then mark the letter (A), (B), (C), or (D) on your answer sheet.

101 The members of the committee will ------- in Heart Lane Hall for the shareholder meeting.

(A) convene
(B) implement
(C) nominate
(D) initiate

102 Employees have been requested to update ------- working hours.

(A) theirs
(B) their
(C) them
(D) they

103 The company's bi-monthly budget report was ------- explained by Mr. Pam Isley.

(A) brief
(B) briefly
(C) briefness
(D) briefing

104 All personal items ------- behind in the lounge are kept for 30 days before being discarded.

(A) left
(B) leave
(C) leaving
(D) leaves

105 Joyce Appliances has recalled this year's line of microwave ovens in ------- to reports of defective components.

(A) response
(B) responsibility
(C) responsible
(D) responsive

106 All workers who ------- electrical equipment must wear hard hats.

(A) are operated
(B) operates
(C) to operate
(D) operate

107 At Shalting Management Consultants, we ------- our ideas to clients as concisely as possible.

(A) believe
(B) insert
(C) decide
(D) explain

108 The structure of the building -------, but the interior has been completely remodeled.

(A) preserving
(B) preserved
(C) had been preserving
(D) has been preserved

109 A ------- the information seemed to be missing from the report at first, but it was quickly identified.
(A) little
(B) few of
(C) few
(D) little of

110 Harleque Industries is currently exploring methods to more ------- manufacture its air conditioning units.
(A) produce
(B) production
(C) productive
(D) productively

111 An increasing ------- of homeowners are refinancing their mortgages to make use of lower interest rates.
(A) number
(B) amount
(C) type
(D) supply

112 Kortra Software has unveiled a music player that can ------- any type of sound file.
(A) dispose
(B) contain
(C) reconcile
(D) accommodate

113 ------- the board comes to a conclusion today, the vote will have to be postponed until next month's meeting.
(A) Whereas
(B) If
(C) Unless
(D) Even

114 Forecasters anticipate an increase in public spending in Lancetown ------- the next three years.
(A) between
(B) upon
(C) against
(D) over

115 Directors of the zoo are predicting an ------- in visitors following the birth of a rare white tiger cub.
(A) insert
(B) effort
(C) increase
(D) array

116 Not many of the consumers questioned were familiar with the product line manufactured by Grantham Cosmetics, ------- advertisement appears in glossy magazines.
(A) whose
(B) what
(C) which
(D) who

117 Mr. Lao from Price Financial Services will be using the main boardroom while he ------- the company's annual reports.
(A) compiles
(B) responds
(C) proceeds
(D) realizes

118 The Fitness for Life promotion DVD will feature a number of exercises for a healthy body, with an ------- on upper body strength.
(A) emphasize
(B) emphasized
(C) emphasis
(D) emphasizes

119 Harris Supermarkets' ------- is to encourage more people to shop at the stores by insisting on better customer service.
(A) inquiry
(B) structure
(C) objective
(D) transfer

120 The town of Santos has been evacuated ------- a bush fire heading towards Netherman Falls.
(A) provided that
(B) owing to
(C) instead of
(D) even if

GO ON TO THE NEXT PAGE

121 ------- a minor decline in kitchen appliance sales, Boldwon Electrical has experienced a surge across all of its industries.

(A) Aside from
(B) Compared to
(C) Although
(D) For instance

122 After discussion with the labor union started, Foxtune Industries ------- to raise wages and reduce working hours for all employees.

(A) permitted
(B) included
(C) consented
(D) complied

123 Customers who purchased the third edition of the Gloria coffee maker are ------- to complete the customer survey card and return it.

(A) circulated
(B) encouraged
(C) conducted
(D) considered

124 Weather forecasters predict five ------- days of sunshine, which should provide a welcome reprieve from recent unprecedented rainfall.

(A) refreshed
(B) atmospheric
(C) deliberate
(D) consecutive

125 With just 2 weeks to go before the start of the annual Glastonbury Festival, the organizers have ------- to decide which act is headlining.

(A) yet
(B) not
(C) finally
(D) already

126 A local oil corporation, Petro Co., plans to start ------- of its new line of oil products.

(A) production
(B) producing
(C) product
(D) productivity

127 The appointment of Russ Heiskell as CEO will ------- Marbeck's position as one of the leading pharmaceutical institutions in Egypt.

(A) incline
(B) accomplish
(C) administer
(D) solidify

128 ------- adopting the Kiving production method, Qantros Corporation has experienced a reduction in product defects.

(A) That
(B) Because
(C) For
(D) Since

129 Although the revised return policy will go into ------- on June 1, customers who made a purchase before May 15 will be exempt from it.

(A) effect
(B) effective
(C) effectively
(D) effectiveness

130 Ucham Construction builds energy-efficient residential structures worldwide and ------- requires skilled and experienced workers.

(A) because
(B) therefore
(C) however
(D) rather

PART 6

Directions: Read the texts that follow. A word, phrase, or sentence is missing in parts of each text. Four answer choices for each question are given below the text. Select the best answer to complete the text. Then mark the letter (A), (B), (C), or (D) on your answer sheet.

Questions 131-134 refer to the following article.

May 1 — Interling Credit Union and Royalwin Credit Union yesterday unveiled ------- plans to
                                                                            131.

merge. The new entity will be named Victory Credit Union. It will become the largest locally

headquartered ------- corporation with a total of 120,000 members, holding over $5 billion in
                             132.
assets.

The boards of both credit unions convened several months ago to consider merging. This past

week, they voted unanimously for the merger. -------.
                                                133.

The ------- of the new joint entity is supposed to take several weeks. During that time, members
      134.
are advised to continue using the services of their respective institutions. However, they will also

be able to access the services of their new partner institution.

---

131 (A) its
    (B) our
    (C) their
    (D) his

132 (A) finance
    (B) financed
    (C) financial
    (D) financially

133 (A) Specifics were first released to the public yesterday.
    (B) The official records show the entity is compliant with all federal regulations.
    (C) Banking is one of the fastest emerging industries.
    (D) Membership is available to certain groups of people.

134 (A) distinction
    (B) assessment
    (C) estimate
    (D) formation

GO ON TO THE NEXT PAGE

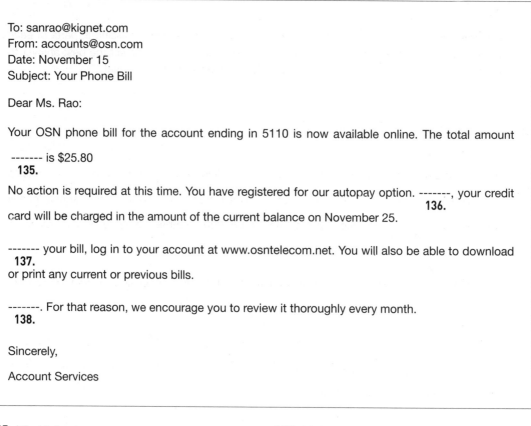

To: sanrao@kignet.com
From: accounts@osn.com
Date: November 15
Subject: Your Phone Bill

Dear Ms. Rao:

Your OSN phone bill for the account ending in 5110 is now available online. The total amount

------- is $25.80
   135.

No action is required at this time. You have registered for our autopay option. -------, your credit
                                                                                136.
card will be charged in the amount of the current balance on November 25.

------- your bill, log in to your account at www.osntelecom.net. You will also be able to download
137.
or print any current or previous bills.

-------. For that reason, we encourage you to review it thoroughly every month.
138.

Sincerely,

Account Services

135 (A) obtained
   (B) due
   (C) kept
   (D) returned

136 (A) In fact
   (B) Otherwise
   (C) Hence
   (D) However

137 (A) Check
   (B) To check
   (C) Checking
   (D) Having checked

138 (A) Enclosed in this e-mail is a special
        coupon for loyal customers.
   (B) Thank you for doing business with OSN
        Telecom.
   (C) Important changes about your account
        may be included on your bill.
   (D) You will be charged an extra fee due to a
        late payment.

Questions 139-142 refer to the following e-mail.

To: harvey@koln.com
From: kyra@koln.com
Subject: Interviews
Date: September 2
Attachment: contact_list.doc

Dear Harvey:

You may remember that the hiring committee I work for is planning to interview some job candidates in the following weeks. I would like to ask you to contact each of the ------- and
139.
schedule their individual interviews. Included is a document containing their names and contact information. It also ------- their preferred dates and times for the interviews. Once you have
140.
scheduled the interviews, please immediately report to me.

-------. Should you have any further inquiries, just let me know. I will be out of town until
141.
tomorrow, ------- I will be checking my e-mail and text messages.
142.

Best,

Kyra

139 (A) employees
(B) acquaintances
(C) applicants
(D) residents

140 (A) lists
(B) would have listed
(C) will list
(D) listed

141 (A) We can meet tomorrow to discuss the details.
(B) I appreciate your patronage as a regular customer.
(C) All you need to do is train new employees.
(D) Thanks for handling this important issue.

142 (A) whereas
(B) although
(C) but
(D) unless

GO ON TO THE NEXT PAGE

Questions 143-146 refer to the following memo.

FROM: Jan Grady

TO: Packaging Department

DATE: December 2

One of the objectives for our department's planning team has been to ------- expenses over
143.
the following year. We have identified three areas for potential cost-cutting: labor, materials,

and processes. -------. Therefore, we have decided to focus on the other two areas. As for the
144.
second area, the department will begin using new, cheaper boxes. Details ------- these and other
145.
new packing materials will be determined soon. As for the third area, we are still evaluating our

current packaging process to identify potential ineffectiveness. As soon as those have been

found, ------- will be made. We should familiarize employees with the new processes. If you have
146.
any questions about these changes, please forward them to your supervisor.

143 (A) evaluate
(B) promote
(C) curtail
(D) calculate

144 (A) New workers are encouraged to attend
the training session.
(B) We already allocate employee work hours
efficiently.
(C) Cutting-edge equipment will be installed
in the coming weeks.
(D) Our success is attributed to your
contributions.

145 (A) regards
(B) regarded
(C) regarding
(D) to regard

146 (A) promotions
(B) transactions
(C) installments
(D) adjustments

PART 7

Directions: In this part you will read a selection of texts, such as magazine and newspaper articles, e-mails, and instant messages. Each text or set of texts is followed by several questions. Select the best answer for each question and mark the letter (A), (B), (C), or (D) on your answer sheet.

Questions 147-148 refer to the following advertisement.

Callan's Seafood

235 Ocean Drive
Monday – Saturday: 8 A.M. – 7 P.M.
Sunday: 10 A.M. – 5 P.M.
339-555-4481

The region's best wholesaler for fresh seafood, including:
squid, fresh fish, and shellfish
cod and haddock
halibut and eel

Weekly special! Save 25 percent on oysters, mussels, crabs and lobsters.
Offer ends on February 2.

147 What is stated about Callan's Seafood?

(A) It sells frozen food.
(B) It is open every day of the week.
(C) It takes orders from overseas.
(D) It specializes in exotic fish.

148 According to the advertisement, what has been discounted?

(A) White fish
(B) Boating equipment
(C) Deep sea fish
(D) Shellfish

GO ON TO THE NEXT PAGE

Questions 149-150 refer to the following receipt.

Welcome to Luigi's Vehicle Service and Repair

Open Monday through Saturday
8:30 A.M. to 5:00 P.M.

Customer: Alex Jang

Order #: 20201187

Wednesday, October 8, 8:37 A.M.

Item	Service	Pick-Up Date/ Time	Cost
Van	Wheel Alignment	Wed. October 8/ 4 P.M.	$8.00
Hatchback	Interior Cleaning	Fri. October 10/ 6 P.M.	$20.00
Motorcycle	Service	Mon. October 13/ 10 A.M.	$30.00
Scooter	Service	Mon. October 13/ 10 A.M.	$30.00

Total cost: $88.00

Amount paid: $88.00

Balance due: $ 0.00

Thank you for choosing Luigi's

Ask about our Monday Interior Cleaning

149 For what vehicle did Ms. Jang receive same-day service?

(A) Motorcycle
(B) Hatchback
(C) Scooter
(D) Van

150 What is indicated in the receipt about Ms. Jang's service?

(A) It will be invoiced
(B) It was billed on October 10.
(C) It was paid for in full.
(D) It contained a number of vans.

Questions 151-153 refer to the following chart.

http://www.appliancereviewer.com

Microwave Appliances Under $200

MODEL	DETAILS	REVIEWER COMMENTS
Access T-L	Weight: 3kg Baking Function: Yes Suggested retail price: $199	Available in stainless steel only Very fast defrost
Vista 4	Weight: 3kg Baking Function: No Suggested retail price: $49	Simple, easy-to-use controls Replacement parts very expensive
Caterham Special	Weight: 5kg Baking Function : No Suggested retail price: $99	Ten-year guarantee on motor Powerful roast facility
Plasma 700	Weight: 6kg Baking Function: Yes Suggested retail price: $99	Very cumbersome High energy-efficiency rating

151 Why would someone refer to the chart?

(A) To learn about microwaves in a certain price range
(B) To find the components of each microwave
(C) To determine how many microwaves a store sells each week
(D) To compare the energy efficiency of microwaves

152 What is a stated advantage of Access T-L?

(A) It is available in several colors.
(B) It defrosts food quickly.
(C) It has a ten-year warranty.
(D) It uses energy efficiently.

153 How are Caterham Special and Plasma 700 similar?

(A) They cost the same amount.
(B) They both have baking capacity.
(C) They are the same weight.
(D) They both received negative reviews.

GO ON TO THE NEXT PAGE ▶

Questions 154-155 refer to the following text message chain.

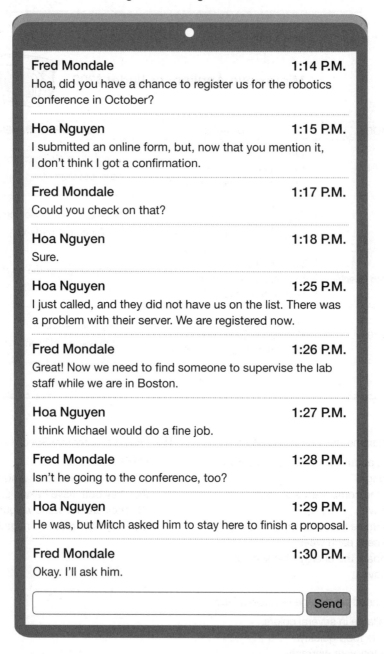

Fred Mondale — 1:14 P.M.

Hoa, did you have a chance to register us for the robotics conference in October?

Hoa Nguyen — 1:15 P.M.

I submitted an online form, but, now that you mention it, I don't think I got a confirmation.

Fred Mondale — 1:17 P.M.

Could you check on that?

Hoa Nguyen — 1:18 P.M.

Sure.

Hoa Nguyen — 1:25 P.M.

I just called, and they did not have us on the list. There was a problem with their server. We are registered now.

Fred Mondale — 1:26 P.M.

Great! Now we need to find someone to supervise the lab staff while we are in Boston.

Hoa Nguyen — 1:27 P.M.

I think Michael would do a fine job.

Fred Mondale — 1:28 P.M.

Isn't he going to the conference, too?

Hoa Nguyen — 1:29 P.M.

He was, but Mitch asked him to stay here to finish a proposal.

Fred Mondale — 1:30 P.M.

Okay. I'll ask him.

Send

154 What is suggested about Michael?

(A) He cannot supervise the lab.

(B) He is a new employee.

(C) He is presenting at a conference.

(D) He will not go to Boston.

155 At 1:15 P.M., what does Ms. Nguyen mean when she writes, "Now that you mention it"?

(A) She is embarrassed that she forgot to check on the registration.

(B) She realizes that she needs to be less forgetful about details.

(C) She just realized something because of what Mr. Mondale said.

(D) She thought Mr. Mondale was going to submit the registration.

Emiron Losing Market Share

By Junaid Kasim

Hong Kong, April 11 — Following recent market research into customer satisfaction, Emiron Energy was ranked the tenth most customer-friendly energy supplier, with 60% of users claiming to be satisfied. -[1]-. The survey was conducted by Aston Research in the previous month and revealed that although Emiron is rated higher than its main rival, Tivol Power, its position has dropped dramatically from last year's survey, which placed Emiron in fourth position. -[2]-.

"Despite the fact that we have fallen behind other competitors, our aim is to concentrate on our customers' needs," comments Adam Rawling, spokesperson for Emiron. -[3]-. "As for next year, we are putting certain changes in place to improve our customer service. For example, we are consolidating all technical service staff in one building for better training and quality-control monitoring. This will be completed by March of next year." -[4]-.

156 What did the customers most likely say about Emiron?

(A) Its energy supply is too slow.
(B) Its prices are too high.
(C) Its call center is short-staffed.
(D) Its technical service is inconsistent.

157 What will Emiron do next year?

(A) It will use new technology.
(B) It will merge with other competitors.
(C) It will place all technical staff in one location.
(D) It will carry out more market research.

158 In which of the positions marked [1], [2], [3], and [4] does the following sentence best belong?

"It is hoped these changes will increase the popularity of Emiron in the customers' opinions."

(A) [1]
(B) [2]
(C) [3]
(D) [4]

GO ON TO THE NEXT PAGE

```
E-Mail Message
```

To: cbowden@washngo.com
From: rmansell@plumbbase.com
Date: June 30
Re: Elite Washer/ Drier

Dear Mr. Bowden,

I'm contacting you regarding one of the washer/ driers your organization manufactures, the Elite Washer Drier. A significant number of customers who bought this item have complained that the internal liquid holder is loose due to a missing screw. Luckily, we have that size of screw available in stock and were able to supply it for customers.

I would be grateful if you would replace the screws that we have had to give to customers so we do not lose any of our stock profits.

Due to the concerns about this fault in the machine, we have decided to delay ordering any additional washer/ driers from you until the matter has been rectified. When we receive assurance that this is resolved, we will be more than happy to resume our orders.

Thank you for assisting me in this matter.

Sincerely,

Raine Mansell
Manager
Plumbbase

159 Why did Ms. Mansell write the e-mail?

(A) To question an invoice
(B) To recommend an appliance
(C) To address a problem
(D) To reply to a customer

160 What does Ms. Mansell ask Mr. Bowden to do?

(A) Explain how to use a machine
(B) Help promote the washer/ drier
(C) Replace some items
(D) Speed up an order

161 What decision has Plumbbase made?

(A) It will postpone placing orders for a particular product.
(B) It will sell a variety of washing machines.
(C) It will charge customers for screws.
(D) It will return some unsatisfactory merchandise.

Weekly Catering News

On Friday, Saloma's nightclub agreed on the terms to purchase three Galant casinos. One of the casinos is located in Antrim and the other two in Belfast. -[1]-.

For the foreseeable future, the venues will continue under the Galant brand name, with nothing announced as yet for a change in name. -[2]-. In a press release, the CEO of Saloma, Ansar Quidar announced: "I am delighted to incorporate these venues under the Saloma brand. We are aiming to become the leading name in entertainment in Antrim and Belfast. Our long-term strategy is to provide these communities with affordable and exciting leisure entertainment." Mr. Quidar also stressed that no jobs were under threat. -[3]-.

Saloma's nightclub was the brainchild of Mr. Quidar's great-grandfather, who opened the first bar in Omaghe over a century ago. Mr. Quidar took over ownership after the death of his father 7 years ago. There are now Saloma bars in many towns and cities in Ireland. -[4]-.

162 What is the purpose of the article?
(A) To announce an acquisition
(B) To report on the gaming market
(C) To recruit new bar staff
(D) To comment on the relocation of a company

163 What does Mr. Quidar say about employment at the Antrim and Belfast branches?
(A) He wants to experiment with new hiring practices.
(B) He expects support within the community.
(C) He intends to retain current employees.
(D) He plans to offer performance-based bonuses.

164 What is indicated about Saloma's Nightclub?
(A) It is a family-owned business.
(B) It has international clubs.
(C) It will soon expand into Scotland.
(D) It offers free gaming.

165 In which of the positions marked [1], [2], [3], and [4] does the following sentence best belong?
"The sale price has not yet been announced."
(A) [1]
(B) [2]
(C) [3]
(D) [4]

GO ON TO THE NEXT PAGE

Questions 166-168 refer to the following online chat discussion.

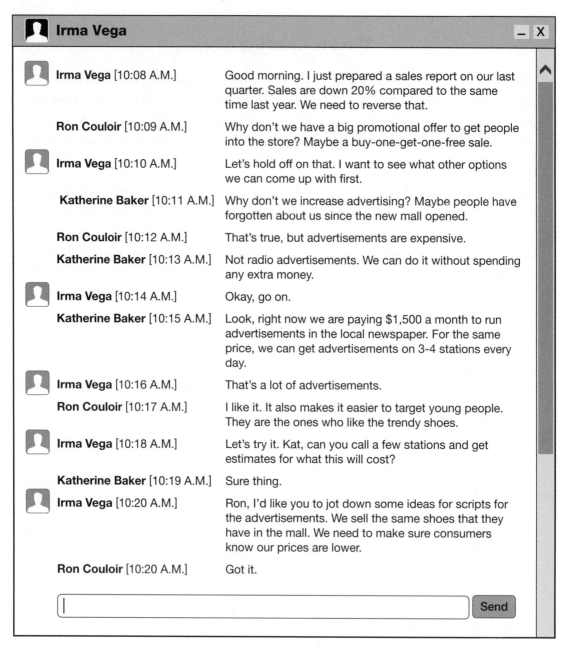

Irma Vega — X

Irma Vega [10:08 A.M.] Good morning. I just prepared a sales report on our last quarter. Sales are down 20% compared to the same time last year. We need to reverse that.

Ron Couloir [10:09 A.M.] Why don't we have a big promotional offer to get people into the store? Maybe a buy-one-get-one-free sale.

Irma Vega [10:10 A.M.] Let's hold off on that. I want to see what other options we can come up with first.

Katherine Baker [10:11 A.M.] Why don't we increase advertising? Maybe people have forgotten about us since the new mall opened.

Ron Couloir [10:12 A.M.] That's true, but advertisements are expensive.

Katherine Baker [10:13 A.M.] Not radio advertisements. We can do it without spending any extra money.

Irma Vega [10:14 A.M.] Okay, go on.

Katherine Baker [10:15 A.M.] Look, right now we are paying $1,500 a month to run advertisements in the local newspaper. For the same price, we can get advertisements on 3-4 stations every day.

Irma Vega [10:16 A.M.] That's a lot of advertisements.

Ron Couloir [10:17 A.M.] I like it. It also makes it easier to target young people. They are the ones who like the trendy shoes.

Irma Vega [10:18 A.M.] Let's try it. Kat, can you call a few stations and get estimates for what this will cost?

Katherine Baker [10:19 A.M.] Sure thing.

Irma Vega [10:20 A.M.] Ron, I'd like you to jot down some ideas for scripts for the advertisements. We sell the same shoes that they have in the mall. We need to make sure consumers know our prices are lower.

Ron Couloir [10:20 A.M.] Got it.

Send

166 Where do the writers most likely work?

(A) At a radio station
(B) At a clothing store
(C) At a shopping mall
(D) At a shoe store

167 What does Mr. Couloir agree to do?

(A) Generate advertising ideas
(B) Check the prices at some competitors
(C) Design a promotional offer
(D) Talk with mall shoppers

168 At 10:14 A.M., what does Ms. Vega mean when she says, "Okay, go on"?

(A) She wants to finish the discussion so she can get going.
(B) She is reconsidering the idea proposed by Mr. Couloir.
(C) She wants Ms. Baker to explain the details of her idea.
(D) She is skeptical that radio advertisements will work.

GO ON TO THE NEXT PAGE

Questions 169-171 refer to the following e-mail.

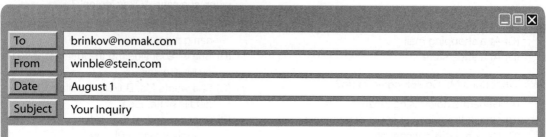

To: brinkov@nomak.com
From: winble@stein.com
Date: August 1
Subject: Your Inquiry

Dear Mr. Brinkov,

Thank you for your e-mail inquiry, which I reviewed today. I can now tell you a bit about how we can help Nomak Print increase traffic through the redesign of your Web site.

Stein Design was established five years ago. We have been appointed as an Internet consultant for a number of large companies, many of which are also overseas. Some of our biggest clients include KKS Clothing of Mombasa, Signet Designs of New York, and Falas Inc. of Hong Kong. As a result of our consulting work, these companies have seen a dramatic increase in visitors to their Web site, many of whom have become interested customers.

If you would like to work with us, I can assure you of the highest possible standards of work. Stein Design has an impressive record of completing projects on time and within budget. I am positive your company will see increased profitability.

Please feel free to call me directly at 901-555-1232 to arrange a meeting during which we will analyze your requirements further. I look forward to hearing from you.

Sincerely,

Lena Wimble
Senior Sales Manager
Stein Design

169 Why does Ms. Wimble send the e-mail?

(A) To confirm an upcoming meeting at Nomak Print
(B) To encourage a company to pursue a business relationship
(C) To give information about a design forum
(D) To describe how to set up a new Web page

170 What is mentioned about Stein Design?

(A) It does business overseas.
(B) Its fees are lower than those of other consultants.
(C) It has recently hired several designers.
(D) Its headquarters are in Mombasa.

171 The word "assure" in paragraph 3, line 1, is closest in meaning to

(A) promise
(B) inform
(C) convince
(D) promote

Questions 172-175 refer to the following article.

SEATTLE(March 3) — Seattle-based Mallins Cosmetics has recently revealed plans to construct another research and development facility. At the moment, the organization's only such facility is situated in Maine, a distance of more than 200 kilometers from its Seattle main headquarters. The cost of the new facility has been announced as $4 million and this move is at the forefront of a new initiative to expand into the European market.

Management executives are hoping this bold move to Berlin, Germany will boost the company's reputation as a major player in the European cosmetics industry. Once the project is completed, the two R&D facilities will easily accommodate the requirements of the American and the European markets. "An important advantage is that we will now have access to European products and ingredients, which previously we had to source and import. This took time and added to our cost margins," said company president Steve Baker.

Mr. Baker's father, David Baker, founded Mallins

Cosmetics in 1981 after graduating from a university in California. When he returned to Seattle, he began a part-time job selling imported cosmetics to students in the region. Within six months, his part-time business had managed to bring in large profits, which increased when he went full time the next year. Today, Mallins Cosmetics is recognized internationally as a quality producer with outlets in more than 20 countries worldwide. Recently, however, sales have fallen off with the new R&D team under Mr. Baker aggressively attempting to find new angles.

The full range of Mallins Cosmetic's existing products should be available in the majority of European countries by the end of the year, according to R&D director Anna Bottram. Ms. Bottram has a long-term vision to introduce a line of anti-ageing creams aimed at the older generation to complement the company's current product line. "Our aim is to grow and develop new items our customers will appreciate," she said.

172 Why is Mallins Cosmetics building a new facility?

(A) Because the production department is too far away from its headquarters
(B) Because operation costs at the current location have increased
(C) Because it needs to introduce modernized equipment
(D) Because its leaders want to sell their products in a new location

173 Where will the new facility be located?

(A) Seattle
(B) Maine
(C) Berlin
(D) California

174 What is mentioned about Mallins Cosmetics?

(A) Sales of its products have stopped growing recently.
(B) It sells more products overseas.
(C) Customers can currently buy its products only in Seattle.
(D) It is planning to fire several executives.

175 What new type of product is Mallins Cosmetics planning to develop?

(A) Lipsticks
(B) Lotions
(C) Creams
(D) Powder

GO ON TO THE NEXT PAGE

Questions 176-180 refer to the following e-mail and online article.

To	Andrea Golding <agolding@coverart.com>
From	Toyah Labon <tlabon@sequencepress.com>
Subject	Ingleton
Date	June 14, 2:44 P.M.
Attachment	Tennis illustration.zip

Hi Andrea,

Earlier today, I received a call from Larss Ingleton about the cover for *Tennis Players through the Ages*, his latest book in what is to be a three-volume series on sports heroes in the modern era. He does not approve of the neutral tone images we were intending to use and wants this cover to be similar in design to his previous book, *Soccer in the Americas*. So as soon as possible, can I rely on you to come up with some initial designs so we can send them for approval to Mr. Ingleton? I've also attached some illustrations of tennis for your reference.

As this is not the only design-related issue that Mr. Ingleton has raised when I spoke to him, I think it would be highly beneficial for everyone in the design department involved in the project to hear what he has to say. So I've arranged a conference call with him on Tuesday at midday from his home in the Austrian Alps. I'll email over the list of recipients for the call. Please let me know if you have any questions.

Toyah

The Art of Covers

www.theaustrianreview.com / book-review

Tuesday August 11

The Austrian Review annually asks prominent artists to vote for their favorite book cover designs. Iliana Drobvik, who is director of art design at the University of Altrecht in Belgium, reveals his favorites this week.

Iliana Drobvik: I love to see book covers that show a myriad of images about the content itself and are interesting enough for me to recognize some of the people mentioned in the book. So when I came across the cover of <Tennis Players through the Ages> designed by Andrea Golding, I was quite taken. The book was written by Mr. Larss Ingleton, an Austrian writer, and it was published by Sequence Press. The cover bears illustrations of tennis stars past and present, with no title or author on the cover itself. Instead, the cover makes use only of black and white drawings with a red background. This cover is remarkably similar in design to the first book in the trilogy planned by Mr. Larss Ingleton; that first book's cover also makes use of black and white drawing but with a blue background. Golding is obviously an expert in line drawing and I applaud her design work.

176 What is one purpose of the e-mail?

(A) To request that a coworker return some books she borrowed

(B) To inform a staff member that adjustments need to be made

(C) To set a deadline for additional work to be done on a project

(D) To announce the publication date of an author's latest book

177 What is implied about Toyah Labon?

(A) She invited Mr. Larss Ingleton to participate in a meeting.

(B) She is an expert on structural engineering.

(C) She will visit the Austrian Alps next week.

(D) She is the author of five books.

178 What is indicated about the cover of *Soccer in the Americas*?

(A) It features only three colors.

(B) Iliana Drobvik designed it.

(C) Larss Ingleton was dissatisfied with it.

(D) It is covered in photographs.

179 In the online article, the word "bears" in paragraph 2, line 5, is closest in meaning to

(A) accepts

(B) requires

(C) displays

(D) fits

180 What is NOT suggested about Andrea Golding?

(A) Her work is on a book published by Sequence Press.

(B) She designed one of the books in the trilogy.

(C) Her work makes extensive use of color.

(D) An art critic named her work as his favorite book cover.

Test 05

GO ON TO THE NEXT PAGE

Questions 181-185 refer to the following press release and e-mail.

---

13 September

Press Release

Luizi Corporation is delighted to announce the unveiling of its new factories in Pampa and Corboba on Saturday, September 13. In addition, we can also reveal the merger with Rassoul Manufacturing, a centrally located organization in Tucuman, has finally been approved this week. According to Luizi's President, Amande Resok, these transactions consolidate the corporation's determination to increase its presence in Argentina.

Luizi was established by Joachim Fillen after he was made redundant at Bolero Industries, five years ago. Having been employed there for a decade, he was ready to return back to his home in Parana, where, in partnership with his family and friends, he began his

fruit wholesale business there. Mr. Fillen's plan was to concentrate on domestic produce using only a local supply network. The strategy was massively lucrative and Fillen's idea was soon adopted by similar wholesalers throughout the country. This led to the company becoming one of the most revered and esteemed firms of its kind.

Even with its unprecedented growth in the market, the company's original office, purpose-built five years ago, is still used as the company's main base, and the business has continued its quest for innovation. The IT team has recently introduced a picking system that can relay orders almost twice as fast as earlier models.

From : Amande Resok [AmandeResok@Luizi.com]
To : Tim Janke [TimJanke@Luizi.com]
Date : September 21
Subject : Good News

Dear Mr. Janke,

I'm delighted to inform you that the Human Resources Department has decided to honor you as a recipient of this year's long service awards. The award was based on your commitment and contribution to the company since you joined Luizi. Since then, you have been consistent in helping Luizi's transition from a local business to one of the leading companies in South American wholesaling. In addition, the work ethic you have displayed as a team leader, particularly as a manager of the shipping division, is exemplary.

In celebration of this year's awards, a gourmet dinner will be held at the company's headquarters on Tuesday, 25 September, 5 P.M., after which, I will present the awards. Thank you again for your hard work and dedication and I'm looking forward to seeing you there.

Amande Resok
Chief Executive Officer

181 According to the press release, why has Luizi Corporation been successful?

(A) It rapidly expanded into the overseas market.
(B) It offered lower prices than its competitors.
(C) It installed a wholesaler system that is widely used.
(D) It formed a partnership with Bolero.

182 What is NOT mentioned as an activity Luizi Corporation is involved in?

(A) Merging with a company
(B) Opening new offices
(C) Introducing an upgraded system
(D) Offering training opportunities

183 How long did Mr. Fillen work at Bolero Industries?

(A) For 2 years
(B) For 5 years
(C) For 10 years
(D) For 15 years

184 Why will Luizi Corporation host a reception?

(A) To celebrate the conclusion of a business deal
(B) To attract more business opportunities in Argentina
(C) To honor the service of several workers
(D) To mark the anniversary of the company's founding

185 Where will Mr. Janke most likely be on September 25?

(A) In Tucuman
(B) In Pampa
(C) In Parana
(D) In Cordoba

GO ON TO THE NEXT PAGE

OFFICE EXPRESS

Store # 840 - San Pedro
555-8203

WEEKLY SPECIALS (March 2 – March 9)

Tax preparation software $25
All laptops 10% off – Starting at just $300 (regular: $330)
All Dextra brand printers 20% off – Starting at just $100 (regular: $120)
Office supplies from 5% – 50% off
SPEND $75 or more and get a complimentary USB drive ($5 value).

Sign up for our rewards card and earn points with both in-store purchases and those made at www.officeexpress.com. For every dollar spent, you get a point. Bonus points can be earned on select purchases. Points cannot be earned on sale items.

Thank you for purchasing a Dextra T950 printer. Included with your printer are one three-color cartridges and one black ink cartridge. Please follow the instructions on the other side of the card when inserting the cartridges into your printer. It is advised that you print a test page before using the printer for the first time. This helps ensure that the print heads are lined up correctly.

Replacement cartridges can be purchased from many retailers. In addition, they are available at our online store at www.dextra.com. Cartridges ordered from our Web site will be shipped within 48 hours at no extra charge. You can use coupon code DT2000 to take an additional 10% off your first order. This discount is only available for purchases made on our Web site.

Feel free to contact us 24 hours a day, 7 days a week if you have any questions about your new printer.

Customer support: 1-800-555-1818 / customersupport@dextra.com

Technical support: 1-800-555-0909 / techsupport@dextra.com

From	Dan Farmer <dfarm@jetmail.net>
To	Dextra, Inc. <customersupport@dextra.com>
Subject	Order #8945
Date	March 25

To Whom It May Concern:

On March 2, I purchased a T950 printer at an Office Express store while I was visiting a friend in San Pedro. The printer is awesome. It is exactly what I needed to print high-quality flyers for my business. I have been using it so much that I have almost run out of ink. There is no Office Express in my area, so I ordered four replacement cartridges (Order #8945) from your Web site with code DT2000. Unfortunately, the ones that were sent to me are the wrong size. I would like to exchange these for correct ones. Please advise me what to do.

Sincerely,

Dan Farmer

---

186 According to the advertisement, what is true about rewards card points?

(A) They can be earned for online purchases.
(B) They can be redeemed for discounts.
(C) They can be earned on discounted items.
(D) They are only available to loyal customers.

187 What is suggested about Mr. Farmer?

(A) He regularly shops at Store #840.
(B) He received a free USB drive.
(C) He signed up for a rewards card.
(D) He paid less than $100 for his printer.

188 What is most likely true about order #8945?

(A) It took four days to arrive.
(B) There was a fee for shipping.
(C) It included a 10% discount.
(D) There was an incorrect address.

189 In the information, the word "ensure" in paragraph 1, line 5, is closest in meaning to

(A) adjust
(B) transmit
(C) measure
(D) confirm

190 What is indicated about Dextra's customer support?

(A) It can be reached by phone on weekends.
(B) It processes orders placed on Dextra's Web site.
(C) Its members prefer being contacted by e-mail.
(D) It can assist with installation issues.

GO ON TO THE NEXT PAGE

From the Office of Dr. Sharron Wilson
27 Mustang Road • Billings, MT 61520
(894) 555-0128
office@doctorwilson.com

Dear Ms. Sainsbury:

Your health is important to us. That's why we would like to remind you that you have scheduled an appointment with us on

Tuesday, October 5, at 8:30 A.M.

If you are a new patient, please arrive ten minutes prior to your scheduled appointment to fill out a patient information form and a payment authorization form.

If, for any reason, you need to cancel or change your appointment, please contact us at least 24 hours in advance to preclude a cancelation fee.

We look forward to seeing you!

From	ms2002@netmail.com
To	office@doctorwilson.com
Date	October 3, 3:45 P.M.

Thank you for sending me the reminder. I had almost forgotten about my appointment. The past few weeks have been very hectic at work. Still, I know how important it is to get my annual physical. Is there any way I could change my appointment to Friday, October 8? Any time will work for me. I will make sure I arrive ten minutes early to fill out the paperwork.

In addition, people at work keep saying it would be a good idea for me to get a flu shot. I'm not sure they are really effective. I would like to discuss this with Dr. Wilson before agreeing to get a shot.

Thanks,
Marsha Sainsbury

PATIENT BILLING STATEMENT

Marsha Sainsbury   Dr. Sharron Wilson
1898 Jasper Canyon Ln.   27 Mustang Road
Billings, MT 61520   Billings, MT 61520

Summary of Services
Physical Examination $125.00
Vaccination, Influenza $ 25.00

Account Summary
Account #: 8093-034
Service Date: October 8
Billed Charges: $150.00
Payment Method: Insurance   Provider Name: Health One

NOTE: All charges billed to an insurance provider must be approved by the provider.
If the provider rejects the charge, the patient will be responsible for the payment in full.
Please check with your insurance provider before authorizing services.

191 What is NOT mentioned in the notice?

(A) The time of the appointment
(B) The location of the appointment
(C) The reason for the appointment
(D) The deadline to cancel an appointment

192 What is suggested about Ms. Sainsbury?

(A) She has had recent health problems.
(B) She is a new patient of Dr. Wilson's.
(C) She frequently gets sick at work.
(D) She had to pay a cancelation fee.

193 Why did Ms. Sainsbury write the e-mail?

(A) To request additional information
(B) To make an appointment
(C) To submit paperwork
(D) To change an appointment

194 What is most likely true about Ms. Sainsbury's visit?

(A) It took place in the morning.
(B) She arrived later than scheduled.
(C) It was on her preferred date.
(D) She decided not to get a flu shot.

195 In the bill, the word "authorizing" in paragraph 4, line 3, is closest in meaning to

(A) allowing
(B) considering
(C) refusing
(D) paying

GO ON TO THE NEXT PAGE

Questions 196-200 refer to the following e-mail, article, and information.

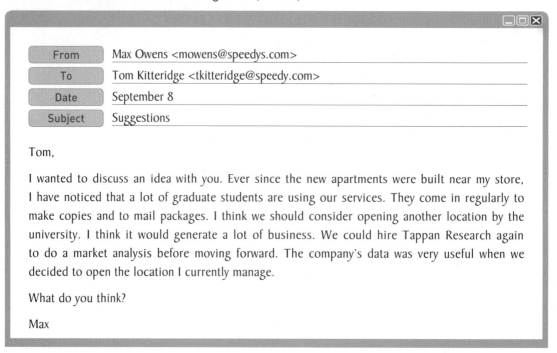

From: Max Owens <mowens@speedys.com>
To: Tom Kitteridge <tkitteridge@speedy.com>
Date: September 8
Subject: Suggestions

Tom,

I wanted to discuss an idea with you. Ever since the new apartments were built near my store, I have noticed that a lot of graduate students are using our services. They come in regularly to make copies and to mail packages. I think we should consider opening another location by the university. I think it would generate a lot of business. We could hire Tappan Research again to do a market analysis before moving forward. The company's data was very useful when we decided to open the location I currently manage.

What do you think?

Max

BURLINGTON — (May 8) Speedy's, the nationwide chain of copying and printing centers, announced that it will be opening a new location in the neighborhood just south of the university campus next month.

The company, which also offers mail services, says it wants to provide students with a faster, more affordable alternative to making photocopies in the library.

"Our market data showed there was tremendous demand for our services in this part of the city," explained regional manager Tom Kitteridge.

The new location on Wheeler Street, next to Java Max coffee shop, will be open 24 hours a day.

Unlike its other Burlington locations, this Speedy's will allow students to open prepaid accounts. Students pay in advance and receive a student PIN. This system avoids the hassle of having to carry cash or a credit card. Students can easily check and add to their account balances in the store.

SELF-SERVICE PRINTERS/ COPIERS

Instruction

1. Insert your credit/debit card OR enter your student PIN.

2. Select the type of service: printing/copying.
   a. If printing, insert your USB drive and follow the prompts on the display to print files on this storage device.
   b. If copying, select the type of copy and size.

3. Indicate the number of pages needed.

4. Press start.

5. When the job is complete, you will be asked if you would like to receive a paper or electronic receipt. If using a credit/debit card, an e-mail address must be provided for e-receipts.

Need help? Ask a friendly associate at the front desk.

196 What is the purpose of the e-mail?

(A) To report on sales
(B) To file a complaint
(C) To make a suggestion
(D) To request data

197 What is most likely true about Mr. Kitteridge?

(A) He will manage the new Speedy's location.
(B) He is one of Mr. Owens's employees.
(C) He is a resident of Burlington.
(D) He hired a marketing research firm again.

198 In the article, the word "hassle" in paragraph 5, line 4, is closest in meaning to

(A) inconvenience
(B) interaction
(C) expense
(D) contradiction

199 What is NOT mentioned in the instructions?

(A) Payments can be made with a credit card.
(B) Printing can be done from a USB drive.
(C) Assistance is available if needed.
(D) Students can print in full color.

200 What is suggested about the self-service copiers?

(A) They are only available at the university location.
(B) Students can send files to them from their phones.
(C) Students with prepaid accounts can use them.
(D) They are identical to the type used in the library.

GO ON TO THE NEXT PAGE

Actual Test

06

⏱	시작 시간	:
	종료 시간	:

LISTENING TEST

In the Listening test, you will be asked to demonstrate how well you understand spoken English. The entire Listening test will last approximately 45 minutes. There are four parts, and directions are given for each part. You must mark your answers on the separate answer sheet. Do not write your answers in your test book.

PART 1

Directions: For each question in this part, you will hear four statements about a picture in your test book. When you hear the statements, you must select the one statement that best describes what you see in the picture. Then find the number of the question on your answer sheet and mark your answer. The statements will not be printed in your test book and will be spoken only one time.

Example

Sample Answer
Ⓐ ● Ⓒ Ⓓ

Statement (B), "The man is working at a desk," is the best description of the picture, so you should select answer (B) and mark it on your answer sheet.

1

2

GO ON TO THE NEXT PAGE ▶

3

4

5

6

GO ON TO THE NEXT PAGE

PART 2

7 Mark your answer on your answer sheet.

8 Mark your answer on your answer sheet.

9 Mark your answer on your answer sheet.

10 Mark your answer on your answer sheet.

11 Mark your answer on your answer sheet.

12 Mark your answer on your answer sheet.

13 Mark your answer on your answer sheet.

14 Mark your answer on your answer sheet.

15 Mark your answer on your answer sheet.

16 Mark your answer on your answer sheet.

17 Mark your answer on your answer sheet.

18 Mark your answer on your answer sheet.

19 Mark your answer on your answer sheet.

20 Mark your answer on your answer sheet.

21 Mark your answer on your answer sheet.

22 Mark your answer on your answer sheet.

23 Mark your answer on your answer sheet.

24 Mark your answer on your answer sheet.

25 Mark your answer on your answer sheet.

26 Mark your answer on your answer sheet.

27 Mark your answer on your answer sheet.

28 Mark your answer on your answer sheet.

29 Mark your answer on your answer sheet.

30 Mark your answer on your answer sheet.

31 Mark your answer on your answer sheet.

PART 3

Directions: You will hear some conversations between two or more people. You will be asked to answer three questions about what the speakers say in each conversation. Select the best response to each question and mark the letter (A), (B), (C), or (D) on your answer sheet. The conversations will not be printed in your test book and will be spoken only one time.

32 Where does the man work?

(A) At a café
(B) At an appliance store
(C) At a repair shop
(D) At a distribution center

33 Why is the woman's order delayed?

(A) A fault has occurred in the factory.
(B) A delivery van has broken down.
(C) A payment was refused.
(D) Her appliance is out of stock.

34 What does the woman say she will do?

(A) Select an alternative appliance
(B) Cancel the order
(C) Use a different credit card
(D) Collect her own order

35 Why is the woman calling?

(A) To ask about a theater schedule
(B) To find out the cost for children
(C) To sign up for membership
(D) To arrange a show

36 What is the theater going to offer during the winter?

(A) Membership packages
(B) Discounted tickets
(C) Free admission
(D) Special shows

37 What does the man recommend?

(A) Purchasing from the Web site
(B) Checking the times of the shows
(C) Arriving early for tickets
(D) Signing up for discounts

38 What does the woman request?

(A) A lab coat
(B) A temporary security pass
(C) An alternative entrance
(D) Directions to a department

39 What does the man ask to see?

(A) A registration form
(B) A driver's license
(C) A safety certificate
(D) A form of identification

40 What does the man suggest?

(A) Contacting a different department
(B) Paying with cash
(C) Changing her ID details
(D) Searching for her wallet

41 What is the man's problem?

(A) He left his confirmation at home.
(B) He cannot attend the exhibition.
(C) He forgot to register.
(D) His name is missing from a list.

42 What does the woman ask to see?

(A) A letter of confirmation
(B) A payment receipt
(C) A form of identification
(D) A coordinators badge

43 What is being offered to some conference participants?

(A) Free entry to an exhibition
(B) A voucher for a meal
(C) Access to a conference
(D) A gift shop coupon

GO ON TO THE NEXT PAGE

44 Where most likely do the speakers work?

(A) At an office
(B) At a jewelry shop
(C) At a supermarket
(D) At a catering business

45 What problem does the man mention?

(A) A delivery did not arrive.
(B) A colleague was late.
(C) A dinner was postponed.
(D) A freezer was faulty.

46 Why will the man make a telephone call?

(A) To find an alternative supplier
(B) To ask for more time
(C) To confirm the status of an order
(D) To check on a client's booking

47 Where do the speakers most likely work?

(A) At a printing company
(B) At a financial institute
(C) At a construction firm
(D) At an office furniture design firm

48 What does the man mean when he says, "You know I really want to be a part of it"?

(A) He needs some part for repairs.
(B) His supervisor didn't give him permission.
(C) He is interested in joining the team.
(D) He will go on a business trip soon.

49 What does the woman suggest?

(A) Talking to a supervisor
(B) Checking schedules
(C) Postponing a deadline
(D) Borrowing some equipment

50 What did the woman do last week?

(A) She spoke at a seminar.
(B) She inspected a college.
(C) She went on a vacation.
(D) She visited a headquarters.

51 What does the man ask the woman to do?

(A) Talk to a superior
(B) Go on a vacation
(C) Attend a workshop
(D) Repeat a seminar

52 What problem does the woman mention?

(A) She cannot travel to the office.
(B) She has forgotten her notes.
(C) She has not received her fee.
(D) She is away for a fortnight.

53 What are the speakers mainly discussing?

(A) A new contract
(B) A marketing report
(C) An employee evaluation
(D) A travel itinerary

54 Why does the man say, "we don't have any specific procedure for this"?

(A) To put off an announcement
(B) To give the woman an approval
(C) To clarify an issue
(D) To suggest a policy change

55 Why is the supervisor unavailable?

(A) She is meeting some clients.
(B) She is training new employees.
(C) She is finalizing a contract.
(D) She is speaking at a convention.

56 Why is the woman calling?

(A) To discuss travel arrangements
(B) To complain about a service
(C) To request a taxi
(D) To inquire about a missing item

57 Where will the woman most likely go in an hour?

(A) To a client's office
(B) To a restaurant
(C) To a taxi firm
(D) To a department store

58 What does the man tell the woman to bring?

(A) A form of identification
(B) An application form
(C) A description of the item
(D) Her car

59 What is mentioned about the products?

(A) They are all the same design.
(B) They can be ordered for a limited time.
(C) They are only available online.
(D) They will not be delivered on time.

60 What does the woman imply when she says, "I'm actually short of cash now"?

(A) She only has credit cards.
(B) She left some money in her car.
(C) She does not have enough money.
(D) She can lend some cash to the man.

61 What will the man probably do next?

(A) Place an order
(B) Borrow some money from the woman
(C) Give the woman a lift
(D) Show the woman around the facility

62 What item are the speakers discussing?

(A) A mobile phone
(B) A child seat
(C) A television
(D) A watch

63 What does the woman suggest?

(A) Reviewing an advertising strategy
(B) Canceling production
(C) Delaying a consumer survey
(D) Altering a product design

64 What topic does the man say he will bring up at the meeting?

(A) A request for funding
(B) More time for research
(C) A changed schedule
(D) An alternative product

GO ON TO THE NEXT PAGE

Vacation Packages	Price (per person)
Single ticket	$700
Couple ticket	$500
Family member	$450
Group of 6 or more	$400

Conference Room A	
Accounting	11:00 A.M.
Marketing	2:00 P.M.
Sales	3:00 P.M.
Advertising	4:00 P.M.

65 What are the speakers talking about?

(A) A vacation
(B) An overseas business trip
(C) A package delivery
(D) An accounting staff

66 Look at the graphic. What ticket price will the speakers most likely pay?

(A) $700
(B) $500
(C) $450
(D) $400

67 What does the man suggest the woman do?

(A) Go to an accounting office
(B) Buy tickets as soon as possible
(C) Work overtime
(D) Call a colleague

68 Where do the speakers most likely work?

(A) At a shipping company
(B) At a pharmaceutical company
(C) At a real estate agency
(D) At a software manufacturer

69 Look at the graphic. In which department does Ron most likely work?

(A) Accounting
(B) Marketing
(C) Sales
(D) Advertising

70 What will the woman probably do next?

(A) Bring some presentation materials
(B) Conduct an online survey
(C) Ask a coworker to change rooms
(D) Reschedule a meeting

PART 4

Directions: You will hear some talks given by a single speaker. You will be asked to answer three questions about what the speaker says in each talk. Select the best response to each question and mark the letter (A), (B), (C), or (D) on your answer sheet. The talks will not be printed in your test book and will be spoken only one time.

Test 06

71 What kind of business is Ziggy's?

(A) A gaming store
(B) A bookstore
(C) A video store
(D) A music store

72 What does Ziggy's offer for families with children?

(A) Free drinks in the evenings
(B) A parental list of safe games
(C) A supervised gaming area
(D) A monthly free workshop

73 What does the advertisement say about online orders?

(A) They are shipped at a small cost.
(B) They are delivered overnight.
(C) They will come with special discounts.
(D) They can be gift wrapped.

74 Where most likely is the announcement being made?

(A) On a tour bus
(B) On an airplane
(C) In a hotel
(D) In a bank

75 What does the speaker apologize for?

(A) Early closure
(B) A cancelled service
(C) Delayed payments
(D) A bomb alert

76 What are customers paying bills assured of?

(A) Their payments will not be accepted.
(B) Their bills will be paid at once.
(C) Another option will be offered.
(D) Refunds will be issued.

77 What is the speaker discussing?

(A) A television program
(B) A theater production
(C) An advertising campaign
(D) A performance competition

78 What does the speaker say happened two years ago?

(A) The company won an award.
(B) A new director was appointed.
(C) The company changed its dance routine.
(D) An alternative schedule was introduced.

79 What are listeners asked to do?

(A) Appoint a trustee
(B) Contact an audience
(C) Make recommendations
(D) Plan a new routine

80 Where most likely does the speaker work?

(A) At a photographic store
(B) At a supermarket
(C) At an art gallery
(D) At a travel agency

81 Why does the speaker ask the listener to come to the business?

(A) To refund a holiday
(B) To enter a competition
(C) To pick up a prize
(D) To retrieve a lost item

82 What does the speaker ask the listener to bring?

(A) An invoice
(B) Holiday brochures
(C) Passport identification
(D) Account details

GO ON TO THE NEXT PAGE

83 What is the purpose of the message?

(A) To provide a referral
(B) To change a date
(C) To provide a driving test
(D) To confirm an appointment

84 What does the speaker remind Mr. Landau to do on Friday morning?

(A) Submit an insurance claim
(B) Bring eye glasses if necessary
(C) Call back for examination results
(D) Arrive half an hour early

85 What information does the speaker need from Mr. Laundau?

(A) The address of his workplace
(B) An alternative contact number
(C) An identification number
(D) A date for a repeat visit

86 Where is the speaker most likely calling from?

(A) An airport
(B) A taxi stand
(C) A bus stop
(D) A pet shop

87 What does the speaker imply when she says, "but it isn't easy thus far"?

(A) She cannot get a taxi.
(B) She is stuck in traffic.
(C) She doesn't know where the taxi stand is.
(D) She thinks the destination is too far away.

88 What does the speaker ask the listener to do?

(A) Call back
(B) Walk the pet
(C) Feed her pet
(D) Close the bedroom door

89 Who most likely are the listeners?

(A) Competition participants
(B) Festival goers
(C) Security guards
(D) Conference attendees

90 What does the speaker imply when she says, "I'm going to need you for a little more time"?

(A) The listeners are in a hurry to leave.
(B) The event will go longer than expected.
(C) The speaker is busy with other projects.
(D) The audience wants the event to end soon.

91 What is the speaker distributing to the listeners?

(A) Brochures
(B) Greeting cards
(C) Survey forms
(D) Vouchers

Types of services	Fastshipping	BSS
Additional charge for an international shipping	O	O
Arrival notification service	O	O
Package pickup	O	O
Breakage insurance		O

92 Who most likely is the speaker?

(A) A business owner
(B) A retiring employee
(C) A technician
(D) A professor in a college

93 What is the main purpose of the meeting?

(A) To recruit more employees
(B) To open a new branch
(C) To improve the service
(D) To analyze a rival company

94 Look at the graphic. What will the speaker most likely discuss next?

(A) Additional charge for international shipping
(B) Arrival notification service
(C) Package pickup
(D) Breakage insurance

Survey Results	
Waste treatment system	35%
Enlarging Parking Lot	30%
Fitness Facility	25%
Repainting work	10%

Departing Flight	Destination	Departure Time
742	London	2:00 P.M.
707	Seattle	3:15 P.M.
747	Los Angeles	3:30 P.M.
778	Hawaii	5:30 P.M.

95 What is the focus on the meeting?

(A) Improving the community center
(B) Meeting residents' requests
(C) Raising money
(D) Remodeling commercial facilities

96 Look at the graphic. What does the speaker want to focus on?

(A) Waste treatment system
(B) Enlarging parking lot
(C) Fitness facility
(D) Repainting work

97 What does the speaker want from the listeners?

(A) A decision on whether to increase rent
(B) A suggestion for a new parking lot
(C) A tentative contract
(D) A new floor plan

98 What is the cause of the delay?

(A) Inclement weather
(B) A mechanical flaw
(C) A human error
(D) A routine maintenance

99 Look at the graphic. What is the updated time for the flight?

(A) 2:00 P.M.
(B) 3:15 P.M.
(C) 3:30 P.M.
(D) 5:30 P.M.

100 What are the listeners asked to do?

(A) Board the airplane in advance
(B) Wait for the announcement
(C) Follow the staff members
(D) Buy some food

Test 06

This is the end of the Listening test. Turn to Part 5 in your test book.

GO ON TO THE NEXT PAGE

READING TEST

In the Reading test, you will read a variety of texts and answer several different types of reading comprehension questions. The entire Reading test will last 75 minutes. There are three parts, and directions are given for each part. You are encouraged to answer as many questions as possible within the time allowed.

You must mark your answers on the separate answer sheet. Do not write your answers in your test book.

PART 5

Directions: A word or phrase is missing in each of the sentences below. Four answer choices are given below each sentence. Select the best answer to complete the sentence. Then mark the letter (A), (B), (C), or (D) on your answer sheet.

101 Sanmark has ------- introduced a new kitchen appliance to the market.

(A) successes
(B) successfully
(C) successful
(D) success

102 Broadband access may be cut off by ------- Manote Communications or the service provider.

(A) either
(B) both
(C) however
(D) plus

103 Carmen Sanchez, a well-known -------, received praise for her campaign to save the polar bear.

(A) environmental
(B) environmentalist
(C) environmentally
(D) environments

104 With such a positive response to the Alansi organic food promotion, the marketing team plans ------- production by 40 percent in the next six months.

(A) increase
(B) increasing
(C) increases
(D) to increase

105 Our partnership on the publicity drive is an example of how efficient teamwork can lead to ------- results.

(A) excellently
(B) excellent
(C) excel
(D) excellence

106 The Reventure software is ------- specifically for organizations that want to monitor workers when they are away from the office.

(A) designed
(B) appointed
(C) accomplished
(D) informed

107 Two days ago, Ms. Hayes told people that the piles of paperwork in the corner were -------.

(A) she
(B) hers
(C) her
(D) herself

108 Reconstruction of the pipeline was ------- planned to be completed by February 11.

(A) originally
(B) extremely
(C) strongly
(D) highly

109 As a response to employee -------, our offices will be opened earlier in the morning.

(A) suggestions
(B) suggest
(C) suggests
(D) suggested

110 As well as soft drinks, a selection of canapés will be provided ------- the employee orientation course.

(A) during
(B) along
(C) onto
(D) about

111 Mr. McBride applauded the workers for ------- dedication during the recent production run.

(A) their
(B) them
(C) theirs
(D) they

112 Laymon's DVD store received positive ------- for its customer service from members of the public.

(A) impact
(B) access
(C) feedback
(D) experience

113 Before ------- the winners of the awards, please make sure that they are all in attendance in the main dining hall.

(A) announcing
(B) announced
(C) announcement
(D) announcer

114 Several efforts were made to ease traffic congestion on the main highway, ------- of which addressed any problems.

(A) none
(B) nothing
(C) nobody
(D) neither

115 The Dunlop County History Museum ------- by the local historical research society.

(A) maintained
(B) is maintained
(C) is maintaining
(D) can maintain

116 Amaize County has attracted a large number of new businesses ------- its low taxes and bountiful workforce.

(A) as a result
(B) owing to
(C) now that
(D) because

117 We will notify you ------- our employment decision on or after November 1st.

(A) to
(B) of
(C) for
(D) from

118 Acquisition of the newest equipment can have a significant impact on a company's overall -------.

(A) profitable
(B) profitability
(C) profitably
(D) profited

119 Our staffing assignments are adjusted ------- to make sure that all employees have an opportunity to work directly with our customers.

(A) previously
(B) accordingly
(C) periodically
(D) extremely

120 ------- the hotel's reception desk is open around the clock, the free shuttle service to and from the airport is only available from 6 A.M. to 10 P.M.

(A) Despite
(B) However
(C) Although
(D) Nevertheless

GO ON TO THE NEXT PAGE

121 ------- that the recent inclement weather will reduce tourism to Sunnyside Island, several local hotel operators have announced special offers.

(A) Concerning
(B) Concerned
(C) Been concerned
(D) To have been concerning

122 ------- company policy, sales associates must obtain a permit from a supervisor before using company equipment personally.

(A) Instead of
(B) As well as
(C) On behalf of
(D) In accordance with

123 At Bergen National Park, you can enjoy a trek up the mountainside and a ------- walk by a lake.

(A) persistent
(B) conclusive
(C) leisurely
(D) tolerant

124 The financial district is located in downtown Starnberg and is easily ------- by public transport.

(A) accessible
(B) active
(C) necessary
(D) transportable

125 ------- Wesler employee revealing confidential company information to others will be terminated.

(A) All
(B) Several
(C) Few
(D) Any

126 Starkland officials and Thronin Construction Engineers are currently engaged in ------- over the proposals to construct a new ring road.

(A) negotiations
(B) receipts
(C) construction
(D) increase

127 The initiative that Mayor Tomlinson ------- to improve the highways, involved sectioning off a part of Route 22 for use by public transport only.

(A) implementing
(B) implement
(C) implemented
(D) implements

128 Employees must have been employed for a minimum of a year to be ------- for the company's pension scheme.

(A) compatible
(B) eligible
(C) responsive
(D) flexible

129 Mr. Khalid has indicated that he is willing to travel abroad ------- it would be of benefit to his organization's future prospects.

(A) somewhere
(B) whenever
(C) himself
(D) whether

130 A reduction in operating costs is one ------- for investing in new technology in the workplace.

(A) justification
(B) condolence
(C) translation
(D) diagnosis

PART 6

Directions: Read the texts that follow. A word, phrase, or sentence is missing in parts of each text. Four answer choices for each question are given below the text. Select the best answer to complete the text. Then mark the letter (A), (B), (C), or (D) on your answer sheet.

Questions 131-134 refer to the following flyer.

Attention Performing Artists!

Are you interested in an exclusive opportunity to perform on stage at our theater? -------, you are
131.
invited to sign up for a chance to display your talent at the York Open Festival on June 23.

Entry forms are available online at www.yorkopen.org and your performance will be judged by

several performers from events staged at our local theater. Together with your completed entry

form, please upload ------- of your specialist area. -------.
132. **133.**

The application deadline is May 1, and the judges' decisions will be made on that day. -------
134.
applicants will have use of the stage facilities and will be expected to stay for the duration of the

event.

---

131 (A) Instead
(B) Even so
(C) If so
(D) After that

132 (A) developments
(B) instructions
(C) details
(D) requirements

133 (A) We have already finished reviewing all of
the entry forms.
(B) This will help the judges to put you into
the correct category.
(C) You need to obtain necessary forms at
the reception desk.
(D) Performing on stage requires courage
and the ability to react instantly.

134 (A) Invited
(B) Invites
(C) Invitation
(D) Inviting

GO ON TO THE NEXT PAGE

Questions 135-138 refer to the following article.

Montana (March 15) — Max-Gas, a popular national chain of gas stations, will be opening its first

two stations in Montana soon. The company's stations feature large 24-hour convenience stores

with a wide array of snacks, beverages, and other daily necessities. -------, Max-Gas stations are
135.
well known for being efficiently managed and having friendly staff. -------.
136.

Montana's first Max-Gas will be constructed at the corner of Lloyd Street and 10th Avenue. The

------- one, to be situated at Kisco Street and 20th Avenue, will be a special Max-Gas station,
137.
equipped with a small kitchen facility. Like other special stations, this one will have tables and

chairs ------- patrons can sit down and eat.
138.

135 (A) Nonetheless
(B) After all
(C) Besides
(D) Namely

136 (A) Improvements of highways are attributed
to government's effort.
(B) They also pride themselves on their safe
and clean amenities.
(C) Commuters are driving their cars less
and less as the price of gasoline rises.
(D) The availability of consumer goods will
increase in the near future.

137 (A) similar
(B) former
(C) rival
(D) second

138 (A) there
(B) whose
(C) which
(D) where

To: dcarlton@jetmail.net
From: jdelphi@houndban.com
Date: April 5
Subject: Your Interview

Dear Mr. Carlton:

I am writing on behalf of the hiring team at Houndban, Inc. The team was very impressed with your

interview on Thursday. -------, you were one of the most promising candidates. -------. Instead
                        139.   **140.**
we would like to invite you to send your résumé to our Fineville office. It is currently looking for a

senior accountant. ------- your experience and knowledge, you would be an asset to Houndban,
                    141.
Inc. If you are willing to consider relocating to Fineville, we would be happy to recommend you

for the ------- there.
            142.

Sincerely,

Joanne Delphi

---

139 (A) Otherwise
    (B) Meanwhile
    (C) In fact
    (D) As always

140 (A) We never received a copy of your
       reference letter.
    (B) We think you don't have enough
       experience.
    (C) We would like you to intern with our
       company.
    (D) Unfortunately, we are unable to offer you
       a position at this time.

141 (A) Now that
    (B) Given
    (C) Unlike
    (D) Also

142 (A) program
    (B) lodging
    (C) vacancy
    (D) training

GO ON TO THE NEXT PAGE

Questions 143-146 refer to the following article.

New Library Opens

September 10 — The city's new library branch at Victory Center began serving patrons two

days ago. The mayor was ------- for the opening ceremony. Moreover, members of several local

                    143.

community groups and schoolchildren ------- in the event.

                        144.

The new 1,200-square-meter library was designed with environmental considerations in mind.

-------. In addition, 60% of the building's electricity comes from solar panels on its roof.

145.

One of the library's objectives is to connect users to cutting-edge -------. While there are plenty

                        146.

of reference materials, there are also lots of computer terminals. Patrons can also bring their own

devices to use the library's free ultra-high-speed Internet.

---

143 (A) presented
    (B) presenting
    (C) present
    (D) presently

144 (A) participated
    (B) participating
    (C) will participate
    (D) would have participated

145 (A) It has five large air-conditioning units.
    (B) A famous architect designed it.
    (C) It is heated entirely by the sun.
    (D) It is close to a subway station.

146 (A) technology
    (B) vehicles
    (C) education
    (D) appliance

PART 7

Directions: In this part you will read a selection of texts, such as magazine and newspaper articles, e-mails, and instant messages. Each text or set of texts is followed by several questions. Select the best answer for each question and mark the letter (A), (B), (C), or (D) on your answer sheet.

Questions 147-148 refer to the following advertisement.

Newhaven Retirement Village

Newhaven Retirement Village is now leasing!

- One-and two-bedroom apartments

- Located in the center of downtown Newhaven, this new 48-unit residential village caters to retired people.

- On-site amenities include two communal lounges, a swimming pool and fitness center, and ample parking, all included in the monthly rental charge.

- This village is in a perfect location, overlooking Waterdown Bridge and close to shops and public amenities.

- Visit our showroom apartments and see what we have available. Our leasing agents are on hand to take prospective tenants around the village.

Newhaven Retirement Village
32 Treetop Road
Newhaven
857-555-4125
www.newhavenretirementvillage.com

147 What does the advertisement describe?

(A) Retirement homes for rent
(B) Corporate relocation service
(C) Local visitors' attractions
(D) Vacation homes for sale

148 What are the readers invited to do?

(A) Purchase a membership
(B) Take a tour
(C) Sign an agreement
(D) Send a deposit payment

GO ON TO THE NEXT PAGE

Questions 149-150 refer to the following e-mail.

```
┌─────────────────────────────────────────────────────────────┐
│                      E-Mail Message                           │
├─────────────────────────────────────────────────────────────┤
│  To:      Kelmer Manufacturing Employees                    ▲ │
│  From:    Sally Arnold <arsally@kelmer.com>                   │
│  Date:    February 12                                         │
│  Subject: Company Information                                ▼ │
├─────────────────────────────────────────────────────────────┤
│                                                             ▲ │
│  Recently, we sent all staff members a copy of our new        │
│  employee manual, together with a separate acknowledgement    │
│  form.                                                        │
│                                                               │
│  The manual contains complete information regarding the       │
│  policies and procedures of Kelmer Manufacturing.            │
│  Additionally, it contains details about job descriptions     │
│  and employee benefits. Please read the manual carefully      │
│  and sign the acknowledgement form enclosed, confirming       │
│  that you have read and understood the rules and procedures   │
│  as described in the manual, and that you undertake to        │
│  follow company rules.                                        │
│                                                               │
│  Please send your signed forms to John Feathers in Human      │
│  Resources.                                                   │
│  Thank you for your cooperation in this matter.               │
│                                                               │
│  Sally Arnold                                                 │
│  Managing Director, Human Resources                         ▼ │
└─────────────────────────────────────────────────────────────┘
```

149 What does Ms. Arnold discuss in the e-mail?

(A) A training course
(B) An employment opportunity
(C) A company publication
(D) A change in employment procedures

150 What does Ms. Arnold ask employees to do?

(A) Sign and send a form
(B) Review their job benefits
(C) Attend a meeting
(D) Return a book

Thank you for purchasing a Mission B-452 laptop computer. Our free anti-virus software is included in your laptop purchase. As this is our introductory version, it is recommended that you purchase the complete edition soon. You can order the full version directly from Mission at our online store, www.missioncomputers.com. We guarantee that you will receive an immediate download and the software package will be delivered to you within five working days. If you do not receive it by that time, we will provide a full refund. As a valued customer, you will receive a 15 percent discount off your first software purchase. Just type in code 41230 when placing your order. If you would prefer to purchase software through a retail outlet, our packages are stocked by all leading computer equipment stores. However, please be aware that most retailers do not allow customers our corporate discount.

Call 800-555-3412, 24 hours a day for technical support or 800-555-3412 Monday through Friday 8 A.M. to 9 P.M. with any questions or feedback about your purchase.

151 For whom was the notice written?

(A) Owners of new laptop computers
(B) Sales advisors
(C) Technical support professionals
(D) Software developers

152 What promise is made about placing orders for software?

(A) The introductory software continues for three months.
(B) The buyer receives the software for free if delivery is late.
(C) The technical department will respond to queries promptly.
(D) Customer service is provided 24/7.

153 How can shoppers receive a discount?

(A) By purchasing items from a computer store
(B) By mailing a voucher
(C) By calling customer support
(D) By entering numbers when ordering online

GO ON TO THE NEXT PAGE

Questions 154-155 refer to the following text message chain.

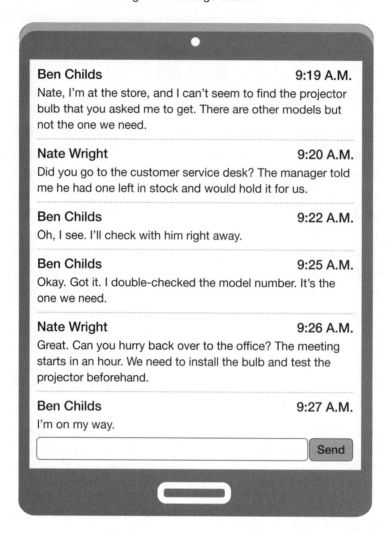

Ben Childs   9:19 A.M.

Nate, I'm at the store, and I can't seem to find the projector bulb that you asked me to get. There are other models but not the one we need.

Nate Wright   9:20 A.M.

Did you go to the customer service desk? The manager told me he had one left in stock and would hold it for us.

Ben Childs   9:22 A.M.

Oh, I see. I'll check with him right away.

Ben Childs   9:25 A.M.

Okay. Got it. I double-checked the model number. It's the one we need.

Nate Wright   9:26 A.M.

Great. Can you hurry back over to the office? The meeting starts in an hour. We need to install the bulb and test the projector beforehand.

Ben Childs   9:27 A.M.

I'm on my way.

Send

154 What is most likely true about Mr. Wright?

(A) He gave Mr. Childs the wrong model number.

(B) He contacted the store about a projector bulb.

(C) He plans to return to the office right away.

(D) He is going to give a presentation.

155 At 9:22 A.M., what does Mr. Childs mean when he writes, "Oh, I see"?

(A) He found the last projector bulb.

(B) He is still looking around the store.

(C) He understands the situation now.

(D) He can see the customer service desk.

A Note from the Editor

This September issue of *Thailand Cuisine* coincides with the magazine's second anniversary. It has been two years since we published our first issue, and since then we have become one of the area's most popular magazines on ethnic cooking. Our circulation recently reached 22,000, and the number continues to rise.

Local food lovers have praised our publication, and we were awarded the accolade of Best New Food Magazine at last month's World Food Festival. As Senior Editor, I would like to express my appreciation for our dedicated staff, our writers, our advertisers, and our growing community of readers, all of whom have contributed greatly to our success.

Stella Morgan

156 What is the purpose of Ms. Morgan's note?

(A) To make an offer available
(B) To ask for contributions
(C) To express appreciation
(D) To introduce a writer

157 What is indicated about *Thailand Cuisine*?

(A) It is becoming increasingly popular.
(B) It has increased its advertising charges.
(C) It will soon be distributed worldwide.
(D) It is seeking additional contributors.

158 Why does Ms. Morgan mention the World Food Festival?

(A) Because the magazine received an award at the event
(B) Because the publishers sponsored the event
(C) Because she recruited extra volunteers there
(D) Because she held a cooking demonstration

GO ON TO THE NEXT PAGE

Questions 159-161 refer to the following memo.

From: Geraldine Compton
To: Bickford Marketing employees
Subject: Stanley Haynes

We are pleased to announce that Mr. Stanley Haynes, Managing Director of our Singapore branch office, is due to visit our office in Washington, D.C., in two weeks' time. Mr. Haynes has worked with Bickford Marketing for five years as a research analyst and Web site designer before transferring to Asia.

Mr. Haynes has successfully worked for the last two years setting up the online division of our Singapore branch. As a result, sales figures have continued to rise significantly, and Bickford has now become an established name in Asia.

Mr. Haynes will be leading a discussion focusing on social media marketing. The presentation, which will be very detailed, will be followed by a question-and-answer session. We encourage participants to take notes during the meeting.

All staff are required to attend, but in the case of a scheduling conflict, please contact Ms. Walker or your office manager.

We look forward to seeing you soon.

Sincerely,
Bickford Marketing

159 What does the memo announce?

(A) An upcoming business presentation
(B) The celebration of a company's five-year anniversary
(C) Employment opportunities in the Singapore office
(D) The appointment of a new company director

160 What is indicated about Mr. Haynes?

(A) He was recently hired by Mr. Bickford.
(B) He referred a client to Bickford Marketing.
(C) He will be managing the Washington office.
(D) He has experience in online marketing development.

161 According to the memo, what should participants bring with them to the meeting?

(A) A sheet of prepared questions
(B) A list of marketing topics
(C) Copies of their résumés
(D) Note-taking materials

Questions 162-164 refer to the following letter.

Sharm Ra Hotels
50 Merino Street
Cairo, Egypt
August 7

To all interested applicants:

Thank you for your inquiry concerning training opportunities at Sharma Ra Hotels. We offer a small number of paid summer traineeships to qualified applicants who wish to make a career in the holiday and hotel industries. Applicants selected to participate in our training scheme gain hands-on experience in a true life working environment and work with tutors on specific projects related to their individual aspirations.

Please find enclosed an application packet and job descriptions for each department. After reading these thoroughly, please apply directly to the section in which you are interested. Completed applications should be received by the end of this month. Interviews will be held with selected applicants during the first week of September. The trainee programs begin February 1 and end on March 10. We look forward to receiving your applications shortly.

Sincerely,

Selma Banks

Selma Banks
Traineeships organizer

Enclosures

162 What is suggested about the recipients of the letter?

(A) They have already contacted Sharm Ra Hotels.
(B) They will be interviewed by Selma Banks.
(C) They are planning their vacations.
(D) They work at tourist offices.

163 What are the recipients of the letter asked to review?

(A) A brochure describing the hotels
(B) The company's financial procedures
(C) A list of changes to a program
(D) Information about training projects

164 When are applications due?

(A) On August 31
(B) On September 4
(C) On February 1
(D) On March 10

GO ON TO THE NEXT PAGE

Questions 165-168 refer to the following online chat discussion.

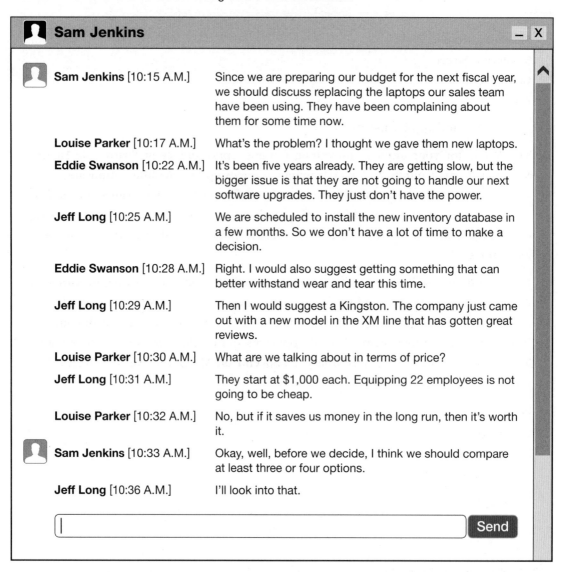

Sam Jenkins   — X

Sam Jenkins [10:15 A.M.]   Since we are preparing our budget for the next fiscal year, we should discuss replacing the laptops our sales team have been using. They have been complaining about them for some time now.

Louise Parker [10:17 A.M.]   What's the problem? I thought we gave them new laptops.

Eddie Swanson [10:22 A.M.]   It's been five years already. They are getting slow, but the bigger issue is that they are not going to handle our next software upgrades. They just don't have the power.

Jeff Long [10:25 A.M.]   We are scheduled to install the new inventory database in a few months. So we don't have a lot of time to make a decision.

Eddie Swanson [10:28 A.M.]   Right. I would also suggest getting something that can better withstand wear and tear this time.

Jeff Long [10:29 A.M.]   Then I would suggest a Kingston. The company just came out with a new model in the XM line that has gotten great reviews.

Louise Parker [10:30 A.M.]   What are we talking about in terms of price?

Jeff Long [10:31 A.M.]   They start at $1,000 each. Equipping 22 employees is not going to be cheap.

Louise Parker [10:32 A.M.]   No, but if it saves us money in the long run, then it's worth it.

Sam Jenkins [10:33 A.M.]   Okay, well, before we decide, I think we should compare at least three or four options.

Jeff Long [10:36 A.M.]   I'll look into that.

                                            Send

165 What is indicated about the sales team?

(A) They recently updated their inventory software.

(B) They have used the same equipment for several years.

(C) They recently submitted a budget request for laptops.

(D) They are having problems processing sales orders.

166 What is suggested about the current laptops?

(A) They cost more than $1,000.

(B) Their power supplies failed.

(C) They will soon be obsolete.

(D) They were bought at a discount.

167 What is implied about Kingston?

(A) Its laptops are durable.

(B) The company cannot afford them.

(C) It makes one model.

(D) It is the top-rated brand.

168 At 10:36 A.M., what does Mr. Long mean when he writes, "I'll look into that"?

(A) He will determine how money can be saved.

(B) He will gather information on different models.

(C) He will ask employees what laptop they prefer.

(D) He will confirm the price of the Kingston.

GO ON TO THE NEXT PAGE

Test 06

Questions 169-171 refer to the following job advertisement.

Integrated Irrigation and Vegetable Production in Brazil (IIVPB)

54 Rua 3
Gravata, Brazil
www.vpb.br

POSITION VACANT

For 10 years, IIVPB has been educating smallholders in the use of organic growing methods. -(1)-. The aim is to increase production while using the latest research in irrigation methods and maintaining the high quality of organic growing methods. -(2)-. We are an independently-funded organization based in São Paolo, with additional locations in the Brazilian states of Paraiba, Bahia, Pernambuco, and Rio Grande do Norte.

-(3)-. The successful candidate will lead the research and act as a liaison between the research team and owners of smallholdings. The successful applicant must have a solid scientific research background, preferably agricultural, and have a minimum of four years of professional managerial experience.

Please submit applications, accompanied by a cover letter and résumé, in person, by e-mail, by regular mail or on our Web site, www.iivpb.br/careers, by November 10. The successful applicant is expected to begin his or her duties on December 10. –(4)–.

169 What is indicated about IIVPB?

(A) It is committed to using modern irrigation procedures.
(B) It is revising its corporate mission.
(C) It sells irrigation equipment.
(D) It receives financial assistance from the government.

170 What is NOT suggested about the position?

(A) It will be filled before the end of the year.
(B) It involves liaison between parties.
(C) It requires experience in project management.
(D) It is restricted to Brazilian nationals.

171 In which of the positions marked [1], [2], [3], and [4] does the following sentence best belong?

"We are looking to fill the position of Project Manager at our Paraiba location."

(A) [1]
(B) [2]
(C) [3]
(D) [4]

Employee Focus: Stacey May

Stacey May, who plans to step down as senior underwriter in March, has served Trafford Insurance in many roles for 25 years. Insurance company president Geoffrey Marks said, "It's seldom that one finds the range of experience at Trafford that Stacey has." –[1]–.

Ms. May began her career in insurance as a temporary administrative assistant at Simpson Insurance Brokers in Harlowe. She found the work to be very satisfying, and at the end of her contract, started to seek a permanent position in the industry. –[2]–. After eighteen months of answering telephones and routine administrative duties, Ms. May was hired as a trainee underwriter at Trafford Insurance's Eggington branch, and in less than just six months, was promoted to junior underwriter. –[3]–.

However, Ms. May continued her climb upwards in the ranks. She explained, "I enjoyed learning about insurance policies and wanted to become a senior underwriter. My manager at the Eggington branch, Craig Ling, gave me advice on how to proceed. On Craig's recommendation, I decided to apply for the insurance studies program at Butterick College in Anderton, just as Craig had done five years before. I financed my course by applying for a student loan and continued to work as a junior underwriter part-time. It took me six years to complete the insurance degree." –[4]–.

Once she had graduated from Butterick College, Ms. May joined the insurance department at Trafford Insurance's headquarters. Two years later, she was appointed assistant to Senior Underwriter Hope Bennett, and when Ms. Bennett transferred to the large claims division, Ms. May was chosen to take her place. "Just think about that," Ms. May said, "I started out doing the filing, and I ended up as senior underwriter at the company's headquarters."

Test 06

172 What is the purpose of the article?

(A) To introduce an employee who is retiring after long years of service
(B) To give information regarding applications for training courses
(C) To describe all the job openings at the insurance company
(D) To report on the varied duties of an employee

173 What is indicated about Mr. Ling?

(A) He was interviewed for the article.
(B) He studied insurance.
(C) He has teaching experience.
(D) He is a part-time underwriter at an insurance company.

174 What is suggested about Trafford Insurance?

(A) It offers its employees discounts on college fees.
(B) It recently merged with Simpson Insurance Brokers.
(C) Its headquarters are in Eggington.
(D) It has a large claims department.

175 In which of the positions marked [1], [2], [3], and [4] does the following sentence best belong?

"She found employment as a permanent administrative officer at Trafford's Anderton branch."

(A) [1]
(B) [2]
(C) [3]
(D) [4]

GO ON TO THE NEXT PAGE

Questions 176-180 refer to the following flyer and e-mail.

The 10th Mansfield Art and Drama Festival

October 10-12

The Mansfield Art and Drama Festival, sponsored by Mansfield Cultural Association, has something for everyone. The events, lasting three days, will feature exhibits by prominent artists and entertainment by local musicians and actors. Refreshments and crafts will be available for purchase and a variety of children's activities are scheduled.

Here are some of the events:

Friday, October 10, 4 PM, Art Gallery Picasso
The opening of Elena Martin's *Portraits of My Family*. Exhibition runs through 17 November. Open Monday to Friday, 10.30 A.M. to 8 P.M., Saturday and Sunday, noon to 6 P.M. Admission is free.

Saturday & Sunday, October 11-12, 11 AM to 7 PM, St. Mary's RC Church
Children's arts and crafts and play activities. Admission is free.

Saturday, October 11, 3 PM, Risedale Open Air Theater
(Rain relocation: Welbury Theater) Concert by the Peruvian Youth Choir (as requested by popular demand). Tickets available at the door.

Saturday & Sunday, October 11-12, 1 PM to 7 PM, McLean Memorial
Ethnic Food and Crafts Fair

Sunday, October 12, 6 PM to 8 PM, Fennymore Theater
The Stowbridge Theater Company presents *Summer at the Farm* by the playwright Stel Gosse. Tickets available at the door.

Pre-booking available beginning October 1. For further details and a complete list of events, please visit us at www.madf.org.

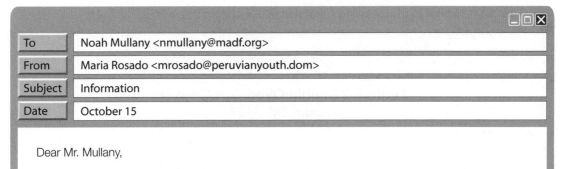

To: Noah Mullany <nmullany@madf.org>
From: Maria Rosado <mrosado@peruvianyouth.dom>
Subject: Information
Date: October 15

Dear Mr. Mullany,

This is to thank you once again for inviting us to perform our Peruvian music at the Mansfield Arts and Drama Festival. It was such bad luck that it rained so heavily that we had to perform indoors, since that meant a much smaller audience could enjoy our performance. However, we were delighted with the ovation we received from the audience. Many people purchased our CDs or asked us whether our music could be downloaded from popular music Web sites.

We hope we will have the privilege of participating in future festivals.

Sincerely,

Maria Rosado

Events manager

Peruvian Youth Choir

176 What event is NOT scheduled to take place at 6 P.M. on Sunday?

(A) A craft-making program
(B) An art showing
(C) An ethnic food market
(D) A ballet performance

177 What is indicated about the Festival?

(A) It is being advertised online.
(B) It starts at 11 A.M. each morning.
(C) It takes place three times a year.
(D) It has the duration of one week.

178 When is a play to be performed?

(A) October 1
(B) October 9
(C) October 10
(D) October 12

179 Why did Ms. Rosado send Mr. Mullany an e-mail?

(A) To express her thanks
(B) To request tickets for a performance
(C) To cancel her reservation
(D) To cancel a performance

180 What is suggested about the Peruvian Youth Choir?

(A) It has more people accessing its Web site.
(B) It is currently on tour in South America.
(C) It performed at Welbury Theater.
(D) It participated in the Festival for the first time.

GO ON TO THE NEXT PAGE

Questions 181–185 refer to the following list of features and Web site.

Eumark 2 Double Oven Gas Cooker
Model EM-3189

FEATURES:

- Extra-large double oven accommodates more cooking than standard cookers.
- Heat-treated steel exterior offers excellent protection from rust and easier cleaning.
- Integral automatic timer lets you know when your food is cooked. Control panel lights indicate the optimum cooking temperature.
- New SaveEnergy technology provides a varied temperature control that uses less gas than most other models.
- A variety of burners for small, medium and large cooking pans
- Three-shelf design enables the cooker to bake, roast and warm food at the same time so your meals are totally coordinated.

WWW.EUMARK.COM

| Review | Products | Terms and Conditions | Locations |

"Great value for money"

Posted by: Abigail Davies
Posted on: September 14
Located in: Berkshire, UK

My previous cooker was manufactured by another company and only lasted three years. I was delighted when Eumark designed this very advanced but inexpensive model. I didn't think it would be as economical as my previous appliance, but I was pleasantly surprised. This appliance cooks all types of food perfectly. The oven has three tiers internally (bake, roast and warm) and four different burners (small, medium and two large) to suit a variety of pot sizes. I am also particularly impressed with the fact that the oven turns itself off when cooking is complete, so that I can leave it and go out. It is also available in a wide range of bright colors. Best of all, Eumark has designed the cooker to be long lasting. My only complaint is that it has so many functions that it took me a long time to figure them out. I had to study the manual very carefully to follow all the instructions.

181 What is indicated in the list of features?

(A) A set of instructions for cooking recipes
(B) The positive characteristics of a product
(C) Information about the various types of oven gas cooker
(D) All types of food which can be made by Eumark 2 Double Oven Gas Cooker

182 According to the list of features, what is an advantage of SaveEnergy technology?

(A) It uses less energy.
(B) It saves the customer time.
(C) It extends the durability of the appliance.
(D) It makes the item easier to clean.

183 In the Web site, the word "suit" in paragraph 1, line 5, is closest in meaning to

(A) accommodate
(B) dress up
(C) qualify
(D) appeal to

184 What criticism does Ms. Davies make about the product?

(A) It is complicated.
(B) It is too heavy.
(C) It is too noisy.
(D) It is expensive.

185 What feature does Ms. Davies like that is NOT mentioned in the product description?

(A) Its number of hobs
(B) Its large oven size
(C) Its variety of appearance
(D) Its cooking settings

GO ON TO THE NEXT PAGE

Upgrade your computer skills with
New Technology Campus
Fall Course Offerings (Term 1)

Working with Databases (Basic-level Course) $975
   8 sessions (9:30 A.M. – 11:45 A.M.)
   Starting: September 3

Word Processing Boot Camp (Intermediate-level Course) $825
   6 sessions (8:30 A.M. – 11:30 A.M.)
   Starting: September 10

Perfecting Presentation Software (Advanced-level Course) $775
   5 sessions (1:00 P.M. – 5:30 P.M.)
   Starting: September 17

Spreadsheet Secrets (Intermediate-level Course) $450
   4 sessions (9:00 A.M. – 12:15 P.M.)
   Starting: September 24

All classes are held on Saturdays at

Lowman Continuing Education Building
8904 Lightfoot Avenue, Vernon
(818) 555-9303

Register at www.newtechnologycampus.com.
A nonrefundable deposit (10% of tuition)
is due at the time of registration.

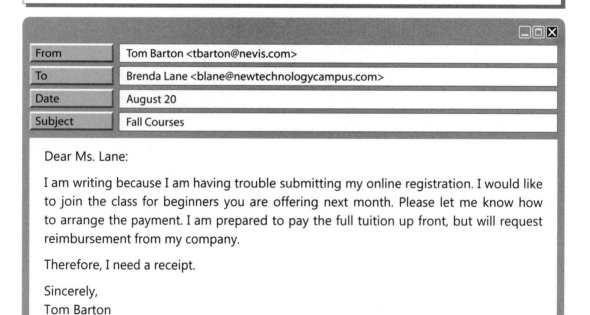

From	Tom Barton <tbarton@nevis.com>
To	Brenda Lane <blane@newtechnologycampus.com>
Date	August 20
Subject	Fall Courses

Dear Ms. Lane:

I am writing because I am having trouble submitting my online registration. I would like to join the class for beginners you are offering next month. Please let me know how to arrange the payment. I am prepared to pay the full tuition up front, but will request reimbursement from my company.

Therefore, I need a receipt.

Sincerely,
Tom Barton

Dear Mr. Barton,

Your course will start next week. Please note that a room has not yet been assigned. Therefore, we ask that you come at least fifteen minutes prior to your class' scheduled starting time. Upon arrival, please check in at the security desk located at the building's east entrance. You will receive a temporary parking permit and ID badge. In addition, you will be directed to your classroom at that time.

If you have not paid the balance of your tuition, you will need to do so on your starting date. A representative from the admissions office will be present in the lobby.

If you have any questions, please feel free to call us at (818) 555-8787.

186 What is indicated about the New Technology Campus courses?

(A) They allow for in-person registration.
(B) They require advanced payment.
(C) They are only offered in the morning.
(D) They limit the number of participants.

187 What is true about the course Mr. Barton wants to take?

(A) It will meet a total of six times.
(B) It will be held in the afternoon.
(C) It will cost his company $450.
(D) It will meet for fewer than three hours.

188 In the e-mail, the word "full" in paragraph 1, line 3, is closest in meaning to

(A) entire
(B) extra
(C) important
(D) overdue

189 According to the postcard, what should Mr. Barton do?

(A) Arrive early for his first class
(B) Bring a form of identification
(C) Park in a special area
(D) Issue a parking permit

190 What is suggested about the postcard?

(A) It was mailed to Mr. Barton's workplace.
(B) It was written by Ms. Lane.
(C) It requires a response from Mr. Barton.
(D) It was sent before September 3.

GO ON TO THE NEXT PAGE

Questions 191-195 refer to the following Web site, article, and e-mail message.

www.fabulousfoods.com

| **About Us** | Products | Branches | Online Sales | Contact Us |

Our Story

Fabulous Foods started in 1920 as Fabulous Bakery in a small town in western New York. Owner and founder David Hecht baked breads and sweets by using his family's secret recipes. The company started making potato chips and other snack foods in the 1950s. Hecht decided to sell the company in 1958 to a group of investors who renamed it Fabulous Foods. The new owners sold the bakery operation and focused exclusively on the development and production of potato chips, corn chips, popcorn, and other tasty snacks, including a popular low-fat line for health-conscious consumers. Today, Fabulous Foods distributes its products to retail stores in all 50 U.S. states, Canada, and Mexico.

BUFFALO (July 16) — On Sunday, July 21, a series of foot races will be held at the city's Burlington Park to raise money for health education. The Race for Your Health features 15 km, 10 km, and 5 km races, with the earliest starting at 7:30 A.M. Participants can compete in six different categories based on age and gender. Prizes will be awarded to the top three finishers in each category. There will also be a noncompetitive 2 km fun walk for people of all ages. Several local businesses, including Burlington Sports Drinks and Fabulous Foods, as well as St. James Hospital are sponsoring the event. To register, visit www.racehealth.org. There is a $25 fee for the fun walk and a $45 fee for the races. Participants will receive a T-shirt, complimentary beverages and promotional items from the sponsors.

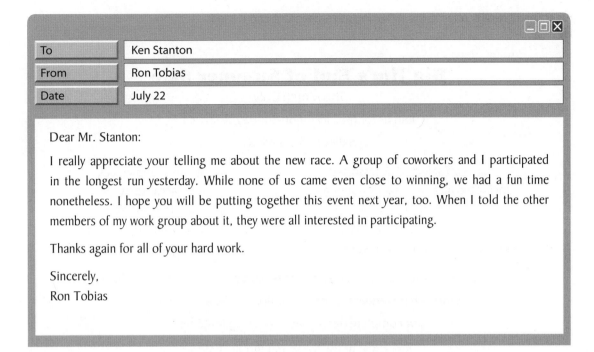

To: Ken Stanton
From: Ron Tobias
Date: July 22

Dear Mr. Stanton:

I really appreciate your telling me about the new race. A group of coworkers and I participated in the longest run yesterday. While none of us came even close to winning, we had a fun time nonetheless. I hope you will be putting together this event next year, too. When I told the other members of my work group about it, they were all interested in participating.

Thanks again for all of your hard work.

Sincerely,
Ron Tobias

On the Web site, the word "operation" in paragraph 1, line 5, is closest in meaning to

(A) business
(B) equipment
(C) procedure
(D) surgery

192 What is indicated about Fabulous Foods?

(A) It regularly sponsors events.
(B) It donates money to schools.
(C) It has a factory in Canada.
(D) It is located in Buffalo.

193 In the article, what is NOT mentioned about the event?

(A) Children are eligible to participate.
(B) A payment is required to register.
(C) Eighteen prizes will be awarded.
(D) All races will be finished by noon.

194 Who most likely is Mr. Stanton?

(A) The winner of the 15 km race
(B) The organizer of the Race for Your Health
(C) A public health worker at St. James Hospital
(D) A colleague at Mr. Tobias's company

195 What is suggested about Mr. Tobias?

(A) He ran in the 10 km event.
(B) He paid $25 to participate.
(C) He received free food.
(D) He was given a prize.

GO ON TO THE NEXT PAGE

Actual Test 06   267

Big Jim's End of Summer Sale

This Month Only

Join us for the kickoff on Sunday, August 1

Balloons for the kids

20% off selected accessories, including all Magic headphones and Blackman camera cases	15% off small appliances manufactured by G5, Livingston, and Ward
10% off large appliances manufactured by Titus, Livingston, and Ward	5% off all TVs, stereos, and LCD projectors

Join our Preferred Buyers Club and earn reward points for every purchase.

Points can be redeemed for promotional gifts and discounts.

For complete details, visit www.bigjims.com.

Offer good at the following Big Jim's stores

88 Reese Road in Marston 555-0340

7816 Eagle Road in Lincoln 555-2149

908 Jasper Ave in Winston 555-3873

Some products are eligible for free delivery. Check with a store manager.

E-Mail Message

To: Sam Long <slong@bigjims.com>
From: Donna Kingsley <dkingsley@netnet.com>
Subject: Delivery
Date: September 2, 8:29 A.M.

Dear Mr. Long:

When I bought my Ward brand dishwasher at your store last week, I originally asked you to deliver it on the third. However, something has come up, and that plan now conflicts with my schedule. Could you deliver it on the sixth at 4:00 P.M. or the seventh at 10:00 A.M.? Please let me know if any of these dates and times work for you. Since your Jasper Avenue store is not that far from my home, I hope that you can do this for me. I'm sorry I was not able to contact you about this matter sooner.

Thanks,

Donna Kingsley

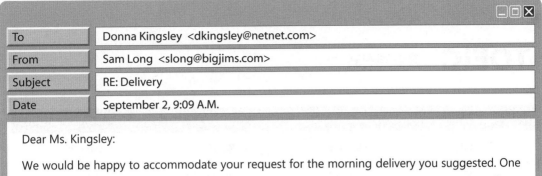

To	Donna Kingsley <dkingsley@netnet.com>
From	Sam Long <slong@bigjims.com>
Subject	RE: Delivery
Date	September 2, 9:09 A.M.

Dear Ms. Kingsley:

We would be happy to accommodate your request for the morning delivery you suggested. One of our drivers will contact you to confirm your address and delivery time. In the meantime, if you have any questions or concerns, feel free to contact us.

Thank you for choosing to do business with us.

Sincerely,

Sam Long

196 What is NOT indicated about Big Jim's?

(A) It has multiple locations.
(B) It carries electronic equipment.
(C) It gives incentives to loyal shoppers.
(D) It sells products online.

197 Why did Ms. Kingsley contact Mr. Long?

(A) To confirm a recent order
(B) To inquire about a discount
(C) To change an appointment
(D) To provide a delivery address

198 What is most likely true about Ms. Kingsley?

(A) She paid for the delivery.
(B) She received a 10% discount.
(C) She lives in Lincoln.
(D) She earned reward points.

199 In the second e-mail, the word "accommodate" in paragraph 1, line 1, is closest in meaning to

(A) accept
(B) adjust
(C) review
(D) shelter

200 When will Ms. Kingsley receive her purchase?

(A) On September 2
(B) On September 3
(C) On September 6
(D) On September 7

Stop! This is the end of the test. If you finish before time is called, you may go back to Parts 5, 6, and 7 and check your work.

GO ON TO THE NEXT PAGE

TOEIC® 점수 환산표

정답수	Listening Comprehension	정답수	Reading Comprehension
96-100	480-495	96-100	460-495
91-95	435-490	91-95	410-475
86-90	395-450	86-90	380-430
81-85	355-415	81-85	355-400
76-80	325-375	76-80	325-375
71-75	295-340	71-75	295-345
66-70	265-315	66-70	265-315
61-65	240-285	61-65	235-285
56-60	215-260	56-60	205-255
51-55	190-235	51-55	175-225
46-50	160-210	46-50	150-195
41-45	135-180	41-45	120-170
36-40	110-155	36-40	100-140
31-35	85-130	31-35	75-120
26-30	70-105	26-30	55-100
21-25	50-90	21-25	40-80
16-20	35-75	16-20	30-65
11-15	20-55	11-15	20-50
6-10	15-40	6-10	15-35
1-5	5-20	1-5	5-20
0	5	0	5

ANSWER SHEET

Actual Test 1

수험번호

응시일자 : 년 월 일

성명	한글	
	한자	
	영자	

좌석번호

Ⓐ Ⓑ Ⓒ Ⓓ Ⓔ
① ② ③ ④ ⑤ ⑥ ⑦

LISTENING (Part I~IV)

NO.	ANSWER	NO.	ANSWER	NO.	ANSWER	NO.	ANSWER	NO.	ANSWER
	A B C D		A B C D		A B C D		A B C D		A B C D
1	Ⓐ Ⓑ Ⓒ Ⓓ	21	Ⓐ Ⓑ Ⓒ Ⓓ	41	Ⓐ Ⓑ Ⓒ Ⓓ	61	Ⓐ Ⓑ Ⓒ Ⓓ	81	Ⓐ Ⓑ Ⓒ Ⓓ
2	Ⓐ Ⓑ Ⓒ Ⓓ	22	Ⓐ Ⓑ Ⓒ Ⓓ	42	Ⓐ Ⓑ Ⓒ Ⓓ	62	Ⓐ Ⓑ Ⓒ Ⓓ	82	Ⓐ Ⓑ Ⓒ Ⓓ
3	Ⓐ Ⓑ Ⓒ Ⓓ	23	Ⓐ Ⓑ Ⓒ Ⓓ	43	Ⓐ Ⓑ Ⓒ Ⓓ	63	Ⓐ Ⓑ Ⓒ Ⓓ	83	Ⓐ Ⓑ Ⓒ Ⓓ
4	Ⓐ Ⓑ Ⓒ Ⓓ	24	Ⓐ Ⓑ Ⓒ Ⓓ	44	Ⓐ Ⓑ Ⓒ Ⓓ	64	Ⓐ Ⓑ Ⓒ Ⓓ	84	Ⓐ Ⓑ Ⓒ Ⓓ
5	Ⓐ Ⓑ Ⓒ Ⓓ	25	Ⓐ Ⓑ Ⓒ Ⓓ	45	Ⓐ Ⓑ Ⓒ Ⓓ	65	Ⓐ Ⓑ Ⓒ Ⓓ	85	Ⓐ Ⓑ Ⓒ Ⓓ
6	Ⓐ Ⓑ Ⓒ Ⓓ	26	Ⓐ Ⓑ Ⓒ Ⓓ	46	Ⓐ Ⓑ Ⓒ Ⓓ	66	Ⓐ Ⓑ Ⓒ Ⓓ	86	Ⓐ Ⓑ Ⓒ Ⓓ
7	Ⓐ Ⓑ Ⓒ	27	Ⓐ Ⓑ Ⓒ Ⓓ	47	Ⓐ Ⓑ Ⓒ Ⓓ	67	Ⓐ Ⓑ Ⓒ Ⓓ	87	Ⓐ Ⓑ Ⓒ Ⓓ
8	Ⓐ Ⓑ Ⓒ	28	Ⓐ Ⓑ Ⓒ Ⓓ	48	Ⓐ Ⓑ Ⓒ Ⓓ	68	Ⓐ Ⓑ Ⓒ Ⓓ	88	Ⓐ Ⓑ Ⓒ Ⓓ
9	Ⓐ Ⓑ Ⓒ	29	Ⓐ Ⓑ Ⓒ Ⓓ	49	Ⓐ Ⓑ Ⓒ Ⓓ	69	Ⓐ Ⓑ Ⓒ Ⓓ	89	Ⓐ Ⓑ Ⓒ Ⓓ
10	Ⓐ Ⓑ Ⓒ	30	Ⓐ Ⓑ Ⓒ Ⓓ	50	Ⓐ Ⓑ Ⓒ Ⓓ	70	Ⓐ Ⓑ Ⓒ Ⓓ	90	Ⓐ Ⓑ Ⓒ Ⓓ
11	Ⓐ Ⓑ Ⓒ	31	Ⓐ Ⓑ Ⓒ Ⓓ	51	Ⓐ Ⓑ Ⓒ Ⓓ	71	Ⓐ Ⓑ Ⓒ Ⓓ	91	Ⓐ Ⓑ Ⓒ Ⓓ
12	Ⓐ Ⓑ Ⓒ	32	Ⓐ Ⓑ Ⓒ Ⓓ	52	Ⓐ Ⓑ Ⓒ Ⓓ	72	Ⓐ Ⓑ Ⓒ Ⓓ	92	Ⓐ Ⓑ Ⓒ Ⓓ
13	Ⓐ Ⓑ Ⓒ	33	Ⓐ Ⓑ Ⓒ Ⓓ	53	Ⓐ Ⓑ Ⓒ Ⓓ	73	Ⓐ Ⓑ Ⓒ Ⓓ	93	Ⓐ Ⓑ Ⓒ Ⓓ
14	Ⓐ Ⓑ Ⓒ	34	Ⓐ Ⓑ Ⓒ Ⓓ	54	Ⓐ Ⓑ Ⓒ Ⓓ	74	Ⓐ Ⓑ Ⓒ Ⓓ	94	Ⓐ Ⓑ Ⓒ Ⓓ
15	Ⓐ Ⓑ Ⓒ	35	Ⓐ Ⓑ Ⓒ Ⓓ	55	Ⓐ Ⓑ Ⓒ Ⓓ	75	Ⓐ Ⓑ Ⓒ Ⓓ	95	Ⓐ Ⓑ Ⓒ Ⓓ
16	Ⓐ Ⓑ Ⓒ	36	Ⓐ Ⓑ Ⓒ Ⓓ	56	Ⓐ Ⓑ Ⓒ Ⓓ	76	Ⓐ Ⓑ Ⓒ Ⓓ	96	Ⓐ Ⓑ Ⓒ Ⓓ
17	Ⓐ Ⓑ Ⓒ	37	Ⓐ Ⓑ Ⓒ Ⓓ	57	Ⓐ Ⓑ Ⓒ Ⓓ	77	Ⓐ Ⓑ Ⓒ Ⓓ	97	Ⓐ Ⓑ Ⓒ Ⓓ
18	Ⓐ Ⓑ Ⓒ Ⓓ	38	Ⓐ Ⓑ Ⓒ Ⓓ	58	Ⓐ Ⓑ Ⓒ Ⓓ	78	Ⓐ Ⓑ Ⓒ Ⓓ	98	Ⓐ Ⓑ Ⓒ Ⓓ
19	Ⓐ Ⓑ Ⓒ Ⓓ	39	Ⓐ Ⓑ Ⓒ Ⓓ	59	Ⓐ Ⓑ Ⓒ Ⓓ	79	Ⓐ Ⓑ Ⓒ Ⓓ	99	Ⓐ Ⓑ Ⓒ Ⓓ
20	Ⓐ Ⓑ Ⓒ Ⓓ	40	Ⓐ Ⓑ Ⓒ Ⓓ	60	Ⓐ Ⓑ Ⓒ Ⓓ	80	Ⓐ Ⓑ Ⓒ Ⓓ	100	Ⓐ Ⓑ Ⓒ Ⓓ

READING (Part V~VII)

NO.	ANSWER	NO.	ANSWER	NO.	ANSWER	NO.	ANSWER	NO.	ANSWER
	A B C D		A B C D		A B C D		A B C D		A B C D
101	Ⓐ Ⓑ Ⓒ Ⓓ	121	Ⓐ Ⓑ Ⓒ Ⓓ	141	Ⓐ Ⓑ Ⓒ Ⓓ	161	Ⓐ Ⓑ Ⓒ Ⓓ	181	Ⓐ Ⓑ Ⓒ Ⓓ
102	Ⓐ Ⓑ Ⓒ Ⓓ	122	Ⓐ Ⓑ Ⓒ Ⓓ	142	Ⓐ Ⓑ Ⓒ Ⓓ	162	Ⓐ Ⓑ Ⓒ Ⓓ	182	Ⓐ Ⓑ Ⓒ Ⓓ
103	Ⓐ Ⓑ Ⓒ Ⓓ	123	Ⓐ Ⓑ Ⓒ Ⓓ	143	Ⓐ Ⓑ Ⓒ Ⓓ	163	Ⓐ Ⓑ Ⓒ Ⓓ	183	Ⓐ Ⓑ Ⓒ Ⓓ
104	Ⓐ Ⓑ Ⓒ Ⓓ	124	Ⓐ Ⓑ Ⓒ Ⓓ	144	Ⓐ Ⓑ Ⓒ Ⓓ	164	Ⓐ Ⓑ Ⓒ Ⓓ	184	Ⓐ Ⓑ Ⓒ Ⓓ
105	Ⓐ Ⓑ Ⓒ Ⓓ	125	Ⓐ Ⓑ Ⓒ Ⓓ	145	Ⓐ Ⓑ Ⓒ Ⓓ	165	Ⓐ Ⓑ Ⓒ Ⓓ	185	Ⓐ Ⓑ Ⓒ Ⓓ
106	Ⓐ Ⓑ Ⓒ Ⓓ	126	Ⓐ Ⓑ Ⓒ Ⓓ	146	Ⓐ Ⓑ Ⓒ Ⓓ	166	Ⓐ Ⓑ Ⓒ Ⓓ	186	Ⓐ Ⓑ Ⓒ Ⓓ
107	Ⓐ Ⓑ Ⓒ Ⓓ	127	Ⓐ Ⓑ Ⓒ Ⓓ	147	Ⓐ Ⓑ Ⓒ Ⓓ	167	Ⓐ Ⓑ Ⓒ Ⓓ	187	Ⓐ Ⓑ Ⓒ Ⓓ
108	Ⓐ Ⓑ Ⓒ Ⓓ	128	Ⓐ Ⓑ Ⓒ Ⓓ	148	Ⓐ Ⓑ Ⓒ Ⓓ	168	Ⓐ Ⓑ Ⓒ Ⓓ	188	Ⓐ Ⓑ Ⓒ Ⓓ
109	Ⓐ Ⓑ Ⓒ Ⓓ	129	Ⓐ Ⓑ Ⓒ Ⓓ	149	Ⓐ Ⓑ Ⓒ Ⓓ	169	Ⓐ Ⓑ Ⓒ Ⓓ	189	Ⓐ Ⓑ Ⓒ Ⓓ
110	Ⓐ Ⓑ Ⓒ Ⓓ	130	Ⓐ Ⓑ Ⓒ Ⓓ	150	Ⓐ Ⓑ Ⓒ Ⓓ	170	Ⓐ Ⓑ Ⓒ Ⓓ	190	Ⓐ Ⓑ Ⓒ Ⓓ
111	Ⓐ Ⓑ Ⓒ Ⓓ	131	Ⓐ Ⓑ Ⓒ Ⓓ	151	Ⓐ Ⓑ Ⓒ Ⓓ	171	Ⓐ Ⓑ Ⓒ Ⓓ	191	Ⓐ Ⓑ Ⓒ Ⓓ
112	Ⓐ Ⓑ Ⓒ Ⓓ	132	Ⓐ Ⓑ Ⓒ Ⓓ	152	Ⓐ Ⓑ Ⓒ Ⓓ	172	Ⓐ Ⓑ Ⓒ Ⓓ	192	Ⓐ Ⓑ Ⓒ Ⓓ
113	Ⓐ Ⓑ Ⓒ Ⓓ	133	Ⓐ Ⓑ Ⓒ Ⓓ	153	Ⓐ Ⓑ Ⓒ Ⓓ	173	Ⓐ Ⓑ Ⓒ Ⓓ	193	Ⓐ Ⓑ Ⓒ Ⓓ
114	Ⓐ Ⓑ Ⓒ Ⓓ	134	Ⓐ Ⓑ Ⓒ Ⓓ	154	Ⓐ Ⓑ Ⓒ Ⓓ	174	Ⓐ Ⓑ Ⓒ Ⓓ	194	Ⓐ Ⓑ Ⓒ Ⓓ
115	Ⓐ Ⓑ Ⓒ Ⓓ	135	Ⓐ Ⓑ Ⓒ Ⓓ	155	Ⓐ Ⓑ Ⓒ Ⓓ	175	Ⓐ Ⓑ Ⓒ Ⓓ	195	Ⓐ Ⓑ Ⓒ Ⓓ
116	Ⓐ Ⓑ Ⓒ Ⓓ	136	Ⓐ Ⓑ Ⓒ Ⓓ	156	Ⓐ Ⓑ Ⓒ Ⓓ	176	Ⓐ Ⓑ Ⓒ Ⓓ	196	Ⓐ Ⓑ Ⓒ Ⓓ
117	Ⓐ Ⓑ Ⓒ Ⓓ	137	Ⓐ Ⓑ Ⓒ Ⓓ	157	Ⓐ Ⓑ Ⓒ Ⓓ	177	Ⓐ Ⓑ Ⓒ Ⓓ	197	Ⓐ Ⓑ Ⓒ Ⓓ
118	Ⓐ Ⓑ Ⓒ Ⓓ	138	Ⓐ Ⓑ Ⓒ Ⓓ	158	Ⓐ Ⓑ Ⓒ Ⓓ	178	Ⓐ Ⓑ Ⓒ Ⓓ	198	Ⓐ Ⓑ Ⓒ Ⓓ
119	Ⓐ Ⓑ Ⓒ Ⓓ	139	Ⓐ Ⓑ Ⓒ Ⓓ	159	Ⓐ Ⓑ Ⓒ Ⓓ	179	Ⓐ Ⓑ Ⓒ Ⓓ	199	Ⓐ Ⓑ Ⓒ Ⓓ
120	Ⓐ Ⓑ Ⓒ Ⓓ	140	Ⓐ Ⓑ Ⓒ Ⓓ	160	Ⓐ Ⓑ Ⓒ Ⓓ	180	Ⓐ Ⓑ Ⓒ Ⓓ	200	Ⓐ Ⓑ Ⓒ Ⓓ

1. 사용 필기구 : 컴퓨터용 연필(연필을 제외한 사인펜, 볼펜 등은 사용 절대 불가)

2. 잘못된 필기구 사용과 〈보기〉의 올바른 표기 이외의 잘못된 표기로 한 경우에는 당 위원회의 OMR기기가 판독하지 결과에 따르며 그 결과는 본인 책임입니다. 1가의 정답만 골라 아래의 올바른 표기대로 정확히 표기하여야 합니다.

〈보기〉올바른 표기: ● 　 잘못된 표기: ⊘ ◐ ◑ ◉

3. 답안지는 컴퓨터로 처리되므로 훼손하거나 더럽혀지지 않도록 하여야 하며, 상단의 타이밍마크(▮▮▮▮)부분을 찢거나, 낙서 등을 하면 본인에게 불이익이 발생할 수 있습니다.

4. 감독관의 확인이 없거나 시험 종료 후에 답안 작성을 계속할 경우 시험 무효 처리됩니다.

* 서약 내용을 읽으시고 확인란에 반드시 서명하십시오.

본인은 TOEIC 시험 문제의 일부 또는 전부를 유출하거나 어떠한 형태로든 타인에게 누설 공개하지 않을 것이며 인터넷 또는 인쇄물 등을 이용해 유포하거나 참고 자료로 활용하지 않을 것입니다. 또한 TOEIC 시험 부정 행위 처리 규정을 준수할 것을 서약합니다.

서 약 인

확 인

ANSWER SHEET

Actual Test 2

응시일자 :   년   월   일

수험번호

성	한글	
명	한자	
	영자	

좌석번호

Ⓐ Ⓑ Ⓒ Ⓓ Ⓔ
① ② ③
④ ⑤ ⑥ ⑦

LISTENING (Part I~IV)

NO.	ANSWER	NO.	ANSWER	NO.	ANSWER	NO.	ANSWER	NO.	ANSWER
	A B C D		A B C D		A B C D		A B C D		A B C D
1	Ⓐ Ⓑ Ⓒ Ⓓ	21	Ⓐ Ⓑ Ⓒ Ⓓ	41	Ⓐ Ⓑ Ⓒ Ⓓ	61	Ⓐ Ⓑ Ⓒ Ⓓ	81	Ⓐ Ⓑ Ⓒ Ⓓ
2	Ⓐ Ⓑ Ⓒ Ⓓ	22	Ⓐ Ⓑ Ⓒ Ⓓ	42	Ⓐ Ⓑ Ⓒ Ⓓ	62	Ⓐ Ⓑ Ⓒ Ⓓ	82	Ⓐ Ⓑ Ⓒ Ⓓ
3	Ⓐ Ⓑ Ⓒ Ⓓ	23	Ⓐ Ⓑ Ⓒ Ⓓ	43	Ⓐ Ⓑ Ⓒ Ⓓ	63	Ⓐ Ⓑ Ⓒ Ⓓ	83	Ⓐ Ⓑ Ⓒ Ⓓ
4	Ⓐ Ⓑ Ⓒ Ⓓ	24	Ⓐ Ⓑ Ⓒ Ⓓ	44	Ⓐ Ⓑ Ⓒ Ⓓ	64	Ⓐ Ⓑ Ⓒ Ⓓ	84	Ⓐ Ⓑ Ⓒ Ⓓ
5	Ⓐ Ⓑ Ⓒ Ⓓ	25	Ⓐ Ⓑ Ⓒ Ⓓ	45	Ⓐ Ⓑ Ⓒ Ⓓ	65	Ⓐ Ⓑ Ⓒ Ⓓ	85	Ⓐ Ⓑ Ⓒ Ⓓ
6	Ⓐ Ⓑ Ⓒ Ⓓ	26	Ⓐ Ⓑ Ⓒ Ⓓ	46	Ⓐ Ⓑ Ⓒ Ⓓ	66	Ⓐ Ⓑ Ⓒ Ⓓ	86	Ⓐ Ⓑ Ⓒ Ⓓ
7	Ⓐ Ⓑ Ⓒ	27	Ⓐ Ⓑ Ⓒ Ⓓ	47	Ⓐ Ⓑ Ⓒ Ⓓ	67	Ⓐ Ⓑ Ⓒ Ⓓ	87	Ⓐ Ⓑ Ⓒ Ⓓ
8	Ⓐ Ⓑ Ⓒ	28	Ⓐ Ⓑ Ⓒ Ⓓ	48	Ⓐ Ⓑ Ⓒ Ⓓ	68	Ⓐ Ⓑ Ⓒ Ⓓ	88	Ⓐ Ⓑ Ⓒ Ⓓ
9	Ⓐ Ⓑ Ⓒ	29	Ⓐ Ⓑ Ⓒ Ⓓ	49	Ⓐ Ⓑ Ⓒ Ⓓ	69	Ⓐ Ⓑ Ⓒ Ⓓ	89	Ⓐ Ⓑ Ⓒ Ⓓ
10	Ⓐ Ⓑ Ⓒ	30	Ⓐ Ⓑ Ⓒ Ⓓ	50	Ⓐ Ⓑ Ⓒ Ⓓ	70	Ⓐ Ⓑ Ⓒ Ⓓ	90	Ⓐ Ⓑ Ⓒ Ⓓ
11	Ⓐ Ⓑ Ⓒ	31	Ⓐ Ⓑ Ⓒ Ⓓ	51	Ⓐ Ⓑ Ⓒ Ⓓ	71	Ⓐ Ⓑ Ⓒ Ⓓ	91	Ⓐ Ⓑ Ⓒ Ⓓ
12	Ⓐ Ⓑ Ⓒ	32	Ⓐ Ⓑ Ⓒ Ⓓ	52	Ⓐ Ⓑ Ⓒ Ⓓ	72	Ⓐ Ⓑ Ⓒ Ⓓ	92	Ⓐ Ⓑ Ⓒ Ⓓ
13	Ⓐ Ⓑ Ⓒ	33	Ⓐ Ⓑ Ⓒ Ⓓ	53	Ⓐ Ⓑ Ⓒ Ⓓ	73	Ⓐ Ⓑ Ⓒ Ⓓ	93	Ⓐ Ⓑ Ⓒ Ⓓ
14	Ⓐ Ⓑ Ⓒ	34	Ⓐ Ⓑ Ⓒ Ⓓ	54	Ⓐ Ⓑ Ⓒ Ⓓ	74	Ⓐ Ⓑ Ⓒ Ⓓ	94	Ⓐ Ⓑ Ⓒ Ⓓ
15	Ⓐ Ⓑ Ⓒ	35	Ⓐ Ⓑ Ⓒ Ⓓ	55	Ⓐ Ⓑ Ⓒ Ⓓ	75	Ⓐ Ⓑ Ⓒ Ⓓ	95	Ⓐ Ⓑ Ⓒ Ⓓ
16	Ⓐ Ⓑ Ⓒ	36	Ⓐ Ⓑ Ⓒ Ⓓ	56	Ⓐ Ⓑ Ⓒ Ⓓ	76	Ⓐ Ⓑ Ⓒ Ⓓ	96	Ⓐ Ⓑ Ⓒ Ⓓ
17	Ⓐ Ⓑ Ⓒ	37	Ⓐ Ⓑ Ⓒ Ⓓ	57	Ⓐ Ⓑ Ⓒ Ⓓ	77	Ⓐ Ⓑ Ⓒ Ⓓ	97	Ⓐ Ⓑ Ⓒ Ⓓ
18	Ⓐ Ⓑ Ⓒ	38	Ⓐ Ⓑ Ⓒ Ⓓ	58	Ⓐ Ⓑ Ⓒ Ⓓ	78	Ⓐ Ⓑ Ⓒ Ⓓ	98	Ⓐ Ⓑ Ⓒ Ⓓ
19	Ⓐ Ⓑ Ⓒ	39	Ⓐ Ⓑ Ⓒ Ⓓ	59	Ⓐ Ⓑ Ⓒ Ⓓ	79	Ⓐ Ⓑ Ⓒ Ⓓ	99	Ⓐ Ⓑ Ⓒ Ⓓ
20	Ⓐ Ⓑ Ⓒ	40	Ⓐ Ⓑ Ⓒ Ⓓ	60	Ⓐ Ⓑ Ⓒ Ⓓ	80	Ⓐ Ⓑ Ⓒ Ⓓ	100	Ⓐ Ⓑ Ⓒ Ⓓ

READING (Part V~VII)

NO.	ANSWER	NO.	ANSWER	NO.	ANSWER	NO.	ANSWER
	A B C D		A B C D		A B C D		A B C D
101	Ⓐ Ⓑ Ⓒ Ⓓ	121	Ⓐ Ⓑ Ⓒ Ⓓ	141	Ⓐ Ⓑ Ⓒ Ⓓ	161	Ⓐ Ⓑ Ⓒ Ⓓ
102	Ⓐ Ⓑ Ⓒ Ⓓ	122	Ⓐ Ⓑ Ⓒ Ⓓ	142	Ⓐ Ⓑ Ⓒ Ⓓ	162	Ⓐ Ⓑ Ⓒ Ⓓ
103	Ⓐ Ⓑ Ⓒ Ⓓ	123	Ⓐ Ⓑ Ⓒ Ⓓ	143	Ⓐ Ⓑ Ⓒ Ⓓ	163	Ⓐ Ⓑ Ⓒ Ⓓ
104	Ⓐ Ⓑ Ⓒ Ⓓ	124	Ⓐ Ⓑ Ⓒ Ⓓ	144	Ⓐ Ⓑ Ⓒ Ⓓ	164	Ⓐ Ⓑ Ⓒ Ⓓ
105	Ⓐ Ⓑ Ⓒ Ⓓ	125	Ⓐ Ⓑ Ⓒ Ⓓ	145	Ⓐ Ⓑ Ⓒ Ⓓ	165	Ⓐ Ⓑ Ⓒ Ⓓ
106	Ⓐ Ⓑ Ⓒ Ⓓ	126	Ⓐ Ⓑ Ⓒ Ⓓ	146	Ⓐ Ⓑ Ⓒ Ⓓ	166	Ⓐ Ⓑ Ⓒ Ⓓ
107	Ⓐ Ⓑ Ⓒ Ⓓ	127	Ⓐ Ⓑ Ⓒ Ⓓ	147	Ⓐ Ⓑ Ⓒ Ⓓ	167	Ⓐ Ⓑ Ⓒ Ⓓ
108	Ⓐ Ⓑ Ⓒ Ⓓ	128	Ⓐ Ⓑ Ⓒ Ⓓ	148	Ⓐ Ⓑ Ⓒ Ⓓ	168	Ⓐ Ⓑ Ⓒ Ⓓ
109	Ⓐ Ⓑ Ⓒ Ⓓ	129	Ⓐ Ⓑ Ⓒ Ⓓ	149	Ⓐ Ⓑ Ⓒ Ⓓ	169	Ⓐ Ⓑ Ⓒ Ⓓ
110	Ⓐ Ⓑ Ⓒ Ⓓ	130	Ⓐ Ⓑ Ⓒ Ⓓ	150	Ⓐ Ⓑ Ⓒ Ⓓ	170	Ⓐ Ⓑ Ⓒ Ⓓ
111	Ⓐ Ⓑ Ⓒ Ⓓ	131	Ⓐ Ⓑ Ⓒ Ⓓ	151	Ⓐ Ⓑ Ⓒ Ⓓ	171	Ⓐ Ⓑ Ⓒ Ⓓ
112	Ⓐ Ⓑ Ⓒ Ⓓ	132	Ⓐ Ⓑ Ⓒ Ⓓ	152	Ⓐ Ⓑ Ⓒ Ⓓ	172	Ⓐ Ⓑ Ⓒ Ⓓ
113	Ⓐ Ⓑ Ⓒ Ⓓ	133	Ⓐ Ⓑ Ⓒ Ⓓ	153	Ⓐ Ⓑ Ⓒ Ⓓ	173	Ⓐ Ⓑ Ⓒ Ⓓ
114	Ⓐ Ⓑ Ⓒ Ⓓ	134	Ⓐ Ⓑ Ⓒ Ⓓ	154	Ⓐ Ⓑ Ⓒ Ⓓ	174	Ⓐ Ⓑ Ⓒ Ⓓ
115	Ⓐ Ⓑ Ⓒ Ⓓ	135	Ⓐ Ⓑ Ⓒ Ⓓ	155	Ⓐ Ⓑ Ⓒ Ⓓ	175	Ⓐ Ⓑ Ⓒ Ⓓ
116	Ⓐ Ⓑ Ⓒ Ⓓ	136	Ⓐ Ⓑ Ⓒ Ⓓ	156	Ⓐ Ⓑ Ⓒ Ⓓ	176	Ⓐ Ⓑ Ⓒ Ⓓ
117	Ⓐ Ⓑ Ⓒ Ⓓ	137	Ⓐ Ⓑ Ⓒ Ⓓ	157	Ⓐ Ⓑ Ⓒ Ⓓ	177	Ⓐ Ⓑ Ⓒ Ⓓ
118	Ⓐ Ⓑ Ⓒ Ⓓ	138	Ⓐ Ⓑ Ⓒ Ⓓ	158	Ⓐ Ⓑ Ⓒ Ⓓ	178	Ⓐ Ⓑ Ⓒ Ⓓ
119	Ⓐ Ⓑ Ⓒ Ⓓ	139	Ⓐ Ⓑ Ⓒ Ⓓ	159	Ⓐ Ⓑ Ⓒ Ⓓ	179	Ⓐ Ⓑ Ⓒ Ⓓ
120	Ⓐ Ⓑ Ⓒ Ⓓ	140	Ⓐ Ⓑ Ⓒ Ⓓ	160	Ⓐ Ⓑ Ⓒ Ⓓ	180	Ⓐ Ⓑ Ⓒ Ⓓ
						181	Ⓐ Ⓑ Ⓒ Ⓓ
						182	Ⓐ Ⓑ Ⓒ Ⓓ
						183	Ⓐ Ⓑ Ⓒ Ⓓ
						184	Ⓐ Ⓑ Ⓒ Ⓓ
						185	Ⓐ Ⓑ Ⓒ Ⓓ
						186	Ⓐ Ⓑ Ⓒ Ⓓ
						187	Ⓐ Ⓑ Ⓒ Ⓓ
						188	Ⓐ Ⓑ Ⓒ Ⓓ
						189	Ⓐ Ⓑ Ⓒ Ⓓ
						190	Ⓐ Ⓑ Ⓒ Ⓓ
						191	Ⓐ Ⓑ Ⓒ Ⓓ
						192	Ⓐ Ⓑ Ⓒ Ⓓ
						193	Ⓐ Ⓑ Ⓒ Ⓓ
						194	Ⓐ Ⓑ Ⓒ Ⓓ
						195	Ⓐ Ⓑ Ⓒ Ⓓ
						196	Ⓐ Ⓑ Ⓒ Ⓓ
						197	Ⓐ Ⓑ Ⓒ Ⓓ
						198	Ⓐ Ⓑ Ⓒ Ⓓ
						199	Ⓐ Ⓑ Ⓒ Ⓓ
						200	Ⓐ Ⓑ Ⓒ Ⓓ

서	명		확 인

1. 시용 필기구 : 컴퓨터용 연필(연필을 제외한 사인펜, 볼펜 등은 사용 절대 불가)
   관도한 경우에 따르며 그 결과는 본인 책임입니다. 1개의 정답만 골라 아래의 올바른 표기대로 정확히 표
   기하여야 합니다.

   〈보기〉 올바른 표기 : ●   잘못된 표기 : ⊘ ⊗ ◍

2. 정못된 필기구 사용과 〈보기〉의 올바른 표기 이외의 잘못된 표기로 한 경우에는 입 위원회의 OMR기기가
   판독한 결과에 따르므로 그 결과는 본인 책임입니다.

3. 답안지는 컴퓨터로 처리되므로 훼손하시면 안 되며, 상단의 타이밍마크(▮▮▮▮)부분을 찢거나, 낙서 등을
   하면 본인에게 불이익이 발생할 수 있습니다.

4. 감독관의 확인이 없거나 시험 종료 후에 답안 작성을 계속할 경우 시험 무효 처리됩니다.

* 서약 내용을 읽으시고 확인란에 반드시 서명하십시오.

본인은 TOEIC 시험 문제의 일부 또는 전부를 유출하거나 이때로 형태로든 타인에게 누설 공개하
지 않을 것이며 인터넷 또는 인쇄물 등을 이용해 유포하거나 참고 자료로 활용하지 않을 것입니다.
또한 TOEIC 시험 부정 행위 처리 규정을 준수할 것을 서약합니다.

ANSWER SHEET

Actual Test 3

좌석번호

Ⓐ Ⓑ Ⓒ Ⓓ Ⓔ
① ② ③ ④ ⑤ ⑥ ⑦

수험번호

응시일자 :   년   월   일

	한글
성 명	한자
	영자

확 인

LISTENING (Part I~IV)

(Columns of answer bubbles numbered 1–20, 21–40, 41–60, 61–80, 81–100, each with A B C D)

READING (Part V~VII)

(Columns of answer bubbles numbered 101–120, 121–140, 141–160, 161–180, 181–200, each with A B C D)

1. 시용 필기구 : 컴퓨터용 연필(연필을 제외한 사인펜, 볼펜 등은 시용 절대 불가)

2. 잘못된 필기구 사용과 〈보기〉의 올바른 표기 이외의 잘못된 표기로 한 경우에는 당 위원회의 OMR기기가 판독한 결과에 따르며 그 결과는 본인 책임입니다. 17개의 정답란 골라 아래의 올바른 표기대로 정확히 표기하여야 합니다.

〈보기〉 올바른 표기 : ●   잘못된 표기 : Ⓧ ⦸ ◍

3. 답안지는 컴퓨터로 처리되므로 훼손하시면 안 되며, 상단의 타이밍마크(▮▮▮▮)부분을 찢거나, 낙서 등을 하면 본인에게 불이익이 발생할 수 있습니다.

4. 감독관의 확인이 없거나 시험 종료 후에 답안 작성을 계속할 경우 시험 무효 처리됩니다.

*서약 내용을 읽으시고 확인란에 반드시 서명하십시오.

서 약

본인은 TOEIC 시험 문제의 일부 또는 전부를 유출하거나 어떠한 형태로도 타인에게 누설 공개하지 않을 것이며 인터넷 또는 인쇄물 등을 이용해 유포하거나 참고 자료로 활용하지 않을 것입니다. 또한 TOEIC 시험 부정 행위 처리 규정을 준수할 것을 서약합니다.

확 인

ANSWER SHEET

Actual Test 4

응시일자 :　　　　년　　　　월　　　　일

수험번호

성	한글
명	한자
	영자

좌석번호

Ⓐ Ⓑ Ⓒ Ⓓ Ⓔ
① ② ③ ④ ⑤ ⑥ ⑦

LISTENING (Part I~IV)

NO.	ANSWER	NO.	ANSWER	NO.	ANSWER	NO.	ANSWER	NO.	ANSWER
	A B C D		A B C D		A B C D		A B C D		A B C D
1	Ⓐ Ⓑ Ⓒ Ⓓ	21	Ⓐ Ⓑ Ⓒ	41	Ⓐ Ⓑ Ⓒ Ⓓ	61	Ⓐ Ⓑ Ⓒ Ⓓ	81	Ⓐ Ⓑ Ⓒ Ⓓ
2	Ⓐ Ⓑ Ⓒ Ⓓ	22	Ⓐ Ⓑ Ⓒ	42	Ⓐ Ⓑ Ⓒ Ⓓ	62	Ⓐ Ⓑ Ⓒ Ⓓ	82	Ⓐ Ⓑ Ⓒ Ⓓ
3	Ⓐ Ⓑ Ⓒ Ⓓ	23	Ⓐ Ⓑ Ⓒ	43	Ⓐ Ⓑ Ⓒ Ⓓ	63	Ⓐ Ⓑ Ⓒ Ⓓ	83	Ⓐ Ⓑ Ⓒ Ⓓ
4	Ⓐ Ⓑ Ⓒ Ⓓ	24	Ⓐ Ⓑ Ⓒ	44	Ⓐ Ⓑ Ⓒ Ⓓ	64	Ⓐ Ⓑ Ⓒ Ⓓ	84	Ⓐ Ⓑ Ⓒ Ⓓ
5	Ⓐ Ⓑ Ⓒ Ⓓ	25	Ⓐ Ⓑ Ⓒ Ⓓ	45	Ⓐ Ⓑ Ⓒ Ⓓ	65	Ⓐ Ⓑ Ⓒ Ⓓ	85	Ⓐ Ⓑ Ⓒ Ⓓ
6	Ⓐ Ⓑ Ⓒ Ⓓ	26	Ⓐ Ⓑ Ⓒ Ⓓ	46	Ⓐ Ⓑ Ⓒ Ⓓ	66	Ⓐ Ⓑ Ⓒ Ⓓ	86	Ⓐ Ⓑ Ⓒ Ⓓ
7	Ⓐ Ⓑ Ⓒ	27	Ⓐ Ⓑ Ⓒ Ⓓ	47	Ⓐ Ⓑ Ⓒ Ⓓ	67	Ⓐ Ⓑ Ⓒ Ⓓ	87	Ⓐ Ⓑ Ⓒ Ⓓ
8	Ⓐ Ⓑ Ⓒ	28	Ⓐ Ⓑ Ⓒ Ⓓ	48	Ⓐ Ⓑ Ⓒ Ⓓ	68	Ⓐ Ⓑ Ⓒ Ⓓ	88	Ⓐ Ⓑ Ⓒ Ⓓ
9	Ⓐ Ⓑ Ⓒ	29	Ⓐ Ⓑ Ⓒ Ⓓ	49	Ⓐ Ⓑ Ⓒ Ⓓ	69	Ⓐ Ⓑ Ⓒ Ⓓ	89	Ⓐ Ⓑ Ⓒ Ⓓ
10	Ⓐ Ⓑ Ⓒ	30	Ⓐ Ⓑ Ⓒ Ⓓ	50	Ⓐ Ⓑ Ⓒ Ⓓ	70	Ⓐ Ⓑ Ⓒ Ⓓ	90	Ⓐ Ⓑ Ⓒ Ⓓ
11	Ⓐ Ⓑ Ⓒ	31	Ⓐ Ⓑ Ⓒ Ⓓ	51	Ⓐ Ⓑ Ⓒ Ⓓ	71	Ⓐ Ⓑ Ⓒ Ⓓ	91	Ⓐ Ⓑ Ⓒ Ⓓ
12	Ⓐ Ⓑ Ⓒ	32	Ⓐ Ⓑ Ⓒ Ⓓ	52	Ⓐ Ⓑ Ⓒ Ⓓ	72	Ⓐ Ⓑ Ⓒ Ⓓ	92	Ⓐ Ⓑ Ⓒ Ⓓ
13	Ⓐ Ⓑ Ⓒ	33	Ⓐ Ⓑ Ⓒ Ⓓ	53	Ⓐ Ⓑ Ⓒ Ⓓ	73	Ⓐ Ⓑ Ⓒ Ⓓ	93	Ⓐ Ⓑ Ⓒ Ⓓ
14	Ⓐ Ⓑ Ⓒ	34	Ⓐ Ⓑ Ⓒ Ⓓ	54	Ⓐ Ⓑ Ⓒ Ⓓ	74	Ⓐ Ⓑ Ⓒ Ⓓ	94	Ⓐ Ⓑ Ⓒ Ⓓ
15	Ⓐ Ⓑ Ⓒ	35	Ⓐ Ⓑ Ⓒ Ⓓ	55	Ⓐ Ⓑ Ⓒ Ⓓ	75	Ⓐ Ⓑ Ⓒ Ⓓ	95	Ⓐ Ⓑ Ⓒ Ⓓ
16	Ⓐ Ⓑ Ⓒ	36	Ⓐ Ⓑ Ⓒ Ⓓ	56	Ⓐ Ⓑ Ⓒ Ⓓ	76	Ⓐ Ⓑ Ⓒ Ⓓ	96	Ⓐ Ⓑ Ⓒ Ⓓ
17	Ⓐ Ⓑ Ⓒ	37	Ⓐ Ⓑ Ⓒ Ⓓ	57	Ⓐ Ⓑ Ⓒ Ⓓ	77	Ⓐ Ⓑ Ⓒ Ⓓ	97	Ⓐ Ⓑ Ⓒ Ⓓ
18	Ⓐ Ⓑ Ⓒ	38	Ⓐ Ⓑ Ⓒ Ⓓ	58	Ⓐ Ⓑ Ⓒ Ⓓ	78	Ⓐ Ⓑ Ⓒ Ⓓ	98	Ⓐ Ⓑ Ⓒ Ⓓ
19	Ⓐ Ⓑ Ⓒ	39	Ⓐ Ⓑ Ⓒ Ⓓ	59	Ⓐ Ⓑ Ⓒ Ⓓ	79	Ⓐ Ⓑ Ⓒ Ⓓ	99	Ⓐ Ⓑ Ⓒ Ⓓ
20	Ⓐ Ⓑ Ⓒ	40	Ⓐ Ⓑ Ⓒ Ⓓ	60	Ⓐ Ⓑ Ⓒ Ⓓ	80	Ⓐ Ⓑ Ⓒ Ⓓ	100	Ⓐ Ⓑ Ⓒ Ⓓ

READING (Part V~VII)

NO.	ANSWER	NO.	ANSWER	NO.	ANSWER	NO.	ANSWER
	A B C D		A B C D		A B C D		A B C D
101	Ⓐ Ⓑ Ⓒ Ⓓ	121	Ⓐ Ⓑ Ⓒ Ⓓ	141	Ⓐ Ⓑ Ⓒ Ⓓ	161	Ⓐ Ⓑ Ⓒ Ⓓ	181	Ⓐ Ⓑ Ⓒ Ⓓ
102	Ⓐ Ⓑ Ⓒ Ⓓ	122	Ⓐ Ⓑ Ⓒ Ⓓ	142	Ⓐ Ⓑ Ⓒ Ⓓ	162	Ⓐ Ⓑ Ⓒ Ⓓ	182	Ⓐ Ⓑ Ⓒ Ⓓ
103	Ⓐ Ⓑ Ⓒ Ⓓ	123	Ⓐ Ⓑ Ⓒ Ⓓ	143	Ⓐ Ⓑ Ⓒ Ⓓ	163	Ⓐ Ⓑ Ⓒ Ⓓ	183	Ⓐ Ⓑ Ⓒ Ⓓ
104	Ⓐ Ⓑ Ⓒ Ⓓ	124	Ⓐ Ⓑ Ⓒ Ⓓ	144	Ⓐ Ⓑ Ⓒ Ⓓ	164	Ⓐ Ⓑ Ⓒ Ⓓ	184	Ⓐ Ⓑ Ⓒ Ⓓ
105	Ⓐ Ⓑ Ⓒ Ⓓ	125	Ⓐ Ⓑ Ⓒ Ⓓ	145	Ⓐ Ⓑ Ⓒ Ⓓ	165	Ⓐ Ⓑ Ⓒ Ⓓ	185	Ⓐ Ⓑ Ⓒ Ⓓ
106	Ⓐ Ⓑ Ⓒ Ⓓ	126	Ⓐ Ⓑ Ⓒ Ⓓ	146	Ⓐ Ⓑ Ⓒ Ⓓ	166	Ⓐ Ⓑ Ⓒ Ⓓ	186	Ⓐ Ⓑ Ⓒ Ⓓ
107	Ⓐ Ⓑ Ⓒ Ⓓ	127	Ⓐ Ⓑ Ⓒ Ⓓ	147	Ⓐ Ⓑ Ⓒ Ⓓ	167	Ⓐ Ⓑ Ⓒ Ⓓ	187	Ⓐ Ⓑ Ⓒ Ⓓ
108	Ⓐ Ⓑ Ⓒ Ⓓ	128	Ⓐ Ⓑ Ⓒ Ⓓ	148	Ⓐ Ⓑ Ⓒ Ⓓ	168	Ⓐ Ⓑ Ⓒ Ⓓ	188	Ⓐ Ⓑ Ⓒ Ⓓ
109	Ⓐ Ⓑ Ⓒ Ⓓ	129	Ⓐ Ⓑ Ⓒ Ⓓ	149	Ⓐ Ⓑ Ⓒ Ⓓ	169	Ⓐ Ⓑ Ⓒ Ⓓ	189	Ⓐ Ⓑ Ⓒ Ⓓ
110	Ⓐ Ⓑ Ⓒ Ⓓ	130	Ⓐ Ⓑ Ⓒ Ⓓ	150	Ⓐ Ⓑ Ⓒ Ⓓ	170	Ⓐ Ⓑ Ⓒ Ⓓ	190	Ⓐ Ⓑ Ⓒ Ⓓ
111	Ⓐ Ⓑ Ⓒ Ⓓ	131	Ⓐ Ⓑ Ⓒ Ⓓ	151	Ⓐ Ⓑ Ⓒ Ⓓ	171	Ⓐ Ⓑ Ⓒ Ⓓ	191	Ⓐ Ⓑ Ⓒ Ⓓ
112	Ⓐ Ⓑ Ⓒ Ⓓ	132	Ⓐ Ⓑ Ⓒ Ⓓ	152	Ⓐ Ⓑ Ⓒ Ⓓ	172	Ⓐ Ⓑ Ⓒ Ⓓ	192	Ⓐ Ⓑ Ⓒ Ⓓ
113	Ⓐ Ⓑ Ⓒ Ⓓ	133	Ⓐ Ⓑ Ⓒ Ⓓ	153	Ⓐ Ⓑ Ⓒ Ⓓ	173	Ⓐ Ⓑ Ⓒ Ⓓ	193	Ⓐ Ⓑ Ⓒ Ⓓ
114	Ⓐ Ⓑ Ⓒ Ⓓ	134	Ⓐ Ⓑ Ⓒ Ⓓ	154	Ⓐ Ⓑ Ⓒ Ⓓ	174	Ⓐ Ⓑ Ⓒ Ⓓ	194	Ⓐ Ⓑ Ⓒ Ⓓ
115	Ⓐ Ⓑ Ⓒ Ⓓ	135	Ⓐ Ⓑ Ⓒ Ⓓ	155	Ⓐ Ⓑ Ⓒ Ⓓ	175	Ⓐ Ⓑ Ⓒ Ⓓ	195	Ⓐ Ⓑ Ⓒ Ⓓ
116	Ⓐ Ⓑ Ⓒ Ⓓ	136	Ⓐ Ⓑ Ⓒ Ⓓ	156	Ⓐ Ⓑ Ⓒ Ⓓ	176	Ⓐ Ⓑ Ⓒ Ⓓ	196	Ⓐ Ⓑ Ⓒ Ⓓ
117	Ⓐ Ⓑ Ⓒ Ⓓ	137	Ⓐ Ⓑ Ⓒ Ⓓ	157	Ⓐ Ⓑ Ⓒ Ⓓ	177	Ⓐ Ⓑ Ⓒ Ⓓ	197	Ⓐ Ⓑ Ⓒ Ⓓ
118	Ⓐ Ⓑ Ⓒ Ⓓ	138	Ⓐ Ⓑ Ⓒ Ⓓ	158	Ⓐ Ⓑ Ⓒ Ⓓ	178	Ⓐ Ⓑ Ⓒ Ⓓ	198	Ⓐ Ⓑ Ⓒ Ⓓ
119	Ⓐ Ⓑ Ⓒ Ⓓ	139	Ⓐ Ⓑ Ⓒ Ⓓ	159	Ⓐ Ⓑ Ⓒ Ⓓ	179	Ⓐ Ⓑ Ⓒ Ⓓ	199	Ⓐ Ⓑ Ⓒ Ⓓ
120	Ⓐ Ⓑ Ⓒ Ⓓ	140	Ⓐ Ⓑ Ⓒ Ⓓ	160	Ⓐ Ⓑ Ⓒ Ⓓ	180	Ⓐ Ⓑ Ⓒ Ⓓ	200	Ⓐ Ⓑ Ⓒ Ⓓ

1. 사용 필기구 : 컴퓨터용 연필(연필을 제외한 사인펜, 볼펜 등은 사용 절대 불가)

2. 정답란 필기구 사용과 〈보기〉의 올바른 표기 이외의 잘못된 표기로 한 경우에는 딤 위원회의 OMR기기가 판독한 결과에 따르며 그 결과는 본인 책임입니다. 1개의 정답만 골라 아래의 올바른 표기대로 정확히 표 기해야 합니다.

〈보기〉 올바른 표기 : ●　잘못된 표기 : ⊘ ◉ ◍

3. 답안지는 컴퓨터로 처리되므로 훼손하거나 더럽히지 않도록 주의하고, 상단의 타이밍마크(∎∎∎∎)부분을 찢거나, 낙서 등을 하면 본인에게 불이익이 발생할 수 있습니다.

4. 감독관의 확인이 없거나 시험 종료 후에 답안 작성란을 계속할 경우 시험 무효 처리됩니다.

*서약 내용을 읽으시고 확인란에 반드시 서명하십시오.

서　약

본인은 TOEIC 시험 문제의 일부 또는 전부를 유출하거나 아래의 형태(음성, 녹음, 동영상 등)로 인터넷 이메일 등을 이용해 유포하거나 참고 자료로 활용하지 않을 것이며, 지 않을 것이며 인터넷 이메일 등을 이용해 유포하거나 참고 자료로 활용하지 않을 것이며, 또한 TOEIC 시험 부정 행위 관련 처리 규정을 준수할 것을 서약합니다.

확　인

ANSWER SHEET

Actual Test 5

수험번호

응시일자 :   년   월   일

성명	한글
	한자
	영자

좌석번호

Ⓐ Ⓑ Ⓒ Ⓓ Ⓔ
① ② ③ ④ ⑤ ⑥ ⑦

LISTENING (Part I~IV)

NO.	ANSWER				NO.	ANSWER				NO.	ANSWER				NO.	ANSWER			
	A	B	C	D		A	B	C	D		A	B	C	D		A	B	C	D
1	Ⓐ	Ⓑ	Ⓒ	Ⓓ	21	Ⓐ	Ⓑ	Ⓒ	Ⓓ	41	Ⓐ	Ⓑ	Ⓒ	Ⓓ	61	Ⓐ	Ⓑ	Ⓒ	Ⓓ
2	Ⓐ	Ⓑ	Ⓒ	Ⓓ	22	Ⓐ	Ⓑ	Ⓒ	Ⓓ	42	Ⓐ	Ⓑ	Ⓒ	Ⓓ	62	Ⓐ	Ⓑ	Ⓒ	Ⓓ
3	Ⓐ	Ⓑ	Ⓒ	Ⓓ	23	Ⓐ	Ⓑ	Ⓒ	Ⓓ	43	Ⓐ	Ⓑ	Ⓒ	Ⓓ	63	Ⓐ	Ⓑ	Ⓒ	Ⓓ
4	Ⓐ	Ⓑ	Ⓒ	Ⓓ	24	Ⓐ	Ⓑ	Ⓒ	Ⓓ	44	Ⓐ	Ⓑ	Ⓒ	Ⓓ	64	Ⓐ	Ⓑ	Ⓒ	Ⓓ
5	Ⓐ	Ⓑ	Ⓒ	Ⓓ	25	Ⓐ	Ⓑ	Ⓒ	Ⓓ	45	Ⓐ	Ⓑ	Ⓒ	Ⓓ	65	Ⓐ	Ⓑ	Ⓒ	Ⓓ
6	Ⓐ	Ⓑ	Ⓒ	Ⓓ	26	Ⓐ	Ⓑ	Ⓒ	Ⓓ	46	Ⓐ	Ⓑ	Ⓒ	Ⓓ	66	Ⓐ	Ⓑ	Ⓒ	Ⓓ
7	Ⓐ	Ⓑ	Ⓒ		27	Ⓐ	Ⓑ	Ⓒ	Ⓓ	47	Ⓐ	Ⓑ	Ⓒ	Ⓓ	67	Ⓐ	Ⓑ	Ⓒ	Ⓓ
8	Ⓐ	Ⓑ	Ⓒ		28	Ⓐ	Ⓑ	Ⓒ	Ⓓ	48	Ⓐ	Ⓑ	Ⓒ	Ⓓ	68	Ⓐ	Ⓑ	Ⓒ	Ⓓ
9	Ⓐ	Ⓑ	Ⓒ		29	Ⓐ	Ⓑ	Ⓒ	Ⓓ	49	Ⓐ	Ⓑ	Ⓒ	Ⓓ	69	Ⓐ	Ⓑ	Ⓒ	Ⓓ
10	Ⓐ	Ⓑ	Ⓒ		30	Ⓐ	Ⓑ	Ⓒ	Ⓓ	50	Ⓐ	Ⓑ	Ⓒ	Ⓓ	70	Ⓐ	Ⓑ	Ⓒ	Ⓓ
11	Ⓐ	Ⓑ	Ⓒ		31	Ⓐ	Ⓑ	Ⓒ	Ⓓ	51	Ⓐ	Ⓑ	Ⓒ	Ⓓ	71	Ⓐ	Ⓑ	Ⓒ	Ⓓ
12	Ⓐ	Ⓑ	Ⓒ		32	Ⓐ	Ⓑ	Ⓒ	Ⓓ	52	Ⓐ	Ⓑ	Ⓒ	Ⓓ	72	Ⓐ	Ⓑ	Ⓒ	Ⓓ
13	Ⓐ	Ⓑ	Ⓒ		33	Ⓐ	Ⓑ	Ⓒ	Ⓓ	53	Ⓐ	Ⓑ	Ⓒ	Ⓓ	73	Ⓐ	Ⓑ	Ⓒ	Ⓓ
14	Ⓐ	Ⓑ	Ⓒ		34	Ⓐ	Ⓑ	Ⓒ	Ⓓ	54	Ⓐ	Ⓑ	Ⓒ	Ⓓ	74	Ⓐ	Ⓑ	Ⓒ	Ⓓ
15	Ⓐ	Ⓑ	Ⓒ		35	Ⓐ	Ⓑ	Ⓒ	Ⓓ	55	Ⓐ	Ⓑ	Ⓒ	Ⓓ	75	Ⓐ	Ⓑ	Ⓒ	Ⓓ
16	Ⓐ	Ⓑ	Ⓒ		36	Ⓐ	Ⓑ	Ⓒ	Ⓓ	56	Ⓐ	Ⓑ	Ⓒ	Ⓓ	76	Ⓐ	Ⓑ	Ⓒ	Ⓓ
17	Ⓐ	Ⓑ	Ⓒ		37	Ⓐ	Ⓑ	Ⓒ	Ⓓ	57	Ⓐ	Ⓑ	Ⓒ	Ⓓ	77	Ⓐ	Ⓑ	Ⓒ	Ⓓ
18	Ⓐ	Ⓑ	Ⓒ		38	Ⓐ	Ⓑ	Ⓒ	Ⓓ	58	Ⓐ	Ⓑ	Ⓒ	Ⓓ	78	Ⓐ	Ⓑ	Ⓒ	Ⓓ
19	Ⓐ	Ⓑ	Ⓒ		39	Ⓐ	Ⓑ	Ⓒ	Ⓓ	59	Ⓐ	Ⓑ	Ⓒ	Ⓓ	79	Ⓐ	Ⓑ	Ⓒ	Ⓓ
20	Ⓐ	Ⓑ	Ⓒ		40	Ⓐ	Ⓑ	Ⓒ	Ⓓ	60	Ⓐ	Ⓑ	Ⓒ	Ⓓ	80	Ⓐ	Ⓑ	Ⓒ	Ⓓ

READING (Part V~VII)

NO.	ANSWER				NO.	ANSWER				NO.	ANSWER				NO.	ANSWER			
	A	B	C	D		A	B	C	D		A	B	C	D		A	B	C	D
101	Ⓐ	Ⓑ	Ⓒ	Ⓓ	121	Ⓐ	Ⓑ	Ⓒ	Ⓓ	141	Ⓐ	Ⓑ	Ⓒ	Ⓓ	161	Ⓐ	Ⓑ	Ⓒ	Ⓓ
102	Ⓐ	Ⓑ	Ⓒ	Ⓓ	122	Ⓐ	Ⓑ	Ⓒ	Ⓓ	142	Ⓐ	Ⓑ	Ⓒ	Ⓓ	162	Ⓐ	Ⓑ	Ⓒ	Ⓓ
103	Ⓐ	Ⓑ	Ⓒ	Ⓓ	123	Ⓐ	Ⓑ	Ⓒ	Ⓓ	143	Ⓐ	Ⓑ	Ⓒ	Ⓓ	163	Ⓐ	Ⓑ	Ⓒ	Ⓓ
104	Ⓐ	Ⓑ	Ⓒ	Ⓓ	124	Ⓐ	Ⓑ	Ⓒ	Ⓓ	144	Ⓐ	Ⓑ	Ⓒ	Ⓓ	164	Ⓐ	Ⓑ	Ⓒ	Ⓓ
105	Ⓐ	Ⓑ	Ⓒ	Ⓓ	125	Ⓐ	Ⓑ	Ⓒ	Ⓓ	145	Ⓐ	Ⓑ	Ⓒ	Ⓓ	165	Ⓐ	Ⓑ	Ⓒ	Ⓓ
106	Ⓐ	Ⓑ	Ⓒ	Ⓓ	126	Ⓐ	Ⓑ	Ⓒ	Ⓓ	146	Ⓐ	Ⓑ	Ⓒ	Ⓓ	166	Ⓐ	Ⓑ	Ⓒ	Ⓓ
107	Ⓐ	Ⓑ	Ⓒ	Ⓓ	127	Ⓐ	Ⓑ	Ⓒ	Ⓓ	147	Ⓐ	Ⓑ	Ⓒ	Ⓓ	167	Ⓐ	Ⓑ	Ⓒ	Ⓓ
108	Ⓐ	Ⓑ	Ⓒ	Ⓓ	128	Ⓐ	Ⓑ	Ⓒ	Ⓓ	148	Ⓐ	Ⓑ	Ⓒ	Ⓓ	168	Ⓐ	Ⓑ	Ⓒ	Ⓓ
109	Ⓐ	Ⓑ	Ⓒ	Ⓓ	129	Ⓐ	Ⓑ	Ⓒ	Ⓓ	149	Ⓐ	Ⓑ	Ⓒ	Ⓓ	169	Ⓐ	Ⓑ	Ⓒ	Ⓓ
110	Ⓐ	Ⓑ	Ⓒ	Ⓓ	130	Ⓐ	Ⓑ	Ⓒ	Ⓓ	150	Ⓐ	Ⓑ	Ⓒ	Ⓓ	170	Ⓐ	Ⓑ	Ⓒ	Ⓓ
111	Ⓐ	Ⓑ	Ⓒ	Ⓓ	131	Ⓐ	Ⓑ	Ⓒ	Ⓓ	151	Ⓐ	Ⓑ	Ⓒ	Ⓓ	171	Ⓐ	Ⓑ	Ⓒ	Ⓓ
112	Ⓐ	Ⓑ	Ⓒ	Ⓓ	132	Ⓐ	Ⓑ	Ⓒ	Ⓓ	152	Ⓐ	Ⓑ	Ⓒ	Ⓓ	172	Ⓐ	Ⓑ	Ⓒ	Ⓓ
113	Ⓐ	Ⓑ	Ⓒ	Ⓓ	133	Ⓐ	Ⓑ	Ⓒ	Ⓓ	153	Ⓐ	Ⓑ	Ⓒ	Ⓓ	173	Ⓐ	Ⓑ	Ⓒ	Ⓓ
114	Ⓐ	Ⓑ	Ⓒ	Ⓓ	134	Ⓐ	Ⓑ	Ⓒ	Ⓓ	154	Ⓐ	Ⓑ	Ⓒ	Ⓓ	174	Ⓐ	Ⓑ	Ⓒ	Ⓓ
115	Ⓐ	Ⓑ	Ⓒ	Ⓓ	135	Ⓐ	Ⓑ	Ⓒ	Ⓓ	155	Ⓐ	Ⓑ	Ⓒ	Ⓓ	175	Ⓐ	Ⓑ	Ⓒ	Ⓓ
116	Ⓐ	Ⓑ	Ⓒ	Ⓓ	136	Ⓐ	Ⓑ	Ⓒ	Ⓓ	156	Ⓐ	Ⓑ	Ⓒ	Ⓓ	176	Ⓐ	Ⓑ	Ⓒ	Ⓓ
117	Ⓐ	Ⓑ	Ⓒ	Ⓓ	137	Ⓐ	Ⓑ	Ⓒ	Ⓓ	157	Ⓐ	Ⓑ	Ⓒ	Ⓓ	177	Ⓐ	Ⓑ	Ⓒ	Ⓓ
118	Ⓐ	Ⓑ	Ⓒ	Ⓓ	138	Ⓐ	Ⓑ	Ⓒ	Ⓓ	158	Ⓐ	Ⓑ	Ⓒ	Ⓓ	178	Ⓐ	Ⓑ	Ⓒ	Ⓓ
119	Ⓐ	Ⓑ	Ⓒ	Ⓓ	139	Ⓐ	Ⓑ	Ⓒ	Ⓓ	159	Ⓐ	Ⓑ	Ⓒ	Ⓓ	179	Ⓐ	Ⓑ	Ⓒ	Ⓓ
120	Ⓐ	Ⓑ	Ⓒ	Ⓓ	140	Ⓐ	Ⓑ	Ⓒ	Ⓓ	160	Ⓐ	Ⓑ	Ⓒ	Ⓓ	180	Ⓐ	Ⓑ	Ⓒ	Ⓓ

NO.	ANSWER			
	A	B	C	D
181	Ⓐ	Ⓑ	Ⓒ	Ⓓ
182	Ⓐ	Ⓑ	Ⓒ	Ⓓ
183	Ⓐ	Ⓑ	Ⓒ	Ⓓ
184	Ⓐ	Ⓑ	Ⓒ	Ⓓ
185	Ⓐ	Ⓑ	Ⓒ	Ⓓ
186	Ⓐ	Ⓑ	Ⓒ	Ⓓ
187	Ⓐ	Ⓑ	Ⓒ	Ⓓ
188	Ⓐ	Ⓑ	Ⓒ	Ⓓ
189	Ⓐ	Ⓑ	Ⓒ	Ⓓ
190	Ⓐ	Ⓑ	Ⓒ	Ⓓ
191	Ⓐ	Ⓑ	Ⓒ	Ⓓ
192	Ⓐ	Ⓑ	Ⓒ	Ⓓ
193	Ⓐ	Ⓑ	Ⓒ	Ⓓ
194	Ⓐ	Ⓑ	Ⓒ	Ⓓ
195	Ⓐ	Ⓑ	Ⓒ	Ⓓ
196	Ⓐ	Ⓑ	Ⓒ	Ⓓ
197	Ⓐ	Ⓑ	Ⓒ	Ⓓ
198	Ⓐ	Ⓑ	Ⓒ	Ⓓ
199	Ⓐ	Ⓑ	Ⓒ	Ⓓ
200	Ⓐ	Ⓑ	Ⓒ	Ⓓ

확 인

1. 시용 필기구 : 컴퓨터용 연필(연필을 제외한 사인펜, 볼펜 등은 사용 절대 불가)

2. 잘못된 필기구 사용과 〈보기〉의 올바른 표기 이외의 잘못된 표기로 한 경우에는 당 위원회의 OMR기기가 판독한 결과에 따르며 그 결과는 본인 책임입니다. 1747개의 정답란 골라 아래의 올바른 표기대로 정확히 표기하여야 합니다.
〈보기〉 올바른 표기 : ●   잘못된 표기 : ⊘ ◐ ◖

3. 답안지는 컴퓨터로 처리되므로 훼손하시면 안 되며, 상단의 타이밍마크(IIII)부분을 찢거나, 낙서 등을 하면 본인에게 불이익이 발생할 수 있습니다.

4. 감독관의 확인이 없거나 시험 종료 후에 답안 작성을 계속할 경우 시험 무효 처리됩니다.

* 서약 내용을 읽으시고 확인란에 반드시 서명하십시오.

서   약

본인은 TOEIC 시험 문제의 일부 또는 전부를 유출하거나 어떠한 형태로든 타인에게 누설 공개하지 않을 것이며 인터넷 또는 인쇄물 등을 이용해 유포하거나 참고 자료로 활용하지 않을 것입니다. 또한 TOEIC 시험 부정 행위 처리 규정을 준수할 것을 서약합니다.

ANSWER SHEET

Actual Test 6

수험번호

응시일자 : 년 월 일

LISTENING (Part I~IV)

NO.	ANSWER	NO.	ANSWER	NO.	ANSWER	NO.	ANSWER	NO.	ANSWER
	A B C D		A B C D		A B C D		A B C D		A B C D
1	Ⓐ Ⓑ Ⓒ Ⓓ	21	Ⓐ Ⓑ Ⓒ	41	Ⓐ Ⓑ Ⓒ Ⓓ	61	Ⓐ Ⓑ Ⓒ Ⓓ	81	Ⓐ Ⓑ Ⓒ Ⓓ
2	Ⓐ Ⓑ Ⓒ Ⓓ	22	Ⓐ Ⓑ Ⓒ	42	Ⓐ Ⓑ Ⓒ Ⓓ	62	Ⓐ Ⓑ Ⓒ Ⓓ	82	Ⓐ Ⓑ Ⓒ Ⓓ
3	Ⓐ Ⓑ Ⓒ Ⓓ	23	Ⓐ Ⓑ Ⓒ	43	Ⓐ Ⓑ Ⓒ Ⓓ	63	Ⓐ Ⓑ Ⓒ Ⓓ	83	Ⓐ Ⓑ Ⓒ Ⓓ
4	Ⓐ Ⓑ Ⓒ Ⓓ	24	Ⓐ Ⓑ Ⓒ	44	Ⓐ Ⓑ Ⓒ Ⓓ	64	Ⓐ Ⓑ Ⓒ Ⓓ	84	Ⓐ Ⓑ Ⓒ Ⓓ
5	Ⓐ Ⓑ Ⓒ Ⓓ	25	Ⓐ Ⓑ Ⓒ	45	Ⓐ Ⓑ Ⓒ Ⓓ	65	Ⓐ Ⓑ Ⓒ Ⓓ	85	Ⓐ Ⓑ Ⓒ Ⓓ
6	Ⓐ Ⓑ Ⓒ Ⓓ	26	Ⓐ Ⓑ Ⓒ	46	Ⓐ Ⓑ Ⓒ Ⓓ	66	Ⓐ Ⓑ Ⓒ Ⓓ	86	Ⓐ Ⓑ Ⓒ Ⓓ
7	Ⓐ Ⓑ Ⓒ Ⓓ	27	Ⓐ Ⓑ Ⓒ	47	Ⓐ Ⓑ Ⓒ Ⓓ	67	Ⓐ Ⓑ Ⓒ Ⓓ	87	Ⓐ Ⓑ Ⓒ Ⓓ
8	Ⓐ Ⓑ Ⓒ Ⓓ	28	Ⓐ Ⓑ Ⓒ	48	Ⓐ Ⓑ Ⓒ Ⓓ	68	Ⓐ Ⓑ Ⓒ Ⓓ	88	Ⓐ Ⓑ Ⓒ Ⓓ
9	Ⓐ Ⓑ Ⓒ Ⓓ	29	Ⓐ Ⓑ Ⓒ	49	Ⓐ Ⓑ Ⓒ Ⓓ	69	Ⓐ Ⓑ Ⓒ Ⓓ	89	Ⓐ Ⓑ Ⓒ Ⓓ
10	Ⓐ Ⓑ Ⓒ Ⓓ	30	Ⓐ Ⓑ Ⓒ	50	Ⓐ Ⓑ Ⓒ Ⓓ	70	Ⓐ Ⓑ Ⓒ Ⓓ	90	Ⓐ Ⓑ Ⓒ Ⓓ
11	Ⓐ Ⓑ Ⓒ Ⓓ	31	Ⓐ Ⓑ Ⓒ	51	Ⓐ Ⓑ Ⓒ Ⓓ	71	Ⓐ Ⓑ Ⓒ Ⓓ	91	Ⓐ Ⓑ Ⓒ Ⓓ
12	Ⓐ Ⓑ Ⓒ Ⓓ	32	Ⓐ Ⓑ Ⓒ	52	Ⓐ Ⓑ Ⓒ Ⓓ	72	Ⓐ Ⓑ Ⓒ Ⓓ	92	Ⓐ Ⓑ Ⓒ Ⓓ
13	Ⓐ Ⓑ Ⓒ Ⓓ	33	Ⓐ Ⓑ Ⓒ	53	Ⓐ Ⓑ Ⓒ Ⓓ	73	Ⓐ Ⓑ Ⓒ Ⓓ	93	Ⓐ Ⓑ Ⓒ Ⓓ
14	Ⓐ Ⓑ Ⓒ Ⓓ	34	Ⓐ Ⓑ Ⓒ	54	Ⓐ Ⓑ Ⓒ Ⓓ	74	Ⓐ Ⓑ Ⓒ Ⓓ	94	Ⓐ Ⓑ Ⓒ Ⓓ
15	Ⓐ Ⓑ Ⓒ Ⓓ	35	Ⓐ Ⓑ Ⓒ	55	Ⓐ Ⓑ Ⓒ Ⓓ	75	Ⓐ Ⓑ Ⓒ Ⓓ	95	Ⓐ Ⓑ Ⓒ Ⓓ
16	Ⓐ Ⓑ Ⓒ Ⓓ	36	Ⓐ Ⓑ Ⓒ	56	Ⓐ Ⓑ Ⓒ Ⓓ	76	Ⓐ Ⓑ Ⓒ Ⓓ	96	Ⓐ Ⓑ Ⓒ Ⓓ
17	Ⓐ Ⓑ Ⓒ Ⓓ	37	Ⓐ Ⓑ Ⓒ	57	Ⓐ Ⓑ Ⓒ Ⓓ	77	Ⓐ Ⓑ Ⓒ Ⓓ	97	Ⓐ Ⓑ Ⓒ Ⓓ
18	Ⓐ Ⓑ Ⓒ Ⓓ	38	Ⓐ Ⓑ Ⓒ	58	Ⓐ Ⓑ Ⓒ Ⓓ	78	Ⓐ Ⓑ Ⓒ Ⓓ	98	Ⓐ Ⓑ Ⓒ Ⓓ
19	Ⓐ Ⓑ Ⓒ Ⓓ	39	Ⓐ Ⓑ Ⓒ	59	Ⓐ Ⓑ Ⓒ Ⓓ	79	Ⓐ Ⓑ Ⓒ Ⓓ	99	Ⓐ Ⓑ Ⓒ Ⓓ
20	Ⓐ Ⓑ Ⓒ Ⓓ	40	Ⓐ Ⓑ Ⓒ	60	Ⓐ Ⓑ Ⓒ Ⓓ	80	Ⓐ Ⓑ Ⓒ Ⓓ	100	Ⓐ Ⓑ Ⓒ Ⓓ

READING (Part V~VII)

NO.	ANSWER	NO.	ANSWER	NO.	ANSWER	NO.	ANSWER	NO.	ANSWER
	A B C D		A B C D		A B C D		A B C D		A B C D
101	Ⓐ Ⓑ Ⓒ Ⓓ	121	Ⓐ Ⓑ Ⓒ Ⓓ	141	Ⓐ Ⓑ Ⓒ Ⓓ	161	Ⓐ Ⓑ Ⓒ Ⓓ	181	Ⓐ Ⓑ Ⓒ Ⓓ
102	Ⓐ Ⓑ Ⓒ Ⓓ	122	Ⓐ Ⓑ Ⓒ Ⓓ	142	Ⓐ Ⓑ Ⓒ Ⓓ	162	Ⓐ Ⓑ Ⓒ Ⓓ	182	Ⓐ Ⓑ Ⓒ Ⓓ
103	Ⓐ Ⓑ Ⓒ Ⓓ	123	Ⓐ Ⓑ Ⓒ Ⓓ	143	Ⓐ Ⓑ Ⓒ Ⓓ	163	Ⓐ Ⓑ Ⓒ Ⓓ	183	Ⓐ Ⓑ Ⓒ Ⓓ
104	Ⓐ Ⓑ Ⓒ Ⓓ	124	Ⓐ Ⓑ Ⓒ Ⓓ	144	Ⓐ Ⓑ Ⓒ Ⓓ	164	Ⓐ Ⓑ Ⓒ Ⓓ	184	Ⓐ Ⓑ Ⓒ Ⓓ
105	Ⓐ Ⓑ Ⓒ Ⓓ	125	Ⓐ Ⓑ Ⓒ Ⓓ	145	Ⓐ Ⓑ Ⓒ Ⓓ	165	Ⓐ Ⓑ Ⓒ Ⓓ	185	Ⓐ Ⓑ Ⓒ Ⓓ
106	Ⓐ Ⓑ Ⓒ Ⓓ	126	Ⓐ Ⓑ Ⓒ Ⓓ	146	Ⓐ Ⓑ Ⓒ Ⓓ	166	Ⓐ Ⓑ Ⓒ Ⓓ	186	Ⓐ Ⓑ Ⓒ Ⓓ
107	Ⓐ Ⓑ Ⓒ Ⓓ	127	Ⓐ Ⓑ Ⓒ Ⓓ	147	Ⓐ Ⓑ Ⓒ Ⓓ	167	Ⓐ Ⓑ Ⓒ Ⓓ	187	Ⓐ Ⓑ Ⓒ Ⓓ
108	Ⓐ Ⓑ Ⓒ Ⓓ	128	Ⓐ Ⓑ Ⓒ Ⓓ	148	Ⓐ Ⓑ Ⓒ Ⓓ	168	Ⓐ Ⓑ Ⓒ Ⓓ	188	Ⓐ Ⓑ Ⓒ Ⓓ
109	Ⓐ Ⓑ Ⓒ Ⓓ	129	Ⓐ Ⓑ Ⓒ Ⓓ	149	Ⓐ Ⓑ Ⓒ Ⓓ	169	Ⓐ Ⓑ Ⓒ Ⓓ	189	Ⓐ Ⓑ Ⓒ Ⓓ
110	Ⓐ Ⓑ Ⓒ Ⓓ	130	Ⓐ Ⓑ Ⓒ Ⓓ	150	Ⓐ Ⓑ Ⓒ Ⓓ	170	Ⓐ Ⓑ Ⓒ Ⓓ	190	Ⓐ Ⓑ Ⓒ Ⓓ
111	Ⓐ Ⓑ Ⓒ Ⓓ	131	Ⓐ Ⓑ Ⓒ Ⓓ	151	Ⓐ Ⓑ Ⓒ Ⓓ	171	Ⓐ Ⓑ Ⓒ Ⓓ	191	Ⓐ Ⓑ Ⓒ Ⓓ
112	Ⓐ Ⓑ Ⓒ Ⓓ	132	Ⓐ Ⓑ Ⓒ Ⓓ	152	Ⓐ Ⓑ Ⓒ Ⓓ	172	Ⓐ Ⓑ Ⓒ Ⓓ	192	Ⓐ Ⓑ Ⓒ Ⓓ
113	Ⓐ Ⓑ Ⓒ Ⓓ	133	Ⓐ Ⓑ Ⓒ Ⓓ	153	Ⓐ Ⓑ Ⓒ Ⓓ	173	Ⓐ Ⓑ Ⓒ Ⓓ	193	Ⓐ Ⓑ Ⓒ Ⓓ
114	Ⓐ Ⓑ Ⓒ Ⓓ	134	Ⓐ Ⓑ Ⓒ Ⓓ	154	Ⓐ Ⓑ Ⓒ Ⓓ	174	Ⓐ Ⓑ Ⓒ Ⓓ	194	Ⓐ Ⓑ Ⓒ Ⓓ
115	Ⓐ Ⓑ Ⓒ Ⓓ	135	Ⓐ Ⓑ Ⓒ Ⓓ	155	Ⓐ Ⓑ Ⓒ Ⓓ	175	Ⓐ Ⓑ Ⓒ Ⓓ	195	Ⓐ Ⓑ Ⓒ Ⓓ
116	Ⓐ Ⓑ Ⓒ Ⓓ	136	Ⓐ Ⓑ Ⓒ Ⓓ	156	Ⓐ Ⓑ Ⓒ Ⓓ	176	Ⓐ Ⓑ Ⓒ Ⓓ	196	Ⓐ Ⓑ Ⓒ Ⓓ
117	Ⓐ Ⓑ Ⓒ Ⓓ	137	Ⓐ Ⓑ Ⓒ Ⓓ	157	Ⓐ Ⓑ Ⓒ Ⓓ	177	Ⓐ Ⓑ Ⓒ Ⓓ	197	Ⓐ Ⓑ Ⓒ Ⓓ
118	Ⓐ Ⓑ Ⓒ Ⓓ	138	Ⓐ Ⓑ Ⓒ Ⓓ	158	Ⓐ Ⓑ Ⓒ Ⓓ	178	Ⓐ Ⓑ Ⓒ Ⓓ	198	Ⓐ Ⓑ Ⓒ Ⓓ
119	Ⓐ Ⓑ Ⓒ Ⓓ	139	Ⓐ Ⓑ Ⓒ Ⓓ	159	Ⓐ Ⓑ Ⓒ Ⓓ	179	Ⓐ Ⓑ Ⓒ Ⓓ	199	Ⓐ Ⓑ Ⓒ Ⓓ
120	Ⓐ Ⓑ Ⓒ Ⓓ	140	Ⓐ Ⓑ Ⓒ Ⓓ	160	Ⓐ Ⓑ Ⓒ Ⓓ	180	Ⓐ Ⓑ Ⓒ Ⓓ	200	Ⓐ Ⓑ Ⓒ Ⓓ

성명
한글
한자
영자

좌석번호
Ⓐ Ⓑ Ⓒ Ⓓ Ⓔ
① ② ③ ④ ⑤ ⑥ ⑦

성 명
한글
한자
영자

서 약

확 인

넥서스

토익 최신 유형을 반영한 최종 마무리 문제집 + 해설집

나혼자 끝내는 新토익

기출모의

1200제

감수 박지은·넥서스토익연구소 지음

LC+RC
실전 모의고사
6회

스크립트+정답 및 해설

Actual Test

01

🎧 Listening Comprehension

PART 1

1 (A)	2 (C)	3 (B)	4 (A)	5 (D)	6 (C)	

PART 2

7 (A)	8 (B)	9 (C)	10 (C)	11 (A)	12 (B)	13 (B)	14 (C)	15 (B)	16 (A)
17 (B)	18 (B)	19 (A)	20 (C)	21 (A)	22 (A)	23 (B)	24 (B)	25 (B)	26 (C)
27 (C)	28 (B)	29 (C)	30 (C)	31 (A)					

PART 3

32 (A)	33 (D)	34 (C)	35 (A)	36 (C)	37 (A)	38 (B)	39 (A)	40 (D)	41 (A)
42 (C)	43 (C)	44 (A)	45 (B)	46 (A)	47 (C)	48 (D)	49 (A)	50 (B)	51 (B)
52 (D)	53 (C)	54 (D)	55 (A)	56 (C)	57 (A)	58 (C)	59 (D)	60 (D)	61 (A)
62 (B)	63 (D)	64 (A)	65 (C)	66 (A)	67 (B)	68 (B)	69 (C)	70 (A)	

PART 4

71 (B)	72 (A)	73 (A)	74 (A)	75 (D)	76 (D)	77 (B)	78 (A)	79 (A)	80 (D)
81 (A)	82 (C)	83 (D)	84 (C)	85 (C)	86 (B)	87 (C)	88 (D)	89 (A)	90 (D)
91 (B)	92 (B)	93 (C)	94 (A)	95 (D)	96 (C)	97 (A)	98 (A)	99 (C)	100 (D)

📖 Reading Comprehension

PART 5

101 (B)	102 (C)	103 (B)	104 (B)	105 (B)	106 (A)	107 (D)	108 (C)	109 (A)	110 (C)
111 (C)	112 (B)	113 (D)	114 (A)	115 (A)	116 (A)	117 (B)	118 (B)	119 (D)	120 (B)
121 (C)	122 (C)	123 (A)	124 (D)	125 (D)	126 (A)	127 (A)	128 (A)	129 (C)	130 (C)

PART 6

131 (B)	132 (D)	133 (B)	134 (B)	135 (C)	136 (C)	137 (B)	138 (A)	139 (C)	140 (B)
141 (A)	142 (D)	143 (D)	144 (B)	145 (A)	146 (B)				

PART 7

147 (B)	148 (A)	149 (C)	150 (C)	151 (B)	152 (D)	153 (A)	154 (A)	155 (D)	156 (A)
157 (D)	158 (C)	159 (A)	160 (D)	161 (D)	162 (B)	163 (A)	164 (B)	165 (B)	166 (C)
167 (A)	168 (B)	169 (A)	170 (B)	171 (D)	172 (A)	173 (D)	174 (C)	175 (B)	176 (A)
177 (D)	178 (A)	179 (A)	180 (A)	181 (A)	182 (B)	183 (A)	184 (D)	185 (C)	186 (B)
187 (D)	188 (A)	189 (D)	190 (C)	191 (A)	192 (A)	193 (B)	194 (D)	195 (D)	196 (C)
197 (D)	198 (A)	199 (B)	200 (A)						

leave 남기다 approach 다가가다 archway 아치형 입구
pavement 보도, 인도 potted plant 화분에 심어진 식물

Part 1

본책 P15

1

미M
(A) He is taking notes.
(B) He is signing a paper.
(C) He is typing on a keyboard.
(D) He is cleaning the computer monitor.

(A) 남자가 필기를 하고 있다.
(B) 남자가 종이에 서명하고 있다.
(C) 남자가 키보드를 두드리고 있다.
(D) 남자가 컴퓨터 모니터를 청소하고 있다.

take a note 필기하다 type 타자를 치다

2

영M
(A) A woman is putting on some boots.
(B) A woman is sweeping the driveway.
(C) A woman is grasping a broomstick.
(D) A woman is standing under the tree.

(A) 여자가 장화를 신고 있다.
(B) 여자가 진입로를 쓸고 있다.
(C) 여자가 빗자루를 잡고 있다.
(D) 여자가 나무 아래에 서 있다.

put on 입다, 착용하다 sweep 쓸다 driveway (차고) 진입로
grasp 잡다 broomstick 빗자루

3

미W
(A) Leaves are being cleared on a path.
(B) Some cars are parked at the side of the street.
(C) Snow is being piled along a walkway.
(D) The vehicles are facing opposite directions.

(A) 낙엽들이 길에서 청소되고 있다.
(B) 차 몇 대가 거리 옆에 주차되어 있다.
(C) 눈이 인도를 따라 쌓이고 있다.
(D) 차들이 서로 다른 방향을 보고 있다.

path 길 pile 쌓이다, 쌓다 walkway 도보, 인도 face (방향을) 향하
다 opposite 반대의 direction 방향

4

호M
(A) Some bicycles have been left on the street.
(B) A vehicle is approaching an archway.
(C) The roof of a building is being fixed.
(D) The pavement is decorated with potted plants.

(A) 몇몇 자전거들이 거리에 남겨져 있다.
(B) 차 한 대가 아치형 입구에 진입하고 있다.
(C) 건물의 지붕이 수리되고 있다.
(D) 보도가 화분으로 장식되어 있다.

5

미M
(A) The seats are being arranged in a semi-circle.
(B) Folding chairs have been set up on the stage.
(C) A concert is being given inside an auditorium.
(D) A man has his back to a group of people.

(A) 좌석이 반원으로 정렬되고 있다.
(B) 접이식 의자들이 무대 위에 놓여 있다.
(C) 연주회가 강당 안에서 진행되고 있다.
(D) 남자가 여러 사람 앞에서 그의 등을 보이고 있다.

semi-circle 반원 folding chairs 접이식 의자 set up 놓다, 설치하
다 auditorium 강당

6

미W
(A) A vehicle is stopped at a stop sign.
(B) Shipping containers are being lifted by a crane.
(C) Rows of containers have been stacked up.
(D) Workers are smoothing the road surface.

(A) 차 한 대가 정지 신호 앞에 멈춰 서 있다.
(B) 수송 컨테이너들이 기중기로 올려지고 있다.
(C) 여러 줄의 컨테이너들이 쌓여 있다.
(D) 인부들이 도로의 표면을 매끄럽게 하고 있다.

stop sign 정지 신호 shipping container 수송 컨테이너 crane
기중기 row 줄 stack up 쌓이다 smooth 매끄럽게 만들다

Part 2

본책 P18

7

미M Where can I find the financial report?
미W (A) I saw it on your desk.
      (B) There was a sale at the store.
      (C) I'm going to Beijing.

재가 어디에서 재정 보고서를 찾을 수 있나요?
(A) 당신 책상 위에서 봤어요.
(B) 상점에서 세일이 있었어요.
(C) 전 북경에 갈 거예요.

financial report 재정 보고서

8

영M Who's in charge of the meeting today?
미W (A) I'll stand over there.
      (B) It's Ms. Cortez.
      (C) Our aim for the next quarter.

오늘 회의는 누가 담당하나요?
(A) 제가 저기에 서 있을게요.
(B) 코르테즈 씨입니다.
(C) 다음 분기를 위한 우리 목표요.

in charge of ~을 담당하는 aim 목표 quarter 분기

9

미W Which train are you catching?
미M (A) Sure, I'll catch it.
      (B) Yes, aren't you?
      (C) The one at noon.

어느 기차를 탈 건가요?
(A) 그럼요, 그걸 탈 거예요.
(B) 네, 당신은 아닌가요?
(C) 정오에 있는 거요.

catch (버스・기차 등을 시간 맞춰) 타다; 잡다

10

미M Where can I get my laptop repaired?
미W (A) I didn't know you were moving.
      (B) It's the newest product.
      (C) I gave mine to Andy's shop.

제 노트북 컴퓨터를 어디에서 수리 받을 수 있나요?
(A) 저는 당신이 이사하셨는지 몰랐어요.
(B) 그건 최신 제품입니다.
(C) 제 것을 앤디의 수리점에 맡겼습니다.

laptop 노트북 컴퓨터 newest 최신의

11

미M Did Mr. Yang talk through our pension benefits with
미W you?
      (A) Very meticulously.
      (B) Yes, she was.
      (C) Thanks, I feel great.

양 씨가 저희와 연금 수당에 대해 설명해 주셨나요?
(A) 매우 꼼꼼히요.
(B) 네, 그녀는 그랬어요.
(C) 고맙습니다. 기분이 매우 좋아요.

talk through ~에 대해 설명하다 pension benefit 연금 수당
meticulously 꼼꼼히, 세심히

12

미W How many people have registered for the team game?
영M (A) It's a new concept.
      (B) About half a dozen.
      (C) There are three different lines.

몇 명의 사람들이 단체 경기를 신청했나요?
(A) 그건 새로운 개념이에요.
(B) 약 12명이요.
(C) 세 가지 다른 라인이 있어요.

register for ~을 신청하다 concept 개념 dozen 12개짜리 한 묶음

(A) 그것은 새로운 개념입니다.
(B) 6명 정도 됩니다.
(C) 세 가지 다른 제품군이 있습니다.
half a dozen 반 다스 여섯 line (상품의) 종류

13 [미M][미W] Let's finish at lunch today.
(A) Stop it at the end.
(B) That's a good idea.
(C) I already ate.
오늘 점심시간에 끝냅시다.
(A) 끝에서 멈추세요.
(B) 좋은 생각입니다.
(C) 저는 이미 먹었어요.
at the end 끝에

14 [미W][미M] Dinner yesterday was delightful, wasn't it?
(A) Sorry, I wasn't available then.
(B) No, she's the new creative director.
(C) Yes, the fish was delicious.
어제 저녁 식사가 매우 마음에 들었어요, 그렇지 않았나요?
(A) 죄송합니다. 저는 그때 시간이 가능하지 않았어요.
(B) 아니요, 그녀는 새로운 광고 제작 감독입니다.
(C) 네, 생선이 맛있었어요.
delightful 정말 기분 좋은, 마음에 드는 creative director 광고 제작 감독, 광고 담당 이사

15 [미W] Would you rather travel on the highway or the scenic route?
(A) It's easier like that.
(B) The quickest route is best.
(C) I've been here twice.
고속도로로 가시겠어요, 아니면 경치가 좋은 길로 가시겠어요?
(A) 그렇게 하면 더 쉽습니다.
(B) 가장 빠른 길이 제일 좋아요.
(C) 저는 여기에 두 번 와 봤습니다.
highway 고속도로 scenic route 경치가 좋은 길

16 [영M][미W] Why is the light on the photocopier red?
(A) Maybe it's out of ink.
(B) Thank you, but I've decided not to.
(C) It is too light in here.
복사기의 불이 왜 빨간색인가요?
(A) 아마 잉크가 없나 봐요.
(B) 감사합니다. 하지만 저는 그러지 않기로 했어요.
(C) 여기 너무 밝아요.
be out of ~이 부족하다, ~이 없다

17 [미W] Isn't Kelvin having an operation soon?
(A) Sure, I'd love to try some.
(B) In March, I believe.
(C) No, it's not too difficult.
켈빈은 곧 수술을 받게 되지 않나요?
(A) 물론이죠, 제가 좀 해 볼게요.
(B) 제 생각엔 3월에 받을 거예요.
(C) 아니요, 많이 어렵지 않습니다.
operation 수술 try 시도하다

18 [미M][미W] When will the debate on human rights be aired?
(A) At the accounting office.
(B) On Wednesday in the daytime.
(C) Yes, it was thought-provoking.
인권에 관한 토론은 언제 방송될 건가요?
(A) 회계 부서에서요.
(B) 수요일 낮에요.
(C) 네, 시사하는 바가 많았어요.
debate 토론 human rights 인권 air 방송하다 accounting office 회계 부서 thought-provoking 시사하는 바가 많은

19 [영M][미W] I'm having difficulty locating Mr. Rozenberg's dinner suit.
(A) Maybe I can be of assistance.
(B) I have twelve in total.
(C) Where did you find it?
로젠버그 씨의 야회복을 찾는 데 어려움을 겪고 있어요.
(A) 어쩌면 제가 도움이 될 수 있겠네요.
(B) 제가 총 12벌을 갖고 있어요.
(C) 어디에서 찾으셨나요?
have difficulty -ing ~하는 데 어려움을 겪다 locate 찾다 dinner suit 야회복 be of assistance 도움이 되다 in total 통틀어

20 [영M][미M] Would you like me to add up your expenses before you hand them in?
(A) Oh, I paid with credit card.
(B) I'd like a little extra, please.
(C) Thanks, but Ms. Washington already helped.
당신이 그것들을 제출하기 전에 당신의 비용을 합계해 드릴까요?
(A) 저런, 저는 신용 카드로 지불했어요.
(B) 좀 더 주세요.
(C) 감사합니다만, 워싱턴 씨가 이미 도왔어요.
add up 합계를 내다 expense 비용 hand in 제출하다

21 [미W][미M] Which pair of shoes did you finally buy?
(A) Actually, I couldn't choose any yet.
(B) Just a small measure, please.
(C) Thanks for your help.
결국 당신은 어떤 신발을 샀나요?
(A) 사실, 어떤 것도 아직 고르지 못했어요.
(B) 소량만 주세요.
(C) 도움에 감사합니다.
measure (몇몇) 양정도

22 [영M][미W] You'll be arriving in Dunkirk on Thursday, won't you?
(A) No, my ferry was cancelled.
(B) Could I use those next week?
(C) Yes, he emailed to say he'd arrived.
당신은 목요일에 됭케르크에 도착할 거예요, 그렇지 않나요?
(A) 아니요, 제 페리는 취소되었습니다.
(B) 제가 그것들을 다음 주에 사용해도 되나요?
(C) 네, 그는 그가 도착했다는 이메일을 보냈습니다.
ferry 연락선, 페리

23 [미W][미M] Isn't the assessor meant to come to lunch today?
(A) Two new assessments.
(B) Yes, he's held up in traffic.
(C) Most days of the year.
평가자가 오늘 점심시간에 오시는 게 아니었나요?
(A) 두 개의 새로운 평가입니다.
(B) 네, 그는 교통 체증으로 꼼짝 못하고 있어요.
(C) 거의 일 년 내내요.
assessor 감정인, 평가자 mean to ~할 셈이다 assessment 평가(한 의견) be held up in traffic 교통 정체로 꼼짝 못하다

24 [미M][미W] I think I left my umbrella in the taxi.
(A) We left after midnight.
(B) You should call them immediately.
(C) We have one just round the corner.
제 우산을 택시에 두고 내린 것 같아요.
(A) 우리는 자정에 떠났습니다.
(B) 당신은 그들에게 즉시 전화해야 해요.
(C) 근처에 하나 있습니다.
midnight 자정 just round the corner 아주 가까운 모퉁이를 돌아

Part 3

25 Why has the transport system been disrupted?

미W (A) A train and a bus.

영M (B) There was an accident.

(C) I've read the comments.

교통 시스템에 왜 지장이 생겼나요?

(A) 기차와 버스입니다.

(B) 사고가 있었어요.

(C) 제가 평들을 읽어 보았어요.

disrupt 방해하다; 지장을 주다 comment 평

26 Could you swap Janghir's shift this Tuesday?

미W (A) I didn't realize that.

미W **(B) Yes, it shifted perfectly.**

(C) Let me check who's working.

이번 주 화요일 장히어의 교대조를 바꿀 수 있나요?

(A) 저는 그걸 몰랐습니다.

(B) 네, 그건 완벽하게 바뀌었습니다.

(C) 누가 일하고 있는지 확인해 볼게요.

swap 바꾸다 shift 교대조(근무); 바꾸다

27 Were you involved in the Millicent fund investigation?

미W (A) That's not her workload.

영M **(B) A vital clue.**

(C) Yes, together with Rachel and Chloe.

당신은 밀리센트 기금 수사에 관련되어 있나요?

(A) 그건 그녀의 작업량이 아니에요.

(B) 중요한 단서입니다.

(C) 네, 레이철과 클로이랑 같이요.

involved in ~에 관련된 fund 자금 investigation 조사, 수사

workload 작업량 vital 중요한; 중요한 clue 단서

28 Have you put the tablecloths in the wash yet?

미M (A) I'll take twenty, thanks.

미W **(B) Actually, I've just dried them.**

(C) Not as often as I would like.

식탁보들을 세탁기에 아직 넣지 않았죠?

(A) 20개를 받겠습니다. 감사합니다.

(B) 실은, 제가 방금 그것들을 말렸어요.

(C) 제가 원하는 만큼 자주는 아니에요.

tablecloth 식탁보 wash 세탁기 dry 말리다

29 Would you prefer to book this hotel or the one in the next town?

미W (A) I've worked as a receptionist for 20 years.

영M (B) I bought them from a street vendor.

(C) Either will be fine.

이 호텔을 예약하는 게 더 좋으세요, 아니면 옆 동네에 있는 호텔에 예약하길 원하세요?

(A) 접수계원으로 20년 동안 근무했습니다.

(B) 거리의 노점상에서 샀습니다.

(C) 어느든 상관없어요.

book 예약하다 receptionist 접수계원 street vendor 거리의 노점상

30 Why don't you ask Larry about the rodent issue?

미M (A) Yes, I brought some poison.

미W **(B) I think you're making a mistake.**

(C) It's already been taken care of.

래리에게 설치류 문제에 관해 문의하는 건 어때요?

(A) 네, 저는 독약을 갖고 있어요.

(B) 제 생각엔 당신이 실수를 저지르고 있는 것 같습니다.

(C) 이미 처리가 되었습니다.

rodent 설치류 take care of ~을 처리하다

31 Who will replace Mr. Landrake as financial officer?

미W (A) It hasn't been confirmed.

영M **(B) That sounds like an excellent start.**

(C) Lisa provided the catering.

랜드레이크 씨의 재무 책임자 자리를 누가 대신하게 되나요?

(A) 결정되지 않았어요.

(B) 좋은 시작처럼 들리네요.

(C) 리사가 음식 공급을 맡았어요.

replace 대신하다; 대체하다 financial officer 재무 책임자

catering 음식 조달; 음식 공급

Questions 32-34 refer to the following conversation. 미M 미W

M Ms. Kitayama, I have an inquiry. ㉜ I have a position for a beautician and I know you recently recruited for a similar job last week. Where did you place the job advertisement?

W ㉝ I emailed the beauty department at Westland College and they put forward a number of graduates for the job.

M That's an excellent idea. Although by now the majority of graduates have probably got jobs. I am going to require an extra person within the next two weeks.

W Then, ㉞ you should post the position on the Health and Beauty Web site. A number of people use the site, amateurs and professionals. You are bound to get a large amount of interest.

남 키타야마 씨, 궁금한 게 있어요. 제게 미용사 자리가 하나 있는데, 당신이 최근에 비슷한 일자리를 지난주에 모집했던 것으로 알고 있습니다. 어디에 채용 광고를 내셨죠?

여 저는 웨스트랜드 대학의 미용부로 이메일을 보냈고, 그들이 그 일자리에 많은 졸업생들을 후보자로 제안했어요.

남 아주 괜찮은 생각이네요. 지금쯤이면 이미 대다수의 졸업생들이 이미 취직 중이겠지만요. 저는 앞으로 2주 이내로 한 명이 더 필요해요.

여 그렇다면 당신은 헬스 앤 뷰티 웹 사이트에 그 자리를 내 보셔야 할 거에요. 아마추어와 전문가 등 많은 사람들이 그 사이트를 이용합니다. 분명 많은 관심을 받으실 거예요.

inquiry 문의 beautician 미용사 recruit 모집하다 place an advertisement 광고를 게재하다 put forward (취업 후보자 등을) 제안하다 majority of 다수의 post 게시하다 professional 전문가 graduate 졸업생 be bound to 반드시 ~할 것이다 navigate 길을 찾다

32 What does the man want to do?

(A) Recruit an assistant

(B) Get a degree

(C) Have a facial

(D) Visit a Web site

남자는 무엇을 하고 싶어 하는가?

(A) 직원 채용하기

(B) 특허 받기
(C) 얼굴 마사지 받기
(D) 웹 사이트 방문하기

33 Why did the woman contact the college?
(A) To locate a suitable salon
(B) To sign up for a college course
(C) To rent some equipment
(D) To find trained job applicants

여자가 대학에 연락했던 이유는?
(A) 알맞은 미용실을 찾기 위해
(B) 대학 강좌를 신청하기 위해
(C) 장비를 빌리기 위해
(D) 훈련된 입자리 지원자를 찾기 위해

34 Why does the woman recommend the Health and Beauty Web site?
(A) It features useful advice.
(B) It is only for professionals.
(C) It has a lot of users.
(D) It is simple to navigate.

여자가 헬스 앤 뷰티 웹 사이트를 추천하는 이유는?
(A) 유용한 팁을 특징으로 한다.
(B) 전문가용 전용이다.
(C) 이용자들이 많다.
(D) 길을 찾기 쉽다.

Questions 35-37 refer to the following conversation. [영M] [미W]

M Hi, Claire. ㉟ Could you let me know when you are available this week? I'd like to arrange a time for a meeting with you. We have to ensure we're organized for the annual tax return.

W Hmm, I can't really arrange anything for the next three days as ㉟ I'm attending a wedding in Las Vegas. Isn't the tax return due next week?

M No, I'm afraid all the revenue forms have to be submitted by Friday at 5 P.M. ㊲ Why don't we arrange an afternoon for a video conference call about the annual submissions when you return from your trip?

남 안녕하세요, 클레어. 이번 주 언제 시간이 가능한지 알려 주실 수 있나요? 당신과 회의할 시간을 마련하고 싶습니다. 우리는 연례 소득세 신고 준비를 확실히 해야 해요.

여 흠, 저는 라스베이거스의 결혼식에 참석해서 다음 3일간은 아무 일정을 잡을 수 없는데요. 소득세 신고는 다음 주가 아닌가요?

남 아니요, 모든 수입에 관한 서류가 금요일 오후 5시까지 제출되어야 합니다. 당신이 돌아오면 연례 제출에 대한 화상 회의를 하도록 오후 시간을 정하는 게 어때요?

tax return 소득세 신고(서) due ~하기로 되어 있는 revenue (정부·기업의) 수익, 수입 video conference call 화상 회의 tax office 세무서 documentation (요구받거나 입증에 필요한) 서류

35 What does the man ask about?
(A) The woman's availability
(B) The amount of tax to be returned
(C) The return from a vacation
(D) The call to a client

남자는 무엇에 관해 묻는가?
(A) 여자의 가능한 시간
(B) 돌려줘야 할 세금의 액수
(C) 휴가에서의 복귀
(D) 고객에게 건 전화

36 What does the woman plan to do this week?
(A) Finalize a seminar
(B) Visit the tax office
(C) Attend a ceremony
(D) Provide some paperwork

여자는 이번 주에 무엇을 할 계획인가?
(A) 세미나 마무리 짓기
(B) 세무서 방문하기
(C) 예식 참석하기
(D) 몇몇 서류 직접 제공하기

37 What does the man suggest doing?
(A) Setting up a conference call
(B) Filling out a registration form
(C) Submitting the required documentation
(D) Making a phone call

남자는 무엇을 하도록 제안하는가?
(A) 화상 회의 잡기
(B) 등록 서류 작성하기
(C) 요청받은 서류 제출하기
(D) 전화 걸기

Questions 38-40 refer to the following conversation. [미W] [영M]

W Hi, ㊳ I am keen on seeing the game at the baseball center on Saturday. I tried to buy four tickets over the phone but my calls weren't being answered. ㊴ We are having some technical issues with the phone company today. Would you like to book the tickets with me?

W Yes, thank you. I'd like four sixth row seats for the Saturday morning match at the Pedusa Stadium. Are there any available?

M Certainly. If you ㊵ let me have your credit card information, I can reserve these straight away.

여 안녕하세요. 저는 토요일 야구 경기장에 너무 가고 싶어요. 전화로 4장의 표를 사려고 했지만 제 전화로는 응답이 없더군요.

남 죄송합니다. 저희가 오늘 전화 회사와 기술적인 문제를 겪고 있습니다. 저와 표를 예매해 드릴까요?

여 네, 감사합니다. 저는 페두사 경기장에서 토요일 아침 경기 6번째 열의 표 4장을 원합니다. 남아 있는 게 있나요?

남 물론이죠. 당신의 신용 카드 정보를 알려 주시면, 그 표를 즉시 예매할 수 있습니다.

keen on ~을 아주 좋아하는, ~에 관심이 많은 row (극장·등의 좌석) 줄 match 시합, 경기 stadium 경기장 straight away 곧바로 premiere 개봉, 초연 representative 대표, 대리인 reference number 조회 번호

38 What event does the woman want to attend?
(A) A movie premiere
(B) A sporting event
(C) A book launch
(D) A theater performance

여자는 어떤 행사에 참석하기를 원하는가?
(A) 개봉 첫 영화
(B) 스포츠 행사
(C) 책 출간
(D) 극장 공연

39 What is the problem?
(A) A phone system is not working.
(B) A representative reserved the wrong tickets.
(C) A credit card was stolen.
(D) A game is sold out.

무엇이 문제인가?
(A) 전화 시스템이 작동하고 있지 않다.
(B) 담당자가 잘못된 표를 예약했다.
(C) 신용 카드가 도난당했다.
(D) 게임이 매진되었다.

40 What information does the man request?
(A) A reference number
(B) A business address
(C) The name of an event
(D) Credit card details

남자가 요청하는 정보는?
(A) 조회 번호
(B) 회사 주소
(C) 행사명
(D) 신용 카드 정보

Questions 41-43 refer to the following conversation. (미M) (미W)

M Hello, Ms. Mayall. This is Mark Tolley. I am calling to introduce myself. I did some freelance design work for your company a year ago and ❹ I believe you are the new head of the technical department. ❷ I was inquiring whether you have any design work I can assist with. I'd appreciate working with you.

W Well, thank you for the call. To be honest, though, Mark, we're keeping the majority of our designing in house for now. That's not to say it won't change in the future though. I'd be happy to file your details in case we need help.

M OK. That would be good. If it's acceptable to you then, ❸ I'd like to email you my updated portfolio. And I hope you bear me in mind if anything turns up.

남 안녕하세요, 마열 씨. 저는 마크 톨리입니다. 제 소개를 하려고 전화했습니다. 저는 1년 전 당신의 회사에서 프리랜서로 디자인 작업을 했고 당신이 기술 부서의 새로운 책임자라고 알고 있습니다. 제가 도움을 줄 수 있는 디자인 작업이 혹시 있는지 문의를 드립니다. 당신과 같이 일하게 된다면 매우 감사하겠습니다.

여 음, 전화해 주셔서 감사합니다. 하지만 솔직히 말하자면 마크, 저희는 현재 대부분의 디자인 작업을 내부에서 처리하고 있어요. 그렇다고 미래에도 변함이 없을 거라는 않는 건 아닙니다. 우리가 도움이 필요할 경우를 대비해, 기꺼이 당신의 정보를 보관하고 있겠습니다.

남 네, 그게 좋겠어요. 언어 괜찮다면 당신에게 제 최근 포트폴리오를 이메일로 보내 드리고 싶습니다. 그리고 어떤 일이든지 생기면 저를 기억해 주시기 바랍니다.

freelance 프리랜서[자유 계약자]로 일하는   head (단체·조직의) 책임자   inquire 문의하다   in house (회사·조직) 내부의   that's not to say ~라고 말하는 것은 아니다   file (문서 등을 정리하여) 보관하다   in case ~할 경우를 대비하여   portfolio 작품집, 포트폴리오   bear in mind 기억하다   updated 최신의   turn up 생기다, 나타나다   reference 추천서   forthcoming 다가오는

41 Who most likely is the woman?
(A) A technical director
(B) A human resources manager
(C) A temporary worker
(D) A factory worker

여자는 누구일 것 같은가?
(A) 기술팀 이사
(B) 인사부 부장
(C) 임시 직원
(D) 공장 근로자

42 Why is the man calling?
(A) To request a reference
(B) To submit his portfolio
(C) To ask about employment
(D) To explain a forthcoming training session

남자가 전화를 건 이유는?
(A) 추천서를 요청하기 위해
(B) 그의 포트폴리오를 제출하기 위해
(C) 고용에 관해 질문하기 위해
(D) 다가오는 교육 과정을 설명하기 위해

43 What does the man offer to send?
(A) An extended contract
(B) A draft design
(C) An upgraded portfolio
(D) An updated résumé

남자는 무엇을 보내겠다고 제안하는가?
(A) 연장된 계약
(B) 디자인 초안
(C) 업그레이드된 포트폴리오
(D) 갱신된 이력서

W Good morning. My name is Marsha Juncker. **㊹ I have made a booking to rent a room.**

M Yes, Ms. Juncker. I have your details here. You booked a single room for three days, right?

W Yes, but I'm thinking about staying an extra night. **㊺ I saw your promotion that promised an extra night's stay free if I book three nights.**

M I'm sorry but **㊻ that promotion only applies to stays that include the weekend and the cost for an extra weekday stay is our normal rate.** Would you like to extend your stay?

여 좋은 아침이에요. 제 이름은 마샤 정커입니다. 방을 빌리려고 예약했어요.

남 네, 정커 씨. 당신의 정보가 제게 있습니다. 3일간 숙박할 1인실로 예약하셨어요, 그렇죠?

여 네, 하지만 저는 하룻밤 더 묵을 생각입니다. 3일간 숙박하면 하룻밤은 공짜로 묵을 수 있다고 약속하는 당신의 광고를 봤거든요.

남 죄송하지만 그 광고는 주말을 포함한 숙박에만 적용되고, 평일 추가 숙박 비용은 정상 가격입니다. 숙박을 연장해 드릴까요?

booking 예약 single room 1인실 promotion 광고 normal rate 정상가 retreat 조용한 곳 public 대중

44 Where does the conversation most likely take place?
(A) At a hotel
(B) At a rental agency
(C) At a weekend retreat
(D) At a conference hall

대화가 어디에서 일어날 것 같은가?
(A) 호텔
(B) 대여점
(C) 주말 여행지
(D) 회의장

45 What does the woman mention about the promotion?
(A) A free bus service
(B) Details of a special offer
(C) The date of a new hotel opening
(D) Discounts at the restaurant

여자가 광고에 대해 언급한 것은?
(A) 무료 버스 서비스
(B) 특별 할인의 세부 정보
(C) 새 호텔의 개장일
(D) 레스토랑에서의 할인

46 What does the man explain to the woman?
(A) The discount applies only on certain days.
(B) There will be a two-hour delay.
(C) The hotel is closed to the public.
(D) The promotion has false information.

남자는 여자에게 무엇을 설명하는가?
(A) 할인은 특정한 날에만 적용된다.
(B) 2시간 지연이 있을 것이다.
(C) 호텔은 대중에게 공개되지 않는다.
(D) 광고에 허위 정보가 있다.

M1 **㊼ Two of our team members called in sick, but we have a big banquet tonight and need to come up with a plan.**

W The guests are going to arrive in two hours.

M2 The good news is that we have most of the food prepared. So maybe I can ask someone on the kitchen staff to help set up the tables.

M1 Good idea. **㊽ What about serving the food?**

W **㊽ Since we are going to need one more person for that, I can help. That means I need to have everything organized perfectly before dinner is served.**

M1 **㊾ If you need someone to help coordinate with the kitchen, I might be able to do it.**

W I don't think you have to worry about that.

남1 팀원들 중 두 명이 오늘 병가를 냈어요. 그런데 우리가 오늘 저녁에 큰 연회를 진행해야 해서 계획을 세워야 합니다.

여 손님들이 2시간 후에 도착할 거예요.

남2 좋은 소식은 대부분의 음식들은 준비가 되어 있다는 것입니다. 그래서 아마도 우리가 주방 직원들 중 한 명에게 우리 테이블을 세팅하는 것을 도와 달라고 할 수 있을 것 같아요.

남1 좋은 생각이네요. 음식 서빙하는 것은 어떻게 하면 좋을까요?

여 우리가 서빙할 한 명이 더 필요한 거니까, 제가 도울게요. 그러면 제가 저녁 식사가 제공되기 전까지 모든 것을 다 완료해야 된다는 얘기가 되는군요.

남1 당신이 주방일을 도울 누군가를 필요로 한다면, 제가 도와 드릴 수 있어요.

여 그건 걱정 안 하셔도 될 것 같아요.

call in sick 전화로 병가를 내다 come up with ~을 제시하다 coordinate 조직하다, 재다

47 What problem are the speakers discussing?
(A) Changing a menu
(B) Rescheduling an event
(C) Being understaffed
(D) Hiring employees

회자들은 어떤 문제에 관한 논의를 하고 있는가?

(A) 메뉴를 바꾸는 것
(B) 행사 일정을 재조정하는 것
(C) 직원이 부족한 것
(D) 직원들을 고용하는 것

48 What does the woman offer to do?

(A) Wash dishes
(B) Meet a client
(C) Move tables
(D) Serve food

여자는 무엇을 해 주겠다고 하는가?

(A) 접시를 닦는다.
(B) 고객을 만난다.
(C) 테이블을 옮긴다.
(D) 음식을 서빙한다.

49 What does the woman mean when she says, "I don't think you have to worry about that"?

(A) She believes she can handle the task.
(B) She is able to help cooking.
(C) She is having some trouble with the customer.
(D) She thinks the men can't solve the problem.

여자는 "그건 걱정 안 하셔도 될 것 같아요"라고 말했을 때 무엇을 의미했는가?

(A) 그녀는 그녀가 그 일을 처리할 수 있다고 믿는다.
(B) 그녀는 요리를 도울 수 있다.
(C) 그녀는 고객과 문제가 있다.
(D) 그녀는 남자들이 문제를 해결할 수 없다고 생각한다.

Questions 50-52 refer to the following conversation. (영M) (미W)

M Good morning, Ms. Jamison. This is Bill Lowell from *Modern Life Magazine.* ⑩ I'm calling to let you know that we would like you to write the article on weekend farms near cities that you proposed.

W That's great news! I'm so glad that you liked my idea. I think your readers will find it as fascinating a topic as I do.

M ⑪ We believe they will be as impressed as we are by your passion for your topics in the writing samples you sent us. How soon do you think you can have a draft ready?

W Hmm... in about a month I believe.

M Great. ⑫ How about if we set March 15 as the deadline? If you have any questions regarding this, just give me a call.

W Absolutely.

남 안녕하세요, 제이슨 씨. 저는 〈모던 라이프 매거진〉의 빌 로웰입니다. 당신이 제안해 주신 도시 근교에 있는 주말 농장에 관한 기사를 써 주실 것을 요청 드리기 위해 전화드립니다.

여 좋은 소식이에요. 제 아이디어가 마음에 드신다니 정말 기쁩니다. 제가 생각하는 것만큼 당신의 독자들도 이 주제를 매력이 있다고 느낄 것이라고 생각합니다.

남 당신이 우리에게 보내 주신 글의 주제에 대한 당신의 열정이 우리가 감명받은 것처럼 독자들도 그럴 거라 믿어요. 언제쯤 원고가 준비될 수 있으신가요?

여 음… 대략 1달 뒤에요.

남 좋습니다. 우리가 3월 15일을 마감 날짜로 잡는 것이 어떠세요? 이에 관련해서 어떠한 질문이라도 있으시면 제게 전화주세요.

여 알겠습니다.

fascinating 매력적인, 관심이 가는   draft 원고, 초안   landscaping 조경

50 What does the woman plan to write about?

(A) Professional landscaping
(B) Farming
(C) Public transportation
(D) Fashion trends

여자는 무엇에 관해 글을 쓸 예정인가?

(A) 전문 조경
(B) 농사
(C) 대중교통
(D) 패션 트렌드

51 What did the man receive from the woman?

(A) A billing statement
(B) Samples of her work
(C) A rental contract
(D) References

남자는 여자로부터 무엇을 받았는가?

(A) 청구 내역서
(B) 작업 샘플들
(C) 임대 계약서
(D) 추천서

52 What does the woman mean when she says, "Absolutely"?

(A) She will answer some questions.
(B) She can't call at the moment.
(C) She will not be able to complete the draft by the deadline.
(D) She agrees to the man's suggestion.

여자는 "알겠습니다"라고 말했을 때 무엇을 의미했는가?

(A) 그녀가 몇몇 질문에 관해 답변할 것이다.
(B) 그녀가 지금은 전화를 할 수 없다.
(C) 그녀는 마감일자까지 원고를 완료할 수 없다.
(D) 여자는 남자의 제안에 동의한다.

Questions 53-55 refer to the following conversation. 미M 미W

M Kaya, Amanda called. She's not going to be able to make it onsite ⑤③ because there's a major traffic accident on the highway. ⑤④ She asked me to find the keys to Jamid's site office but I can't find them on her desk.

W Oh, I'm sorry. I have them here. I took them off her desk meaning to get another duplicate set of keys cut. Should we wait until she gets here before we head over to the site?

M No, Amanda said carry on with the plans. We don't want to delay work anymore. ⑤⑤ I'll just get my hard hat from the office.

남 카야, 아만다가 전화했었어요. 고속도로에서 대형 교통사고가 있었기 때문에, 그녀는 제시간에 현장에 도착하지 못할 것 같아요. 그녀가 자미드의 현장 사무소의 열쇠를 찾아달라고 요청했는데, 책상 위에 보이질 않네요.

여 오 죄송해요. 제가 여기 갖고 있어요. 열쇠들을 복사하기 위해서 그녀의 책상에서 가져갔거든요. 우리가 현장으로 가기 전에 그녀가 이곳에 도착할 때까지 기다려야 할까요?

남 아니요. 이만다가 계획대로 진행하라고 말했어요. 우리는 더 이상 작업 지연하고 싶지 않네요. 제 사무실에서 안전모를 갖고 올게요.

make it (어떤 곳에) 간신히) 시간 맞춰 가다   onsite 현지의, 현장의   major 큰   site office 현장 사무소   mean to ~하려 하다   duplicate 복사(본)   head 가다   site현장   carry on with ~을 계속하다   fetch 데리고 오다   hard hat 안전모

53 Why will Amanda be late for the meeting?
(A) She is still on site.
(B) She has to make a phone call.
(C) She is caught in traffic congestion.
(D) She has lost the keys to the office.

아만다가 회의에 늦게 되는 이유는?
(A) 그녀는 아직 현장에 있다.
(B) 그녀는 전화를 한 통 해야 한다.
(C) 그녀는 교통체증에 걸렸다.
(D) 사무실 열쇠를 잃어버렸다.

54 What did Amanda ask the man to do?
(A) Fetch a hard hat
(B) Drive straight to the office
(C) Take notes at a meeting
(D) Get some keys from her desk

이만다는 남자에게 무엇을 해달라고 요청했는가?
(A) 안전모 가져다주기
(B) 운전해서 사무실로 곧장 가기
(C) 회의에서 메모하기
(D) 그녀의 책상에서 열쇠 가져가기

55 What does the man say he will do next?
(A) Pick up some work supplies
(B) Contact a supervisor
(C) Link up his computer
(D) Call the site manager

남자는 다음에 무엇을 가지러 하겠다고 하는가?
(A) 직업 장비 가지러 가기
(B) 관리자에게 연락하기
(C) 그의 컴퓨터 연결하기
(D) 현장 관리자에게 전화하기

Questions 56-58 refer to the following conversation. 미W 영M

W That's all the interview questions that I have, Robert. Do you have any questions for me?

M Actually, yes. You asked me about my availability. ⑤⑦ However, I am still not clear what you had in mind for the starting date.

W Well, we need someone right away. ⑤⑥ So, ideally, we would like to hire a new assistant for my stationery store no later than next week. We could be a little flexible with the starting date though. Are you still interested?

M Yes, I am. I was afraid you needed someone this week. I already committed to help my cousin's shop this week.

W Great. Then I would like to offer you the job. ⑤⑧ Can you start on Monday next week?

M Not a problem.

여 거기까지가 제가 준비한 인터뷰 질문들이에요, 로버트. 저에게 질문 있으세요?

남 사실, 있어요. 제게 언제 일을 시작할 수 있을지에 관해 질문하셨잖아요. 그런데, 아직 당신이 언제를 업무 시작일자로 생각하고 계시는 건지 잘 모르겠어요.

여 음, 저희가 지금 당장 사람이 필요해요. 그래서, 가능하다면, 다음 주 전에 제 문구점에 새로운 보조원을 고용하고 싶어요. 그래도 업무 시작일자에 대해서는 좀 더 변화를 줄 수 있어요. 여전히 관심이 있으신가요?

남 네, 그렇습니다. 이번 주에 사람이 필요하신가 해서 좀 신경이 쓰였어요. 제가 이미 제 사촌의 가게에서 이번 주에 일을 도와주기로 약속을 했거든요.

여 좋습니다. 그럼 저희가 당신을 고용하고 싶어요. 다음 주 월요일부터 일을 시작하실 수 있을까요?

남 네, 문제없습니다.

availability 유용성, 이용 가능성   ideally 이상적으로   flexible 유연한   commit 약속하다   stationery 문구류

56 Where does the woman work?
(A) At an educational institute
(B) At a convention center
(C) At a stationery store
(D) At a staffing agency

여자는 어디에서 일을 하는가?
(A) 교육 기관
(B) 컨벤션 센터
(C) 목구점
(D) 직원 채용 대행사

57 What does the man ask about the job?
(A) The starting date
(B) The salary
(C) The duration
(D) The location

남자는 직업에 관해 무엇을 질문하는가?
(A) 업무 시작일자
(B) 급여
(C) 기간
(D) 위치

58 Why does the man say, "Not a problem"?
(A) He doesn't have any questions at the moment.
(B) He wants to start on a different date.
(C) He can start working on Monday.
(D) He can take the job right away.

남자는 왜 "문제없습니다"라고 말했는가?
(A) 그는 현재 질문할 것이 없다.
(B) 그는 다른 날 시작하고 싶어 한다.
(C) 그는 월요일부터 일을 시작할 수 있다.
(D) 그는 즉시 일을 맡을 수 있다.

Questions 59-61 refer to the following conversation. 미W 영M

W Hello, I'm contacting you because ⑤⑨ I'd like to have a studio specially designed for dance club activities. You don't build custom constructions, do you?

M No, we don't. But we occasionally subcontract them from a building firm. If you can tell me what you want, ⑥⓪ I can get a quote for you.

W Thanks, but I would rather do it myself. ⑥① If you'd care to give me the contact details and Web site, I'll be happy to contact them directly.

여 안녕하세요. 댄스 클럽 활동을 위해 특별히 제작된 연습실을 연계해서 당신에게 연락을 합니다. 당신은 주문 공사는 하지 않죠. 그렇죠?

남 네, 하지 않습니다. 하지만 저희는 때때로 건설 회사에 하청을 맡긴다. 원하는 바를 제게 말씀해 주시면, 당신을 위해 견적을 낼 수 있습니다.

여 감사하지만 차라리 제가 직접 하는 게 좋겠습니다. 연락처와 웹 사이트를 알려 주신다면 그룹에게 직접 연락하면 되겠어요.

studio 연습실 custom 맞춤의, 주문의 occasionally 가끔, 때때로 subcontract 하청을 주다, 하도급을 주다 quote 견적 approximate 거의 정확한

59 What does the woman want to do?
(A) Request a collection service
(B) Hold a new dance class
(C) Alter a previous order
(D) Have an area specially designed

여자가 하고 싶어 하는 것은?
(A) 수거 서비스 요청하기
(B) 새 무용 강좌 시작하기
(C) 이전 주문 변경하기
(D) 공간을 특별하게 제작하기

60 What does the man say he can do?
(A) Comment on her work
(B) Design a dance stage
(C) Check a building guarantee
(D) Obtain an approximate estimate

남자가 할 수 있다고 말한 것은?
(A) 여자의 작업에 대해 의견 달기
(B) 댄스 무대 디자인하기
(C) 건물 보증서 확인하기
(D) 대략적인 견적 알아내기

61 What does the woman request?
(A) Contact information
(B) Design samples
(C) Blueprint drawings
(D) A stock catalog

여자가 요청한 것은?
(A) 연락처
(B) 디자인 견본
(C) 청사진 도안
(D) 재고 카탈로그

Questions 62-64 refer to the following conversation. 미W 미M

W Hi, Titan. I'm hoping you would give me some suggestions. ⑥② I want to buy some security cameras for my factory. I know you install a lot of security equipment, and I was wondering what you'd suggest.

M Well, I just read a review in a magazine about the new ultra sensitive sensors from Jeynes Office Security Company. Apparently, they've been receiving positive customer feedback.

W Oh, really? I've seen that brand advertised. ⑥③ Could you tell me which issue of the magazine the feature is in so I can read more about them?

M Sure, I'd be happy to. But while you're here, ⑥④ why don't I give you my copy instead?

여 안녕하세요, 타이탄. 저는 당신이 제안을 좀 해길 바라고 있어요. 저는 제 공장에 설치할 감시 카메라를 사고 싶어요. 당신이 감시용 기기를 많이 설치한다고 알고 있는데, 어떤 것을 추천할지 궁금하네요.

남 음, 저는 방금 잡지에서 제이스 사무 안전 용품 회사에서 나온 새로운 초강력 센서기에 대한 평을 읽었어요. 확실히 긍정적인 고객의 반응을 받고고 있나 봐요.

여 오, 그래요? 그 브랜드가 광고된 것을 본 적이 있어요. 그것들에 대해 더 읽어볼 수 있도록 그 특집이 잡지의 어떤 호에 실렸는지 알려 줄 수 있으요?

남 물론입니다. 기꺼이 알려 드리죠. 하지만 당신이 여기 있는 동안인 제 잡지를 대신 드리는 건 어떨까요?

Actual Test 01   010 • 011

security camera 감시 카메라, 보안용 카메라 **ultra sensitive** 초감각
sensor 센서기 **apparently** 명백히 **issue** (잡지·신문 같은 정기 간행물의)
호 **feature** 특징·특장 **copy** 한 부

62 What are the speakers mainly discussing?
(A) Factory installations
(B) Security systems
(C) A new brand launch
(D) A fashion magazine

화자들이 주로 논하고 있는 것은?
(A) 공장 설비
(B)보안용 시스템
(C) 새 브랜드 출시
(D) 패션 잡지

63 What does the woman ask for?
(A) A list of security cameras
(B) An Internet address
(C) A purchase order number
(D) Details of a magazine

여자가 요청한 것은?
(A) 감시 카메라 목록
(B) 인터넷 주소
(C) 구매 주문 번호
(D)잡지의 세부 사항

64 What does the man offer to do?
(A) Give the woman his magazine
(B) Install a security device
(C) Review a feature
(D) Purchase products online

남자는 무엇을 하겠다고 제안하는가?
(A) 여자에게 그의 잡지 주기
(B) 보안 장치 설치하기
(C) 기능 검토하기
(D) 온라인으로 제품 구매하기

Questions 65-67 refer to the following conversation and floor plan.
[영M] [미W]

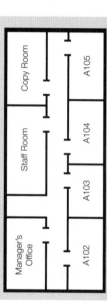

| Manager's Office | Staff Room | | Copy Room |
| A102 | A103 | A104 | A105 |

M **65** Hi. I'm calling to let you know that the LCD computer monitor and color printer that you ordered just arrived. Where do you want them delivered?

W **66** Well, the LCD computer monitor is for Mr. Wilcox. His office is immediately across from the manager's office. As for the color printer, it goes in the copy room.

M Okay. I should be able to drop by this afternoon. Will you be there to let me into the office?

W I'm going out for lunch meeting with a client and should be back by 2:30 P.M. So as long as you come after that time and before 6:00 P.M., then yes.

M **67** Let's tentatively say 3:00 P.M. then. If I come any later, I might not have enough time to help you set everything up.

W That works for me. Thanks.

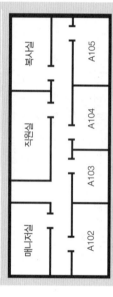

| 매니저실 | 직원실 | | 복사실 |
| A102 | A103 | A104 | A105 |

남 안녕하세요. 당신이 주문한 LCD 모니터와 컬러 프린터가 막 도착했습니다. 이 사람들을 어디로 보내 드릴까요?
여 음, LCD 모니터는 윌콕스 씨를 위한 것이에요. 그의 사무실은 매니저 사무실의 바로 맞은편에 위치해 있습니다. 컬러 프린터는 바로 복사실로 가져가면 됩니다.
남 네, 제가 오후에 방문할게요. 제가 사무실에 들어갈 수 있도록 계실 수 있나요?

여 제가 고객과 점심 미팅이 있어서 오후 2시 30분은 되어야 사무실로 돌아올 거예요. 그러니까 그 시간 이후에 오시기만 한다면, 그리고 오후 6시 이전이라면, 괜찮아요.
남 그럼 잠정적으로 오후 3시로 하죠. 더 늦게 도착하게 되면 장비들을 모두 설치하는 데 있어 시간이 좀 부족할 수도 있겠네요.
여 그 정도는 괜찮습니다. 감사합니다.

immediately 즉시, 바로 **tentatively** 잠정적으로, 시험삼아

65 Why is the man calling?
(A) To cancel an appointment
(B) To place an order
(C) To arrange a delivery
(D) To obtain contact information

남자는 왜 전화하고 있는가?
(A) 약속을 취소하기 위해서
(B) 주문을 하기 위해서
(C)배송 계획을 잡기 위해서
(D) 연락 정보를 얻기 위해서

66 Look at the graphic. Where is the LCD computer monitor supposed to go?
(A) A102
(B) A103
(C) A104
(D) A105

그래픽을 보시오. LCD 컴퓨터 모니터는 어디로 보내져야 하는가?
(A) A102
(B) A103
(C) A104
(D) A105

67 When will the speakers most likely meet?
(A) At 2:00 P.M.
(B) At 3:00 P.M.
(C) At 4:00 P.M.
(D) At 5:30 P.M.

화자들은 아마도 언제 만나게 될 것 같은가?
(A) 오후 2시
(B) 오후 3시
(C) 오후 4시
(D) 오후 5시 30분

Questions 68-70 refer to the following conversation and inventory.
미W 미M

Inventory	
Item	Quantity
Dining table	6
Stool	5
Table cloth	2
Small-sized rug	7

W Wow! The sale was a huge success. 68 It looks like we sold out of several items. There are no more dining tables, stools, table cloths or small-sized rugs in the store displays.

M 68 According to the inventory, we still have some extras in the storeroom.

W That's good news. Can you restock the displays then? Put 5 of each of the missing items out. We'll need them just in case new customers come in next week.

M Okay. 69 But what if we don't have 5?

W 69 Then put out what we have and order more of those items right away. I just want to make sure we have the minimum that we need for now. 70 I will take complete inventory in a few weeks anyway.

M You've got it.

재고 목록	
품목	수량
식탁	6
의자	5
식탁보	2
작은 사이즈의 양탄자	7

여 와! 판매가 아주 성공적이에요. 우리의 여러 제품이 완판된 것으로 보입니다. 진열대에 식탁, 의자, 식탁보 또한 작은 사이즈의 양탄자들이 안 보이네요.

남 재고 목록에 따르면, 우리가 아직 창고에 재고를 좀 가지고 있어요.

여 좋은 소식이네요. 그럼 진열대를 다시 채워주시겠어요? 현재 보이지 않는 물건들을 5개씩 꺼내 주세요. 다음 주에 새로운 고객들이 혹시 올지 모르니까 우리가 그것들을 준비해 둬야 합니다.

남 네, 그런데 만약 우리에게 5개가 없다면 어떻게 하죠?

여 그럼 일단 가진 것들을 진열하고 모자라는 것들을 바로 주문해요. 저는 우리가 현재 필요한 최소량을 보유하고 있기를 원해요. 제가 몇 주 후에는 어쨌거나 완전히 완전히 재고 조사를 실시할 거예요.

남 네, 알겠습니다.

inventory 재고 목록　storeroom 창고　right away 바로

68 What are the speakers discussing?
(A) The duration of a promotional event
(B) The recent inventory
(C) Sales figures of a new product
(D) Strategies for promoting the business

화자들은 무엇에 관해 이야기하고 있는가?
(A) 판촉 행사 기간
(B) 최근 재고 목록
(C) 새로운 제품의 판매 수치
(D) 사업 홍보를 위한 전략

69 Look at the graphic. Which item will the man order right away?
(A) Dining table
(B) Stool
(C) Table cloth
(D) Small-sized rug

그래픽을 보시오. 어느 물건을 남자가 바로 주문하겠는가?
(A) 식탁
(B) 의자
(C) 식탁보
(D) 작은 사이즈의 양탄자

70 What does the woman say she will do in a few weeks?
(A) Make a list of items
(B) Repair a broken display
(C) Invite customers to the shop
(D) Promote an event

여자는 몇 주 후에 무엇을 할 것인가?
(A) 물건들의 목록을 만든다.
(B) 고장 난 전시물을 고친다.
(C) 고객들을 상점으로 초대한다.
(D) 행사를 홍보한다.

Part 4

Questions 71-73 refer to the following telephone message. [미M]

Hello, ⑦ this is Cal Khan calling from Poco Building Supplies. We processed the order you placed through our Web site yesterday but ⑫ I have a question about one of the items you asked for. You stated that you required 200 PVC window panels. Before we approve the delivery, I wanted to check the amount and confirm that you actually want 200 items and not 2 or 20. ⑬ Please email me to verify the quantity of items in your order. You can reach me on ckahn@pbsupplies.com. I'll be on the shop floor until the store closes tonight at 8 P.M. Thank you.

안녕하세요, 포코 빌딩 서플라이즈에서 전화하고 있는 칼 칸입니다. 우리는 어제 당신이 웹 사이트를 통해 주문한 것을 처리했지만, 당신이 요청한 물건들 중 하나에 대해 질문이 있습니다. 당신은 200개의 PVC 창문 판이 필요하다고 언급하셨습니다. 우리가 주문을 승인하기 전에 저는 양을 확인하고 당신이 실제로 2개나 20개가 아닌 200개를 원하는 전지 확실히 하고 싶었습니다. 당신의 주문에 있는 양의 맞는지 확인해 주기 위해 제게 이메일을 보내 주세요. 당신은 ckahn@pbsupplies.com으로 연락하시면 됩니다. 저는 오늘 밤 오후 8시에 가게 문을 닫을 때까지 생산 현장에 있을 것입니다. 감사합니다.

building supplies 건축 자재 state 언급하다 panel (문이나 벽에 붙이는 독재) 금속으로 된 사각형) 판 verify (맞는지) 확인하다, 입증하다 quantity 양 shop floor 생산 현장

71 Where does the speaker work?
화자는 어디에서 일하는가?
(A) At an accounting firm
(A) 회계법인
(B) At a construction materials supplier
(B) 건축 자재 공급업체
(C) At an office supply store
(C) 사무용품 매장
(D) At a window replacement company
(D) 창문 교체 회사

72 Why is the speaker calling?
화자가 전화하고 있는 이유는?
(A) To query an order
(A) 주문에 대해 물어보기 위해
(B) To offer a discount
(B) 할인을 제공하기 위해
(C) To explain shipment costs
(C) 배송 비용에 대해 설명하기 위해
(D) To cancel a delivery
(D) 배달을 취소하기 위해

73 What is the listener asked to do?
청자는 무엇을 하도록 요구받는가?
(A) Email a reply
(A) 이메일로 답변하기
(B) Return a phone call
(B) 전화 회신하기
(C) Check an estimate
(C) 견적서 확인하기
(D) Provide a credit card
(D) 신용 카드 제공하기

Questions 74-76 refer to the following tour information. [영M]

Hi! ⑭ I'm Hugh Dancy from Last Minute Cruises. Welcome to our cruise ship, The Age of the Ocean. This evening, we will be hosting a talent show as well as karaoke, which commences at 8 PM. Before that, ⑮ we have a gala barbecue on the Main Deck and ⑯ a special event, an after-dinner solo by international singer, Caitlin Mariel, who is a special guest on the ship for the summer season. Now if you follow me, we will settle you in.

안녕하세요! 저는 라스트 미닛 크루즈의 휴 댄시입니다. 저희 유람선 '에이지 오브 디 오션'에 오신 것을 환영합니다. 오늘 저녁, 저희는 오후 8시에 시작하는 가라오케뿐 아니라 장기자랑을 개최하겠습니다. 그 전에, 주 갑판에서 바비큐가 있고, 여름 시즌을 위해 배의 특별 손님으로 세계적인 가수 케이틀린 마리엘이 저녁 식사 후 솔로곡을 노래하는 특별 행사가 있습니다. 이제 저를 따라오시면 자리를 잡도록 도와 드릴 것입니다.

cruise ship 유람선 host 개최하다 talent show 장기자랑 A as well as B A뿐만 아니라 B karaoke 가라오케, 노래방 commence 개시하다, 시작하다 gala 경축 행사 main deck 주 갑판 settle in (새 집·직장 등에) 자리를 잡다(정착) park attendant 주차 단속 요원 welcome speech 환영사

74 Who most likely is the speaker?
화자는 누구일 것 같은가?
(A) A ship employee
(A) 선박 직원
(B) A local singer
(B) 지역 가수
(C) A park attendant
(C) 주차 단속 요원
(D) An entertainer
(D) 엔터테이너

75 According to the speaker, where will dinner be served?
화자에 따르면, 저녁 식사는 어디에서 제공될 것인가?
(A) On the beach
(A) 해변
(B) In the lobby
(B) 로비
(C) In the cafeteria
(C) 카페테리아
(D) On the deck
(D) 갑판 위

76 What will the listeners attend after dinner?
청자들은 저녁 식사 후에 무엇에 참석할 것인가?
(A) A play
(A) 연극
(B) A welcome speech
(B) 환영사
(C) A film
(C) 영화
(D) A concert
(D) 콘서트

Questions 77-79 refer to the following talk. (미W)

I hope you all benefit from our first ⑦ IT training session at Barrats. Remember that you can perform all of these tasks at your own workstations so don't forget to practice during your breaks. Before you leave the classroom, ⑦ please fill out the questionnaire that is given to each of you. We would like to know what you learned in the training and any further areas that you would like to cover in future training sessions. If you would like to be contacted about advanced classes, please ⑦ state your e-mail address on the test form and we will get back to you with a proposed timetable.

benefit 혜택을 보다, 도움을 받다 work station 작업 장소 practice 연습하다 questionnaire 설문지 further 추후의 advanced 상급의, 고급의 state 밝히다; 명하다, 쓰다 proposed 제안된 first aid 응급 처치 consent form 동의서

저는 여러분이 모두 배럿츠의 첫 IT 교육 과정에서 도움을 받을 수 있길 바랍니다. 당신의 직업 공간에서 이 모든 과제를 수행할 수 있다는 것을 기억하고, 휴식 시간에 연습하는 것을 잊지 마세요. 교실을 나가기 전에 여러분에게 나눠 준 설문지를 작성해 주시기 바랍니다. 우리는 여러분이 교육에서 무엇을 배웠는지, 그리고 추후 교육 시간에 더 다루면 좋겠다고 바라는 것들은 무엇인지를 알고 싶습니다. 만약 당신이 상급 수업에 관해 연락을 받고 싶다면, 당신의 이메일 주소를 시험지 위에 적으면 우리가 예정 시간표와 함께 연락드리겠습니다.

77 What have listeners been learning?
(A) New employee orientation
(B) Technology training
(C) First aid in the office
(D) Improving production techniques

청자들은 무엇을 배워 왔는가?
(A) 신입 직원 오리엔테이션
(B) 기술 교육
(C) 사무실 내의 응급 처치
(D) 제작 기법 향상

78 What does the speaker ask listeners to complete?
(A) A questionnaire
(B) A timetable
(C) A consent form
(D) A test

화자는 청자들이 무엇을 완료하기를 요구하는가?
(A) 설문지
(B) 시간표
(C) 동의서
(D) 시험

79 Why would listeners provide an e-mail address?
(A) To receive a list of advanced classes
(B) To apply for employment opportunities
(C) To cancel a reservation
(D) To get details of trainer's notes

청자들이 이메일 주소를 제공하게 되는 이유는?
(A) 상급 수업의 목록을 받기 위해
(B) 고용 기회에 지원하기 위해
(C) 예약을 취소하기 위해
(D) 강사의 메모의 세부 내용을 얻기 위해

corporate 기업의 consultancy service 상담 서비스 expert 전문적인 consultation 상담 dedicated 헌신적인 individual 개인의, 개별의 consultant 상담사 skilled with ~에 숙련된

Questions 80-82 refer to the following advertisement. (미M)

Do you have a corporate sales business in the Sao Paulo region? ⑧ Do you often require training and consultancy services? Sales Training is here to assist. We provide expert consultation packages by the day, week or month. You will have a dedicated expert individual consultant for your organization, skilled with the latest corporate knowledge. Book one of our trainers today to take advantage of this new service. We provide training for staff in sales techniques, customer service and ⑧ we have recently added online selling. Also, if you are in the sales business in the Rio area, visit our Web site now to see ⑧ our new facility to open next month. Find us on the web at www.salestraining.com.

귀하는 상파울루 지역에 판매 기업을 가지고 계십니까? 교육 훈련과 상담 서비스를 자주 필요로 하세요? 세일즈 트레이닝이 도움을 주러 이곳에 있습니다. 저희는 전문적인 상담 패키지를 일일, 주간, 월별로 제공하고 있습니다. 귀하는 귀하의 사업체를 위한 헌신적인 개별 전문 상담사를 만날 수 있습니다. 이 새로운 서비스를 이용하기 위해 저희 트레이너 중 한 명을 예약하세요. 저희는 판매 기법과 교객 서비스에 대한 직원 훈련을 제공하고, 최근에는 온라인 판매를 추가해 놓았습니다. 또한, 만약 귀하가 리오 지역에 판매 사업을 하고 있다면, 다음 달에 개장할 새 시설을 확인하러 지금 저희 웹 사이트에 방문해 주세요. 웹 사이트 주소는 www. salestraining.com입니다.

80 What is being advertised?
(A) Retail opportunities
(B) Offices for hire
(C) Sports training
(D) Sales consulting

무엇이 광고되고 있는가?
(A) 소매업 기회
(B) 임대용 사무실
(C) 스포츠 훈련
(D) 판매 상담

81 What new service did the company recently add?
(A) Internet selling
(B) Web page design
(C) Facility management
(D) Mail handling

회사가 최근에 추가한 새 서비스는?
(A) 인터넷 판매
(B) 웹 페이지 디자인
(C) 시설 경영
(D) 우편 취급

82 What will happen next month?
(A) Prices will increase.
(B) More staff will be recruited.
(C) A new location will open.
(D) An online seminar will be offered.

다음 달에 무슨 일이 있을 것인가?
(A) 가격이 오를 것이다.
(B) 더 많은 직원들이 채용될 것이다.
(C) 새 지점이 개장할 것이다.
(D) 온라인 세미나가 제공될 것이다.

Questions 83-85 refer to the following excerpt from a talk. 영W

Next, I've got some thrilling news. ⓑ Our digital illustration company is going to begin work in a brand-new field of industry. We will be entering the fitness and sports business. In fact, ⓑ we've just signed the deal this morning to create cartoon characters for Health Comes First, a fitness company based in Hamburg. This means that ⓑ we'll be spending the next few weeks creating animated characters to show our new customers.

다음으로, 제가 신나는 소식을 갖고 있습니다. 우리 디지털 일러스트 회사가 새로운 산업 분야에서 일을 시작할 것입니다. 우리는 건강 관리와 스포츠 사업에 진출할 것입니다. 사실, 우리는 함부르크에 본사를 둔 건강 관리 회사인 헬스 컴스 퍼스트를 위한 만화 캐릭터를 제작하겠다는 계약서에 오늘 아침 서명했습니다. 이는 우리가 새 고객에게 보여 줄 만화 캐릭터를 제작하기 위해 앞으로 몇 주를 보낸다는 것을 의미합니다.

thrilling 신나는 illustration 삽화 brand new 새로운 field 분야 enter 들어서다; 진출하다 sign a deal 계약을 맺다 create 제작하다, 만들다 cartoon 만화 based in ~에 본사를 둔 animated 만화 영화로 된 launch 출시하다

83 What kind of company does the speaker work for?
(A) A retail store
(B) A packaging company
(C) A fitness corporation
(D) An illustration company

화자는 어떤 종류의 회사를 위해 일하는가?
(A) 소매점
(B) 포장 회사
(C) 건강 관리 기업
(D) 삽화 회사

84 What has the company recently done?
(A) Moved to Germany
(B) Opened a new branch
(C) Signed a contract
(D) Launched a new product range

회사가 최근에 한 일은?
(A) 독일로 이전
(B) 새 지사 개장
(C) 계약에 서명
(D) 새 제품군 출시

85 According to the speaker, what will listeners do over the next few weeks?
(A) Recruit new employees
(B) Design a building
(C) Prepare work samples
(D) Join a health club

화자에 따르면, 청자들은 앞으로 몇 주 동안 무엇을 할 것인가?
(A) 신입 직원 모집하기
(B) 건물 설계하기
(C) 견본 준비하기
(D) 헬스클럽 가입하기

Questions 86-88 refer to the following advertisement. 호M

Energy costs are on the rise. That's why smart consumers are shifting to Ultimate Solar Heating Systems. ⓑ Our systems utilize the power of the sun to heat your home and provide you with hot water constantly. ⓑ You might be surprised to know that after paying for the installation, you will need to pay almost nothing to use and maintain an Ultimate Solar Heating System. That's right. You will see your heating and hot water utility bills disappear. Plus, if you order a system with us, we will provide you with a free energy inspection of your home, a service that our competitors charge at least $300 to do. So give us a call today and find out how we can help you save money. This is as good as it gets. Call us at 555-7828.

에너지 비용이 상승하고 있습니다. 그것이 바로 현명한 소비자들이 얼티밋 솔라 히팅 시스템으로 전환하고 있는 이유입니다. 저희 시스템은 태양 에너지를 이용하여 당신의 집에 난방과 뜨거운 물을 지속적으로 제공합니다. 당신은 설치비를 지불하시고 나서는 놀라실 수도 있는데 얼티밋 솔라 히팅 시스템을 이용하고 유지하는 데 들어가는 비용이 거의 없기 때문입니다. 맞습니다. 당신은 당신의 난방비와 뜨거운 물에 대한 청구서가 사라지는 것을 알게 되실 겁니다. 게다가 저희에게 시스템을 주문하시면, 저희는 당신의 집에 대해 무료로 에너지 검사를 제공해 드립니다. 이는 우리의 경쟁업체가 최소한 300달러에 제공하고 있는 서비스이죠. 그래서, 오늘 전화하셔서 저희가 어떻게 여러분들이 비용을 절약해 드리는지에 관해 확인해 보세요. 이보다 더 나은 조건은 없습니다. 555-7828로 전화주세요.

shift 바꾸다, 전환하다 utilize 활용하다, 이용하다 constantly 지속적으로 utility bill 공과금 inspection 검사 insulation 단열 공과금이 없음

86 What products are being discussed?
(A) Solar cells
(B) Heating systems
(C) Computer programs
(D) Home insulation

어떤 제품들이 논의되고 있는가?
(A) 태양 전지
(B) 난방 시스템
(C) 컴퓨터 프로그램
(D) 주택 단열

87 According to the speaker, what might surprise listeners about these products?
(A) They are cheap to install.
(B) They are selling very well.
(C) They cost little to maintain.
(D) They teach directions to use.

화자에 따르면, 제품들에 관한 무엇이 청자들을 놀라게 할 수도 있는가?
(A) 설치 비용이 저렴하다.
(B) 아주 잘 팔린다.
(C) 유지 비용이 거의 들지 않는다.
(D) 스스로 사용 방법을 알려 준다.

88 What does the speaker mean when he says, "This is as good as it gets"?
(A) The system is in good condition.
(B) He can't make the system better.
(C) His staff is very knowledgeable.
(D) He thinks he is offering a good deal.

화자가 "이보다 더 나은 조건은 없습니다"라고 말한 것은 무엇을 의미하는가?
(A) 시스템이 좋은 상태이다.
(B) 그는 시스템을 더 좋게 만들 수 없다.
(C) 그의 직원들이 아주 해박하다.
(D) 그는 아주 좋은 조건을 제공한다고 생각한다.

Questions 89-91 refer to the following telephone message. (호W)

Hi, Kevin. **89** This is Mary from City Residence. We met last week when you signed the rental contract for a two-bedroom apartment in the building I manage. Well, I know that I said you could move in before the end of this month. But I have to say that's not an option anymore. While performing an inspection of the unit you will be renting, it was determined that the flooring and the refrigerator need to be replaced. **90** So it will take us a bit longer to make those upgrades. I promise that the unit will be ready by the first of next month. **91** If we are able to have it ready a day or two early, I will certainly let you know. I'm sorry things didn't work out as I had promised.

안녕하세요, 케빈. 저는 시티 레지던스의 매리입니다. 우리는 지난주에 제가 관리하는 건물에 있는 방이 두 개 있는 아파트에 대한 임대 계약을 할 때 만났습니다. 제가 이번 달 말 전에 당신이 이곳으로 이사를 올 수 있다고 말한 것을 기억하고 있어요. 그런데 그렇게 할 수 없을 거 같아요. 당신이 임대하게 될 방에 대한 검사를 진행하는 동안 바닥재와 냉장고를 교체해야 된다는 결정이 내려졌습니다. 그래서 이런 작업을 하는 데에 시간이 좀 더 필요할 것 같습니다. 당신의 방이 다음 달 1일까지는 준비가 될 수 있도록 약속드리겠습니다. 만약 하루나 이틀 정도 더 성향이 진행되지 않은 부분에 대해 죄송하다는 말씀을 드립니다.

rental contract 임대 계약 inspection 조사 contractor 시공업자 lease 임대 계약 terminate 종료하다

89 Who is the speaker?
화자는 누구인가?
(A) A building manager
(B) A contractor
(C) A mover
(D) An inspector
(A) 건물 관리인
(B) 시공업자
(C) 이사업체 직원
(D) 검사관

---

90 What does the woman mean when she says, "that's not an option anymore"?
여자가 "그렇게 할 수 없을 거 같아요"라고 말한 것은 무엇을 의미하는가?
(A) A service is no longer available.
(B) A lease has been terminated.
(C) A building failed to pass inspection.
(D) A date needs to be changed.
(A) 서비스가 더 이상 불가하다.
(B) 임대 계약이 종료되었다.
(C) 건물이 검사를 통과하지 못했다.
(D) 날짜가 변경되어야 한다.

91 What does the woman offer to do?
여자는 무엇을 해 주겠다고 하는가?
(A) Arrange a moving service
(B) Contact the listener under certain conditions
(C) Supervise an installation
(D) Give a discount
(A) 이사 서비스를 준비해 준다.
(B) 특정한 조건 하에 청자에게 연락한다.
(C) 설치를 감독한다.
(D) 할인을 해 준다.

Questions 92-94 refer to the following telephone message and receipt. (호M)

Receipt	
Doughnut	$1.75
Chocolate cake	$2.50
Apple pie	$3.00
Pastry	$4.25
Total	$11.50

Hi. This is Paulo. I bought some bread from your bakery about half an hour ago. **93** Well, when I got home, I realized that one of the items that I bought —an apple pie, — **92** was not in my shopping bag, but there is a charge for it on my receipt. The cashier probably forgot to put it in my shopping bag. Could you kindly see if it is still there? If not, could I stop by and get a replacement? I need it to prepare a small dinner party. **94** Please let me know as soon as possible. My name, again, is Paulo. My number is 555-3457. I look forward to hearing from you.

영수증	
도넛	1.75달러
초콜릿 케이크	2.50달러
애플 파이	3.00달러
페스트리	4.25달러
합계	11.50달러

안녕하세요. 저는 파울로입니다. 제가 30분쯤 전에 당신의 빵집에서 빵을 좀 구매했습니다. 그런데 집에 도착했을 때 제가 구매한 빵 중의 하나인 애플 파이가 제 쇼핑백에 들어 있지 않다는 것을 알게 되었어요. 그러나 제 영수증에는 청구가 되어 있네요. 아마도 계산원이 제 기방에 집어넣는 것을 잊었나 봅니다. 혹시 아직 거기 있는지 한 번 봐 주실래요? 만약 없다면, 제가 잠깐 들러서 대체품으로 가져가도 될까요? 제가 오늘 소규모로 저녁 파티를 준비해야 해서 그 파이가 필요하거든요. 가능한 한 빨리 제게 알려주세요. 제 이름은 파울로입니다. 제 번호는 555-3457이에요. 연락을 기다리고 있겠습니다.

replacement 교체, 대체물

Actual Test 01   016 • 017

improve 개선하다   purifier 정화 장치   pay off 성과를 올리다   flat 평평한
incentive 인센티브, 장려금

92 Why is the speaker calling?
(A) To cancel an order
(B) To report a missing item
(C) To arrange a delivery
(D) To request a refund
화자는 왜 전화하고 있는가?
(A) 주문을 취소하기 위해
(B) 잃어버린 물건을 알리기 위해
(C) 배송을 준비하기 위해
(D) 환불을 요청하기 위해

93 Look at the graphic. What is the price of the item the speaker refers to?
(A) $1.75
(B) $2.50
(C) $3.00
(D) $4.25
그래픽을 보시오. 화자가 언급하는 물건의 가격은 얼마인가?
(A) 1.75달러
(B) 2.50달러
(C) 3.00달러
(D) 4.25달러

94 What does the speaker want the listener to do?
(A) Get in touch with him
(B) Give him a refund
(C) Email the list
(D) Upgrade the shipping method
화자는 청자가 무엇을 하기를 원하는가?
(A) 남자에게 연락하기
(B) 남자에게 환불해 주기
(C) 리스트를 이메일로 보내기
(D) 배송 방법을 업그레이드하기

Questions 95-97 refer to the following excerpt from a meeting and chart. 🔊W

Sales(millions)
1st quarter 2nd quarter 3rd quarter 4th quarter

I want to move on to some good news. ⑨⑤ I know all of you worked very hard to improve the design of our company's line of water purifiers. Well, it appears that your hard work paid off. If you look at the chart by the sales division, you can see that the month after the new designs were released onto the market, sales started to rise. ⑨⑥ For the first six months of the year, they had been flat at around $100 million. Then, they jumped by $200 million during the month of the release and have continued to increase since then. You've done a great job, everyone! To celebrate, I would like to invite all of you out to Marilyn Hotel this Friday evening. ⑨⑦ Dinner is on me!

95 Where most likely does the speaker work?
(A) At a phone company
(B) At an accounting firm
(C) At a lighting maker
(D) At an appliance manufacturer
화자는 아마도 어디서 일하는 것 같은가?
(A) 전화 회사
(B) 회계 회사
(C) 조명 제조업체
(D)가전제품 제조업체

96 Look at the graphic. When did the company release the new products?
(A) 1st quarter
(B) 2nd quarter
(C) 3rd quarter
(D) 4th quarter
그래픽을 보시오. 언제 회사가 새로운 제품들을 출시했는가?
(A) 1분기
(B) 2분기
(C) 3분기
(D) 4분기

97 What does the speaker say she will do for the listeners?
(A) Treat them to dinner
(B) Give them a financial incentive
(C) Present an award
(D) Let them take a vacation
화자는 청자들을 위해 무엇을 할 것이라고 이야기하는가?
(A) 저녁을 대접한다.
(B) 금전적인 혜택을 준다.
(C) 상을 준다.
(D) 휴가를 준다.

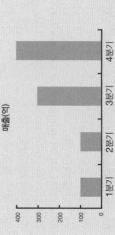

매출(억)
1분기 2분기 3분기 4분기

이제 좋은 소식을 전해드리겠습니다. 저는 여러분들이 우리 회사의 정수기 제품군의 디자인을 개선하기 위해서 아주 열심히 일을 했다는 것을 잘 알고 있습니다. 여러분들이 노고가 성과를 올리고 있는 것으로 보여집니다. 영업부서 바로 옆에 있는 차트를 보시면, 우리의 새로운 디자인이 시장에 풀린 다음 달부터 매출이 증가하기 시작했다는 것을 알 수 있습니다. 올해 상반기 동안에는 매출이 1억 달러로 매출이 2억 달러로 대략 상승했고, 그때부터 지속적으로 증가해 왔습니다. 여러분 모두 수고하셨습니다. 이를 축하하기 위해 이번 주 금요일 저녁에 여러분 모두를 마릴린 호텔로 초대합니다. 저녁은 모두 제가 사겠습니다!

Questions 98-100 refer to the following radio broadcast and map.
혼M

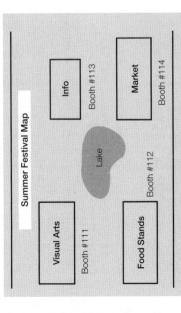

Summer Festival Map

Visual Arts
Booth #111

Info
Booth #113

Lake

Market
Booth #114

Food Stands
Booth #112

Before we get back to listening to the music, I want to remind you that this weekend is the 10th annual Summer Festival. It will take place on Saturday from 9 A.M. to 10 P.M. in Bryant Park. It's a great place to see the work of artists, both locals and those from out of town. You can also sample food from a variety of restaurants. Plus, there will be great musical performances. That's what I am looking forward to most of all. Be sure to stop by to meet your favorite Rock musicians broadcasting live during the fair. 98 99 Our booth will be next to the information tent on the eastern side of the lake. 100 For more information, visit the festival's Web site at www. summerfestival.org. There, you can download maps and a schedule of performances.

broadcast 방송하다   challenging 도전적인, 어려운   certificate 증명서

98 What does the speaker say about the Summer Festival?
(A) He plans to attend it.
(B) There is not much room to park cars.
(C) He will perform there.
(D) He is one of the sponsors.

화자는 여름 축제에 대해 무엇을 언급하는가?
(A) 그는 행사에 참여할 예정이다.
(B) 주차 장소가 충분하지 않다.
(C) 그는 행사에서 공연할 것이다.
(D) 그는 스폰서 중 한 명이다.

99 Look at the graphic. Where will the radio station be broadcasting from?
(A) Booth #111
(B) Booth #112
(C) Booth #113
(D) Booth #114

그래픽을 보시오. 라디오 방송은 어디서 진행되겠는가?
(A) 부스 번호 111
(B) 부스 번호 112
(C) 부스 번호 113
(D) 부스 번호 114

100 According to the speaker, what can listeners do at the Summer Festival's Web site?
(A) Buy tickets
(B) Reserve seats
(C) Get a certificate
(D) Obtain maps

화자에 따르면, 청자들은 여름 축제 웹 사이트에서 무엇을 할 수 있는가?
(A) 티켓을 구매한다.
(B) 좌석을 예매한다.
(C) 증명서를 받는다.
(D) 지도를 얻는다.

여름 축제 지도
시각 예술 부스 번호 111
정보 부스 번호 113
호수
음식 가판대 부스 번호 112
시장 부스 번호 114

다시 음악 감상을 하시기 전에, 이번 주말에 10번째 연례 여름 축제가 있을 것임을 상기시켜 드리고 싶습니다. 행사는 토요일 오전 9시부터 오후 10시까지 브라이언트 공원에서 열립니다. 그 공원은 지역 내외를 불문한 다양한 예술가들의 작품을 볼 수 있는 훌륭한 장소입니다. 여러분들은 또한 다양한 식당들의 음식을 시식해 보실 수 있습니다. 게다가 아주 멋진 음악 공연도 있을 것입니다. 저는 그 공연들이 무엇보다 가장 기대되는 부분입니다. 이 행사 기간 동안에 막 방문하셔서 라이브로 방송되는 여러분들이 가장 좋아하는 음악가들을 만나 보세요. 저희 부스는 호수 의 동쪽 편에 자리하고 있는 인포메이션 텐트 바로 옆에 있습니다. 더 많은 정보를 원하신다면, 축제 웹 사이트인 www.summerfestival. org로 방문하시면 됩니다. 거기서 행사 장소 지도와 공연 스케줄을 다운받아 보실 수 있습니다.

Part 5

101 해설 빈칸은 관사(the) 뒤에 funding과 함께 '재정 지원 결정'이라는 의미 명사가 되어야 하므로 (B)가 정답이다. deciding은 '라는 의미 명사가 되므로 decide를 수식하는 동사로, 명사와 함께 복합명사로 쓸 수 없다.

이모티 매니지먼트의 경영진들은 연구 부서 팀의 재정 지원 결정을 옹호하기로 결정했다.

executive 경영진 uphold 옹호하다; 인정하다 funding 재정 지원
자금 제공 research 연구

102 해설 before 뒤에 오면서 목적어(the workplace)를 받아 쓸 수 있는 것은 동명사 (C)이다. before는 전치사 혹은 부사절 접속 사로 뒤에 -ing 형태를 쓸 수 있다.

에너지를 보존하기 위해 작업장을 떠나기 전에 전기 기구의 스위치를 끄세요.

conserve 보존하다 switch off (스위치 등을 눌러서) 끄다 electrical appliance 전기 기구 workplace 작업장

103 해설 명사 어휘 문제로 문맥상 '구체적인 조언을 들을 수 있는 기회가 지년스러우므로 정답은 (B)이다.

내세설 페인팅 엔 데코레이팅 소는 숙련된 공예가들로부터 구체적인 조언을 들을 수 있는 기회를 특징으로 한다.

decorate 장식하다 feature 특별히 포함하다, 특징으로 삼다 specific 구체적인, 세부적인 craftsman 공예가

104 해설 일맞은 전치사를 고르는 문제로 문맥상 '관리 회계사 자리에 공석이 있다'가 자연스러우므로 정답은 (B)이다. '~대한 공석이'라는 표현 vacancy for를 알아 두자. across(~에 걸쳐), through(통과하여), off(떨어져, 벗어나), into도 자주 출제되는 전치사들이다.

KKL 그룹은 경력이 풍부한 관리 회계사 자리에 공석이 있다.
have a vacancy 공석이 있다 experienced 경험이 있는, 능숙한 management accountant 관리 회계사

105 해설 숙어 be likely to부정사 정답은 (B)로 고를 수 있다. likely는 생김새와 달리 형용사로 쓰이므로 꼭 외워 두자.

국내 소비의 급증으로 인해 이번 분기에는 금여가 독일이 유지될 것 같다.
plunge 급락 consumption 소비

106 해설 전치사 문제로 '월말까지'라는 해석이 어울리므로 정답의 후보는 by와 until이다. by는 일사적으로 완료되는 행위(complete, register, pay, submit)와 어울려 쓰고, until을 지속되는 행위 (wait, stay, continue)와 어울려 쓰는 것을 알아 두자. 정답은 (A) by이다.

루카스 씨는 전체적인 세션 프로그램이 월말까지 연료될 것으로 예측했다.

forecast 예측하다 entire 전체의 regeneration (정신적·도덕적인) 갱생 신생

107 해설 빈칸 뒤에 목적어 역할을 하는 명사 broadband connection이 있으므로 빈칸 앞에 쓰이는 소유격 자리이다. theme은 목적어 자리에, theirs는 소유 대명사로 주어, 목적어, 보어 자리에, they도 주어 자리에 오므로 명사 앞에는 따라서 정답은 (D)이다.

최근 설문조는 온라인 고객의 50퍼센트 이상이 길은 회사에서 광대역 접속 서비스를 갱신할 계획이라는 것을 보여 주었다.

questionnaire 설문지 reveal 공개하다, 보여 주다 renew 갱신하다
전기 기구 broadband connection 광대역 접속

108 해설 뒤에 목적어가 없으므로 자동사가 들어가야 한다. 또한 자동사로 쓰이는 타동사이므로 정답은 when이다. 보기 3, 4형식으로 쓰이는 타동사이고 mention은 3형식 타동사이다. inform(알리다)은 바로 뒤에 일일 대상을 놓는 3, 4형식 동사이다. 정답은 자동사인 (C) speak이다.

고객 서비스 직원에게 이야기하기 위해서는 이 양식 아래에 있는 번호로 전화를 걸어 주세요.

representative 직원

109 해설 Even though가 이끄는 절이 끝나고, 빈칸은 새로운 주절의 주어가 들어갈 자리이다. 인청대명사 중에서 주어 자리에 들어갈 수 있는 것은 주격(she)과 소유대명사(hers)인데, 의미상 '그녀가 그녀의 것보다 어울리므로 정답은 주격인 (A) she이다.

오나이씨스 씨는 이번 주 세미나에는 참석할 수 없지만, 다음 주에는 모든 부서 매니저들과 함께 참석할 것이다.

along with ~와 함께

110 해설 help의 목적격 보어가 들어갈 자리이다. help가 동사원형과 to부정사를 모두 목적어로 취할 수 있으므로 정답은 동사인 (C) diversify이다.

타이탄 산업을 인수한 것은 파이퍼 홀딩스가 사업 전략을 다각화하는 데 도움이 될 것이다.

acquisition 인수

111 해설 선택지 네 개가 모두 형용사이므로 해석으로 푸는 문제이다. superior(우수한), exemplary(모범적인), cautious(조심성 있 느는 모두 의미상 맞지 않으므로 정답은 (C) vulnerable(취약한)이다. 참고로 be vulnerable to(~에 취약하다, 민감하다)를 관용 표현으로 외워 두자.

최신 보안 소프트웨어가 없으면, 컴퓨터 시스템은 수많은 바이러스에 취약하다.

루카스 씨는 전체적인 세션 프로그램이 월말까지 연료될 것으로 예측했다.

112 해설 빈칸 앞에 자동사 react가 있으므로 부사인 (B)가 가장 적절하다. prompt는 명사, 형용사 혹은 동사이고, prompting은 동명사나 분사, promptness는 명사이므로 동사를 수식할 수 없 있는데 모두 전치사 to와 함께이므로 쓰는 것을 알아 두자.

엘리어스 스토어의 경비원은 의심스러운 우편물에 대한 직원들이 우려 에 즉시 대응했다.

security department 경비실 react 반응하다, 대응하다 prompt 즉각적인 suspicious 의심스러운, 미심쩍은 promptly 즉시

113 해설 접속사 수식 문제로 Travelers ~ identification까지 필 수 성분을 모두 갖춘 완전한 문장이므로 빈칸 ~ flights까지는 수 식 역할을 한다. 빈칸 뒤에 -ing 형태를 받으면서 수식하는 것은 전치사와 부사절 접속사이므로 정답의 후보는 although, when 이다. 문맥상 국내선을 탑승할 때가 적절하므로 (D)가 정답이 다. although는 의미상 적절하지 않고, in addition은 부사로 다. such as는 앞 명사의 구체적인 예를 제시할때 사용하므로 적절 하지 않다.

appropriate 적절한 identification 신분증 board 탑승하다
domestic flight 국내선

여행객들은 국내선에 탑승할 때 적절한 신분증을 꼭 보여 줘야 한다.

114 해설 be동사 뒤에 올 수 있는 것은 형용사나 형용사이며, 부사 too 뒤에 올 수 있는 형용사 narrow와 비교급 narrower 중에서 모 맥상 '도로가 너무 좁기 때문에'가 적절하므로 (A)가 정답이다. narrowly는 부사, narrowst는 동사이므로 보어 역할을 할 수 없 다.

장거리 대형 트럭 운전자들을 도로가 너무 좁기 때문에 파크 애비뉴의 출입이 금지된다.

long-distance 장거리의 lorry 대형 트럭 forbidden 금지된
narrowly 가까스로, 간신히

115 해설 빈칸은 명사구를 이끄는 전치사 자리이다. close와 next는 형용사/부사로 쓰이는 단어이므로 오답이다. 전치사인 near(~ 근처에)와 besides(~외에) 중에서 의미상 어울리는 것은 (A) near 이다. 참고로 besides는 부사로 쓰일 때는 '게다가'라는 의미로 쓰인다.

이코호 인터내셔널의 본사는 스프링힐의 우체국 근처에 위치해 있다.

headquarters 본사

116 해설 경영 적품을 좀 더 평가해야 한다는 것은 승진가 결정되지 않았다는 말이므로 정답은 (A) decided이다.

승자가 아직 결정되지 않았기 때문에 심사위원들은 경쟁 적품들을 좀 더 평가해야 할 것이다.

judge 심사위원 assess 평가하다 entry 출품작

117 해설 부사 어휘 문제로 정관로 '당신의 이름으로 대기 명단에 올라갈 것이다'가 적절하므로 (B)가 가장 정답이다.

만약 당신이 지엔한 대화에 정원이 명단에 당신의 이름은 자동으로 올라갈 것이다. 생황 경우를 대비한 대기자 명단 in case ~할 경우를 대비하여 drop out 중퇴하다 intermittently 간헐적으로 progressively 계속적으로 considerably 상당히

waiting list 대기자 명단

118 해설 전치사 뒤에 올 수 있는 것은 명사이므로 정답의 후보는 replacement와 replacing이다. 둘 중에 뒤에 목적어 old buses를 받을 수 있는 것은 동명사인 (B)이다. replaced(대체된), 교체된는 형용사로 뒤에 명사를 수식할 수 있으나 '더 연료 효율성이 뛰어나 교체된 오래된 버스들로'라는 의미가 되므로 적절하지 않다. 'A를 B로 교체하다'라는 의미로 replace A with B도 알아 두자.

오래된 버스들을 새롭고 더 연료 효율성이 뛰어난 모델로 교체함으로 써, 캐나딕은 유지 보수비와 수리비를 절약할 수 있었다.

fuel-efficient 연료 효율적인, 연료 절약형인 maintenance 유지 보수 replacement 대체, 교체

119 해설 명사 어휘 문제로 문맥상 심사 위원단에게 수신되어야 하는 것은 올해의 예술가 추천이므로 알맞은 선택지는 (D)이다.

올해의 예술가 추천은 심사 위원단에게 알맞은 오후 3시 전에 수신되어야 한다.

judging committee 심사 위원단 authority 권한; 권위; 권위자 occurrence 발생 존재 nomination 지명, 추천

120 해설 조동사(can)는 동사원형(look forward to) 사이는 부사 자리이다. another, any는 형용사, 대명사이고 which는 관계대 명사/부사로 쓰이는 단어이므로 오답이다. 대명사, 대명사 부사 자리에 쓰일 때는 '운동,' 부사로 쓰일 때는 '게다가'라는 의미로 쓰이므로 (B)가 정답이다.

뛰어난 판매 기록 덕분에 우리 판매원들은 모두 이번 달에 보너스를 기대할 수 있게 되었다.

record 기록 sales executive 판매원

121 해설 선택지 모두 p.p이므로 해석으로 풀어야 하는 문제이다. total은 '합계를 내다', alleviate는 '완화시키다', consist는 전치 사 of와 함께 쓰여 '~로 구성되다'의 의미로 모두 의미상 맞지 않다. 배운 명사로는 '청구서'의 의미지만, 동사로는 '모사하다'의 의 미가 있음을 알아 두자. 따라서 정답은 (C) billed이다.

리차드 K. 노스의 미스터리 소설이 〈하우스 인 더 미스트〉는 10년 동안의 최고의 소설로 묘사되어 왔다.

total 합계를 내다 alleviate 완화시키다 bill 묘사하다

122 해설 빈칸이 이끄는 부분(~ appliance까지)에는 동사가 없기 때문에 절이 아니라 분사구문(given)으로 축약된 구조로 보아야 한 다. 따라서 부사절 접속사인 (C) when이 정답이다.

대부분의 소비자들은 새 가전제품과 고품질의 가전제품 사이에서 선택 권이 주어졌을 때 상품의 품질을 우선시한다.

123 해설 be pleased to부정사(~하게 되어서 기쁘다)를 숙어로 외워 두자. 여기서 to부정사는 부사 역할로서 감정의 원인을 나타내는 to부정사로 쓰인 것이다. 비슷한 표현으로 be delighted to 도 알아 두자. 따라서 정답은 (A)이다.

하퍼드 파이낸셜은 단골 고객들에게 이 지역에서 이용 가능한 최고의 컨설팅 서비스를 제공하게 되어서 기쁩니다.

loyal customer 단골 손님

124 해설 가정법 if절 안에 과거완료시제(had agreed)가 쓰였으므로, 주절에는 조동사의 과거완료시제(B와 D) 중에 수동태 형태인 (A)가 없으므로 빈칸 뒤에 목적어가 없으므로 빈칸 뒤에 형태인 (D) would have been sent가 정답이다.

만약 복스 테크 시가 계약을 체결하는 것에 동의했었더라면, 필요한 자금이 보내졌을 테인요.

125 해설 When 또는 By the time절 안에 과거시제가 있을 때, 주 절에는 똑같이 과거시제나 과거완료시제가 와야 한다. (C) were spreads는 시제는 맞지만, 수가 맞지 않으므로 오답이다. 따라서 정답은 (D) had spread이다. 참고로 When 또는 By the time 절 안에 현재시제가 있을 때는 실제로는 미래를 의미하는 것이므 로, 주절에 미래/미래완료시제가 와야 한다.

바드시도 레인의 화재가 보고되었을 때쯤에, 그 불은 인근 지역까지 퍼 진 상태였다.

126 해설 형용사 어휘 문제로 문맥상 '유명한 화가'인 제임스 매닝이 가장 자연스러우므로 (A)가 정답이다. distinguished는 '구별된' 으로 해석될 수도 있지만 '유명한, 뛰어난'이라는 의미도 있다는 것 을 알아두자.

8월에 코너스 갤러리는 유명한 화가인 제임스 매닝의 많은 작품을 전시 할 것이다.

distinguished 유명한 founded 설립된 estimated 추정된 allocated 할당된

127 해설 문장에 동사가 두 개(was scheduled와 was put off) 있 으므로 빈칸에는 접속사가 들어가야 한다. 선택지에서 접속사로 쓰일 수 없는 (B) this도 오답이다. 나머지 선택지는 모두 접속사 인데, (D) that은 콤마 뒤에 쓸 수 없으므로 오답, (C) what은 명 사절 접속사로서 명사(The training) 뒤에 쓸 수 없으므로 오답이다. 빈칸이 이끄는 절은 명사를 뒤에서 수식하는 형용사절이 므로 형용사절 접속사로 쓰일 수 있는 (A) which가 정답이다.

6월 20일에 시작될 예정이었던 훈련은 3주 동안 연기되었다.

put off 연기하다

128 해설 빈칸 뒤에 절이 있으므로 접속사가 들어갈 자리이다. (B) nevertheless는 부사, (C) regardless of는 전치사이므로 오답 이다. (A)와 (D) 중에서 의미상 '~라고 할지라도'를 뜻하는 (A)가 정답이다.

내일 전산스 공원에서 열릴 음악 축제들은 오늘 밤 날이 개더 라도 그 행사를 연기할 것을 고려하고 있다.

129 해설 수동태(be p.p.) 동사 뒤에 형용사(unreliable)가 남아 있는 것으로 보아 빈칸에는 형용사를 목적격 보어로 취하는 5형식 동사 가 들어가야 한다. 따라서 정답은 (C) deemed(간주되는)이다.

클리머짓 정수기는 올 여름 성공적이었지만, 품질 기준 협회에 의해서 신뢰할 수 없는 것으로 간주되었다.

bank account 은행 계좌 fee 요금 비용 statement 명세서, 내역 payment 지불(액) revise 수정하다 accordingly 그에 따라, 적절히 guarantee 보증하다 sign up for ~을 신청하다, ~에 등록하다 automatic debit 자동 이체 결제 amount due 지불해야 할 금액 on a regular basis 정기적으로 of good standing 신용도가 높은 reimburse 환급하다 waive 철회하다, 보류하다

unreliable 신뢰할 수 없는

130

해설 동사 어휘 문제로 문맥상 '소음 문제와 씨름해야 했다고 보고했다'는 내용이므로 고생하다가 가장 자연스러우므로 정답은 (C)이다.

센드린 빌딩의 몇몇 세입자들은 종종 많은 소음 문제와 씨름해야 했다고 보고했다.

tenant 세입자 report 신고하다, 보고하다 put forth 내뻗다 contend with (문제와) 씨름하다 aspire to ~을 갈망하다

Part 6

문제집 P29

[131-134]

수신: service@blueoceanair.com
발신: james.gimbel@cmail.com
제목: 예약 오류

안녕하세요, 저는 제임스 김벨입니다. 제가 시드니에서 워싱턴으로 가는 비행편을 7월 12일 화요일에 예약했어요, 아내와의 10주년 기념일을 축축하기 위해서 워싱턴으로 동이갈 계획이었거든요. **131** 예약 번호는 5774001입니다. 7월 15일 출발일에 제가 공항에 한 시간 일찍 도착했어요. 그리고 **132** 독서 블루오션 항공사의 체크인 키오스크로 갔어요. 키오스크에 예약 정보를 입력했더니 제 체크인 상태가 유효하지 않다고 나오는 겁니다. 키오스크 직원 중 한 명에게 제가 문제가 있다고 했고 이메일을 보여주면서 어떤 일이 있는지를 물어봤습니다. 그분이 제 항공편을 철회했다고 했지만 저는 그렇지 않았는데도 그것이 취소되었습니다. **133** 그랬더니, 그분이 저를 대기 명단에 올려 놓았습니다. 저는 비행기 탑승 전 2시간 넘게 대기 명단 가운데 순간가지 마지막 앞에서 긴장한 상태로 서 있었습니다.

저는 너무 당황스러웠고, 귀사의 시스템에 정말 실망했습니다. 이 문제에 대한 설명을 원합니다. 가능한 한 빨리 제 휴대폰으로 전화주세요.

감사합니다.

제임스 김벨

134 문제 뒤에 this issue가 있으므로 이 문제에 '문의' 설명이 적절하다. 따라서 (B)가 정답이다.

status 상태 invalid 무효의, 오류가 있는 representative 직원, 대표자 nervously 긴장하며 embarrassed 당황한 as soon as possible 가능한 한 빨리

131

해설 '예약 번호(booking number)'를 하나의 복합명사로 이루 두자. booking은 동명사나 분사보다도 일반명사로 자주 쓰인다. 따라서 정답은 (B)이다.

132

해설 줄거리를 보면 공항에 도착하자마자 '즉시' 체크인 키오스크로 간 것으로 볼 수 있다. 따라서 정답은 (D)이다. (A) 점차적으로 / (C) 공평하게 / (B) 정확히

133

(A) 따라서 저는 추가 요금을 내야 했습니다.
(B) 그랬더니, 그분이 저를 대기 명단에 올려 놓았습니다.
(C) 인터캠케도 그 프린터기가 작동하지 않았어요.
(D) 그후에 그분은 저에게 장기발을 열라고 요청했어요.

해설 빈칸 뒤에 저리가 날 때까지 기다려야 한다는 내용이 있으므로 대기 명단에 올렸다는 (B)가 정답이다.

134

해설 빈칸 뒤에 this issue가 있으므로 이 문제에 '문의' 설명이 적절하다. 따라서 (B)가 정답이다.

[135-138]

안나 루벤
윈스턴 플랫츠 80-5
우디 거리 2917
리버사이드, 캘리포니아 89723

루벤 씨께,

고객님의 은행 계좌에 대한 정보 요청에 감사드립니다. 8월에 결제될 또한 것은 저희에게 있습니다. 8월에 결제될 **135** 그러나 저조한 고객님의 장기 우수 고객이라는 것을 알고 있습니다. 때문에 정상 청구액을 **136** 철회합니다. 고객님의 계좌는 이에 따라 수정되었습니다.

월별 결제가 **137** 항상 제때 이루어지는 것을 확실히 하기 위해 우리는 고객님께 자동 이체 결제 서비스를 신청하도록 권장하는 바입니다. 이 서비스로 고객님은 정기적으로, 영 시면 금액으로 손쉽한 요금을 지불할 수 있습니다. 좀 더 자세한 정보를 알고 싶으시면 www. chvasbankingservice.com/payments를 방문해 주세요.

궁금하거나 우려되는 점이 있다면 d,adelaide@chvasbankingservice. com으로 제게 연락하실 수 있습니다.

거래에 감사드립니다.

다나 아델레이드
계정 담당자

135

(A) 이 연체료를 전자 방식이나 또는 직접 납부할 수 있습니다.
(B) 새로운 자축 계좌를 여실 것을 권장합니다.
(C) 그러나 저조는 고객님이 장기 우수 고객이라는 것을 알고 있습니다.
(D) 월말까지 환급받으시려면 양식을 작성해 주셔야 합니다.

해설 빈칸 앞에는 수수료를 내야 한다고 했고 뒤에는 이를 철회하겠다는 내용이 나오므로 그 원인이 되는 장기 우수 고객이라는 (C)가 정답이다.

136

해설 첫 단락은 제조에 돈이 늦게 들어와서 결제를 제때 못해 20 달러의 연체금이 붙었지만, 우수 고객이기 때문에 이 금액을 먼저 해 준다는 내용이 적절하다. 따라서 (C)가 적절하다. (A) 기대하다 / (B) 부과하다 / (D) 영예를 주다

137

해설 결제가 '항상' 제때 이루어지는 것을 확실히 하기 위해 자동 이체 결제 신청을 해 보라는 내용이 자연스러우므로 (B)가 정답이다. (A) 이미 / (C) 균등하게 / (D) 곧

138

해설 관사와 명사 사이에는 형용사가 와야 하므로 일단 (C)는 제외한다. 문맥상 '명세된'이라는 의미가 되어야 하므로 과거분사 (A)가 정답이다.

146

(A) 다음 달부터 그는 해외에서 근무하게 될 것입니다.
(B) 그는 앤디 그리피스 씨의 업무들을 인수인계할 것입니다.
(C) 이것은 최고 재무 책임자로서의 그의 직무에 추가될 것입니다.
(D) 그는 회사의 모든 예산 견적을 다루게 될 것입니다.

해설 빈칸 앞 문단에서 국내 영업 부장이었던 그리피스 씨가 새로운 직무를 맡게 되었다고 했다. 빈칸 바로 앞 문장에서 존 월튼 씨가 국내 영업 부장으로 승진했다고 했으므로 그리피스 씨의 업무를 인계받을 것이라는 (B)가 정답이다.

[143-146]

수신: 전 직원
발신: 인사부장
제목: 인사 이동

2월 10일 이사회 회의에서 **143** 결원이 통과된 후, 헬로스 시스템은 다음과 같은 인사 변화에 돌입하게 기쁩니다. 저희 센터 **140** 고객들의 의견들을 고려한 끝에, 더 많은 단체운동 공간과 사우나 시설들을 추가할 것입니다. 2층에 추가 단체운동 공간이 생길 것이고, 벤치 프 레스나 러닝 머신 같은 많은 웨이트 장비들은 1층으로 옮겨질 것입니다.

다음의 지점들은 계속해서 사용하실 수 있습니다.

근거 지점을 찾아보시려면 www.acebodyfit.com에 방문하셔서 온 라인 채널 서비스로 저희 체육관 직원에게 얘기해 보십시오.

143
board meeting 이사회 회의   personnel changes 인사 이동   steadily
꾸준히   appoint 임명하다   domestic 국내의   oversee 총괄하다   in
charge of 책임지는   short-term 단기간의   long-term 장기간의

After 절이 주어가 필요한 자리이므로 반드시 명사가 들어가야 한다. 따라서 정답은 (D) resolution(결의안)이다.

144
최고 재무 책임자로서 '주로' 맡게 될 직무를 소개하는 문장이므로 정답은 (B) primarily이다. (A) 장기적으로 / (C) 상대적으로 / (D) 긍정적으로

145
반갑게는 부사절 접속사가 들어가야 한다. 선택지에서 부사절 접속사인 것은 Now that(~이므로) 뿐이므로 정답은 (A)이다. 참고로 Whether는 명사절과 부사절을 모두 이끌 수 있는데, 부사절 접속사로 쓰이려면 뒤에 or이나 or not이 반드시 있어야 하므로 오답이다.

[139-142]

피트니스 센터 폐점

에이스바디 피트니스 센터의 대부분 지점들이 **139** 광범위한 보수 공사로 8월 14일 일요일부터 폐점합니다. 주요 업그레이드는 최신식 운동 장비, 새로운 내부 페인트칠, 새 바닥재와 가구들을 포함합니다. 저희 센터 **140** 고객님들의 의견들을 고려한 끝에, 더 많은 단체운동 공간과 사우나 시설들을 추가할 것입니다. 2층에 추가 단체운동 공간이 생길 것이고, 벤치 프레스나 러닝 머신 같은 많은 웨이트 장비들은 1층으로 옮겨질 것입니다.

폐점하는 몇 개월 지속될 수도 있습니다. **141** 12월 1일에 개점하는 것을 예상하고 있습니다.

다음의 지점들은 계속해서 사용하실 수 있습니다.

- 윌러스 지점 (메인대로 25)
- 파라다이스 지점 (브레이 드라이브 8)
- 아쿠아틱 지점 (이스트 거리 110)

근거 지점을 **142** 찾아보시려면 www.acebodyfit.com에 방문하셔서 온라인 채팅 서비스로 저희 체육관 직원에게 얘기해 보십시오.

renovation 보수 공사   coat (페인트 따위의) 칠   flooring 바닥재   fixtures 기구   GX(group exercise) 단체 운동   bench presses 벤치 프레스(역기 를 들어올리는 운동)   treadmills 러닝 머신

139
관사와 명사 사이에서 명사를 수식하는 형용사 자리이다. 선택지에서 형용사 역할을 할 수 있는 것은 (C) extensive(광범위한)와 (D) extending(연장하는)인데, '광범위한 보수 공사'가 의미상 어울리므로 정답은 (C)이다.

140
피트니스 센터의 시설에 대해서 의견을 낼 수 있는 사람들은 고객들(patrons)이라고 볼 수 있으므로 정답은 (B)이다. (A) 후보자들 / (C) 보행자들 / (D) 승객들

141
(A) 12월 1일에 재개점하는 것을 예상하고 있습니다.
(B) www.acebodyfit.com에서 댄스 수업에 등록하실 수 있습니다.
(C) 규칙적인 운동은 당신의 건강을 위해 필수로 간주됩니다.
(D) 체육관은 내일 오전 10시에 열 예정입니다.

해설 빈칸 앞에 몇 개월 동안 폐쇄될 수도 있다고 했으므로 12월 1일에 재개점하는 것을 예상한다는 (A)가 정답이다.

142
가까운 지점을 '찾으려면'이라는 의미가 적절하므로 to부정사 (D) 가 정답이다.

[147-148]

수신: 해밀턴 하산 오후 2시 46분
발신: 나이마 항공 승객 서비스

[147] 긴급 메시지: 나이마 항공 4492 항공편인 시간표 변경을 위한 메시지를 확인하세요.

4492 항공편

[148] 브리스톨 지역 공항에서
액세티 성 데이비드 공항

지연

예정 출발 시간 - 오후 4시 20분
실제 출발 시간 - 오후 4시 50분
예정 도착 시간 - 오후 7시 30분
추정 도착 시간 - 오후 7시 40분

탑승 게이트: 31

수하물 수취: 수하물 컨베이어 벨트 4번

연결 항공편을 예약하셨으면, 환승 정보를 위해 항공사에 확인해 주세요.

alert 주의 flight 항공편 regional 지역의 departure 출발 estimated 추정되는 baggage claim 수하물 수취 carousel 수하물 컨베이어 벨트 connecting flight 연결 항공편 transfer 환승 status 상태

147 문자가 보내진 이유는?
(A) 항공편 예약을 확인하기 위해
(B) 비행 변경을 발표하기 위해
(C) 승객에게 탑승 게이트를 알리기 위해
(D) 연결 항공편의 업데이트된 내용을 제공하기 위해

148 하산 씨에 관해 언급된 것은?
(A) 브리스톨에서 출발할 것이다.
(B) 액세티에서 그의 비행 요금을 지불했다.
(C) 가방 두 개를 수하물로 부쳤다.
(D) 비행 정보를 분실했다.

[149-151]

4월 18일 잭슨즈 개업식에 오세요!

[150] 개점을 축하하기 위해 잭슨즈는 개장 첫 주에 "하나 사면, 하나 반값" 행사를 제공하고 있습니다. [149] 그러니 오셔서 저희 기방과 신발을 구경하세요. 아래 브랜드들을 포함한 20개 이상의 브랜드 중에서 선택하세요.

• 얀토
• 지그리드
• 라 망수
• 인디그
• 파지 맘마

[151] 잭슨즈는 체리슈 베일 쇼핑센터의 웰든 으로에 위치해 있습니다. 지하며, 일주일 내내 정상 영업시간 동안 열립니다.

3월 30일자 <체리슈 베일 헤럴드>에서 새로운 잭슨즈 매장 관리자 엘리 주노의 프로필을 확인해 주세요.

할인은 손님 1인당 5개 품목으로 제한됩니다.

grand opening 개장, 개점 trading 거래, 영업 be located 위치하다 take a look at ~을 보다 issue (정기 간행물의) 호 be situated 위치하다

149 잭슨즈에서는 무엇이 판매되는가?
(A) 음식
(B) 의류
(C) 패션 액세서리
(D) 스포츠 장비

150 전단지에 따르면 손님들이 4월 18일에서 24일 사이에 할 수 있는 것은?
(A) 무료 <체리슈 베일 헤럴드>를 한 부 받기
(B) 신규 점포 개장을 위한 기자 회견 참석하기
(C) 물건 한 개를 구매하고 다른 한 개를 반값에 구매하기
(D) 추가 할인을 위해 전단지 제시하기

151 잭슨즈에 대해 언급된 것은?
(A) 직원을 구하고 있다.
(B) 쇼핑몰에 위치하고 있다.
(C) 엘리 주노가 소유주를 인터뷰할 것이다.
(D) 3월 30일에 개장할 것이다.

[152-153]

나마스키

나마스키 그룹은 환경 보호에 헌신하고 쓰레기가 매립지에 보내지는 것을 방지하기 위해 모든 노력을 기울입니다. 저희는 고객들이 제품의 수명이 다할 때 책임 있게 폐기하도록 정책적으로 장려합니다. [152] 나마스키 매장 중인 곳에서 제품을 구매하셨다면 저희는 기까이 제품을 배달해 드립니다. 동시에 저희는 오래된 가전제품을 수거하여 저희 폐기 시설로 가져갑니다. 아니면 고객님께서 오래된 가전제품을 저희 폐기 시설로 보내도록 조치하실 수 있습니다. [153] 고객님의 지역에 있는 나마스키 매장은 인근 지역의 전자제품이든 비슷한 크기의 가전제품이든 환경경적 방식을 제공하는 인의 폐기 시설 목록을 드릴 수 있습니다.

be dedicated to ~에 전념하다 attempt 시도, 노력 prevent 예방하다 waste 쓰레기 landfill 쓰레기 매립지 dispose of ~을 처분하다 lifecycle (상품 등이 개발되고 사용되는) 제품 주기 gladly 기꺼이 appliance 가전제품 collect 수거하다 disposal facility 폐기 시설 alternatively 그 대신에 environmentally friendly 친환경적인 method 방식 depot 창고

152 공지의 목적은?
(A) 새 전자제품 라인을 홍보하기 위해
(B) 배송 지연을 알리기 위해
(C) 고객에게 할인을 알리기 위해
(D) 이용 가능한 서비스를 설명하기 위해

153 공지에 따르면 나마스키가 제공하는 정보는?
(A) 근처의 폐기 센터의 이름
(B) 고객의 공개된 제품 후기
(C) 환경적인 폐기 방식에 관한 최근의 연구
(D) 회사의 생산 창고에 대한 설명

[154-156]

클리어뷰 영화 촬영소
웨일 거리 686, 서리, 영국

3월 30일

이모젠 크렌포드 씨
뱁츠 스트리트 34, 클래런던 아파트 121호
서리, 영국

크렌포드 씨께,

클리어뷰 영화 촬영소에 대한 관심에 감사드립니다. 저희 고객인 이안 블레어 씨가 귀하 요리 조달사의 직책에 적극적 후보자로 당신을 언급했고, 당신의 지원서를 받으셨습니다. (154) 4월 17일 수요일, 오후 1시에 면접을 보고 싶습니다. (155) 이 날이 가능한지 확인하기 위해 제 비서인 쉼라 헤네시로 연락해서 알려주세요. 그녀는 010-555-9234로 연락 가능합니다.

또한, 이력서를 이메일로 보내줄 수 있다면 감사하겠습니다. (156) 저희 웹 사이트를 통해 온라인으로 제출한 이력서 오류가 나서 문서의 마지막 절을 볼 수 없었습니다.

마지막으로, 면접 시 먹 그 기관에 지원하셔야 할 몇 가지 필수 서류들을 동봉합니다. 연락 기다리겠습니다.

에드워드 트렌트

인사 부장

동봉

suitable 적당한 candidate 후보자 catering 음식 공급업 assistant 조수 acceptable 수락할 수 있는 reach (전화 등으로) 연락하다 corrupted (컴퓨터 파일에) 오류가 있는 enclosed 동봉한 mandatory 의무적인 enclosure 동봉된 것 alteration 변경 glitch 결함 vacancy 공석 reference 추천인

154 트렌트 씨가 크렌포드 씨에게 편지를 쓰는 이유는?
(A) 약속을 잡기 위해
(B) 추천을 요청하기 위해
(C) 채용 공고에 관해 문의하기 위해
(D) 온라인 양식 수정을 요청하기 위해

155 크렌포드 씨가 연락하도록 요구된 사람은?
(A) 블레인 씨
(B) 생산 관리 책임자
(C) 영화사 임원
(D) 쉼 씨

156 트렌트 씨가 문제로 언급하는 것은?
(A) 그는 전자문서의 일부분을 확인할 수 없었다.
(B) 크렌포드 씨가 지원한 공석이 이미 채용 마감되었다.
(C) 크렌포드 씨가 추천인으로 언급한 사람이 연락이 되지 않았다.
(D) 크렌포드 씨가 보낸 지원서가 마감일 이후에 수신되었다.

[157-158]

베스 챈들러 [14:21]	짐, 센트럴에서 린 씨를 데리러 좀 와 줄 수 있어요?
짐 로저스 [14:24]	당신이 데리러 간다고 생각했어요.
베스 챈들러 [14:25]	(158) 그러려고 했는데, 린 씨가 탄 기차가 늦게 도착할 것 같다고 문자가 왔어요. 제가 그 시간에는 약속이 있거든요.
짐 로저스 [14:27]	알겠어요. 제가 몇 시에 거기 가면 될까요?
베스 챈들러 [14:28]	(157) 보스턴에서 출발하는 그 기차는 5시 30분에 도착하기로 되어 있어요. 그래도 가기 전에 한 번 더 확인해 보셨으면 좋겠어요.
짐 로저스 [14:29]	회사 차를 가져가도 되나요?
베스 챈들러 [14:30]	그럼요, 좋은 길로 가져가세요. 좋은 인상을 심어주고 싶다면요. 그로부터 회사는 저희의 가장 중요한 바 이어 중 하나거든요.

head over ~로 가다   get in touch with ~와 연락하다

157 린 씨에 대해서 사실인 것은?
(A) 그는 회의의 일정을 다시 잡았다.
(B) 그는 기차에 늦게 탑승했다.
(C) 그는 챈들러 씨의 상사이다.
(D) 그는 보스턴을 출발하여 이동하고 있다.

158 14시 27분에 로저스 씨가 "알겠어요"라고 했을 때 그 의미는 무엇인가?
(A) 그는 센트럴역이 어디에 있는지를 안다.
(B) 그는 린 씨와 연락할 것이다.
(C) 그는 요청의 이유를 이해한다.
(D) 그는 기차가 때때로 늦는다는 것을 알게 되었다.

[159-161]

발신: 유기 사토 <ysatou@tabe.org>
수신: 이지 야마모토 <iyamamoto@antifren.org>
날짜: 8월 3일
제목: 귀하의 등록 요청

야마모토 씨께,

9월 15일로 예정된 건설 선업 엽얍이트 컨벤션에 대한 관심에 감사드립니다. 유감스럽게도 행사의 표가 매진되었기 때문에 더 이상 참석 요청을 받지 않습니다. 대기자 명단에 올라가길 바라신다면 명단에 입력 주세요. 등록된 분들 중 참석할 수 없는 분이 개시된 명단에 있는 분들께 자리를 제공할 것입니다. 이번에 참석하실 수 없게 되면, (159) 건설 선업 엽얍이트 컨벤션은 매분기마다 열리고, 다음 행사는 1월에 있다는 것을 유념해 주십시오.

(160) 이번 기회를 통해 도쿄 건축 기사 협회의 회원이 되시도록 권해 드려도 괜찮겠습니까? 회원연은 연간 300달러이며, 여러 가지 혜택을 받으실 것입니다. 선엄 영부 등록과 지역 건설 자체 엽체의 할인 가드, (161) 분기 별 간테임마테에 참석할 기회 등이 포함됩니다. 회원 신청을 위해 회원 등록 부서인 (440) 555-9943으로 전화하시거나, 웹 사이트 www.tabe.org의 관련 페이지를 방문해 주세요.

다가오는 컨벤션에 참석하실 수 있길 바라며, TABE의 회원이 되는 것도 고려해 보시길 바랍니다.

유기 사토
도쿄 건축 기사 협회
www.tabe.org
전화번호: (440) 555-9943
팩스: (440) 555-4631

registration 등록 convention 회의 regrettably 유감스럽게도 note 염두에 두다 attendance 참석 sold out 매진된 cancellation 취소 quarter 분기 association 협회 building engineer 건축 기사 inclusion 포함 directory 명부 relevant 관련 있는 chair 의장을 맡다 venue 개최 예정지 advance registration 사전 등록

159 건설 선업 엽얍이트 컨벤션에 관해 언급된 것은?
(A) 1년에 4번 개최된다.
(B) 사토 씨가 의장을 맡는다.
(C) 새로운 개념이다.
(D) 더 큰 장소로 이전한다.

160 사토 씨가 야마모토 씨에게 제안하는 것은?
(A) 환불 요청하기
(B) 그의 연락처 정보를 그녀에게 보내기
(C) 그녀와 약속 잡기
(D) 단체에 가입하기

161. TABE 회원들에게 제공되는 혜택으로 언급된 것은?
(A) 추천인 사전들의 명단
(B) 세미나 사전 등록
(C) 세미나 지정 좌석
(D) 사교 행사 초대

[162-164]

수산 S&L 제조 그룹
발신: 금융 전망 위원회
날짜: 4월 14일
제목: 분석 보고서

[162] S&L은 수년간 대량 음식 공급업에 종사하면서 고품질의 포장 음식을 생산하는 것으로 명성을 얻어왔습니다. 그러나 우리는 현재 위기에 직면해 있습니다. 여러분도 아시다시피, [163] 포장평가 지난 3년간 12퍼센트나 올랐습니다. 우리는 이 비용을 충당할 수 있도록 수많은 대안을 의논했습니다. 전반적으로 일치되는 의견은 제품군의 가격을 인상하는 것이지만, 가격 인상은 고객을 낙담 또는 위협할 수밖에 없습니다.

우리가 매우 효과적인 사업 전략을 갖고 있다는 점을 명심하세요. 우리의 소셜 미디어 홍보는 널리 노출되고 있고, 그것에게 좋은 반응을 얻고 있습니다. 광고비는 독립이 유지할 것을 제안합니다. 그러나 우리는 [164] 제품고 비 포장 설정에 되는 포장 디자인을 찾아야 합니다. 이런 식으로 잠재 고객을 실망시키지 않으면서 가격 전략을 유지할 수 있고, 이것이 어떠한 손실을 회복하는 데 도움이 될 것입니다.

제안 묵스

forecast 예측 analysis 분석 well-established 정착된 reputation 명성 mass 대량의 face 직면하다 crisis 위기 significantly 상당히 numerous 수많은 consensus 의견 일치 bear in mind 명심하다 view 보다 advocate 옹호하다 discourage 단념시키다 potential 잠재적인 recoup 만회하다 universally 일반적으로 economical 경제적인 shut down 휴업하다

162. S&L 제조 그룹에 관해 언급된 것은?
(A) 음식 공급 산업의 포장재를 제조한다.
(B) 그들의 분야에서 좋은 평가를 받고 있다.
(C) 세계적인 기업이다.
(D) 신제품 연구에 투자를 했다.

163. S&L 제조 그룹에 문제가 있는 이유는?
(A) 생산 비용이 올랐다.
(B) 사업 전략들이 거의 성공하지 못했다.
(C) 제품의 품질이 떨어졌다.
(D) 광고가 유명하지 않다.

164. 위원회가 S&L 제조 그룹에 추천하는 것은?
(A) 전반적으로 가격 인상하기
(B) 더 경제적인 포장에 투자하기
(C) 생산 중단하기
(D) 신제품 개발 늘리기

165. 기사는 누구를 대상으로 하는가?
(A) 후시마 엄 이나니
(B) 현지 사업주들
(C) 요리 전문가
(D) 주 광장 사업 협회의 직원들

166. 관심 있는 노점상이 해야 할 행동으로 언급되지 않은 것은?
(A) 일정 금액을 선물로 지불하기
(B) 양식 작성하기
(C) 제품 견본 제출하기
(D) 세부 사항을 이메일로 보내기

167. 공개 행사에 관해 언급된 것은?
(A) 두 개의 기관이 행사를 후원한다.
(B) 방문객은 참석하기 위해 돈을 내야 한다.
(C) 그럴 대여할 수 있는 기판대가 넘어설 것이다.
(D) 행사는 과거에 참석률이 높았다.

168. [1], [2], [3], [4]로 표기된 위치 중 다음 문장이 들어가기 적절한 것은?
"게다가 아마추어 공연인들과 예술가들은 행사 내내 공연을 할 것이다."
(A) [1]
(B) [2]
(C) [3]
(D) [4]

[165-168]

알렉산드리아의 비즈니스에 주목하다

[167] 메인 스퀘어 사업 협회와 알렉산드리아 지역 단체가 첫 번째 알렉산드리아 사업 물산품을 개최하기 위해 뭉쳤다. -[1]-. 행사는 8월 24일 토요일, 오전 11시 30분부터 오후 8시 / 30분까지 주 광장에서 열리고, [165] 현지 기업들에게 그들의 상품과 서비스를 전시할 기회를 제공할 것이다. 지역 사회에서 인지도를 높이고 싶은 어느 기업에게나 이상적인 공개 행사가 될 것이다.

다양한 알렉산드리아 현지 기업들과 공연인들에게 그들의 제품을 강조할 수 있는 자리를 제공하자는 데 목적이 있다. [166] 지역 상점들은 상품을 전시할 것이고, 식당과 카페들은 일부의 경우 아예에서 요리도 하면서 시식용 음식을 제공할 것이다. -[2]-.

행사는 무료이고, 대중에게 공개될 것이다. [166] 판매지들을 위한 부스는 하루에 100유로의 대여비로 사용할 수 있다. 이웅 가능한 노점의 수가 한정되어 있으니 노점상들은 가급적 빨리 예약하는 것이 좋다. -[3]-. [165] 지원자는 행사 지원서를 작성하고 환불이 되지 않는 50유로의 보증금과 함께 후시마 엄 이나니에게 henani@alex.org로 7월 3일까지 보내야 한다. -[4]-.

spotlight 조명 amalgamate 합병하다 display 전시하다 raise one's profile 인지도를 높이다 showcase 공개 행사 performer 공연인 highlight 강조하다 boutique 부티크(값비싼 옷이나 선물을 파는 작은 가게) in the open air 야외에서 interested party 관계자 rental fee 대여비 vendor 판매 회사, 노점상 non-refundable 환불이 불가능한 deposit 보증금 up front 미리, 선불로 cookery 요리 surplus 잉여

exclusively 독점적으로 savory 식전 또는 식후에 구미를 돋우는 자극적인 요리 foodstuff 식품 ingredient 재료 inspector 검독관 pre-packaged 미리 포장된 range from A to B 범위가 A에서 B에 이르다 upwards 위로 commission 수수료 brisk 빠른 height 최고조 administrator 관리인 handmade 손으로 만든 complimentary 무료의

172 이메일의 목적은?
(A) 행사가 어떻게 운영되는지 설명하기 위해
(B) 던페어 크래프트 이벤트을 홍보하기 위해
(C) 수석업 제품을 주문하기 위해
(D) 요리 대회를 홍보하기 위해

173 맥켄지 씨는 누구인가?
(A) 가공업
(B) 관광객
(C) 식당 직원
(D) 요리사

174 던페어 아일랜드 음식 축제에서 판매되는 모든 항목들에 대해 언급된 것은?
(A) 100파운드 이상 가격이 책정된 것은 없다.
(B) 가격은 6월, 7월, 8월에 30퍼센트 할인된다.
(C) 던페어 아일랜드 주민에 의해 만들어진다.
(D) 전 세계의 재료들을 사용한다.

175 [1], [2], [3], [4]로 표시된 위치 중 다음 문장이 들어가기 적절한 것은?
"노점상은 판매 음식에 대해 10퍼센트의 수수료를 지불하셔야 합니다."
(A) [1]
(B) [2]
(C) [3]
(D) [4]

170 오전 10시 20분에 파커 씨가 "제가 켄의 말에 덧붙이자면"이라고 했을 때 그 의미는 무엇인가?
(A) 그녀는 이전에 독별 씨의 조언을 따랐다.
(B) 그녀는 인맥을 만드는 것이 중요하다고 생각한다.
(C) 그녀는 현재 제약회사에서 일하고 있다.
(D) 그녀는 새로운 사람들을 만나고 싶어 한다.

171 아벨 씨에 대해서 암시된 것은?
(A) 그녀는 이전 고용주에게 돌아갈 것이다.
(B) 그녀는 최근에 이력서를 수정했다.
(C) 그녀는 학교로 돌아갈 계획이다.
(D) 그녀는 병원에 있는 일자리에 지원했다.

[172-175]

발신: hamish@dunfair.com
수신: lmckenzie@hotline.com
제목: 던페어 아일랜드 음식 축제
날짜: 6월 2일

맥켄지 씨께,

172 던페어 아일랜드 음식 축제에 대해 문의 주셔서 감사합니다. **174** 던페어 아일랜드의 주민들에 의해 독점적으로 —[1]— 저희는 5년 동안 이 축제를 주최해 오고 있습니다. 제공되는 식품은 모두 현지 요리사들이 만든 케이크와 잼뿐만 아니라, 사탕, 특별한 향신료 등입니다. 저희는 전 세계로부터 재료를 사용해 축제 당일에 갓 요리된 음식 만 하용하며, 음식을 점검하기 위해 검독관을 보냅니다. 사전 포장된 음식은 허용하지 않습니다. **175** 가격대는 1파운드에서 100파운드 이상의 헤딩 케이크에도 있습니다. —[2]—

또 매달 첫 토요일에 던페어 크래프트 이벤트을 개최하는데, 현지 주민들과 기업들이 만든 상품을 선보이고, 오후 4시에서 6시 사이에 무료 다과를 제공합니다. —[3]— 이 행사는 항상 성황을 이루고 평균 50명 이상의 관광객과 주민들이 옵니다. 판매는 관광 성수기인 여름 내내 특히 바쁜 경향이 있습니다.

172 던페어 아일랜드 음식 축제의 일원이 되고 싶으시면 전문으로 하는 음식 사진을 0메일로 보내 주시고 사용된 재료의 목록도 포함해 주세요. **[4]** 또한 보내주신 공이 음식 공급 지역증인 무엇이든지 말씀해 연락드리겠습니다.

해미쉬 그린
던페어 아일랜드 음식 축제 관리자

[169-171]

모리 아벨 오전 8:45
저는 2년 전에 생물학 학사로 졸업했고, 그 이후로 식품에서 시사 시 중을 느는 일을 해 왔습니다. 일은 힘들고 급여는 적습니다. 저는 저의 대학교 보건소에서 주로 연구실 일을 하면서 일을 하곤 했는데, 다시 비들로 현자를 찌르고 싶지는 않습니다. 사람들은 제가 제약 보 일을 알아봐야 한다고 말합니다. 제가 어디에서 시작하면 좋을까요?

켄 툭벨 오전 9:01
어떤 업계가 채용 중인지 알아보려면 당신이 사는 지역의 구인란을 살펴보세요. 관심이 가는 회사들을 조사해 보세요. **170** 그러고 나서 그곳에서 일하는 사람들과 인적 네트워크를 형성하려고 노력하세요.

폴 스미스 오전 10:10
저는 몇몇 인기 있는 전통제의 제조업체인 근래러스에서 약사로 일했었어요. 이 회사의 다른 주요 화사에 지원하려면 단탄한 실험 실 경력이 있을 거예요. 당신이 약간의 실험실 경력이 있기 때문에 먼저 병원 연구실에 있는 일자리를 찾아볼 것을 제안 드려요. 일단 이 닥터부터 만드세요.

캐디스 파커 오전 10:20
170 제가 켄의 밀에 덧붙이자면 당신이 관심 있는 분야의 사람들의 일이가 드는 것이 첫 번째 단계에요.

켄 툭벨 오전 11:01
만약 당신이 지역에서 회사를 찾을 수 없다면, 새로운 커리어를 시작하기 위해서 이사를 해야 할지도 몰라요.

캐디스 파커 오후 12:20
누자지로 이사하는 것을 고려해 보시겠어요? 그곳에 몇몇 주요 제약 회사들이 본사를 두고 있거든요.

모리 아벨 오후 4:45
여러분 모두의 조언들에 감사해요 **171** 그분이 지역에 제브는 제임스 병원에 공석이 있다고 **170** 일러주셨어요. **171** 그분이 지역에 제브는 제임스 병원에 공석이 있다고 내일 인터뷰가 있어요. 행운을 빌어 주세요.

---

pharmaceutical 제약의   chemist 약사   point 일러주다

169 스미스 씨에 대해서 암시된 것은?
(A) 그는 제약 업계에서 일했었다.
(B) 그는 실험실을 관리하곤 했었다.
(C) 그는 현재 누자시에 살고 있다.
(D) 그의 회사는 지원서를 받고 있다.

real estate 부동산 square meter 평방 미터 purpose-built 특별한
목적으로 건립된 complex 복합 건물, 단지 entire 전체의 ground floor
1층 upmarket 상류층을 대상으로 하는 double tiered 2단의, 두 줄의
fixture 설비, 장치 marble 대리석 sumptuous 호화로운 generosity
너그러움 adjacent 인접한 invaluable 매우 귀중한 fervent 열렬한
councilor 의원 strike up a relationship 관계를 정립하다 secure 확보
하다 enhance 향상시키다 profile 프로필을 올려 주다

176 우탐바 부동산에 대해 알 수 있는 것은?
(A) 여러 도시에서 건물을 판매한다.
(B) 임대 시장에 집중한다.
(C) 현재 4개의 건물만 판매 중이다.
(D) 판매 회사와 직접 만나 거래하는 것을 선호한다.

177 기사의 주요 목적은?
(A) 전통 태국 요리를 가르치기 위해
(B) 지역 식당의 메뉴를 발표하기 위해
(C) 브리지번 시 공무원의 프로그램을 알리기 위해
(D) 업계의 행사에 대해 보고하기 위해

178 기사에 따르면 자스민 팰리스가 이전한 이유는?
(A) 새 임대가 거절되었다.
(B) 주인이 브리지번으로 이사하기로 했다.
(C) 이전 장소가 너무 작았다.
(D) 새로운 건물이 더 현대적인 시설을 갖추었다.

179 자스민 팰리스는 이전에 어디에 위치했을 것 같은가?(연계 지문 문제)
(A) 베이랜드 뷰
(B) 이틀레이드 스트리트
(C) 와타마 애비뉴
(D) 리온즈 플레이스

180 용 씨 가족에 대해 알 수 있는 것은?
(A) 태불라 의원의 지인이다.
(B) 음악 연주자이다.
(C) 자스민 팰리스의 단골 고객이다.
(D) 골드 코스트 출신이다.

[176-180]

우탐바 부동산

(176) 브리지번, 케언스, 골드 코스트 일대에서 10년 이상 영업

특별 목록

리온즈 플레이스 395: 170평방 미터, 특별히 지어진 복합 건물에 위치한
최상의 사무실 공간. 메인 입주 구역, 여러 개의 사무실과 3개의 중간 규
모 회의실. 건물 공용 주차장. 최상의 골드 코스트에 위치

(179) 베이랜드 뷰 229: 280평방 미터. 브리지번의 조지 왓소롱 건물의 1
층 전체. 음식 조달업을 위한 장비 완비. 양호한 상태. 전시제품 포함

와타마 애비뉴 12: 320평방 미터. 브리지번 번경 구역 중심부의 고급 2
층 상점 건물. 상이 장식이 까가져 있는 20미터 길이의 대리석 바닥물 포
함한 새 설비와 부속물

이틀레이드 스트리트 7: 320평방 미터. 식당이나 음식 조달업에 적합하지
만, 소매업 목적으로 사용 가능. 중상가의 분주한 지점에 위치. 케언스
와 근접

(176) 매매 또는 임대 사무실과 점포 공간을 더 많이 보유하고 있습니다!
전체 리스트를 보시려면 www.wotambarealty.com에 방문하시거나
(330) 555-3593으로 전화 또는 properties@wotambarealty.com으
로 이메일 보내 주세요.

식당이 새 위치를 발표하다

12월 1일 – **(177)** 인기 있는 태국 식당인 자스민 팰리스가 어제 마틴 대로
211번지에서 재개장했다. 현지 포크 그룹인 스카가 비트가 음악을 제공
했고, 가게 주인인 차이 용마 란 용이 손님들에게 그들의 고향인 방콕에서
특별한 날에 제공하는 요리로 호화로운 연회를 제공했다. 손님 명단이 단
골손님들을 시작으로, 수백 명의 손님이 왔다. 차이 용은 지역 사회의 관
대함과 지원에 감사하는 짧은 연설을 했다. "저희가 태국에서 왔을 때 한
영원히 주고 계속해서 저희 식당에 지속적인 지지를 보내주신 브리지번 주
민들께 감사드립니다."

자스민 팰리스는 7년 전에 열었고, 그 이후로 너무나도 유명해져 **(178)** 기
존 장소는 손님들을 수용할 수 없었다. **(179)** "이전 식당은 매장 면적이
300평방 미터 이하였고, 손님들이 인근 주차장을 이용해야 했기 때문에
주차 문제가 있었습니다."라고 용 씨가 말했다. "우탐바 부동산은 이전 가
게를 특별 목록에 올려 관리해 주었고, 차이 용은 지역 사회에 위치를 뿐
아니라 훌륭한 시서 공간과 케이터링 시설이 있는 이곳을 찾는 데 매우
큰 도움을 주셨습니다."

자스민 팰리스를 가장 열렬히 지지하는 손님 중에는 **(180)** 용 씨 가족과 친밀한 관계
를 시작한 제임스 테불라 의원이 있는데, 그는 손님들에게 젊은 연설을 했
다. 재개장에 대한 질문에 답하면서 테불라 의원은 "자스민 팰리스는 브리
즈번에서 입지를 굳혔습니다. 새로운 장소로 인해 인기가 더 높아질 거라
고 확신합니다."라고 말했다.

[181-185]

수신: 지타 리토빅 〈glitovic@voicedesign.com〉
발신: 사샤 티모비스 〈stimovis@manatidesign.com〉
제목: 디자인 밸리드
날짜: 12월 12일

지타 리토빅 씨께,

(181) 마나티디자인의 단골 고객으로서 귀하는 디자인 밸리드의 새로 업데
이트된 버전의 출시에 관심이 있으실 겁니다. 시장에 나와 있는 디자인 솔
루션 소프트웨어의 가장 진보하고, 효율적인 패키지가 이제는 더 많은 옵
션을 갖추게 되었습니다!

(182) 디자인 밸리드는 기술적인 도안과 모양, 로고, 애니메이션을 제작하
는 그림 도구와 같은 이전 버전에 포함되었던 모든 표준 사양을 갖추고
있습니다. 하지만 최신 버전은 복잡한 벡터 예과 효과와 색상, 3D 효과를
위한 고급 옵션을 포함하고 있습니다. 덧붙여, 소프트웨어는 지속적으로
업데이트되도 있기 때문에 디자인 밸리드에 새 기능을 업그레이드하고 주
가할 수 있습니다.

전문 감사가 소프트웨어를 어떻게 사용하는지에 대한 조언과 시연을 제
공함 무료 온라인 교육 강좌에 귀하를 초대합니다. 더불어, **(183)** 이 워크숍
에 참여한 하시면 추후에 구매하시는 마나티디자인의 제품은 어느 것이든
10퍼센트의 할인이라 무료 설치를 받으실 것입니다. 등록을 위해 웹 사이
에 가셔서 온라인 등록에 연결된 링크를 따라가세요. 전 품목이 포트물리
에 가셔서 보실 수도 있습니다.

사샤 티모비스
기술 서비스 부장

시예로 이미지

예약 양식

이름: 메리언 존스
전화번호: (412) 555-6736
(188) (187) 예약 일자: 5월 1일 토요일
예약 시간: 오후 2시 - 오후 7시
장소: **(189)** 빅포드 파크 시드베리 코드 리셉션 센터

귀하가 필요하신 것: 자와 와줄지는 귀사에게 저희 결혼식과 피로연의 피로연의
(190) 촬영을 부탁드리고 싶습니다. 저희는 영상 촬영이 가능성 또한 어쩐지 논의 중이온데, 먼저 귀사와 비용부터 논의하고싶습니다. 기능하다면, 귀사의 작품 샘플을 좀 볼 수 있을까요?

premier 최고의 reception 결혼 피로연 bridal shower 신부 파티 tentatively 잠정적으로 nonrefundable 환불 불가능한 deposit 예치금 staff 직원을 제공하다

---

186 시예로 이미지에 대해서 암시된 것은? (연계 지문 문제)
(A) 조기 상담 비용을 청구한다.
(B) 5월 1일에 있을 행사에 직원을 제공할 수 있다.
(C) 10명의 직원들을 보낼 수 있다.
(D) 존스 씨를 위한 영상을 만들 것이다.

187 존스 씨에 대해서 사실인 것은? (연계 지문 문제)
(A) 그녀는 실내에서 결혼을 할 것이다.
(B) 그녀는 큰 피로연 행사를 열 것이다.
(C) 그녀는 저녁에 테일러 씨에게 전화했다.
(D) 그녀는 4월에 시예로를 만날 것이다.

188 이메일에 따르면, 존스 씨는 시예로가 그녀의 행사를 촬영하게 하려면 무엇을 해야 하는가?
(A) 조기 지불을 해야 한다.
(B) 작정한 신분증을 제출해야 한다.
(C) 웨딩 플래너에게 연락해야 한다.
(D) 테일러 씨의 사무실을 방문해야 한다.

189 빅포드 파크에 대해서 암시된 것은? (연계 지문 문제)
(A) 그곳은 대여하기에 비싸지 않은 장소이다.
(B) 그곳은 1년에 많은 결혼식을 개최한다.
(C) 그곳은 많은 손님들을 수용할 수 있다.
(D) 그곳은 로하트에서 200킬로미터 이내에 있다.

190 양식의 5번째 줄에 있는 "촬영"과 가장 비슷한 의미의 단어는?
(A) 참석하다
(B) 기록하다
(C) 사진을 찍다
(D) 서비스하다

[186-190]

시예로 이미지

최고의 웨딩 사진 및 영상 업체

전통적이든 현대적이든, 또는 그 중간 어디인가이든, 당신의 결혼식은 매우 특별합니다. 시예로 이미지는 당신만의 특별한 방식으로 그림을 기록하기 위해서 같이 작업할 수 있습니다. 지난 10년간, 기억에 남는 사진과 영상을 제작하기 위해서 자herot 수백 쌍의 커플들과 작업해 왔습니다. **(189)** 로하트에 본사를 두고 있는 저희의 재능 있는 전문가들을 이루어진 팀은 **(187)** 200킬로미터 이내의 장소까지 이동할 수 있습니다. 결혼식과 피로연뿐만 아니라, 신부 파티나 총각/처녀 파티, 그리고 결혼 다음 날의 브런치까지 가능합니다. info@cieloimages.com으로 연락주세요.

수신: mjones@mail.com
발신: info@cieloimages.com
날짜: 1월 28일
제목: 이용 가능성
첨부 문서: 예약 양식

존스 씨에게,

시예로 이미지에 관심을 보여주셔서 감사합니다. **(186)** 귀하의 결혼식날 저희 장소로 저희에게 관심을 보여주신 점 감사합니다. 만약 예약을 하고 싶으시면, 잠정적으로 날짜를 정하기 위해서 첨부된 양식을 작성하셔서 저에게로 이메일로 답신을 보내주세요. 그리고 난 뒤 저희가 사진 회의를 잡기 위해서 연락을 드릴 겁니다. 그 회의에서 저희는 귀하의 필요한 사항과 예산에 대해서 논의할 겁니다. **(188)** 예약을 확정하시려면, 회의 날 200달러의 환불 불가능한 예치금을 요청할 겁니다. 실제 결혼식날로부터 **(187)** 약 2주 전에, 계획을 검토하기 위해서 최종 약속을 잡을 겁니다. 만약 질문이 있으시면, 이 이메일로 또는 555-9090으로 자유롭게 연락주세요.

로나 테일러

송장

발신: 마나티 디자인
9사 로드 11
뉴로브니 34963
불가리아

수신: 지타 리토닉
보이스 디자인 스튜디오
메이페어 스트리트 992
런던 서부11
영국

(183) 주문일: 1월 6일
배송일: 1월 7일
예상 배송일: 1월 11일

품목	수량	설명	비용
AC41	1	디자인 엘리트(업무용)	525달러
	1	**(184)** 10퍼센트 할인	-52달러 50센트
	1	배송비	0달러

모든 판매는 취소가 불가능합니다. 환불이나 교환은 불가능합니다. **(185)** 기술 지원은 www.manatidesign.com/support을 방문하세요.

launch 출시 package 패키지, 일괄 프로그램 drawing tool 그림 도구 drawing 그림 standard feature 표준 사양 intricate 복잡한 add-on 추가하다 constantly 끊임없이 demonstration 시연 register 등록하다 description 서술, 기술 accounting 회계 release 출시하다 residential 주거용의

181 왜 티모버스 씨는 리토닉 씨에게 이메일을 보냈는가?
(A) 새 제품을 추천하기 위해
(B) 설치에 대해 조언해 주기 위해
(C) 워크숍 피드백을 요청하기 위해
(D) 회의 참석을 상기시키기 위해

182 디자인 엘리트에 대해 사실인 것은?
(A) 회계 데이터베이스를 만들 수 있다.
(B) 이전에 출시된 제품의 업데이트 된 버전이다.
(C) 온라인으로만 구매가 가능하다.
(D) 경쟁사의 유사 제품보다 두 배로 효율적이다.

183 리토닉 씨가 구매한 날짜는?
(A) 1월 6일
(B) 1월 7일
(C) 1월 11일
(D) 1월 14일

184 리토닉 씨에 대해 알 수 있는 것은? (연계 지문 문제)
(A) 익일 배달을 위해 돈을 지불했다.
(B) 주거용 목적으로 소프트웨어를 구매했다.
(C) 같은 소프트웨어를 두 개 이상 주문했다.
(D) 교육 강좌에 참여했다.

185 마나티 디자인에 대해 언급된 것은?
(A) 일대일 교습을 제공한다.
(B) 소프트웨어에 대한 환불 및 교환을 해 준다.
(C) 온라인 고객 지원을 제공한다.
(D) 우편으로 등록할 수 있다.

수신: 모든 세입자들
제목: 곧 오픈하는 놀이방

프레셔스 위시스는 버튼 빌딩에 놀이방을 오픈하기 위한 계약서에 서명했습니다. 그 시설은 3층에 위치할 것입니다. 이 3개월부터 5살까지의 아이들을 위해서 [197] 하기범은 보육 전문가들이 주간 돌봄 서비스를 제공할 것입니다. 월 [192] 식사 시간, 신청 양식 등을 알고 싶으시면 www. preciouswishes.com으로 방문하세요.

프레셔스 위시스

이름: 로리 위터스
고용주: [193] 잭슨 컨설팅
전화번호(직장): (505) 555-0334
전화번호(개인): (505) 555-2217
이메일: lwaters@jacksonconsulting.com

등록될 아이 나이: 147H월, 4살
필요한 날짜: [✓]월요일 [✓]화요일 [✓]수요일 [✓]목요일 [✓]금요일
필요한 시간: [ ]반나절(5시간 미만) [✓]종일(5시간 이상)
추가 정보: 제 딸이 땅콩 알레르기가 있습니다.

수신: lwaters@jacksonconsulting.com
발신: poliver@preciouswishes.com
제목: 귀하의 신청서
날짜: 2월 8일

위터스 씨에게,

[191] 자녀의 새로 생긴 지점에 신청해 주셔서 감사합니다. 시설에 대한 관심이 저희 수용력을 훨씬 뛰어 넘었습니다. 따라서 저희는 신청서들을 받은 순서대로 아이들을 배치하고 있습니다.

[194] 비록 이번에는 귀하에게 공간을 제공해 드릴 수 있지만, 대기 명단에 올려드렸습니다. 귀하께서는 현재 42명 중에서 7번입니다. 공석이 생기면 알려드리겠습니다. 그리고 나서 귀하는 이 자리를 승낙할지 거절할지를 결정하기 위한 48시간을 가지게 될 것입니다.

만약 언제라도 이 명단에서 빼지기를 원하신다면, 저희에게 친절하게 알려주세요. [195] 그러나 귀하의 신청서와 함께 내신 1인당 신청비 50달러는 환불해 드릴 수 없습니다.

진심을 담아,
페트리샤 올리버

---

195 위터스 씨에 대해서 사실인 것은 무엇인가? (연계 지문 문제)
(A) 그녀는 다른 팀이 서비스 제공업체를 찾을 것이다.
(B) 그녀는 업무 일에 4일 일한다.
(C) 그녀는 신청을 취소할 것이다.
(D) 그녀는 프레셔스 위시스에 100달러를 주었다.

[196-200]

근면 (7월 1일) – 지난 주말, 선시인 마켓의 개업을 축하하기 위해서 수천 명이 린우드 주민들이 있었습니다. 최근에 개조된 6층짜리 렌싱 빌딩 1층에 5,000 평방 미터를 차지하고 있는 이 새로운 식료품점은 이주 다양한 신선한 농산물, 고기, 빵 등을 제공합니다.

[196] 린우드 지역이 지난 10년간 상당한 성장을 경험한 반면, 부족했던 딱 하기지는 바로 식료품점이었습니다. 사실 주민들은 식품을 구매하기 위해서 최소 5킬로미터를 이동해야 했습니다. 린우드 중심부에 위치한 이 새로운 생긴 가게는 1킬로미터 반경 이내에 거주하는 주민이 15,000명이 나 됩니다.

[197] 자네에 사는 시장 저스틴 벤딕스 씨의 다운타운 앤 바운드 기획의 일환으로서 렌싱 빌딩 개발을 구매했습니다. 2년 전에 취임한 이래로, 시장은 시내와 그 주변 지역의 경제 발전을 그의 최우선 순위로 삼아 왔습니다.

수신: 킬리 제이스 〈kchase@sunshinemarket.com〉
발신: 저스틴 벤딕스 〈jbendix@cityofdanton.gov〉
제목: 주차 문제
날짜: 8월 28일

제이스 씨에게,

[200] 메인가가 주차에 대한 귀하의 걱정에 대해서 저에게 연락주셔서 감사합니다. 저는 귀하와 귀하의 고객들이 겪고 있는 불만을 이해하고 있습니다. 시에서 이 상황을 해결하는 데 전념하고 있으니 믿으셔도 됩니다. [197] 저희는 현재 개발 계획의 두 번째 단계를 추진하고 있습니다. [197] 그것은 귀하의 가게에서 약 500미터 떨어진 곳 10번가와 메인가의 코너에 새로운 주차장을 건설하는 것을 포함하고 있습니다. 귀하의 고객들은 무료로 주차할 수 있게 될 것입니다.

진심을 담아,
저스틴 벤딕스 드림

---

component 구성 allergic 알레르기가 있는 exceed 초과하다 capacity 수용력 status 상태

191 프레셔스 위시스에 대해서 암시되지 않은 것은? (연계 지문 문제)
(A) 새로운 시설을 확장할 것이다.
(B) 다수의 지점을 가지고 있다.
(C) 훈련받은 직원들을 데리고 있다.
(D) 영유아를 위한 돌봄을 제공한다.

192 공지의 3번째 문단, 1번째 줄에 있는 '요금'과 가장 비슷한 의미의 단어 는?
(A) 비용
(B) 숫자
(C) 순위
(D) 속도

193 잭슨 컨설팅에 대해서 암시된 것은? (연계 지문 문제)
(A) 3층에 있다.
(B) 버튼 빌딩에 공간을 임차하고 있다.
(C) 직원들 상담수가 아이가 있다.
(D) 프레셔스 위시스의 건물주이다.

194 올리버 씨는 위터스 씨에게 왜 글을 썼는가?
(A) 그녀에게 새로운 장소의 공간을 제공하기 위해서
(B) 딸에게 대해서 지불을 요청하기 위해서
(C) 프레셔스 위시스의 건물주이다.
(D) 명단에서 그녀를 앞으로 이동시켜 주기 위해서

공지

수신: 모든 고객분들게

저희는 가게 앞 주차 상황에 대해서 많은 불평을 받았습니다. 그곳에 주차하지 않아 주세요. **196** 대신, 가게 뒤편에 있는 골판이나 근처 공영주금을 이용해 주세요. 만약 귀하의 차량까지 식료품들을 나를 수 없다면, 저희 직원이 기꺼이 도와 드리겠습니다.

198 저에서 차량에게 이 긴급한 문제에 대한 해결책을 찾기 위해 **199** 열심히 노력하고 있다고 확실히 약속했습니다. 그 동안에, 조금 참이 주시고 이해해 주시면 대단히 감사하겠습니다.

진심을 담아,

관리팀

200 선사인 마켓

---

ground floor 1층　significant 상당한　rest assured that ~임을 확신해도 된다　pressing 긴급한

196 안우드에 대해서 암시된 것은?

(A) 시내 버스가 그 지역에 서비스를 제공하지 않는다.
(B) 많은 주민들이 시내에서 일한다.
(C) 선사인 마켓이 있기 전에는 제대로 된 식료품점이 없었다.
(D) 그곳 경제 성장이 제한되었다.

197 다음타운 앤 비요드 기획에 대해서 사실인 것은? (연계 지문 문제)

(A) 더 많은 주택을 추가하는 것을 제안한다.
(B) 2년 안에 완료될 것이다.
(C) 이전 시장에 의해서 시작되었다.
(D) 이용 가능한 주차 공건을 확장할 것이다.

198 공지의 목적은 무엇인가?

(A) 상황을 설명하기 위해서
(B) 불평을 제기하기 위해서
(C) 고객들을 비판하기 위해서
(D) 새로운 서비스를 제안하기 위해서

199 공지의 2번째 문단, 1번째 줄에 있는 '열심히'와 가장 비슷한 의미의 단어는?

(A) 강하게
(B) 부지런하게
(C) 단호하게
(D) 주로

200 선사인 마켓에 대해서 암시된 것은? (연계 지문 문제)

(A) 메인가에 위치해 있다.
(B) 약 5,000명의 고객이 있다.
(C) 자가용을 가진 손님들이 거의 없다.
(D) 새로운 주차장을 지을 것이다.

Actual Test

02

🎧 Listening Comprehension

PART 1

1 (B)	2 (A)	3 (C)	4 (D)	5 (C)	6 (C)

PART 2

7 (B)	8 (A)	9 (B)	10 (B)	11 (C)	12 (C)	13 (C)	14 (A)	15 (A)	16 (A)

7 (B)	8 (A)	9 (B)	10 (B)	11 (C)	12 (C)
13 (C)	14 (A)	15 (A)	16 (A)		
17 (C)	18 (C)	19 (C)	20 (C)	21 (B)	22 (B)
23 (A)	24 (B)	25 (B)	26 (A)		
27 (A)	28 (C)	29 (B)	30 (A)	31 (C)	

PART 3

32 (A)	33 (A)	34 (C)	35 (D)	36 (B)	37 (D)
38 (A)	39 (C)	40 (C)	41 (A)		
42 (C)	43 (B)	44 (C)	45 (D)	46 (C)	47 (D)
48 (B)	49 (C)	50 (C)	51 (A)		
52 (D)	53 (B)	54 (B)	55 (A)	56 (C)	57 (B)
58 (A)	59 (C)	60 (A)	61 (C)		
62 (A)	63 (C)	64 (D)	65 (C)	66 (D)	67 (C)
68 (A)	69 (D)	70 (B)			

PART 4

71 (A)	72 (C)	73 (A)	74 (D)	75 (A)	76 (B)
77 (A)	78 (B)	79 (C)	80 (B)		
81 (A)	82 (D)	83 (A)	84 (D)	85 (C)	86 (A)
87 (D)	88 (C)	89 (D)	90 (B)		
91 (D)	92 (C)	93 (A)	94 (B)	95 (C)	96 (A)
97 (B)	98 (B)	99 (A)	100 (B)		

📖 Reading Comprehension

PART 5

101 (A)	102 (A)	103 (B)	104 (A)	105 (B)	106 (B)
107 (B)	108 (C)	109 (C)	110 (C)		
111 (D)	112 (B)	113 (A)	114 (C)	115 (D)	116 (D)
117 (D)	118 (A)	119 (B)	120 (B)		
121 (A)	122 (D)	123 (A)	124 (C)	125 (D)	126 (D)
127 (D)	128 (A)	129 (C)	130 (B)		

PART 6

131 (D)	132 (B)	133 (C)	134 (B)	135 (C)	136 (B)
137 (A)	138 (C)	139 (D)	140 (A)		
141 (B)	142 (A)	143 (A)	144 (B)	145 (B)	146 (B)

PART 7

147 (A)	148 (D)	149 (B)	150 (D)	151 (B)	152 (C)
153 (C)	154 (A)	155 (B)	156 (C)		
157 (B)	158 (C)	159 (C)	160 (A)	161 (D)	162 (D)
163 (B)	164 (C)	165 (A)	166 (C)		
167 (A)	168 (D)	169 (A)	170 (D)	171 (A)	172 (A)
173 (A)	174 (B)	175 (C)	176 (D)		
177 (A)	178 (D)	179 (D)	180 (B)	181 (A)	182 (D)
183 (A)	184 (A)	185 (A)	186 (D)		
187 (B)	188 (A)	189 (D)	190 (C)	191 (D)	192 (B)
193 (A)	194 (C)	195 (C)	196 (C)		
197 (D)	198 (B)	199 (D)	200 (A)		

Part 1

본책 P59

1 미M
(A) He is moving some furniture.
(B) He is handling some boxes.
(C) He is opening a cabinet.
(D) He is setting up a sign.

(A) 남자가 가구를 옮기고 있다.
(B) **남자가 상자를 다루고 있다.**
(C) 남자가 캐비닛을 열고 있다.
(D) 남자가 표지판을 설치하고 있다.

handle 다루다; 들다, 옮기다   cabinet 보관함, 캐비닛   set up 설치하다   sign 표지판

2 미W
(A) They are working on the floor.
(B) They are measuring a wall.
(C) They are rolling up their sleeves.
(D) They are sweeping the sidewalk.

(A) 사람들이 바닥에 작업을 하고 있다.
(B) 사람들이 벽을 측정하고 있다.
(C) 사람들이 그들의 소매를 걷고 있다.
(D) 사람들이 보도를 쓸고 있다.

measure 재다, 측정하다   roll up one's sleeves 소매를 걷다
sweep (빗자루로) 쓸다   sidewalk 보도

3 영M
(A) The fruits are being placed in bags.
(B) Plants are growing in pots.
(C) Apples have been piled in the baskets.
(D) Crates of fruit are being delivered.

(A) 과일들이 가방에 담기고 있다.
(B) 식물들이 화분에서 자라고 있다.
(C) **사과가 바구니에 쌓여 있다.**
(D) 과일 상자들이 배달되고 있다.

place 놓다   plant 식물   pot 화분   pile 쌓다   crate 나무 상자

4 미W
(A) A mirror is being adjusted on a shelf.
(B) Some items are being removed from a case.
(C) A woman is polishing some glass cabinets.
(D) A woman is examining a pair of sunglasses.

(A) 거울이 선반 위로 조정되고 있다.
(B) 몇몇 물건들이 케이스에서 치워지고 있다.
(C) 여자가 유리 보관함을 닦고 있다.
(D) **여자가 한 쌍의 선글라스를 살펴보고 있다.**

adjust 조정하다   shelf 선반   polish 윤을 내다   examine 살펴보다

5 호M
(A) Shoppers are lining up to buy some products.
(B) A customer is winding a watch.
(C) Some merchandise is displayed for sale.
(D) Some vendors are standing inside the shop.

(A) 쇼핑객들이 제품을 사기 위해 줄을 서고 있다.
(B) 손님이 손목시계의 태엽을 감고 있다.
(C) **일부 상품이 판매를 위해 진열되어 있다.**
(D) 일부 노점상들이 가게 안에 서 있다.

line up 줄을 서다   wind (태엽을) 감다   merchandise 상품
display 진시하다   vendor 노점상

6 미W
(A) A row of plants have been placed on a shelf.
(B) Potted plants are hanging from the ceiling.
(C) She is holding a watering can with both hands.
(D) She is pouring the soil into a container.

(A) 한 줄로 늘어선 식물들이 선반 위에 놓여 있다.
(B) 화분들이 천장에 매달려 있다.
(C) 여자가 두 손으로 물뿌리개를 들고 있다.
(D) 여자가 용기에 흙을 붓고 있다.

a row of 한 줄의   place 놓다   potted plant 화분 식물   hang
걸다, 걸리다   ceiling 천장   hold 들다   watering can 물뿌리개
pour 붓다, 따르다   soil 흙   container 컨테이너, 용기

Part 2

본책 P62

7 미W
Who will I need to speak to?
(A) Kathleen Moore was.
(B) You should contact Janine.
(C) It was signed last week.

제가 누구에게 이야기해야 하나요?
(A) 캐슬린 무어였어요.
(B) **재닌에게 연락하셔야 합니다.**
(C) 지난주에 서명되었어요.

sign 서명하다

8 미W
The album got a good review, didn't it?
(A) Yes, and it deserved it.
(B) The apartment has a great view.
(C) She went too late.

그 음반은 좋은 평을 받았어요, 그렇죠?
(A) **네, 그리고 충분히 그럴 만했어요.**
(B) 그 아파트는 좋은 경관을 가졌어요.
(C) 그녀는 너무 늦게 갔어요.

review 평, 논평   deserve ~을 받을 만하다

9 영M
Why did Damson Inc. relocate their offices?
(A) She never offered.
(B) They needed more room.
(C) Not too long.

댐슨 주식회사는 왜 그들의 사무실을 이전했나요?
(A) 그녀는 한 번도 권하지 않았어요.
(B) **그들은 공간이 더 필요했어요.**
(C) 너무 길지 않아요.

relocate 이전하다   offer 제안하다, 권하다
faulty 결함이 있는, 고장 난

10 미W
Do you know if Mr. Chilt is arriving this afternoon?
(A) Not every one of them.
(B) I believe so.
(C) Sorry, it's faulty.

칠트 씨가 오늘 오후에 도착하는지 알고 있나요?
(A) 모두는 아니에요.
(B) **그렇다고 알고 있어요.**
(C) 죄송하지만, 고장이 났어요.

11 미M
The session has been changed to a new location.
(A) They're leaving on Monday.
(B) I saw that film.
(C) Yes, it's in the main convention hall.

회의는 새로운 장소로 변경되었습니다.
(A) 그들은 월요일에 떠납니다.
(B) 저는 그 영화를 봤어요.
(C) **네, 그건 중앙 컨벤션 홀에서 열립니다.**

session (특정한 활동을 위한) 시간   location 위치, 장소
convention hall 회의장

12 미W
When can we expect the documents?
(A) The shipping merchandise.
(B) In dreadful condition.
(C) Within 48 hours.

우리는 언제 서류를 받을 것으로 예상할 수 있나요?
(A) 선적하는 상품이요.
(B) 끔찍한 상태입니다.
(C) **48시간 이내요.**

shipping 배송   dreadful 끔찍한

13 How many people will be attending the seminar?
영M (A) It went well, thank you.
미W (B) Because it's undersubscribed.
(C) Most of our team.

몇 명이 세미나에 참석할 건가요?
(A) 잘 진행되었습니다, 감사합니다.
(B) 신청자가 부족해서요.
(C) 팀원 대부분이요.

go well 잘 되다 undersubscribed 신청참가 응모자가 불충분한

14 What is the precise time now in Tokyo?
미W (A) A quarter to four.
미M (B) Another 25 kilometers or so.
(C) Yes, many times.

도쿄의 정확한 시간은 몇 시인가요?
(A) 3시 45분이요.
(B) 약 25킬로미터쯤 더요.
(C) 네, 여러 번이요.

precise 정확한 a quarter to 시간 ~시가 되기 15분 전 or so ~쯤, ~가량

15 Would you like to buy two jars of sauce as they're reduced?
미W (A) I think I'll just buy one for now.
미M (B) No, I didn't get that.
(C) A ticket for one, please.

할인되었으니 소스를 두 병 사실래요?
(A) 지금은 한 병만 살까 해요.
(B) 아니요, 저는 그걸 받지 않았어요.
(C) 표 한 장 주세요.

jar 병, 단지 reduced 할인된 감소된 for now 지금은, 현재로선

16 Do you want the first contract or can I send you the amended one?
미W (A) The latter will do.
영M (B) A manager's signature.
(C) It's out of control.

첫 번째 계약서를 원하나요, 아니면 수정된 걸 보내 드릴까요?
(A) 후자면 됩니다.
(B) 과장님의 서명이요.
(C) 통제 불능입니다.

amend 수정하다 latter 후자 manager 과장, 관리자 signature 서명 out of control 통제가 불가능한

17 When did you return to Singapore?
미M (A) No, it's in Malaysia.
미W (B) Please put it there.
(C) Four years ago.

언제 싱가포르로 돌아오셨나요?
(A) 아니요, 그건 말레이시아에 있어요.
(B) 거기에 두세요.
(C) 4년 전이요.

return 돌아오다, 돌아가다

18 Where can I find a list of our past customers?
미W (A) That's not good for me.
미W (B) I'll have one, thanks.
(C) It's in our internal archives.

어디에서 과거 손님 명단을 찾을 수 있나요?
(A) 그건 제게 좋지 않아요.
(B) 한 개 주세요, 감사합니다.
(C) 그건 내부 기록 보관소에 있습니다.

past 과거의, 지난 internal 내부의 archive 기록 보관소

19 Who is in charge of choosing the product color?
미M (A) A new blender.
미W (B) It was commissioned three years ago.
(C) The team leader is.

누가 제품의 색을 선택하는 것을 담당하나요?
(A) 새 믹서기요.
(B) 3년 전에 임명되었습니다.
(C) 팀 리더입니다.

in charge of ~을 담당하다 blender 믹서기, 분쇄기 commission 임명하다

20 I heard you've been put forward for promotion.
미W (A) He didn't tell us his details.
미W (B) Why don't you book it now?
(C) Yes, it was unexpected.

저는 당신이 승진 대상자로 추천되었다고 들었어요.
(A) 그는 우리에게 그의 정보를 알리지 않았어요.
(B) 지금 예약하는 건 어때요?
(C) 네, 예상치 못했어요.

put forward (후보로) 추천하다, 제안하다 unexpected 예상치 못한

21 Should we label the last bottles in the morning?
영M (A) Look in the closet on the left.
미W (B) I'd rather do it this evening.
(C) We can always check again.

우리 마지막 병의 라벨은 아침에 붙일까요?
(A) 왼쪽의 벽장을 찾아보세요.
(B) 저는 차라리 오늘 저녁에 하겠습니다.
(C) 우리는 언제든지 다시 확인할 수 있어요.

label 표/라벨을 붙이다 rather 차라리

22 How did you learn about this recruitment fair?
미W (A) We close at 9.
영M (B) From the newspaper advertisement.
(C) Yes, it was very tidy.

당신은 이 채용 박람회를 어떻게 알게 되었나요?
(A) 우리는 9시에 문을 닫습니다.
(B) 신문 광고에서요.
(C) 네, 그건 매우 깔끔했습니다.

recruitment fair 채용 박람회 tidy 깔끔한, 잘 정돈된

23 Aren't you supposed to be in the meeting upstairs?
미W (A) No, Alexis went in my place.
미M (B) It's my phone number.
(C) I think I missed her.

당신은 위층에 있는 회의에 있어야 하는 것 아닌가요?
(A) 아니요, 알렉시스가 대신해요.
(B) 그건 제 전화번호예요.
(C) 제 생각엔 저는 그녀를 놓친 것 같아요.

go in one's place 자리를 대신하다 miss 놓치다; 그리워하다

24 Where do you place the completed samples when we're done?
영M (A) Sit anywhere you like.
미W (B) There's a container on the floor.
(C) No, I'm not finished yet.

우리가 끝나면 완성된 샘플은 어디에 놓나요?
(A) 앉고 싶은 곳에 앉으세요.
(B) 바닥에 용기가 있어요.
(C) 아니요, 아직 끝나지 않았어요.

place 두다 complete 완료하다 container 용기

Part 3

Questions 32-34 refer to the following conversation. 미M 미W

M Excuse me, ㉜ do you know where I can find the Porter History Exhibition? I've been looking all over but the information I was given at the coach station seems to be incorrect.

W Actually, I'm going there now. I help out at the place where the exhibition is being held. We can go over there together.

M Would it be better to take public transport? ㉝ I'm meeting a colleague there in 20 minutes and I don't want to miss him.

W Don't worry, ㉞ the exhibition is just around the corner. It would take us longer to find public transport than it would to walk as it's less than ten minutes away.

남 실례합니다, 포터 역사 전시회를 어디에서 찾을 수 있는지 알려 주실 수 있으세요? 여기저기 다 찾아보았지만 버스 정류장에서 받은 정보가 올바르지 않은 것 같아요.

여 실은, 제가 그곳으로 갈 거예요. 제가 전시회가 열리는 곳에서 일을 돕고 있어요. 저와 같이 가면 됩니다.

남 대중교통을 이용하는 것이 더 나을까요? 제가 20분 후에 동료를 만날 건데, 그를 놓치고 싶지 않아요.

여 걱정하지 마세요, 전시회는 근처에 있으니까요. 10분도 안 되는 거리 니까, 걸어가는 것보다 대중교통을 찾는 것이 더 오래 걸릴 거예요.

exhibition 전시 │ look all over 모든 곳을 찾아보다 │ coach station 버스 정류장 │ incorrect 틀린, 올바르지 않은 │ help out 돕다 │ colleague 동료 │ just around the corner 근처에 │ 가까이에 │ venue 개최 장소

32 Where are the speakers going?

(A) To an exhibition
(B) To a museum
(C) To a taxi stand
(D) To a friend's house

화자들은 어디로 가고 있는가?

(A) 전시회
(B) 박물관
(C) 택시 승강장
(D) 친구의 집

---

25 The train I take to get home is cancelled for the foreseeable future.
미M 미W

(A) By next week.
(B) What transport are you taking then?
(C) It's not that close.

제가 집으로 갈 때 타는 기차가 당분간 취소되었습니다.

(A) 다음 주까지요.
(B) 그럼 이제 어떤 교통수단을 이용하실 건 같아요?
(C) 그렇게 가깝진 않아요.

cancel 취소하다 │ foreseeable future 가까운 미래에 │ transport 교통수단

26 Why don't you find out if Mr. Eyres can approve the students' request?
영M 영M

(A) He is busy, regrettably.
(B) A student loan.
(C) No, I couldn't find it.

에일스 씨가 학생들의 요청을 승인할 수 있는지 알아보시는 건 어때요?

(A) 안타깝게도, 그는 바쁩니다.
(B) 학생 융자요.
(C) 아니요, 저는 찾을 수 없었어요.

regrettably 안타깝게도 │ student loan 학생 융자

27 Was this order placed online or over the phone?
미W 미M

(A) It was an online order.
(B) A new project.
(C) Please order more boxes.

이 주문은 온라인으로 받은 건가요, 아니면 전화로 받은 건가요?

(A) 온라인 주문이었어요.
(B) 새로운 프로젝트예요.
(C) 박스를 더 주문해 주세요.

over the phone 전화상으로

28 Why was the delivery early this week?
미M 미W

(A) In June, I believe.
(B) I'll have time to do it.
(C) The order was completed.

이번 주에 왜 배달이 일찍 왔나요?

(A) 6월일 거예요.
(B) 저는 그것을 할 시간이 있어요.
(C) 주문이 완료되었어요.

complete 완료하다

29 Isn't anyone working late in the laboratory?
미W 미W

(A) I don't have much left.
(B) Maybe they're at dinner.
(C) The experiment procedures.

실험실에서 늦게까지 일하고 있는 사람이 아무도 없나요?

(A) 저에겐 많이 남아 있지 않아요.
(B) 그들이 아마 저녁 식사 중인 것 같아요.
(C) 실험 절차요.

laboratory 실험실 │ procedure 과정

30 I might have left my phone in your taxi.
영M 미W

(A) Okay, I'll hunt for it.
(B) There's a problem with the car.
(C) No, I'll be here all evening.

당신의 택시에 제 전화기를 두고 내렸을 수도 있어요.

(A) 알겠어요, 제가 찾아볼게요.
(B) 차에 문제가 있어요.
(C) 아니요, 저는 저녁 내내 여기 있을 거예요.

hunt for ~을 찾다; ~을 사냥하다

31 Should we give the manager our resignation letters now?
미W 미M

(A) Until the middle of the week.
(B) The residential building on Kings Street.
(C) Let's wait for the meeting in the morning.

과장님께 우리의 사직서를 지금 드려야 할까요?

(A) 주 중반까지요.
(B) 킹스 가의 주거용 건물이요.
(C) 아침 회의 때까지 기다립시다.

resignation letter 사직서 │ residential building 주거용 건물

33 What will happen in 20 minutes?

(A) A meeting
(B) A bus ride
(C) A talk
(D) A display

20분 후에 무슨 일이 있을 것인가?
(A) 만남
(B) 버스 승차
(C) 발표
(D) 전시회

34 Why does the woman suggest that she and the man walk?

(A) There are no available taxis.
(B) The walk would do them good.
(C) They are close to the venue.
(D) Buses are expensive.

여자는 왜 그녀와 남자가 걷는 것을 제안하는가?
(A) 탈 수 있는 택시가 없다.
(B) 산책이 그들에게 좋을 것이다.
(C) 목적지가 가까이 있다.
(D) 버스는 요금이 비싸다.

Questions 35-37 refer to the following conversation. [미W] [영M]

W Mr. Foucault, here is the confirmation for your new table. Now, ⑯ when would you prefer us to deliver it? We do local deliveries from Sunday to Monday.

M Well, ⑯ the only time I'll be able to take off work is Thursday. It will have to be on that day. Is there anything extra to pay?

W No, delivery is free of charge. But ⑰ if you want us to remove your old table, you'll have to pay a minimal amount.

M I'll have to get back to you on that. My co-worker might want it, as it's still in excellent condition.

여 포컬트 씨, 당신의 새 테이블을 위한 확인서입니다. 언제 이것을 배송하시길 원하세요? 저희는 일주일 내내 배송을 해 드립니다.

남 음, 제가 근무를 쉴 수 있는 날은 목요일뿐입니다. 그날로 해야 할 것 같아요. 추가로 내야 할 비용이 있나요?

여 아니요, 배송은 무료입니다. 하지만 만약 당신이 우리가 오래된 테이블을 치우길 원하시면, 최소 요금을 지불하셔야 합니다.

남 그건 제가 알아보고 나중에 다시 알려드릴게요. 그것이 아직 좋은 상태여서, 제 동료가 그걸 원할 수도 있거든요.

confirmation 확인서 시항 local delivery 시내 배달 take off work 휴가를 낸다. 근무를 쉬다 minimal 최소의 get back to ~에게 나중에 다시 연락하다 co-worker 동료 extended 길어진, 늘어난 overnight shipping 당일 배송 bespoke 맞춤형 removal 제거

35 What are the speakers mainly discussing?

(A) Returning an item
(B) Repairing an item of clothing
(C) Hiring a furniture maker
(D) Arranging a delivery

화자들이 주로 이야기하고 있는 것은?
(A) 제품 반품
(B) 의류 제품 수선
(C) 가구 제조업체 고용
(D) 배송 준비

36 What day will the man be available?

(A) Monday
(B) Thursday
(C) Friday
(D) Sunday

남자는 어느 요일에 시간이 가능한가?
(A) 월요일
(B) 목요일
(C) 금요일
(D) 일요일

37 According to the woman, what requires an extra fee?

(A) An extended guarantee
(B) Overnight shipping
(C) A bespoke design
(D) Removal of the existing item

여자에 따르면, 추가 비용이 필요한 것은?
(A) 연장된 보증서
(B) 익일 배송
(C) 맞춤형 디자인
(D) 기존 물건 제거

Questions 38-40 refer to the following conversation. [미M] [미W]

M Hey, Ruth. Some of us from the sports center are booking tickets for ㉟ the Slingbacks game next week. Are you available to come with us?

W Oh, the Slingbacks are one of my favorite teams. ㊴ I'm amazed tickets are still on sale, though. I imagined they were sold out.

M Yes, they had to change the venue to accommodate demand. I'm going to book seats online for everyone tomorrow, so we can all sit together. I can reserve one for you as well, but ㊵ please tell me by later this evening if you'd like to go to see them or not.

남 루스, 스포츠 센터에서 몇 명이 다음 주 슬링백 경기 표를 예매하고 있어요. 당신도 우리와 함께 갈 수 있으세요?

여 오, 슬링백은 제가 가장 좋아하는 팀 중 하나예요. 그런데 아직도 그 표가 판매 중이라니 놀랍네요. 이미 매진되었다고 생각했거든요.

남 네, 그들은 수요를 맞추기 위해 경기 장소를 변경해야 했어요. 저는 모두 다 같이 앉을 수 있도록 전체 인원의 좌석을 내일 예매할 겁니다. 당신을 위한 표도 예매할 수 있지만, 가서 볼 건지 아닌지 저녁까지 저에게 알려주세요.

be amazed 깜짝 놀라다 sold out 표가 매진된, 품절인 venue 〈콘서트 · 스포츠 경기 · 회담 등의〉 장소 accommodate 수용하다 seat 좌석 as well 〈~뿐만 아니라〉 ~도 mid 중간, 중반 relocate 이전하다 charge 청구하다 intention 의사

38 What event does the man plan to attend?

(A) A sports event
(B) A concert
(C) A theater performance
(D) A school play

남자가 참석할 계획인 행사는?
(A) 스포츠 행사
(B) 콘서트
(C) 극장 공연
(D) 학교 연극

39 Why is the woman surprised?

(A) A performance has been relocated.
(B) An event has been cancelled.
(C) Space is available.
(D) Parking is charged.

Questions 44-46 refer to the following conversation. 미W 영M

W Well, this has been a beneficial meeting, Andrew, and ㊹ ㊺ I'd like to offer you the opportunity of a franchise with the Chinese Chicken. Now, as you are aware, there's a probation period for six months but after that, there'll be the opportunity for you to take over the franchise permanently.

M Thank you, Ms. Jackson. I'm pleased you agreed to give me a chance even though I am new to the fast food industry.

W Well, ㊻ I was particularly impressed with the portfolio of successful businesses you have managed in the past. We're looking forward to working with you.

여 음, 이번 회의는 매우 유익했어요, 앤드류. 그리고 저는 당신에게 차이 니즈 치킨 프랜차이즈 기회를 제안하고 싶습니다. 현재 당신이 알다 시피, 6개월 동안은 수습 기간이지만, 그 후에는 당신이 앞으로도 계 속 그 프랜차이즈를 맡게 될 기회가 있을 겁니다.

남 감사합니다, 잭슨 씨. 제가 패스트푸드 업계가 처음임에도, 기회를 주 신 데 대해 매우 기쁩니다.

여 음, 저는 특히 당신이 과거에 관리해 온 성공적인 사업들의 포트폴리 오에 매우 깊은 인상을 받았어요. 우리는 당신과 같이 일하게 된 것 을 매우 기대하겠습니다.

beneficial 유익한, 도움이 되는   franchise 프랜차이즈   probation period 수습기간   take over 맡다; 인수하다   permanently 영구적으로 particularly 특히   be impressed 깊은 인상을 받다, 감명을 받다 portfolio (특히 구직 때 제출하는 사진·그림 등의) 작품집[포트폴리오] manage 운영하다   in the past 과거에   apprenticeship 견습직

44 Where does the woman work?
(A) At a travel agency
(B) At an employment agency
(C) At a fast food chain
(D) At a clothing store

여자는 어디에서 일하는가?
(A) 여행사
(B) 직업소개소
(C) 패스트푸드 체인점
(D) 옷 가게

---

storage 창고   unit 구성단위   lease 임대하다   rental agreement 임대 계약   exterior 외관   clear out 치우다, 청소하다   current 현재의   stock 재고   extend 연장하다   vendor 행상인, 판매 회사   rearrange 재조정하다

41 What has the woman decided to do?
(A) Sell a building
(B) Extend the lease
(C) Increase the rent
(D) Renovate a house

여자는 무엇을 하기로 결정했는가?
(A) 건물 판매하기
(B) 임대 연장하기
(C) 임대료 인상하기
(D) 집 개조하기

42 According to the woman, who will come to the unit on Saturday?
(A) A contracting team
(B) A vendor
(C) A few of friends
(D) A work crew

여자에 따르면, 토요일에 누가 건물로 올 것인가?
(A) 계약 팀
(B) 판매 회사
(C) 몇몇 친구들
(D) 직업반

43 What request does the man make?
(A) That a contract be renewed
(B) That the dates be rearranged
(C) That the rent be reduced
(D) That the exterior be painted

남자가 요청하는 것은?
(A) 계약을 갱신해 달라고
(B) 날짜를 재조정해 달라고
(C) 임대료를 낮춰달라고
(D) 외관을 페인트 칠해 달라고

여자가 놀란 이유는?
(A) 공연 장소가 이전되었다.
(B) 행사가 취소되었다.
(C) 좌석이 남아 있다.
(D) 주차 비용이 청구된다.

40 What should the woman do by the end of the day?
(A) Contact the booking desk
(B) Change a schedule
(C) Confirm her intention to attend
(D) Issue an invitation

여자가 오늘 저녁까지 해야 하는 것은?
(A) 예약 창구에 연락하기
(B) 일정 변경하기
(C) 그녀의 참석 의사 확인해 주기
(D) 초청장 발부하기

Questions 41-43 refer to the following conversation. 미W 미M

W Kolen, this is Ann. I am the owner of the storage unit you are leasing. I just wanted to tell you that ㊶ I've made a decision to sell the unit.

M Oh, really? My rental agreement doesn't end until March. Will I be able to use it until then?

W Of course, that's not an issue. But ㊷ on Saturday, some of my friends will be repairing the exterior and repairing some small damage on the roof. Just a few repairs to prepare it for sale.

M ㊸ Is there any possibility this can be done at the end of next week? I'll be clearing my current stock out before then. So they could do the work when the unit is empty.

여 콜렌, 앤이에요. 저는 당신이 임대하고 있는 창고의 소유주입니다. 그 건물을 팔기로 결정을 내렸어요.

남 오, 정말인가요? 제 임대 계약은 3월이 되어야 끝나요. 그때까지는 제 가 사용할 수 있는 건가요?

여 그럼요, 그건 문제가 되지 않습니다. 하지만 토요일에 제 친구들이 외 관을 수리하고 지붕 위의 손상된 부분을 수리할 것입니다. 판매 준비 를 위해 조금만 수리를 해야 합니다.

남 혹시 이 작업을 다음 주말에 하실 수 있을까요? 그 전에 제가 현재 있는 재고품을 치울 거예요. 그러면 건물이 비었을 때 그들이 작업을 할 수 있겠네요.

45 What does the woman offer the man?

(A) An apprenticeship
(B) Some food samples
(C) Travel opportunities
(D) A franchise

여자는 남자에게 무엇을 제안하는가?

(A) 견습직
(B) 음식 샘플
(C) 여행 기회
(D) 프랜차이즈

46 What was the woman particularly interested in?

(A) A résumé
(B) A reference letter
(C) A portfolio
(D) A travel schedule

여자가 특히 관심을 가진 것은?

(A) 이력서
(B) 추천서
(C) 포트폴리오
(D) 여행 일정

Questions 47-49 refer to the following conversation with three speakers. (영M) (미W) (영W)

M ❼ I'm expecting another patient in a few minutes. Could one of you please prepare examining room three?

W1 That would be Mr. Todd Atkinson. I'll get it ready for him.

M Thanks. ❽ I also need to review his medical file before I see him.

W2 I have been looking for it, but it isn't in the cabinet where it is supposed to be.

W1 Sorry, I got busy and forgot to tell you that I already took it out. I put it in room three.

W2 Please tell me next time. I was worried it had gotten lost under all these billing statements.

M No harm done. Please take Mr. Atkinson to room three as soon as it is ready.

W1 Sure.

남 몇 분 후에 또 다른 환자가 오는 걸로 알고 있어요. 누가 3번 진찰실을 좀 준비해줄 수 있나요?

여1 그 환자 이름은 토드 앳킨슨입니다. 진찰실은 제가 준비할게요.

남 고마워요. 그리고 만나기 전에 그 환자의 의료 기록을 확인해 보고 싶어요.

여2 제가 기록을 찾아 봤거든요. 그런데 그게 있어야 할 캐비닛 안에 없어요.

여1 죄송합니다. 제가 바빠서 그 기록을 벌써 꺼내 뒀다는 것을 말한다는 걸 깜박했어요. 3번 방에 뒀어요.

여2 다음 번에는 제게 얘기해 주세요. 제가 좀 걱정했거든요, 이 청구서 더미 아래에서 잃어버린 줄 알았어요.

남 큰 문제될 거 없어요. 준비가 되는 대로 토드 앳킨슨 씨를 3번 방으로 모셔다 드리세요.

여1 네.

examining room 진찰실 billing statement 거래 내역서

47 Where do the speakers most likely work?

(A) At a pharmacy
(B) At a fitness center
(C) At a copy center
(D) At a doctor's office

화자들은 어디서 일할 것 같은가?

(A) 약국
(B) 피트니스 센터
(C) 복사 가게
(D) 개인 병원

48 What does the man say he needs to see?

(A) A bill
(B) Medical information
(C) A billing statement
(D) A label

남자는 무엇을 보고자 하는가?

(A) 청구서
(B) 의료 정보
(C) 거래 내역서
(D) 라벨

49 Why does the man say, "No harm done"?

(A) He is glad the bills are found.
(B) He has an idea to organize files.
(C) He is not concerned about the issue.
(D) He is satisfied with the women's performance.

왜 남자는 "큰 문제될 거 없어요"라고 말했는가?

(A) 청구서를 찾아서 기쁘다.
(B) 파일을 정리할 아이디어가 있다.
(C) 그 문제에 대해서 걱정하지 않는다.
(D) 여자의 성과에 만족한다.

Questions 50-52 refer to the following conversation. (미W) (영M)

W Hi. This is Beth Rivers calling. I rented one of your pensions in Miami last month. ⑩ I just received an e-mail from one of your staff saying that I owe $200. I thought I paid the bill.

M Let me check our computer system. It says here that you were charged a damage fee.

W ⑪ I don't get it.

M According to the employee who inspected the property after you left, ⑪ the door to the terrace was cracked.

W I don't know what you are talking about. I never even went into the terrace during my stay. If there was a problem, I would have reported it when I checked out.

M Let me get my supervisor. Only he can process this type of issue. Hold on, please.

pension 펜션 terrace 툴 마당 crack 금가게 하다; 금, 틈 dispute 이의를 제기하다

50 Why is the woman calling?

(A) To return a key
(B) To change a reservation
(C) To dispute a charge
(D) To inform the man of the payday

여자는 왜 전화하는가?

(A) 열쇠를 반납하려고
(B) 예약을 변경하려고
(C) 부과금에 관해 이의를 제기하기 위해
(D) 남자에게 부과일자를 알리기 위해

51 What does the man say happened?

(A) A door was damaged.
(B) A reservation was canceled.
(C) A key was lost.
(D) All pensions were already rented out.

남자는 무슨 일이 일어났다고 이야기하는가?

(A) 문에 손상이 생겼다.
(B) 예약이 취소되었다.
(C) 열쇠를 잃어버렸다.
(D) 모든 펜션이 이미 임대되었다.

52 What does the woman mean when she says, "I don't get it"?

(A) She was lost in the area.
(B) She never received an inspection report.
(C) She thinks the door is too expensive.
(D) She doesn't understand the reason for the fee.

여자가 말한 "이해가 안 되네요"는 무엇을 의미하는가?

(A) 여자가 길을 잃었다.
(B) 여자가 검사보고서를 받지 못했다.
(C) 여자는 문이 비싸다고 생각한다.
(D) 여자는 비용의 이유에 관해 이해를 하지 못한다.

여 안녕하세요. 전화드리는 저는 베스 리버스입니다. 제가 마이애미에 있는 귀사의 펜션 중 하나를 지난달에 임대했어요. 제가 얼마 전에 귀사의 직원 중 한 명으로부터 이메일을 받았는데요, 제가 200달러를 지불해야 한다고 나와 있네요. 저는 지불했다고 기억하고 있거든요.

남 제가 컴퓨터로 한 번 확인해 보겠습니다. 확인해 보니 파손비 부분에 관해서 부과되신 내역이 있네요.

여 이해가 안 되요.

남 귀하께서 퇴실하고 나서 저희 직원이 펜션을 확인해 본 결과, 테라스로 향하는 문에 금이 가 있는 것을 확인했습니다.

여 무슨 이야기를 하시는지 잘 모르겠어요. 저는 머무르는 동안 테라스에 나간 적도 없어요. 만약에 문제가 있었다면, 제가 확인했을 때 일 저만 처리될 권한이 있거든요. 잠시만 기다려 주세요.

남 제가 매니저와 함께 나올 수 있도록 해 드릴게요. 이러한 문제는 매니저만 처리할 권한이 있거든요. 잠시만 기다려 주세요.

Questions 53-55 refer to the following conversation. (미M) (미W)

M Hi, Shelley. ⑬ Have you heard any news about the bid you submitted to Patriot Corporation for the construction contract?

W We didn't get it.

M Oh, that's a shame. I know you put a lot of effort into it, but I hope you don't see it as wasted effort.

W It certainly feels like I wasted a lot of time since we didn't get the contract.

M Remember that this was your first time preparing a bid. There will be many more contracts to try. ⑮ Now you have some solid experience that will help you next time.

W Thanks, Donald. That's a better way to look at the situation. I'll keep that in mind.

bid 입찰, 입찰가격

53 What are the speakers mainly discussing?

(A) A construction material
(B) A bid for a contract
(C) An affected deadline
(D) A completed task

화자들은 무엇에 관한 논의를 하고 있는가?

(A) 건설 자재
(B) 계약 입찰
(C) 영향이 있는 마감일
(D) 완료된 업무

남 안녕, 셀리. 네가 패트리어트 사에 건설 계약 건에 대해 제출한 입찰에 관해서 들은 소식이 있니?

여 우리 입찰에서 떨어졌어.

남 아런다. 네가 노력 많이 한 거 내가 알고 있는데, 그래도 나는 네가 그 노력이 헛수고라고는 생각하지 않았으면 해.

여 사실 내가 시간을 많이 낭비했다고 생각하고 있긴 해, 계약을 못 따내긴 했으니까.

남 잊지 마. 이번이 네가 입찰을 준비한 첫 시도였다는 것을 말이야. 시도할 낢은 계약들이 있을 거야. 이제 너는 다음번 시도 때 네게 도움이 될 제대로 된 경험이 있잖아.

여 고마워, 도널드. 그렇게 생각하는 것이 좋겠다. 꼭 기억하고 있을게.

54 Why does the man say, "that's a shame"?

(A) He is not proud of what the woman did.

(B) He is expressing sympathy.

(C) He expected the result.

(D) He is excited to hear the news.

왜 남자는 "이럼이다"라고 말하는가?

(A) 남자는 여자가 한 일이 자랑스럽지 않다.

(B) 남자는 동정을 표현하고 있다.

(C) 남자는 결과를 예상했다.

(D) 남자는 소식을 듣게 되어 기쁘다.

55 What does the man remind the woman about?

(A) She has gained experience.

(B) She will need his help soon.

(C) She has to put in a higher bid.

(D) She was recently hired.

남자는 여자에게 무엇을 상기시키는가?

(A) 경험을 얻었다.

(B) 곧 남자의 도움을 필요로 할 것이다.

(C) 더 높은 금액을 제시해야 한다.

(D) 최근에 고용되었다.

Questions 56-58 refer to the following conversation. 미W 미M

W So, Miguel! ⑤⑥ Thanks for applying for Colonel in chief. I see from your credentials that you served abroad before. Why don't we begin by discussing your most recent army position?

M Sure, my last posting was at the Mozambique Barracks. ⑤⑦ I was in charge of training a number of military divisions, and we protected a number of important military installations.

W That's impressive. But it appears you only served there for three months. Why did you have to leave?

M Well, ⑤⑧ it was only a temporary posting. I was covering the absence of the chief lieutenant who was on sick leave. So he returned and I had to go back to my unit.

colonel in chief 명예 연대장 람·조직·국가 등을 위해 일하다, 근무하다 abroad 해외에, 해외로 posting 배치, 파견 barrack 막사 be in charge of ~을 담당하다 division 부서, 사단 a number of 많은 military installation 군사 시설 impressive 인상 깊은 temporary 임시의 cover (자리를 비운 사람의 일을) 대신하다 absence 부재 lieutenant 중위 sick leave 병가 unit (특정 임무를 위한) 부대 second in command 부사령관 diversify 다각화하다 credentials 자격, 자격증 serve (어떤 사

56 What position is the man applying for?

(A) Second in command

(B) Company engineer

(C) Colonel in chief

(D) Chief lieutenant

남자는 어느 직책에 지원하고 있는가?

(A) 부사령관

(B) 회사 기사

(C) 명예 연대장

(D) 선임 중위

57 What does the man say he was in charge of?

(A) Planning a campaign

(B) Training army personnel

(C) Teaching at a school

(D) Constructing a building

남자는 그가 무엇을 담당했었다고 말하는가?

(A) 캠페인 기획

(B) 군사 인력 훈련

(C) 학교 교육

(D) 건물 건설

58 Why did the man leave his last post?

(A) He was employed on a temporary basis.

(B) He was offered a better position.

(C) He wanted to diversify.

(D) He moved to a different city.

남자가 그의 최근 배치를 떠난 이유는 무엇인가?

(A) 임시로 고용되었다.

(B) 더 좋은 직책을 제안받았다.

(C) 다양한 경험을 하고 싶었다.

(D) 다른 도시로 이사했다.

Questions 59-61 refer to the following conversation. 영M 미W

M Leanne, ⑥⑩ do you know where Simon Jack's application form is? He is the third interviewee this afternoon.

W Yes, I took out all the files for the applicants invited to come in today. ⑥⑨ They should be on your desk next to the pile of employer files.

M Oh, okay. You're one step ahead of me, thanks.

W No problem. ⑥⑪ Today is the date of decorating the administration department office. Remember? The filing system is in a bit of disarray. So when I arrived, I took out all the application forms we need today from the office.

남 리앤, 오늘 세 번째 면접자인 사이먼 잭의 지원서가 어디에 있는지 아시나요? 그는 오늘 세 번째 면접자입니다.

여 네, 제가 오늘 면접 보러 올 지원자들 파일을 모두 꺼내 놓았습니다. 서류들은 고용주 파일 옆의 당신 책상에 있을 거예요.

남 오, 알겠습니다. 당신은 저보다 한 발 앞서 있군요. 감사합니다.

여 괜찮습니다. 오늘이 행정부에 도배 작업이 있는 날이에요. 기억하세요? 파일이 조금 어지럽혀졌어요. 그래서 제가 도착했을 때, 오늘 필요한 모든 지원서를 사무실에서 꺼내 놓았어요.

application form 지원서 take out 꺼내다 paperwork 서류 작업 ahead of ~에 앞에 decorate 장식하다; 도배하다 administration department 행정부 in a disarray 어지럽혀진 refurbish 새로 꾸미다, 재단장하다

59 Where do the speakers most likely work?

(A) In a doctor's office

(B) In a decorating shop

(C) In an employment agency

(D) At a music store

화자들은 어디에서 일할 것 같은가?

(A) 개인 병원
(B) 장식품 매장
(C) **직업소개소**
(D) 음반 가게

60 What does the man ask the woman about?
(A) The location of some information
(B) The time of an interview
(C) The contact details of a painter
(D) The cost of an item

남자가 여자에게 무엇에 관해 물어보는가?
(A) **어떤 자료의 위치**
(B) 면접 시간
(C) 페인트공의 연락처
(D) 제품의 가격

61 What does the woman say is happening today?
(A) A business is relocating.
(B) New equipment is being installed.
(C) An office is being refurbished.
(D) A filing system is being updated.

여자는 오늘 무슨 일이 있을 것이라고 말하는가?
(A) 사업체가 이전할 것이다.
(B) 새 장비가 설치될 것이다.
(C) **사무실이 재단장될 것이다.**
(D) 파일 시스템이 갱신될 것이다.

Questions 62-64 refer to the following conversation. 미W 미M

W Zack, how is the design of ⓺ **the new suction cleaner progressing?** I noticed your department has been working hard these past few months.

M Well, ⓺ we devised a powerful wireless cleaner that can be operated without a cable. People will be able to clean easily to reach places, even outdoors.

W I'm a gardener, and I'd certainly want to try a product like that. When do you anticipate it'll be ready for launch?

M Later this week, ⓺ we're going to ask some volunteers to try out a prototype as members of a research group so that we can make any required changes. With luck, we'll start manufacturing within the next six months.

여 잭, 새로운 진공청소기의 디자인이 어떻게 진행되어 가고 있나요? 지난 몇 달간 당신 부서가 열심히 작업해 오는 것을 봤어요.

남 음. 저희는 전선 없이 작동되는 강력한 무선 청소기를 고안해 냈어요. 사람들은 심지어 야외에서도 손쉽게 청소할 수 있을 것입니다.

여 저는 정원사이고, 저라면 확실히 그런 제품을 사용해 보고 싶을 거예요. 출시 준비가 되는 시점은 언제로 예상하나요?

남 이번 주에에 저희는 필요한 수정을 할 수 있도록 몇몇 지원자들에게 연구 그룹의 일원으로서 그 시제품을 시험해 보도록 요청할 것입니다. 운이 좋으면 저희는 다음 6개월 이내에 제조를 시작할 것입니다.

62 What type of work does the man most likely do?
(A) He designs products.
(B) He coordinates training sessions.
(C) He provides landscape services.
(D) He heads advertising campaigns.

남자는 어떤 종류의 일을 할 것 같은가?
(A) **제품을 디자인한다.**
(B) 교육 수업을 짠다.
(C) 조경 서비스를 제공한다.
(D) 광고 캠페인을 이끈다.

63 What are the speakers mainly discussing?
(A) Sports equipment
(B) Gardening clothing
(C) A cleaning product
(D) A wireless computer

화자들은 주로 무엇에 관해 이야기하는가?
(A) 운동 기구
(B) 정원 작업복
(C) **청소 제품**
(D) 무선 컴퓨터

64 According to the man, what will happen this week?
(A) A marketing campaign will be launched.
(B) A manufacturing process will start.
(C) A product will be ready for sale.
(D) A research study will take place.

남자에 따르면, 이번 주에 무슨 일이 일어날 것인가?
(A) 마케팅 캠페인이 시작될 것이다.
(B) 제조 과정이 시작될 것이다.
(C) 제품 판매가 준비될 것이다.
(D) **연구 조사를 할 것이다.**

suction cleaner 진공청소기 progress 진행하다 notice 알아차리다 department 부서 devise 고안하다 powerful 강력한 wireless 무선 cable 전선 anticipate 예상하다 launch 출시하다 volunteer 지원자 try out 사용해 보다 prototype 원본 research group 연구 그룹 with luck 운이 좋으면 manufacture 제조하다 coordinate 조직화하다 landscape 풍경

Staff	Extension
Paul Smith	234
Ronny Hanks	235
Ginger Harrison	236
Kelly Shaffer	237

M Kelly, now that I am a full-time employee, am I eligible for the company's health insurance plan?

W Of course. ⑥ You have 45 days from the date of your promotion to decide if you want to enroll. The same goes for the other benefits available only to full-time employees. Any benefits you received as a part-time employee, you can keep.

M 45 days? I'd better make a decision soon. ⑥ Do you know how I can get more information about the insurance plan?

W You need to contact Human Resources. ⑥ The benefits specialist for our department is Ginger Harrison. I suggest you call his extension. You can find his number in the employee phone directory.

M Thanks, I'll do that.

직원	내선번호
폴 스미스	234
로니 행크스	235
진저 해리슨	236
켈리 셰퍼	237

남 켈리, 이제 제가 정규 직원이 되었으니, 회사가 제공하는 건강 보험을 이용할 수 있나요?

여 물론이죠. 승진한 날로부터 45일간 보험에 등록할지 독 그러지 않을지 결정할 수 있는 시간이 있어요. 정규 직원들에게만 제공되는 다른 혜택들 또한 마찬가지입니다. 파트타임 직원으로서 받았던 혜택도 유지할 수 있어요.

남 45일이요? 그럼 순 결정을 해야 겠네요. 제가 보험에 관한 정보를 더 많이 얻을 수 있나요?

Lunch Menu	
Fresh Salad	$8
Hearty Soup	$9
Personal Pizza	$12
Salmon Sandwich	$7

W Hello. My name is Linzie, and I will be your server today. Could I get you something to drink to get you started?

M Yes, please. I'd like a glass of wine.

W Okay. Do you need some time to look at the menu?

M No, I'm actually kind of in a hurry. ⑥ I have to meet with a client at 12:00. ⑥ So could you please bring me a grilled salmon sandwich?

W Would you like it on white or wheat bread? And would you like anything on it?

M I'd like wheat bread, and please add honey-mustard, mayonnaise, lettuce, tomatoes, and onions.

W Got it. ⑦ I'll be back with your drink in a moment.

점심 메뉴	
신선한 샐러드	8달러
따뜻한 수프	9달러
1인용 피자	12달러
연어 샌드위치	7달러

여 안녕하세요. 제 이름은 린지이고, 제가 오늘 서빙을 해 드릴 것입니다. 우선 마실 것 좀 가져다 드릴까요?

남 네, 저는 와인 한 잔 부탁해요.

여 네. 메뉴 고르실 시간 좀 드릴까요?

남 아뇨. 제가 좀 급해요. 제가 12시 정각에 고객을 만나기로 되어 있거든요. 구운 연어 샌드위치로 할게요.

여 화이트 혹은 밀빵 중에 어떤 게 좋으세요? 그리고 빵에 무엇을 올려 드릴까요?

남 밀빵이 좋겠고, 허니 머스터드, 마요네즈, 상추, 토마토, 그리고 양파를 올려주세요.

여 알겠습니다. 음료 먼저 바로 가져다 드릴게요.

in a hurry 바쁜   grilled 구운   salmon 연어

여 인사부서에 연락하셔야 합니다. 우리 부서 복지 혜택 담당자는 진저 해리슨입니다. 그의 내선번호로 연락해 보시라고요. 그의 내선번호는 직원 전화번호부에 나와 있어요.

남 고마워요. 그럴게요.

now that ~이므로   eligible for ~에 대해 자격이 있는   enroll 등록하다
benefit 혜택   extension 내선   directory 안내책자

65 According to the woman, what does the man have 45 days to do?

(A) Apply for a promotion
(B) Register his driving license
(C) Enroll in an insurance plan
(D) Hire a full-time employee

여자에 따르면, 남자는 45일간 무엇을 할 수 있는가?

(A) 승진에 지원한다.
(B) 운전면허증을 등록한다.
(C) 보험에 등록한다.
(D) 정규 직원을 고용한다.

66 What does the man want to obtain?

(A) An insurance card
(B) A list of entire staff
(C) A new phone number
(D) Information about specific benefits

남자는 무엇을 얻기를 원하는가?

(A) 보험 카드
(B) 모든 직원들의 명부
(C) 새로운 전화번호
(D) 특정한 복지에 관한 정보

67 Look at the graphic. What number will the man call?

(A) 234
(B) 235
(C) 236
(D) 237

그래픽을 보시오. 어느 번호로 남자가 전화할 것인가?

(A) 234
(B) 235
(C) 236
(D) 237

68 What does the man say he needs to do at noon?
(A) Have a business meeting
(B) Take a bus
(C) See a friend
(D) Return to the office

남자는 정오에 무엇을 해야 한다고 하는가?
(A) 업무상 미팅을 한다.
(B) 버스를 탄다.
(C) 친구를 만난다.
(D) 사무실로 돌아간다.

69 Look at the graphic. How much will the man pay for his food?
(A) $8
(B) $9
(C) $12
(D) $7

그래픽을 보시오. 남자는 음식에 대해 얼마를 지불하겠는가?
(A) 8달러
(B) 9달러
(C) 12달러
(D) 7달러

70 What does the woman say she will do next?
(A) Set the man's table with dishes
(B) Return with a part of the man's order
(C) Bring the check
(D) Buy a bottle of wine

여자는 다음에 무엇을 할 것이라고 하는가?
(A) 남자의 테이블에 접시를 정리한다.
(B) 남자가 주문한 것의 일부를 가져온다.
(C) 계산서를 가져온다.
(D) 와인 한 병을 구매한다.

Part 4

문제 P67

Questions 71-73 refer to the following announcement. 미M

In regional news, **71** today the municipal library opened its newly built media center. The first visitors to the new space is a group of school children from St. Monarch School, whose fundraising helped to build the extension to the building. **72** Library curator, Richard Blaine, says that he is pleased to welcome the pupils of St. Monarch. To commemorate the opening, **73** the library is providing free refreshments to the general public this Sunday from 10 A.M. to 4 P.M.

지역 뉴스에서, 오늘 시립 도서관이 새로 지어진 미디어 센터를 개장했습니다. 새로운 공간의 첫 번째 방문객들은 그 건물의 증축을 도와 모금을 기부한, 성 모나크 학교의 학생들이었습니다. 도서관 큐레이터인 리처드 블레인은 성 모나크의 학생들을 맞이하게 되어 반갑다고 말했습니다. 개장을 기념하기 위해, 도서관은 무료 다과를 일반 대중에게 이번 주 일요전 10시부터 오후 4시까지 제공합니다.

regional 지역의 municipal library 시립 도서관 newly 새롭게 fundraising 모금 extension 확대 curator 큐레이터 pupil 학생(어린) commemorate 기념하다 refreshments 다과 general public 일반 대중 instructional 교육용의

71 What happened today at the municipal library?
(A) An extension was opened.
(B) A new curator was appointed.
(C) An exhibit space closed.
(D) Some media were invited.

오늘 시립 도서관에서 무슨 일이 있었는가?
(A) 증축 건물이 개장했다.
(B) 새 큐레이터가 임명되었다.
(C) 전시 공간이 문을 닫았다.
(D) 일부 매체가 초대받았다.

72 Who is Richard Blaine?
(A) A teacher
(B) A librarian
(C) A curator
(D) An architect

리처드 블레인은 누구인가?
(A) 교사
(B) 도서관 사서
(C) 큐레이터
(D) 건축가

73 According to the speaker, what will the library offer on Sunday?
(A) Free food and drink
(B) Free computer access
(C) Instructional videos
(D) Library vouchers

화자에 따르면, 도서관은 일요일에 무엇을 제공할 것인가?
(A) 무료 음식과 음료
(B) 무료 컴퓨터 이용
(C) 교육용 비디오
(D) 도서관 할인권

Questions 74-76 refer to the following recorded message. 미W

Hello, **74** you've reached the Government Customs Department. **75** We are currently unavailable due to the Queen's Birthday holiday. If this is an emergency and you wish to speak to someone urgently, please call Sir Andre Wilson at 20-555-2121. Otherwise, if you'd like to speak personally to an advisor or make an inquiry, **76** call back tomorrow during our working hours of 08:00 A.M. to 7:00 P.M.

안녕하세요, 당신은 정부 관세국에 전화하셨습니다. 저희는 국경일인 여왕 탄생일로 인해 현재 전화를 받을 수 없습니다. 만약 비상사태이고 급히 누군가와 이야기하길 원하신다면, 앤드레 윌슨 경에게 20-555-2121로 전화 주세요. 그렇지 않을 경우, 개인적으로 상담을 원하시거나 문의를 하고 싶으시다면, 내일 저희 근무 시간인 오전 8시에서 저녁 7시 사이에 다시 전화해 주세요.

reach (특히 전화로) 연락하다 customs department 관세국 currently 현재 unavailable (시간이나 이용이) 가능하지 않은 Queen's Birthday 여왕 탄생일(6월 둘째 토요일인 영국의 공휴일) emergency 비상 (사태) urgently 급히 personally 개인적으로 advisor 고문 inquiry 질문 solicitor 사무 변호사 residence 거주지 observe 축하[기념]하다 merge 합병하다

Questions 77-79 refer to the following advertisement. (미국)

Every year, home owners throw away hundreds of pounds by not maintaining their oven appliances. Why not make sure that your oven is working to its full capacity? Call Acoven Services at 070-555-9464 and arrange a free call-out, by ⑰ one of our repair experts who will check your appliance and explain exactly how our maintenance programs work. And ⑱ from the beginning of this month, there's a 15 percent discount on any service agreement that you take out with us. So call today!

매년, 주택 소유주들은 그들의 오븐 장치를 유지하지 않음으로 인해 수백 파운드를 버립니다. 당신의 오븐이 최대치로 기능하고 있는지 확실히 하는 게 어때요? 070-555-9464로 Acoven 서비스에 전화하셔서 당신의 가전기기를 점검하고 저희 유지 보수 프로그램이 어떻게 운영되는지 정확히 설명해 드릴 수리 전문가 중 한 명을 호출하세요. 그리고 이번 달 초부터, 당신이 받게 되는 모든 서비스 계약에 대해 15퍼센트의 할인이 있습니다. 그러니 오늘 전화 주세요!

home owner 주택 소유주 / throw away 버리다 / appliance 가전제품 / capacity 용량; 능력 / call-out 호출 / expert 전문가 / arrange 마련하다, 준비하다 / maintain 유지하다 / take out 신청하다 (공식적 문서·서비스를) 받다 / agreement 동의, 합의 / sign up for 신청하다 / inspection 점검 / scheme 계획, 제도 / come into force 발효[시행]되다 / collect 수금하다

77 What is being advertised?
(A) Appliance maintenance
(B) Residential repairs
(C) Technician training
(D) Cooking classes

무엇이 광고되고 있는가?
(A) 가전제품 유지 보수
(B) 주택 수리
(C) 기술자 훈련
(D) 요리 수업

78 Why are listeners asked to call?
(A) To reach an agreement
(B) To arrange an inspection
(C) To receive a new oven
(D) To sign up for discounts

청자들이 전화해 달라고 요청받는 이유는?
(A) 합의에 도달하기 위해
(B) 점검을 처리하기 위해
(C) 새 오븐을 받기 위해
(D) 할인을 신청하기 위해

79 What will happen at the beginning of the month?
(A) Payments will be collected.
(B) A program will start.
(C) A discount scheme comes into force.
(D) A report will be issued.

월초에 무슨 일이 있을 것인가?
(A) 지불액이 수금될 것이다.
(B) 프로그램이 시작될 것이다.
(C) 할인 정책이 시행될 것이다.
(D) 보고서가 발부될 것이다.

Questions 80-82 refer to the following talk. (영국)

⑳ Welcome to the 20th annual award ceremony for creative writing. We were overwhelmed to see applications from so many talented writers. People whose creativity challenges a conservative way of writing. After hours of reflection, ㉑ we unanimously awarded Ms. Femke Jukkin the Newcomer of the Year. Her latest, the Life Choices to be Made, showed incredible imagination and skill. Before we invite Ms. Jukkin to the podium, ㉒ I would like you to open the brochure that you received when you arrived. We have included in it a short excerpt from Ms. Jukkin's novel.

창의적인 글쓰기 20주년 시상식에 오신 것을 환영합니다. 재능 있는 작가들이 지원서가 쇄도해서 압도당했습니다. 보수적인 방식의 글쓰기에 도전하는 창의력이 있는 사람들 말입니다. 몇 시간 동안 숙고한 후, 저희는 만장일치로 해외 신인 작가상을 팜케 주킨 씨에게 수여했습니다. 그녀의 최신작인 (결정해야 할 삶의 선택)은 믿기 어려운 상상력과 기량을 보여 주었습니다. 주킨 씨를 연단에 불러오기 전에, 저는 여러분이 주킨 씨에 소설에서 발췌 문구를 포함했습니다.

award ceremony 수상식 / creative writing 창작 / overwhelm 압도하다 / talented 재능 있는 / creativity 창의력 / conservative 보수적인 / reflection 반성; 심사숙고 / unanimously 만장일치로 / newcomer 신인자, 신참자 / incredible 믿기지 않을 정도의 / podium 연단, 지휘대

74 What kind of business did the caller reach?
(A) A department store
(B) A solicitor's firm
(C) A royal residence
(D) A governmental department

발신자는 어떤 종류의 회사에 전화를 했는가?
(A) 백화점
(B) 사무 변호사 회사
(C) 국왕의 거주지
(D) 정부 부처

75 Why is the business closed?
(A) A national holiday is observed.
(B) Some departments have merged.
(C) A ceremony is taking place.
(D) The office has shut down.

회사가 문을 닫은 이유는 무엇인가?
(A) 국경 공휴일을 기념하고 있다.
(B) 일부 부서가 통합되었다.
(C) 의식이 진행되고 있다.
(D) 사무실이 문을 닫았다.

76 When will the business reopen?
(A) After a few hours
(B) Tomorrow
(C) In two days
(D) Next week

회사는 언제 문을 다시 열 것인가?
(A) 몇 시간 후
(B) 내일
(C) 이틀 후
(D) 다음 주

brochure 안내 책자 excerpt (글·음악·영화 등의) 발췌 (부분)

80 What type of event is being held?
(A) An art gallery opening
(B) An awards ceremony
(C) A conservative meeting
(D) A play preview

어떤 종류의 행사가 개최되고 있는가?
(A) 미술 갤러리 개장
(B) 시상식
(C) 보수당의 회의
(D) 공연 시사회

81 What field does Ms. Jukkin work in?
(A) Writing
(B) Teaching
(C) Catering
(D) Publishing

쥬킨 씨가 일하고 있는 분야는?
(A) 집필
(B) 강의
(C) 출장 요리업
(D) 출판

82 What will listeners most likely do next?
(A) Watch a video
(B) Hear a speech
(C) Eat a meal
(D) Pick up a brochure

청자들은 다음에 무엇을 할 것 같은가?
(A) 비디오 관람
(B) 연설 듣기
(C) 식사하기
(D) 책자 챙기기

Questions 83-85 refer to the following telephone message. 호M

Hi, Mr. Ubamo. **83** This is Mtama from MJ's Vehicle Exchange. **84** I'm calling about the second hand truck you wanted us to look at. Well, I have an offer for you as we'd like to take it off your hands. Because of the damage to the paintwork, we can't offer you your asking price. In the past, we purchased similar models for about 300 euros. However, **85** we are willing to negotiate if you find a better offer. Give me a call so we can discuss this. This is Mtama and you can reach me at 44-555-6687.

안녕하세요, 우바모 씨. MJ 자동차 거래소의 음타마입니다. 당신이 저희가 봐주길 바라셨던 중고 트럭에 관해 전화 드렸습니다. 저희가 그것을 사길 원하기 때문에 제안을 하나 드리려고 합니다. 페인트칠에 비손 때문에, 당신이 요구하는 가격으로 할 수 없습니다. 과거에, 저희는 비슷한 모델을 약 300유로에 구매했습니다. 그러나 저희는 당신이 더 좋은 가격을 제시하신다면, 협의를 할 의향이 있습니다. 이것에 대해 이야기할 수 있도록 전화 주세요. 저는 음타마이고 44-555-6687로 전화 주시면 됩니다.

vehicle 차량 second hand 중고의, 헌 take ~ off a person's hand 떠맡다, 인수하다, 사다 paintwork 페인트 작업 asking price 요청 가격 negotiate 협상하다 lot 부지, 지역 outlet 직매점, 전문 매장 estimate 견적서

83 Where most likely does the speaker work?
(A) At a used car lot
(B) At a gas station
(C) At a supermarket
(D) At a vehicle repair outlet

화자는 어디에서 일할 것 같은가?
(A) 중고차 거래장
(B) 주유소
(C) 슈퍼마켓
(D) 자동차 수리점

84 What does Mr. Ubamo want to do?
(A) Ask for a job
(B) Repair his truck
(C) Advertise a business
(D) Sell a vehicle

우바모 씨는 무엇을 하고 싶어 하는가?

(A) 일자리 요청
(B) 그의 트럭 수리
(C) 업체 광고
(D) 자동차 판매

85 What should Mr. Ubamo do when he returns the call?
(A) Speak to a manager
(B) Ask for an estimate
(C) Negotiate the price
(D) Provide credit card details

우바모 씨는 전화를 회신할 때 무엇을 해야 하는가?
(A) 책임자와 이야기하기
(B) 견적 요청하기
(C) 가격 흥정하기
(D) 신용 카드 세부 사항 제공하기

Questions 86-88 refer to the following talk. 영M

Good morning, and welcome to Yellow Stone State Park. My name is Mark Williams. **86** I'll be leading today's hike. Right now, we are standing in front of the information center. In a moment, we'll stroll along the pond, cross over a bridge, and climb a small hill. The park is a habitat for hundreds of types of native plants. We also have dozens of species of birds, small mammals, and other wildlife that make their home here. If we are quiet, we might get to see them. No one can guarantee anything, though. **88** We recommend that all of you bring a water bottle. Although this is just a one-hour walk, it can get quite warm this time of the year.

안녕하세요, 옐로우 스톤 주립공원에 오신 것을 환영합니다. 제 이름은 마크 윌리엄스입니다. 제가 오늘의 하이킹을 이끌 예정입니다. 지금 저희는 안내소 앞에 서 있습니다. 곧 저희는 연못을 따라 걷게 되고, 다리를 건너 뒤, 작은 언덕을 오르게 됩니다. 이 공원은 수백 종이 넘는 야생식물들의 서식지입니다. 또한 수십 종의 새들, 작은 포유동물들, 그리고 또 다른 야생물들이 이곳을 생활의 터전으로 하고 있습니다. 만약 우리가 소음을 내지 않을 경우, 그들을 볼 수 있을지도 모릅니다. 그러나 누구도 이러한 것을 보장해 줄 수는 없습니다. 모두 물병을 가지고 다니기를 권장합니다. 한 시간 정도밖에 걷지 않아도 연중 이맘때는 꽤 더울 수 있습니다.

stroll 한가롭게 거닐다, 산책하다 habitat 서식지, 산지 mammal 포유류 guarantee 보장하다 logger 벌목꾼

86 Who most likely is the speaker?
(A) A guide
(B) An animal activist
(C) A fitness trainer
(D) A logger

화자는 누구일 것 같은가?
(A) 가이드
(B) 동물 보호운자
(C) 운동 트레이너
(D) 벌목가

87 What does the man mean when he says, "No one can guarantee anything, though"?
(A) He is uncertain if they are going in the right direction.
(B) He is uncertain if the weather will be good.
(C) He cannot be sure this hike is not hard.
(D) He cannot be sure they will see any animals.

남자는 "그러나 누구도 이러한 것을 보장해 줄 수 는 없습니다"라고 말했을 때 무엇을 의미했는가?
(A) 남자는 그들이 제대로 된 방향으로 가고 있는지 확신하지 못한다.
(B) 남자는 날씨가 좋을지에 대해 확신하지 못한다.
(C) 남자는 이 하이킹이 힘이 들지 않을지에 대해 확신하지 못한다.
(D) 남자는 동물을 볼 수 있을지에 대해 확신하지 못한다.

88 What does the speaker suggest the listeners do?
(A) Wear warm clothes
(B) Bring a map
(C) Carry water
(D) Stay with a group

화자는 청자들에게 무엇을 할 것을 제안하는가?
(A) 따뜻한 옷을 입어라.
(B) 지도를 가져와라.
(C) 물을 가지고 다녀라.
(D) 일행에서 떨어지지 마라.

Questions 89-91 refer to the following excerpt from a seminar.
[98W]

Well, that's all we have for today. **(89)** I hope that this seminar on prioritizing tasks has been useful to you. We discussed several techniques for helping you and your employees to plan strategically. It has been my experience that if you practice these strategies, you will get work done more efficiently. **(90)** The handouts I just gave you summarize the key points we went over today. They also include a list of Web sites with additional resources. Make sure to go over all of these. I think you will find them useful. Before you leave, please take a moment to complete the comment card on your table. Your feedback will help us improve this and other seminars. Thanks again for taking part in the seminar.

오늘은 이게 전부입니다. 업무의 우선순위를 정하는 것에 관한 이 세미나가 여러분들께 도움이 되었기를 바랍니다. 우리는 당신과 당신 직원들이 보다 전략적으로 계획을 짜는 것에 도움을 줄 수 있는 여러가지 기술에 관한 논의를 했습니다. 제 경험상으로 볼 때 이 전략들을 실행한다면 여러분들은 이게 보다 효율적으로 업무를 완수할 수 있으실 것입니다. 방금 제가 여러분들께 제공한 안내 자료는 우리가 오늘 진행했던 해당 내용을 요약한 것입니다. 그 안내 자료에는 추가 자료에 관한 웹 사이트들이 정리되어 있습니다. 자료를 꼭 검토해 보시기를 바랍니다. 여러분들 모두 가 유용하다고 생각하실 것입니다. 나가시기 전에, 시간을 좀 내셔서 테이블 위에 있는 의견 카드를 작성해 주세요. 여러분들의 의견이 이 세미나를 비롯하여 다른 세미나까지 개선하는 데 도움이 될 것입니다. 다시 한 번 이 세미나에 참석해 주셔서 감사합니다.

prioritize 우선순위를 매기다, 우선적으로 처리하다 strategically 전략적으로 summarize 요약하다 task force 대책 위원회 coordinate 조직화하다

89 What most likely was the topic of the seminar?
(A) Organizing a task force
(B) Cooperating with colleagues
(C) Coordinating a hiring process
(D) Arranging assignments effectively

세미나의 주제는 무엇이었을 것 같은가?
(A) 대책 위원회를 조직하는 것
(B) 동료들과 협동하는 것
(C) 고용 절차를 조직화하는 것
(D) 업무를 효율적으로 정리하는 것

---

90 What did the speaker pass out to the listeners?
(A) A recent article
(B) A list of resources
(C) An enrollment form
(D) A list of attendees

화자는 청자들에게 무엇을 나눠 주었는가?
(A) 최근 기사
(B) 자료 리스트
(C) 등록 서류
(D) 참가자 리스트

91 Why does the speaker say, "Make sure to go over all of these"?
(A) To celebrate a product launch
(B) To give an assignment
(C) To promote other seminars
(D) To recommend Web sites

화자는 왜 "자료를 꼭 검토해 보시기를 바랍니다"라고 말했는가?
(A) 제품 론칭을 축하하기 위해
(B) 업무를 주기 위해
(C) 다른 세미나를 홍보하기 위해
(D) 웹 사이트를 추천하기 위해

Questions 92-94 refer to the following news report and map. 호M

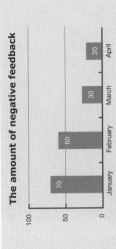

1	2	3	4
Rose Street	Pine Street	Broadway	Hillside Street	Nassau Street

It's time for our 7 A.M. traffic update. Commuters planning to take the highway into the city today might want to consider avoiding exit number 4. ❾❷ Work crews are filling up a huge sink hole near the exit ramp. As a result, you will experience delays if you have to use this exit. If you can use another exit to get where you need to go, ❾❸ then the Transportation Department recommends taking exits 6 or 9 instead. If you are going to be downtown today, ❾❹ please use extra caution at the intersection of Pine Street and Broadway. The traffic lights there are not working due to a temporary power outage. Police are stationed to help direct traffic until an electrical utility crew can get power restored.

commuter 통근자　fill up 메우다, 메꾸다, 채우다　ramp 경사로　caution 주의, 조심　temporary 일시적인, 임시　power outage 정전　station 배치하다　utility 공익사업, 공공요금, 공공시설　slippery 미끄러운　detour 우회

92 What is causing traffic delays at exit number 4?

(A) A car accident
(B) A slippery road
(C) Road repair work
(D) A scheduled town event

무엇이 4번 출구에서의 정체를 야기하고 있는가?

(A) 자동차 사고
(B) 미끄러운 도로
(C) 도로 보수 작업
(D) 예정된 마을 행사

93 What does the Transportation Department recommend?

(A) Using detours
(B) Commuting by public transportation
(C) Not passing through downtown
(D) Avoiding a certain bridge

교통당국에서 무엇을 추천하는가?

(A) 우회로 이용하기
(B) 대중교통으로 출퇴근하기
(C) 도심 통과하지 않기
(D) 특정 다리 피하기

94 Look at the graphic. What traffic light is not working?

(A) 1
(B) 2
(C) 3
(D) 4

그래픽을 보시오. 어느 교통 신호등이 작동하지 않는가?

(A) 1
(B) 2
(C) 3
(D) 4

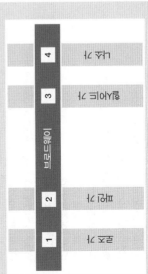

1	2	3	4
로즈 가	파인 가	브로드웨이	힐사이드 가	나소 가

오전 7시 교통 업데이트 시간입니다. 오늘 고속도로를 통해 도심으로 들어오시려는 분들은 4번 출구를 피하는 것이 좋을 듯 합니다. 출구 경사로 근처에 있는 매우 큰 싱크홀을 작업자들이 메우고 있는 중입니다. 그래서 4번 출구로 나오셔야 되면 정체를 겪게 되실 것으로 보입니다. 여러 분들의 목적지로 가실 때 이외 다른 출구를 이용하셔도 괜찮으시다면 6번 출구나 9번 출구를 대신 이용하실 것을 교통당국에서 권

당합니다. 오늘 시내를 향하신다면, 파인 가와 브로드웨이 교차로에서 특히 주의를 기울이셔야 합니다. 교통 신호등이 현재 작동하지 않고 있습니다. 경찰이 배전 직원들이 전기를 복구할 때까지 교통 정리를 돕기 위해 파견돼 있을 것입니다.

Questions 95-97 refer to the following excerpt from a meeting and chart. 영W

The amount of negative feedback

January	February	March	April
70	60	30	20

The next topic on today's meeting is customer service. Overall, I want to point out that our customer service team is exceptional. ❾❺ They are extremely efficient, and the additional associates who were hired to join the team earlier this year have done a great job. Nevertheless, we saw an increase in negative feedback a few months ago. ❾❻ We determined that the cause was an unclear return and exchange policy. To address this problem, we simplified the policy and retrained all the customer service representatives. ❾❼ Well, if you take a look at the chart on the screen, you can see that the amount of negative feedback decreased from 60 to 30 in the month after the training session. And it is continuing to fall.

부정적인 피드백 수

1월	2월	3월	4월
70	60	30	20

오늘 회의의 다음 주제는 고객 서비스입니다. 전체적으로, 우리 고객 서비스팀이 아주 출하고 있다고 말하고 싶어요. 팀원들은 아주 효율적으로 일하고 또한 올해 초에 고용되어 팀에 추가된 직원들도 아주 일을 잘했습니다. 그럼에도, 우리는 몇 달 전에 부정적인 내용의 피드백이 증가했다는 것을 알 수 있었습니다. 우리는 그 원인이 모호한 반품과 교환 정책에 있다고 결론을 내렸습니다. 이 문제를 처리하기 위해 우리는 정책을 간소화하고, 고객 서비스 직원들을 다시 교육하기로 교육 과정 이후에 600에서 30으로 줄 보시면, 부정적인 피드백의 수가 교육 과정 이후에 600에서 30으로 줄었다는 것을 확인해 볼 수 있습니다. 그리고 계속해서 감소하고 있습니다.

95 What does the speaker say about the customer service team?

(A) It was recently transferred.
(B) It received a pay increase.
(C) Its workforce has been expanded.
(D) It still needs to improve.

화자는 고객 서비스팀에 관해서 무엇을 언급하는가?

(A) 최근에 전근되었다.
(B) 임금 인상을 받았다.
(C) **인력이 충원되었다.**
(D) 아직 개선을 필요로 한다.

96 What was the cause of negative comments?

(A) An ambiguous policy
(B) An expensive service price
(C) Untrained staff
(D) A defective product

부정적인 의견의 원인은 무엇이었는가?

(A) **모호한 정책**
(B) 비싼 서비스 가격
(C) 교육받지 않은 직원
(D) 결함 있는 제품

97 Look at the graphic. When was the training session held?

(A) In January
(B) In February
(C) In March
(D) In April

그래픽을 보시오. 언제 교육 과정이 열렸는가?

(A) 1월
(B) **2월**
(C) 3월
(D) 4월

Questions 98-100 refer to the following telephone message and invoice. (호M)

INVOICE	
Product Number	Description
P365	Soccer ball (# 3)
P345	Basketball (# 2)
P443	Running shoes (# 2 pairs)
P334	Track Jacket (# 1)

Hello, Ms. Williams. This is Paul Grey at East Athletics. You placed an order on our Web site yesterday. ⑨ I am just calling to let you know that one of the items on your order, the soccer ball, is currently out of stock. We expect to receive a new shipment and to fully restock the item at our warehouse within 5-6 days. If you would like, we can send you the other items first and send the soccer ball to you later. ⑩ There will be no additional shipping costs for you. Otherwise, we can wait until we have all the items and ship them to you together. The ⑨ Please let me know which option you prefer. The number is 555-5783. Thanks and have a great day!

송장	
제품 번호	제품
P365	축구공(3개)
P345	농구공(2개)
P443	운동화(2족)
P334	트랙 재킷(1개)

안녕하세요, 윌리엄스 씨. 저는 이스트 애슬레틱스 사의 폴 그레이입니다. 어제 당신이 저희 웹 사이트에서 주문을 해 주셨어요. 주문하신 물건 중에 하나인 축구공이 현재 재고가 없다는 사실을 알려드리기 위해 전화를 드립니다. 저희는 새로운 배송이 들어와 창고에 있는 재고를 다시 채우게 되는 것이 5~6일 안에 이루어지리라 예상하고 있습니다. 원하신다면 다른 제품들을 먼저 보내 드리고, 후에 축구공을 보내 드리도록 하겠습니다. 추가적인 배송비는 발생하지 않을 것입니다. 혹은, 모든 제품이 다 들어오기를 기다렸다가 한번에 보내드릴 수도 있습니다. 어떻게 하시기를 원하시는지 알려주세요. 연락주실 번호는 555-5783입니다. 감사드리며, 좋은 하루 되세요!

---

98 Why is the speaker calling?

(A) To cancel an order
(B) To ask a preference
(C) To ask for a payment
(D) To sell a product

왜 화자는 전화를 하고 있는가?

(A) 주문을 취소하기 위해
(B) **선호 사항을 물어보기 위해**
(C) 지불을 요청하기 위해
(D) 제품을 판매하기 위해

99 Look at the graphic. Which item is currently out of stock?

(A) P365
(B) P345
(C) P443
(D) P334

그래픽을 보시오. 어느 항목이 현재 재고가 없는가?

(A) **P365**
(B) P345
(C) P443
(D) P334

100 What does the speaker offer to do?

(A) Refund some money
(B) Waive a shipping fee
(C) Upgrade a shipping method
(D) Cancel an order

화자는 무엇을 해 주겠다고 하는가?

(A) 돈을 환불해 준다.
(B) **배송비를 면제해 준다.**
(C) 배송 방법을 업그레이드해 준다.
(D) 주문을 취소해 준다.

Part 5

문제 P70

101

해설 빈칸은 동사(has not yet finished)의 목적어 자리이다. 주격 she를 제외하고는 모두 목적어 역할을 할 수 있지만 문맥상 앵커 씨가 그녀의 비용 청구서를 아직 끝내지 못한 것이므로 앞의 비용 청구서를 대신 받는 소유대명사 (A)가 적절하다.

린 씨는 그의 비용 청구서를 제출했지만, 앵커 씨는 아직 자신의 것을 끝내지 못했다.

hand in 제출하다   expense claim 비용 청구서

102

해설 빈칸은 명사(wireless service)를 수식하는 자리이므로 형용사가 들어가야 한다. 선택지에 있는 형용사 (A) reliable(믿을 수 있는)과 (B) reliant(의존적인) 중에 의미상으로 (A)가 적절하다.

HTR 회사는 저렴한 연간 비용으로 믿을 수 있는 무선 서비스를 제공한다.

wireless 무선의   affordable 저렴한

103

해설 주어는 Fun & Turn이고 빈칸은 문장의 동사 자리이므로 (B)가 정답이다. 주어가 단수이므로 (C)는 오답이다.

편 앤 턴인 고객들에게 이메일로 보내지는 온라인 소식지를 출판한다.

newsletter 소식지   publisher 출판인   publish 출판하다
publishable 발행할 수 있는, 출판할 수 있는

104

해설 부사절 접속사 문제로 주절 many people now join online forums는 필수 성분을 모두 갖춘 완벽한 절이므로 the Internet ~ ideas는 수식 역할을 한다. 빈칸 뒤에 절을 받으면서 수식 역할을 하는 부사절 접속사가 정답이므로 Because, After 가 정답의 후보이다. 문맥상 ~ 때문에가 자연스러우므로 (A)가 정답이다. So는 등위 접속사로 문장과 문장을 연결할 수는 있지만 문장의 맨 앞에는 쓸 수 없다.

인터넷은 생각을 교환할 수 있는 훌륭한 장소이기 때문에 많은 사람들이 현재 온라인 포럼에 가입한다.

exchange 주고받다, 교환하다   forum 포럼, (토론의) 장, 토론회

105

해설 원래 부사절(When you choose a removal company)이었던 부분을 분사구문으로 축약한 구조이다. 주어 (you)를 생략하고 동사를 분사로 축약하는데, 능동태 동사이므로 (B)가 정답이다.

이사 업체를 선택할 때는 정확한 이사 견적을 요청해야 한다.

moving company 이사 업체   accurate 정확한

106

해설 a welcome addition(환영받는 추가되는 것 추가된 시설/추가된 사람)을 관용 표현으로 외워 두자. 정답은 (B)이다.

도슨 씨는 그 분야의 광범위한 지식 때문에 재무팀의 환영받는 추가 인원으로 간주된다.

extensive 광범위한

107

해설 of가 소유의 의미로 쓰일 때는 뒤에 소유대명사(yours)를 넣어서 표현한다. (소유격+own)이 소유대명사를 대신할 수 있으므로 정답은 (B)이다.

당신의 인상적인 이력서를 만드는 것은 전합트 프로그램의 도움이 있으면 쉽고 간단할 수 있다.

impressive 인상적인

108

해설 조동사(can) 뒤에는 동사원형이 들어가야 한다. 선택지에서 동사원형은 (B) have extended과 (C) be extended인데, 이 둘은 태의 차이이다. (B)는 능동태 동사이므로 뒤에 목적어가 있어야 하고, (C)는 수동태 동사이므로 뒤에 목적어는 없지 때문에 정답은 (C)이다.

노트북 컴퓨터를 사용하지 않을 때는 끄는 붕음으로써 배터리 수명을 연장할 수 있다.

extend 연장하다

109

해설 빈칸은 뒤에 명사를 이끄는 수식어구 자리이므로 전치사가 들어와야 한다. (D) next는 형용사 또는 부사로 쓰이므로 오답이며 나머지 전치사 선택지 중에서 의미상 가장 적절한 ~ 동안이라는 (C) during이 정답이다.

공휴일에 사무실에 들어가고 싶은 직원들은 미리 허가를 요청해야 한다.

110

해설 전치사(in)과 명사(effort) 뒤에서 수식하는 자리이다. 명사 effort는 to부정사의 수식을 받는 명사 중 하나이므로 (C)가 정답이다. '~하기 위한 노력으로'라는 의미의 (in an effort to부정사)와 '노력하다'라는 의미의 (make an effort to부정사)는 자주 쓰이는 표현이므로 암기해 둔다. 또한, to부정사의 수식을 받는 명사 chance, opportunity, right, ability, way, plan, time, effort를 외워 두면 편리하다.

규정을 준수하고 있는지 확인하기 위한 노력의 일환으로, 회계 감사관들은 모든 공장의 모든 구역을 점검해야 한다.

ensure 반드시 ~하게 하다, 보장하다   compliance 준수   auditor 회계 감사관

111

해설 빈칸은 2형식 동사인 become이 주격 보어가 들어갈 자리이다. 주격 보어 자리에는 명사나 형용사가 들어갈 수 있는데, 부사 (thoroughly)가 명사를 수식할 수 없으므로 형용사인 (thorough)가 올 수 있다. 따라서 정답은 (D)이다.

당신은 온라인 수업을 듣기 전에 그 소프트웨어에 대해서 철저히 익숙해져야 한다.

throughly 완전히

112

해설 빈칸 뒤는 절(s+v)이 아닌 명사구이므로 빈칸에는 접속사가 아니라 전치사가 들어갈 자리이다. 선택지에서 전치사로 쓸 수 있는 것은 (B) regardless of(~와 관계없이) 뿐이다.

JPR 모기지 사는 당신의 현재 재정 상태와 관계없이 주택 융자를 받는 것을 쉽게 만들어 준다.

housing loan 주택 융자   status 상태

113

해설 선택지가 모두 부사이므로 의미상 어울리는 단어를 고르는 문제이다. 전치사 Following(~ 후에)의 해석과 가장 잘 어울리는 부사로서 정답은 (A) finally(마침내)이다.

오랜 토론 후에, 로비 비품들을 최신으로 바꾸자는 제안이 마침내 수락되었다.

proposal 제안   furnishing 비품

114

해설 빈칸은 명사(Reservations)를 수식할 형용사 자리이다. 선택지에서 형용사 역할로 쓰일 수 있는 것은 made(과거분사) 뿐이 없으므로 (C)가 정답이다. 나머지 선택지는 모두 동사이므로 오답이다.

호텔 웹 사이트를 통해서 이루어진 예약들은 체크인하기 12시간 전에 반드시 확인되어야 한다.

115

해설 Bashir ~ celebrities는 문장의 필수 성분을 모두 갖춘 완벽한 문장이므로 뒤가 이후는 앞의 내용을 수식한다. 동사를 받으면서 앞에 명사를 수식하는 것은 관계대명사이므로 (D)가 정답이다. since는 전치사 혹은 부사절 접속사로 전치사일 경우 과거 시점이나 시간을 나타내는 명사가 오고, 부사절 접속사일 경우 완전한 문장이 온다. recently는 부사, where는 관계부사로 둘 다 뒤에 완전한 정접속사로 두 경우 모두 완전한 문장이 온다.

올해 초, 바시르 칸은 (스타 온 스테이지) 잡지의 표지에 등장했던 여러 유명 인사들을 인터뷰했다.

earlier 초기의   celebrity 유명 인사

116 해설 뒤에 명사구를 이끌고 있는 수식어구 자리이므로, 빈칸에는 전치사가 들어야 한다. (A), (B), (C)는 모두 접속사이므로 오답이고, 유일한 전치사인 (D) notwithstanding(~에도 불구하고)이 정답이다.

몇몇 지역 가게들과 대표자들은 그 지역의 쇠약한 경제에도 불구하고 올해 뛰어난 매출을 보고했다.

remarkable 뛰어난

117 해설 동사 어휘 문제로 문맥상 '전례 없는 수요를 수용하다'가 자연스러우므로 (D)가 정답이다.

마스틴 맥주 공장은 영업 기간 내해 전체 없는 수요를 수용하기 위해 추가 직원들을 모집했다.

brewery 맥주 공장 recruit 모집하다 unprecedented 전례 없는 throughout ~동안 죽, 내내 period 기간 estimate 추산하다

118 해설 빈칸은 명사(attention)를 수식할 자리이므로 형용사가 들어가야 한다. 따라서 정답은 (A)이다.

당신의 질문들은 즉각적인 관심을 받을 것이고 당신은 영업일 기준 3일 이내에 전화를 받게 될 것이다.

business day 영업일

119 해설 선택지가 모두 동사이므로 앞뒤에 맞는 동사 어휘를 선택하는 문제이지만 전치사 in과 함께 사용할 수 있는 동사는 자동사로 제로되므, should postpone은 능동이고 will be postponed는 수동이다. 빈칸 뒤에 목적어가 없으므로 (B)가 정답이다.

쓰리 코너스 호텔을 위해 계획된 모든 행사들은 중앙 복도의 손상이 수리될 때까지 지연될 것이다.

plan 계획하다 main hall 중앙 복도

120 해설 주어가 All events이고 planned ~ Hotel은 수식어이므로 빈칸은 동사 자리이다. postponing은 분사 혹은 동명사이므로 제외되고, are postponing, should postpone는 능동이고 will be postponed는 수동이다. 빈칸 뒤에 목적어가 없으므로 (B)가 정답이다.

121 해설 선택지 어휘가 혼동될 수 있지만 '명사를 다듬어 받건게 들어갈 작성한 형태를 찾아야 한다; become과 focused 사이는 분사를 수식하는 부사 자리이므로 (A)가 정답이다. narrowing은 분사 혹은 동명사이고 narrowest는 비교급, narrowed는 동사로 동사로 부사 자리에 쓸 수 없다.

122 해설 선택지 모두 형용사이므로 해석으로 푸는 문제이다. 행사 장소는 사람들을 수용하기에 '넓다'는 듯이 적절하므로 (D)가 정답이다. (A) '포함된', (B) '전반적인', (C) '불충분한'은 모두 문맥에 맞지 않으므로 오답이다.

그 행사 장소는 도시 전역에서 오는 1,000명 이상의 사람들을 수용하기에 충분히 넓다.

venue 장소 accommodate 수용하다

123 해설 문장에 동사가 begins와 is 두 개이므로 빈칸은 접속사 자리이고, 빈칸부터 in Japan까지가 문장의 주어 역할을 해야 하므로 명사절 접속사 (A)가 정답이다. although, while은 부사절 접속사이고, despite는 전치사이다.

얌타 무역사가 일본에서 무역 거래를 시작했지는 그들의 재무 상담사들이 착수한 실행 기능성 보고서에 달려 있다.

trading 거래, 무역 feasibility 실행 가능성 undertake 착수하다 financial consultant 재무 상담사

124 해설 빈칸 앞에 전치사 in이 있으므로 동명사 (C)가 정답이다.

고페미 셰프스 식당은 조리법을 배우는 데 큰 관심이 있는 견습생을 구하고 있다.

apprentice 견습생 culinary art 조리법

125 해설 전치사의 목적어가 필요한 자리이므로 명사가 들어가야 한다. 따라서 정답은 (D)이다.

126 해설 부사 어휘 문제로 해석을 통해 문맥상 가장 자연스러운 부사를 골라야 한다. 여기서는 (D)가 가장 내용과 잘 어울리며 '생산제조하다'라는 표현과 exclusively(오직)가 함께 잘 사용된다는 것을 알아 된다.

프로템 유한회사에서는 제조된 기침약은 오직 성인들만을 위해 만들어졌으며, 어린이이들에게 주어서는 안 된다.

cough 기침 medication 약 manufacture 제조하다. 생산하다 formulate 만들다 alternatively 그 대신에, 그렇지 않으면 partially 부분적으로 mutually 상호간에, 서로 exclusively 오직, 오로지

127 해설 준동사 boost의 목적어가 필요한 자리이므로 명사가 들어가야 한다. 따라서 정답은 (D)이다. 참고로 이 문장의 본동사는 helped인데, help는 목적어를 생략하고 바로 뒤에 목적격 보어를 붙을 수 있는 동사이므로 바로 뒤에 동사원형(원형부정사) 형태인 boost가 따라오는 구조이다. help는 목적격 보어로 동사원형이나 to부정사를 취한다.

특정 크기와 모양의 컨테이너 개념은 전체 해운업에 걸쳐 표준화를 신장시키는 데 도움을 주었다.

standardization 표준화

128 해설 원래 부사절(Before you use our online bill payment system)이었던 부분을 분사구문으로 축약한 형태이다. 따라서 정답은 (A)이다. (B) So that은 부사절 접속사이고 뒤에 반드시 절 형태를 이뤄야야 하므로 오답이고, (C) In order to부정사가 와야 하므로 오답이며, (D) According to는 전치사이므로 뒤에 명사(구)로는 동사(using) 형태를 이끌 수 없지만, '~에 따라서는 의미상 어울리지 않으므로 오답이다.

우리의 온라인 지불 시스템을 사용하기 전에, 당신은 먼저 등록 양식을 작성해야 한다. 작성하라

fill in 작성하다

129 해설 distinguish A from B를 B로부터 구별해 내다를 숙어처럼 암기해 두면 편하다. 따라서 정답은 (C)이다. (A) integrate는 보통 integrate A into B(A를 B로 통합시키다)라는 숙어로 활용된다. (B) suppose는 '가정하다, 추측하다'라는 의미이고 (D) modify는 '수정하다'라는 의미로 의미상 어울리지 않는다.

진품인 공동품 가구와 모조품인 것을 구별하는 것은 점점 더 어려워지고 있다.

increasingly 점점 authentic 진품의 imitation 모조품

130 해설 (A) proceed(나아가다, 진행하다)는 자동사로서 뒤에 전치사 to나 with가 오고 그 뒤에 이어서 목적어가 와야 하므로 오답 이다. (C) retrieve(되찾다)와 (D) convince(확신시키다)는 타동사이기 하지만 의미상 맞지 않으므로 오답이다. 협력과 팀워크를 '촉진시키기 위해서가 적절하므로 (B)가 정답이다.

밀리 사는 전 직원들간의 협력과 팀워크를 촉진시키기 위해서 회사 아유회를 개최하고자 한다.

cooperation 협력

Part 6

문제 P73

[131-134]

공지

수신: 모든 기술 지원 직원들
발신: 피오나 노튼
제목: 훈련 과정

향후 2주 동안, 우리 부서에 있는 직원들에게 몇몇 **131** 선택적인 훈련 과정을 제공할 것입니다. 이 프로그램의 목표는 직원들에게 그들의 전문성과 지식을 향상시킬 수 있는 기회를 제공하는 것입니다. 6시간의 워크숍을 반복한 기술 문제들을 해결하는 것, 특별한 고객의 니즈를 충족시키는 것, 그리고 생산성을 향상시키는 것을 포함하여 다양한 주제를 다룰 것입니다. **132** 비록 그 교육 과정들은 필수적이진 않지만, 직원들은 참가할 것을 강력히 권장합니다. 모든 교육과 관련된 비용은 회사에 의해서 **133** 충당될 것입니다.

이 교육 과정들은 조이스 트레이닝(www.joicetraining.com)에 의해서 조직될 것입니다. **134** 관심 있는 사람들은 이 회사 웹 사이트에서 일정을 찾아볼 수 있습니다.

objective 목표 enhance 향상시키다 expertise 전문성 an array of 다수의 address 해결하다 productivity 생산성 mandatory 필수의

131

(A) '필수적인', (B) '무준한', (C) '기', (D) '선택적인' 중에서 의미상 어울리는 어휘를 고르는 문제이다. 4번째 문장에서 '비록 교육 과정은 필수적이진 않지만 ~'이라고 했으므로 정답은 (D)이다.

132

뒤에 절(S+V)이 있으므로 접속사가 들어가야 한다. (A) Due to는 전치사이므로 오답이다. 부사절은 '강하게 권장된다는 내용이므로 이럴 땐 내용상으로는 주절은 '참석이 강하게 권장되는 부사절 접속사는 (B) Even though(비록 ~이지만)이다. So that은 '~하기 위해서'라는 의미이고 While은 '~ 동안에, 반면에'라는 의미이다.

133

동사의 태와 시제를 묻는 문제이다. 반칸 뒤에 목적어가 없으므로 수동태 동사가 들어가야 한다. (A)와 (C)가 답의 후보가 된다. 맨 첫 문장에서 '향후 2주 동안' 교육 과정을 제공할 것이라고 했으므로 앞으로 미래에 관련 비용이 충당될 것이라는 사실을 알 수 있다. 따라서 미래시제인 (C)가 정답이다.

134

(A) 저희는 이것이 야기할 수도 있는 불편함이 있다면 사과 드립니다.
(B) 관심 있는 사람들은 이 회사 웹 사이트에서 일정을 찾아볼 수 있습니다.
(C) 오직 교육 과정을 완수한 관리자들만이 자격증을 획득할 수 있습니다.
(D) 이 어려운 상황을 해결하는 데 도움을 주셔서 감사합니다.

해설 빈칸 바로 앞에 조이스 트레이닝이라는 회사가 언급되었으므로 '이 회사 웹 사이트에서 일정을 찾아볼 수 있다'는 (B)가 정답이다.

[135-138]

모스엔젤레스 — 토컴 파이낸셜은 월급까지 소매 고객들을 위한 새로운 투자 지원 서비스를 **135** 공개하겠다고 발표했다. 이 새로운 서비스는 전문 지원위원의 전문성과 모바일 어플리케이션의 편리함을 경험할 것이다.

그것은 다음 절차로 진행된다. **137** 먼저 사용자들은 그들의 스마트폰에 어플리케이션을 다운로드받아야 한다. 일반이 질문에 답하고 재무 정보를 입력한 후에, 사용자들은 각자의 독특한 상황에 맞춰 도움을 제공해 줄 것이다. 사용자들은 연락 단계 할 것이다. 사용자들은 연락 후에 제3 자문위원에게 연락을 받게 될 것이다. 사용자들은 24시간 내내 이야기를 나눌 수 있다.

이 서비스에 대한 비용은 연 관리 자산의 대략 0.5% 정도가 될 것으로 **138** 예상된다. 사용자들의 자산은 반드시 토컴 파이낸셜에 개설해 보유되어야 하고, 그 계정에서 수백 가지의 투자 옵션들이 이용 가능하다.

advisory 자문 retail client 소매 고객 combine 결합하다 expertise 전문성 convenience 편리함 a series of 일련의 customized 개개인의 요구에 맞춘 assigned 할당된 around the clock 24시간 내내 assets 자산

135

(A) '포기하다', (B) '모방하다', (C) '공개하다', (D) '취소하다' 중에 서 문맥적으로 어울리는 어휘를 고르는 문제이다. 이 글의 내용은 한 업체가 새로운 서비스에 대해서 소개하는 내용이므로 정답은 (C) unveil(공개하다)이다.

136

관사(a)와 명사(advisor) 사이에서 명사를 수식할 형용사 자리이 므로 정답은 (B) professional(전문적인)이다.

[137]

137
(A) 먼저 사용자들은 그들의 스마트폰에 어플리케이션을 다운로드 받아야 한다.
(B) 고객들은 개인 정보 유출에 대해서 걱정한다.
(C) 추가 제품들을 보시려면 우리 웹 사이트를 살펴보세요.
(D) 컴퓨터 소프트웨어는 최근에 상당히 발전되었다.

해설 빈칸 바로 앞에서 절차에 대해서 일적 준다고 했고 빈칸 뒤 로드 절차에 대한 내용이 나오므로 (A)가 정답이다.

138

동사의 태를 묻는 문제이다. 비용(The cost)은 예상하는 존재가 아니라 예상되어지는 존재이므로 수동태 동사가 들어가야 하는 자리이다. 따라서 정답은 (C) is expected(예상된다)이다.

[139-142]

수신: 캔버라 재무부
발신: 브렛 링
날짜: 8월 12일
제목: 법률 문서 정리

여러분께,

제가 이 글을 쓰는 것은 정부의 재무부에서 나온 소식과 최근 정보 때문 입니다. **139** 듣자 하니, 모든 세금 계산서와 기업 문서들을 컴퓨터로 제출 하기를 요구하는 새로운 법이 나왔다고 합니다.

저는 우리들 중 일부가 이미 www.canberracorp/govfiling의 온라인 시 스템에 익숙하지만, 꽤 복잡함을 느끼고 있다는 것을 알고 있습니다. **140** 당신은 일단 정보를 입력하기 위한 관련 페이지를 처음 열 필요가 있습니다. 그리고 비밀번호를 입력한 후, **141** 여러분의 자세한 개인 정보가 올바른 곳에 입력될 수 있도록 정확한 조회 번호를 꼭 입력하셔야 합니다.

이 **142** 절차에 대해 기타 의문 사항이 있다면, 제게 이메일로 연락해 주세요.

브렛 링

Finance Department 재무부 legal 법적인 filing 서류 정리 tax invoice 세금 계산서 corporation 기업 electronically 컴퓨터 로 familiar with ~에 익숙한 complex 복잡한 access 접속하다 reference 참조 via ~을 통해 relevant 관련된 impose 부과하다

139

해설 빈칸 앞에서 최근 정보에 대해서 알려준다고 했고 뒤에는 그 정보가 어떤 것인지 알려주고 있다. 따라서 '~ 사실에 근거해서 ~인 것 같다'는 뜻의 (D)가 정답이다. (A) 제다가 / (B) 처음에 / (C) 반대로

Part 7

[147-148]

147 다음 페이지는 단백 프린터를 작동하는 방법과 집에 있는 전자 기기
와 연결하는 방법을 보여 줍니다. **147** 설명서에 흔동되는 것이 있다면, 영
업시간 중에 단백 고객 서비스 팀원에게 전화 주세요. 서비스 센터와 모든
연락 정보는 4쪽에 일괄벳순으로 열거되어 있습니다.

illustrate 보여 주다 work 작동하다 electronic device 전자 기기
instruction 설명, 지시 사항 confuse 흔란스럽게 하다 contact detail
연락 정보 list 열거하다 alphabetically 일괄벳순으로 return policy 반
품 규정 process 처리하다 clarify 뚜렷하게 설명하다

147 정보가 나오는 것은?
 (A) 사용자 안내서
 (B) 제품 카탈로그
 (C) 전화번호부
 (D) 직원 수칙

148 정보에 따르면 단백이 직원은 어떻게 도울 수 있는가?
 (A) 반품 규정을 설명함으로써
 (B) 송장을 처리함으로써
 (C) 서비스 전화 일정을 잡음으로써
 (D) 설명을 명확히 함으로써

[149-150]

라이스 헤리티지 센터

149 라이스 헤리티지 센터는 우리 지역의 역사적 문화재 보존에 관련한 권
이상의 책과 사진, 공예품을 보유하고 있습니다. 센터에서는 우리의 전통
을 형성해 온 역사적이고 중대한 사건들에 관한 정보와 자료를 제공합니
다. 서적과 사진의 표괄적인 역사적 수집과 함께, 우리 유산에 영향을 끼
친도 다른 지역 사용이 나레도로부터 온 사진과 그룹을 소장하고 있습니
다. 방대한 양의 출판물과 기록 보관소는 관광객들과 방문객들뿐만 아니
라 지역 주민들도 이용이 가능합니다. 전시관의 역사 구역에는 지역민들
이 책은 일부 사진 및 수천 장의 그룹을 포함하는 사진 전시와 많은 고대
의 유물을 보유하고 있습니다. **150** 소량의 금액으로 사진 복사본을 받으
실 수 있습니다. 기록 보관소를 이용하시려는 분은 뜻을 위한 역속 및 조회 지
원은 요청 이용이 가능합니다.

heritage 유산, 유물 artifact 공예품 historic 역사적인 significant 중대
한 shape 형성하다 comprehensive 포괄적인 종합적인 influence 영
향을 끼치다 extensive 광범위한, 방대한 archive 기록 보관소 access
접근하다 display 전시 charge 요금 reference 참조, 조회 replica 복
제품 reprint 재인쇄

submission 제출 제출물 issue 호 accompany 동반하다 as
indicated 명시된 바와 같이 deposit 예금하다 checking account 당좌
예금계좌 renegotiate 재협상하다 verify 확인하다

149 무엇에 관한 정보인가?
(A) 지역 사회의 행사
(B) 연구 도서관
(C) 지역 사진 강좌
(D) 관광 정보 센터

150 구매가 가능한 것은?
(A) 전통 선물
(B) 문서 복사본
(C) 잡지 기사의 복사본
(D) 사진의 재판

[151-152]

entrepreneur 기업가   acquaintance 지인   audiovisual 시청각의

151 환영회에 대해서 암시된 것은?
(A) 이사회 멤버가 연설자가 될 것이다.
(B) 음식이 예상되었던 것보다 비용이 더 들지 않을 것이다.
(C) 장비는 이미 설치되었다.
(D) 카모 씨는 신입사원이다.

152 오전 9시 37분에 피셔스 씨가 "그래야 할 것 같네요"라고 썼을 때 그 의미는 무엇인가?
(A) 그는 카모 씨가 장비를 수령해 오기를 원한다.
(B) 그는 환영회가 좋은 생각이라고 동의한다.
(C) 그는 카모 씨가 가게에 연락해 보기를 원한다.
(D) 그는 대화를 즉시 끝내야 한다.

셈 피셔스 [오전 9:29]	안녕하세요, 라니. 신입사원 환영회 계획은 어떻게 진행되고 있나요?
래니 카모 [오전 9:30]	당신이 요청했던 요리를 준비해 줄 수 있는 음식 공급업체를 찾았어요. 그리고 그 업체가 우리의 예산 범위 내에서 준비해 줄 수 있다고 하네요.
셈 피셔스 [오전 9:32]	좋은 소식이네요. 조청 연설자는 찾으셨나요?
래니 카모 [오전 9:33]	지역 기업가 중 한 분이 저희 이사회 멤버의 지인인데, 네, 그분이 해 주기로 동의했어요.
셈 피셔스 [오전 9:34]	당신이 거의 모든 걸 다 처리하신 것 같네요.
래니 카모 [오전 9:35]	모든 것은 아니에요. 아직 시청각 장비를 준비해야 해요. 이미 지금 제가 업체에 연락해 봐야 할 것 같아요.
셈 피셔스 [오전 9:37]	그래야 할 것 같네요.

[153-155]

목차

613호

체중 감량   11
이메일이 스파스가 생식으로 하는 효과적인 다이어트 법을 설명한다.

모두를 위한 운동   15
편집자들이 최상의 운동 순서를 찾는 필수적인 조언을 한다.

자가 재배   20
가게 키로바기 당신이 직접 기른 건강한 채소로 맛있는 요리를 만드는 방법을 보여 준다.

얼굴의 가치   25
리아 케드리라가 당신의 외모 개선을 위한 성형 수술에 대해 이야기한다.

좋은 아이디어   29
팔로미 그리그가 불가리에 도모하여 찍은 사진들을 공유한다.

마사 프롤리오 요리장   34
마사스 디너의 요리장이 어떻게 지저방 재료를 이용하여 완벽한 식단을 준비하는지 설명한다.

전기로 소화시키기   39
로베나 소드 건기로 운동이 최고의 운동인 이유에 대해 설명한다.

다음 호   45
9월 호 예고편

153 잡지의 주요 초점은?
(A) 운동과 스포츠
(B) 정원 가꾸기와 농사
(C) 건강과 미용
(D) 음식과 요리

154 목차에 따르면 최근에 해외여행을 한 사람은?
(A) 그레그 씨
(B) 키로바 씨
(C) 마사 씨
(D) 소 씨

155 잡지의 어디에서 요리법을 찾을 수 있을 것 같은가?
(A) 15쪽
(B) 20쪽
(C) 25쪽
(D) 45쪽

weight loss 체중 감량   effectively 효과적으로   essential 필수적인   routine 정해진 순서   home grown 집에서 재배한   cosmetic surgery 성형 수술   low fat 저지방   preview 예고편   editor 편집자   raw 날것의

[156-158]

블랜라타 장기 대회

다른 사람들이 보고 싶어 할 장기를 갖고 있나요? 그렇다면 블랜라타 장기 대회에 신청하세요.

블랜라타 장기 대회는 무엇인가요?
[156] 대회는 하이 스트리트에서 레드 라이온 술집을 소유하고 있고 그곳에서 공연하기 위한 연기자를 찾던 블랜라타 술집 주인인 일체스 밴드에 의해 시작되었습니다. -[1]-. 수상자는 공연 경력을 시작할 수 있도록 100곡을 ... 지역에서 매진된 공연을 받게 됩니다. 예를 들어, 작년 수상자는 영국 전역에서 매진된 공연을 했습니다. 수상자는 8월 21일에 지역 주민과 성 앤드루 뮤지컬 하고 지역에 의해 블랜라타 주민 센터에서 결정될 것입니다. -[2]-.

제가 지원 자격이 되나요?
[156] 대회는 나이나 지위, 능력에 관계없이 모든 스코틀랜드 국민에게 열려 있습니다. 아마추어와 반 전문 예술가들의 참가를 환영합니다. -[3]-.

어떻게 신청할 수 있나요?
참가 신청은 우편이나 이메일로 7월 2일까지 제출해야 합니다. 신청서와 참가 서류는 저희 웹 사이트 www.blenratha/sc/entry_form에서 찾으실 수 있습니다. 문의할 내용은 담당자이신 헤라러 로스코에게 (050) 555-0258로 연락하세요. -[4]-. [157] 심사 위원단을 신청하시려면 평가 진행 지인 브렌다 라이스에게 (050) 555-0259로 연락하세요

talent contest 장기 대회   public house 술집   venue (회합의) 장소   competition 경연   reward 상을 주다   eligible 적임의   regardless of ~에 관계없이   semi-professional 반 직업적인   entry 출전   previous 이전의   put forward 제시하다   judging panel 심사 위원단   evaluation 평가   coordinator 진행자   solicit 요청하다   inquire about ~에 관해 묻다

156 레드 라이온에 관해 언급된 것은?
(A) 매주 장기 대회를 개최한다.
(B) 블랜라타의 외부에 위치한다.
(C) 일체스 밴드의 소유이다.
(D) 성 앤드루 뮤지컬 하고 옆에 있다.

157 공지에 따르면 라이스 씨에게 연락해야 하는 이유는?
(A) 마감일 연장을 요청하기 위해
(B) 경연 대회의 수상자 결정을 돕는 데 지원하기 위해
(C) 참석을 확인하기 위해
(D) 공지 규정에 관해 문의하기 위해

158 [1], [2], [3], [4]로 표시된 위치 중 다음 문장이 들어가기 적절한 곳은?
"이전에 경연에 참가했던 사람들도 환영합니다."
(A) [1]
(B) [2]
(C) [3]
(D) [4]

[159-162]

도시 내 반사회적 행동 금지

그레이스 길렌토

엔테베 거리의 반사회적인 행동을 줄이려는 노력으로 시 위원회는 범정 음주 시간을 변경해 계획 중이다. -[1]- "우리 시는 0간에 가장 시끄럽고 소란스럽습니다."라고 엔테베 시 위원회의 대변인인 아더바 처리스 씨가 말했다. "지역social과 관광객들이 술집 나이트클럽, 카지노 등에 제공하는 오락에 참여하기 위해 시내로 가기 때문입니다. 방문객들이 시내로 올 때 보통 무료 공공 버스를 타고 와서 음주 운전을 걱정할 필요가 없습니다. 이는 거리에 훈련을 가중시킵니다." -[2]-

현재 어떤 술집들은 오후 6시부터 오후 8시까지 술을 반값으로 제공하고, 일부 술집들은 밤새 싼 주류를 제공한다. "이는 바꿔야야 합니다."라고 처리스 씨가 말했다. "모든 장소가 가격이 같은 도시들처럼 공통된 가격 구조를 도입하고 싶습니다. -[3]-

제안된 변경안이 발효되면 최근 도입된 여러 가지 제안들 중 하나가 될 것이다. 5월에는 새로운 카드시스템으로 오후 6시부터 오후 8시까지 한 사람당 살 수 있는 술의 양이 제한되었다. -[4]-

anti-social 반사회적 ease (고통, 불편 등을) 덜다 rowdy 소란스러운 소동을 벌이는 spokesperson 대변인 alike 돌다, 똑같이 head to ~을 향하다 participate in ~에 참여하다 entertainment 오락 disruption 혼란, 붕괴 go into effect 효력이 발생하다 stamp out 근절하다 surcharge 추가 요금 disorderly 무질서한 measure 기준, 방안

159 엔테베에 관해 알 수 있는 것은?
(A) 오락 장소가 너무 많다.
(B) 술에 추가 요금을 지불해야 한다.
(C) **무질서한 행동으로 문제를 겪고 있다.**
(D) 음주 운전으로 문제를 겪고 있다.

160 시 위원회가 고려 중인 것은?
(A) **술 가격 인상**
(B) 새 주차장 만들기
(C) 술집에 입장 가능한 인원 줄이기
(D) 보안 요원 도입

161 엔테베에서 최근에 있었던 일은?
(A) 시내의 가게들 일부가 손상되었다.
(B) 술집을 열 수 있는 허가를 받기가 더 어려워졌다.
(C) 더 많은 술집과 클럽이 문을 열었다.
(D) **음주자들을 위한 새 감시 방안이 도입되었다.**

162 [1], [2], [3], [4]로 표시된 위치 중 다음 문장이 들어가기 적절한 곳은?
"카드는 출입문에서 나뉘 주며, 각 구매품에 도장을 찍어 준다."
(A) [1]
(B) [2]
(C) [3]
(D) [4]

[163-165]

폴 가렌터	오전 11:35
누마크 기념이 직원 감사 행사를 열 건데, 그래서 그쪽에서는 우리가 에피타이저랑 관광객들이 술집, 나이트클럽, 카지노 등에 제공하는 오락에 참여하기 위해 메뉴인 아더바 처리스 씨가 말했다. "지역social과 관광객들이 음료, 디저트를 제공해 주기를 원합니다, 문제는 파이저랑 이번 주 금요일 저녁이라는 건데요. **164** 이미 우리는 그 행사가 이번 주 개의 저녁와 저녁에 하나의 행사가 더 있거든요	
켄 대비	오전 11:37
바빠지겠네요! 제가 직원들한테 연락해서 누가 시간이 되는지 알아볼까요?	
폴 가렌터	오전 11:38
네, 그렇게 해 주세요.	
미아 친	오전 11:39
음식은 어째요? 모든 걸 다 준비하기에는 시간이 맞지 않을데요.	
켄 대비	오전 11:40
수요일, 목요일에 미리 몇몇 음식은 준비해 놓을 수 있을 것 같아요.	
폴 가렌터	오전 11:41
그렇지 않아요. 음식은 신선해야만 해요. 누마크는 우리의 중요 고객 중 하나이고, 그 회사는 매우 까다롭거든요.	
미아 친	오전 11:42
주방 직원들을 일부 우리고 해서 초과 근무하도록 하는 건 어때요?	
켄 대비	오전 11:43
165 제가 딴한테 얘기해서, 주방 직원들을 그렇게 하게끔 설득할 수 있을지 알아볼게요	
폴 가렌터	오전 11:45
이미 그들은 그렇게 해야 할 거에요.	
미아 친	오전 11:46
메뉴는 최종 결정되었나요?	
폴 가렌터	오전 11:47
그건 제가 해결했어요. 누마크와의 계약서 한 부를 이메일로 보낼게요. 요, 필요한 모든 행사 정보가 들어 있을 거에요.	

appetizer 에피타이저 entrée 주요리 demanding 요구가 많은 convince 설득하다

163 대화 참여자들은 어떤 종류의 회사에서 일할 것 같은가?
(A) 식당
(B) **출장 음식 서비스 업체**
(C) 식료품점
(D) 호텔

164 대화 참여자들은 왜 추가 직원이 필요한가?
(A) 한 고객이 추가 서비스을 요청했다.
(B) 주문이 제시간에 완료되지 않았다.
(C) **한 행사가 그들의 일정에 추가되었다.**
(D) 일정을 조정하는 데 실수가 있었다.

165 오전 11시 45분에 가렌터 씨가 "이미 그들은 그렇게 해야 할 거에요."
라고 했을 때 그의 의도는 무엇인가?
(A) **그는 주방 직원들이 추가 근무를 할 것을 요구하고 있다.**
(B) 그는 그 고객이 특별히 신경 써서 대우받기를 원한다.
(C) 그는 단에게 상황을 설명할 시간이 없다.
(D) 그는 서방 직원들이 일부 올 것을 원한다.

[166-167]

수산: 마크 레도
발신: 마가렛 킴
날짜: 9월 10일 토요일
제목: 작은 문제

마크 씨에게,

월요일 오후에 있을 회의를 위한 당신의 문서를 검토해 보고, 어떻게 하면 당신의 발표를 강화시킬수 있을지에 대해서 조언을 해 드리고 요청하셨
조, 그런데 제가 오늘 밤에 제 이메일에 대해서 확인했을 때, **166** 제가 당신에게 제 개인 이메일이 아니라 업무용 계정을 알려드렸다는 걸 깨달았어요. 제가 지금 알려드리는 오늘 밤에 너무 늦은 것 같고, 이참에 우리가 구나가 지금 **167** 구내식당에서 그냥 그 문서를 저녁할 수신을 될 것 같지 아니라 요, 그럼 제가 회의 전에 그 문서를 검토를 충분한 시간이 있을 것 같습니다. 즐거운 저녁 시간 보내세요.

안녕히 가세요.
마가렛 킴 드림

166 킴 씨는 어떤 문제를 겪었는가?
(A) 그녀는 레도 씨의 문서를 읽어버렸다.
(B) 그녀는 레도 씨를 만날 시간이 없었다.
(C) **그녀는 잘못된 연락처를 제공했다.**
(D) 그녀는 그녀의 이메일을 확인하는 것을 잊어버렸다.

aside from ~을 제외하고 prestige 위신, 명망 profile 인지도, (대중의) 관심 nominee 지명된 사람, 후보 inundated 감당 못할 정도로 몰리는 commission (일을) 의뢰하다 meet demand 요구에 응하다 precisely 정확히 prestigious 명망 있는

172 기사의 목적은?
(A) 회사의 성취를 강조하기 위해
(B) 유명한 아티스트를 설명하기 위해
(C) 사진 대회에 출전하도록 촉청하기 위해
(D) 수상자로 간주를 지명하기 위해

173 슈퍼상에 관해 알 수 있는 것은?
(A) 세계적으로 영향력이 있는 명망 있는 상이다.
(B) 전에 카리자에 본사를 둔 회사가 수상했었다.
(C) 한 명의 개인에 의해 설립되었다.
(D) 처음에 사진 회사가 상을 받았다.

174 액시스 24의 사진들이 다루는 분야로 언급되지 않은 것은?
(A) 스포츠 행사
(B) 광고판
(C) 자연
(D) 사람

175 기사에 따르면 미너사 씨가 계획하는 일은?
(A) 홍보용 예산 늘리기
(B) 사진 촬영소를 하나 더 열기
(C) 추가로 직원 고용하기
(D) 카리자에서 있을 기념식에 참석하기

[172-175]

7월 15일 — 172 찬사를 받고 있는 컴페티브 TV캠페인을 위해 사진을 제공한 화사인 액시스 24가 출판된 사진과 그래픽 일러스트레이션 분야에서 탁월함을 보여준 데 대해 173 20년 이상 상을 수여해 온 국제적인 슈퍼상에 지명되었다. 3천 명 이상의 참가자를 중에서 선택된 액시스 24는 지명된 곳 중 유일하게 카리자에 본사를 둔 촬영소이다. 8월 20일 독일의 뮐른에서 올해의 슈퍼상 수상자들이 발표될 것이다.

"화사 내의 전문성, 전문 지식, 창의력에 대한 한사인 이 지명이 매우 자랑스럽습니다."라고 화사의 청립자이자 최고경영자인 이슬람 미너사 씨가 발표했다.

174 슈퍼상 심사 위원은 전 세계 광고 화사와 최고 간부들 6명으로 구성된다. 그들은 사진 포트폴리오의 품질과 혁신으로 액시스 24가 선택되었다고 평했다.

"지혜는 야생 동물부터 스포츠 행사, 사람, 자연까지 모든 것을 다룹니다. "그리고 최종 결과물이 소렴없이 소통합니다."

"지명되는 것만으로도 미너사 씨가 이끌 수 있도록 도와주고, 액시스 24는 대중의 인지도가 높아져 사업이 번창하고 있다. 지명작들의 이름이 발표되었을 때 촬영소는 그림에 대한 일을 의뢰하기를 원하는 관심 있는 사람들로부터의 요청이 쇄도했다. 175 증가된 수요를 충족시키는 유일한 방법으로 더 많은 전문 사진작가와 기술자를 고용하는 것이고, 이는 바로 우리가 다음에 취할 행동입니다."라고 미너사 씨는 말했다.

액시스 24에 관한 더 많은 정보는 www.axis24.co.pk에서, 슈퍼상에 관한 한 세부 내용은 www.schifferprize.org에서 찾을 수 있다.

acclaimed 찬사를 받는 nominate 지명하다 illustration 삽화 entrant 참가자 tribute 헌사 professionalism 전문성 expertise 전문지식 creativity 창의력 judge 심사원 심사위원 comprise ~으로 구성되다 founder 청립자 top executive 최고 간부 innovation 혁신 portfolio 작품집 wildlife 야생 동물 liaise 연락을 취하다 end product 최종 결과물

(C) 206호
(D) 204호

170 마이애미 오리엔테이션이 위원회에 관해 언급된 것은?
(A) 방문객들에게 무료 교통을 제공한다.
(B) 좀 더 다양한 서비스들을 제공한다.
(C) 여러 장소에 사무실이 있다.
(D) 여러 언어로 된 자료를 제공한다.

171 전단지에 따르면 참석자들이 발표 후에 할 수 있는 것은?
(A) 도시 투어하기
(B) 회원권 정보 요청하기
(C) 공개 행사의 좌석 예약하기
(D) 무료 점심 즐기기

167 김 씨는 레노 씨에게 무엇을 하라고 요청하는가?
(A) 그에게 직접 자료를 담라고
(B) 다른 직원한테 도움을 요청하라고
(C) 문서를 팩스로 보내라고
(D) 이침에 그녀의 사무실에 들르라고

[168-171]

168 최근에 마이애미로 이사하셨나요? 오리엔테이션에서 마이애미에서 살기

발표 일정

오전 10시: 168 169 도시에서 이동하기 - 대중교통 선택 (212호)	
오전 11시: 168 169 마이애미에서 아파트 또는 집 대여하기 (212호)	오전 11시: 금융 및 은행 거래하기 (206호)
12시 정오: 마이애미에서 실기 찾기 (208호)	12시 정오: 마이애미에서 일자리 찾기 (206호)
오후 1시: 마이애미 돌아다니기 - 지역 행사와 명소 요약 (204호)	

일부 발표들이 시간이 겹친다는 점을 기억하시고 가장 유용한 것을 결정하셔서 참석하셔야 합니다. 169 대중교통에 관한 얘기나 212호에 적절한 숙소 찾는 가는 매우 인기가 높은 자리 둘 다를 위해서 일찍 도착하십시오.
170 발표는 영어로 진행됩니다만, 프랑스어, 스페인어, 이럽어로 번역된 버전이 있습니다. 음사와 음료도 구매 가능합니다.
171 마지막 발표 후, 주요 명소를 안내하는 관광이 있습니다. 마이애미에 해변의 장기 거주자와 오리엔테이션 위원회 회원이 관광을 이끌 것입니다. 더 많은 정보를 위해 거주자 오리엔테이션 www.miamiwelcoming.com을 방문해 주세요.

orientation 예비 교육 presentation 발표 public transport 대중교통 rent 임대하다 condominium 아파트 finance 금융 banking 은행 업무 get to know 알게 되다 round-up 종합, 요약 attraction 명소 clash 충돌하다 겹치다 time-wise 시간에 관하여 suitable 적합한 accommodation 숙박 시설 translate 번역하다 transcript 글로 옮긴 기록 resident 거주자

168 전단지는 누구를 대상으로 하는가?
(A) 마이애미 지역 공무원들
(B) 미국을 방문하는 관광객들
(C) 마이애미 관광 이사회 회원들
(D) 지역에 새로 온 주민들

169 가장 인기가 높은 발표들이 열리는 곳은?
(A) 212호
(B) 208호

홈	연락처	주문	고객평

이촌인제노아에 광고하기: **176** 이촌인제노아는 오랫동안 지ہ리 잡아 온 웹사이트로, 거의 2만 명의 팔로워가 제노아 지역의 오락과 명소에 대한 민을 만하고 상세한 정보를 위해 방문하고 있습니다.

저희 웹 사이트의 광고는 다음과 같은 형식으로 보입니다:

형식 1
수직 배너가 오른쪽 또는 왼쪽에 나타납니다. **177** 많은 글을 포함할 수 없습니다. 영상을 나올 수 없습니다.

형식 2
중간 크기의 광고가 페이지 시작 시 중앙에 나타납니다. 한 개의 이미지와 한 개의 영상이 문자와 함께 포함될 수 있습니다.

형식 3
페이지 상단으로 스크롤 하는 수도 표시 배너입니다. 음량이 포함될 수 있습니다.

형식 4 **178**
가장 큰 규모의 광고로, 사진 10장까지 가능하며, 동영상, 음향, 문자가 포함된 박스형 광고입니다.

광고 구매를 위해 엘로이즈 르준에게 ellejeune@artsingenoa.com으로 연락해 주세요.

이그리드 블루멘
블로렌스 갤러리 사장

발신: 잉그리드 블루멘 [admin@florensgallery.com]
수신: 엘로이즈 르준 [ellejeune@artsingenoa.com]
제목: 블로렌스 갤러리 광고
날짜: 4월 23일

르준 씨께,

179 이촌인제노아와 다시 광고를 진행하는 것에 관해 문의하려고 편지를 씁니다. **178** 다시 한 번 박스형 광고를 선택하고 싶습니다. 지난번과 같은 사진들과 녹음을 사용하고 싶습니다. 그래나 문자는 바뀌어야 합니다. 곧 있을 전시회와 관련하여 제가 원하는 문구를 보내 드리겠습니다. 문구가 는 예 잘 띄게 강조되도록 제작부에 확인해 좀 좋을 수 있나요? 또, **180** 최대 단어 수도 알려 주실 수 있나요?

이그리드 블루멘
블로렌스 갤러리 사장

review 평 long-established 설립된 지 오래된 reliable 믿을만한 format 형식 vertical 수직의, 세로의 banner 배너 광고 audio 녹음 visual 영상 medium-sized 중형 규모의 text 문자 horizontal 수평의, 가로의 scroll (마우스로) 스크롤하다 exhibition 전시(회) prominence 중요성 font 서체 length 길이

애니스턴 과실 재배원
과일과 채소
위스테리아 로드 87, 솜머셋 YL3
(013) 90 72 65 58
www.aniston.co.uk

저희는 과일과 채소를 재배하고 싶다면 애니스턴 과실 재배원으로 오세요. 각종에서 온 다양한 식물의 재배원으로 오세 **176** 60에이커의 농장을 운영하시고 어떤 과일과 채소를 재배하고 싶은지 결정하세요. 제공하는 제품은 4가지로 분류됩니다.

181
구역 1: 땅에 열리는 과일과 채소
구역 2: 나무에 열리는 과일
구역 3: 근채류
구역 4: 전 세계에서 온 외래 과일과 채소

182 정원사들이 많은 다른 언어를 사용하므로 과일과 채소를 재배하고 보살피고 수확하는 최선의 방법에 대해 어떤 문의든지 기까이 답할 것입니다.

183 이국적이고 색다른 것을 찾고 있나요? 입주에서 세계적인 농산물을 보여 드릴 수 있 정원사를 불러 주세요. 선택하시고 나서는 애니스턴 과실 재배원이 영국 내에서 어디든지 주문을 배달할 수 있습니다.

애니스턴 과실 재배원 주문서

종류	양
184 1. 빨간 고추	100
2. 파란 고추	100
3. 과일나무: 사과	1
4. 산딸기 식물	300
5. 딸기 식물	200

고객: 안젤라 스틸턴드
185 배송 날짜: 3월 12일
주소: 힐 라이즈 26, 여빌, 솜머셋
전화: (01398) 319553

주문서를 작성하시면 서비스 데스크에 주세요. 직원이 주문을 확인하고 질문에 답해 드리며, 품목이 재고에 있는지 확인할 것입니다. 고객은 최초 주문으로부터 일주일 이내로 배달받으실 것입니다. **185** 손상을 입은 식물이나 나무는 배달된 지 하루 이내로 알려 주셔야 합니다.

root vegetable 근채류 exotic 외래의 nurture 보살피다 ship 수송하다 bulk 큰 규모의 negotiable 협의할 수 있는 raspberry 산딸기 hand in 건네주다 damaged 손상을 입은 orchard 과수원 flourish 무성하게 자라다 geographical 지리적인 origin 기원 plus 더하여

---

176 르준 씨는 어디에서 일하는가?
(A) 광고 대행사
(B) 마케팅 연구 회사
(C) 제노아에 있는 갤러리
(D) 미술 관련 웹 사이트

177 형식 1에 관해 언급된 것은?
(A) 영상은 허용하지 않는다.
(B) 가장 비싸다.
(C) 가장 많은 글을 포함할 수 있다.
(D) 빨리 준비될 수 있다.

178 어느 광고 형식에 블로렌스 씨가 가장 관심을 가질 것 같은가? (연계 지문 문제)
(A) 형식 1
(B) 형식 2
(C) 형식 3
(D) 형식 4

179 블로렌스 갤러리에 관해 알 수 있는 것은?
(A) 개조 중에 있다.
(B) 최근에 새 전시회를 열었다.
(C) 추후 공자가 있을 때까지 문을 닫을 것이다.
(D) 이전에 이촌인제노아에 광고했었다.

180 블루멘 씨가 문자에 대해 묻는 것은?
(A) 서체의 크기가 얼마나 되어야 하는지
(B) 길이가 얼마나 되어야 하는지
(C) 어떤 형식이 최상인지
(D) 출판하는 데 비용이 얼마나 드는지

181. 애니스턴 과실 재배원에 관해 알 수 있는 것은?
(A) 손님들이 정원을 견학하도록 허용한다.
(B) 외래 채소를 종종 해외로 배송한다.
(C) 대부분의 농산물을 현지 농장과 과수원에 판매한다.
(D) 열리지 않는 과일 나무는 교체해 줄 것이다.

182. 광고에 따르면 직원들이 손님들에게 줄 수 있는 정보는?
(A) 외래 농산물을 위한 최고의 요리별 선정
(B) 각각의 과일과 채소의 원산지
(C) 다른 주문에 대한 가격 할인
(D) 과일과 채소 재배법에 관한 조언

183. 손님들은 특이한 식물을 어떻게 요청해야 하는가?
(A) 수석 정원사에게 말함으로써
(B) 우편으로 개별 신청서를 보냄으로써
(C) 과실 재배원의 웹 사이트를 방문함으로써
(D) 정원 직원 전문가에게 주문서를 줌으로써

184. 과실 재배원의 직원들은 스탠리드 씨의 주 대부분을 주로 어디에서 찾을 것인가? (연계 지문 문제)
(A) 구역 1
(B) 구역 2
(C) 구역 3
(D) 구역 4

185. 양식에 따르면 스탠리드 씨가 3월 13일까지 해야 하는 일은?
(A) 구매품에 대한 문제를 회사에 알리기
(B) 과일 나무 주문 비용과 배달 요금 지불하기
(C) 잘못 배달된 여분의 식물 반품하기
(D) 구매한 품목 심기

[186-190]

http://www.sandeventcontest.com

행사 이름: 여름 모래 조각 대회
장소: 노바스코샤의 마르카스 해변
날짜: 8월 15일~18일
연락: 제레미 첸

내용: 올해로 5년째인 이 연간 행사는 (188) 전 세계에서 80명 이상의 모두 또는 아마추어 참가자들을 참여하게 만듭니다. 1인 부문과 단체 부문 둘 다 있는데, (188) 작년에는 약 12,000명의 방문객들이 있었습니다. 이 대회는 노바스코샤에서 가장 인기 있는 해변 이벤트 중 하나가 되었습니다. 캐나다의 이 지역에서 가장 큰 모래 해변 중 하나인 마르카스 해변은 힐리팩스 시에서 약 40분 정도 떨어져 있습니다. 조각뿐이 아니라, 4일 동안 진행되는 이 축제는 음식 공연이나 다양한 음식 업체들, 그리고 방문자들을 위한 모래 조각 수업들을 지원합니다. 입장은 무료지만, 주차는 10달러입니다.

제5회 연간 여름 모래 조각 대회 우승자들

순위	이름	국적	제목
1등	레이첼 무르타프	호주	초록색 언어
2등	엘리다 그래햄	뉴질랜드	돌고래 떼
3등	자바리 오네다	미국	하스트 섬
4등	존 피터스	브라질	해적선
5등	(190) 자마르 귀몬드	캐나다	해양 생물들

* 개인 부문

힐리팩스의 새로운 소식!

에일린 티오

연간 여름 모래 조각 대회가 지난주에 개최되었는데. 그것은 (188) 여름 시즌을 마나 보내는 완벽한 방법이었다. 특히 좋았던 날씨 덕분에, (188) 방문객들의 숫자가 지난해에 비해서 두 배로 증가했다.

이 대회는 개인 부문과 단체 부문에 대해서 조각상들을 (187) 가득들였다. 조계 경탄, 해조, 부두와 다른 자연에서 온 재료들이 해양 생물 관련 디자인부터 저 수위 배를 묘사하는 것을 모두 포함했다.

(189) 호주에서 온 레이첼 무르타프 씨는 그녀의 초록색 언어 작품으로 두 번이나 우승했던 뉴질랜드에서 온 엘리다 그래햄 씨를 이겼는데, 그 작품은 바다에서 나온 유리들로 화려하게 장식되었다. (190) 모든 조각들이 훌륭했지만 나의 개인적인 최고의 작품은 해안선이었다. 그 작품의 독대를 위해서 부두를 사용한 것은 이전에 본 적이 없는 것이었다.

관람객들도 제외들을 즐길 수 있었다. 대회에 참가하지 않은 많은 조각 전문가들이 모두가 참여 가능한 무료 수업을 진행했다. 오늘 이름과 음식들만 아니라 이것도 여름의 끝을 즐길 수 있는 완벽한 방법을 선사했다.

preceding 이전의, 앞선　boast 뽐내다, 자랑하다　an array of 다양한
incorporate 포함하다　depict 묘사하다　beat 이기다　richly 화려하게
ornament 장식하다

186. 대회 참가자들에 대해서 암시된 것은?
(A) 그들은 모두 아마추어이다.
(B) 그들은 미리 등록할 것을 요청받는다.
(C) 그들은 개인적으로 전 세계 참여한다.
(D) 그들은 다양한 방문객들을 나타내게 했다.

187. 기사의 2번째 문단, 1번째 줄에 있는 "가득들였다"와 가장 비슷한 의미의 단어는? (연계 지문 문제)
(A) 철회했다
(B) 끓어들었다
(C) 옮겼다
(D) 상상했다

188. 올해 행사에 대해서 암시된 것은? (연계 지문 문제)
(A) 20,000명 이상의 방문객들이 왔다.
(B) 참가하기 위해서는 1인당 10달러가 든다.
(C) 작년 행사보다 기간이 더 길었다.
(D) 마르카스 해변에서 처음으로 개최되었다.

189. 그래함 씨에 대해서 언급된 것은?
(A) 그는 작품에 조개 껍데기를 사용했다.
(B) 그는 모래 조각 수업을 제공했다.
(C) 그는 이전에 대회에서 우승했었다.
(D) 그는 최근에 뉴질랜드로 이사를 갔다.

190. 타오 씨는 누구의 작품을 가장 좋아했는가? (연계 지문 문제)
(A) 무르티프 씨의 것
(B) 오베다 씨의 것
(C) 피터스 씨의 것
(D) 귄모드 씨의 것

[191-195]

파인탑 파이낸셜에 지인들을 추천해 주시면 모두가 혜택을 받을 수 있습니다!*

자회 파인탑 파이낸셜에 보내주신 신뢰에 감사드립니다. 190 193 우수 회원으로서, 당신은 저희의 모든 금융 상품을 이용하실 수 있고 최고의 가 혜택들을 누리실 수 있습니다.

진심 어린 감사를 표현하기 위해서, 지회의 계좌를 오픈하거나 기존을 추천해 주시면 20달러를 드리고자 합니다. 또한 추천받은 그분들에게도 파인탑 온라인 예금 계좌나 파인탑 투자 증권 계좌에 200달러 이상 예금하시면 즉시 www.PineTop.com에 등록하시고 특별 코드 PP880을 입력하시기만 하면 됩니다.

* 193 이 제안은 오직 우량한 자산 상태에 있는 우수 회원에게만 해당됩니다. 추천받는 분은 반드시 신규 고객이어야 합니다. 기존 또는 이전 파인탑 파이낸셜의 직원은 지원이 되지 않습니다.

refer 추천하다 acquaintance 지인 initial 최초의 deposit 예금
referral 추천인의 사람 ineligible 지격이 없는

191. 공지는 누구를 위해 쓰였는가?
(A) 파인탑 파이낸셜 직원들
(B) 잠재 투자자들
(C) 주주들
(D) 기존 계좌 소유자들

192. 나롤스 씨는 왜 로페즈 씨에게 글은 썼는가?
(A) 투자에 대한 조언을 하려고
(B) 그녀에게 특별한 혜택에 대한 정보를 제공하려고
(C) 최근의 계좌 입금을 확인하려고
(D) 재무 상담사를 소개해 주려고

193. 나롤스 씨에 대해서 사실인 것은 무엇인가? (연계 지문 문제)
(A) 그는 파인탑 파이낸셜의 우수 고객이다.
(B) 그는 로페즈 씨를 거의 모른다.
(C) 그는 파인탑 파이낸셜의 직원이다.
(D) 그는 최근에 신규 계좌를 열었다.

수신: 미란다 로페즈 (mlopez@networkone.com)
발신: 조 니콜스 (jnichols@networkone.com)
제목: 193 파인탑 파이낸셜의 특별 혜택
날짜: 2월 2일

안녕하세요, 미란다.

당신이 퇴직 연금 계좌를 시작하는 것에 대해서 걱정하고 있었던 것이 194 지난번 기억이 나요. 자, 여기 당신에게 도움이 될 만한 것이 있어요. 192 파인탑 파이낸셜이 계좌를 개설하는 것만으로 20달러를 준다고 합니다. 193 저는 이 회사의 서비스를 올해도 6년째 이용해 오고 있는데, 만족했던 경험밖에는 없어요. 온라인 계좌 개설이 정말 쉬워요. 194 그들은 안전하고 사용하기 쉬운 신청 방법이 나와 있는 전단지를 동봉했어요.

조

미란다 로페즈
201 뉴포트 로드
살렘, MA 50084
4월 25일

195 로페즈 씨에게

파인탑 파이낸셜에 회원이 되신 것을 환영합니다. 저희는 4월 15일에 귀하의 성함으로 파인탑 온라인 예금 계좌를 개설했습니다. 첨부된 계약 조건들과 수수료 표를 확인해 주세요.

195 신규 가입에 대해서 감사드리며, 저희는 귀하의 계좌에 20달러를 입금해 드릴 것입니다. 계좌 오픈일로부터 30일 이내에 입금이 이뤄질 것입니다.

www.PineTop.com에 방문하시면 귀하의 계좌에 접속 가능합니다. 이래에 나와 있는 계좌번호와 임시 비밀번호를 입력해 주세요. 일단 로그인하시고 나서, 사용자 이름과 임시 비밀번호를 다시 설정해야 합니다.

계좌 번호: 78082210
임시 비밀번호: jj99-0dff-8822-ss

만약 질문이 있으시면, 1-600-555-6690로 주저말고 연락주세요.

진심을 담아,

리 카드나
신규 계좌 담당자

194. 이 이메일의 2번째 문단, 1번째 줄에 있는 '건단지와 가장 비슷한 의미의 단어는?
(A) 신청서
(B) 신문
(C) 인세블
(D) 영수증

195. 로페즈 씨에 대해서 암시된 것은? (연계 지문 문제)
(A) 그녀는 파인탑 파이낸셜의 기존 고객이다.
(B) 그녀는 리 카드나와 같은 곳에서 일한다.
(C) 그녀는 계좌에 200달러 이상을 예금했다.
(D) 그녀는 가까운 미래에 은퇴할 계획이다.

[196-200]

관리자 교육 세미나
이번 봄 새로운 세미나!
전략의 기본

관리직으로 승진한 것을 축하드립니다. 귀하는 이제 총핵을 맡은 사람이 되었습니다.

이 세미나 어려운 직위에서 성공하기 위해 필수적인 스킬들을 배우세요. 우리의 관리의 기본 세미나는 시작하기 위해서 필요한 것들을 가르처 드립니다. 다음은 같은 방법들을 배우게 될 것입니다.

- 업무 효율적으로 위임하기
- 직원들에게 동기 부여하기
- 198 비판 가하기
- 198 마감 기한 기록하고 충족시키기
- 198 신입사원 교육하기

이 하루 동안의 세미나는 귀하가 효율적인 관리자가 되기 위해서 필요한 많은 스킬들을 소개할 것입니다. 하습하게 될 스킬들은 귀하에게 도움이 될 뿐만 아니라, 조직 안에서 귀하의 업무 효율성을 199 향상시키는 데도 도움이 될 것입니다. 안내서를 다운받으시려면 www.abc.com으로 방문해 주세요.

196 공지글의 4번째 문단, 2번째 줄에 있는 '향상시키다'와 가장 비슷한 의미의 단어는?

(A) 보충하다
(B) 열망하다
(C) 개선시키다
(D) 이끌다

197 도베 세미나에 대해서 암시된 것은?

(A) 후일에 다시 반복될 것이다.
(B) 할인된 가격으로 제공되고 있다.
(C) 사전 등록이 요구된다.
(D) 참가자들에게 학습 자료를 나눠 준다.

198 4월 7일 세미나에서 배울 수 있는 스킬이 아닌 것은? (연계 지문 문제)

(A) 신입사원들을 교육하는 방법
(B) 승진을 요청하는 방법
(C) 시간을 관리하는 방법
(D) 다른 사람들을 지휘하는 방법

199 가터 씨는 도베에서 어떤 세미나를 이끌었을 것 같은가? (연계 지문 문제)

(A) 관리의 기본
(B) 리더십과 팀 단합
(C) 건설적인 비판
(D) 관리직 마스터하기

200 바카 씨에 대해서 암시된 것은? (연계 지문 문제)

(A) 그는 다른 직원들을 관리하고 있다.
(B) 그는 무료로 세미나에 참석했다.
(C) 그는 발렌자 디자인의 사장이다.
(D) 그는 가터 씨와 함께 일했었다.

관리직 교육 세미나

발리웨어 도베 4월 7일-10일

[198] 관리의 기본	4월 7일 화요일 오전 9시 – 오후 5시 효율적인 관리자가 되기 위해 필요한 스킬 배우기
리더십과 팀 단합	4월 8일 수요일 오전 8시 30분 – 오후 4시 30분 생산적인 팀을 만들고 이끌기 위한 일련의 전략 세우기
건설적인 비판	4월 9일 목요일 오전 9시 – 오후 5시 직원들에게 긍정적인 변화를 가져 올 수 있는 방법 배우기. 이 세미나는 작을 만들지 않고 건설적인 비판을 기울수 있는 효과적인 기술들을 다룹니다.
[199] 관리직 마스터하기	4월 10일 금요일 오전 8시 30분 – 오후 4시 30분 당신이 필요 할 수 있는 최고의 매니저가 되세요. 오늘날 전문 직장에서 입증된 방법들을 어떻게 실행할 수 있는지에 대해서 배우세요. [199] 선행 학습: 상급 관리직 과정

[197] 세미나들에는 강의 자료가 포함되어 있습니다. 또한, 참가자들은 온라인 자료 도서관에 대한 접근권도 얻을 수 있습니다.

발신: vincent.baca@valenza.com
수신: mpoplar@abc.com
제목: 도베 관리직 세미나
날짜: 4월 15일

포플라 씨에게,

저희 발렌자 디자인에게 훌륭한 훈련을 해 주셔서, 저희 직원 9명이 지난 주 우리 시에서 열린 귀하의 세미나에 참가할 수 있었음에 다시 한 번 감사드리고 싶습니다. 저를 포함한 모든 참가자들이 지난주 교육 시간에 일어나 많이 배웠느느지를 계속 얘기하고 있습니다. [199] 지난 세미나에서처럼 저는 제자신도 가터 씨에게 많은 것을 배웠습니다. 그분으 아는 것이 많은 강사일 뿐만 아니라, 또한 그분이 가르치시는 리더십 능력에 모범을 보이는 분이시다. [199] [200] 그분의 상급 관리직 과정에서 제가 배울 수 있는 모든 것을 다 배웠다고 생각했습니다. 그러나 제가 틀렸어요!

진심을 담아,
빈센트 바카

supervisory 관리의　challenging 어려운　delegate 위임하다　constructive 건설적인　cover 다루다　implement 실행하다　prerequisite 선행 학습, 전제 조건　generous 후한　model 모형을 만들다

Actual Test

03

🎧 Listening Comprehension

본책 P100

PART 1

1 (B)	2 (C)	3 (C)	4 (D)	5 (A)	6 (B)			

PART 2

7 (A)	8 (A)	9 (A)	10 (C)	11 (C)	12 (B)	13 (B)	14 (C)	15 (B)	16 (B)
17 (C)	18 (A)	19 (B)	20 (B)	21 (C)	22 (B)	23 (A)	24 (C)	25 (A)	26 (A)
27 (A)	28 (C)	29 (C)	30 (C)	31 (B)				

PART 3

32 (A)	33 (C)	34 (D)	35 (B)	36 (D)	37 (A)	38 (B)	39 (C)	40 (C)	41 (D)
42 (C)	43 (D)	44 (C)	45 (B)	46 (D)	47 (A)	48 (A)	49 (C)	50 (B)	51 (C)
52 (A)	53 (B)	54 (A)	55 (C)	56 (B)	57 (A)	58 (D)	59 (C)	60 (D)	61 (B)
62 (C)	63 (D)	64 (A)	65 (A)	66 (C)	67 (D)	68 (D)	69 (B)	70 (A)	

PART 4

71 (D)	72 (A)	73 (D)	74 (B)	75 (B)	76 (B)	77 (A)	78 (D)	79 (A)	80 (D)
81 (C)	82 (A)	83 (D)	84 (B)	85 (B)	86 (B)	87 (D)	88 (A)	89 (A)	90 (C)
91 (B)	92 (C)	93 (B)	94 (A)	95 (C)	96 (E)	97 (C)	98 (D)	99 (A)	100 (A)

📖 Reading Comprehension

본책 P112

PART 5

101 (D)	102 (A)	103 (C)	104 (A)	105 (D)	106 (D)	107 (B)	108 (A)	109 (D)	110 (C)
111 (C)	112 (B)	113 (D)	114 (C)	115 (D)	116 (A)	117 (C)	118 (D)	119 (C)	120 (B)
121 (D)	122 (B)	123 (C)	124 (D)	125 (D)	126 (A)	127 (B)	128 (B)	129 (B)	130 (C)

PART 6

131 (B)	132 (D)	133 (B)	134 (C)	135 (A)	136 (C)	137 (B)	138 (A)	139 (B)	140 (D)
141 (B)	142 (B)	143 (C)	144 (B)	145 (B)	146 (D)			

PART 7

147 (D)	148 (A)	149 (B)	150 (A)	151 (B)	152 (C)	153 (A)	154 (D)	155 (A)	156 (B)
157 (D)	158 (C)	159 (B)	160 (C)	161 (D)	162 (A)	163 (A)	164 (B)	165 (B)	166 (A)
167 (B)	168 (D)	169 (C)	170 (C)	171 (D)	172 (D)	173 (A)	174 (D)	175 (D)	176 (D)
177 (C)	178 (C)	179 (B)	180 (C)	181 (D)	182 (B)	183 (A)	184 (C)	185 (B)	186 (D)
187 (B)	188 (D)	189 (C)	190 (C)	191 (A)	192 (D)	193 (B)	194 (A)	195 (B)	196 (D)
197 (B)	198 (D)	199 (C)	200 (C)					

Part 1

본책 P.101

1 미M
(A) People are entering the train station.
(B) Passengers are waiting to board the train.
(C) Some workers are repairing railway tracks.
(D) Pedestrians are crossing a busy street.

(A) 사람들이 기차역으로 들어서고 있다.
(B) 승객들이 기차에 탑승하기 위해 대기하고 있다.
(C) 몇몇 인부들이 철도 선로를 수리하고 있다.
(D) 보행자들이 혼잡한 거리를 건너고 있다.

board 탑승하다 railway track 철도 선로 pedestrian 보행자 busy street 혼잡한 거리, 번화가

2 미W
(A) Plants are growing in pots.
(B) Some trees are growing next to a column.
(C) The worker is raking the soil.
(D) The gardener is trimming bushes.

(A) 식물들이 화분에서 크고 있다.
(B) 몇몇 나무들이 기둥 옆에서 자라고 있다.
(C) 인부가 갈퀴로 흙을 긁어모으고 있다.
(D) 정원사가 관목을 손질하고 있다.

pot 화분 column 기둥 rake 갈퀴질하다, 긁어모으다 trim 자르다, 손질하다 bush 관목, 덤불

3 영M
(A) Some people are walking down a hallway.
(B) Some people are glancing at a statue.
(C) A bridge leads to some buildings.
(D) Banners have been suspended from some lampposts.

(A) 몇몇 사람들이 복도를 따라 내려가고 있다.
(B) 몇몇 사람들이 조각상을 보고 있다.
(C) 다리가 몇몇 건물들로 이어져 있다.
(D) 현수막이 가로등 기둥에 걸려 있다.

hallway 복도 glance 흘깃 보다 statue 동상 lead to ~로 이어지다 banner 현수막 suspend 매달다, 걸다 lamppost 가로등 기둥

4 호M
(A) Some merchandise is being displayed for sale.
(B) Some books are being distributed in a store.
(C) Shoppers are waiting in line to make purchases.
(D) Bookshelves have been filled with reading materials.

(A) 몇몇 상품이 판매를 위해 전시되고 있다.
(B) 몇몇 책들이 가게에 배부되고 있다.
(C) 쇼핑객들이 구매를 위해 줄을 서서 기다리고 있다.
(D) 책꽂이가 읽을거리로 채워져 있다.

merchandise 상품 distribute 나눠 주다, 배부하다 wait in line 줄을 서서 기다리다 make a purchase 구매하다 bookshelf 책꽂이 reading material 읽을거리

5 영M
(A) They are collaborating on a project.
(B) One of the workers is taking off his tool belt.
(C) One of the workers is plugging in some equipment.
(D) They are moving some wooden materials into a warehouse.

(A) 사람들이 어떤 일에 협력하고 있다.
(B) 인부들 중 한 명이 그의 공구 벨트를 벗고 있다.
(C) 인부들 중 한 명이 장비에 플러그를 꽂고 있다.
(D) 사람들이 나무 자재를 창고로 옮기고 있다.

collaborate 협력하다 take off 벗다 tool belt 공구 벨트 plug in 플러그를 꽂다 wooden 나무로 된 warehouse 창고

6 미W
(A) The building overlooks the mountain.
(B) Mountains can be seen from an outdoor pool.
(C) Swimmers are stepping down into a pool.
(D) A pool is surrounded by trees.

(A) 건물이 산을 내려다보고 있다.
(B) 야외 수영장에서 산이 보인다.
(C) 수영하는 사람들이 수영장 안으로 들어가고 있다.
(D) 수영장이 나무로 둘러싸여 있다.

overlook 내려다보다 step down 단을 내려가다 be surrounded by ~으로 둘러싸이다

Part 2

본책 P.104

7 미M How long will it take to cycle to the stadium?
영M (A) About half an hour.
(B) By bus, I think.
(C) Maybe tomorrow.

경기장까지 자전거로 얼마나 걸릴까요?
(A) 약 30분 정도요.
(B) 제 생각엔 버스로요.
(C) 어쩌면 내일이요.

cycle 자전거를 타다 stadium 경기장 half an hour 30분

8 You two haven't worked together, have you?
미M (A) No, not yet.
미M (B) I have too many.
(C) The day before.

당신 둘은 같이 일해 본 적이 없죠, 그렇죠?
(A) 네, 아직이요.
(B) 저는 너무 많아요.
(C) 그 전날이요.
the day before 그 전날

9 Didn't you want to catch a faster flight?
영M (A) Yes, but I missed it.
미W (B) The east terminal.
(C) I took some back.

더 빠른 비행 편 탑승을 원하지 않았나요?
(A) 네, 하지만 제가 놓쳤어요.
(B) 동부 터미널이요.
(C) 제가 몇 개 다시 가져갔습니다.
catch a flight 비행기에 탑승하다 take back 다시 가져가다

10 Where's a cheap place to get breakfast?
미W (A) Let's line up for it.
(B) I can't lend you any money.
(C) At the café downtown.

아침에서 아침 식사를 저렴하게 먹을 수 있나요?
(A) 그것을 기다리기 위해 줄을 섭시다.
(B) 당신에게 돈을 조금도 빌려 줄 수 없어요.
(C) 시내에 있는 카페에요.
downtown 시내에

11 When will your driving license expire?
미M (A) It's right along the sidewalk.
미W (B) Return it by secure delivery, please.
(C) Not until March.

당신의 운전 면허증은 언제 만료되나요?
(A) 그것은 바로 보도를 따라가 있습니다.
(B) 안전 배송으로 반품해 주세요.
(C) 3월까지는 유효해요.
expire 만료되다, 만기하다 sidewalk 인도, 보도 secure delivery 안전 배송

12 Shouldn't we try going in the main entrance?
미M (A) We don't check any more.
영M

13
Did the Cairo office call today?

(B) No, it's locked as well.
(C) There's a trial download.

중앙 출입구로 가는 걸 시도해 봐야 하지 않을까요?
(A) 우리는 더 이상 확인하지 않아요.
(B) 아니요, 그쪽 또한 잠겨 있습니다.
(C) 시험 다운로드가 있습니다.
main entrance 중앙 출입구   trial 시험,실험

13 Did the Cairo office call today?
[미M] (A) No, that will suffice.
[미W] (B) Yes, Ms. Jenkins left a contact number for you.
(C) Try this one as an alternative.

카이로 사무실에서 오늘 전화가 왔나요?
(A) 아니요, 충분할 거예요.
(B) 네, 젠킨스 씨가 당신에게 전화번호를 남겼습니다.
(C) 이것을 대안으로 시도해 보세요.
suffice 충분하다   contact number 전화번호   alternative 대안

14
14 Let's see if another shop has these glasses at a lower price.
[미W] (A) The window exhibit.
[영M] (B) Thanks. I bought them last summer.
(C) Yes, it's worth looking.

다른 가게에 그 안경이 더 낮은 가격으로 나와 있는지 봅시다.
(A) 창문 진열대요.
(B) 고맙습니다. 지난여름에 샀어요.
(C) 네, 살펴볼 가치가 있어요.
exhibit 전시   worth ~할 가치가 있는

15
15 Who can I speak to about selling my stocks and shares?
[영M] (A) Yes, marketing is on the second floor.
[미M] (B) Mr. Ypres can guide you.
(C) You can email it now.

제 주식과 지분을 매도하는 것에 대해 누구와 이야기할 수 있나요?
(A) 네, 마케팅 부서는 2층에 있습니다.
(B) 이프레스 씨가 안내해 줄 수 있습니다.
(C) 당신은 지금 이메일로 보낼 수 있습니다.
stocks and shares 주식과 지분   guide 안내하다

16
16 Which design did the research group prefer?
[미M] (A) I thought that, as well.
[미W] (B) The one A-One Design created.
(C) Four males and six females.

연구 그룹은 어느 디자인을 선호했나요?
(A) 저도 그렇게 생각했어요.
(B) 에이-원 디자인이 만든 것이요.
(C) 4명의 남성과 6명의 여성이요.
research group 연구 그룹   male 남성   female 여성

17
17 Have you finished the clients' details?
[영M] (A) No, I just rented it.
[미W] (B) I saw it on the morning bulletin.
(C) Not quite, but they'll be completed soon.

고객의 세부 정보를 완성했나요?
(A) 아니요, 그것을 방금 빌렸어요.
(B) 아침 뉴스에서 보았습니다.
(C) 다 하지는 못했지만, 곧 끝날 것입니다.
client 고객   morning bulletin 아침 뉴스   not quite 완전히 ~하지는 않은

18
18 Here, you left your wallet in the café.
[미W] (A) Thanks for returning it.
(B) It's at one o'clock.
(C) Please call Sammi.

여기요, 당신은 카페에 지갑을 놓고 갔어요.
(A) 돌려주셔서 감사합니다.
(B) 한 시 정각에 있습니다.
(C) 새미에게 전화해 주세요.
leave 남기다   wallet 지갑

19
19 Wasn't that documentary program fascinating?
[미W] (A) Directly to your television.
(B) I haven't watched it yet.
[영M] (C) On the second page.

그 다큐멘터리 프로그램이 대단히 흥미롭지 않나요?
(A) 당신의 텔레비전에 직접이요.
(B) 아직 보지 못했습니다.
(C) 두 번째 페이지이요.
documentary 다큐멘터리, 기록물   fascinating 매우 흥미로운

20
20 How was the play you saw at the NY Theater?
[미W] (A) I tried the new recipe.
(B) We've really enjoyed it.
[미M] (C) By the end of today.

NY 극장에서 본 연극은 어땠나요?
(A) 새로운 조리법을 시도해 봤어요.
(B) 정말 재미있었어요.
(C) 오늘까지요.

21
21 Why does Mr. Planter look tanned today?
[영M] (A) We tried on many occasions.
[미W] (B) Because it's in the morning.
(C) He just came back from vacation.

플랜터 씨는 오늘 왜 햇볕에 탄 것처럼 보이나요?
(A) 우리는 다양한 상황을 시도해 보았습니다.
(B) 아침이라서요.
(C) 그는 이제 막 휴가에서 돌아왔거든요.
tan 햇볕에 타우다, 햇볕에 타다   occasion 상황 (~을 하기에) 적절한 때

22
22 What should we buy for a wedding gift?
[미W] (A) Around 8 PM.
(B) Why don't you ask Katy?
[영M] (C) The food is excellent here.

우리는 결혼 선물로 무엇을 살까요?
(A) 오후 8시 경에요.
(B) 케이티에게 물어보는 건 어때요?
(C) 이곳의 음식은 훌륭해요.
wedding gift 결혼 선물

23
23 We could place the item in the local shop window.
[미W] (A) And advertise it on a Web site, too.
[미W] (B) Several different offers as well.
(C) She's advertised there every year.

우리는 그 물건을 지역 매장의 창가에 진열할 수 있습니다.
(A) 그리고 웹 사이트에 광고를 해도 되죠.
(B) 다른 여러 제안들도요.
(C) 그녀는 그곳에서 매년 광고를 했습니다.
place 배치하다, 놓다

24
24 Who's going to pick up Ms. Lejeune from the bus station?
[미W] (A) A domestic journey.
[미M] (B) From the 6th to the 12th.
(C) I nominated Pierre to do it.

누가 그 중 씨를 버스 정류장에서 데리러 올 건가요?
(A) 국내 여행이요.
(B) 6일에서 12일까지요.
(C) 제가 피에르에게 하라고 지명했습니다.
pick up 데리러 가다   domestic journey 국내 여행   nominate 지명하다

Part 3

25 Do you think Mark will rent a larger van or transport everything in his car?
영M (A) Hiring a removal van would be easier.
(B) It's quite a few miles away.
(C) Were you pleased with them?

마크가 더 큰 승합차를 빌릴 것 같나요, 아니면 그의 차로 모든 것을 운송할 것 같나요?
(A) 이삿짐 트럭을 빌리는 것이 더 쉬울 것 같아요.
(B) 상당히 멀리 떨어져 있어요.
(C) 당신은 그것들에 만족했나요?

van 승합차 removal van 이삿짐 트럭 be pleased with ~에 만족하다

26 The last assembly of the convention starts at 5.
미W (A) I might not be on time.
영M (B) Dr. Karacki will.
미M (C) Could you pass me one, please?

컨벤션의 마지막 집회는 5시에 시작합니다.
(A) 저는 제시간에 못 갈 수도 있어요.
(B) 카락키 박사님이 할 거예요.
(C) 하나 건네주시겠어요?

assembly 의회, 집회 convention 컨벤션, 협의회 be on time 제시간에 오다

27 Would you like me to sort out the basement later?
영M (A) Karen Lasorda said she'd do it.
미M (B) It lasts twenty minutes.
미M (C) He usually cycles to work.

제가 나중에 지하실을 정리하길 원하세요?
(A) 카렌 라소다가 자기가 하겠다고 했다고 했습니다.
(B) 20분간 유지됩니다.
(C) 그는 보통 자전거로 출근합니다.

sort out 정리하다 basement 지하실 last 지속하다, 지속되다

28 There's a discount on everything at Klein's Hardware Store all week.
영M (A) I applied two days ago.
(B) But I shipped it yesterday.
(C) I read about it in the newspaper.

클라인의 철물점에서 모든 물품이 일주일 내내 할인됩니다.
(A) 이틀 전에 지원했어요.
(B) 하지만 제가 어제 발송했어요.
(C) 신문에서 읽었어요.

hardware store 철물점 all week 일주일 내내

29 Would you rather eat Cantonese or Italian?
미W (A) I like this option.
미M (B) You should sign up for this course.
(C) Which one would you choose?

광둥식 요리를 먹겠어요, 이탈리아 음식을 먹겠어요?
(A) 저는 이 선택권이 좋아요.
(B) 이 과정에 등록하셔야 해요.
(C) 당신이라면 무엇을 선택하겠어요?

Cantonese 광둥어; 광둥어 사용자(본화권)의 option 선택권, 옵션

30 Please look over this company handbook before the training starts.
영M (A) Yes, but there are not enough questionnaires.
미W (B) At the resource center.
(C) I'll make sure I do that.

훈련이 시작되기 전에 이 회사의 편람을 살펴봐 주세요.
(A) 네, 하지만 질문자가 충분하지 않아요.
(B) 자원 센터에서요.
(C) 확실히 그렇게 하도록 하겠습니다.

look over 살펴보다 handbook 편람, 안내서 resource 자원, 재원
make sure 확실하게 하다

31 You don't mind if I switch the lights on, do you?
미M (A) Change direction at the corner.
영M (B) Not in the least.
(C) In fair condition.

불을 스위치를 켜도 상관없죠, 그렇죠?
(A) 모퉁이에서 방향을 바꾸세요.
(B) 전혀 그렇지 않아요.
(C) 양호한 상태입니다.

mind 신경 쓰다 direction 방향 not in the least 적어도, 조금도
fair condition 비교적 괜찮은 상태, 양호한 상태

Questions 32-34 refer to the following conversation. 미M 미W

M Hello, this is Mr. Allison, in room 3219. ㉜ My heating system isn't working too well. The radiators turn on, but the air coming out of it isn't warm.

W I'm sorry about that, sir. Unfortunately, all our heating engineers are unavailable at present. I can offer you an alternative room. In fact, ㉝ I'll upgrade you to a family room at the same cost as your single room.

M That would be ideal. ㉞ But could you send a porter to bring my cases to the new room straight away? I don't have time to do it. A taxi is picking me up in fifteen minutes to take me to a concert.

남 안녕하세요. 저는 3219호에 있는 앨리슨입니다. 난방 시스템이 제대로 작동하지 않아요. 난방 기구들은 켜지는데, 나오는 바람이 따뜻하지 않습니다.

여 그것에 대해 사과드립니다. 안타깝게도, 저희 모든 난방 기구 기사들이 현재 시간이 안 됩니다. 제가 이용하실 대체 객실을 제공해 드릴 수 있습니다. 고객님의 1인용 객실 비용으로 가족용 객실로 업그레이드 해드리겠습니다.

남 그게 좋겠어요. 하지만 새 객실로 제 짐들을 가지고 갈 짐꾼을 당장 불러 주시겠어요? 제가 그럴 시간이 없어요. 저를 콘서트로 데려다 줄 택시가 15분 후에 올 거라서요.

heating system 난방 시스템 work 작동하다 radiator 난방 기구
unfortunately 안타깝게도, 불행하게도 engineer 기사 unavailable 시간이
가능하지 않은; 이용 가능하지 않은 at present 현재 alternative 대체
의, 대안의 upgrade (비행기 좌석·호텔 객실 등급 상하 등급으로 높여 주
다 single room 1인실 porter 집꾼; 수위 straight away 당장 즉시
pick up 데리러 가다 complimentary 무료의 accommodation 숙소
partial 부분적인 assistance 도움, 지원

32 What is the man's complaint?
(A) His heating system does not work.
(B) His booking was cancelled.
(C) His taxi was late.
(D) His luggage is missing.

남자의 문제는?
(A) 난방 시스템이 작동하지 않는다.
(B) 예약이 취소되었다.
(C) 택시가 늦었다.
(D) 짐이 분실되었다.

33 What does the woman offer the man?
(A) A free lift to the concert
(B) A complimentary meal
(C) An upgraded accommodation
(D) Early check-in options

여자가 남자에게 제의하는 것은?
(A) 콘서트까지 무료 승차
(B) 무료 식사
(C) 숙소 업그레이드
(D) 조기 체크인 옵션

34 What does the man request?
(A) An apology
(B) A partial refund
(C) Free taxi rides
(D) Assistance with his bags

남자가 요청하는 것은?
(A) 사과
(B) 일부 환불
(C) 무료 택시 승차
(D) 그의 가방 운반의 도움

Questions 35-37 refer to the following conversation. 미W 미M

W ㉟ I'm trying to get a doctor's appointment. I've only recently moved into the area.

M OK, I can assist you with that. ㊱ I just have to see your health card with your new address. A doctor or nurse will be able to see you once you have registered here at the St. Johns Surgery.

W Oh, I don't remember where I put that document. I suppose I had better go and look for it.

M Well, just remember that you can't register without it. Meanwhile, ㊲ here's a list of our regular doctors.

---

doctor's appointment 병원 진료 예약 health card 의료보험증 surgery 병원; 수술 meanwhile 그동안에; 한편 regular 정규의 undergo surgery 수술을 받다 contribution 기부 disclaimer 권리 포기 각서

35 What does the woman want to do?
(A) Volunteer at a gallery
(B) Register for health care
(C) Get some legal advice
(D) Undergo surgery

여자는 무엇을 하길 바라는가?
(A) 갤러리에 자원봉사하기
(B) 의료 서비스 등록하기
(C) 법적 자문 구하기
(D) 수술하기

36 What does the man say the woman has to do?
(A) Provide her date of birth
(B) Make a contribution
(C) Attend a medical test
(D) Present her health card

남자는 여자에게 무엇을 해야 한다고 요청하는가?
(A) 그녀의 생년월일 제공하기
(B) 기부하기
(C) 건강 검진 참석하기
(D) 그녀의 의료보험증 제시하기

37 What does the man give the woman?
(A) A list of staff
(B) A policy document
(C) A disclaimer
(D) A replacement card

남자는 여자에게 무엇을 주는가?
(A) 직원들의 목록
(B) 규정 문서

여 병원 진료를 예약하려 합니다. 저는 최근에 막 이 지역으로 이사 왔어요.

남 알겠어요. 제가 도와 드리겠습니다. 당신의 새로운 주소가 있는 의료보험증만 보면 됩니다. 당신이 성 존스 병원에 등록되면 바로 의사나 간호사를 만나실 수 있습니다.

여 오, 제가 그 증서를 어디에 두었는지 기억을 못하네요. 다시 돌아가서 찾아봐야 할 것 같아요.

남 음, 그것 없이는 등록을 할 수 없다는 걸 기억해 두세요. 그동안에, 이곳의 정규 의료진들 목록이 여기 있습니다.

Questions 38-40 refer to the following conversation. 영M 미W

M Carol, were you able to check the computers in the Marketing Department?

W Yeah, I just got back from there. They all still have the outdated version of the data management software.

M Okay. ㊳ In that case, we need to make time on Thursday to install the new version. Can you do that?

W I'm sorry. I'm going to be at our branch office on Parker Avenue for training that day. ㊴ Can you ask Mike if he can do the work?

M Right. I forgot about that. ㊴ Can you ask Mike if he can do the work?

W Sure, I can ask him. I'm heading back to the office right now. The marketing manager asked me when they will be getting new computer keyboards.

M ㊵ I'd say that's not anytime soon. We don't have money in the budget right now. Maybe in the spring.

남 캐롤, 마케팅 부서에 있는 컴퓨터를 확인해 볼 수 있었나요?

여 네. 방금 확인하고 돌아왔어요. 컴퓨터의 데이터 관리 시스템 소프트웨어가 아직 다 오래된 버전이에요.

남 그렇군요. 그렇다면, 우리가 목요일에 시간을 좀 내서 새로운 버전을 설치해야겠어요. 가능하신가요?

여 죄송해요. 그날은 제가 파커 거리에 있는 지점에 교육 때문에 나가 있어야 해요.

여 맞네요. 제가 잊고 있었어요. 마이크가 그 작업을 할 수 있는지 물어봐 줄래요?

남 그럼요. 제가 물어볼게요. 제가 지금 사무실로 돌아가는 중이에요. 참 한 가지 더요. 마케팅 부서 매니저가 언제 그들이 새로운 컴퓨터 키보드를 받게 되는지 제게 물어봤어요.

여 금방 될 것이라고 생각하진 않아요. 현재 우리가 예산이 없거든요. 아마도 봄이나 되지 않을까 싶네요.

outdated 낡은, 오래된 구식의 management 경영, 관리, 경영진

38 What are the speakers discussing?
(A) Ordering supplies
(B) Installing software

(C) 권리 포기 각서
(D) 대체 카드

(C) Scheduling an event
(D) Buying devices

화자들은 무엇에 관해 논의를 하고 있는가?
(A) 비품을 주문하는 것
(B) 소프트웨어를 설치하는 것
(C) 행사 스케줄을 잡는 것
(D) 기기를 구매하는 것

39 What does the woman say she will do next?
(A) Meet with a superior
(B) Finish her work
(C) Speak with a coworker
(D) Check her schedule

여자는 다음에 무엇을 할 것이라고 이야기하는가?
(A) 상관을 만난다.
(B) 일을 마무리한다.
(C) 동료와 이야기한다.
(D) 스케줄을 확인한다.

40 What does the man mean when he says, "I'd say that's not anytime soon"?
(A) They are too busy to meet with the manager.
(B) They have other projects to focus on now.
(C) They are unable to purchase keyboards now.
(D) They have not received the keyboards yet.

남자가 '금방 될 것이라고 생각하지 않아요'라고 말했을 때 무엇을 의미했는가?
(A) 그들은 매니저를 만나기에는 너무 바쁘다.
(B) 그들은 현재 집중해야 하는 다른 프로젝트들이 있다.
(C) 그들은 현재 키보드를 구매할 수 없다.
(D) 그들은 아직 키보드를 받지 못했다.

---

two-story 2층 package 꾸러미 collect 수거하다, 가지고 가다 porter 짐꾼

41 Where is the conversation taking place?
(A) At a warehouse
(B) At a delivery office
(C) At a florist shop
(D) At a hospital

대화는 어디에서 일어나고 있는가?
(A) 창고
(B) 택배 사무소
(C) 꽃 가게
(D) 병원

42 According to the woman, why is the room number wrong?
(A) The room is occupied by a male.
(B) The patients are not allowed packages.
(C) The building only has a small number of rooms.
(D) The street name is incorrect.

여자에 따르면, 방의 번호가 잘못된 이유는?
(A) 그 방은 남자가 쓰고 있다.
(B) 환자들은 택배를 받을 수 없다.
(C) 건물은 객실이 적다.

(D) 거리의 이름이 틀렸다.

43 What does the woman say she will do next?
(A) Arrange for a delivery
(B) Order some food
(C) Call for a porter
(D) Contact Ms. Callard

여자는 다음에 무엇을 하겠다고 말하는가?
(A) 배달 준비하기
(B) 음식 주문하기
(C) 짐꾼 부르기
(D) 칼라드 씨에게 연락하기

Questions 44-46 refer to the following conversation. 미W 미M

W Hi, Kenny. This is Sharon. How are things going this morning?

M Everything's good. I came in early so I could get ahead start on the report.

W Great. Actually that's the reason I am calling. Yesterday, I reviewed the first chapters you wrote. The writing is exactly what we have wanted. ㊹ However, I was wondering if you could make some revisions to the graphs.

M Sure. What about them?

W ㊺ Well, the client asked for full-color graphs, but you made them in black and white. Do you think you could change them to the client's requests?

M That's not an issue. I just need a couple of hours.

W That's fine. We are still ahead of schedule.

여 안녕하세요, 케니. 저는 샤론입니다. 오전 상황이 어떤가요?

남 모든 것이 좋아요. 제가 일찍 도착해서 업무 보고서 작업을 사전작업 할 수 있었습니다.

여 좋네요. 사실 그것 때문에 제가 전화드리는 거예요. 어제, 제가 당신이 작성한 첫 번째 챕터를 검토했어요. 그 내용은 정확히 우리가 원하는 것이었어요. 그런데 그래프를 일부 수정해주면 좋겠다고 생각했어요.

남 그럼요. 어떤 부분이에요?

여 음, 고객이 완전히 컬러로 구성된 그래프를 원했는데, 당신은 흑백으로 작성했어요. 고객의 요청대로 변경해줄 수 있나요?

남 문제 없죠. 두 시간 정도면 될 것 같습니다.

여 좋아요. 아직 지하가 시간이 좀 있어요.

---

revision 수정, 변경, 검토 black and white 흑백 go over 검토하다

Questions 41-43 refer to the following conversation. 영M 미W

M Hello, I have a food basket ㊶ here for a patient in room 312.

W That can't be the right room. ㊷ We are a two-story building with only 20 rooms. What's the name on the delivery?

M The package is for Anita Callard. Someone ordered it last week and wanted it delivered today.

W Oh! Ms. Callard is in room 12. If you leave the basket over there, ㊸ I'll get her to come and collect it.

남 안녕하세요, 312호 환자 분께 온 음식 선물 바구니가 있습니다.

여 그 방일 리가 없어요. 우리 건물은 오직 20개의 방이 있는 2층 건물입니다. 누구 이름으로 온 배달인가요?

남 택배는 아니타 칼라드에게 온 것입니다. 누군가가 지난주에 주문해서 오늘 배달되길 원한 거고요.

여 아! 칼라드 씨는 12호실에 있습니다. 바구니를 저쪽에 두시면, 그녀가 와서 가져가도록 할게요.

44 Why is the woman calling?
(A) To report to a customer
(B) To propose a project
(C) To request some changes
(D) To ask for information

여자는 왜 전화하고 있는가?
(A) 고객에게 보고하기 위해
(B) 프로젝트를 제안하기 위해
(C) 변경 사항들을 요청하기 위해
(D) 정보를 요청하기 위해

45 What does the woman ask the man to do?
(A) Go over her work
(B) Add color to visual aids
(C) Contact a client
(D) Remove some colors on the graphs

여자는 남자가 무엇을 하기를 원하는가?
(A) 여자의 작업을 검토해 주기
(B) 시각 자료에 색 입히기
(C) 고객에게 연락하기
(D) 그래프에서 몇 가지 색 제거하기

46 Why does the man say, "That's not an issue"?
(A) He currently has been assigned a lot of projects.
(B) He is worried about a deadline being affected.
(C) He is almost finished writing a report.
(D) He has no problem meeting the woman's request.

남자는 왜 "문제없죠"라고 말하는가?
(A) 남자가 최근에 많은 프로젝트를 배정받았다.
(B) 남자는 마감 기한에 영향이 있을 것을 걱정한다.
(C) 남자는 보고서 작성을 거의 끝냈다.
(D) 남자는 여자의 요청을 수행하는 데 있어 문제가 없다.

47 What does the woman ask the man to do?
(A) Bring an item from stock
(B) Contact some students
(C) Turn out the lights
(D) Rearrange a cupboard

여자는 남자에게 무엇을 해 달라고 요청하는가?
(A) 재고에서 물건 가져다주기
(B) 몇몇 학생들에게 연락하기
(C) 불 끄기
(D) 찬장 다시 정돈하기

48 Why is the man unable to help?
(A) A delivery has been delayed.
(B) Some equipment has been damaged.
(C) A student requires his assistance.
(D) A lab has been closed down.

남자가 도와줄 수 없는 이유는?
(A) 배달이 지연되었다.
(B) 일부 장비가 손상되었다.
(C) 한 학생이 그의 도움을 필요로 한다.
(D) 실험실이 문을 닫았다.

49 What will happen at 12:00?
(A) A replacement tutor will be sent.
(B) The man will buy some light bulbs.
(C) The woman's students will arrive.
(D) Different equipment will be used.

12시에 무슨 일이 일어날 것인가?
(A) 대체 교사가 보내질 것이다.
(B) 남자가 몇몇 전구를 살 것이다.
(C) 여자의 학생들이 도착할 것이다.
(D) 다른 장비가 사용될 것이다.

Questions 47-49 refer to the following conversation. 〔미W〕〔미M〕

W Hi, Jason. It's Margot. The light on the optic laser in the laboratory has broken. ❹ Could you get me a new one from the stock cupboard?

M Unfortunately, I can't do that at the moment. We've run out. I ordered some more bulbs two days ago but ❹ the delivery hasn't arrived yet. The wholesalers promised me that the shipment with a new batch of specialist lights will arrive within an hour.

W Well, I sincerely hope that's the case and the delivery comes soon. ❹ My students are arriving at midday to practice on the equipment.

여 안녕하세요, 제이슨. 마고예요. 연구실 음식 레이저의 전구가 고장 났어요. 재고 찬장에서 새것을 하나 가져다 줄 수 있어요?

남 안됐지만, 저는 지금 그걸 해 줄 수가 없어요. 다 떨어졌거든요. 이틀 전에 제가 전구를 더 주문했는데, 아직 배달이 도착하지 않았어요. 도매업자들이 새 특별 전등 묶음이 한 시간 이내에 도착할 거라고 약속했어요.

여 음, 저는 정말 상황이 이러하니 배송이 빨리 왔으면 해요. 제 학생들이 그 장비로 실습하기 위해 정오에 도착할 거거든요.

optic laser 광 레이저 run out (공급품이) 다 떨어지다 bulb 전구 wholesaler 도매업자 shipment 수송품, 배송 batch 집단, 무리 specialist 전문의 sincerely 진심으로 case 상황

Questions 50-52 refer to the following conversation. 〔미M〕〔미W〕

M Hi, Lisa. Do you have a minute to talk about the Carstairs Inc. account? ❺ They want to initiate a marketing campaign for one of their plumbing products, Linked Rollers. It appears that it hasn't been selling much, but they believe it will be well accepted once it is publicized.

W Have they thought of relevant advertising? ❺ Maybe they could put out an advertisement in trade magazines to boost its familiarity with customers.

M ❺ They actually trialed that two months ago and didn't have much response. They are looking for something totally different this time.

남 안녕하세요, 리사. 카스테어스 사에 관해 잠시 이야기 나눌 수 있을까요? 그들은 그들의 배관류 제품 중 하나인 링크드 롤러스를 위한 마케팅 캠페인을 개시하고 싶어 합니다. 많이 팔리고 있는 것처럼 보이지는 않지만, 일단 홍보가 되면 잘 팔릴 것으로 입습니다.

여 그들이 관련 광고를 생각해 보셨을까요? 어쩌면 그들은 고객들에게 더 많이 알려지기 위해 잡지에 업계 광고를 내 볼 수도 있어요.

남 실제로 그들은 그것을 두 달 전에 시험해 보았으나, 큰 반응이 없었습니다. 이번에는 완전히 다른 것을 찾고 있어요.

Do you have a minute ~? 잠시 시간 좀 내 주실 수 있나요? account 계정, 단골, 고객 initiate 시작하다 plumbing 배관 배관 작업 publicize 홍보하다 relevant 관련 있는 작정된 put out an advertisement 광고를

내다 trade 특정 업계 영업 boost 신장시키다, 북돋우다 familiarity 친숙함, 낯익음 trial (능력 등의) 시험하다 warehouse 창고

50 What does Carstairs Inc. want to advertise?
(A) A job opportunity
(B) A product
(C) An event
(D) A warehouse

카스테어스 사는 무엇을 광고하고 싶어 하는가?
(A) 채용 기회
(B) 제품
(C) 행사
(D) 창고

51 What does the woman suggest?
(A) Offering online discounts
(B) Hiring a marketing expert
(C) Advertising in specialist media
(D) Advertising on the radio

여자는 무엇을 제안하는가?
(A) 온라인 할인 제공
(B) 마케팅 전문가 고용
(C) 전문 미디어 광고
(D) 라디오 광고

52 What does the man say about the woman's suggestion?
(A) It was unsuccessful in the past.
(B) It will take too long.
(C) It was not possible for the company.
(D) It was too expensive to run.

남자는 여자의 제안에 대해 무엇이라고 말하는가?
(A) 과거에 성공을 거두지 못했다.
(B) 너무 오랜 시간이 걸릴 것이다.
(C) 회사에서는 불가능한 일이었다.
(D) 운영하기에 너무 비쌌다.

Questions 53-55 refer to the following conversation. 미W 영M

W Hi, I bought a long sleeved dress from your online store last week, only when I went to fasten it up, **53** the zipper broke.

M Oh, it's not difficult to return faulty items. **54** I'll send you a returns form. What you must do is fill in the form with your reference number, and enclose it in the original packaging. If you do that, there won't be a fee to mail it back to us. Would you like us to send a replacement dress or do you want to choose a different one from the site?

W **55** I'd like to get my money back if that's possible. I had to have a new dress for a wedding yesterday, so I ended up borrowing one from a friend.

여 안녕하세요, 지난주에 당신의 온라인 상점에서 긴 소매 드레스를 샀는데, 지퍼를 올려려 할 때 그게 그저 고장이 나서요.

남 오, 결함이 있는 상품을 반품하는 것은 어렵지 않습니다. 당신에게 반품 양식을 보내 드리겠습니다. 당신이 해야 하는 일은 양식에 조회 번호를 기입한 뒤, 원래의 포장에 동봉하는 것입니다. 그렇게 하면, 저희에게 보내는 데 요금은 들지 않으실 것입니다. 저희가 대체 상품을 보내 드리길 원하신요, 아니면 현장에서 다른 상품으로 고르실 건가요?

여 가능하다면 제 돈을 돌려받고 싶습니다. 어제 결혼식에 갈 옷이 필요해서, 결국 친구에게 옷을 빌려왔거든요.

long sleeved 긴 소매의   fasten up 묶다(잠그다)   faulty 결함이 있는, 고장 난   fill in 기입하다, 채워 넣다   reference number 참조 번호   enclose 동봉하다   packaging 포장   mail 우편으로 보내다   replacement 대체물   end up 결국 ~이 되다

53 According to the woman, what is the problem with the dress?
(A) The dress didn't fit.
(B) The fastener was faulty.
(C) The size is too small.
(D) The price is too high.

여자에 따르면, 드레스에는 어떤 문제가 있는가?
(A) 드레스가 맞지 않았다.
(B) 잠금 장치에 결함이 있다.
(C) 사이즈가 너무 작다.
(D) 가격이 너무 비싸다.

54 What will the man send to the woman?
(A) A document
(B) A new dress
(C) A discount voucher
(D) A full refund

남자는 여자에게 무엇을 보낼 것인가?
(A) 서류
(B) 새 드레스
(C) 할인 쿠폰
(D) 전액 환불

55 What does the woman say she would prefer?
(A) To change the color of the dress
(B) To choose a different item
(C) To receive a refund
(D) To wait for a replacement

여자는 자신이 어느 쪽으로 하겠다고 하는가?
(A) 드레스의 색을 바꾸는 것
(B) 다른 물건을 고르는 것
(C) 환불받는 것
(D) 대체 상품을 기다리는 것

Questions 56-58 refer to the following conversation. 미W 미M

W Mr. Hawkins, I've just been looking at our employee criminal record check certificate, and I realized that ⓺ some of our workers' certificates are out of date.

M Really? But I thought we had notification two months ago so that all of our workers will have regular checks. Aren't the certificates valid for six months?

W They are, but that legislation is just for new employees. We need another check for those workers who have been here for more than a year. ⓹ They just need to update their current details to get recertified.

M Okay, ⓽ could you give me a list of workers who need to be recertified? Then we can send off their details.

여 호킨스 씨, 직원들의 전과 기록 확인 증명서를 보고 있었는데, 몇몇 직원들의 증명서가 유효 기간이 만료된 것을 알아챘습니다.

남 정말요? 하지만 저는 모든 직원들이 정기 검사를 받도록 두 달 전에 직원들에게 통보를 보냈어요. 증명서는 6개월 동안 유효한 것 아닌가요?

여 맞아요, 하지만 그 법은 신규 직원들에게만 해당돼요. 우리는 이곳에 온 지 1년 이상 되는 직원들을 위한 다른 검사가 필요합니다. 그들은 재증명 받기 위해, 그들의 현재의 새로 정보를 갱신하기만 하면 됩니다.

남 알겠습니다. 재증명되어야 하는 직원들의 명단을 주실 수 있나요? 그러면 그들의 정보를 보내줄 수 있습니다.

criminal record 전과 기록 certificate 증명서; 자격증 out of date 유효 기간이 지난 notification 통보, 통지 regular checks 정기 검사 valid 유효하다 legislation 제정법 recertify 재증명하다 send off 발송하다 collect 모으다, 수집하다 resubmit 다시 제출하다 tuition 수업료 archive 기록 보관소에 보관하다

56 What problem has the woman identified?
(A) A training session has not been finished.
(B) Some documents are out of date.
(C) Some registration forms have not been collected.
(D) Some employees have given false information.

여자는 무슨 문제점을 발견했는가?
(A) 교육이 끝나지 않았다.
(B) 일부 서류가 유효 기간이 지났다.
(C) 일부 신청서가 수거되지 않았다.
(D) 일부 직원들이 거짓 정보를 제공했다.

57 What does the woman say about workers who were certified more than a year ago?
(A) They need to resubmit their details.
(B) They need to undergo a written test.
(C) They have to pay for extra tuition.
(D) They must contact their supervisors.

여자는 증명 받은 지 1년 이상이 직원들에 대해 무엇을 말하는가?
(A) 그들의 세부 정보를 다시 제출해야 한다.
(B) 필기시험을 가져야 한다.
(C) 추가 수업료를 지불해야 한다.
(D) 그들의 상사에게 연락해야 한다.

58 What does the man ask the woman to do?
(A) Archive some documents
(B) Send some warnings
(C) Organize a workshop
(D) Provide names of workers

남자는 여자에게 무엇을 해 달라고 요청하는가?
(A) 기록 보관소에 서류 보관하기
(B) 경고 보내기
(C) 워크숍 준비하기
(D) 직원들의 이름 제공하기

Questions 59-61 refer to the following conversation with three speakers. 미W 미M 영M

M1 ⓾ So we got approved to open six new retail locations in the southern part of the United States.

W That's great news. So I guess that means we need to narrow down where exactly we want to open the new stores.

M2 Well, most of our sales growth has been coming from consumers in their 30s.

W It would make sense then to target cities with the largest populations of that consumer group.

M1 ⓺⓵ We don't just want spots that have lots of people in their 30s, but those who have decent salaries.

M2 ⓺⓵ So cities with lots of professionals.

M1 That's what I am talking about. Well, we have collected lots of market data. I can analyze them and put together a list for the best locations.

W ⓺⓵ While you do that, I'll talk with our architectural team about building designs.

남1 우리가 6개의 새로운 소매점들을 미국 남쪽 지역에 여는 것에 관한 승인을 받았어요.

여 잘 되었네요. 그럼 추측건대, 우리가 새로운 소매점들을 정확히 어디에 열어야 할지에 대해 추려내야 한다는 걸 의미하겠네요.

남2 음, 우리 판매의 대부분의 증가가 30대 고객들에게서 나오고 있어요.

여 그 고객층이 가장 많은 인구를 차지하는 도시들을 타깃으로 하는 것이 맞을 것 같네요.

남1 우리는 단지 30대가 많은 지역만을 원하는 것은 아니고, 꽤 괜찮은 연봉을 받고 있는 30대가 많은 지역을 원하는 것이죠.

남2 그럼, 전문 직종에 종사하는 30대가 많은 도시로 해야겠네요.

남1 그게 제가 이야기하는 바예요. 우리는 많은 시장 데이터를 모았어요. 제가 그것들을 분석해서 최고로 괜찮은 위치들을 모아 볼게요.

여 당신이 그 일을 하는 동안에, 저는 건축팀과 건물 디자인에 관해서 얘기를 해 볼게요.

retail 소매 decent 꽤 괜찮은 professional 전문가 put together 준비하다, 모으다

59 What are the speakers discussing?
(A) A growing population in certain areas
(B) An industry's hiring trend
(C) Business expansion
(D) A popular city for sales people

화자들은 무엇에 관한 논의를 하는가?
(A) 특정한 지역에 늘어나는 인구
(B) 업계의 고용 추세
(C) 사업 확장
(D) 영업자들에게 인기 있는 지역

60 What is implied about professionals in their 30s?
(A) They are willing to relocate for work.
(B) They want to live in cities.
(C) They are a new market.
(D) They are paid well.

30대의 전문 직종에 있는 사람들에 대해 암시된 것은?
(A) 그들은 일을 위해 기꺼이 이동한다.
(B) 그들은 도시에 살기를 원한다.
(C) 그들은 새로운 시장이다.
(D) 그들은 높은 급여를 받는다.

61 What does the woman offer to do?
(A) Collect market data
(B) Speak with building designers
(C) Put together a report
(D) Tour some buildings

여자는 무엇을 해 주겠다고 하는가?
(A) 시장 정보를 모은다.
(B) 건물 디자이너들과 이야기한다.
(C) 보고서를 준비한다.
(D) 건물을 투어한다.

Questions 62-64 refer to the following conversation.
영M 미W

M Hi, Bella. It's Ramon. I'm sorry to let you down at the last minute, but 62 I won't be able to perform in the play this evening. 63 I've got a domestic crisis and I don't want to leave my family.

W Oh, I'm sorry to hear that, Ramon. You're right to stay and sort it out though. Have you contacted your understudy to let him know he is to take your part?

M I just spoke to Miguel. He said he'd be delighted to do it. But he doesn't have a costume that will fit him.

W That's okay. I'll give him a call and ask him to come in early. 64 That would give us time to find a costume for him that fits.

남 안녕하세요, 벨라. 라몬입니다. 마지막에 당신을 실망시켜 죄송하지만, 저는 오늘 저녁 공연에서 연기를 할 수 없을 것 같습니다. 집에 위급한 상황이 생겨서 가족을 남겨둘 수가 없어요.

여 오, 그 소식을 듣게 되어 유감입니다 라몬. 그래도 당신이 남아서 해결하는 것이 맞습니다. 당신의 대역 배우가 당신의 배역을 대신해야 한다는 것을 알리기 위해 그에게 연락했나요?

남 방금 막 미구엘에게 이야기했습니다. 그는 기꺼이 하겠다고 말했습니다. 하지만 그는 그에게 맞는 복장이 없어요.

여 괜찮습니다. 그에게 전화해서 더 일찍 나오라고 요청할게요. 그러면 그에게 맞는 의상을 찾을 시간이 있을 거예요.

let someone down 누군가를 실망시키다   at the last minute 막판에, 마지막에   play 연기하다   domestic 가정의, 집 안의   crisis 위기   sort out 해결하다; 정리하다   understudy 대역 (배우)   part 배역   be delighted to ~을 하다   costume 복장, 의상   fit 맞다   lose one's voice 목소리가 안 나오다   reliable 믿을 수 있는

62 Where do the speakers work?
(A) At a fitness club
(B) At a doctor's surgery
(C) At a theater
(D) At a police station

화자들은 어디에서 일하는가?
(A) 헬스클럽
(B) 병원
(C) 극장
(D) 경찰서

---

63 Why will the man miss work today?
(A) He is not feeling well.
(B) He has lost his voice.
(C) He does not have a car.
(D) He has a crisis at home.

남자가 왜 오늘 일하러 나오지 못할 것인가?
(A) 몸 상태가 좋지 않다.
(B) 목소리가 나오지 않는다.
(C) 차가 없다.
(D) 집에 위급 상황이 생겼다.

64 What do the speakers say about Miguel?
(A) He needs to be fitted for a costume.
(B) He is always reliable.
(C) He needs some additional training.
(D) He is not happy about the role.

화자들은 미구엘에 관해 뭐라고 하는가?
(A) 의상의 치수를 맞춰야 한다.
(B) 항상 믿을 만하다.
(C) 추가 훈련이 필요하다.
(D) 그의 배역에 만족하지 않는다.

Questions 65-67 refer to the following conversation and schedule.

[미W] [미M]

Room	Day of reservation
4A	Monday
7B	Tuesday
4C	Wednesday
㉖ 2D	Thursday

W The orientation for new hires is next week. How are things coming along?

M I have almost everything done that I had planned. ㉕ I dropped off the information packets at the printer this morning. They should be ready by tomorrow. I'm almost finished preparing my part of the presentation.

W Me, too. I just need to add a few more graphs to my part. ㉗ Were you able to reserve the second floor conference room for next Thursday?

M Unfortunately, ㉖ it's already booked.

W Really? That's not good. I like the video projector and screen in that room. They are easy to use.

M I was able to reserve a room on the third floor though. It's not as big as the one on the second floor, but it still has everything that we need.

W Then, it's going to be fine.

방	예약 날짜
4A	월요일
7B	화요일
4C	수요일
2D	목요일

여 신입 직원들을 위한 오리엔테이션이 다음 주입니다. 잘 진행되어 가고 있나요?

남 계획했던 것들은 거의 완료했습니다. 오늘 오전에 자료 묶음을 인쇄 업체에 맡겨 놓았습니다. 내일까지는 준비가 될 거예요. 저는 제가 진행하는 부분의 프리젠테이션 준비도 거의 마무리했어요.

여 저도요. 저는 단지 몇 개의 그래프만 제 발표 자료에 추가하면 됩니다. 2층 컨퍼런스 룸을 다음 주 목요일을 위해서 예약할 수 있었나요?

남 아쉽게도 벌써 예약이 되었더라고요.

여 그래요? 안됐네요. 그 컨퍼런스 룸 안에 있는 비디오 프로젝터와 스크린이 참 마음에 드는데 말이죠. 사용하기 편하거든요.

남 그래도 제가 3층에 있는 룸은 예약할 수 있었어요. 2층에 있는 룸 보다 크지는 않지만 우리가 원하는 모든 것이 맞추어져 있어요.

여 그럼, 괜찮을 것 같네요.

come along 진행되다 | packet 꾸러미, 소포 | malfunction 오작동하다 | put off 연기하다

65 What most likely will the man do tomorrow?
남자는 내일 무엇을 할 것 같은가?
(A) Pick up some materials
(A) 자료를 가지러간다.
(B) Meet a client
(B) 고객을 만난다.
(C) Test some devices
(C) 기기를 테스트한다.
(D) Finish a presentation
(D) 발표를 완료한다.

66 What problem does the man mention?
남자는 어떤 문제를 언급하는가?
(A) A screen is malfunctioning.
(A) 스크린이 오작동하고 있다.
(B) An event needs to be put off.
(B) 행사를 연기해야 한다.
(C) A room is not available.
(C) 방이 이용 불가하다.
(D) Some equipment is not working.
(D) 장비가 작동하지 않는다.

67 Look at the graphic. What room did the man reserve?
그래픽을 보시오. 남자는 어느 방을 예약했는가?
(A) Room 4A
(A) Room 4A
(B) Room 7B
(B) Room 7B
(C) Room 4C
(C) Room 4C
(D) Room 2D
(D) Room 2D

Questions 68-70 refer to the following conversation and map.

[영M] [미W]

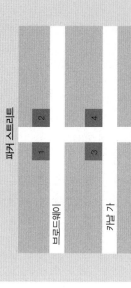

Parker Street

Broadway

Canal Avenue

M Excuse me. I was wondering if you could help me. ㉘ I'm trying to find where to catch a bus that goes to Shelton Hotel.

W You mean the one on Wellington Road?

M Yes, that's correct. My hotel is also on that road.

W The number 21 bus will take you to where you want to go. The nearest bus stop is right in front of the National Museum.

M I'm not familiar with this area of the city. Is it close by?

W Well, I'm afraid you're going to have to do some walking. ㉙ The museum is on the corner of Broadway and Parker Street. You are on Canal Avenue now. Walk down this street about 100 meters. Then, turn left on Parker Street. Walk along the street about 50 meters. Then you will find it on your right at the intersection.

M I hope I can remember all of that.

W ㉚ How about if I write it down for you?

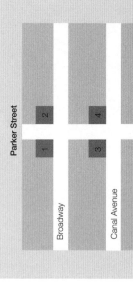

파커 스트리트

브로드웨이

캐널 가

Part 4

본책 P109

Questions 71-73 refer to the following announcement. [미M]

Ladies and gentlemen, this is your tour guide. If you take a look to your right, facing southeast, you should be able to spot Blackstone Castle. This Castle is the oldest structure in the country and has become a shrine for the more superstitious in the local community who believe it is haunted. 72 Oh look, we can clearly see the eagles at their nest on top of the tower. This is a treat as most of the time, the eagles' nest is hidden away. 71 I have been a bus tour guide for many years and I've only seen the birds nesting a couple of times. If you have access to a camera, 73 I recommend you take a picture as a keepsake.

신사 숙녀 여러분, 저는 투어 가이드입니다. 오른쪽으로 방향을 틀어서 남동쪽을 보시면, 여러분께서는 블랙스톤 성을 발견하실 수 있습니다. 이 성은 국내에서 가장 오래된 건축물이고, 귀신이 나온다고 믿는 지역 주민들에게 더 미신적인 성지가 되었습니다. 오 보세요, 우리는 타워 꼭대기의 둥지에서 독수리를 확실히 볼 수 있습니다. 주로 독수리의 둥지는 숨겨져 있기 때문에 이것은 특별한 즐거움입니다. 저는 수년간 버스 관광 안내원이었지만, 그 새들의 둥지를 트는 모습을 두 번밖에 보지 못했습니다. 카메라에 접근이 가능하시다면, 기념이 되도록 사진을 찍으실 것을 추천합니다.

tour guide 관광 안내원　take a look (한번) 보다　face ~을 향하다　spot 발견하다　structure 구조물　shrine 성지　superstitious 미신적인　local community 지역 사회　haunted 귀신이 나오는　clearly 명백히　treat 특별한 즐거움　hide away 숨기다　have access to ~의 접근이 가능하다　keepsake 기념품　ruined 폐허가 된

71 Where does the announcement most likely take place?
(A) On a train
(B) On a boat
(C) On a plane
(D) On a bus

발표는 어디에서 일어나고 있겠는가?
(A) 기차
(B) 보트
(C) 비행기
(D) 버스

72 What does the speaker point out as unusual?
(A) An animal at the castle
(B) A ruined tower structure
(C) A treat for the local community
(D) An unusual weather pattern

화자가 특이한 것으로 가리키는 것은?
(A) 성에 있는 한 종류의 동물
(B) 파괴된 탑 구조물
(C) 지역 주민을 위한 선물
(D) 특이한 날씨 패턴

73 What does the speaker recommend the listeners do?
(A) Book a meal
(B) Watch the birds
(C) Listen to music
(D) Take pictures

화자는 청자들에게 무엇을 추천하는가?
(A) 식사 예약하기
(B) 새 구경하기
(C) 음악 감상하기
(D) 사진 찍기

남 실례합니다. 혹시 저 좀 도와주실 수 있으요? 쉘튼 호텔로 가는 버스를 어디서 탈 수 있을까요?
여 웰링턴 가에 있는 거 말씀하시는 건가요?
남 네, 맞습니다. 제 호텔 포함 그곳에 있어요.
남 21번 버스가 원하시는 곳까지 갑니다. 가장 가까운 정류장이 국립 박물관 바로 앞에 있어요.
남 제가 이 도시에 익숙하지 않아서요, 가까운가요?
여 음, 좀 걸으셔야 할 거예요. 박물관은 브로드웨이와 파커 스트리트의 코너에 위치해 있어요. 지금 당신은 카날 거에 있어요. 이 거리를 따라서 100미터 정도 쭉 걸어 가세요. 그리고 파커 스트리트에서 왼쪽 방향으로 도세요. 길을 따라 500미터 정도 걸어 가세요. 그러면 교차로에서 당신의 오른쪽에 보일 거예요.
여 제가 기억할 수 있으려나 모르겠네요.
남 제가 적어 드릴게요.

familiar 익숙한　intersection 교차로

68 What does the man want to do?
(A) Visit an exhibit
(B) Book a room
(C) Park his car
(D) Take a bus

남자는 무엇을 하고자 하는가?
(A) 전시관 방문
(B) 방 예약
(C) 자동차 주차
(D) 버스 타기

69 Look at the graphic. Where is the national museum?
(A) 1
(B) 2
(C) 3
(D) 4

그래픽을 보시오. 국립 박물관은 어디에 있는가?
(A) 1
(B) 2
(C) 3
(D) 4

70 What does the woman offer to do?
(A) Write down directions
(B) Walk the man to his destination
(C) Give the man a map
(D) Call a taxi

여자는 무엇을 해 주겠다고 하는가?
(A) 가는 길을 적어 준다.
(B) 남자를 목적지까지 데려다준다.
(C) 남자에게 지도를 준다.
(D) 택시를 부른다.

Questions 74-76 refer to the following excerpt from a meeting. 미W

Thank you all for attending this extraordinary general meeting. As you are aware, ⑦④ our winter range of women's coats, dresses and tunics hasn't been selling in stores as we had anticipated. We have surplus clothing in all store locations. So in an attempt to work out how to increase sales, we gave customers a questionnaire to survey what category of outfits or accessories they are most prone to purchase and under what circumstances. And ⑦⑤ I'm going to distribute some of the completed questionnaires now for you to have a look. For the remainder of the meeting, let's use this information to dream up ⑦⑥ new tactics to encourage our shoppers, especially women between the ages of 35 and 55.

모두 이 임시 총회에 참석해 주셔서 감사드립니다. 알고 계시는 바와 같이, 우리 겨울 상품 내 여성 코트, 드레스, 튜닉 드레스는 예상했던 만큼 매장에서 팔리고 있지 않습니다. 모든 지점마다 남은 의류 상품이 있습니다. 그래서 판매를 높이기 위한 방법을 알아내려는 시도로 어떤 카테고리 의류 또는 액세서리들을 구매하는 경향이 가장 높은지와 어떤 상황에서 구매하게 되는지를 조사하기 위해 손님들에게 설문지를 드렸습니다. 그리고 지는 여러분들이 살펴볼 수 있도록 완성된 설문지를 몇 장 나눠 줄 것입니다. 나머지 회의 시간에는 이들 정보를 이용해 우리 쇼핑객들, 특히 35세에서 55세까지의 여성을 지극할 새로운 전략을 생각해 내기 위해 이들 정보를 활용해 봅시다.

extraordinary (회의 등이) 임시의 general meeting 총회 range of ~의 범위 tunic 튜닉 anticipate 예상하다, 기대하다 surplus 잉여, 과잉의 in an attempt to ~하기 위해서 work out 계산하다, 산출하다 questionnaire 설문지 category 범주 outfit 의류 prone to ~을 잘 하는, ~의 경향이 있는 under the circumstance 그런 상황에 distribute 나눠 주다 have a look 관찰하다, 살펴보다 remainder 나머지 dream up 생각해내다 tactics 전략, 전술

74 What type of product is being discussed?
어떤 유형의 제품이 이야기되고 있는가?
(A) Electronic devices
(B) Clothing
(C) Athletic equipment
(D) Office supplies
(A) 전자 제품
(B) 의류
(C) 운동 장비
(D) 사무실 용품

75 What does the speaker say she will give the listeners?
화자가 그녀가 청자들에게 줄 것이라고 말하는 것은?
(A) A product sample
(B) Completed questionnaires
(C) Sales updates
(D) A revised budget
(A) 제품 견본
(B) 완성된 설문지
(C) 판매 업데이트
(D) 수정 예산

76 What are listeners asked to think about?
청자들은 무엇에 관해 생각할 것을 요청받는가?
(A) Ideas for cutting costs
(B) Strategies for attracting customers
(C) Locations for a new shopping center
(D) Names for new products
(A) 비용 삭감 아이디어
(B) 고객 유치 전략
(C) 새 쇼핑센터 위치
(D) 새 제품 이름

Questions 77-79 refer to the following telephone message. 영M

Hi, Moritz. This is Haman. I'm organizing a group of colleagues ⑦ to go ice-skating at Elmer Outdoor Park next weekend. The weather is forecast to be sunny. Would you care to join us? So far, 12 people have said they'd like to come along. If we can persuade a few more people, so ⑦⑧ we have twenty minimum, we qualify for a discount on boots and helmet hire. ⑦⑨ I want to make the booking first thing on Monday morning, so please get back to me and let me know if you're able to come.

안녕하세요, 모리츠, 하만입니다. 저는 다음 주말에 엘마 아웃 공원에서 아이스 스케이팅을 가려고 그룹을 짜고 있습니다. 날씨는 화창할 것으로 예보되었습니다. 저희와 동참하시겠습니까? 지금까지 12명의 사람들이 갈 것이고 싶다고 말했습니다. 만약 당신이 조금 더 사람들을 설득할 수 있다면, 그래서 인원이 최소 20명이 된다면, 우리는 부츠와 헬멧 대여를 할인 받을 자격이 됩니다. 월요일 오전에 맨 먼저 예약을 하고 싶으므로, 연락 주셔서 갈 수 있는지 알려 주세요.

colleague 동료 forecast 예측하다, 예보하다 Would you care to ~? ~하시겠어요? so far 이때까지 come along 함께 가다 persuade 설득하다 minimum 최소한으로 qualify for ~의 자격을 얻다 booking 예약 get back to ~에게 나중에 다시 연락하다 voucher 할인의 쿠폰

77 What is the speaker planning to do this weekend?
화자는 이번 주말에 무엇을 할 계획 중인가?
(A) Go on a sporting trip
(B) Purchase some ice skates
(C) Visit a sporting event
(D) Attend a convention
(A) 스포츠 여행 가기
(B) 아이스 스케이트 구매하기
(C) 스포츠 행사 방문하기
(D) 대회 참석하기

78 According to the speaker, what must people do to receive a discount?
화자에 의하면, 사람들이 할인을 받기 위해 무엇을 해야 하는가?
(A) Arrive by bus
(B) Show a membership card
(C) Present a discount voucher
(D) Make a group booking

Questions 83-85 refer to the following excerpt from a meeting.
［미M］

And last, I want to remind you that ⑧ the 10th anniversary of our organization is approaching. Temp Workers Limited started with just three employees and a handful of clients and ⑧ it's astonishing to see how big a business we've become since then. It's especially inspiring when you consider how much time it takes for the majority of new companies to become established. I am pleased to announce that our office coordinator, Mel Cushing, has agreed to organize the anniversary festivities but we'll require many more people to help out with the preparations. So ⑧ please send Mel an e-mail if you are able to help.

그리고 마지막으로, 우리 회사의 10주년 기념이 다가오고 있다는 사실을 상기시키고 싶습니다. 템프 워커스 주식회사는 오직 세 명의 직원과 소수의 고객으로 시작했는데, 그 이후로 얼마나 큰 사업이 되었는지를 보면 놀랍습니다. 대다수의 회사들이 설립되는 데 걸리는 시간을 고려해 본다면 이는 특히 고무적입니다. 우리 사무 조정자인 멜 쿠싱이 우리 기념 행사를 준비하는 데 동의한 것을 알리게 되어 다행이지만, 준비를 돕는 데 훨씬 더 많은 사람들이 필요할 것입니다. 그러니 당신이 도움을 줄 수 있다면 멜에게 이메일을 꼭 보내세요.

approach 다가가다, 다가오다 temp 임시 직원 a handful of 소수의 astonishing 놀라운 inspiring 고무하는, 자극하는 majority 다수 established 인정받는, 확실히 자리를 잡은 office coordinator 사무 조정자 festivity 축제 행사 help out with ~을 도와주다

83 What is being discussed?
    (A) A press conference
    (B) A client seminar
    (C) A product launch
    (D) A company anniversary
    무엇이 이야기되고 있는가?
    (A) 기자 회견
    (B) 고객 세미나
    (C) 제품 출시
    (D) 회사 기념일

84 According to the speaker, what is surprising?
    (A) Rapid decrease of competitors
    (B) The growth of the business

Actual Test 03 072 • 073

(C) The success of the advertising
(D) A change in a work schedule

화자에 따르면, 무엇이 놀라운가?
(A) 경쟁업체의 급속한 감소
(B) 사업의 성장
(C) 광고의 성공
(D) 업무 일정의 변화

85 Why are listeners asked to email Mel Cushing?
(A) To take part in a survey
(B) To assist with preparations
(C) To distribute leaflets
(D) To book a conference room

청자들은 왜 멜 쿠싱에게 이메일을 보내도록 요청받는가?
(A) 설문 조사에 참여하기 위해
(B) 준비를 돕기 위해
(C) 전단지를 받부하기 위해
(D) 회의실 예약을 위해

Questions 86-88 refer to the following talk. 영W

⑧ Today, I'm going to talk with you about some techniques team leaders can use to improve their employees' productivity. Nearly every company I have worked with has said that this is one of their top priorities. Yet, they often fail to get their workers to be more motivated or more efficient. Now, here's my understanding. The goals are good, but the implementation is often not good enough. And, as a result, they often blame the employees. But there are better ways, and that's what we are going to talk about today. ⑧ Before I do that, I want each of you to write down your ideas for what you think makes some employees more productive than others. There are a notepad and a pen in front of you.

오늘, 제가 팀 리더들이 직원들의 생산성을 향상시키기 위해서 사용할 수 있는 기술들에 관해서 이야기를 해 보겠습니다. 제가 같이 일을 해 보았던 대부분의 회사들이 이것을 최우선 과제라고 말해 있었습니다. 그러나 그들은 종종 그들의 직원들에게 동기를 부여하거나, 보다 그들을 효율적으로 만드는 데 실패하고 있었습니다. 자, 이제 제가 깨달은 바입니다. 목표 들은 좋습니다. 그러나 그것들을 이행하는 데에 있어서는 종종 미흡 습니다. 그리고, 그 결과로 팀 리더들은 종종 직원들을 탓했습니다. 그러 나 여기 더 나은 방법들이 있는데 그것이 오늘 우리가 할 이야기가 되겠 습니다. 그 전에, 저는 여러분들 각자가 생각하기에 어떤 방법이 분별이 직원들 의 생산성을 높게 만들 수 있는지에 관한 아이디어를 적어주시기를 바랍 니다. 여러분들 앞에 공책과 펜이 놓여 있습니다.

productivity 생산성 priority 우선 과제, 우선사항 implementation 이행, 실행, 완성 summary 요약본 work station 작업 장소

86 What topic will the woman talk about?
(A) Hiring team leaders
(B) Raising productivity
(C) Improving sales
(D) Transferring employees

여자는 어떤 주제에 관해 이야기할 것인가?
(A) 팀 리더들을 고용하는 것
(B) 생산성을 높이는 것
(C) 판매를 증가시키는 것
(D) 직원들을 전근시키는 것

---

87 Why does the woman say, "Now, here's my understanding"?
(A) She recently presented some findings.
(B) She wants to write a summary.
(C) She trained her staff.
(D) She is going to tell her opinion.

왜 여자는 "자, 이제 제가 깨달은 바입니다"이라고 말했는가?
(A) 그녀는 최근에 결과들을 발표했다.
(B) 그녀는 요약본을 작기를 원한다.
(C) 그녀는 직원들을 교육했다.
(D) 그녀는 그녀의 생각을 말할 것이다.

88 What are listeners asked to do?
(A) Write down some thoughts
(B) Talk with their coworkers
(C) Read some information
(D) Change their work station

청자들은 무엇을 하라고 요청받는가?
(A) 생각들을 적는다.
(B) 동료들과 이야기한다.
(C) 정보를 읽는다.
(D) 작업 장소를 바꾼다.

Questions 89-91 refer to the following excerpt from a meeting.

호M

There is one more item on our agenda. **❽** As you may have heard, we are getting ready to launch a new line of stain remover for all types of vehicles. They were designed to remove tough stains on cars like tar. We have tested these new products with customer focus groups, and they are well liked. I have prepared information packets to familiarize you with the products. They were supposed to be ready for me to hand out today, but we encountered a production delay. **❾** So you can pick them up from my office next Tuesday. I would have liked to go over them with you, but we are not able to do that today. So this is it then. The next meeting is on the twenty-fifth.

의제가 하나 더 있습니다. 들으셨겠지만, 우리는 모든 종류의 자동차에 쓸 수 있는 새로운 얼룩 제거제 제품군을 론칭하기 위해 준비하는 중입니다. 그 제품들은 타르처럼 차에서 제거하기 어려운 얼룩을 없앨 수 있도록 고안됐습니다. 우리는 이 제품을 고객 포커스 그룹과 테스트를 해 보았고, 좋은 반응을 얻었습니다. 제가 여러분들이 제품에 익숙해질 수 있도록 정보 패킷을 준비해 뒀습니다. 패킷들이 오늘 제가 여러분들께 나눠드릴 수 있도록 준비될 예정이었으나, 생산에 문제가 생겨서 지연되었습니다. 그래서 여러분들은 그 패킷을 다음 주 화요일 제 사무실에서 가져가실 수 있습니다. 제가 여러분들과 패킷 내용을 검토하고 싶었으나 오늘은 불가능하게 되었습니다. 그래서 이게 마지막입니다. 다음 미팅은 25일이 되겠습니다.

stain 얼룩, 오점 tar 타르 familiarize 익숙하게 만들다 encounter 직면하다 commercial 민간의 demonstrate 시연하다

89 Where does the speaker most likely work?
(A) At a cleaning product manufacturer
(B) At a commercial airline
(C) At a car dealership
(D) At a food market

화자는 어디서 일할 것 같은가?
(A) 청소용품 제조업체
(B) 민간 항공사
(C) 자동차 대리점
(D) 식료품점

90 When can listeners get the information packets?
(A) Today
(B) Tomorrow
(C) Next week
(D) In two weeks

청자들은 언제 정보 패킷을 얻을 수 있는가?
(A) 오늘
(B) 내일
(C) 다음 주
(D) 2주 후

91 What does the man mean when he says, "So this is it then"?
(A) He will demonstrate how the product works.
(B) He is ready to end the meeting.
(C) He will go over the packets next time.
(D) He wants listeners to design some ideas.

남자가 "그래서 이제 마지막입니다"라고 말한 것은 무엇을 의미하는가?
(A) 그는 제품이 어떻게 작동하는지 시연할 것이다.
(B) 그는 회의를 마무리할 준비가 되었다.
(C) 그는 패킷을 다음에 검토할 것이다.
(D) 그는 청자들이 아이디어를 구상하기를 원한다.

Questions 92-94 refer to the following announcement and schedule.

영W

Train	From	Arriving at
121	JFK	Platform 2
141	Newark	Platform 7
161	Union	Platform 1
171	Jay	Platform 10

Attention, passengers. **❸** This train will be arriving at Platform 7 in Penn Station in about fifteen minutes. This is our final destination. All passengers must exit the train at Penn Station. **❷** Please check the overhead compartments and luggage areas for any personal items before exiting the train. Once you enter the station, you will not be able to return to the train. For passengers transferring to other trains, please check the departure board inside the station to check on your connecting train. Staff members are also available to assist you at the information desk. **❸** Please note that due to maintenance work, the station's main doors are closed. Please use the rear doors on Pine Street to exit the station. Thank you.

기차	출발	도착
121	JFK	플랫폼 2
141	뉴어크	플랫폼 7
161	유니온	플랫폼 1
171	제이	플랫폼 10

승객 여러분. 이 열차는 펜 역의 7번 플랫폼에 약 15분 후에 도착하겠습니다. 이 역은 우리의 최종 목적지가 되겠습니다. 모든 승객 여러분들께서는 펜 역에서 하차하셔야 합니다. 하차하시기 전에 머리 위 보관함 및 짐 칸에 개인 물건이 남아 있지 않은지 확인하시기 바랍니다. 역으로 들어가시고 나면, 다시 기차로 나오실 수 없습니다. 다른 기차로 갈아타시는 승객분께서는 역 안에 위치한 출발 안내 전광판을 참고하셔서 연결편을 확인하시기 바랍니다. 안내 데스크에 있는 직원들이 또한 여러분들을 도와 드릴 것입니다. 보수 작업으로 인해 역의 정문이 폐쇄되었습니다. 역에서 나가실 때에는 파인 스트리트에 있는 후문을 이용해 주시기 바랍니다. 감사합니다.

compartment 구획, 칸, 짐칸　maintenance 관리, 유지, 보수　rear 후방의, 뒤의　belongings 소지품　disembark 내리다　routine 정기적인

92 What are the listeners asked to do?
(A) Store their belongings properly
(B) Not get off the train before an announcement
(C) Check their belongings before disembarking
(D) Move to a different platform

청자들은 무엇을 하라고 요청받는가?
(A) 그들의 개인 소지품을 제대로 보관한다.
(B) 공지 이전에 기차에서 내리지 않는다.
(C) 하차하기 전에 개인 소지품을 확인한다.
(D) 다른 승강장으로 이동한다.

93 Look at the graphic. Where did the train leave from?
(A) JFK
(B) Newark
(C) Union
(D) Jay

시각 자료를 보시오. 기차는 어디서 출발했었는가?
(A) JFK
(B) 뉴어크
(C) 유니온
(D) 제이

94 Why can't passengers use the main entrance?
(A) Improvement work is being done.
(B) The place is too crowded at the moment.
(C) It has been shut down for a routine inspection.
(D) Cleaning work is taking place.

승객들은 왜 정문을 이용할 수 없는가?
(A) 수리 작업이 진행 중이다.
(B) 현재 너무 붐빈다.
(C) 정기 검사로 인해 폐쇄되었다.
(D) 청소 중이다.

Questions 95-97 refer to the following broadcast and map. 호M

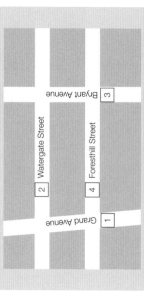

This is Sam Smith with your 6 o'clock traffic news. Everything looks good on the city's main streets and highways. That should make it easier for everyone heading back home this evening. I have a reminder for all of you who use Bryant Avenue to get downtown. Starting tomorrow, that street will be closed between Watergate Street and Foresthill Street. Work crews will be doing maintenance work on electric cables under the Avenue. They are going to use the opportunity to repave the surface of the area. Construction is expected to last for three days at the most. During that time, commuters should follow the yellow signs to detour the site. They will direct you to safely bypass the work area to your downtown destination.

작업을 할 것입니다. 이 기회에 그 구간의 도로도 재포장하려고 할 것입니다. 공사는 최대 3일 동안 지속될 것입니다. 이 동안에 통근자들은 노란색 선을 따라서 이곳을 우회해야 합니다. 그럼 안전하게 작업 지역을 우회해서 시내 목적지로 갈 수 있습니다.

crew 직원, 승무원　repave 재포장하다　surface 표면　bypass 우회하다

95 What is the broadcast about?
(A) Building maintenance
(B) Traffic congestion
(C) A road closure
(D) A new bus schedule

방송은 무엇에 관한 것인가?
(A) 건물 관리
(B) 교통 체증
(C) 도로 폐쇄
(D) 새로운 버스 일정

96 What are commuters advised to do?
(A) Leave earlier
(B) Take a detour
(C) Avoid using public transportation in the area
(D) Drive slowly

통근자들은 무엇을 하라고 충고받는가?
(A) 일찍 떠난다.
(B) 우회를 한다.
(C) 이 지역에서 대중교통을 이용하지 않는다.
(D) 천천히 운전한다.

97 Look at the graphic. What number shows where the construction will take place?
(A) 1
(B) 2
(C) 3
(D) 4

시각 자료를 보시오. 어떤 번호가 공사가 진행 중인 곳을 보여 주는가?
(A) 1
(B) 2
(C) 3
(D) 4

6시 교통 뉴스의 샘 스미스입니다. 시내 중심가와 고속도로 모두 좋아 보입니다. 이로 인해 오늘 저녁 집으로 돌아가는 모두가 편안하실 겁니다. 시내로 가는 데 브라이언트 가를 이용하시는 모든 분들을 주목해 주세요. 내일부터 워터게이트 도로와 포레스트힐 도로 구간 사이의 브라이언트 가가 폐쇄될 예정입니다. 작업자들이 그 구간 아래의 전기 케이블 배선에 대해 정비

Part 5

Questions 98-100 refer to the following announcement and schedule. 영W

New Work Schedule	
Area	Day
Cafeteria	Monday
Breakroom	Tuesday
	Thursday
Storage space	Wednesday
	Friday
Lobby	Saturday

Okay, before we get started working this morning, I just want to let everybody know about the new interior flooring material that we will be using. Our supplier recently let us know that they were planning to discontinue the material we normally use. They were kind enough to send us some samples of their new one to try out. Now, it's really important to understand that the new flooring material is thicker in consistency than the stuff you are familiar with. ⑱ So it takes a little longer to apply, and it also needs more time to settle down. ⑲ As a result, we have to adjust our schedule slightly. ⑳ Initially, we had planned to start on the lobby of the building and then work on other places. But we have to change that as we need more time. So the lobby should be the last.

자, 오전 근무를 시작하기 전에, 제가 앞으로 우리가 사용하게 될 새로운 내부 바닥재에 관해서 모두에게 알려 드리겠습니다. 최근에 우리 공급업체가 지금 우리가 사용하고 있는 재료를 단종시킬 계획이라고 알려왔습니다. 공급업체는 친절하게도 우리가 시도해 볼 만한 새로운 샘플들을 보내주었습니다. 이제 우리는 새로운 재료가 우리가 익숙한 재료보다 두께가 밀도가 가지고 있다는 것을 알고 있어야 합니다. 그래서 재료를 작용하는 데에 좀 더 많은 시간이 걸리고, 자리를 잡는 데에도 보다 많은 시간이 필요합니다. 그 결과, 우리는 우리 스케줄을 조정해야 합니다. 처음에는, 우리가 건물 로비에서 작업을 시작하는 것으로 계획을 잡았었습니다. 그렇기 때문에 보다 많은 시간이 더 필요하기 때문에 변경을 해야 합니다. 그렇기 때문에 로비는 마지막이 되겠습니다.

discontinue 단종시키다, 중단하다 consistency 농도, 밀도, 일관성

---

98 What is the purpose of the announcement?

(A) To get feedback
(B) To assign a task
(C) To promote a product
(D) To change a plan

공지의 목적은 무엇인가?

(A) 피드백을 얻기 위해
(B) 업무를 배정하기 위해
(C) 제품을 홍보하기 위해
(D) 계획을 변경하기 위해

99 What is mentioned about the new material?

(A) It takes longer to settle in.
(B) It is less expensive.
(C) It is more durable.
(D) It is easier to use.

새로운 재료에 관해 무엇이 언급되었는가?

(A) 자리잡는 데에 보다 긴 시간이 걸린다.
(B) 보다 저렴하다.
(C) 보다 내구성이 좋다.
(D) 보다 사용하기 편리하다.

100 Look at the graphic. What day was the lobby originally scheduled to be worked on?

(A) Monday
(B) Tuesday
(C) Wednesday
(D) Saturday

시각 자료를 보시오. 로비는 원래 언제 작업이 진행되기로 되어 있었는가?

(A) 월요일
(B) 화요일
(C) 수요일
(D) 토요일

---

101 해설 주어가 Mr. Kim이고 빈칸은 문장의 동사 자리이므로 finishing과 to finish는 제외된다. 문장 맨 뒤에 있는 next Wednesday 때문에 미래 시제인 (D)가 정답이다. 미래를 나타내는 단서로 next ~, by[until]+미래 시점, as of+미래 시점, soon, shortly 등이 있다.

김 씨는 자동차 산업의 재정 상태에 관한 논문을 다음 주 수요일에 끝낼 것이다.

thesis 논문 financial 재정의 state 상태 automobile 자동차

102 해설 앞급 비교급 문제로 as와 as 사이에 들어갈 것은 형용사와 부사의 원형이므로 flexible, flexed, flexing 모두 빈칸에 들어갈 수 있다. 문맥상 '융통성이 있는'이 적절하므로 (A)가 정답이다. flexed는 '몸이 풀어진', flexing은 '몸을 푸는'이라는 의미로 의미상 적절하지 않다.

영업 직원은 고객과 가격을 흥정할 때 최대한 융통성이 있어야 한다.

flexible 유연한; 융통성 있는 flex (준비 운동으로) 몸을 풀다 flexibility 유연성

103 해설 문맥상 상품과 관련하여 가장 적절한 어휘는 (C)이다. 참고로 allow의 5형식 구조, 〈allow+목적어+to+동사원형〉와 〈be allowed to+동사원형〉을 알아 두자.

귀하의 주문이 배달되는 데 최소한 2~3주는 기다려 주세요.

quantity 양

104 해설 형용사(widest) 전치사(of) 사이에 올 수 있는 것은 명사이다. 선택지 중 명사 역할을 할 수 있는 것은 selection과 selecting인데 문맥상 '그 지역의 가장 다양한 거울 선발류를 제공한다'가 적절하므로 (A)가 정답이다. selecting은 동명사가 될 수 있지만 형용사의 수식을 받지 못하며 동명사는 부사의 수식을 받는다는 것을 알아 둔다.

클라스는 지역에서 가장 독보한 성인과 젊은 사람들용 거울 선발류를 제공한다.

region 지역 footwear 선발류 selection 선택; 선발 selector 선발기

105

해설 문맥상 '리셉션 데스크에 도착하는 즉시 보고해야 한다'가 되어야 자연스러우므로 정답은 (D)이다. 참고로 timely나 ly로 끝나지만 형용사라는 것들도 알아 둔다.

쿠바 태양 에너지 발전소의 모든 손님들은 접수 데스크에 도착하는 즉시 보고해야 한다.

solar 태양열 power plant 발전소

106

해설 형용사 어휘 문제로 문제로 가장 어울리는 형용사는 (D)이다. blank는 빈칸 뒤의 absence와 비슷한 의미인 '비어 있는'이라는 의미의 형용사이다.

휴가를 갈 때, 동료들에게 부재 시 당신의 고객 요청에 어떻게 대처해야 하는지 명확한 지시 사항을 남기세요.

take a holiday 휴가를 가다 instruction 지시 사항 regarding ~와 관련하여 absence 부재 whole 전체의 blank 빈 repetitive 반복적인

107

해설 전치사(for)와 전치사(of) 사이는 명사자리이므로 정답이다. submit 동사, submitted는 동사나 부사로 명사 역할을 할 수 없다.

사업 제안서 제출의 마감 기한은 6월 6일 수요일 오후 5시이다.

deadline 기한, 마감 시간 business proposal 사업 제안 submission 제출

108

해설 알맞은 전치사를 고르는 문제로 'A에게 B를 제공하다'라는 표현은 provide A with B 또는 provide A (A)가 정답이다.

미국 승마 협회 웹 사이트는 회원들의 말에 대한 최신 소식을 쉽게 볼 수 있도록 한다.

equestrian 승마의 association 협회 grant 승인[허락]하다 access 접근

109

해설 빈칸은 동사(requires)를 수식하는 부사 자리이므로 (D)가 정답이다. normal은 형용사나 부사, normality는 명사, norm은 명사로 모두 동사를 수식할 수 없다. 〈require+목적어+to do〉가 '~가 ~하도록 요청하다'라는 의미인 것도 알아 둔다.

야마하에서는 보통 5명 이상의 단체가 공장 견학을 사전에 신청하도록 요청한다.

sign up 등록하다, 신청하다 in advance 사전에 normal 정상인; 평범한 normality 정상 상태 norm 표준, 일반적인 것; 기준 normally 보통은, 보통

110

해설 부사 어휘 문제로 문맥상 어떤 역할을 '공식적으로' 맡았다가 자연스러우므로 가장 적절한 선택지는 (C)이다.

조잉가 멀리오타는 10월 9일 공식적으로 한시르 전지의 정보 통신 담당 최고 책임자 역할을 맡았다.

assume (권력·책임을) 맡다 chief information officer 정보 통신 최고 책임자 collectively 집합적으로, 총괄하여 officially 공식적으로 namely 즉, 다시 말해 densely 빽빽이, 밀집하여, 밀집되게

111

해설 대명사 문제로 빈칸 뒤에 명사(cable)가 있으므로 부사 (there)는 정답에서 제외되고, 복수 명사가 와야 하는 those 역시 제외된다. which는 관계대명사나 명사절 접속사로 위치가 적절하지 않다. 따라서 대명사의 소유격인 (C)가 정답이다.

영사기를 작동시키기 전에, 그것이 선물 당신의 장치에 단단히 연결하세요.

activate 작동시키다; 활성화시키다 projector 영사기 firmly 단단히 device 장치

112

해설 동사 어휘 문제로 문맥상 '연례 정보 모임에 참석하기로 되어 있다는 뜻이 적절하므로 정답은 (B)이다. (A) contributed는 뒤에 전치사 to가 와야 하므로 오답이다.

민발로 스낵스 앤 드링크스의 모든 시간제 직원들이 사장의 연례 정보 모임에 참석할 것으로 예상된다.

gathering (특정 목적을 위한) 모임 conduct 행동하다

113

해설 적절한 전치사를 고르는 문제로 문맥상 '회의 내내 시의회 웹 사이트에서 이용 가능할 것이다'가 가장 자연스러우므로 (D)가 정답이다. since가 와서 전치사로 쓰이면 뒤에 과거 시점 명사나 과거 시점 부사가 와서 '이래로'라는 의미로 쓰이며, between으로 '(둘) 사이'라는 뜻이므로 단수 명사인 meeting과는 어울리지 않는다.

공청회를 녹음한 것이 회의 내내 시의회 웹 사이트에서 이용 가능할 것이다.

recording 녹음[된 것]; 기록 public hearing 공청회

114

해설 장소 앞에 오면서 문맥상 '임시로 다른 작업장으로 이동될 수 있다'가 자연스러우므로 정답은 (C)이다. as가 전치사로 쓰이면 '~로서'라는 의미이므로 여기서는 적절하지 않다.

건물이 수리되는 동안, 직원들 몇 몇은 임시로 다른 작업장으로 이동될 수 있다.

temporarily 임시적으로, 임시로 relocate 이전하다; 이동시키다 workspace 작업 공간

115

해설 빈칸 앞에 동사 visit과 등위접속사 and로 연결되는 동사 원형 자리이므로 (D)가 정답이다. registering은 현재분사나 동명사, registered는 과거분사나 동사, registration은 명사로 정답이 될 수 없다. '~에 등록하다'라는 의미의 register, sign up for, enroll in을 알아 둔다.

자라 플레이스먼트 프로젝트 웹 사이트를 방문하여 컴퓨터 프로그래밍 세미나를 위해 오늘 등록하세요.

placement (흔히 수습 과정의 일부로 하는) 현장 실습 registration 등록

116

해설 선택지 모두 동사로 알맞은 동사 어휘를 고르는 문제이다. 문맥상 방송에서 할 수 있는 행위를 찾으므로 쉽게 정답을 고를 수 있다. '방송 뉴스에서 그의 노력을 일일 것이다'가 가장 자연스러우므로 정답은 (A)이다.

국회의원 로베토 스미스는 내일 오후 7시에 방송 뉴스에서 재선거를 위한 그의 노력을 일일 것이다.

bid 노력; 입찰 reelection 재선거 interfere 참견하다, 간섭하다 level 평평한[반듯하게 하다

117

해설 빈칸은 동사(has been ranked)를 수식하는 부사 자리이므로 (C)가 정답이다. consistency는 명사, consistent는 형용사로 부사 자리에 쓸 수 없다.

《대바게스 워클리》는 우드랜드 힐 지역에서 가장 인기 있는 중간물 중 하나로 꾸준하게 매거져 왔다.

rank 순위를 매기다 publication 출판물 consistency 일관성 consistently 끊임없이, 지속적으로 consistent 한결같은, 일관된

118

해설 that 이후에 빈칸 앞뒤로 완전한 절(all ~ properly)과 완전한 절(they ~ warehouse)이 있으므로 받아야 와야 하는 것은 부사절 접속사 혹은 등위 접속사이다. as much as, whether, before이는 모두 부사절 접속사로 쓸 수 있지만 문맥상 '그것들이 운송되기 전에'가 적절하므로 (D)가 정답이다, such as 〈명사+such as A〉의 형태로 쓰여 'A와 같은 명사'라는 의미로 사용되므로 오답이다.

창고가 운송되기 전에, 모든 소포들이 적절하게 포장되었는지 확인해 주세요.

property 올바르게, 적절히 ship 운송하다 warehouse 창고 as much as ~이지만

119
해설 빈칸은 형용사 자리로 부사인 probablly는 정답이 될 수 없다. 문맥상 '~할 것 같다'라는 의미로 쓰였으므로 빈칸은 형용사 자리인 (D)가 정답이다. likely는 〈be likely to+동사원형〉이지만 '~할 것 같은'이라는 의미의 형용사로도 쓰인다.

복도 개조는 다음 달 조 전까지는 끝나지 않을 것 같다.
renovation 개조 typical 전형적인

120
해설 명사 어휘 문제로 문맥상 '전자부품에 사용되는 철강의 ~가 향후 10년 동안 최고 절정에 달할 것이라고 전망한다'에 들어갈 가장 적절한 선택지는 (B)이다. 명사 demand, request, need 는 뒤에 전치사 for와 함께 쓰이는 것도 알아 둔다.

〈오퍼레이팅 시스템〉 장치는 전자 부품으로 사용되는 철강의 수요가 향후 10년 동안 절정에 달할 것이라고 전망한다.
forecast 예고하다 iron and steel 철강 electronic parts 전자 부품 appliance 가전제품 material 자재 peak 절정에 달하다 resource 자원, 재원

121
해설 전치사 뒤에는 명사나 동명사가 들어갈 수 있는데, 빈칸 뒤의 목적어를 취할 수 있는 것은 동명사이다. 따라서 (D)가 정답이다.
네오컨트리 클럽은 고객이 자신의 물건을 회수할 때 신분증 제시를 요구할 수도 있다.
identification 신분증 belongings 소지품 retrieve 되찾다

122
해설 문장에 동사가 wishes와 must contact 두 개이므로 빈칸은 이를 연결해 주는 접속사가 와야 한다. Nobody, Somebody는 대명사이므로 제외되고, 빈칸부터 seminar까지가 문장에서 주어 역할을 해야 하기 때문에 빈칸은 명사절 접속사 자리이다. whoever, whatever 둘 다 명사절 역할을 할 수 있으며 whatever 절은 불완전한 절을 받으므로 해석을 통해 정답을 선택해야 하는데 뒤에 올해 마케팅 세미나를 기준 사람은 누구든지가 적절하므로 (B)가 정답이다. Whatever는 문맥상 적절하지 않다.
올해 마케팅 세미나에 기관는 사람들은 누구든지 8월 1일까지 구내사 씨에게 연락해야 한다.

123
해설 명사 어휘 문제로 문맥상 '비용을 줄이는 방법에 대한 아이디어를 게시한 모든 사람들에게 감사를 표했다'는 의미가 적절하므로 정답은 (C)이다.
재무 담당 최고 책임자 로버 얀스볼트는 비용을 줄이는 방법에 관한 아이디어를 게시한 모든 사람들에게 감사를 표했다.
CFO 재무 담당 최고 책임자(Chief Financial Officer) post 게시하다, 게시물 lessen 줄이다 imitation 모조품, 모방 exposure 노출 abundance 풍부

124
해설 빈칸 앞까지가 완전한 문장이므로 빈칸부터는 수식 어구가 와야 한다. will regulate은 동사이므로 제외되고, regulated는 과거분사로 뒤에 목적어(the flow of liquid)가 있으므로 올 수 없다. 따라서 정답은 to부정사 형태인 (D)이다.
에어컨은 액체의 흐름을 조절하는 밸브 없이는 작동하지 않을 것이다.
operate 작동하다 valve 밸브 flow 흐름 regulate 조절하다

125
해설 The training ~ all employees까지가 완전한 문장이므로 빈칸 이후는 앞의 내용을 수식하는 표현이 와야 한다. 빈칸 뒤에 명사구(training meetings)가 있으므로 빈칸은 명사를 받아 수식할 수 있는 전치사 자리이다. 따라서 전치사 following, concerning 중에서 빈칸 뒤 내용을 교육 세미나에 관한 메모를 보냈다가 적절하므로 (D)가 정답이다. 참고로 '~에 관하여'라는 의미의 전치사 about, on, over, as to, as for, regarding, concerning을 위해 두자.
교육 직원은 모든 직원들에게 곧 있을 교육 세미나에 관한 메모를 보냈다.
representative 직원 upcoming 곧 있을 result 발생하다, 생기다

126
해설 빈칸은 관사(a)와 형용사(local) 뒤 명사 자리이다. 문맥상 앞의 매퍼 벤드을 가리키는 것이므로 사람 명사인 (A)가 정답이다. enthusiasm 또한 명사이나 의미상 부적절하다.
래시 커뮤니티 공항은 지역 항공의 열렬한 매퍼 벤드가 그린 작품을 전시한다.
aviation 항공 enthusiast 열광적인 팬 enthuse 열변을 토하다, 열광시키다 enthusiastically 열광적으로 enthusiasm 열정, 열광

127
해설 빈칸 뒤에 동명사(investing)가 왔으므로 전치사가 와야 한다. (A) near(~ 근처의), (D) along(~을 따라서)는 전치사이기는 하지만 해석이 맞지 않으므로 오답이다. trend는 '추세, 동향'의 의미가 있으므로 방향성을 나타내는 전치사(B)와 어울릴 수 있다.
보석에 투자하는 쪽으로의 최근의 추세는 계속될 것으로 예상된다.

128
해설 선택지 모두 부사절 접속사이므로 해석으로 풀어야 하는 문제이다. 부사절 접속사 so that은 보통 뒤에 조동사 can이나 may를 이끌면서 '~할 수 있도록'이라는 뜻이므로 정답은 (B)이다.
블루오션 파이낸셜 서비스를 이용하는 신규 고객들은 온라인에서 그들의 계좌 정보에 접속하기 위해서는 바이러스 방어 소프트웨어를 설치해야 한다.
antivirus 바이러스 퇴치용인

129
해설 형용사 어휘 문제로 문맥상 '예상보다 높은 수익 때문에 낙관적이라는 것이 적절하므로 (B)가 정답이다.
지난 9개월 동안의 예상보다 높은 수익으로 인해 지암파-네도우 디자인스는 당연하게도 그들의 확장에 대해 낙관적이다.
understandably 당연하게도, 당연히 expansion 확장 devoted 헌신적인 optimistic 낙관적인 impressive 인상적인 ample 충분한

130
해설 If Starship Entertainment had not given the actor a chance였던 가정법 과거완료에서 if를 생략하고 주어와 동사를 도치한 구조이다(가정법 과거완료(had not given) 시제가 쓰였으므로 주절에도 조동사의 과거완료 형태가 들어가야 한다. 따라서 정답은 (C) would have done이다.
만약 스타십 엔터테인먼트가 그 배우에게 기회를 주지 않았더라면 다른 회사가 그렇게 했을 것이다.

Part 6

[131-134]

자연 공원의 개장

시에 새로운 자연 공원의 개장 **131** 행사가 4월 2일 일요일에 개최될 것이다. 시장, 시의원들, 기자들, 그리고 몇몇 지역 유명 인사들이 참석할 것이다. 공식 리본 커팅식은 오전 10시 30분으로 예정되어 있다 **132** 뒤따라 시장이 환영 연설이 있을 것이다. 지역 식당에서 간식과 음료가 지원될 것이다. 또한 댄스 공연과 마술 쇼를 포함한 오락 행사들도 있을 것이다. **133** 비록 입장은 무료이고 대중들에게 개방되지만, 사전에 온라인으로 등록을 해야 한다. 관심 있는 사람들은 www.naturepark opening. com에서 세부 사항을 볼 수 있다. 좌석 수가 제한되어 있으므로, 그러니 일찍 도착하는 것이 좋다.

celebrity 유명 인사 be in attendance 참석하다 registration 등록 in advance 사전에

131 해설 (A) '발언/연급'. (B) '행사'. (C) '설명/입증'. (D) '발표' 중에서 문제에 어울리는 명사 어휘를 고르는 문제이다. 동사 will be held(개최되다)의 주어로 어울리려 하고, opening(개장)과 나열되어서 복합명사로 어울리므로 정답은 (B) ceremony이다.

132 해설 이미 동사(is scheduled)가 있고, 접속사가 따로 없으므로 더 이상 동사는 들어갈 수 없는 자리이다. 이 자리는 분사구문으로 뒤에 목적어가 없으므로 p.p.가 들어가야 한다. 따라서 정답은 (D) followed이다.

133 해설 빈칸 뒤에 2개의 절이 있으므로 접속사가 들어갈 자리이다. Now that(~이므로), Although(비록 ~이지만), As though(마치 ~인 것처럼) 중에서 해석이 어울리는 것은 (B) Although이다.

134 해설 (A) 지역을 보존하는 것은 중요하다.
(B) 구매 가능한 음식이 있을 것이다.
(C) 좌석의 수가 제한되어 있다.
(D) 그 행사는 궂은 날씨 때문에 연기되었다.
해설 빈칸 바로 뒤에 일찍 오라는 내용이 있으므로 좌석의 수가 제한되어 있다는 (C)가 정답이다.

[135-138]

자회가 정기적으로 마련하는 자전거 투어 중 하나를 통해 버트 마을을 탐험해 보세요. 버트 투어에서 이가데미의 휴양림을 받는 **135** 각 투어는 전문 자전거 선수에 의해 인솔되고 특별히 마을의 서로 다른 조망을 포함하고 있습니다.

가장 인기 있는 루트는 마을의 선명 **136** 지역인 다운베일 밸리를 포함합니다. 세 개의 재분소와 하나의 공장 외에도, 다운베일 밸리는 이 지역 역사를 상징하는 현재는 가동 중인 주석 광산과 여러 공예품점이 본고장입니다. **137** 투어는 대략 세 시간 지속됩니다. 버트의 가장 오래된 선술집 중 하나인 그린 맨 펍에서 원기를 북돋우는 시사로 **138** 을 맞습니다.

다운베일 밸리 투어를 신청하시거나 다른 투어들에 대해 더 알아보시려면, 버트 투어리즘 이가데미 050-555-6939로 전화해 주세요.

sponsor 후원하다 tourism 관광 head 이끌다 expert 전문가, 전문적인 cyclist 자전거 선수, 사이클리스트 feature 특별히 포함하다 perspective 조망, 경치 route 길 encompass 포함하다 industrial 산업의, 공업의 in addition to ~에 더하여 mill 제분소 tin mine 주석 광산 crafts shop 공예품 가게 refreshing 원기를 북돋우는 represent 대표하다 register for ~을 신청하다 find out 알아내다 pub 술집 public house 선술집

135 해설 선택지 모두 명사를 수식할 수 있는 형용사로 쓰이기 때문에 답을 고르기가 까다로운 문제이다. 우선 whose는 관계대명사의 소유격으로 쓰이고, either는 둘 중 하나를 선택할 때 쓰이므로 여기에는 맞지 않다. 빈칸 문장 뒷부분이 different에서 '정해진 하나의 투어가 아니라 '각각의 투어'임을 알 수 있으므로 정답은 (A)이다.

136 해설 다운베일 밸리가 어떤 곳인지를 파악하면 정답을 찾을 수 있다. 빈칸 뒤 문장에서 재분소, 공장, 주석 광산, 공예품점이 밀집해 있음을 알 수 있으므로 선정 지역'이 어울린다. 따라서 정답은 (C)이다. (A) 공장 / (B) 프로그램 / (D) 향형

137 해설 (A) 방문객들은 안전 장비를 착용해야 합니다.
(B) 투어는 대략 세 시간 지속됩니다.
(C) 자전거를 타는 것은 건강에 좋습니다.
(D) 이 가이드가 마을의 역사를 설명해 줄 겁니다.
해설 빈칸 뒤에 투어가 끝나는 것에 대한 내용이 있으므로 투어가 3시간 정도 된다는 정보를 주는 (B)가 정답이다.

138 해설 우선 빈칸 뒤에 with가 있으므로 타동사로 사용되는 (C)와 (D)는 일단 제외한다. 문맥상 '마무리 짓다'라는 의미의 (A)가 적절하다. (B) 나가다 / (C) 주문하다 / (D) 예약하다

[139-142]

수신: muamba@nigermail.com
발신: subscriptions@befitmagazine.com
주제: 구독 갱신
날짜: 9월 20일

무암바 씨께,

귀하의 〈비 피트〉 잡지 구독이 9월 30일에 **139** 만료될 것입니다. 일반적인 연장은 다르지만 주제로 하여 상기시 받은 저희 기사를 하나도 빠뜨림없이 정가률 수 있도록, 특별히 저렴한 가격으로 30일권레 12개월 더 구독 연장하시는 길 잊지 마시기 바랍니다. **140** 게다가, 구독을 이달 앞까지 갱신하시면, 조지 랜드 출판사의 다른 간행물들을 할인가로 받을 수 있는 저렴을 드립니다. 이는 〈엑사사이즈 루틴〉과 〈드레스 투 임프레스〉를 포함합니다.

귀하의 구독을 연장하실 것을 고려하는 내용의 이메일이다. 이 금융 쓴 날짜가 9월 20일이고, 두 번째 문장부터 계속 구독 연장을 권하고 있는 것으로 보아 아직 구독 만기가 되지 않았음을 알 수 있다. 따라서 9월 30일에 구독 만기일이며, 빈칸에는 미래 시제가 와야 하므로 (B)가 정답이다.

www.befitmagazine.com/subscription에 들어오셔서 온라인으로 갱신 양식란 9월 23일 **142** 까지 작성해 주세요.

구독 관리부

subscription renewal 구독 갱신 ensure 확실하게 하다 award-winning 상을 받은 entitle 자격을 주다 publication 간행물 complete 작성하다 valid 유효한 cordially 정중하게

139 해설 독자에게 잡지 구독을 연장할 것을 권하는 내용의 이메일이다. 이 금융 쓴 날짜가 9월 20일이고, 두 번째 문장부터 계속 구독 연장을 권하고 있는 것으로 보아 아직 구독 만기가 되지 않았음을 알 수 있다. 따라서 9월 30일에 구독 만기일이며, 빈칸에는 미래 시제가 와야 하므로 (B)가 정답이다.

140 해설 빈칸 뒤 문장은 빈칸 앞 문장과 마찬가지로 구독 연장을 함으로써 얻게 되는 혜택을 설명하고 있다. 즉, 뒤 문장은 앞 문장에 대해 '추가'의 의미를 지니고 있으므로 두 문장을 잇는 접속사로 쓰는 '게다가, 덧붙여'라는 뜻의 (D)가 적절하다. (A) 결과적으로 / (B) 하지만 / (C) 대신에

141 해설 (A) 이 할인은 첫 구독자들에게만 유용합니다.
(B) 저희는 11월호를 위한 당신의 제출들을 받으셨습니다.
(C) 이것은 〈엑사사이즈 루틴〉과 〈드레스 투 임프레스〉를 포함합니다.
(D) 당신들을 사상성에 정중하게 초대합니다.
해설 빈칸 바로 앞에 조지 랜드 출판사의 간행물에 대해 언급했으므로 이에 해당하는 것을 나타내는 (C)가 정답이다.

Part 7

142 해설 앞엣 것은 전치사를 고르는 문제이다. 이 문장은 9월 23일까지 구독 갱신 양식을 작성하라는 말이므로 ~까지에 해당하는 by와 until이 답이 후보가 된다. by는 일회적인 행동일 때, until은 계속적인 행위일 때 쓰는데 complete(작성하다)라는 행위는 일회적인 행위이므로 정답은 (B) by이다.

[143-146]

공지

수신: 박물관 직원들

3월 5일부터, 메인 박물관 건물의 동쪽 별관이 (143) 공사 때문에 폐쇄될 것입니다. 그 건물의 엘리베이터와 조명 스위치가 낡아서 교체될 필요가 있습니다.

고객들에게 이 구역이 출입금지라는 것을 알리는 표지판이 붙게 될 것입니다. 건물의 일부에 들어갈 필요가 있는 직원들은 제한적으로 가능합니다. (144) 상인으로부터 반드시 허가를 받아야 합니다.

마지막으로, 보통 동쪽 별관에 하역장에 배달되던 물건들은 (145) 일시적으로 북쪽 별관의 우편실로 보내질 것입니다. 일단 작업이 완료되면 우리는 정상 배송 관행으로 돌아갈 것입니다. (146)

여러분의 인내심에 미리 감사드립니다.

에밀 야스코
골드선 박물관 관장

wing 별관 owing to ~ 때문에 alert 알리다 patron 고객 off-limits 출입금지의 on a limited basis 제한적으로 loading dock 하역장 reroute 바꾸다 protocol 절차 in advance 미리, 사전에

143 해설 전치사(owing to)의 목적어 자리이므로 명사가 들어가야 한다. 선택지에서 명사는 constructor(건설사)와 construction(공사)인데, 건설사 때문이 아니라 공사 때문에 별관이 폐쇄되는 것이므로 정답은 (C) construction이다.

144 해설
(A) 직원들은 공사 기간 동안 휴가를 가질 것을 권장받습니다.
(B) 상인으로부터 반드시 허가를 받아야 합니다.
(C) 몇몇 행사들은 여전히 동쪽 별관에서 개최될 것입니다.
(D) 기입 문서들을 보호 상자에 저장될 것입니다.
빈칸 앞에서 직원들은 제한적으로 입장할 수 있다고 했으므로 입장 전에 상인의 허가를 받아야 한다는 (B)가 정답이다.

145 해설 공사 중에만 동쪽 별관으로 배송이 되지 않는다고 했으므로 북쪽 별관으로 '일시적으로' 배송된다고 볼 수 있다. 따라서 정답은 (B) temporarily(일시적으로)이다. (A) 거의 ~ 않다 / (C) 공식적으로 / (D) 영구적으로

146 해설 뒤에 절을 이끄는 자리이므로 접속사인 (D) once(일단 ~하면)가 정답이다. (A) ~ 후에(전치사) / (B) 즉시(부사) / (C) 나중에(부사)

[147-148]

수신: 조수아 이즈마일
발신: 블루 힐 병원

카자나스 의사 선생님으로부터의 메시지입니다. (147) 당신의 예약을 1월 13일, 수요일 오전 9시로 잡아 놓았습니다. 이 예약을 수락하신다면, 확인을 위해 1번을 눌러 주세요.

(148) 지정된 시간에 오실 수 없다면, 일정을 다시 잡기 위해, 사무실 143-555-1856으로 전화 주세요. 감사합니다.

surgery 진료소, 수술(실) make an appointment 예약을 하다 confirm 확인하다 specify 명기하다 reschedule 일정을 다시 잡다 procedure 수술

147 메시지가 보내진 이유는?
(A) 절차에 대해 문의하기 위해
(B) 취소를 알리기 위해
(C) 예약을 변경하기 위해
(D) 승인을 요청하기 위해

148 이즈마일 씨가 예약을 변경하기 위해서 해야 할 일은?
(A) 진료실로 전화하기
(B) 진료실 방문하기
(C) 문자 발송하기
(D) 팩스 발송하기

발신: alerts@dacklonbank.com
수신: 지나 트레이스〈gtrace@budsandbows.com〉
제목: 자동 공지 – 답신하지 마세요.
날짜: 6월 8일

149 저희는 귀하의 택크론 은행 당좌 예금 계좌에서 지금 이체되는 공지를 받으셨습니다.

날짜와 시간: 6월 8일 오전 10시 30분
이체 금액: 250달러
수신 계좌 유형: 당좌 예금

150 귀하가 이 거래를 승인하지 않았다면, 네크론 은행에 즉시 전화해 주세요. 사기 방지 부서는 7일 내내 하루 24시간 1-901-555-1544로 연락이 가능합니다. 또한 antifraud@dacklonbank.com으로 이메일을 보내실 수 있습니다.

automatic 자동의 notification 공지 fund transfer 자금 이체 checking account 당좌 예금 계좌 authorize 승인하다 at once 즉시, 바로 anti-fraud 사기 방지 reach (전화로) 연락이 닿다 outstanding 미결제의 accessible 이용 가능한 alter 바꾸다

149 이메일의 목적은?
(A) 트레이스 씨가 예금을 하도록 설득하기 위해
(B) 트레이스 씨에게 금융 거래에 관해 알리기 위해
(C) 미지불액의 지불을 요청하기 위해
(D) 새로운 사기 예방 계획을 설명하기 위해

150 택크론 은행에 관해 암시된 것은?
(A) 언제든지 이용 가능하다.
(B) 영업시간이 변경되었다.
(C) 우편으로 연락할 수 있다.
(D) 새로운 웹 사이트 주소를 갖게 되었다.

조안 델피 [오후 3:47]	**149** 갈튼 씨, 귀찮게 해서 죄송한데요, 우리 회사 로고가 새겨져 있는 종이랑 봉투가 다 떨어져 가요. 수납장에 각각 조금밖에 안 남있네요.
조지 갈튼 [오후 3:49]	발견했다니 다행이에요. 지금 바로 더 주문해 주세요.
조안 델피 [오후 3:53]	케이시 페이퍼 프로덕츠에서 주문할까요?
조지 갈튼 [오후 3:54]	네. 그리고 향후 3개월은 넘아 있을 수 있게 충분히 주문해 주세요. 그때가 우리가 새로운 예산을 받게 될 때거든요.
조안 델피 [오후 3:57]	**151** 그럼 큰 박스로 각각 세 박스씩 주문할까요?
조지 갈튼 [오후 4:02]	**151** 적당해 보이네요. **152** 주문을 신속히 처리해 주세요. 새로운 게 도착하기 전에 이게 떨어지면 안 되거든요.
조안 델피 [오후 4:07]	**152** 제가 바로 처리할게요.

run out of ~을 다 써버리다 a handful of 소수의 right away 바로 expedite 더 신속히 처리하다 stationery 문구류

151 오후 4시 02분에 갈튼 씨가 "적당해 보이네요"라고 썼을 때 그 의미는 무엇인가?
(A) 그는 델피 씨가 그 문제를 그에게 보고해 준 것에 대해서 고마워하고 있다.
(B) 그는 델피 씨가 정확한 수량을 추천했다고 생각한다.
(C) 그는 델피 씨에게 추가 정보를 말해주려한다.
(D) 그는 델피 씨가 지시사항에 집중해 주기를 바란다.

152 델피 씨는 다음에 무엇을 할 것 같은가?
(A) 배송 일정 다시 잡기
(B) 몇몇 편지들 보내기
(C) 문구류 주문하기
(D) 예산 준비하기

10월 3일

체종 관리 회의 공지

153 지역 주민과 인근 지역 거주자는 체종 체종 관리 그룹의 다음 회의에 참석하실 수 있습니다.

• 날짜: 10월 22일 토요일
  식단 위원회, 오후 6시
• **154** 날짜: 10월 29일 토요일
  운동 위원회, 오후 6시 30분

• 장소:
  더 씨 뷰, 3층
  시맨 홀
  루 드 라 그린빌 2018, 체미스

시간표와 훈련 일정은 10월 4일, 화요일에 공용 도서관 및 시맨 홀과 미스 수영장의 로비에서 확인하실 수 있습니다. 체종 감량 프로그램을 위한 제안이 있는 지역민들은 주최자에게 회의 최소 3일 전에는 연락해 주셔야 합니다.

155 요청 사항 보내실 곳:
재니스 그루쏜, 주최자
체미스 체종 관리 그룹
루 드 라 그린빌 2018, 체미스
jgrousson@chamis.fr

weight 몸무게 management 관리 local resident 지역 주민 surrounding 주변의 committee 위원회 dietary 식단의 venue 장소 foyer 현관, 로비 weight loss 체중 감량 organizer 주최자 publicize 알리다 inaugurate 개시하다 regimen 식이 요법 recruitment 신규 모집 drive 운동 sign up 신청하다

153 공지의 목적은?
(A) 다가오는 행사를 홍보하기 위해
(B) 체중 증가 식이 요법을 개시하기 위해
(C) 새로운 장소를 광고하기 위해
(D) 신입 회원 모집 운동을 발표하기 위해

154 운동에 관한 논의는 언제 하는가?
(A) 10월 3일
(B) 10월 4일
(C) 10월 22일
(D) 10월 29일

155 위원회에 의견을 제안하고 싶다면 무엇을 해야 하는가?
(A) 그룹 씨에게 이메일 보내기
(B) 위원회에 전화하기

(C) 첫 회에 참석하기
(D) 시앤 폴에서 신청하기

[156-157]

JB 스포츠
엘 마리나
스페인 1139

당신의 온라인 스포츠 및 레저 용품점

고객: 사미라 라룬
배송지: 루마고 스트리트 301, 세빌, 스페인 1295
주문 번호: 99842(11월 11일 오전 10시 32분 주문)

수량	품목	가격
1	[156] 파란 디자이너 스니 커즈 (제조사: 그립로)	소계: 58달러 제품: 5달러 80센트 [157] 빠른 배송: 11달러
1	녹색 슬링백 샌들 (제조사: 그란다사모)	주문 함계: 74달러 80센트 빠른 지불금: 74달러 80센트 신용 카드 샌들 잔액: 0

11월 11일 오후 3시 5분 주문품 배송

*구매해 주셔서 감사합니다. 물건이 만족하지 않으시면 입으시면 입지 않은 상태 또는 원래의 포장과 함께 14일 이내로 반품해 주세요. 반품 또는 교환에 관해 더 많은 정보를 원하시면 www.jbsports/sp/returns를 확인해 주세요.

vendor (특정한 제품의) 판매 회사 gear 소지품, 물품 shipping address 배송지 manufacturer 제조업체 slingback 슬링백(뒤트임) unworn 입지 않은 expedited shipping 긴급 배송 accompany 수반(동반)하다 packaging 포장 literary 문학의 material 자료 footwear 신발 parcel 소포

156 JB 스포츠는 어떤 종류의 제품을 파는가?
(A) 문화 자료
(B) 신발류
(C) 읽기
(D) DVD

157 라룬 씨에 관해 언급된 것은?
(A) 11월 11일에 소포를 받았다.
(B) JB 스포츠에서 정가적으로 구매를 한다.
(C) 신발을 더 살 계획이다.
(D) 빠른 배송을 위해 지불했다.

[158-160]

www.raphaelcomputers.com

홈	서비스	추천	예약 요청	연락처

라파엘 컴퓨터 수리점

고객 의견
평가: ★★★★★
서비스 날짜: 8월 7일
서비스 유형: RZ 33 홈 자동화 시스템의 설치

지난주에 저는 제 홈 자동화 시스템을 위한 컴퓨터 단말기에 결함이 있다는 것을 깨달았습니다. -[1]- 라파엘 컴퓨터 수리점의 전단지가 앞문에 붙어 있던 것을 기억하고 그 번호로 전화를 걸었습니다. -[2]- 늦은 오후이고 가게가 기억하지 않아 오전 9시까지 기다려야 할 거라 생각했는데, 주인인 라파엘 씨는 가게 문을 닫은 뒤 곧바로 저의 집에 와주기로 했습니다. 그는 컴퓨터 단말기를 살피고 나서, 업그레이드하거나 수리를 할 수 있다고 했습니다. 몇 년이 지난 컴퓨터이기에 저는 업그레이드하기로 했습니다. 라파엘 씨는 많은 다양한 모델을 시연했고, 저는 저장 용량이 훨씬 더 큰 것으로 결정했습니다. -[3]- 주문과 배달까지 꽤 시간이 걸릴 것으로 생각했지만, 라파엘 씨가 그의 승합차에 하나를 갖고 있어서 그 당일에 설치해 주었습니다. 그의 비자가 시스템이 제대로 작동하는지 확인하기 위해 다음 날 전화를 했습니다. [158] 이 경험은 라파엘 컴퓨터가 수리점에서 보여주는 고객 서비스를 나타내며, 저는 분명히 그의 서비스를 다시 추천할 것입니다. -[4]-

라라 라모스

testimonial 추천서 faulty 결함이 있는 recall 기억하다 leaflet 전단지 post 게시하다 rating 순위, 평가 installation 설치 terminal 단말기 come round to (누구의 집에) 오다, 가다 straight 곧장, 똑바로 demonstrate 시연하다, 보여 주다 memory capacity 기억 용량 bill 청구서, 계산서 out of hours 근무 시간 외에 entire 전체의 present 보이다, 나타내다 extra fee 추가 요금 professional 전문가

158 정보가 웹 사이트에 포함되어 있는 이유는?
(A) 회사의 정책을 설명하기 위해
(B) 설치 과정을 설명하기 위해
(C) 전체 손님을 유치하기 위해
(D) 새 제품을 광고하기 위해

159 라파엘 씨에 관해 언급된 것은?
(A) 라모스 씨와 우편함을 같이 사용한다.
(B) 라모스 씨를 위한 작업을 그녀가 요청한 당일에 완료했다.
(C) 큰 컴퓨터 단말기를 설치하는 데 추가 비용을 청구했다.
(D) 그의 비자가 8월 7일에 라모스 씨에게 연락했다.

160 [1], [2], [3], [4]로 표시된 위치 중 다음 문장이 들어가기 적절한 곳은?

"그는 심지어 근무 시간 외에 한 작업에 대한 추가 청구도 하지 않았습니다."

(A) [1]
(B) [2]
(C) [3]
(D) [4]

[161-164]

전셀 DVD가 이전합니다!

지역에서 가장 많은 비디오와 DVD를 판매하는 것으로 잘 알려진 전셀 DVD가 확장합니다. [161] 저희는 6년 전에 단 하나의 파라마 스트리트 자리에서 시작했고, 이제 블릭스 제과점이 있었던 331 세틀러스 루우로 이전하게 되었습니다. [162] 저희는 계속해서 인화색뿐이 아니라 DVD와 비디오, CD를 판매할 것이지만, 이번어 공간은 전자 게임 시장으로 사업을 성장할 수 있도록 해 줄 것입니다.

파라마 스트리트의 가게는 5월 18일 금요일에 문을 닫을 것이며, 5월 19일 토요일 오전 9시부터 오후 5시까지 새 가게의 개장을 축하하는 파티를 엽니다. 저희의 새 이웃인 퀸진 카페에서 음식을 제공하는 이 행사에 모든 고객들을 초대합니다.

오셔서 새로운 상품을 구경하시고, 퀸진 카페의 맛있는 센두위치와 음료를 맛보세요. 또한 [163] 새로운 독립 영화인 <트레이싱 제임스>까지의 주연 배우, 렌디 글로비 씨가 참석하여 사인을 하고 여러분을 만날 것입니다. [164] 4월 동안 이전 준비를 위해 오래된 재고 일부를 처리할 것입니다. 가장 좋아하는 영화를 할인가로 가격이 언어 갈 수 있는 이 기회를 잡으세요

collection 수집품, 소장품 former 이전의 host 주최하다 cater 음식을 조달하다 present 참석한 indie film 독립 영화 autograph 사인 relocation 재배치, 이전 get rid of ~을 처리하다 seize 잡다 bargain 싸게 사는 물건 amalgamate 합병하다 flyer 전단지 inventory 재고

161 전셀 DVD에 관해 언급된 것은?
(A) 인력을 늘리고 있다.
(B) 블릭스 제과점 옆으로 이사할 것이다.
(C) 퀸진 카페와 유지하기 위해
(D) 6년 동안 영업을 해 왔다.

162 전셀 DVD가 현재 판매하고 있지 않은 것은?
(A) 비디오 게임
(B) 인화책
(C) CD
(D) DVD

메시지 대화 [169-171]

필라 오르테가 오전 8:48
팀원들 안녕하세요. 새로운 이메일 프로그램이 어떻게 작동되고 있는지 알고 싶어서 여러분과 함께 확인해 보려고 합니다. 지금까지 혹시 문제가 있나요?

빈센트 윌리엄스 오전 8:50
저는 좋아요. (169) 메시지가 수신함에 도착하자마자 핸드폰으로 바로 알림이 오니까 제가 고객들에게 더 빨리 응답할 수 있어요.

낸시 도트먼 오전 8:51
제 핸드폰에서는 그게 안 돼요

빈센트 윌리엄스 오전 8:52
핸드폰이 문제가 아니에요. 프로그램 자체의 일환이에요. 그렇게 설정 해 봐요.

낸시 도트먼 오전 8:53
그거 어떻게 할 수 있나요?

빈센트 윌리엄스 오전 8:54
옵션 탭으로 들어가세요. 알림을 설정할 수 있는 부분이 있을 거예요. 거기에서 신규 메시지에 대한 박스에 체크를 누르세요.

낸시 도트먼 오전 8:55
고마워요 전반적으로, 저는 이 프로그램이 고박스보다 더 사용하기 쉽다고 생각해요. 추천해 준 데이빗에게 감사해야 할 것이에요.

이담 폴라 오전 8:59
저는 정부 문서를 업로드하는 데 문제를 겪고 있어요. 누가 도와 줄 수 있나요?

필라 오르테가 오전 9:01
물론이죠. (170) 저도 똑같은 문제를 겪었어요. 그래서 맵테일 기술 연된에게 전화했더니 누군가가 차에게 모든 것을 설명해 줬어요. 어 쩌면 당신엔 고박스랑의 절차가 좀 달라요. (171) 내일 부서 점심 회의 시간에 제가 제까 어떻게 하는지 보여 주면 좋겠요 올 수 있어요?

이담 폴라 오전 9:02
네, 일찍 가도록 할게요. 모든 것을 다 실매불 시간이 있도록요

---

notification 알림 inbox 수신함 overall 전반적으로 attachment 첨부 파일 adjust 조정하다

169 오전 8시 51분에 도트먼지 씨가 "제 핸드폰에서는 그게 안 돼요"라고 했을 때 그 의미는 무엇인가?
(A) 그녀는 핸드폰 설정을 조정하기를 원한다.

---

163 클로제 씨는 누구인가?
(A) 배우
(B) 가게 관리자
(C) 가게 주인
(D) 사진작가

164 진단지에 따르면 4월에 무슨 일이 있을 것인가?
(A) 개장 축하식이 있을 것이다.
(B) 할인이 제공될 것이다.
(C) 공짜 DVD를 나눠줄 것이다.
(D) 새 제고가 배달될 것이다.

[165-168]

165 이 직책의 자격 요건으로 언급된 것은?
(A) 경영학 학위
(B) 자동차 보수에 관한 면밀한 지식
(C) 고객을 다룬 업무 경험
(D) 유효한 운전 면허증

166 지원하기 위해 후보자가 해야 할 일은?
(A) 요청된 문서를 낸 씨에게 보내기
(B) 관리자가 후보를 추천하게 하기
(C) 지원서 작성하기
(D) 2월 11일까지 면접 일정 잡기

167 공자는 어디에서 찾아볼 수 있는가?
(A) 자동차 관련 직종의 공용 데이터베이스
(B) 벤제마 모토 케어 직원에게 보내는 메모
(C) 신문의 채용 공고란
(D) 정비 책임자에게 보내는 편지

168 정비 책임자가 하게 될 업무로 언급되지 않은 것은?
(A) 자동차 제조사와 연락하기
(B) 자동차 결함 진단하기
(C) 자동차 서비스 착수하기
(D) 회사의 고객 명단 갱신하기

[165-168]

벤제마 모토 케어 – 사내 일자리 공고

(167) 이 직책은 이번 달 알까지 내부 직원들에게 열려 있습니다. 그 후, 이 직책은 외부 후보자들에게 광고될 예정입니다.

직악: 정비 책임자

직무 기술:
• 회사의 세 가지 주요 영역인 유지 보수, 수리, 서비스를 더 많은 고객의 차에 제공함으로써 벤제마 모토 케어를 지원
• 모든 유형의 차량에 자동차 안전 검사, 문제 수리, 차량 보수 실시.
• 주요 고객층과 고객 서비스 유지

주요 업무:
• (168) 차량 점검 및 문제 부분 진단
• 엄선된 회사 차량에 컴퓨터 분석 수행
• (168) 복합 수리 시스템을 이용한 세부적인 서비스 준비
• (168) 차 제조사와 정비소 직원의 중간 담당자 역할

자격 요건:
• 차량 유지 보수 분야에 최소 3년간의 경험
• (169) 자동차의 유지 보수에 관한 상세한 이해
• (166) 이 직책에 지원하기 위해서는 이력서와 자기소개서, 추천인 2명의 연락처를 2월 11일까지 정비소 관리자인 케이드 낸에게 knahn@benzema.org로 제출하세요

---

internal 내부의 job posting 일자리 공고 subsequently 그 후에 external 외부의 chief mechanic 정비 책임자 description 설명 MOT 자동차 안전 검사 analytic 분석 clientele 모든 고객 principal 주 된 (주요) duty 업무 diagnose 진단하다 multiple 복합적인 liaison (두 집 단 간의) 연락 담당자 understanding 이해력 cover letter 자기소개서 minimum 최소의 degree 학위 in-depth 상세한 reference 보증인 valid 유효한 supervisor 감독자 liaise 연락하다 undertake 착수하다

169
(B) 그녀는 핸드폰에서 이메일을 확인할 수 없다.
(C) 그녀는 윌리엄스 씨가 알림을 받는다는 것에 놀랐다.
(D) 그녀는 고객의 이메일에 더 빨리 응답하고 싶다.

170 오르타가 씨는 왜 기술 지원부에 연락했는가?
(A) 핸드폰에 알림을 설정하기 위해서
(B) 새로운 이메일 프로그램을 설치하기 위해서
(C) 파일을 첨부하는 방법을 알기 위해서
(D) 고박스 소프트웨어를 업그레이드하기 위해서

171 졸라 씨에 대해서 암시된 것은?
(A) 그는 팔메일을 팀에게 추천할 것이다.
(B) 그는 회의에서 발표를 하게 될 것이다.
(C) 그는 오늘 점심 약속이 있다.
(D) 그는 내일 오르타가 씨로부터 도움을 받게 될 것이다.

[172-175]

3월 30일

최고경영자 던컨 카밀
에런 콜 센터

스프린트 로드 1000
밸링햄, 엘라배마, 미국

카밀 씨에게,

169 템포스 투데이가 임시 직원들을 공급하는 업체로 가장 이름이 알려진 업체 중 하나임을 알려 드리기 위해 편지를 씁니다. 템포스 투데이는 계속해서 같은 이름으로 운영될 것이지만, **172** 일부 기존이 영향을 받을 것입니다. -[1]- **171** 저희의 가장 귀중한 고객 중 한 분이시기 때문에 이번에 이러한 변경 사항들을 개인적으로 알려 드리고자 합니다.

172 임시직 직원의 공급 비용은 대체로 걸릴 것이지만, 콜 센터 직원의 시간 당 급여는 수정되었습니다. -[2]- 새로운 시간 당 급여는 다음과 같습니다.

직원 4명까지 1인당 1시간에 15달러
직원 5~9명 1인당 1시간에 11달러
직원 10~24명 1인당 1시간에 10달러
직원 25~49명 1인당 1시간에 9달러
직원 50명 이상 1인당 1시간에 8달러

새로운 가격 시스템에서 월별 요청하신 인원을 토대로 콜 센터 직원을 공급한 비용을 계산합니다. -[3]- 그러므로 다음 요청에서 2월에 요청했던 같은 인원의 직원을 요청하시면, 가격 면에서 예전 가격보다 단지 50센트가 높지만 가장 낮은 월 요금(1인당 1시간에 8달러)이 청구될 것입니다.

169 WRE 임플로이먼트 사는 또한 숙련된 임시 직원들을 제공합니다. -[4]- 더불어, 저희 웹 사이트는 이제 거래 내역과 개인 기술 저작 요건을 포함해 수많은 편리한 부가 서비스를 제공합니다.

변경 사항에 관한 문의는 주저하지 마시고 저희에게 연락해 주세요. 저희는 계속해서 귀사가 수년간 누리셨던 것과 동급의 질 높은 서비스를 제공할 것입니다. 지속적인 거래에 감사합니다.

일렉시스 찬
템포스 투데이 고객 서비스부 부원장

172 편지의 목적은?
(A) 직원 부족을 보고하기 위해
(B) 새로운 훈련 계획을 발표하기 위해
(C) 새 웹 사이트의 개시 사용하기 위해
(D) 요금 구성의 변경 사항을 설명하기 위해

173 편지에 따르면 WRE 임플로이먼트가 최근에 한 일은?
(A) 다른 회사 인수
(B) 회사의 위치 변경
(C) 새로운 부원장 채용
(D) 엘라배마로 이전

174 카밀 씨는 누구인가?
(A) 콜 센터 임시 직원
(B) WRE 임플로이먼트 사의 사장
(C) 개인 재정 고문
(D) 템포스 투데이의 고객

175 [1], [2], [3], [4]로 표시된 위치 중 다음 문장이 들어가기 적절한 곳은?
"예를 들어, 저희는 그 어떤 행사의 음식 조달도 즉시 제공할 수 있습니다."
(A) [1]
(B) [2]
(C) [3]
(D) [4]

take over (기업 등을) 인수하다 temporary staff 임시 직원 operate 운영하다 valued 귀중한 personally 개인적으로 largely 대체로 hourly rate 시간 급여 operative 전화 직원 revise 수정하다 calculate 계산하다 additional 추가의 skilled 능숙한, 숙련된 at a moment's notice 즉시 numerous 수많은 convenient 편리한 account history 거래 내역 upmarket 고급품의 shortage 부족 scheme 계획, 제도 fee 요금 advisor 고문 accommodation 시설

[176-180]

스페인 별장

●건물: 마드리드 2619 전용 침실 3개가 딸린 도시 주택 최소 4박 더 많은 정보를 원하시면 여기를 클릭해 주세요. ●**180** 건물: 카스티야 4716 침실 2개 아파트 도시 인접이며 현대적인 도시 생활 을 하기에 좋은 입지 더 많은 정보를 원하시면 여기를 클릭해 주세요.	●건물: 이라군 9110 **176** 3년 연속 숙박하고 분주한 일상에서 한적한 안식처로 탈출하고 싶은 이에게 적합 해변 전망 더 많은 정보를 원하시면 여기를 클릭해 주세요. ●건물: 인팔루시아 6130 개인 부두 포함 **179** 1주당 1400달러 더 많은 정보를 원하시면 여기를 클릭해 주세요.

수신: 엘베르토 우에무라(auemura@spholidayrentals.co.esp)
발신: 기얼 인스(jince@ckalltd.co.esp)
날짜: 9월 21일
제목: 건물 4716

안녕하세요 우에무라 씨,

지난여름에 이촌자와 인달루시아로 휴가를 갈 때 당신을 만났고, 당신을 만났을 때 당신을 만났습니다. 이 제공해 준 숙박 시설과 서비스 수준에 매우 만족했습니다. **178** 하지만 목자는 제 취향에는 맞지 않았습니다. 너무 조용했고 외진 곳에 있었습 니다. 그래서 올해에는 마드리드와 카스티야 중 한 곳에 머물고 싶 어요. 2개 이상의 침실이 있습니다. 또한 **177** 일주일에 900~1,000달러 이상을 쓰려고 싶지는 않습니다. **180** 4716 건물에 관심이 있는데, 이용 가능 여부와 세부 사항을 알려 주실 수 있으요? 제가 원하는 것을 찾은 것 같습니다.

답변을 기다리겠습니다.

기얼 인스

176 어느 건물이 무료 1박을 제공하는가?
(A) 2619 건물
(B) **9110 건물**
(C) 4716 건물
(D) 6130 건물

177 인스 씨는 왜 이메일을 보냈는가?
(A) 보증금을 취소하기 위해
(B) 예약에 대한 지불을 하기 위해
(C) **정보를 요청하기 위해**
(D) 여행 조언을 구하기 위해

178 인스 씨는 이전 휴가의 어느 면을 만족스러워하지 않았는가?
(A) 임대한 아파트의 청결
(B) 예약 직원의 제공된 서비스
(C) **근처 지역의 느릿한 생활 페이스**
(D) 임대한 건물로 가는 거리

179 6130 건물은 왜 인스 씨에게 적합하지 않은가? (연계 지문 문제)
(A) 2개 이상의 침실이 있는 숙박 시설을 원한다.
(B) **더 저렴한 것을 찾는다.**
(C) 도시 주택에 머물고 싶어 한다.
(D) 해안으로 여행하고 싶어 하지 않는다.

180 인스 씨가 관심을 가지는 위치는? (연계 지문 문제)
(A) 마드리드
(B) 이라군
(C) **카스티야**
(D) 인달루시아

[181-185]

수신: 전 직원
발신: 인사 부장 안가리도 리스
제목: 설문 조사 피드백
183 날짜: 12월 30일

11월에 **184** 인사부에서는 회사의 여러 분야를 다룬 종합적인 고객 설문 조사를 실시했습니다. 결과를 보면, 대수수의 고객이 고객의 특히 다른 대출 승인 회사와 비교해 보았을 때 전반적으로 서비스에 만족하고 있는 것으로 나 타났습니다. 하지만 개선이 필요한 몇몇 부문이 발견되었습니다.

일반적인 불만은 새 계좌를 처리하는 데 있어 받아들이기 어려울 정도로 시간이 오래 걸린다는 것이었습니다. 현재, 고객 방문 시 첫 대출 과정은 매출 부서의 재정 확인 부서에서 3개의 서명을 필요로 합니다. 그러므로 도이 은행 개좌들 이 0개되기가지 보통 3주가 걸립니다. **182** 이 정 **181** **183** 그러므로 다음 달에 시작되는 1,000달러 미만의 대출 승인 과 정은 선임 대출 담당자부터 1개의 서명만 필요하게 됩니다. **182** 이 정 책으로 진행 시간이 단축될 것이고 고객에게 더 나은 서비스를 제공할 수 있을 것입니다.

문의 사항이 있다면, 주저하지 말고 저에게 연락 주세요.

발신: 알렌 윌러
수신: 인가리도 리스
날짜: 12월 31일
제목: 회람

안녕하세요, 인가리도 씨.

보내 주신 회람을 어제 보았고, 새 제안이 훌륭하다고 생각합니다. **184** 지 히 부서가 설문 조사의 결과를 수렴하고 있었기에, 많은 고객들이 승인을 받기 위해 몇 주를 기다렸다고 말했습니다. 당신의 생각에 덧붙여, 저는 컴퓨터를 통해 서명을 받는 것으로 승인 과정을 더 가속화할 수 있다고 생각합니다. **185** 저희 공급업체 중 하나인 아센트 & 존스는 최근에 대부 분의 거래를 온라인으로 처리할 수 있도록 해 주는 소프트웨어를 설치했 습니다. 저희도 비슷한 시스템을 고려해 보아야 한다고 생각합니다. 제가 한번 조사해 보겠습니다.

알렌

Vocabulary

vacation home 별장 property 건물 부동산; 건물 exclusive 독점적인; 전 용의 consecutive 연속적인 suitable 적합한 pace 속도 haven 안 식처 base 기지, 본거지 vibrant 활기찬 jetty 부두, 둑 fiancé (남자) 약 혼자 be to one's taste 취향에 맞다 remote 외진, 먼 preferably 가 급적이면 access 접근 nightlife 야간 활동 reluctant 꺼리는 meet one's needs ~의 요구를 충족시키다 deposit 보증금 cleanliness 청결 nearby 근처의 coast 해안

carry out 수행하다 comprehensive 포괄적인; 종합적인 questionnaire 설문지 loan approval 대출 승인 improvement 개선 firm 회사 identify 발견하다 unacceptably 받아들이기 어려울 정도로 process 처 리(진행)하다 signature 서명 transfer 시행 옮기다 loan officer 대출 담당 자 hesitate 주저하다 issue 발부하다 compile (여러 출처에서 자료를) 모으다, 편집하다 electronically 전자적으로, 컴퓨터로 handle 취급하다 look into ~을 조사하다 workload 작업량 eliminate 제거하다

181. 리스 씨가 회원에서 발표하는 것은?
(A) 다른 회사와의 합병
(B) 선임 영업 직원을 위한 더 많은 설문 조사
(C) 추가 재무부 직원 고용
(D) 계약 승인을 위한 새로운 절차

182. 회원에 따르면 변화의 목적은?
(A) 대출 담당자의 직업량을 줄이기 위해
(B) 불필요한 지연을 없애기 위해
(C) 조직 내 의사소통을 개선하기 위해
(D) 인력 규모를 확장하기 위해

183. 변화는 언제 시행될 것인가?
(A) 1월
(B) 2월
(D) 11월
(C) 12월

184. 윌러 씨는 어느 부서에서 일하는가? (연계 지문 문제)
(A) 재무부
(B) 영업부
(C) 인사부
(D) 고객 관리부

185. 윌러 씨는 무엇을 추천하는가?
(A) 설문에 참여하는 것
(B) 컴퓨터 소프트웨어 프로그램을 써 보는 것
(C) 고객의 요금을 줄이는 것
(D) 대출 승인 한도를 높이는 것

[186-190]

키 빌딩
190 건물 관리인 일정
9월 1일 – 10월 4일

지역	요일(시간)
186 톰 잭슨	월요일 – 금요일 (오전 9시 30분 – 오후 1시 30분)
일란 친	월요일 – 금요일 (오후 6시 30분 – 오후 10시 30분)
제임스 쿠마	월요일, 수요일, 금요일 (오후 2시 30분 – 오후 8시 30분)
190 로드니 레인하르트	화요일, 목요일 (오후 2시 30분 – 오후 8시 30분) 토요일 (오전 8시 – 오후 2시)

187 만약 할당된 근무시간에 일을 할 수 없다면, 가능한 한 빨리 당신의 상사에게 연락하세요.

수신: **187** 일란 친 (achin@keybuilding.com)
발신: **187** 조 앤더슨 (janderson@keybuilding.com)
날짜: 8월 19일
제목: 일정 변경

일란 씨,

186 187 9월 1일부터 7일까지의 주 동안 당신의 가족이 당신을 방문할 것으로 예상된다고 저에게 알려줘서 고마워요. 톰 씨가 그 주주일 동안 당신의 일정과 바꿔주겠다고 동의했으니, 그 다음 주부터는 9월 넘은 기간 동안 두 분 다 할당된 근무시간으로 다시 돌아가게 될 겁니다.

이 요청된 변경이 **188** 평소의 일이 아니기 때문에 어떤 구체적인 직업이 완료되어야 하는지에 대해서 톰 씨에게 얘기해 주세요. 점겨 있는 방에 당신이 청소하도록 들어 보내 주려면, 보인부서에 연락해야 할지도 몰라요.

추가 질문이 있으면 알려주세요.

감사합니다.

조

새로운 시간 입력 시스템

9월 29일부터 10월 4일이 걸쳐 있는 주부터 모든 키 빌딩 직원들은 시나리오 일지는 새로운 웹 기반의 시간 입력 시스템을 사용할 것이 요구됩니다. 어떤 모바일 장비로도 시나리오에 접속할 수 있기 때문에 직원들은 더 이상 중이로 된 시간표를 제출하기 위해서 인사부로 올 필요가 없을 겁니다. 대신, 직원들은 사용자 이름과 비밀번호로 로그인을 하고 일한 시간을 입력하면 됩니다.

189 직원들에게 시나리오를 사용하는 방법을 보여주기 위해서 데이빗 해리슨 씨가 다음 날짜에 교육 시간을 제공할 겁니다:

보안부서	9월 22일 월요일(오전 10시) – 오전 11시 (30분)
회계부서	9월 23일 화요일(오후 3시) – 오후 4시 30분
190 관리부서	9월 24일 수요일(오후 2시) – 오후 3시 (30분)
행정부서	9월 25일 목요일(오전 8시 30분) – 오전 10시)

직원들은 본인 부서의 예정된 날짜에 교육에 참여할 점으로 예정된 시간에 반드시 교육에 참여해야 합니다.

만약 꿀가능하다면, 다른 시간에 참석을 일정을 점을 수 있도록 내선번호 1212로 헤리슨 씨에게 연락하십시오.

janitor 관리인 assigned 할당된 remainder 나머지 access 접속하다 obtain 얻다

186. 잭슨 씨에 대해서 암시된 것은?
(A) 그는 보통 토요일마다 일한다.
(B) 그의 가족은 키 빌딩에 살고 있다.
(C) 그는 한 달 동안 일정을 바꿀 것이다.
(D) 그는 9월에 주 5일 저녁에 일할 것이다.

187. 앤더슨 씨에 대해서 암시된 것은? (연계 지문 문제)
(A) 그는 시나리오 교육 시간을 이끌 것이다.
(B) 그는 친 씨의 매니저이다.
(C) 그는 일주일을 쉴 것이다.
(D) 그는 키 빌딩을 소유하고 있다.

188. 이메일의 2번째 문단, 1번째 줄에 있는 '평소의'와 가장 비슷한 의미의 단어는?
(A) 할당된
(B) 긴
(C) 훈련된
(D) 보통의

189. 직원들은 왜 교육시간에 참석할 것을 요청받는가?
(A) 그들의 사용자 이름과 비밀번호를 얻기 위해서
(B) 새로운 프로그램을 배우기 위해서
(C) 그들의 인사 관리자를 만나기 위해서
(D) 그들의 시간표를 업데이트하기 위해서

[191-195]

190 테인하르트 씨는 시나지를 사용하기 위한 교육을 어떤 날짜에 받게 될 것인가? (연계 지문 문제)

(A) 9월 22일
(B) 9월 23일
(C) 9월 24일
(D) 9월 25일

피플 무버가 확장합니다!

191 국내에서 가장 빠르게 성장하고 있는 도시간 버스 서비스 업체인 피플 무버가 블룸, 뉴포트, 웨스트벨, 알렌타운 그리고 그레버 시티를 포함해서 19개의 새로운 목적지로 서비스 제공을 시작할 계획입니다. 피플 무버는 4월 15일에 블룸과 뉴포트에서 서비스를 제공하기 시작할 것입니다. **191** 더 작은 도시들로의 서비스는 5월과 6월에 선보일 예정입니다.

확장을 기념하기 위해 저희는 어떤 새로운 목적지로도 오고 갈 수 있는 100장의 왕복 티켓을 나눠줄 예정입니다. 참여하기 위해서 어떠한 구매도 필요하지 않습니다. **192** 단지 저희 웹 사이트 www.peoplemover.com으로 오셔서 양식을 작성해 주시면 됩니다. 참가 신청은 반드시 3월 31일까지 제출되어야 합니다.

참스타운 (6월 3일) - **192** 참스타운 주민들은 도시간 직행버스 서비스의 복구를 거의 3년 동안 기다려 왔다. **191 193** 토요일에 첫 번째 피플 무버 버스가 지금은 폐쇄된 유니온 스트리트 터미널 옆에서 28명의 승객을 태웠을 때 모든 것이 변했다.

"저는 리치몬드에 있는 제 친척들을 보는 것을 고대하고 있어요"라고 똑 기대하며 버스에 탑승한 다니카 베이커 씨가 말했다. 중간이 이래로, 베이커 씨는 그 도시로 가는 내내 시내 버스와 택 라인의 이용에 **192** 내서널 버스 시를 이용해 왔다. "이제 피플 무버가 47로 와서 너무 기뻐요"라고 그녀는 덧붙였다.

193 시장 직무실의 직원들은 올해 말에 시에서 유명한 도시간 버스 터미널을 개조해서 다시 오픈할 예정이라고 말한다. 그동안에 피플 무버는 그 건물 바로 옆에 헬로버스 스트리트에 정차할 것이다. 현재 일정표는 www.peoplemover.com으로 들어가거나 1-888-555-8399로 전화하면 얻을 수 있다.

엘리자베스 루이스
873 히퍼 로드
참스타운
6월 28일

194 루이스 씨에게,

축하합니다! 당신이 선택하는 어떤 목적지라도 피플 무버로 갈 수 있는 티켓에 당첨되셨습니다. 피플 무버에 의해서 서비스가 제공되는 이무 버스 터미널나 이 편지를 가져오시거나, 1-888-555-8789로 전화하시면 티켓을 **195** 요청할 수 있습니다. 티켓은 발행일로부터 12개월간 유효할 것입니다.

당신을 모시게 될 것을 기대하고 있겠습니다.

개런 콜먼
고객 서비스 부장
피플 무버

---

roll out 시작하다 　 round-trip 왕복의 　 simply 그저 　 entry 참가
restoration 복구 　 shuttered 문을 닫은 　 claim 요청하다 　 valid 유효한
acquire 인수하다 　 remarkably 매우 　 inspiration 영감 　 media-
saturated 미디어로 포화된

191 새로운 버스 라인에 대해서 암시된 것은? (연계 지문 문제)

(A) 뉴포트보다 인구가 적다.
(B) 블룸보다 먼저 새로운 버스 서비스를 받았다.
(C) 피플 무버에 의해서 서비스를 제공받는 최초였다.
(D) 더 이상 대중교통이 없다.

192 내서널 버스 라인에 대해서 암시된 것은?

(A) 블룸으로 서비스를 제공했다.
(B) 피플 무버에 의해서 최근에 인수되었다.
(C) 현재 리치몬드로 바깥 지역에서 운영하고 있다.
(D) 3년 전에 폐업했다.

193 참스타운의 지방 자치단체에 대해서 암시된 것은?

(A) 현재 버스 노선을 직접으로 대립으로 하고?
(B) 유니온 스트리트 터미널을 수리할 계획이다.
(C) 택시 서비스를 운영하고 있다.
(D) 피플 무버와의 계약서에 사인했다.

194 루이스 씨에 대해서 사실인 것은 무엇인가? (연계 지문 문제)

(A) 그녀는 피플 무버 콘테스트에 온라인으로 참여했다.
(B) 그녀는 우편으로 티켓을 받았다.
(C) 그녀는 때때로 리치몬드로 여행을 간다.
(D) 그녀는 연말 전에 여행을 갈 것이다.

195 편지의 1번째 문단, 2번째 줄에 있는 '요청하다'와 가장 비슷한 의미인 단어는?

(A) 주장하다
(B) 얻다
(C) 구매하다
(D) 예약하다

[196-200]

수신: 회원분들께
발신: 빈센트 지알스
제목: 다가오는 행사들
날짜: 8월 18일

196 이번 달 초에 있었던 "와일드 엣 하트" 오프닝 행사에 와 주신 모든 분들께 감사드립니다. 청솔하지 못했던 문들을 위해서 이번 순회 회에 전시회는 언제든지 사라디로 ... 100장 이상의 사진들을 특별히 포함합니다. **196** 그의 작품은 내년 2월까지 쪽 뉴베리 박물관에서 전시될 것입니다. **199** "와일드 엣 하트"는 **200** 브라질의 풍경 사진들을 특색으로 합니다. 꼭장히 이름다운 흑백 인물 사진과

사라디고 씨의 특별 강연뿐만 아니라, 누베리 박물관은 9월에 몇몇 웹 사이트를 방문해 주세요, **197** 회원분들은 셋째 주 목요일 행사에 대해서는 입장료를 안 내셔도 됩니다.

---

http://www.newberrymuseum.org

| 전시 | 방문 계획 | 행사 | 회원 |

9월 3일 가족의 날: 오전 10시 - 오후 5시
196 부모와 아이들이 같이 오시면 무료 입장. 아트리움에서 아이들을 위한 미술 공예 활동들

9월 10일 책 사인회: 정오 - 오후 2시
지역 역사가 매니얼 콜튼 씨가 그의 최신 작품 <체이스 모드: 과거와 현재>에 대한 사인회를 엽니다. 그 책은 박물관 기프트숍에서 살 수 있습니다.
(회원 10% 할인)

197 **9월 22일 셋째 주 목요일: 오후 6시 - 오후 9시**
사람들과 어울리고, 갤러리를 거닐고, 어쨌 시즌즈의 라이브 재즈도 즐기세요. 박물관 카페에서 음식과 음료를 구매할 수 있습니다.

198 **9월 25일 특별 행사: 오후 2시 - 오후 4시**
알레한드로 사리고사 씨의 강연에 함께하세요 사리고사 씨는 그의 일생과 작품에 대해서 얘기할 거고, 그의 작품들은 현재 박물관에 전시 중입니다.

영혼이 담긴 사진들, 뉴베리에 오다

(198) 리처드 딘

화가 마누엘 솔라레스 씨는 훌륭한 예술은 영혼을 울린다고 말한 적이 있다. 아마도 그는 언제든지도 사리그씨의 사진을 생각하고 있었던 것 같다. 사리그씨의 사진들은 몹시 아름답다. **(196)** 내가 지난 주말 뉴베리 박물관에 방문했을 때, 사리그씨 씨는 그의 예술에 대한 열정. 여행에 대한 애정. 오늘날 미디어로 포화된 세상에서 예술 작가가 직면한 도전 과제들에 대해서 얘기했다. 설사 당신이 이 강의를 **(200)** 놓쳤다고 해도 지난 10년간 그가 가장 좋아했던 사진들. **(199)** 주로 그의 모국에서 온 사진들의 전시회를 볼 수 있는 시간이 아직 있다. 세부 사항은 www.newberrymuseum.com에서 확인 가능하다.

traveling 순회하는   on display 전시 중인   stunning 굉장히 아름다운
portrait 인물 사진   up-to-date 최신의

196 "외일드 앳 하트"에 대해서 암시되지 않은 것은?
(A) 인물 사진을 특색으로 한다.
(B) 예술가의 강의를 포함한다.
(C) 8월에 오픈했다.
(D) 뉴베리 박물관에 영구적으로 남게 될 것이다.

197 뉴베리 박물관 회원들에게 대해서 암시된 것은? (연계 지문 문제)
(A) 그들은 특별 초대권을 받는다.
(B) 그들은 어슨 사운즈를 무료로 볼 수 있다.
(C) 그들은 기프트샵에서의 모든 구매에 대해서 할인을 받는다.
(D) 그들은 월 회비를 낸다.

198 단씨는 언제 뉴베리 박물관을 방문했을 것 같은가? (연계 지문 문제)
(A) 9월 3일
(B) 9월 10일
(C) 9월 22일
(D) 9월 25일

199 사라고스 씨에 대해서 암시된 것은? (연계 지문 문제)
(A) 그는 5개월 동안 여행을 할 것이다.
(B) 그의 커리어는 10년 전에 시작되었다.
(C) 그는 브라질에서 태어났다.
(D) 그의 작품은 온라인에서 볼 수 있다.

200 기사의 1번째 문단, 8번째 줄에 있는 '놓쳤다'와 가장 비슷한 의미의 단어는?
(A) 늦게 도착했다
(B) 보는 것을 피했다
(C) 참석하지 못했다
(D) 슬픔을 느꼈다

Actual Test

04

🎧 Listening Comprehension

PART 1

1 (B)	2 (A)	3 (C)	4 (B)	5 (A)	6 (D)

PART 2

7 (A)	8 (A)	9 (C)	10 (C)	11 (B)	12 (B)	13 (B)	14 (A)	15 (C)	16 (A)
17 (A)	18 (C)	19 (A)	20 (A)	21 (A)	22 (C)	23 (C)	24 (A)	25 (C)	26 (B)
27 (C)	28 (B)	29 (B)	30 (B)	31 (C)					

PART 3

32 (B)	33 (D)	34 (C)	35 (A)	36 (D)	37 (A)	38 (B)	39 (D)	40 (C)	41 (A)
42 (D)	43 (A)	44 (A)	45 (B)	46 (A)	47 (C)	48 (B)	49 (C)	50 (C)	51 (C)
52 (B)	53 (C)	54 (B)	55 (B)	56 (D)	57 (D)	58 (A)	59 (C)	60 (B)	61 (C)
62 (B)	63 (C)	64 (A)	65 (C)	66 (C)	67 (B)	68 (A)	69 (B)	70 (C)	

PART 4

71 (D)	72 (A)	73 (C)	74 (B)	75 (C)	76 (D)	77 (C)	78 (B)	79 (D)	80 (D)
81 (A)	82 (B)	83 (A)	84 (C)	85 (A)	86 (D)	87 (B)	88 (C)	89 (C)	90 (C)
91 (B)	92 (D)	93 (C)	94 (D)	95 (D)	96 (C)	97 (B)	98 (C)	99 (C)	100 (C)

📖 Reading Comprehension

PART 5

101 (D)	102 (A)	103 (B)	104 (D)	105 (A)	106 (B)	107 (A)	108 (C)	109 (C)	110 (C)
111 (D)	112 (A)	113 (B)	114 (A)	115 (A)	116 (C)	117 (D)	118 (B)	119 (A)	120 (B)
121 (B)	122 (C)	123 (B)	124 (C)	125 (A)	126 (A)	127 (D)	128 (C)	129 (D)	130 (B)

PART 6

131 (D)	132 (B)	133 (C)	134 (A)	135 (B)	136 (B)	137 (C)	138 (C)	139 (D)	140 (C)
141 (A)	142 (C)	143 (A)	144 (D)	145 (C)	146 (D)				

PART 7

147 (B)	148 (B)	149 (C)	150 (A)	151 (B)	152 (B)	153 (C)	154 (C)	155 (B)	156 (A)
157 (C)	158 (B)	159 (C)	160 (A)	161 (D)	162 (B)	163 (C)	164 (D)	165 (C)	166 (D)
167 (D)	168 (B)	169 (B)	170 (C)	171 (A)	172 (B)	173 (B)	174 (A)	175 (B)	176 (C)
177 (C)	178 (B)	179 (D)	180 (B)	181 (A)	182 (B)	183 (A)	184 (C)	185 (B)	186 (C)
187 (A)	188 (D)	189 (C)	190 (B)	191 (C)	192 (D)	193 (D)	194 (B)	195 (A)	196 (D)
197 (C)	198 (B)	199 (B)	200 (C)						

Part 1

본책 P145

1 영M
(A) Some people are entering a restaurant.
(B) A waiter is serving some customers.
(C) A woman is sipping from a glass.
(D) A woman is ordering from a menu.

(A) 몇몇 사람들이 레스토랑에 들어가고 있다.
(B) 웨이터가 손님들에게 음식을 서빙하고 있다.
(C) 여자가 유리잔에서 음료를 마시고 있다.
(D) 여자가 메뉴에서 주문하고 있다.

serve (식당 등에서 음식을) 제공하다 sip (조금씩) 마시다

2 미M
(A) An arched bridge stands over the waterway.
(B) Rowboats are lined up along the edge of the water.
(C) A staircase reaches to the doorway.
(D) Some people are sitting on a seashore.

(A) 아치형 다리가 수로 위로 서 있다.
(B) 노 젓는 보트가 가장자리를 따라 정렬되어 있다.
(C) 계단이 출입구까지 닿아 있다.
(D) 몇몇 사람들이 해변가에 앉아 있다.

arched bridge 아치형 다리 waterway 수로 rowboats (노로 젓는) 보트 line up 줄을 서다 edge 가장자리, 모서리 staircase 계단 doorway 출입구 seashore 해변가

3 미W
(A) The man is lifting a tray.
(B) The man is holding a plate of food.
(C) Some food is being prepared on a stove.
(D) Some kitchen utensils are being washed.

(A) 남자가 쟁반을 들고 있다.
(B) 남자가 음식 한 접시를 들고 있다.
(C) 일부 음식이 스토브 위에서 준비되고 있다.
(D) 몇몇 부엌 조리기구가 씻기고 있다.

lift 들어 올리다 tray 쟁반 plate 접시 stove 가스난로, 스토브 kitchen utensil 주방용구, 부엌용 조리기구

4 호M
(A) A woman is arranging bags in the window display.
(B) A woman is pointing at some merchandise.
(C) They are looking at themselves in a mirror.
(D) Some items are hanging near the bulletin board.

(A) 여자가 창가 진열장 안의 가방을 정리하고 있다.
(B) 여자가 상품을 손가락으로 가리키고 있다.
(C) 사람들이 거울에 비친 자신들의 모습을 보고 있다.
(D) 몇몇 물건들이 게시판 가까이에 걸려 있다.

window display 창가 진열 point at ~을 향해 손가락을 가리키다 merchandise 상품 bulletin board 게시판

5 영M
(A) The woman is using a sponge to wipe off a plate.
(B) The woman is putting the dishes in the sink.
(C) Some dishes are being passed in a kitchen.
(D) Some water is being poured from the pitcher.

(A) 여자가 접시를 닦는 데 스펀지를 사용하고 있다.
(B) 여자가 접시를 싱크대에 놓고 있다.
(C) 몇몇 접시들이 부엌에서 건네지고 있다.
(D) 물이 물주전자에서 따라지고 있다.

wipe 닦다 sink 싱크대 pitcher 물주전자

6 미W
(A) Lines are being painted on the road.
(B) There is a big house at the top of the hill.
(C) Vehicles are parked in a row on the sand.
(D) Pointed roofs are visible in the distance.

(A) 도로 위에 선이 칠해지고 있다.
(B) 언덕 꼭대기에 큰 집이 한 채 있다.
(C) 차들이 모래사장 위에 한 줄로 주차되어 있다.
(D) 멀리에 뾰족한 지붕이 보인다.

vehicle 차 in a row 한 줄로 pointed 뾰족한, 뾰족한 visible 보이는, 눈에 띄는 in the distance 멀리에, 먼 곳에

Part 2

본책 P148

7 미M / 미W
Do you need your oil changed?
(A) Yes, please.
(B) I'm a little bit exhausted.
(C) No, they haven't yet.

엔진 오일 교환이 필요한가요?
(A) 네, 해 주세요.
(B) 저는 조금 지쳤습니다.
(C) 아니요, 그들은 아직 안 했어요.

oil change (자동차의) 엔진 오일 교환 exhausted 기진맥진한, 진이 다 빠진 just 막, 방금

8 미W / 미M
How much are two tickets to the game?
(A) About 30 dollars, I think.
(B) I just heard about that.
(C) At 5:30.

경기 입장권 두 장은 얼마인가요?
(A) 30달러 정도 될 거예요.
(B) 그것에 관해 방금 들었어요.
(C) 5시 30분예요.

9 미M / 미W
When are the guests coming?
(A) At the local airport.
(B) A very tight schedule.
(C) Tomorrow at midday.

손님들은 언제 오나요?
(A) 현지 공항에요.
(B) 매우 빡빡한 일정이에요.
(C) 내일 정오에요.

tight (일정 등이) 빡빡한, 꽉 찬 midday 정오, 한낮

10 미M / 영M
Who's the manager in your department?
(A) They are in a meeting right now.
(B) That's a brilliant idea.
(C) It's Mr. Omata.

당신 부서의 관리자는 누구인가요?
(A) 그들은 지금 회의 중입니다.
(B) 멋진 생각입니다.
(C) 오마타 씨입니다.

manager 과장; 관리자 brilliant 훌륭한, 멋진

11 미W / 미M
Would you rather work the weekend or the weekday shift?
(A) We're going after training.
(B) Weekend is the best.
(C) 30 minute breaks.

당신은 주말 교대조 아니면 평일 교대조로 일하길 원하나요?
(A) 우리는 교육 후에 갑니다.
(B) 주말이 가장 좋습니다.
(C) 30분 휴식이요.

weekday 평일 shift 교대조; 교대 근무 (시간) break (짧은) 휴식

12 영M / 미W
Have you visited the new annex yet?
(A) No, it's on Birch Street.
(B) I haven't had a chance.
(C) That book was fascinating.

새로운 별관을 아직 방문해 보지 못했나요?
(A) 아니요, 버치 가에 있어요.
(B) 기회가 없었습니다.

(C) In the top drawer.
어느 곳이 데이브의 자리인가요?
(A) 그는 여기에 앉습니다.
(B) 온라인에서 하나 보았습니다.
(C) 맨 위 서랍에요.
workstation 사무실에서 근로자 한 사람에게 주어지는 직업 장소

22 Shouldn't the food have been delivered by now?
음식이 지금쯤이면 배달되었어야 하지 않나요?
(A) The delivery man did.
(B) Actually, I'm not very hungry.
(C) Yes, it's usually here by noon.
(A) 배달부가 그랬어요.
(B) 사실, 저는 별이 배고프진 않습니다.
(C) 네, 보통 정오에 이곳에 오던데요.
delivery man 배달부

23 Why don't we evaluate the formula again?
그 공식을 한 번 더 평가해 보는 건 어때요?
(A) No, he didn't.
(B) It probably will.
(C) That sounds like an excellent idea.
(A) 아니요, 그는 그렇게 하지 않았어요.
(B) 아마 그럴 거예요.
(C) 훌륭한 생각인 것 같아요.
evaluate 평가하다 formula 공식

24 These new cafeteria seats are comfortable.
이 새로운 구내식당의 좌석들은 편안하네요.
(A) I prefer the old ones.
(B) A really low price.
(C) It's on Mark Turner's chair.
(A) 이전 것이 더 좋아요.
(B) 매우 낮은 가격이요.
(C) 마크 터너의 의자 위에 있습니다.
cafeteria 구내식당

25 Are you going away for the weekend or staying at home?
당신은 주말여행을 떠날 건가요, 아니면 집에 있을 건가요?
(A) At the end of the week.
(B) Please rest a while.
(C) I'm travelling to Brisbane.

(C) 그 책은 매우 흥미진진했어요.
annex 별관, 부속 건물 fascinating 매우 흥미로운, 매력적인

13 Where is that large vessel going?
저 큰 선박은 어디로 가고 있나요?
(A) They should be here soon.
(B) On a fishing trip.
(C) The coat's too large.
(A) 그들이 곧 올 겁니다.
(B) 낚시 여행이요.
(C) 그 코트는 너무 커요.
vessel (대형) 선박, 배

14 Emma made the lunch booking, right?
엠마가 점심 예약을 했어요, 그렇죠?
(A) Yes, she called yesterday.
(B) I haven't seen his schedule.
(C) Actually, it's at the end.
(A) 네, 그녀가 어제 전화했어요.
(B) 아직 그의 일정을 못 봤어요.
(C) 사실, 그건 끝에 있어요.
booking 예약

15 Will you be on sick leave all week?
당신은 일주일 내내 병가 중일 건가요?
(A) A round trip tour.
(B) Medication is included.
(C) No, I'll be in the office.
(A) 왕복 여행이요.
(B) 약물 치료가 포함됩니다.
(C) 아니요, 사무실에 있을 거예요.
be on sick leave 병가 중이다 round trip 왕복 여행 medication 약(물) (치료)

16 Have you considered hiring a freelance supplier?
프리랜서 공급자 채용을 고려해 보셨어요?
(A) I've been meaning to.
(B) Just a little lower.
(C) Yes, two or three business days.
(A) 네, 그럴 셈이었습니다.
(B) 조금만 더 낮게요.
(C) 네, 2일이나 3일의 영업일이요.
freelance 프리랜서로 일하는 supplier 공급자, 공급업체 mean to ~할 셈이다 business days 영업일, 평일

---

17 Why did the restaurant close so early?
그 레스토랑은 왜 이리 일찍 문을 닫았어요?
(A) To prepare for a banquet.
(B) Because it's not far away.
(C) Well, he is normally late.
(A) 연회를 준비하기 위해서요.
(B) 멀리 있지 않아서요.
(C) 글쎄요, 그는 평상시 늦습니다.
banquet 연회, 만찬 far away 멀리 normally 평상시, 보통

18 How was your trip to Atlanta?
애틀랜타 여행은 어땠어요?
(A) He arrives on Monday.
(B) I left it on the plane.
(C) The weather was fantastic.
(A) 그는 월요일에 도착합니다.
(B) 비행기에 놓아두었습니다.
(C) 날씨가 매우 좋았습니다.
leave 놓아두다 fantastic 기막히게 좋은, 환상적인

19 Why wasn't Ajmal at the training session?
아즈말은 왜 교육 시간에 없었나요?
(A) He had a scheduling conflict.
(B) A new staff member told us.
(C) In section 4.
(A) 그는 일정이 겹쳤어요.
(B) 신입 직원이 우리에게 얘기했어요.
(C) 4번 구역에요.
conflict 갈등, 충돌 section 부분, 구획, 구역

20 Who's doing the math seminar today?
누가 오늘 수학 세미나를 맡고 있나요?
(A) A guest lecturer.
(B) In the lobby.
(C) No, he is not available.
(A) 초청 강사요.
(B) 복도에서요.
(C) 아니요, 그는 시간이 가능하지 않습니다.
guest lecturer 초청 강사 lobby 복도

21 Which workstation is Dave's?
(A) He sits here.
(B) I saw one online.

Part 3

Questions 32-34 refer to the following conversation. 영M 미W

M Hello, my friends and I are camping in this area, so I'm here to check out some local attractions. I'm most interested in activities that would appeal to teenagers.

W Well, ㉝ the River Yeo is close and they organize numerous water sports for young adults. It also has a white water rafting course suitable for teenagers.

M That sounds like just what we want. Can you give me directions to the river?

W Yes, of course. ㉜ ㉞ Here's a brochure listing various summer activities in the surrounding region.

남 안녕하세요, 제 친구들과 저는 이 지역에 캠핑을 와서 일부 지역 명소들을 살펴보러 여기에 와 있습니다. 저는 십 대들에게 매력적인 활동에 가장 관심이 있어요.

여 음, 여 강이 가까이 있고 그곳은 청소년들을 위한 많은 수상 스포츠를 준비합니다. 또한, 십 대들에게 적합한 급류 타기 강좌도 있습니다.

남 저희가 딱 원했던 것 같은데요. 강으로 가는 방향을 알려 주실 수 있나요?

여 네, 물론이죠. 주변 지역 내 다양한 여름 활동이 열거된 책자가 있습니다.

camping 캠핑, 야영　check out 확인하다, 살펴보다　local attraction 지역 명소　appeal to ~에 호소하다　young adult 청소년　white water rafting 급류 타기　suitable 적합한　give directions 길을 가르쳐 주다　list 열거하다　surrounding 주위의, 인근의　brochure 책자　booklet 소책자　general store 잡화점

32 Where is the conversation most likely taking place?
(A) At an outdoor concert
(B) At a tourist information office
(C) At a riverside
(D) At a general store

대화는 어디에서 일어나고 있을 것 같은가?
(A) 야외 콘서트장
(B) 관광 정보 센터
(C) 강가
(D) 잡화점

(A) 이번 주말이요.
(B) 담분간 쉬세요.
(C) 브리즈번으로 여행 갑니다.
go away for the weekend 주말여행을 떠나다　a while 잠시, 잠깐

26 Would you like me to email you a meeting reminder?
미W (A) In the newspaper.
영M (B) No, I'll remember without one.
(C) Very upsetting.

제가 회의 알림용 이메일을 보내 주길 원하나요?
(A) 신문에요.
(B) 아니요, 그것 없이도 기억할 것입니다.
(C) 매우 속상하게 해네요.
reminder 상기시키는 것, 상기시켜 주는 편지나 메모　upsetting 속상하게 하는

27 Didn't you sign the treaty?
미M (A) Sure, I will call him.
영M (B) You're welcome to join us.
(C) It hasn't been completed.

조약에 서명하지 않았나요?
(A) 그럼요, 제가 그에게 전화할게요.
(B) 우리와 함께해도 됩니다.
(C) 그건 아직 완료되지 않았어요.
treaty 조약　welcome to ~을 자유로이 할 수 있는

28 Alan did a good job with that negotiation.
영M (A) The job's still open.
미W (B) Yes, I was impressed, too.
(C) When will that happen?

앨런은 그 협상을 잘 해냈어요.
(A) 그 일자리는 아직 공석이에요.
(B) 네, 저도 매우 감명받었어요.
(C) 그게 언제 일어날 건가요?
do a good job 잘하다　negotiation 협상　open (일자리가) 비어 있다　impressed 감명(감동)을 받은

29 How about getting a drink before the match?
미W (A) The parking is expensive.
미M (B) Do we have time?
(C) Their latest game.

시합 전에 한잔하는 건 어때요?
(A) 주차는 비쌉니다.
(B) 우리 시간이 있나요?
(C) 그들의 최근 경기요.
match 시합, 경기　latest 최신의, 최근의

30 Do you think the head of department made the wrong decision?
영M (A) I don't know whether he attends the meeting.
미W (B) It's too soon to tell.
(C) They already have.

당신은 그 부서장이 옳지 않은 결정을 내렸다고 생각하세요?
(A) 그가 회의에 참석하는지는 모르겠어요.
(B) 아직 말하기는 일러요.
(C) 그들은 이미 했어요.
head of department 부서장　make a decision 결정을 내리다

31 What's Martina planning to do with her apartment when she relocates to Madrid?
미M (A) She's having a clearance sale here.
미W (B) Maybe she's going to go at once.
(C) She's trying to rent it out.

마티나는 마드리드로 이사할 때, 그녀의 아파트를 어떻게 할 계획인가요?
(A) 그녀가 여기에서 재고정리 세일을 할 거예요.
(B) 이마 그녀는 바로 갈 거예요.
(C) 임대하려 해요.
relocate 이전하다, 이사하다　clearance sale 재고정리 세일　at once 즉시, 바로　rent out 임대하다

33 What does the woman recommend?
(A) Walking along the hillside
(B) Swimming in the local pool
(C) Exploring the environment
(D) Experiencing water sport activities

여자는 무엇을 추천하는가?
(A) 산비탈 산책
(B) 지역 수영장에서 수영
(C) 환경 탐험
(D) **수상 스포츠 활동 경험**

34 What does the woman give the man?
(A) An invoice
(B) A map
(C) A booklet
(D) A ticket

여자가 남자에게 주는 것은?
(A) 송장
(B) 지도
(C) **소책자**
(D) 티켓

Questions 35-37 refer to the following conversation. 미W 미M

W Mr. Hunt, this is Tanya Bouchon from Skylight TV. I'm calling to tell you that ㉟ ㊱ we'd like to accept your film script about your whale watching experiences in Alaska.

M That's fantastic news. I've been a supporter of your nature programs for many years. You featured some of my favorite locations. So I was eager for you to realize my script would fit into your programming.

W We do think it's a relevant idea. In fact, ㊲ I'd like to arrange a meeting with you to discuss a series of programs about whale activity in other locations. There's great interest in this topic right now.

script 대본 whale watching 고래 관찰 supporter 지지자, 후원자 feature 특징으로 다루다 be eager for ~을 갈망하다 fit into ~에 꼭 들어맞다 relevant 관련 있는, 적절한 come along 도착하다, 함께 오다 a series of 일련의 Alaskan 알래스카의, 알래스카 사람 film rights 상영권

35 What did the man write about?
(A) His unique tours
(B) Working with Alaskans
(C) His favorite TV film
(D) Writing for television

남자는 무엇에 관해 글을 썼는가?
(A) **그의 독특한 투어**
(B) 알래스카인들과의 업무
(C) 그가 가장 좋아하는 TV 영화
(D) 텔레비전용 글

36 Why is the man pleased?
(A) He was offered a job in Alaska.
(B) His idea will be published.
(C) His television will be replaced.
(D) His script has been accepted.

남자가 기뻐하는 이유는?
(A) 알래스카의 일자리를 제안받았다.
(B) 그의 생각이 출판될 것이다.
(C) 그의 텔레비전이 교체될 것이다.
(D) **그의 대본이 받아들여졌다.**

37 Why does the woman want to meet with the man?
(A) To talk about some programs
(B) To perform an audition
(C) To take part in a documentary
(D) To discuss film rights

여자가 남자를 만나고 싶어 하는 이유는?
(A) **몇몇 프로그램들에 대해 이야기하기 위해**
(B) 오디션을 하기 위해
(C) 다큐멘터리에 참여하기 위해
(D) 상영권을 논의하기 위해

Questions 38-40 refer to the following conversation with three speakers. 미W 영M 영W

W1 Hi, Mike and Helen. I am glad I caught you two! Do you happen to know where Jorge might be?

M Unfortunately, I don't. Is there anything you need from him? ㊳ I can call him on his mobile phone if you'd like.

W1 ㊵ Yeah, apparently there's a problem with the printers on the third floor.

M You know, Haley in our office is pretty good at office equipment.

W2 I fix all the machines on my floor. Would you like me to take a look at it right now?

여1 안녕하세요, 마이크, 헬렌. 두 분을 만나게 되어서 다행이네요. 혹시 호르헤가 어디에 있는지 알고 계신가요?

남 안타깝지만, 저는 모르겠네요. 그로부터 뭐 필요한 것이 있나요? 원하시면 휴대폰으로 전화해 볼게요.

여1 네, 사실 3층에 있는 프린터기에 문제가 생겨서요.

남 우리 사무실의 헤일리가 사무실 장비를 꽤 잘 다뤄요.

여2 제가 근무하는 층에 있는 종이 기계들은 제가 다 수리하고 있어요. 제가 고장난 3층 프린터기를 지금 봐 드릴까요?

happen to 우연히 ~하다 apparently 명백히, 보아하니

38 What does the man offer to do?
(A) Replace an old machine
(B) Call a coworker
(C) Email an acquaintance
(D) Look up the schedule

남자는 무엇을 해주겠다고 하는가?
(A) 오래된 기계를 교체한다.
(B) **동료에게 전화한다.**
(C) 지인에게 이메일을 보낸다.
(D) 스케줄을 자세히 살펴본다.

39 Why is Jorge needed?
(A) To install a program
(B) To make photocopies
(C) To call technical support
(D) To make some repairs

호르헤는 왜 필요한가?
(A) 프로그램을 설치하기 위해
(B) 복사하기 위해
(C) 기술 지원부에 전화하기 위해
(D) 수리하기 위해

40 Why does the man say, "Haley in our office is pretty good at office equipment"?
(A) To revise some schedule
(B) To recommend Haley for a promotion
(C) To suggest that Haley help with some machines
(D) To propose using another piece of equipment

왜 남자는 "우리 사무실의 할리 씨가 사무실 장비를 꽤 잘 다뤄요"라고 말했는가?
(A) 일정을 변경하기 위해
(B) 할리를 승진에 추천하기 위해
(C) 할리가 기계에 관한 도움을 주는 것을 제안하기 위해
(D) 다른 장비를 사용하는 것을 제안하기 위해

Questions 41-43 refer to the following conversation. [영M] [미W]

M I understand ㊶ you attended the conference for computer updates yesterday. Can I ask you to prepare a short presentation for our new apprentices?

W Sorry, but I'm not much of a public speaker. How about I write up what I learnt from the conference and ㊷ give you the information so you can get someone else to do the presentation?

M Well, why don't I just ask you about the latest updates? Then I'll be able to prepare a presentation myself for tomorrow. ㊸ When are you available today?

W OK. That sounds like a good plan. ㊸ Let's meet later over coffee.

남 저는 당신이 어제 있었던 컴퓨터 업데이트 회의에 참석했다고 알고 있어요. 저희 견습생들을 위해 짧은 발표를 준비해 주실 것을 부탁해도 될까요?

여 죄송합니다. 하지만 저는 좋은 연설자가 아닙니다. 제가 회의에서 배운 것을 적고 당신이 다른 사람에게 발표를 시킬 수 있도록 그 정보를 주는 건 어떤가요?

남 음, 그냥 제가 최신 업데이트에 대해 물어보는 건 어때요? 그러면 저 스스로 내일 할 발표를 준비할 수 있을 거예요. 오늘 언제 시간이 가능하세요?

여 좋아요. 좋은 계획 같네요. 이따 커피를 마시며 봅시다.

apprentice 견습생 ~ write up ~을 완전히 작성하다 public speaker 연설자 meet over coffee 커피를 마시면서 만나다 external 외부의 adjust 조정하다, 조절하다 layout 레이아웃, 배치

41 What event has the woman recently attended?
(A) A computer seminar
(B) A fund-raising lunch
(C) A presentation
(D) A writing conference

여자가 최근에 참석한 행사는?
(A) 컴퓨터 세미나
(B) 모금 활동 점심
(C) 발표
(D) 집필 회의

---

42 What alternative does the woman suggest?
(A) Hiring an external consultant
(B) Producing an updated memo
(C) Adjusting the layout of a brochure
(D) Getting someone else to prepare a presentation

여자가 제안하는 대안은?
(A) 외부의 자문 위원 고용
(B) 업데이트된 메모 작성
(C) 책자의 배치 조정
(D) 다른 사람에게 발표 준비시키기

43 What do the speakers agree to do?
(A) Meet today
(B) Talk with a manager
(C) Arrange a date
(D) Present a paper

화자는 무엇을 하겠다고 동의하는가?
(A) 오늘 만나기
(B) 관리자와 대화하기
(C) 날짜 정하기
(D) 문서 제출하기

Questions 44-46 refer to the following conversation. [미W] [미M]

W Hi, ㊹ I'm calling because I'm painting my garden furniture and I've been searching for the right coating to protect the furniture from bad weather. Would you be able to give me some suggestions?

M Yes, we have a technical department available to advise you. Which brand of coating do you prefer?

W ㊺ I'd like to see a sample of the metallic color product I saw in your brochure. I think it's coating number 5.

M Okay, and if you like what we send you, ㊻ you can fill in an order form which is available on the Web site when you've made a decision of what you want to purchase.

Questions 47-49 refer to the following conversation. 미W 영M

W I'm glad I ran into you. ⑰ How is the accounting class going for you?

M It's now progressing quite fast ⑱ since we've learned all of the basic skills.

W Good luck with that! It should give you a lot of good practice.

M Definitely. ⑲ We're going to take part in a project where we can show off our skills. Our teacher is going to use this project as a way to evaluate us.

W Is accounting easy to learn?

M There's an open house where we'll demonstrate what we're learning if you're interested.

W I think I'll go to that. Thanks for the tip!

여 이렇게 보게 되어서 다행이네요. 회계 수업은 어때요?

남 수업은 이제 아주 빠르게 진행되고 있어요. 우리가 기본적인 기술은 모두 배웠거든요.

여 잘 되었네요! 그 수업이 충분히 좋은 연습이 되겠어요.

남 물론이죠. 우리는 우리 기술들을 보여줄 수 있는 프로젝트에 참가하게 될 거예요. 우리 선생님이 그 프로젝트를 우리의 평가 기준으로 사용하실 거예요.

여 회계가 배우기 쉬운가요?

남 관심이 있으시다면, 우리가 함께 배우고 있는 것을 설명하는 공개 강좌가 있다는 것을 알려 드리고 싶어요.

여 거기 가봐야겠어요. 정보 감사합니다!

47 What did the man do recently?
(A) He set up a new establishment.
(B) He developed new software.
(C) He signed up for a course.
(D) He demonstrated a new product.

남자는 최근에 무엇을 했는가?
(A) 새로운 업체를 설립했다.
(B) 새로운 소프트웨어를 개발했다.
(C) 수업에 등록했다.
(D) 새로운 제품을 시연했다.

48 What does the man mean when he says, "It's now progressing quite fast"?
(A) He has become busy recently.
(B) The class is picking up speed.
(C) He thinks the course is easy.
(D) The class is very difficult to follow.

남자는 "수업은 이제 아주 빠르게 진행되고 있어요"라고 말했을 때 무엇을 의미했는가?
(A) 남자는 최근에 많이 바빠졌다.
(B) 수업이 속도를 내고 있다.
(C) 남자는 수업이 쉽다고 생각한다.
(D) 수업이 따라가기 어렵다.

49 What is the man going to participate in?
(A) An upcoming lecture
(B) His favorite show
(C) A project
(D) A professional workshop

남자는 무엇에 참여하겠는가?
(A) 향후 있을 강연
(B) 그가 가장 좋아하는 공연
(C) 프로젝트
(D) 전문 워크숍

여 안녕하세요, 제 정원용 가구를 페인트 칠하려고 하는데, 야외용으로 보호할 코팅을 찾고 있어서 전화 드렸어요. 의견을 좀 주실 수 있나요?

남 네, 저희에게 조언을 드릴 수 있는 기술 부서가 있습니다. 어떤 브랜드의 코팅을 원하시나요?

여 당신의 책자에서 보았던 금속 색상의 전문을 보고 싶네요. 코팅 5번이었던 것 같은데요.

남 알겠습니다. 그리고 저희가 보낸 것이 마음에 드시면, 어떤 것을 구입하실지 결정하셨을 때 저희 웹 사이트에서 기능한 물품으로 주문서를 작성해 주시면 됩니다.

44 Who most likely is the woman contacting?
(A) A paint supplier
(B) A clothing designer
(C) A garden expert
(D) A furniture manufacturer

여자는 누구에게 연락을 하고 있는 것 같은가?
(A) 페인트 공급업체
(B) 의상 디자이너
(C) 전문 정원사
(D) 가구 제조업자

45 What does the woman want to do?
(A) Select a decorator
(B) See a product sample
(C) Speak to a designer
(D) Receive an estimate

여자는 무엇을 하고 싶어 하는가?
(A) 도배업자 선택하기
(B) 제품 견본 확인하기
(C) 디자이너와 대화하기
(D) 견적서 받기

46 According to the man, how can the woman place a future order?
(A) By completing an online form
(B) By calling directly
(C) By sending an e-mail
(D) By mailing a request

남자에 따르면, 여자는 추후에 어떻게 주문을 할 수 있는가?
(A) 온라인 주문서를 작성함으로써
(B) 직접 전화함으로써
(C) 이메일을 보냄으로써
(D) 우편으로 요청을 보냄으로써

Questions 50-52 refer to the following conversation. 미M 미W

M Hi, Louisa. Is everything prepared for when the guests arrive?

W Yes, I've double checked and everything's going as planned. 50 The guests will arrive by 12:30 as scheduled so you can set the table at 1.

M Excellent! The dining hall is all prepared for me to serve the new healthy menu. Oh, 51 are this evening's drinks reception ready? I also need to prepare some food.

W Yes, I was able to contact a supplier that will provide the champagne you requested. 52 I just have to contact them to confirm the delivery time.

Questions 53-55 refer to the following conversation. 영M 미W

M I met with 53 a possible buyer for Bill's Automobile Center yesterday. She is a business owner who manages similar garages in the town and she wants to expand her business.

W Well, we have had that business on sale for a long time now. Other interested parties said that the location was too remote. I know 54 the owner, Mr. Graston is becoming worried about his rising debts.

M You are right. This must be the perfect time to 55 suggest to Mr. Graston that he reduce the selling price of the business.

남 인녕하세요, 루이사. 손님들이 도착할 때를 위해 모든 것이 준비되었나요?

여 네, 두 번 확인했고, 모든 것이 계획한 대로 진행되고 있어요. 손님들은 예정대로 12시 30분에 도착할 테니, 당신은 1시에 식사를 준비해 주시면 됩니다.

남 훌륭해요! 식당은 제가 새롭고 건강한 메뉴를 제공할 수 있도록 모두 준비되어 있어요. 아, 저녁에 있을 음료 연회를 위한 준비는 다 되었나요? 저도 음식 준비를 좀 해야 하거든요.

여 네, 당신이 요청한 샴페인을 제공할 공급업체에 연락할 수 있었어요. 배달 시간을 확인하기 위해 그들에게 연락만 하면 됩니다.

double check 두 번 점검하다 as scheduled 예정대로, 계획대로 dining hall 식당 reception 연회 supplier 공급업체 champagne 샴페인 applicant 지원자 enthusiast 열광적인 팬 luncheon 오찬 merchandise 물품, 상품

---

50 Who are the speakers expecting?
(A) Business customers
(B) Job applicants
(C) Health enthusiasts
(D) Luncheon guests

화자들은 누구를 기다리는가?
(A) 비즈니스 손님들
(B) 취업 지원자들
(C) 건강 애호가들
(D) 오찬 손님들

---

51 What will the man do later this evening?
(A) Present some merchandise
(B) Give a tour of the hotel
(C) Organize a party
(D) Change a schedule

남자는 오늘 저녁에 무엇을 할 것인가?
(A) 일부 상품 보여 주기
(B) 호텔 구경시켜 주기
(C) 파티 준비하기
(D) 일정 변경하기

---

52 What does the woman say she needs to do?
(A) Contact a supplier
(B) Meet the guests
(C) Prepare a menu
(D) Call a colleague

여자는 무엇을 해야 한다고 말하는가?
(A) 공급업체에 연락하기
(B) 손님들 만나기
(C) 메뉴 준비하기
(D) 동료에게 전화하기

남 저는 어제 빌즈 자동차 센터를 살 가능성이 있는 분을 만났어요. 그녀는 마을 내에 비슷한 카센터를 운영하는 가게 주인이고, 자신의 사업을 확장하고 싶어 하거든요.

여 음, 우리는 그 사업을 꽤 오랜 시간 동안 시장에 내 놓았어요. 관심 있어 한 다른 사람들은 위치가 너무 외졌다고 했어요. 그 소유주인 그라스톤 씨가 늘어나는 빚에 대해 걱정하고 제가 알고 있습니다.

남 맞습니다. 이것이 아마도 그라스톤 씨에게 그 사업체의 판매가를 낮추라고 제안할 완벽한 타이밍이네요.

possible buyer 잠재 구매자 automobile 자동차 garage 카센터, 차고 business owner 사업 소유주 interested party 관심자, 이해 당사자 remote 외진, 먼 potentially 잠재적으로, 어쩌면 selling price 판매가 property 재산 reluctant to ~을 주저하는 mount 서서히 증가하다 expire 만료되다 inspection 시찰, 점검 take out a loan 대출하다

---

53 What are the speakers discussing?
(A) A commercial property sale
(B) A building program
(C) Travel schedules
(D) Financial matters

화자들은 무엇에 관해 이야기하는가?
(A) 상업적인 자산 매각
(B) 건축 프로그램
(C) 여행 일정
(D) 재정 문제

---

54 What does the woman mention about Mr. Graston?
(A) He is reluctant to sell.
(B) His debts are mounting.

Questions 56-58 refer to the following conversation. 미M 미W

M Hi, Naomi. I was just told that ⑤⑥ my get-together with our German counterparts has been rearranged, so I have to travel there earlier than expected. Could you please give me your proposal for the campaign I'll be discussing with them in Hamburg? I need to receive it in two hours.

W I'm sorry, but regrettably ⑤⑦ I'll be at the hospital all morning. But I can work on it when I return and email you all the information in time for the meeting.

M That would be good. It's a long drive, so ⑤⑧ you have plenty of time to get it to me before I arrive.

남 안녕하세요, 나오미. 저는 독일 쪽 담당자와의 모임이 재조정되었다고 들어서 예상보다 일찍 그곳으로 가야 해요. 함부르크에서 그들과 함께 이논할 당신의 캠페인 제안서를 주시겠어요? 두 시간 이내로 받아야 해요.

여 죄송하지만 안타깝게도 저는 오전 내내 병원에 있을 거예요. 하지만 돌아오면 작업할 수 있고, 회의 시간에 맞춰 모든 정보를 당신에게 이메일로 보낼 수 있습니다.

남 그러면 되겠네요. 오랜 시간 동안 운전할 테니, 제가 도착하기 전에 보내기까지 충분한 시간이 있겠네요.

get-together 모임 counterpart 상대 rearrange 재조정하다 earlier than expected 예상보다 일찍 proposal 제안서 regrettably 안타깝게 도 terms 조건

56 According to the man, what has changed?
(A) A travel plan
(B) The availability of a client
(C) The terms of a contract
(D) A meeting time

남자에 따르면, 무엇이 변했는가?
(A) 여행 계획
(B) 고객의 가능한 시간
(C) 계약 조항
(D) 회의 시간

57 What problem does the woman mention?
(A) She has booked the wrong flight.
(B) She is going on a vacation.
(C) Her computer keeps breaking down.
(D) She has an appointment in the morning.

여자가 언급하는 문제는 무엇인가?
(A) 다른 비행 편을 예약했다.
(B) 휴가를 간다.
(C) 컴퓨터가 계속 고장이 난다.
(D) 아침에 약속이 있다.

58 What does the man say the woman will have time to do?
(A) Send over a document
(B) Drive around
(C) Reserve a lunch
(D) Return to the office

남자는 여자가 무엇을 할 수 있는 시간이 있다고 말하는가?
(A) 서류 보내기
(B) 운전하기
(C) 점심 예약하기
(D) 사무실로 돌아가기

(C) His lease has expired.
(D) He is moving abroad.

여자가 그라스톤 씨에 대해 언급하는 것은?
(A) 그는 팔기를 주저한다.
(B) 그의 빚이 쌓이고 있다.
(C) 그의 임대 기간이 만료되었다.
(D) 그는 해외로 이사 간다.

55 What does the man say he will suggest to Mr. Graston?
(A) Performing an inspection
(B) Reducing the price
(C) Purchasing an automobile
(D) Taking out a loan

남자는 그라스톤 씨에게 무엇을 제안하겠다고 말하는가?
(A) 순찰 시행
(B) 가격 인하
(C) 자동차 구매
(D) 융자 대출

Questions 59-61 refer to the following conversation. 미W 영M

W Hi. I saw the promotional poster for this laptop on your window, but I don't see it displayed anywhere. Which one are you looking for?

M Ah, we have several promotions going on right now. Which one are you looking for?

W The model SP50T. ⑥⑩ I can't seem to find any information about it.

M ⑥⑩ The reason is that the promotion is currently online only. What do you want to know?

W I want to read more about the specifications.

M Let me walk you through our Web site now. Please come this way.

여 안녕하세요. 제가 창문에 붙어 있는 노트북 컴퓨터 홍보용 포스터를 봤는데요. 어디에도 전시되어 있는 제품이 안 보이네요.

남 아, 저희가 현재 여러 종류의 맞춤 행사를 진행하고 있어요. 어떤 것을 찾고 계시나요?

여 SP50T요. 제가 그 제품에 관한 정보를 어디에서도 찾을 수 없네요.

남 정보를 찾으실 수 없는 이유는 그 판촉 행사가 온라인 전용이라서 그렇습니다. 무엇을 알고 싶으세요?

여 제품의 세부 사항에 관해서 읽어보고 싶어요.

남 제가 웹 사이트를 보면서 설명해 드릴게요. 이쪽으로 오시겠어요?

laptop 노트북 컴퓨터 promotion 홍보, 판촉 specification 설명서, 사양, 설명

59 What does the woman want to know?
(A) The period of the promotion
(B) The price of a product
(C) Information about a specific item
(D) Directions to the store

여자는 무엇을 알고 싶어 하는가?
(A) 판촉 행사의 기간
(B) 제품의 가격
(C) 특정한 물건의 정보
(D) 상점으로 가는 길

60 What does the man say about the promotion?
(A) It will last until the end of the week.
(B) It is only available online.
(C) It is only for a specific product.
(D) It hasn't started yet.

남자는 판촉 행사에 관해 무엇을 언급하는가?
(A) 주문까지 진행될 것이다.
(B) 온라인에서만 진행된다.
(C) 특정한 제품만 해당된다.
(D) 아직 시작되지 않았다.

61 Why does the man say, "Let me walk you through our Web site now"?
(A) To make an online order
(B) To negotiate a price
(C) To show some information
(D) To explain some download methods

남자는 왜 "제가 웹 사이트를 보면서 설명해 드릴게요"라고 말하는가?
(A) 온라인 주문을 하기 위해서
(B) 가격을 협상하기 위해서
(C) 정보를 보여주기 위해서
(D) 다운로드하는 방법을 설명해 주기 위해서

Questions 62-64 refer to the following conversation. 미W 영M

W: Hi, 62 I'm hosting a party next month and I'd like to book a room to accommodate all my guests. Will you have any suitable rooms available on the 23rd?
M: Well, 63 how many guests will be in your party? That will give us an idea of how much catering is required and the size of the venue you need to book.
W: Okay. I have invited 200 people and expect between 100 and 150 will attend.
M: In that case, you probably need one of our mid-sized rooms. I know two are reserved for events on that day, but I am sure one is available on the 23rd. Please give me a minute and 64 I'll check the advanced bookings.

여: 안녕하세요. 다음 달에 파티를 여는데, 제 모든 손님들을 수용할 객실을 예약하고 싶습니다. 23일에 이용 가능한 적합한 객실이 있나요?
남: 음, 파티에 손님이 몇 분 오시게 되나요? 얼마나 많은 필요한 음식 공급과 예약하셔야 할 장소의 규모를 알 수 있습니다.
여: 알겠어요. 200명을 초대했고, 100명에서 150명 사이에 있는 인원이 참석할 것으로 예상해요.
남: 그런 경우라면 손님께서는 아마 저희의 중간 규모 객실들이 필요할 겁니다. 그날 행사로 두 개의 객실이 예약되어 있다고 알고 있지만, 하나는 확실히 23일에 이용 가능할 겁니다. 잠시 시간을 주시면 제가 사전 예약을 확인해 보겠습니다.

host 개최하다 book a room 객실을 예약하다 accommodate 수용하다 suitable 적합한 catering 요리 조달·출장 요리 required 필요한 venue (콘서트·스포츠 경기·회담 등의) 장소 in that case 그런 경우에는 advanced booking 사전 예약 possibly 아마 middle sized 중형의 breakdown 명세(서)

62 What does the woman say she needs?
(A) A booking form
(B) An entertainment room
(C) A price breakdown
(D) Rented accommodation

여자가 그녀가 필요하다고 말하는 것은?
(A) 예약 양식
(B) 오락 공간
(C) 가격 내역
(D) 임대한 숙박 시설

63 What does the man ask the woman about?
(A) Her date of birth
(B) Her passport number
(C) The size of her party
(D) The location of her venue

남자는 여자에게 무엇에 대해 묻는가?
(A) 그녀의 생일
(B) 그녀의 여권 번호
(C) 파티의 규모
(D) 그녀의 행사 장소의 위치

64 What will the man most likely do next?
(A) Check prior bookings
(B) Speak to a colleague
(C) Provide an estimate
(D) Source alternative arrangements

남자는 다음에 무엇을 할 것 같은가?
(A) 사전 예약 확인하기
(B) 동료와 대화하기
(C) 견적 제시하기
(D) 대안 제공하기

Questions 65-67 refer to the following conversation and chart. 미M 미W

Discount code
(Available only from 10/3 to 10/13)

Items	Discount Rates
Table	50%
Chair	40%
Sofa	30%
Bed frame (Cherrywood)	25%
Bed mattress (Memory form)	20%
67 Bed frame (Cherrywood) & Bed mattress (Memory form) as a set	30%

M: 65 Hello. I'm looking for a bed frame and mattress set, please.
W: We have a wide selection you can choose from! Do you have a specific material and style you want?
M: Hmm... Well, 66 I haven't purchased from your store before, but I'd like something in Cherrywood for the frame and a memory form for the mattress.
W: You're in luck! 67 We are currently offering a limited-time discount on our entire Cherrywood bed frame and memory form sets. The promotional code will be automatically added to your order when you pay.
M: That's great. Where can I see the products?

할인 코드
(10월 3일부터 10월 13일까지만 이용 가능)

품목	할인율
테이블	50%
의자	40%
소파	30%
침대 프레임(체리우드)	25%
침대 매트리스(메모리폼)	20%
침대 프레임(체리우드) & 침대 매트리스(메모리폼) 세트	30%

남: 안녕하세요. 제가 침대 프레임과 매트리스 세트를 좀 보고 싶습니다.
여: 저희는 선택할 수 있는 다양한 종류의 제품군을 가지고 있습니다. 원하시는 특정한 소재 및 스타일이 있으신가요?

Questions 68-70 refer to the following conversation and catalog page. (영M)(미W)

Product Number	Descriptions	Price
CM1350	High speed with 13-inch monitor	$125
CM1550	High speed with 15-inch monitor	$150
70 CM1750	High speed with 17-inch monitor	$185
CM1950	High speed with 19-inch monitor	$230

M 68 How are the preparations for our new associate coming along?

W So far, so good. She is going to start next Monday. We have a space for her office. There is a desk already in there. I was able to find a phone and a printer, too. But I couldn't find a computer anywhere.

M 69 Did you ask the Maintenance Department? Sometimes they have unused computers in storage.

W 69 I did, but they don't have any.

M We'll just have to buy one. Our budget is pretty limited though. 70 Get one with the largest monitor you can find for under $200. Oh, and make sure it has a lock. She needs to keep her files secure.

남 그럼 우리가 하나 구매해야겠어요. 우리 예산이 꽤나 타이트하긴 해요. 가장 큰 모니터를 가진 것으로, 200달러 이하인 것으로 구매해 보세요. 그리고 잠금장치가 있는지도 확인하세요. 그녀가 파일들을 안전하게 보관하고 싶어할 테니까요.

associate 동료 | storage 창고 | secure 안전한 | transfer 전송하다 | furnish (가구를) 비치하다 | locate ~의 위치를 찾아내다

68 What are the speakers mainly discussing?
(A) Preparing for a new staff member
(B) Replacing computers
(C) Transferring important files
(D) Furnishing a lobby
화자들은 무엇에 관한 논의를 하고 있는가?
(A) 신입 직원을 위한 준비를 하는 것
(B) 컴퓨터를 교체하는 것
(C) 중요한 파일을 전송하는 것
(D) 로비에 가구를 비치하는 것

69 What does the woman say she did?
(A) Rescheduled a date
(B) Contacted another department
(C) Replaced some furniture
(D) Located missing files
여자는 무엇을 했다고 말하는가?
(A) 날짜를 재조정했다.
(B) 다른 부서에 연락했다.
(C) 가구를 교체했다.
(D) 잃어버린 파일들을 찾았다.

70 Look at the graphic. What product will the woman most likely purchase?
(A) CM1350
(B) CM1550
(C) CM1750
(D) CM1950
시각 자료를 보시오. 여자는 어느 제품을 구매하겠는가?
(A) CM1350
(B) CM1550
(C) CM1750
(D) CM1950

제품 번호	설명	가격
CM1350	초고속 13인치 모니터	125달러
CM1550	초고속 15인치 모니터	150달러
CM1750	초고속 17인치 모니터	185달러
CM1950	초고속 19인치 모니터	230달러

남 신입 사원을 위한 준비는 어떻게 되어 가나요?
여 지금까지는 잘 진행되고 있어요. 그녀가 다음 주 월요일에 업무를 시작합니다. 우리는 그녀의 사무실로 쓸 공간이 있어요. 이미 책상은 그 공간 안에 구비돼 있습니다. 전화기와 프린터기도 확보할 수 있었어요. 그런데, 제가 컴퓨터는 어디에서도 찾을 수가 없었어요.
남 관리부서에 문의해 봤어요? 가끔씩 그들이 쓰지 않는 컴퓨터를 창고에 보관하곤 하던데요.
여 해봤죠. 그러나 가진 것이 없다고 했습니다.

남 음... 제가 이전에는 이 점포에서 구매해 본 적이 없지만 프레임으로 된 제트리우드 그리고 매트리스는 메모리폼으로 된 것을 원합니다.
여 운이 좋으시네요. 자화가 현재 정해진 시간 동안에 힐인기에 제공하는 제트리우드 프레임 그리고 메모리폼 매트리스 세트가 있습니다. 판촉 행사 할인 반응는 지름이신 때에 자동으로 주문에 적용될 게예요.
남 잘 되었네요. 어디서 제품을 볼 수 있나요?

specific 특정한, 구체적인, 문형별 | automatically 자동으로

65 What is the man planning to do?
(A) Use a discount coupon
(B) Move out of a current apartment
(C) Purchase some furniture
(D) Find more information about the promotion
남자는 무엇을 할 계획인가?
(A) 할인 쿠폰을 사용한다.
(B) 현재 아파트에서 이사한다.
(C) 가구를 구매한다.
(D) 판촉 행사에 관련 정보를 찾는다.

66 What does the man indicate about the business?
(A) It offers only a few kinds of products.
(B) It is popular.
(C) This is his first time to purchase from the business.
(D) All kinds of items are on sale.
남자는 업체에 관해서 무엇을 암시하는가?
(A) 얼마 안 되는 종류의 제품을 보유하고 있다.
(B) 유명하다.
(C) 남자는 이 매장에서 처음 구매한다.
(D) 모든 종류의 제품들이 할인 중이다.

67 Look at the graphic. Which discount will the man receive?
(A) 40%
(B) 30%
(C) 25%
(D) 20%
시각 자료를 보시오. 남자는 어떤 할인을 받겠는가?
(A) 40%
(B) 30%
(C) 25%
(D) 20%

Part 4

Questions 71-73 refer to the following telephone message. 영M

Hello, this is Mario Cobiella calling from the Cretol Conference Center. 72 I'm scheduling an international convention and 71 would like to place an order of 2,000 name tags for all delegates. The convention is about three months from now but I'd like to finalize all the details by April 23. 73 Could you inform me of the cost for this amount? Please call me back at 555-5629, so we can discuss the details of the order. Thank you.

안녕하세요. 저는 크레톨 회의 센터의 마리오 코비에라입니다. 저는 국제 컨벤션의 일정을 잡으려 하고, 모든 대표자들을 위한 명찰을 2,000개 주문하고 싶습니다. 그 컨벤션은 지금으로부터 약 3달 정도 후이지만, 4월 23일까지는 모든 세부 사항들을 마무리 짓고 싶습니다. 이 액수가 포함된 비용이 얼마인지 알려 주실 수 있으신가요? 주문의 세부 사항을 이야기할 수 있도록, 555-5629로 전화 주세요. 감사합니다.

schedule 일정을 잡다 name tag 명찰 delegate 대표자 finalize 마무리 짓다, 완결하다 gathering 모임 estimate 견적서

71 Why is the speaker calling?
(A) To approve a design
(B) To arrange a meeting
(C) To extend a deadline
(D) To place an order

화자가 전화하는 이유는?
(A) 디자인을 승인하기 위해
(B) 회의를 준비하기 위해
(C) 마감일을 연장하기 위해
(D) 주문하기 위해

72 What event is the speaker planning?
(A) A global gathering
(B) An advertising presentation
(C) A construction project
(D) A store renovation

화자가 계획 중인 행사는?
(A) 국제 모임
(B) 광고 발표
(C) 건설 프로젝트
(D) 매장 리모델링

73 What information does the speaker request?
(A) Expected time
(B) A printing deadline
(C) A cost estimate
(D) A meeting agenda

화자가 요청하는 정보는?
(A) 예상 시간
(B) 인쇄 마감일
(C) 가격 견적
(D) 회의 안건

Questions 74-76 refer to the following recorded message. 미W

You've reached 74 Hannaford beauty technicians. We are situated on the Hannaford's Main Street next to the Iris coffee shop. The store is closed at the moment but our beauticians are available Tuesday through Saturday from 8 A.M. to 5 P.M. We also have 75 late opening on Thursdays until 10 P.M. Advance bookings are preferred to ensure you get full attention. To arrange an appointment, 76 please leave a message after the tone.

하나포드 미용사입니다. 저희는 하나포드 중심가의 아이리스 커피숍 옆에 위치합니다. 가게는 현재 문을 닫았지만, 저희 미용사는 화요일부터 토요일, 오전 8시부터 오후 5시까지 이용 가능합니다. 저희는 또한 목요일은 오후 10시까지 늦게 영업합니다. 고객님께 최고의 서비스를 약속드리기 위해 사전 예약이 선호됩니다. 예약하기 위해, 신호음이 끝나면 메시지를 남겨 주세요.

beauty technician 미용사 situate 위치하다 at the moment 미침, 지금 beautician 미용사 advance booking 사전 예약 attention 관심 appointment 약속, 예약 tone 신호음

74 What type of business is Hannaford's?
(A) A travel agency
(B) A beauty shop
(C) A dental clinic
(D) A café

하나포드는 어떤 종류의 사업인가?
(A) 여행사
(B) 미용실
(C) 치과
(D) 카페

75 What day is the business open late?
(A) On Tuesday
(B) On Wednesday
(C) On Thursday
(D) On Saturday

가게가 문을 늦게까지 여는 날은 무슨 요일인가?
(A) 화요일
(B) 수요일
(C) 목요일
(D) 토요일

76 What does the speaker recommend?
(A) Asking for a discount
(B) Visiting another salon
(C) Changing an appointment
(D) Leaving a message

화자가 추천하는 것은?
(A) 할인 요청하기
(B) 다른 미용실 방문하기
(C) 예약을 바꾸기
(D) 메시지 남기기

Questions 77-79 refer to the following announcement. 미M

Attention, ladies and gentlemen. 77 We'll be landing at La Manche Airport in ten minutes. Please make sure you take all of your hand luggage with you when you exit the plane. 78 For passengers travelling onto Switzerland, please leave through terminal 1 exit and proceed to terminal 3 for your connecting flight. 79 For those who are unable to walk, there is transport to take you to the customs hall. Thank you for flying with us.

주목해 주세요. 신사 숙녀 여러분. 우리는 10분 후에 라 망쉬 공항에 착륙할 것입니다. 비행기에서 내릴 때, 기내 반입용 짐을 모두 챙겨서 내리세요. 스위스로 여행을 가는 승객들은 연결 항공편을 위해 1번 터미널 출구로 나가 3번 터미널로 가 주세요. 도보가 힘드신 분들을 위해 공항 내로 이용 운송해 줄 교통편이 준비되어 있습니다. 저희 비행 서비스를 이용해 주셔서 감사합니다.

attention 주목하세요 hand luggage 기내 반입용 수하물 exit 퇴장하다, 나가다: 출입구 travel onto ~을 가져 여행하다 proceed 계속 가다 connecting flight 연결 비행 be unable to ~을 할 수 없다 transport 교통수단 customs hall 세관 refreshment stand 다과 판매점

77 Where most likely is the announcement being heard?
(A) In a train station
(B) At the airport
(C) In a plane
(D) In a bus

이 공지는 어디에서 들을 수 있는가?
(A) 기차역
(B) 공항
(C) 비행기
(D) 버스

78 What should people traveling to Switzerland do?
(A) Take transport to the customs hall
(B) Go to another terminal
(C) Wait for luggage removal
(D) Exit via the main hall

스위스로 가는 사람들이 해야 하는 것은?
(A) 세관으로 가는 교통수단 이용하기
(B) 다른 터미널 가기
(C) 수화물을 치울 때까지 기다리기
(D) 중앙 복도를 통해 나가기

79 According to the announcement, what is offered to some passengers?
(A) Car park payment
(B) Ticket machines
(C) Refreshment stands
(D) Transportation

공지에 따르면, 일부 승객에게 제공되는 것은?
(A) 주차 비용
(B) 표 판매기
(C) 간식 판매점
(D) 교통편

Questions 80-82 refer to the following instructions. 영W

So ⑧⓪ this is the end of the tour of the Kalua Zoo Nature Trail. For those people who wish to remain, we will now have a simple test. Here's what we are going to do. I'll provide the Latin names of some animals and a map of the zoo. Whoever can ⑧① accurately translate the names of the corresponding animal, using the map to help you, will be awarded a free pass to the zoo's reptile house. Just ⑧② make sure you don't stray out of the marked areas while you're investigating. I hope you all decide to take part.

이것이 칼루아 동물원 자연 탐사 산책 투어의 마지막입니다. 남아 있길 바라는 사람들을 위해, 지금 간단한 테스트를 하겠습니다. 우리가 할 것은 다음과 같습니다. 제가 일부 동물들의 라틴어 명칭과 동물원의 지도를 드릴 것입니다. 지도를 이용해 해당 동물의 이름을 정확하게 번역할 수 있는 사람은 누구든지 동물원의 파충류 우리의 무료 출입증을 상으로 받게 됩니다. 탐험을 하는 도중 표시된 지역만 벗어나지 않도록 해 주세요. 여러분 모두가 참여해 주시길 희망합니다.

nature trail 자연 탐사 산책로 translate 통역하다, 번역하다 accurately 정확히 Latin 라틴어; 라틴계 corresponding 해당되는 stray 벗어나다 award 수여하다 pass 출입증 reptile 파충류 investigate 수사하다; 조사하다 take part 참여하다 mark 표시하다 identify 확인하다, 알아보다 diagram 도표 demonstration 시연 designated 지정된 enclosure 울타리를 친 장소

80 What event is ending?
(A) A company picnic
(B) A computer demonstration
(C) A sporting event
(D) A nature tour

어떤 행사가 끝나고 있는가?
(A) 회사 야유회
(B) 컴퓨터 시연
(C) 스포츠 행사
(D) 자연 관람

81 What must participants in the competition do?
(A) Translate names correctly
(B) Identify wild flowers
(C) Map out a route
(D) Draw a diagram

대회의 참가자들이 해야 하는 것은?
(A) 이름들을 정확하게 번역하기
(B) 야생화 구분하기
(C) 노선 계획하기
(D) 도표 그리기

82 What are the listeners cautioned about?
(A) Feeding the animals
(B) Getting out of the designated paths
(C) Leaving trash
(D) Walking through the enclosures

청자들은 무엇에 관해 주의를 받는가?
(A) 동물들에게 먹이 주는 것
(B) 지정된 길 벗어나는 것
(C) 쓰레기 버리는 것
(D) 울타리가 처진 곳을 통해 지나가는 것

Questions 83-85 refer to the following announcement. 영M

Hello, everyone, and welcome to The Whale Sanctuary. Regrettably, we'll have to line up for the next available transport. ⑧③ ⑧④ The scheduled boat had a minor fault but as soon as the replacement arrives, we will go aboard. ⑧⑤ Remember there are two different viewpoints of whale watching available, one from the top deck, and the other from below the water. Underwater viewers, please come forward as you will board first, everyone else please wait until called. Thanks and please enjoy your tour.

안녕하세요, 여러분. 고래 보호 구역에 오신 것을 환영합니다. 유감스럽게도, 다음에 이용 가능한 교통편을 위해 줄을 서야 합니다. 예정된 보트는 작은 결함이 있었습니다만, 다른 보트가 오면 어느 즉시 탑승할 것입니다. 상부 갑판과 물 아래의 두 개의 다른 방향에서 고래를 구경할 수 있음을 명심하세요. 수중 관람객들은 먼저 승선할 테니 앞으로 나와 주시고, 다른 분들은 모두 부를 때까지 대기해 주세요. 감사합니다, 즐거운 관람되세요.

sanctuary 보호 구역 regrettably 유감스럽게, 애석하게 line up 줄을 서다 minor 작은 fault 결함 replacement 대체물 top deck 상부 갑판 below the water 수면 아래에 underwater 물속의, 수중의 viewer 구경 꾼; 시청자 come forward 앞으로 나오다 harbor 항구 inclement 좋지 못한, 궂은 in an orderly manner 질서 정연하게

83

Where is the announcement being made?

(A) At a harbor
(B) At a theme park
(C) At a lake
(D) At a museum

어디에서 발표되고 있는가?

(A) 항구
(B) 테마공원
(C) 호수
(D) 박물관

84

Why are listeners told they will need to wait?

(A) A tour guide is delayed.
(B) A dinner has not been delivered.
(C) The transport has not arrived.
(D) The weather is inclement.

청자들이 대기해야 한다고 말하는 이유는?

(A) 여행 가이드가 늦는다.
(B) 저녁 식사가 배달되지 않았다.
(C) 교통편이 도착하지 않았다.
(D) 날씨가 좋지 않다.

85

What are listeners asked to do?

(A) Form two separate groups
(B) Return at another time
(C) Find a viewpoint as quickly as possible
(D) Board the boat in an orderly manner

청자들이 요청받는 것은?

(A) 두 개의 분리된 그룹으로 모이기
(B) 다른 시간대에 돌아오기
(C) 최대한 빨리 구경할 지점 찾기
(D) 질서 정연하게 배에 탑승하기

Questions 86-88 refer to the following telephone message. [호M]

Hi, Emily. This is Pablo from Parco, Inc. ⑧ I just received the file with the sample logo that one of your designers prepared for my company. I think it's a good start. But it's not what we were expecting. When we spoke a few weeks ago, I explained that we are looking for a logo with bright colors but also simple. The logo I received is very bright. The red and yellow look great, but the text is too complicated. Can you replace it with something a little more basic? I remember you mentioning that you had catalogs with sample text. ⑧ Could we meet to review those? I'm free afternoons next week. Let me know what your schedule looks like.

안녕하세요, 에밀리. 저는 파코 사의 파블로입니다. 제가 당신 디자이너들 중의 한 명이 우리 회사를 위해서 만들어 준 샘플 로고가 들어간 파일을 막 받았어요. 시작은 꽤 괜찮은 것 같습니다. 그런데 우리가 기대하는 것과는 좀 다른 것 같아요. 우리가 몇 주 전에 이야기를 나누었을 때, 우리는 밝은색이지만 단순한 디자인을 원한다고 말씀드렸어요. 제가 받은 로고는 아주 밝아요. 빨간색과 노란색은 아주 좋아 보여요, 그런데 글자들이 너무 복잡해 보여요. 글자를 보다 단순한 것들로 교체해 주실 수 있나요? 당신이 샘플 글자들을 포함하고 있는 카탈로그가 있다고 말씀하신 것이 기억나거든요. 이것들을 검토하기 위해 만날 수 있을까요? 저는 다음 주 오후에는 시간이 됩니다. 당신 스케줄이 어떤지 알려 주세요.

basic 기본적인   stationary store 문구점   scheme 배열, 배색

86

Where does the listener most likely work?

(A) At a gallery
(B) At a stationary store
(C) At a paint manufacturer
(D) At a graphic design firm

청자는 어디서 일하는 것 같은가?

(A) 미술관
(B) 문구점
(C) 페인트 공장
(D) 시각 디자인 회사

87

What does the man imply when he says, "it's not what we were expecting"?

(A) He was surprised with a quick response.
(B) He wants a better result.

(C) He doesn't like the color scheme.
(D) He wants to cancel the order.

남자는 "우리가 기대하는 것과는 좀 다른 것 같아요"라고 말했을 때 무엇을 암시했는가?

(A) 빠른 응대에 놀랐다.
(B) 더 나은 결과를 원한다.
(C) 색 배열을 좋아하지 않는다.
(D) 주문을 취소하기를 원한다.

88

What does the speaker want to do?

(A) Reschedule the appointment
(B) Order more products
(C) Arrange a meeting
(D) Change the colors

화자는 무엇하기를 원하는가?

(A) 약속 다시 잡기
(B) 제품을 더 주문하기
(C) 미팅 잡기
(D) 색 변경하기

Questions 89-91 refer to the following instructions. [영W]

Good afternoon, and welcome to the grand opening party of Sunrise Gallery's SoHo location. ⑧ We hope that you enjoy the refreshments provided by Gourmet Catering, located in the reception hall right next to this room. In conjunction with this event, we are showing our special painting selection, aptly named Modern Precious, which is also available for purchase at discounted prices; however, please remember the Modern Precious collection is not expected to last very long, so guests are encouraged to peruse them throughout the event. ⑨ Let's take a look at our special selection.

안녕하세요, 선라이즈 갤러리의 소호 지점 오프닝 행사에 오신 것을 환영합니다. 저희는 여러분들이 이 방 바로 옆에 위치한 리셉션홀에 준비되고 매 케이터링이 제공해 드리는 다과를 즐기시기를 바랍니다. 이와 함께, 저희는 소장하고 있는 특별히 그림 수집품들을 공개하겠습니다. 모던 프레셔스라고 명명되고 또한 할인가에 구매가 가능하답니다. 그러나 모던 프레셔스 수집품들은 오래 남아 있지 않을 거라는 것을 유념하세요. 그러니 손님들께서는 행사가 진행되는 동안에 수집품들을 잘 감상하시기 바랍니다. 이제 특별 수집품들을 감상하도록 하겠습니다.

refreshments 다과류 in conjunction with ~와 함께 aptly 적절히
pursue ~을 추진하다 throughout 기간 내내 souvenir 기념품

in spite of ~에도 불구하고 unfavorable 불리한 domestic 국내
의 circumstance 환경, 상황 offering 제공되는 것 boost 신장시키다
profit 수익, 이익 exclusive 독점적인 distributor 유통업자 expand 확
장하다, 확대하다 in-store 매장 내의 when it comes to ~에 관한 한
stock 주식 retailer 소매상

89 What is available in the reception hall?
(A) Brochures
(B) Maps
(C) Food and drinks
(D) A gift shop

리셉션홀에서 무엇이 있는가?
(A) 안내서
(B) 지도
(C) 음식과 마실 것
(D) 선물 가게

90 What does the speaker imply when she says, "Please remember the Modern Precious collection is not expected to last very long"?
(A) The product sale has ended recently.
(B) Many people are waiting to buy items.
(C) People need to purchase the items quickly.
(D) There is only a small selection of artwork.

화자는 "모던 프레셔스 수집품들은 오래 남아 있지 않을 거라는 것을 기억해주세요"라고 말했을 때 무엇을 암시했는가?
(A) 제품 세일이 최근에 끝났다.
(B) 많은 사람들이 물건들을 사려고 기다린다.
(C) 사람들이 서둘러 물건들을 사야 한다.
(D) 예술 작품들이 많지 않다.

91 What will the listeners do next?
(A) Buy some souvenirs
(B) Look over a special collection
(C) Introduce themselves to each other
(D) Leave the building

청자들은 이제 무엇을 하겠는가?
(A) 기념품을 구매한다.
(B) 특별 수집품들을 감상한다.
(C) 서로에서 각자를 소개한다.
(D) 건물에서 나온다.

Questions 92-94 refer to the following excerpt from a meeting and agenda. 호M

Agenda	
Welcoming speech	Paul Baker
Financial report	Yohey Ogawa
⑬ New product	Beda Hari
Team restructuring	Lisa Whang

In spite of unfavorable domestic industrial circumstances, our company's profits continue to grow, which makes the shareholders happy. Today I would like to let you know about some new offerings that we expect will help boost profits. ⑫ ⑬ As you may know, Top Technologies released a new line of tablet PCs. ⑬ Well, I am pleased to report that we have signed a contract to be the exclusive online distributor of these products. ⑭ We will begin selling them on our Web site in two weeks. In addition, we are expanding our in-store offerings of accessories to include several new brands of headphones, data storage drives, and security software. Our marketing researchers say that customers are interested in having more options when it comes to these types of products.

의제	
환영 연설	폴 베이커
재정 보고	요헤이 오가와
신제품	베다 하리
팀 재구성	리사 황

92 Where does the speaker most likely work?
(A) At a stock trading company
(B) At a computer manufacturer
(C) At an Internet service provider
(D) At an electronics retailer

화자는 어디에서 일하겠는가?
(A) 주식 거래 회사
(B) 컴퓨터 제조업체
(C) 인터넷 서비스 제공자
(D) 전자제품 판매업체

93 Look at the graphic. Who is most likely speaking?
(A) Paul Baker
(B) Yohey Ogawa
(C) Beda Hari
(D) Lisa Whang

시각 자료를 보시오. 누가 연설하고 있는 것 같은가?
(A) 폴 베이커
(B) 요헤이 오가와
(C) 베다 하리
(D) 리사 황

94 According to the speaker, what will the business do in two weeks?
(A) Sign an exclusive deal
(B) Open a new branch
(C) Release new software
(D) Begin selling new items online

화자에 따르면, 업체는 2주 후에 무엇을 하게 될 것인가?
(A) 독점 계약을 한다.
(B) 새로운 지점을 연다.
(C) 새로운 소프트웨어를 출시한다.
(D) 새로운 제품들을 온라인에서 판매한다.

좋지 않은 국내업계 환경에도 불구하고, 우리 회사의 수익은 지속적으로 증가하고 있으며 이는 우리 주주들을 기쁘게 만들고 있습니다. 오늘 저는 여러분들께 우리 수익을 증가시켜 줄 것이라 예상되는 새롭게 제공될 제품에 관해 말씀드리겠습니다. 이미 아실거라 생각하지만, 탑 테크놀로지가 새로운 태블릿 PC 제품군을 출시했습니다. 저는 우리 회사가 이 제품의 독점 온라인 유통업자로 계약하게 되었음을 기쁘게 공지드립니다. 우리는 이 제품을 우리 웹 사이트에서 2주 후부터 판매를 개시합니다. 그리고 우리는 우리 매장 내에서 판매하는 액세서리 제품들의 범위를 새로운 브랜드의 헤드폰, 데이터 저장 드라이브, 그리고 보안 소프트웨어까지 확장할 계획입니다. 우리 마케팅 연구원들은 고객들이 이러한 종류의 제품에 대해서는 다양한 옵션을 갖는 것에 관심이 있다고 설명했습니다.

Questions 98-100 refer to the following excerpt from a meeting and chart. 호M

Survey Result

	New York New York	Starry Night	Poppins	Summer Beach
	●	●●	●●●●●	●●●

I'd like to present the results of last month's survey to everyone before making a final decision. As you may remember, we asked our members to indicate which production we should perform next, and ❾❽ it looks like there is a clear preference for what we should do. ❾❾ Oh, and there are countless responses to Sophia for giving out teasers on social media; it's thanks to her that we had many people call and reserve tickets ahead of time. There's a lot of work ahead of us, but ❿❿ remember to keep our fans updated!

설문 조사 결과

	뉴욕 뉴욕	별이 빛나는 밤	포핀스	여름 해변
	●	●●	●●●●●	●●●

최종 결정을 내리기 전에 제가 지난달 설문조사 결과를 여러분께 알려 드리고자 합니다. 아마 기억하시겠지만, 우리는 우리 회원들에게 어떤 작품을 다음에 공연 올려야 할지에 관해 의견을 답라는 요청을 했고, 우리가 어떤 작품을 할 것인지에 관해 아주 명확한 선호 사항이 있는 것으로 나타났습니다. 그리고 아주 많은 응답이 음악이 소피아가 소셜 미디어에 올리돌은 티저 광고를 통해 들어 있었습니다. 그녀 덕분에 많은 사람들이 전화를 해 왔고 사전에 티켓을 예약했습니다. 우리가 헤야할 일들이 많이 산적해 있지만, 잊지 말고 저희 팬들에게 진행 상황을 알려줄수 있도록 하세요.

Questions 95-97 refer to the following talk and map. 영W

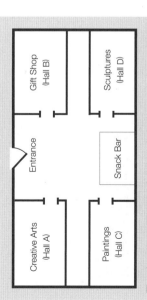

Creative Arts (Hall A)	Entrance	Gift Shop (Hall B)
Paintings (Hall C)	Snack Bar	Sculptures (Hall D)

Thank you, everyone, for your interest and cooperation on our tour of the Wesley Museum. ❾❺ We apologize that our wooden sculptures were made unavailable to the public as many of you expressed interest in seeing them before the tour. The room will be reopened once renovations are completed. ❾❻ ❾❼ However, I urge all of you to attend the live demonstration today at one o'clock for this month's pottery display, produced by John Grisham, a local artist and environmental activist.

창조 예술 (A홀)	입구	기념품점 (B홀)
화화 (C홀)	스낵바	조각룸 (D홀)

여러분의 웨슬리 박물관 투어에 대한 관심과 협조에 감사드립니다. 여기 계신 분들 중 많은 분들이 투어를 시작하기 전에 저희의 나무로 만들어진 조형물들을 보시고자 하는 관심을 보여 주셨는데, 저희가 그 작품들을 여러분들께 보여드릴 수 없었음을 사과드립니다. 그 전시관은 보수 작업이 끝나는대로 다시 개장될 예정입니다. 그 대신, 저는 여래 모두가 오늘 1시에 지역 예술가이자 환경 운동가인 존 그리샴에 의해 실행으로 진행되는 이달의 도자기 전시 시연에 참여하시기를 권유드립니다.

cooperation 협동, 협력 wooden 나무로 된 sculpture 조각품 urge 권유하다 demonstration 시범, 시연, 설명 potter 도예가 curator 큐레이터, 전시 기획자

---

95 Look at the graphic. Which area is unavailable to the public?

(A) Hall A
(B) Hall B
(C) Hall C
(D) Hall D

시각 자료를 보시오. 어느 장소가 대중에게 공개되지 않는가?

(A) A홀
(B) B홀
(C) C홀
(D) **D홀**

96 What does the speaker recommend the listeners do?

(A) Visit another museum
(B) Meet a painter
(C) See a live demonstration
(D) Purchase some gifts

화자는 청자들이 무엇하는 것을 권유하는가?

(A) 다른 박물관을 방문한다.
(B) 화가를 만난다.
(C) **실황으로 진행되는 시연을 본다.**
(D) 선물을 구매한다.

97 Who is John Grisham?

(A) A collector
(B) A local potter
(C) A museum curator
(D) The tour guide

존 그리샴은 누구인가?

(A) 수집가
(B) **지역 도예가**
(C) 박물관 큐레이터
(D) 투어 가이드

indicate 나타내다 countless 셀 수 없이 많은 teaser 예고 광고/정보를 최소화해서 종종을 유발시키는 형태의 광고 ahead of time 사전에

98 Look at the graphic. Which production will be selected?
(A) New York New York
(B) Starry Night
(C) Poppins
(D) Summer Beach
시각 자료를 보시오. 어느 작품이 선택되겠는가?
(A) 누욕 누욕
(B) 별이 빛나는 밤
(C) 포핀스
(D) 여름 해변

99 Why does the speaker praise Sophia?
(A) She wrote scripts well.
(B) She performed her role well.
(C) She made social media updates.
(D) She sold lots of tickets.
왜 화자는 소피아를 칭찬하는가?
(A) 그녀가 대본을 잘 썼다.
(B) 그녀가 그녀의 역할을 잘 연기했다.
(C) 그녀가 소셜 미디어에 정보를 올렸다.
(D) 그녀가 티켓을 많이 팔았다.

100 What does the speaker remind the listeners to do?
(A) Cast actors for roles
(B) Call Sophia
(C) Inform people of updates
(D) Buy many tickets
화자는 청자들이 무엇하기를 상기하는가?
(A) 배역을 위해 배우를 캐스팅한다.
(B) 소피아에게 전화한다.
(C) 사람들에게 새로운 정보를 알린다.
(D) 많은 티켓을 산다.

Part 5

101 해설 상관 접속사 문제로 and와 함께 'A와 B 둘 다'의 의미로 쓰이는 것은 (D)이다. 참고로 상관 접속사 either A or B나 B는 'A 혹은 B', neither A nor B는 'A와 B 둘 다 아닌', not only A but also B는 'A뿐만 아니라 B'(=B as well as A), not A but B는 'A가 아니라 B'라는 의미이다.
조나스 애견용품점은 큰 네덜란드의 스페인 두 곳에서 공장을 개정할 것이다.
Holland 네덜란드 pet supply 애견용품

102 해설 대명사 문제로 명사 앞 대명사의 소유격 자리이므로 (A)가 정답이다.
문레이크 갤러리에 돈을 기부하고 시각 예술에 대한 지지를 보여 주세요.
gallery 갤러리, 미술관 support 지원 visual art 시각 예술

103 해설 형용사 어휘 문제로 빈칸 뒤의 rates와 잘 어울리는 어휘는 (B)이다. 가격을 수식하는 형용사로 많이 출제되는 reasonable(합리적인), affordable(비싸지 않은), moderate(적당한)도 참고로 알아 두자.
누 에이지 이야의 고객들은 저희의 플라스틱 렌즈에 대한 새 인하 가격을 알게 되면 매우 좋아하실 겁니다.
delighted 아주 기뻐하는 find out 알게 되다 louder 소리가 더 큰 rate 요금, 가격 비율

104 해설 조동사(can)와 동사(design) 사이는 동사를 수식하는 부사 자리로 (D)가 정답이다. skillful은 형용사, skill은 명사이므로 동사를 수식할 수 없다.
바르망 머시너리의 전문가들은 귀하의 생산 수요를 맞춤 특별 주문인 솔루션들을 능숙하게 제작할 수 있다.
professional 전문가 custom-tailored 특별 주문인 solution 해결책 suit 맞추다 skillfully 솜씨 있게, 교묘하게

105 해설 all participants ~ next door는 문장의 필수 성분을 모두 갖춘 완벽한 문장이므로 빈칸부터 over까지는 수식 역할이다. 빈칸 뒤에 절을 받아서 수식 역할을 하는 것 중 부사절 접속사로 부사 Still, Soon은 제외되고, 부사절 접속사 When과 Though 중 문맥상 '워크숍이 끝날 때가 작정하므로 (A)가 정답이다.
워크숍이 끝나면, 모든 참가자들은 엽에서 무료 다과를 즐기셔도 됩니다.
be over 끝나다 participant 참가자 refreshments 다과

106 해설 동사 어휘 문제로 문맥상 '항병이 8월 30일까지 완료되어야 한다고 일렀다'에서가 가장 적절한 것은 (B)이다.
로지 씨는 그녀의 동업자들에게 항병이 8월 30일까지 완료되어야 한다고 일렀다.
business associate 사업 동료, 동업자 merger 합병 state 언급하다 inform 알리다 confirm 확인하다

107 해설 알맞은 전치사를 고르는 문제로 빈칸 뒤에 나오는 선임 세무 '전문가들로부터 피드백을 받는 것이므로 (A)가 적절하다.
프랑크 교수는 선임 세무 전문가들로부터 피드백을 받기 위해 종합을 제출 중이다.
general meeting 총회 obtain 얻다, 획득하다 senior 상임의, 고위의 tax professional 세무 전문가

108 해설 부사 어휘 문제로 문맥상 도움을 제공하는 것자가 가장 잘 어울리는 부사는 (C)이다.
한 씨는 친절하게도 그의 동료들이 네트워크 소프트웨어를 사용하는 것을 도와줄 수 있도록 도와주겠다고 제안했다.
co-worker 동료 variably 일정치 않게 accurately 정확하게 generously 친절하게 entirely 전적으로, 완전히

109 해설 관사(the)와 명사(cost) 사이는 명사를 수식하는 형용사 자리로 (C)가 정답이다. totaling이 현재분사로 형용사 역할을 할 수 있으나 '총 ~또는, 합계를 내는'이라는 의미이므로 문맥상 적절하지 않다.
저희 컴퓨터 매장은 새 소프트웨어에 대해 총 가격의 30퍼센트 할인을 보장합니다.
secure 획보하다, 얻어내다

110 해설 help는 목적어 다음에 목적격 보어로 동사원형 혹은 to부정사를 취하는 동사이다. 따라서 빈칸은 목적격 보어로 (C)가 적절하다. <help+목적어+(to) 동사원형에서 목적어가 생략돼 있을 수 있으며 그럴 경우 help 뒤에 또 동사원형이 올 수도 있다는 것을 알아 둔다.
매리 재무 상담사들은 소매상들이 새로 개설한 사업들을 더 수익성 높은 대규모 사업으로 발전시키도록 도울 수 있다.
financial consultant 재무 상담사 retailer 소매상 launch 출시하다; 시작하다 lucrative 수익성 높은 enterprise 대기업; 대규모 사업

111

해설 The urban ~ House는 문장의 필수 성분을 모두 갖춘 완전한 문장이므로 빈칸 이하는 수식 역할을 한다. 빈칸 뒤에 명사(concerns)가 있으므로 빈칸에는 전치사가 들어가야 하고 문맥상 '우리 사항에도 불구하고'가 적절하므로 (D)가 정답이다.

도시 위원회는 바른 유선 위원회에서 제기된 우려 사항에도 불구하고 역사적인 인체스터 하우스의 판매를 확인했다.

urban 도시의, 도회지의 committee 위원회 confirm 확인[인정]하다 raise 제기하다 legacy 유선 historic 역사적인

112

해설 형용사 어휘 문제로 '비즈니스 상인들에게 가치 있는 정보를 제공한다'가 가장 적절하므로 (A)이다.

500만 부 이상을 판매하면서, 〈준 데밀리스 파이낸셜 가이드〉는 비즈니스 상인들에게 가치 있는 정보를 제공한다.

financial 재정의, 금융의 business marketer 사업 상인 eager 열렬한 numerous 수많은 valuable 가치 있는

113

해설 〈be p.p.〉 뒤는 동사를 수식하는 부사 자리로 (B)가 정답이다. directed는 동사 혹은 분사, direction은 명사, direct는 동사로 빈칸에 들어갈 수 없다.

패블러스 드레이프스에서 모든 주간 금액은 은행 계좌로 직접 예치된다.

fabulous 멋진 drape 걸치다 deposit 예치하다 bank account 은행 계좌 direct ~에게 보내다

114

해설 소유격(her)과 명사(path) 사이는 명사를 수식하는 형용사 자리로 (A)가 정답이다. challenge는 동사, challenger는 명사로 형용사 역할을 할 수 없다.

그녀의 고별사에서 브누 씨는 유명 기자가 되기까지의 그녀의 도전적인 행로를 기술했다.

farewell speech 고별사 well-known 잘 알려진 journalist 기자 challenging 도전적인 challenger 도전자

115

해설 전치사(in)와 전치사(of) 사이는 명사 자리로 observance와 observer가 정답 후보인데, in observance of는 '~을 기념하여, 축하하여'라는 불가산명사가 와야 하므로 오답이다. 따라서 정답은 뒤에 가산복수명사/불가산명사가 모두 올 수 있는 (A) some이다.

제임스 컴퓨터스는 공휴일을 기념하여 내일 문을 닫을 것이다.

public holiday 공휴일, 국경일 observance (법률·규칙 등의) 준수; (축제·생일 등의) 축하, 기념 observant 관찰력 있는, 준수하는 observe 관찰[관측]하다 observer 관찰자

116

해설 문장에 동사가 세 개(owns, maintains, have)이므로 접속사가 두 개 필요하다. 등위 접속사 and가 이미 있었고, 빈칸에 하나 더 접속사가 와야 한다. 따라서 정답의 후보는 접속사인 (C) which와 (D) that이 된다. 접속사 뒤에는 들어갈 수 없으므로 정답은 (C) which이다. 참고로 빈칸 앞뒤만 보고 (B) them을 고르지 않도록 주의하자. 접속사 역할과 대명사 역할(them)을 동시에 해야 하는 자리이므로 관계대명사가 들어가야 한다.

리드빌 시는 20개의 공원을 소유하고 관리하고 있는데 그중 여섯 곳은 수영 시설이 있다.

public park 공공 주차장 facility 시설

117

해설 빈칸은 that 절 안의 동사 자리로, 동사가 아닌 having been approved는 제외된다. 빈칸 뒤에 목적어가 없으므로 수동형 have been approved, approved와 수동형 have been approved 중 (D)가 정답이다. 참고로 4행시 문장에서 두 번째 목적어로 that절을 취하는 동사에는 inform, tell, advise, assure, convince 등이 있다.

레이놀즈 씨는 내일 배송 시간이 나도 통의 발전용 터빈이 완료될 수 있도록 보장하기 위해 직원들에게 시간 외 근무를 보장한다.

overtime hours 시간 외 근무 guarantee 보장하다 wind turbine 풍력용 터빈 in time 제시간에 shipment 배송

118

해설 (A) approval은 '승인'이라는 의미인데, 대중들이 승인하는 입장이 아니라 시 의회나 정부 기관이 승인하는 입장이므로 오답이다. (C) display(전시)와 (D) creation(창조)은 의미상 어색하다. 따라서 정답은 (B) response(반응)이다. 참고로 response to(~에 대한 반응)를 세트 표현으로 외워 두자.

그 아이디어에 대한 압도적으로 긍정적인 대중들의 반응에도 불구하고, 새로운 공원을 짓기 위한 자금을 조달하는 것은 어려웠다.

overwhelmingly 압도적으로

119

해설 빈칸은 has recruited의 목적어가 들어갈 자리이므로 형용사로만 쓰이는 (B) every와 (C) other는 오답이다. 명사/형용사로 모두 쓰이는 (A) some과 (D) much가 답이 후보가 되는데, much of 뒤에는 불가산명사가 와야 하므로 오답이다. 따라서 정답은 뒤에 가산복수명사/불가산명사 모두 올 수 있는 (A) some이다.

인스파트 테크놀로지는 이 지역의 최고의 소프트웨어 엔지니어들 몇몇을 공격적으로 채용했다.

aggressively 공격적으로

120

해설 빈칸은 명사(brand)를 수식할 형용사 자리이다. 선택지에는 일반 형용사는 없지만, 현재분사와 과거분사 형태인 (B)와 (D)가 있다. 자기가 인정하는(recognizing) 브랜드가 아니라 인정받는(recognized) 브랜드기 적절하므로 정답은 (B) recognized이다.

작은 지역 가게로 시작했던 세븐 스타 채용사는 이제 국제적으로 인정받는 브랜드가 되었다.

internationally 국제적으로

121

해설 be reminded to부정사(~할 것을 상기받다, 주의받다)를 세트 표현으로 외워 두자. 따라서 정답은 (B)이다. inquire(문의하다)는 about과 함께 쓰이는 자동사이므로 오답이고, deny(부인하다)는 의미상 맞지 않아 오답이며 to부정사가 아닌 전치사 to가 와야 하므로 오답이다.

청소 직원들이 언제 사무실이 비는지 않 수 있도록, 모든 직원들은 하루가 끝날 때 서명하는 퇴실을 잊지 않도록 주의받는다.

sign out 퇴실하다 ※ 이름을 기록하다

122

해설 전치사 문제로 빈칸 뒤에 기간(six-week time period) 명사가 있으므로 기간 명사 앞에 쓸 수 있는 전치사 (C)가 정답이다. 기간 명사 앞에 쓸 수 있는 전치사 for, during, within, throughout, in, after 등도 함께 알아 둔다.

갤러리 전시실의 개조는 6주의 기간 동안 점차적으로 완료될 것이다.

renovation 보수, 개조 showroom 전시실 gradually 점차적으로 period 기간

123

해설 명사와 문제로 판매상/복구가 이달 남은 기간 동안 지속될 것으로 예상된다가 가장 자연스러우므로 정답은 (B)이다.

장기간의 일기예보 보도에 따르면, 이달에 남은 기간 동안 복우가 지속될 것으로 예상된다.

long-term 장기간의 last 계속되다, 지속되다 remainder 나머지 boundary 경계 anticipation 예상; 기대

124

해설 동사 문제로 'A와 B를 비교하다'라는 표현으로 compare A with[to] B를 쓰는데, 문맥상 '두 곳의 최근 성과를 비교했다'가 되어야 하므로 앞 명사(performance)를 받을 수 있는 that이 있는 (C)가 정답이다. 앞에 나온 명사가 반복될 때 이를 대신해 받을 수 있는 대명사에는 단수 that과 those가 있으며 단수, 복수의 차이에 따라 구분해서 사용한다.

부수성 메일 콜럼는 그의 연설에서 콜럼스 엔 터미크 사의 최근 성과를 HG 컨설팅 그룹의 성과와 비교한다.

address 발표, 연설 **what is more** 더욱이, 게다가

125
해설 형용사 어휘 문제로 문맥상 '재선출될 가능성이 있다'가 자연스러우므로 자연스러우므로 (A)가 알맞다.
마케이 일문이 민방위 이것으로 재선출될 가능성이 있다.
Civil Defense 민방위 probable 가능성이 있는 qualified 자격이 있는 constant 끊임없는 endless 무한한

126
해설 접속사 문제로 콤마 뒤에 동사현행(ensure)으로 시작하는 안전한 문장이 앞으로며 받쳐져서 course가지는 수식 어구이다. 문맥상 '회계부에 입하 시험을 완료하는 동안에'가 적절하므로 (A)가 정답이다. 빈칸 뒤 completing은 동명사가 아니라 분사구문을 이루는 분사이다. In addition뒤 Assuming that을 부사절 접속사로 뒤에 완전한 절이 와야 한다.
건물에 대한 꼼꼼한 점검 후에, 우리는 목록 피해가 처음에 예상한 것보다 더 심각하다는 것을 알게 되었다.
entrance test 입학 시험 accounting 회계 ensure 확실히 하다 fill in 작성하다 current 현재의 employer 고용주

127
해설 주어인 '목록 피해'의 어울릴 만한 형용사를 골라야 한다. effective(효과적인), accurate(정확한), apparent(분명한)는 의미상 어울리지 않으므로 오답이다. 참고로 When/By the time절 안에 현재시제가 있을 때는 실제로는 미래를 의미하는 것이므로, 주절에 미래/미래완료 시제가 와야 한다.
meticulous 꼼꼼한, 세심한 accurate 정확한 apparent 분명한

128
해설 When/By the time절 안에 과거시제나 과거완료시제가 있을 때, 주절에는 과거시제나 과거완료시제가 와야 한다. 따라서 정답은 (C) had begun이다. 참고로 When/By the time절 안에 현재시제가 있을 때는 실제로는 미래를 의미하는 것이므로, 주절에 미래/미래완료 시제가 와야 한다.
인수가 발표되었을 때 즘에, 임파 케이머는 이미 새로운 사업 전략들을 개발해 내기 시작했다.
acquisition 인수

129
해설 선택지 모두 전치사이므로 해석으로 풀어야 하는 문제이다. social media marketing campaign은 홍보의 수단이므로 '~을 통하여'라는 뜻의 전치사 (D) through가 정답이다. 참고로 among(~ 사이에)은 뒤에 복수명사가 온다.
사인 미디어 사는 광범위한 소셜 미디어 마케팅 광고를 통해서 새로운 온라인 음악 서비스인 젤리 뮤직을 홍보할 것이다.
extensive 광범위한

130
해설 형용사 어휘 문제로 문맥상 '50퍼센트의 놀라운 기부 성장을 이가졌다'가 가장 자연스러우므로 (B)가 정답이다.
동물 복지 홍보 캠페인은 지난 3개월 동안 50퍼센트의 놀라운 기부 성승의 결과를 보았다.
animal welfare 동물 복지 promotional 홍보의 receptive 수용적인 remarkable 놀라운 tedious 지루한 perpetual 끊임없이 계속되는

Part 6

본책 P159

[131-134]
증가하는 비용 때문에 우리는 공급업체들과의 계약을 재검토하게 되었습니다. 그 결과, 입하 공급업체를 바꾸기로 결정했습니다.
8월 1일부로 모든 향후 입하 주문은 도리 잉크사에게 가야 할 것입니다. 기존의 잉크 재고가 다 소진될 때까지 사용해야 합니다. 그러나 직원들은 새로운 잉크를 사용하기 전에 모든 지침과 절차에 익숙해져야 합니다. 반드시 각각의 제품군에 맞는 적절한 절차들이 적용되어야 합니다.
도리 잉크사는 제품 사용법이 나와 있는 교육용 소책자를 가지고 있습니다. 새 잉크의 첫 발송분이 도착하자마자 이 소책자들은 전 직원들에게 배포될 것입니다. 지침들을 철저하게 검토해 주십시오, 새 제품 사용에 관한 어떤한 문의라도 저희 헬리 씨(1-200-555-0444)에게 보내 주십시오.

expense 비용 as of ~부로, 부터 existing 기존의 run out 다 떨어지다 familiarize 익숙하게 하다 procedure 절차 respective 각각의 instruction 지시사항 application 적용, 응용 thoroughly 철저히 undergo 겪다

131
해설 앞뒤 문장의 의미를 적절하게 연결시켜 줄 접속부사를 고르는 문제이다. 앞 문장에서 공급업체를 바꾸기로 결정했다고 했으니 인과관계로 붙을 수 있다. 따라서 정답은 (D) Consequently(그 결과)이다. (A) 달리, 그렇지 않으면 / (B) 그럼에도 불구하고 / (C) 즉, 다시 말해

132
해설 각각의 제품군에 맞는 '적절한' 절차들이 적용되어야 한다는 말이 가장 어울리므로 정답은 (B) appropriate이다. (A) 구식의 / (C) 수동의 / (D) 명백한

133
(A) 도리 잉크사는 가장 잘 팔리는 성성을 잉크 브랜드 중 하나입니다.
(B) 직원들은 프린터기를 적절히 사용하는 방법에 관해서도 특별 교육을 받아야 합니다.
(C) 도리 잉크사는 제품 사용법이 나와 있는 교육용 소책자를 가지고 있습니다.
(D) 잉크를 덜 쓰고 양면 복사를 함으로써 우리는 비용을 줄일 수 있습니다.
해설 빈칸 뒤에서 These가 나오고 전 직원에게 배포된다고 했으므로 These에 해당하는 brochures가 나오는 (C)가 정답이다.

134
해설 sales representative(영업 사원)를 하나의 복합명사로 위 두자. 참고로 representation은 '묘사, 표현'이라는 의미이다.
정답은 (A)이다.

[135-138]
미키 오벤 이사
클리어 워터 낚시용품
헨조 로드 89
데이턴, 오하이오 45377
오벤 씨에게,

제 상사인 주디 페트리에 씨가 최근에 제게 저희 로스엔젤레스 영업소에 자리를 제공했습니다. 그래서 저의 로스엔젤레스 영업소에서의 135 그러므로 저의 로스엔젤레스 영업소에 자리를 고려해 주셨으면 합니다.

이번에 전근이 된다면, 로스엔젤레스에서 활동 중인 실내 디자인 책임자인 제가 인츠와 제가 다시 한번 어울릴 수 있는 기회를 136 갖게 될 것입니다. 그러나 이것 메이트와에 근무할 때, 저희 두 사람은 전국 플러이 파싱 프로젝트에 공동 작업을 펼친 바 있습니다. 페트리에 씨는 전근에 전적인 지지를 137 표현했고, 규모를 위해 승인을 서면화하겠다고 제안했습니다. 제 이력서를 동봉했으며, 귀하이 138 고려에 미리 감사드립니다.

제이슨 테이트
제품 디자인 전문가
동봉

director 중역, 이사 fishing supply 낚시용품 supervisor 관리자, 감독 transfer 전근 associate with ~와 어울리다 collaborate 공동 작업하다, 협력하다 full support 전적인 지지 in advance 미리, 사전에 enclosure 동봉 application 지원

135

(A) 게다가 그녀는 디자인 회사에서 이미 인턴십을 완료했습니다.

(B) 그러므로 저희 로스엔젤레스 영업소로의 전근 신청을 고려해 주셨으면 합니다.

(C) 그러나 해외 근무 경력에 비추어 봤을 때 제가 그 직무에 적임 자입니다.

(D) 그렇지 않으면 저는 다른 나라로 이주하기로 결정할 것입니다.

해설 빈칸 앞에서 자신이 로스엔젤레스 영업소의 적임자가 될 것 이라는 상사의 의견을 언급했으므로 전근 신청을 한다는 (B)가 정 답이다.

136

해설 빈칸에는 상상하는 일의 결과에 대해 말할 때 쓰는 단어가 필요하므로 would(~할 것이다)로 시작하는 (B)가 정답이다.

137

해설 문제상 빈칸에는 감정이나 의견을 '나타내다[표현하다]'라는 뜻으로 쓰이는 단어가 지앤스러우므로 (C)가 정답이다. (A) 의지하 다 / (B) 이룸을 제기하다 / (D) 원하다

138

해설 이 글은 전근을 가고 싶어서 신청하는 글이므로 마지막 인사 말로 '당신이 고려해 주시면 감사하겠습니다'라는 말이 어울린다. 따라서 정답은 (C) consideration(고려)이다. (A) 아이디어 / (B) 진전 / (D) 인내심

[139-142]

발신: 코디 얼렌
수신: 모든 KPN 직원들

모두 아시다시피, KPN은 지난 6개월 동안 주요 보수 공사를 진행해 왔습니다. 그 시간 동안 우리 인사부는 여전히 뛰어난 서비스를 제공하려 고 노력하는 **139** 동시에 몇몇 조정을 기했습니다. 직원들이 우리 회사에 가장 귀중한 자산이기 때문에 이 변화에 대한 여러분의 경험에 대해서 의 견을 듣고 싶습니다.

140 동봉된 것은 한 페이지짜리 설문조사 설문지입니다. 이 기밀 설문조사는 수피 브 라사치에 의해서 시행될 것이고, 이 기록은 우리 KPN에게 100년 넘간 마케팅 조사의 분석을 제공해 왔던 기관입니다. 여러분은 솔직하고 빠른 응답을 인사부가 독표를 결정하는 데 도움이 될 것입니다. 모든 응답은 **141** 익명으로 유지될 것입니다. 작성된 양식을 6월 10일 월요일까지 인사부서로 제출해 주세요.

142 여러분의 시간과 한신에 대해 미리 감사드립니다. 저희는 항상 KPN에 대한 여러분의 의견과 한신에 감사하고 있습니다.

---

aware 알고 있는 undergo ~을 경험하다 renovation 보수 공사
adjustment 조정, 변화 outstanding 뛰어난 confidential 기밀의
straightforward 솔직한 timely 적시의 determine 결정하다
dedication 헌신 considerable 상당한

139

해설 인사부가 뛰어난 서비스를 제공하면서 '동시에' 몇몇 조정 을 가했다고 모든 것이 자연스러우므로 정답은 (D) while(~하는 동안에/하면서)이다. (A) ~후에 / (B) ~없이 / (C) ~와 달리

140

해설 be동사를 기준으로 앞뒤가 도치된 문장구조이다. 원래 문 장은 'A single-page survey is enclosed'인데, 동물물이 라는 것을 강조하기 위해서 도치한 것이다. 따라서 정답은 (C) Enclosed이다.

141

해설 앞에서 기밀 설문조사라는 내용이 나왔으므로 모든 답변은 '익명으로 유지될 것이다'라고 하는 것이 적절하다. 따라서 정답은 (A) anonymous(익명의)이다. (B) 주인 없는, 방치된 / (C) 지속 가능한 / (D) 의존적인

142

(A) 저희는 직원 만족을 개선하고자 상당한 노력을 해 왔습니다.

(B) KPN의 전 직원들에게 서비스를 제공하게 되어서 영광이었습 니다.

(C) 여러분의 시간과 의견에 미리 감사드립니다.

(D) 여러분의 제안들을 저희 웹 사이트에 올려주세요.

해설 빈칸 뒤에 당신에 대해 감사한다고 했으므로 이와 같은 맥락 의 (C)가 정답이다.

[143-146]

수신: 출장 요리부 직원
발신: 노벨 이바노빅
날짜: 4월 22일
제목: 새 커피 기기
직원 등록 여러분께

오늘 휴게실에 플럼없이 고장 나던 옛 커피 기기를 대신해 새 커피 기기가 **143** 설치되었습니다. 우리는 이 모델이 더 **144** 을을 만할 것이기를 바랍니다.

이것은 평판이 좋은 대용량의 커피 메이커입니다. **145** 품질 보증서에 이 제품이 적어도 10년은 갈 것이라고 나와 있습니다. 이 커피 기기를 효율 적으로 관리하기 위해 **146** 예를 들어 종이팔과 우유 봉지 같은 제조 또는 부대물이 사용되도록 하고 다른 것들은 사용하지 마십시오.

기기 사용 시, 처음에 문제들을 겪을 수 있습니다. 만약 그럴 경우 공기 옆 게시판에 붙어 있을 예정인 설명서를 **146** 참고하세요.
노벨

catering 출장 요리 colleague 동료 common room 휴게실
replacement 대체품 constantly 끊임없이 break down 고장 나다
large-capacity 대용량의 reputable 명성 있는 maintenance 유지 보수
accessory 부대물 sachet (샴푸·설탕 등의 1회분을 넣는) 작은 봉지
initially 처음에 if so 만일 그렇다면 instructions 설명서 notice board
게시판 decent 괜찮은 warranty 품질 보증서

143

해설 회사 휴게실의 낡은 커피 기기를 새 기기로 교체했다는 내용 이므로 빈칸의 문장은 새 기계가 좀 더 만을 만한 제품이기를 바란 다는 의미가 자연스럽다. 따라서 정답은 '믿을 만한이라는 의미의 (A)가 알맞다. (B) 달성할 수 있는 / (C) 휴대용의 / (D) 탐지할 수 있는

144

(A) 우리는 최신 기계를 살 필요가 있습니다.

(B) 다음은 제대로 된 커피를 만드는 방법입니다.

(C) 전 직원들은 요리 수업에 참석할 것이 요구됩니다.

(D) 품질 보증서에 이 제품이 적어도 10년은 갈 것이라고 나와 있 습니다.

해설 빈칸 앞에서 새로 구매한 커피 기기에 대한 설명이 나오므로 이어서 적어도 10년은 문제 없을 거라는 (D)가 적절하다.

145

해설 빈칸 이하는 기계를 살 때 원래 제공되는 부품들에 예를 들 고 있으므로 '부대물'을 가리키는 (C)가 적절하다.

146

해설 정보를 얻기 위해 무엇을 찾아보거나 참고한다는 뜻에 해당 하는 말은 (D)이다. (A) 수정하다 / (B) 바라다 / (C) 승인하다

Part 7

[147-148]

11월 5~9일 8호실 예약				
	11월 5일 월요일	11월 6일 화요일	11월 7일 수요일	11월 8일 목요일	11월 9일 금요일
오전 10시	어린이를 위한 이야기		어린이를 위한 이야기		청년 전문 협회
오전 11시		작가 대릴 돌라지의 강연		공상 과학 소설 독서	
정오			여름 도서 프로그램 파티		**148** 문학 친구들 모임
오후 1시	어린이를 위한 이야기			시 클럽 모임	
오후 2시				이사회 회의	
오후 3시			구직 및 면접 요령 수업		

youth 어린 시절, 청춘 society 협회 lecture 강연 author 저자, 작가 science fiction 공상 과학 board meeting 이사회 job application 구직 interviewing skill 면접 요령

147 8호실은 어디에 위치할 것 같은가?
(A) 박물관
(B) 공공 도서관
(C) 미술 전시관
(D) 직업소개소

148 청년 직문 협회와 같은 날로 일정이 잡힌 행사는?
(A) 어린이를 위한 이야기
(B) 문학 친구들 회의
(C) 공상 과학 독서
(D) 시 클럽 회의

[149-151]

헤이즐 스펜서 [오후 3:51]	마이클, 인턴을 위해서 새로운 이메일 계정을 만들어 줄 수 있어요? **149** 그 인턴은 다음 주 월요일부터 일을 시작할 거예요. 제가 출장 가기 전에 이걸 얘기 했어야 했는데, 완전히 잊어버렸어요.
마이클 헌터 [오후 3:52]	그럼요. 그 인턴 이름이랑 인턴실 기간 좀 알려주시 겠어요?
헤이즐 스펜서 [오후 3:53]	**149** 그의 이름은 드레이시 헤이즈이고 4개월 정도 일할 거예요. 연구 프로젝트 수행을 도와줄 거예요.
마이클 헌터 [오후 3:54]	**150** 그녀의 이메일 주소는 intern. 일겠어요 hayes@kingston.com이 될 거예요. **151** 이 건에 대해서는 프리다 싸한테 공식 승인을 받을 거예요. 기다려야 해요. 그분이 오늘 쉬는 날이라서. 제가 내일 이 이메일 계정을 생성할게요. 그래도 괜찮을까요?
헤이즐 스펜서 [오후 3:55]	이번 주까지만 준비된다면 이주 좋습니다. 감사합니다, 마이클.

duration 기간 carry out ~을 수행하다 formal 공식적인 approval 승인

149 트레이시 헤이즈 씨에 대해서 암시된 것은 무엇인가?
(A) 그녀는 출장 중이다.
(B) 그녀는 지금 이메일을 보내야 한다.
(C) 그녀는 곧 인턴십을 시작할 것이다.
(D) 그녀는 인턴십 이후에 일할 것이다.

150 오후 3시 54분에 헌터 씨가 "알겠어요"라고 썼을 때 그 의미는 무 엇인가?
(A) 그는 새로운 이메일 계정을 만들 것이다.
(B) 그는 누군가에게 이메일을 보낼 것이다.
(C) 그는 연구 프로젝트를 이끌 것이다.
(D) 그는 인턴에게 오리엔테이션을 해줄 것이다.

151 헌터 씨는 무엇을 기다려야 하는가?
(A) 네트워크 엔지니어
(B) 한 사람의 승인
(C) 공식 문서
(D) 면접

[152-154]

수신: 카틸다 덴쉬 (katilda_densch@smail.com)
발신: 브록스 카플란 <kaplanb@smail.com>
날짜: 1월 9일 월요일
제목: 소식

카틸다에게,

제가 지난달에 멤피스 사무실로 방문할 수 있도록 준비해 주셔서 다시 한 번 감사합니다. 매우 유익하고 즐거웠으며 곧 다시 방문하기를 기대합니 다. 제가 그곳에 있는 동안 **153** 당신은 어머니와 가까이 있기 위해 프랑스 로 옮기는 것에 관심이 있다고 했습니다. **152** 현재 파리 사무실의 회계 직무상이 있는지 것을 알려 드리고 싶습니다. 지금는 당신이 매우 적합할 것이라고 생각되는 직책인 세금 전문가를 찾고 있습니다. 직무는 멤피스 에서 당신이 담당하고 있는 관리 회계와와 매우 비슷합니다. 공석은 다음 달 말에 공개적으로 홍보될 것입니다. 지원서를 제출하는 데 관심이 있으시다면, 제게 알려 주 세요. **154** 제가 직책에 대한 세부 사항과 지원서를 이메일로 바로 보내겠 습니다.

브룩스 카플란

fruitful 유익한 accounting 회계 highly 매우 qualified 자격이 있는 opening 공석 publicly 공개적으로 solicit 권유하다 restructuring 구 조 조정 collaborate 공동으로 작업하다

152 이메일의 목적은 무엇인가?
(A) 여행 준비를 의논하기 위해
(B) 덴쉬 씨가 직책에 지원하도록 장려하기 위해
(C) 덴쉬 씨에게 다가오는 업무 회의를 알리기 위해
(D) 회사의 최근 구조 조정에 대해 설명하기 위해

153 이메일에 따르면, 덴쉬 씨가 파리로 이사하는 것에 관심이 있는 이유는?
(A) 카플란 씨와 그 지역을 여행하기 위해
(B) 책무가 더 많은 자리에서 일하기 위해
(C) 가족의 일원과 더 가까이 살기 위해
(D) 카플란 씨와 프로젝트를 공동으로 작업하기 위해

154 카플란 씨가 덴쉬 씨를 위해 차인하는 것은?
(A) 그녀가 프로젝트 관리자를 만날 수 있도록 준비하기
(B) 그녀가 묵을 장소 찾기
(C) 그녀에게 추가 정보 보내기
(D) 그녀의 문의에 답하기

[161-163]

주디 존스
헤사 스트리트 20
제퍼슨, 메인 04348
9월 20일

책임자 폴 두베시니
올 패션 매거진
테니스 로드
제퍼슨, 메인 04348

두베시니 씨,

10월 30일에 채용될 수 있도록, **[161]**(올 패션 매거진)의 사진작가 지의 사직서를 알려 드립니다. 계약에 따라 한 달 전에 말씀 드리는 것입니다.

엄마 전부터 창업을 생각하고 있었습니다. 한 달 전에 **[162]** 마스터 사진전가 협회에서 개인 사진작가로 성을 받았고, **[163]** 제 사업을 시작할 수 있게 최종 승인이 포함되어 있었습니다.

잡지에 있는 동안 이 분야에 대해 많이 배웠습니다. 사진부 동료들은 제가 예술가로썬반이 아니라, 사진가로도 새로운 경험을 쌓아 가졌지만, 인생에서 새로운 이 시간과 여러분 전심으로 연락하고 지내는 것이 저의 바람입니다.

함을 하면서 여러분과 여러분의 지속적으로 그림을 것입니다. 여러분과 회사의 성장을 바랍니다.

주디 존스

161 존스 씨가 두베시니 씨에게 편지를 쓴 이유는 무엇인가?
(A) 전근을 요청하기 위해
(B) 승진을 요청하기 위해
(C) 채용 지원 프로그램을 신청하기 위해
(D) 결정에 대해 알리기 위해

162 존스 씨가 최근에 받은 것은?
(A) 저명한 시간 예술가에게 훈련받을 기회
(B) 그녀의 우수한 직업에 대한 인정
(C) 독립 사진작가에게서 온 특별한 도움에 대한 감사의 편지
(D) 사진부 책임자로서 3건의 계약

163 마스터 사진작가 협회는 존스 씨가 무엇을 하는 데 도움을 주었는가?
(A) 정규직 대신 시간제로 일하도록 결정하도록
(B) 사진부서의 책임자 직책 시작하기

resign 사임하다   take effect 효력이 발생하다   notify 알리다, 통보하다   outline 개요를 서술하다   venture 모험적 사업   field 분야   colleague 동료   funding 자금 지원   advise 통지하다   outstanding 뛰어난   supervisor 관리자   loan 대출

[155-157]

존스 앤 바고스 주식회사

별도의 표시가 없으면, 저녁 교대 근무(오후 5시 ~ 오후 10시) 직책임

창고 담당자

고등학교 졸업장이 있고, 재고 관리 절차에 대해 정통해야 하며, 바쁜 생산 환경에 대한 경험이 있어야 한다. **[155]** 기술과 금속에 관한 기본적 지식 또한 갖추어야 한다. 이전 관리 업무는 선호되지만 필수는 아니다.

공장 기술자

관련 지격을 소지하고, 최소 2년의 공장 근무 경험이 있어야 한다. 중장비 직동이 기능해야 한다. **[156]** 아근이 필수이다.

개인 비서

고등학교 졸업장과 뛰어난 타자 기술, 소매 시설에서의 경력이 있어야 한다. **[156]** 때로 아근해야 한다.

유통 관리자와 재고 관리 보조

성실하고 신뢰할 수 있어야 한다. **[156]** 재고 관리 보조의 경우, 때로 아근 해야 한다.

[157] 이력서는 이곳으로 보내 주세요.

인사부
존스 앤 바고스 주식회사
유통 센터
케임브리지 로드 1415
매사추세츠 보스턴 02109

[157] 전화나 이메일은 사절

shift 교대 근무   unless otherwise indicated 별도의 표시가 없으면   warehouse 창고   diploma 졸업장   awareness 의식   desirable 선호하는   relevant 관련이 있는   qualification 자격(증)   heavy equipment 중장비   retail 소매의   establishment 시설, 기관   distribution 유통   diligent 성실한   reliable 신뢰할 만한   willingness 의지   in person 직접

155 창고 담당직의 필수 조건은?
(A) 마케팅 학위
(B) 금융에 대한 일부 지식
(C) 이전의 관리 경력
(D) 아근을 할 의지

156 아근이 포함되지 <u>않는</u> 직책은?
(A) 유통 관리자
(B) 개인 비서
(C) 공장 기술자
(D) 재고관리 보조

157 지원자가 직책에 지원하는 방법은?
(A) 온라인으로
(B) 직접 찾아가서

(C) 우편으로
(D) 전화로

[158-160]

제임스 마케팅 학교

마케팅 하위 프로그램을 찾고 계신가요? **[158]** -[1]-.

이 프로그램은 12개월 과정으로 2월, 6월, 10월에 등록되고 있고, 다음과 마케팅이 국제 홍보에 대한 폭넓은 지식가 강화가 있습니다. **[159]** 모든 강의는 약령 인사들에 의해 진행되는데, 그들은 대부분 공업계로 회사와 무역 회사의 상급 자리에 있으며, 실무적인 정보를 강의실로 가져올 것입니다. -[2]-. 국제적인 선두 기업들에서의 인터넷 웹셋반이 아니라 **[160]** 이것으로 마케팅 전국 협회에서는 항상 저체 프로그램 국내 3주년 내로 선정하고 있습니다.

내로반들이 등록하는 100달러이며, 해외 신청자는 120달러입니다. -[3]-. 이 광고를 언급하시면 10월 30일 전가지 신청 서류가 제출되는 조건에 등록해 내지 않아도도 됩니다. 정규 등록 마감일은 11월 30일 입니다. **[160]** 지원자들도 정하금 및 후원을 찾아볼 것을 권장합니다. -[4]-.

문의 사항 및 더 많은 정보는 www.jamesmarketing.edu을 방문해 주세요.

제임스 존스

institute 기관   entry 가입; 등록   cross-cultural 다문화   distinguished 유명한, 성공한   personnel 인원, 인사   reputable 평판이 좋은   trading 무역   real-work 실무   consistently 지속적으로   rate 순위, 비율   resident 주민   provided ~라면   scholarship 장학금   sponsorship 후원, 협찬   enrollment 등록   faculty 교수진

158 액셀런스 마케팅 프로그램에 관해 알 수 있는 것은?
(A) 완공하려면 2년이 걸린다.
(B) 뛰어난 명성을 갖고 있다.
(C) 등록 시기가 두 번이 있다.
(D) 최근에 교수진을 추가했다.

159 광고에 따르면 학생들이 이용할 수 <u>없는</u> 것은?
(A) 전문성을 가진 교수들과의 만남
(B) 해외에서 경험을 쌓을 수 있는 기회
(C) 온라인 강좌를 들을 수 있는 기회
(D) 재정적 지원을 받을 기회

160 [1], [2], [3], [4]로 표시된 위치 중 다음 문장이 들어가기 적절한 것은?
"그렇다면 멀리서 찾거 마시고, 제임스 마케팅 학교의 액셀런스 마케팅 프로그램을 선택하세요."
(A) [1]
(B) [2]
(C) [3]
(D) [4]

(C) 개인적인 목표에 집중하는 것을 선택하기
(D) 소기업 대출 신청하기

[164-166]

로사 패턴	**오전 10:03**
안녕, 제가 지금 회계 매니저 직무를 위한 면접을 보고 있는데, 이번 달 일까지 직원자를 채용하기를 원해요. 이번 달 말까지 직원자를 채용할 것으로 예상하고 있어요. 새로운 직원을 위한 컴퓨터를 준비해 줄 수 있나요?	
안단 로스	**오전 10:04**
164 제 생각엔 영업부서에 남는 데스크톱이 있는 것 같아요. 지난주에 한 계약업자가 프로젝트를 마쳤거든요. 제가 하워드를 대화에 포함할게요.	
《 하워드 포스터 씨가 채팅방에 입장했습니다. 》	
안단 로스	**오전 10:05**
하워드, 제시 월터 씨의 기계가 아직 이용 가능한가요?	
하워드 포스터	**오전 10:06**
아니요, 우리 연구 인턴 중 한 명에게 할당되었어요.	
안단 로스	**오전 10:08**
사무용 어딘가에 이용 가능한 다른 컴퓨터가 없나요?	
하워드 포스터	**오전 10:08**
네, 일반 사무 업무를 하기에 거의 새 것이에요.	
로사 패턴	**오전 10:09**
이메일, 스프레드시트, 그리고 프레젠테이션 파일을 다루기에 충분한가요?	
하워드 포스터	**오전 10:11**
데스크톱은 없지만, 월슨 지사에서 회수한 두 대의 휴대용 컴퓨터는 있어요.	
로사 패턴	**오전 10:13**
좋네요. 하워드, **166** 새로운 직원을 위해서 하나 설치해 주실 수 있을까요? **165** 이 직원이 첫날부터 생산적이었으면 좋겠거든요	
하워드 포스터	**오전 10:14**
직장 마세요. 제가 처리할게요	

on board 승선한, 합류한 contractor 계약자 assign 할당하다 retrieve 회수하다

164 로스 씨는 왜 포스터 씨를 초대했는가?
(A) 그녀가 무엇을 주문하고 싶어하는지 설명하기 위해서
(B) 새로운 직원에 대해서 물어보기 위해서
(C) 그에게 몇몇 컴퓨터들을 회수해 오라고 요청하기 위해서
(D) 사무용 장비의 이용 가능성에 대해서 물어보기 위해서

165 패턴스 씨에 대해서 암시된 것은?
(A) 그녀는 몇몇 인턴들을 채용할 것이다.
(B) 그녀는 직원을 위해 몇몇 컴퓨터를 업그레이드하기를 원한다.
(C) 그녀는 새로운 직원이 바로 일하기를 원한다.
(D) 그녀는 윌슨 지사에서 일하고 했었다.

166 오전 10시 14분에 포스터 씨가 "제가 처리할게요"라고 했을 때 그 의미는 무엇인가?
(A) 그는 재무 보고서를 검토할 것이다.
(B) 그는 회의실을 예약할 것이다.
(C) 그는 온라인으로 컴퓨터를 주문할 것이다.
(D) 그는 컴퓨터를 설치할 것이다.

[167-168]

지역 주민들께,

167 다음 주부터 라 알메드 로드 애브뉴 로드 비스트로로 알려질 것입니다. **168** 식당은 포함 더 많은 공간을 제공하기 위해 아래 테라스 확장과 메인 식당의 재단장을 포함하여 여러 가지 수리를 할 것입니다. 새 정원인 폼 가든의 관리하에, 식당은 전과 같은 낮은 가격에 맛 좋은 프랑스 요리를 제공할 것입니다. 변함없는 서비스를 즐겨 주세요.

bistro 작은 식당 undergo (경험을) 겪다 modification 수정, 변경 enlargement 확장, 확대 patio 테라스 refurbish 재단장하다 assure 보장하다 seating capacity 좌석 수

167 광고에 따르면 식당의 무엇이 바뀔 것인가?
(A) 제공되는 음식의 종류
(B) 음식의 가격
(C) 식당의 위치
(D) 식당의 이름

168 간트 씨에 관해 알 수 있는 것은 무엇인가?
(A) 인근의 다른 사업체들을 소유한다.
(B) 식당의 좌석 수를 늘릴 계획이다.
(C) 애브뉴 로드에서 여러 해 해 왔다.
(D) 라 알메드에서 근무했었다.

[169-171]

기업 도서관 카드

169 주립 대학 도서관이 대여 특권을 사용체로 확장합니다. 우리 시에 사무실이 있는 회사의 직원이든 누구라도 기업 도서관 카드를 소지할 자격이 있습니다.

170 기업의 직원 한 명에게 발부되는 카드 한 장이 연회비는 40달러입니다. 정부와 비영리 단체는 이러한 자질에서 면제됩니다.

기업 도서관 카드는 기업을 위해 연구하는 직원들을 위한 것입니다. 이 직원들은 빌려 가는 모든 자료에 대한 책임을 져야 합니다. 연체나 분실 자료에 대해 도서관이 부과하는 벌금은 카드 소지자에 직접 부과됩니다.

기업 카드를 받기 위해서 직원들은 대화 도서관에 직접 와서 신청하여야 합니다. **171** 신청자들은 사진이 있는 신분증과 함께 비용은 신청서와 함께 제출하기 위해 기업 고용주의 편지를 제시해야 할 수 있습니다. 영수증은 환급의 목적으로 제시될 수 있습니다.

기업 카드에 대한 문의는 대출대 855-555-3001로 연락해 주세요.

state university 주립 대학 extend 확장하다 privilege 특권 issue 발행하다 nonprofit 비영리 entity 독립체 be exempt from ~에서 면제되다 fine 벌금, 연체료 impose 부과하다 overdue 기한이 지난 liability 법적 책임 employer 고용주 proof 증명 employment 고용 reimbursement 환급 query 문의 circulation desk 대출대 put forward 제시하다 applicable 적용할 수 있는 relinquish 포기하다

169 공지의 목적은?
(A) 실수를 바로잡기 위해
(B) 서비스를 설명하기 위해
(C) 아이디어를 제시하기 위해
(D) 행사를 발표하기 위해

170 연회비에 대해 언급된 것은?
(A) 신용 카드로 지불할 수 있다.
(B) 오늘 가능성이 낮다.
(C) 일부 유형이 기관에는 적용되지 않는다.
(D) 지역 외 기업은 비용이 더 높다.

171 신청 시 필요요건이 않는 것은?
(A) 서명된 계약서
(B) 신분 증명
(C) 지불금
(D) 고용 세부 사항

[172-175]

6월 5일 — 🔲 식물학자 리바 더복체 씨는 타니 내추럴 헤리티지 프로젝트를 2년에 걸쳐 100만 달러를 기부할 것이라고 어제 발표했다. 프로젝트 또는 지난 3년간 재정적으로 어려움을 겪었기 때문에 기부는 매우 중요한 시점에 일어난 것이다. -[1]-.

"더복체 씨의 후한 선물을 받게 되어 매우 기쁩니다. 타니 내추럴 헤리티지의 회장인 제임스 맥널티 씨가 말했다. "지역 사회의 자연보존 기반을 보존하는 데 큰 도움이 될 것입니다."

내추럴 헤리티지는 10년 전에 지역자연보존회(NRS)에 의해 마을 조기의 자연 휴양지를 보존하고 회복하기 위해 시작되었다. 🔲 🔲 원래 시즘은 지즘이 마련되었던 3년 전 마을 시 의회는 지금에 많은 부분을 지연 보존회에서 신증 토지 개발 프로젝트로 옮기도록 결정했다. -[2]-.

5개월 전 지연보존회는 지역 사회의 개인적인 기부를 마을에 대기엽들로부터 개인적인 기부를 요청하기 시작했다. "기부를 요청하는 편지와 함께 관리가 필요한 자연 경관 사진들을 여러 장 보냈습니다. 그중 하나가 경관 시즘을 여러 장 보냈습니다. 🔲 더복체 씨가 자주 방문하기도 하던 지역이었다." 🔲 전 주민인 리바 더복체 씨가 어떻게 도움 수 있는지 듣기 전까지, 그녀가 개인적으로 그곳과 관련이 있다는 것은 몰랐습니다." 맥널티 씨가 말했다.

타니의 주민들과 지도부는 기부 소식에 크게 기뻐했다. 짐 코너 시장과 시 의 명소에 명예들 기리는 명판을 놓도록 그래하고 있다. -[3]-.

"어렸을 때 자는 타니의 자연 경관에 경험을 받았습니다. 🔲 그곳의 식물을 연구하는 제 직업을 선택한 데 중대한 영향을 줬습니다. 이 기부는 단순히 마을의 자연을 보존하기 위한 것이 아니라다. -[4]-. 이것은 마을의 미래에 투자하는 것입니다."라고 더복체 씨가 말했다.

botanist 식물학자 heritage 유산 crucial 중대한 strain 부담을 주다 thrilled 신난 go a long way toward ~에 도움이 되다 conserve 보존하다 cornerstone 기본이 되는 중요한 것 decade 10년 restore 회복시키다 preserve 지키다 tax revenue 세제 수입 solicit 간청하다 honorary 명예의 plaque 명판 landmark 주요 지형물 appealing 호소력 있는, 매력적인 instrumental 중대한 contributor 기여자

172 기사에 따르면 프로젝트가 지원을 잃었던 이유는 무엇인가?
(A) 건물 가격이 올라갔기 때문에
(B) 지역 정부가 재정 지원을 줄였기 때문에
(C) 개조 작업이 연료되었기 때문에
(D) 타니의 인구가 줄었기 때문에

173 현재 타니의 주민이 아닌 사람은?
(A) 제임스 맥널티
(B) 리바 더복체
(C) 짐 코너
(D) 리처드 돔스

174 더복체 씨가 타니의 자연 보호 구역에 관해 언급한 것은?
(A) 그녀가 식물학자가 되기로 결심하게 했다.
(B) 유지하기에 비용이 많이 든다.
(C) 각자 설립 연도를 알리는 명판이 있어야 한다.
(D) 지역 기반들이 그것들의 회복을 위해 도움 내야 한다.

175 [1], [2], [3], [4]로 표시된 위치 중 다음 문장이 들어가기 적절한 것은?
"그때부터 천면자연 보존을 위한 재정적 지원은 제한되었었다."
(A) [1]
(B) [2]
(C) [3]
(D) [4]

[176-180]

발신: 제니 리 <jli@edumail.com>
수신: 펜튼 루이스 <flewis@springlink.net>
제목: 견적서
날짜: 10월 8일

루이스 씨에게,

이타카 동네의 이웃인 리벤 뷰엔비스 씨가 저희 제게 당신을 추천했습니다. 정원의 어전 문제가 되어버린 레이턴리 삼나무 몇 그룹을 제거하는 데 대한 견적서를 얻고 싶습니다. 🔲 그것들은 높이가 13미터 정도 되는데, 🔲 두 그루도 지즘이 약 45센티미터이며, 나머지 두 그루도 지즘이 약 75센티미터 정도 됩니다. 집에서 40미터 정도 떨어진 곳에 있으며, 올타리로부터 20피트 내에 있습니다. 🔲 10월 15일 금요일 오전 11시에 작업이 가능할까요? 🔲 저희 길이 곧 만광엽에 종사하는 사람들은 10월 11월 12월이 가장 바쁜 시기입니다. 🔲 제가 시간을 낼 수 있는 유일한 날은 다음 주 금요일입니다.

연락 기다리겠습니다.

제니 리

estimate 견적서 refer to 추천하다 cypress 삼나무 diameter 지름 hedge 울타리 afford 여유(형편)가 되다 rest assured 확신해도 된다 premises 구역 sustain (피해 등을) 입다, 당하다 slot 자리; 시간; 틈 presently 현재 initial 처음의 quote 견적 measure 측정하다, 재다 applicable 적용되는 consequently 그 결과, 따라서 calculate 계산하다 associate 동료 property 건물

176 리 씨가 루이스 씨에게 보내는 이메일에 제공하지 않은 정보는?
(A) 그녀의 정원에 있는 식물들의 높이
(B) 그녀의 직업 유형
(C) 그녀가 사는 거리
(D) 그녀가 휴가를 낼 수 있는 날

177 리 씨에 관해 암 수 있는 것은? (연계 지문 문제)
(A) 그녀는 이전에 루이스 트리 서비스에게 일을 맡긴 적이 있다.
(B) 그녀는 3월에 휴가를 갈 계획이다.
(C) 그녀는 루이스 트리 서비스 사무실에서 40킬로미터 이상 떨어진 거리에 산다.
(D) 그녀는 루이스 트리 서비스에서 할인을 받을 것이다.

발신: 펜튼 루이스 <flewis@springlink.net>
수신: 제니 리 <jli@edumail.com>
제목: 귀하의 견적서 요청
날짜: 10월 9일

리 씨에게,

루이스 트리 서비스를 고려해 주셔서 감사합니다. 저희는 서비스를 위한 최선의 장비를 갖추고 있으므로 작업이 필요할 때 구역에 어떤 피해도 🔲 입지 않을 것을 확신하셔도 됩니다. 🔲 저희 고객들이 서비스에 대해 어떻게 말하는지 보시려면, www.fentontreeservice.com/customerreports.com을 방문해 주세요.

🔲 귀하께서 요청하신 날짜와 시간에 작업이 가능합니다. 오전 11시 시간이 현재 비어 있습니다. 보내주신 정보에 기초하여, 서비스를 위한 비용의 첫 견적서를 드릴 수 있습니다. 지름이 20에서 55센티미터인 나무는 400달러를, 지름이 55센티미터를 초과하는 나무는 600달러를 청구합니다. 🔲 또한, 저희 회사의 둔 사무실로부터 40킬로미터 이상 떨어진 장소나 작업은 70달러의 이동 요금이 추가되는 점을 참고하시기 바랍니다. 따라서 총액은 약 2,070달러가 될 것입니다. 정확한 비용을 계산하기 위해, 저희 직원이 이 댁을 방문하여 제거하시기 원하시는 나무들을 측정할 수 있습니다.

준비되시면, 최대한 빨리 연락 주십시오.

펜튼 루이스

178 두 번째 이메일에서 첫째 단락, 둘째 줄의 단어 sustain과 가장 가까운 의미를 가진 단어는?

(A) 평가하다
(B) 겪다
(C) 지지하다
(D) 유발하다

179 루이스 씨는 리 씨에게 무엇을 하라고 추천하는가?

(A) 그녀의 정원을 위한 새 장비를 구매하기
(B) 그에게 오전 11시에 전화하기
(C) 나무들의 정확한 측정치를 가지고 그의 사무실 방문하기
(D) 그의 서비스에 대한 온라인 고객 평 읽기

180 루이스 씨는 언제 직원을 하기로 동의하는가? (연계 지문 문제)

(A) 11월 10일
(B) 10월 15일
(C) 10월 3일
(D) 10월 2일

[181-185]

헤이워스 하우스
렌슨 중심가에 위치

2월 1일에 공개되는 다음도 목적의 새 건물 입대

주거용, 사무용, 상업용 공간 입대

가게와 카페로 둘러싸인 현대적이고, 초현대의 건물. **181** 버스 정류장과 인접.

헤이워스 호수 앤 하이킹을 건너면, 샘이 있는 호수와 등산로 근처.

아파트 (4-8층): 부엌과 욕조가 딸린 욕실, 거실 겸 식사 공간, 넓직한 벽 장이 있는 침실이 한 개 또는 두 개. 세 개 있는 아파트, 지하실의 지장실로 소액의 월 사용료로 이용 가능. 세입자와 방문객을 위한 무료 지하 주차장: 6층과 8층의 공용 세탁 시설 **182** 옥상 정원 조항 예정.

185 사무실 (2-3층): 필요에 따라 분리되는 탄력적인 사무 공간, 1인용 사무실과 안전한 회사 사무실로 작접. 선택 기능한 여러 배치 구조.

소매업 (1층): 가게 앞의 두 개의 공간 제품 둘 다 500평방 미터, **183** 소 매점으로만 사용 가능.

요청하시면 가격과 입대 정보를 제공합니다.

주거용 문의는 레오나르 딘, (080) 555-6705 또는 ldean@hayworth. com으로 보내 주세요.

상업용 문의는 지나 피츠제럴드, (080) 555-6707 또는 gfitz@hayworth. com으로 보내 주세요.

발신: 마이클 펙(mpeck@plaw.com)
수신: 지나 피츠제럴드 (gfitz@hayworth.com)
제목: 헤이워스 하우스
날짜: 11월 21일, 14:23

피츠제럴드 씨께,

185 헤이워스 하우스에 광고하신 것이 가능하다면, 최대한 빨리 그 건물을 방문하길 원합니다.

헤이워스 하우스로부터 단지 몇 블록 떨어진 현재 부지는 추가 인력을 수 용할 수 없을 만큼 작습니다. **184** 저희 사업이 급속도로 성장하여, 늘어난 업무량을 다룰 새 직원들을 가까운 시일 내로 고용할 것입니다.

펙

181 헤이워스 하우스에 관해 언급된 것은?

(A) 버스 노선에 있다.
(B) 지역의 전문가에 의해 지어졌다.
(C) 강가가 자연되었다.
(D) 도시의 가장자리에 있다.

182 광고에 따르면 주거 세입자에게 추가 요즘으로 이용 가능한 것은?

(A) 지하 주차장
(B) 지하 창고
(C) 공용 정원의 사용
(D) 공용 세탁 시설

183 건물에 거주하면 안 되는 세입자의 유형은?

(A) 도매업체
(B) 의류점
(C) 광고 회사
(D) 3인의 가족

184 펙 씨에 회사에 관해 알 수 있는 것은?

(A) 최근에 비용을 인상했다.
(B) 렌슨도 이전한다.
(C) 사업이 번창하고 있다.
(D) 상업용 건물을 사서 리조한다.

185 헤이워스 하우스의 어느 부분이 펙 씨의 관심을 끌 것 같은가? (연계 지 문 문제)

(A) 4-8층
(B) 2-3층
(C) 1층 공간
(D) 지하실

[186-190]

발신: 마이클 윙 영업 부장
발신: 마사 그린, 홍보 부장
날짜: 5월 5일
제목: KTLV 주간 경쟁

마이클 씨에게,

'TV 방송국에서 당신에게 연락했는 걸 저한테 알려주셔서 감사합니다. 당신이 제출하신 그 프로그램에 대한 요약을 검토해 봤는데, 당신의 **187** 전문 지식 때문에 그들이 당신을 원하는 것 같아요. 로렌 파커 부사 장님과 이 문제에 대해서 논의해 봤는데, 그 방송에 출연하는 것을 허락해 주셔요. **186** 일반 행정부서의 제레미 디어츠 씨가 이 방송을 위해 준비 하는 것을 도와줄 거예요. 방송에 필요한 물품 목록을 그에게 전달해 주 세요.

방송 전에, 언론과 대화할 때 당신이 지켜야 할 다음의 규칙들을 명심하세요.

• 회사의 인사 관련 문제에 대해서 언급하지 않기

• **189** 언론 보도자료에 언급되지 않은 어떠한 향후 사업 계획에 대해서도 언급하지 않기

• 회사 고객들과 연관된 민감한 정보를 발설하지 않기

• 회사의 어떠한 비상 상황이나 위기에 대해서 긍정적으로 나타내 주기를 바랍니다.

우리 브랜드의 제품의 제품에 대해서 꼭 이야기 바랄게요.

잘 되길 바랍니다.

행운을 빌며,

마사 그린

KTLV 주간 경쟁에 출연하는 우리 직원

188 5월 24일 토요일, 마케팅 부서의 마이클 윙 씨가 TV 쇼 주간 경쟁에 게스트로 출연합니다. 그 선임 영업 부장은 캠핑 시장의 최근 경향에 대해 서 얘기할 것입니다. 방송에서 그는 캠핑에 대한 조언을 하면서 우리의 텐 트, 침낭, 그리고 조리도구에 대해서 언급할 것입니다. 주간 경쟁은 가장 인기있는 방송 중 하나이고, 18세에서 49세까지의 성인들 사이에서 12.3 의 시청률을 가진 방송입니다. 그의 방송 출연이 우리의 브랜드와 제품을 홍보하는 데 도움이 되기를 바라고 있습니다. 또한, 방송은 15분 채널에서 저녁 8시에서 9시 사이에 방송됩니다. **190** 먼저 제시간에 보지 못하거나 다시 보고 싶다면 KTLV.com에서 스 트리밍할 수 있습니다. 방송은 매주 토요일입니다. **188** 자세한 내용은 KTLV 웹 사이트에 방문하세요.

5월 28일
마이클 윙
올리언스 스포츠 주식회사
1610 위스콘신 애버뉴
밀워키, 위스콘신주 53233

윙 씨에게,

저희 방송에 귀하를 게스트로 모시게 되어서 정말 기쁩니다. 5월 24일 방송은 성공적이었고 저희 예상보다 시청률이 더 높았습니다. 저희 시청자들로부터 많은 긍정적인 반응을 얻었습니다. 시청자들이 이의 캠핑에 대한 귀하의 조언들이 매우 유용하고 유익했다고 말했습니다. 귀하의 노력과 기여에 감사드립니다.

귀하께서 요청하신 것을 했지만, 저희는 귀하가 몇 달 후에 있을 신제품 런칭에 관해 얘기하셨던 부분을 편집하지 않았습니다. 귀하의 우려에도 불구하고, 그 새로운 조리도구 장비는 귀사에 의해서 언론 보도자료에 공식적으로 언급된 적이 있었습니다. 저희가 귀사의 마사 그린 제품을 으로 언급된 적이 있었습니다. 저희가 귀사의 마사 그린 제품을 했습니다.

7월에 한 번 더 저희 방송에 나와 주시기를 부탁드리고 싶습니다. 7월 19일에 아의 활동에 관한 여름 특별 방송을 내보낼 계획입니다. 그 방송은 오후 8시에 시작해서 2시간 정도 방영될 겁니다. 그때 다시 모시게 되기를 진심으로 바랍니다. 가능한 한 빨리 연락 주시기를 기다리겠습니다.

진심을 담아,
브라이언 덥
선임 프로듀서, KTLV

expertise 전문 지식 keep in mind 명심하다 disclose 발설하다 sensitive 민감한 portray 묘사하다 cookware 조리도구 rating 시청률 informative 유익한 edit out ~을 잘라내다

186 이 이메일에 따르면, TV 출연에 대해서 누가 윙 씨를 도와줄 것인가?
(A) 마사 그린
(B) 로렌 파커
(C) 제퍼미 디아즈
(D) 브라이언 덥

187 이 이메일의 1번째 문단, 3번째 줄에 있는 '전문 지식'과 가장 비슷한 의미의 단어는?
(A) 지식
(B) 인상
(C) 외모
(D) 의견

188 발표문의 목적은 무엇인가?
(A) 새로운 캠핑 장비를 홍보하기 위해서
(B) 사람들을 위해 캠핑 팁을 제공하기 위해서
(C) TV 방송의 시청률을 알려주기 위해서
(D) 사람들에게 TV 프로그램을 보라고 권장하기 위해서

189 윙 씨는 왜 그가 방송에서 말한 것을 편집해 달라고 요청했는가? (연계 지문 문제)
(A) 고객에 대한 민감한 정보를 발설해서
(B) 동료에 대한 인사 관련 문제를 얘기해서
(C) 그의 회사의 향후 사업 계획을 언급해서
(D) 그의 회사가 재정적인 어려움을 겪고 있다고 언급해서

190 특별 방송은 정규 방송과 어떻게 다른가? (연계 지문 문제)
(A) 오후 9시에 시작할 것이다.
(B) 한 시간 더 길게 방송될 것이다.
(C) 일요일에 방영될 것이다.
(D) 16번 채널에서 방영될 것이다.

[191-195]

온라인 비즈니스 컨퍼런스

저희의 연례 컨퍼런스가 열리기 때문에 10월을 온라인 비즈니스 컨퍼런스의 참석자들에게 가장 중요한 달입니다. 그러나 참석자들에게 가장 중요한 달은 6월입니다. 다가오는 27번째 OOBC를 위한 조기 등록 달이기 때문입니다. 이것은 7월 1일부터 거의 1년이 연장된다는 것을 의미합니다. 지금의 등록료를 절약할 수 있는 최적의 시기입니다. 특히 단체로 사람들을 보낼 회사들에게는 더욱 많이죠. 만약 당신이 이번 달에 등록한다면, 1인당 100달러를 절약할 수 있습니다. 이 뿐만 아니라 로얄 호텔, 에스트 호텔 또는 넥스트 호텔에서 사용할 수 있는 50달러짜리 기프트 카드도 드립니다. 6월에 등록하시는 모든 분들께 가장 좋은 소식은 할인이 한 명의 컨퍼런스 동안 3박 무료 호텔 숙박권을 받을 수 있다는 것입니다. 당첨자가 될 기회를 얻으려면 6월 30일까지는 반드시 등록해야 합니다.

온라인 비즈니스 컨퍼런스에서 당신을 빨리 보고 싶습니다. 또한 온라인 비즈니스 실무에 대해서 배울 수 있는 최고의 기회가 당신을 기다리고 있습니다. 최고의 가격 혜택을 위해 오늘 등록하세요.

수신: reservations@royalhotel.com
발신: richard.morris@estrada.com
날짜: 6월 28일
제목: Re: 예약

안녕하세요. 제 이름은 리차드 모리스이고, 에스트라다 주식회사에서 일하고 있습니다. 저희 회사는 10월에 열릴 27번째 온라인 비즈니스 컨퍼런스에 몇몇 직원들을 보낼 계획입니다. OOBC측 사람들과 얘기해봤더니 위치와 직원들의 서비스 때문에 귀 호텔을 추천하더군요. 우리 직원들이 이용할 방이 있는지 알고 싶습니다. 귀사의 웹 사이트에서 예약을 해보려고 시도했으나 단체 예약 옵션을 찾을 수가 없었습니다.

11명의 직원들이 10월 12일부터 14일까지 머무를 예정이고, 3개의 1인실과 4개의 2인실이 필요합니다. 만약 가능하다면, 같은 층에서 머물기를 연합니다. 그리고 또한 OOBC 기프트 카드도 쓸 수 있는지 확실하고 싶습니다.

만약 방이 있다면, 연락 주시고 예약하려면 어떻게 해야 하는지 알려주세요.

리차드 모리스
총무부
에스트라다 주식회사

수신: olga.carter@estrada.com
발신: james.stanley@royalhotel.com
날짜: 10월 22일
제목: 예약

카터 씨에게,

오타와의 로얄 호텔에 연락 주셔서 감사합니다. 10월 20일에 보내주신 이메일에 대한 답장을 드립니다. 귀하가 요청하신 대로, 즉시 귀사의 계정을 살펴봤는데 저희가 실제로 귀하에게 금액을 많이 청구한 것을 알게 되었습니다. 저희 직원이 귀하가 제424하신 OOBC 기프트 카드 서비스 업체를 고용해서, 몇몇 자료 다. 저희가 그 새로운 시스템에 익숙하지 않았던 것 같습니다. 실수에 대해서 진심으로 사과 드립니다. 귀하께서 100달러의 요금으로 1인 실에서 3박동안 머무셨으므로, 기프트 카드를 적용하고 나면 250달러를 청구했어야 합니다.

저희가 이 오류를 수정하기 위해 최선을 다하고 있다는 것을 재차 확인시켜 드리고 싶으며 이것은 전체에 로얄 호텔에 있는 지점에서나 무료로 하룻밤을 머무는 데 사용하실 수 있습니다. 파잉 청구된 금액은 영업일 기준 이틀 이내에 귀하의 신용카드 계좌로 환불될 것입니다. 사과의 표시로서, 무료 1박 숙박권을 드리고 싶으며 이것은 전세계 어느 호텔에서나 무료로 하룻밤을 머무는 데 사용하실 수 있습니다.

다시 한 번, 이번 문제가 귀하에게 야기된 모든 불편함에 대해서 사과 드립니다. 다시 또 모시게 되기를 바라겠습니다.

제임스 스탠리
총지배인
로얄 호텔 오타와

191. 오타와 온라인 비즈니스 컨퍼런스에 대해서 암시된 것은?
(A) 직원들이 6월에 가장 바쁘다.
(B) 6월에 5일 동안 지속될 것이다.
(C) 6월에 등록하기가 가장 싸다.
(D) 모든 참가자들이 북권에 당첨될 기회를 가지게 된다.

192. 광고의 2번째 문단, 2번째 줄에 있는 "지속"과 가장 비슷한 의미의 단어는?
(A) 일어날 것 같은
(B) 현실에서 존재하는
(C) 쉽게 이동될 수 있는
(D) 계속될 수 있는

193. 에스트라다 주식회사의 직원들에 대해서 언급되지 않은 것은?
(A) 11명이 컨퍼런스에 참석할 것이다.
(B) 그들은 호텔에서 7개의 방을 필요로 한다.
(C) 그들은 같은 층에서 머물고 싶어 한다.
(D) 그들은 전망이 좋은 방을 원한다.

194. 스탠리 씨는 문제의 원인에 대해서 뭐라고 말했는가?
(A) 지불 시스템이 일시적으로 고장 났다.
(B) 직원이 새로운 시스템에 익숙하지 않았다.
(C) 기프트 카드가 10월에 만기되었다.
(D) 손님의 이름이 목록에 바뀌었다.

195. 호텔은 카터 씨에게 얼마를 청구했는가? (연계 지문 문제)
(A) 300달러
(B) 350달러
(C) 400달러
(D) 500달러

공청회 공지

이 공지는 공청회에 대해서 알려 드리기 위함입니다. 공청회 후에 리치먼드 시 도시 기획부서는 제안된 계획을 채택할지 말지 결정할 것입니다. 모든 관심 있는 분들은 참여하시면 됩니다. 제안된 프로젝트에 대해서 들을 수 있고, 방안에도 의견을 얼을 수 있습니다.

공청회 주제: 파멜라 대로 프로젝트
파멜라 대로의 하수 시스템 복원, 도로 포장 공사와 신호등 업그레이드를 포함한 도로 개선을 위한 제안

장소: 리치먼드 시청
523 웨스트 8번가
리치먼드 시, 조지아주 30003

공청회 날짜: 9월 9일 목요일
시간: 오후 6시 – 오후 8시
추가 정보를 위한 연락: 리치먼드 도시 기획부서 555-3217

파멜라 대로 프로젝트 승인되다

조지아주 리치먼드 시 – 리치먼드 시는 주민들에게 중요한 도로인 파멜라 대로에 대한 120만 달러짜리 보수 공사를 승인했다. 시 공무원들이 알라 대로에서 내낸 조세 공사가 시작될 예정이라고 한다. 이 공사는 지난 여름 목요 기간 동안에 심하게 침수되어 파괴되었기 때문이다.

리치먼드 시의 오래된 하수도가 복수를 대비해 설계되지 않았기 때문에 하수 시스템 또한 손상되었다. 이 프로젝트에는 도로 포장 공사와 신호등 업그레이드도 포함된다.

"폭우 때문에 도로가 통행 불가능한 상태가 되면, 시의 남쪽 지역에 사는 사람들은 주요 도로에 접근할 수 없게 됩니다"라고 시장 제임스 노 리스 씨는 말했다. "도로 개선 프로젝트는 장마철에 주요 고속도로 입구의 접근연을 향상시켜 줄 것입니다."

시는 9월 9일에 공청회를 개최했고, 200명 이상의 시민들이 그룹의 목소리를 내고자 참가했다. 그들 중 오래된 하수 시스템을 교체하는 데에 지금이 바로 투입돼야 한다고 말했다.

"우리는 시민들의 의견을 들었고, 그들이 가장 큰 걱정은 파멜라 도로의 복원이었습니다. 그것은 중요한 일이어서, 우리는 시 예산의 대부분을 투자하기로 한 결정이었다"라고 시장은 말했다.

196 파멜라 대로 프로젝트를 위해서 제안되지 않은 것은 무엇인가?

(A) 도로 포장 공사
(B) 신호등 설치
(C) 하수관 교체
(D) 인도 수리

197 공청회에 대해서 옳은 것은? (연계 지문 문제)

(A) 교량 수리 프로젝트에 관한 것이었다.
(B) 목요일로 인해 시장이 참석하지 않았다.
(C) 시청에서 개최되었고 몇몇 명의 인원이 참석했다.
(D) 시민들이 그 프로젝트에 대해서 못마땅해 했다.

198 기사에 따르면, 파멜라 대로에 대해서 어떤 문제가 언급되었는가?

(A) 차를 몰고 가기에는 너무 어두웠다.
(B) 여름에 침수되었다.
(C) 차량들이 지나가기에 너무 좁았다.
(D) 겨울에 미끄러웠다.

199 기사의 2번째 문단. 1번째 줄에 있는 '통행 불가능한'과 가장 비슷한 의미의 단어는?

(A) 개조된
(B) 패쇄된
(C) 더러운
(D) 들어올려진

200 웹 페이지의 목적은 무엇인가?

(A) 지역 사회 행사를 알리기 위해
(B) 다가오는 폭풍에 대해 경고하기 위해
(C) 교통 정체에 대한 정보를 주기 위해
(D) 건설사를 채용하기 위해

---

www.RichmondCity.gov/notice

2월 1일부터 10월 31일까지 다음과 같은 도로 수리로 인해 노선의 감소나 폐쇄가 있을 수 있습니다. 도시 기획부서는 가능한 한 빨리 필요한 작업을 완료할 수 있도록 모든 노력을 할 것입니다. 이 공사가 완료되면 리치몬드 시민분들이 개선된 것들을 즐기시기를 희망합니다.

파멜라 대로 프로젝트
• 시기: 2월 – 6월
• 설명: 파멜라 대로의 하수 시스템 개선과 신호등 업그레이드

헤이먼 도로 프로젝트
• 시기: 3월 – 9월
• 설명: 헤이먼 도로에 자전거 도로 추가 및 횡단보도 개선

웨스트필드 브릿지 프로젝트
• 시기: 5월 – 10월
• 설명: 교량 및 교량 난간의 수리

아나폴리스 도로 프로젝트
• 시기: 6월 – 10월
• 설명: 교차로 복원

200 예상 교통 체증과 우회로에 대한 정보는 시 웹페이지에 게시될 예정입니다. 모든 최신 소식에 대한 자동 알림을 받으시려면, 저희의 이메일 알림과 문자 알림에 등록하세요. <u>이곳을 클릭</u>

public hearing 공청회 adopt 채택하다 sewage 하수 critical 중요한 sewer 하수관 aging 늙어 가는 impassable 지나갈 수 없는 pedestrian crossing 횡단보도 railing 난간 intersection 교차로 disruption 중단, 두절 detour 우회 alert 알림 disapprove 못마땅해 하다

Actual Test

05

🎧 Listening Comprehension

본책 P.188

PART 1

1 (B)	2 (A)	3 (C)	4 (A)	5 (D)	6 (D)

PART 2

7 (A)	8 (A)	9 (B)	10 (C)	11 (A)	12 (B)	13 (C)	14 (B)	15 (C)	16 (B)
17 (B)	18 (A)	19 (B)	20 (A)	21 (C)	22 (B)	23 (B)	24 (B)	25 (C)	26 (A)
27 (A)	28 (A)	29 (B)	30 (A)	31 (C)					

PART 3

32 (B)	33 (D)	34 (D)	35 (D)	36 (A)	37 (D)	38 (D)	39 (A)	40 (C)	41 (A)
42 (D)	43 (A)	44 (B)	45 (A)	46 (B)	47 (B)	48 (D)	49 (B)	50 (C)	51 (A)
52 (D)	53 (C)	54 (C)	55 (A)	56 (D)	57 (C)	58 (D)	59 (A)	60 (D)	61 (C)
62 (D)	63 (B)	64 (A)	65 (C)	66 (C)	67 (C)	68 (A)	69 (C)	70 (D)	

PART 4

71 (A)	72 (D)	73 (A)	74 (A)	75 (D)	76 (B)	77 (A)	78 (C)	79 (C)	80 (A)
81 (D)	82 (A)	83 (C)	84 (A)	85 (D)	86 (A)	87 (C)	88 (B)	89 (D)	90 (D)
91 (B)	92 (B)	93 (C)	94 (C)	95 (D)	96 (D)	97 (B)	98 (D)	99 (C)	100 (C)

📖 Reading Comprehension

본책 P.200

PART 5

101 (A)	102 (B)	103 (B)	104 (A)	105 (A)	106 (D)	107 (D)	108 (D)	109 (D)	110 (D)
111 (A)	112 (D)	113 (C)	114 (D)	115 (C)	116 (A)	117 (A)	118 (C)	119 (C)	120 (B)
121 (A)	122 (C)	123 (B)	124 (D)	125 (A)	126 (A)	127 (D)	128 (D)	129 (A)	130 (B)

PART 6

131 (C)	132 (C)	133 (A)	134 (D)	135 (B)	136 (C)	137 (B)	138 (C)	139 (C)	140 (A)
141 (D)	142 (C)	143 (C)	144 (B)	145 (C)	146 (D)				

PART 7

147 (B)	148 (D)	149 (D)	150 (C)	151 (A)	152 (B)	153 (A)	154 (D)	155 (C)	156 (D)
157 (C)	158 (D)	159 (C)	160 (C)	161 (A)	162 (A)	163 (C)	164 (A)	165 (A)	166 (D)
167 (A)	168 (C)	169 (B)	170 (A)	171 (A)	172 (D)	173 (C)	174 (A)	175 (C)	176 (A)
177 (A)	178 (A)	179 (C)	180 (C)	181 (C)	182 (D)	183 (C)	184 (C)	185 (D)	186 (A)
187 (B)	188 (C)	189 (D)	190 (A)	191 (C)	192 (B)	193 (D)	194 (C)	195 (A)	196 (C)
197 (D)	198 (A)	199 (D)	200 (C)						

Part 1

1
미M
(A) A display case is being cleaned out.
(B) A woman is helping customers.
(C) Some people are looking out the window.
(D) Some people are entering a restaurant.

(A) 진열장이 청소되고 있다.
(B) 여자가 고객들을 도와주고 있다.
(C) 몇몇 사람들이 창밖을 보고 있다.
(D) 몇몇 사람들이 레스토랑에 들어가고 있다.

display case 진열장; 진열대　clean out 청소하다

2
영M
(A) A wall borders a walking path.
(B) A walkway protrudes into the water.
(C) Some buildings overlook the train tracks.
(D) People are strolling through the tunnel.

(A) 담이 산책로를 경계 짓는다.
(B) 보도가 물가로 튀어나와 있다.
(C) 몇몇 건물들이 기찻선로를 내려다보고 있다.
(D) 사람들이 터널을 통과하며 산책하고 있다.

border 경계를 짓다　walking path 산책로　walkway 통로, 보도　protrude 튀어나오다　overlook 내려다보다　train track 기찻선로　stroll 거닐다, 산책하다

3
미W
(A) She is stretching out on the chair.
(B) She has her hand on the back of a bench.
(C) She is throwing away a piece of paper.
(D) She is raising the blinds.

(A) 여자가 의자 위에서 몸을 뻗고 있다.
(B) 여자가 그녀의 손을 벤치 뒤쪽에 놓고 있다.
(C) 여자가 종이 하나를 버리고 있다.
(D) 여자가 블라인드를 올리고 있다.

stretch out 몸을 뻗다　throw away 버리다　blind (창문에 치는) 블라인드

4
호M
(A) A lounge is divided by partitions.
(B) Vases are arranged on the window ledges.
(C) There are plants near the steps.
(D) An awning has been stretched across the door.

(A) 휴게실이 칸막이로 분리되어 있다.
(B) 화병들이 창턱 위에 정렬되어 있다.
(C) 계단 가까이에 식물이 있다.
(D) 차양이 문을 가로질러 뻗어 있다.

lounge (호텔, 클럽 등의) 휴게실, (공항의) 대합실　partition 칸막이　window ledge 창턱　step 계단　awning (창이나 문 위의) 차양　stretch 뻗다

5
미W
(A) A rider is removing a helmet.
(B) Some tires are being rolled up a ramp.
(C) A walkway is being resurfaced.
(D) A bicycle is casting a shadow.

(A) 기수가 헬멧을 치우고 있다.
(B) 몇몇 타이어들이 경사로 위로 올려지고 있다.
(C) 보도가 재포장되고 있다.
(D) 자전거가 그림자를 드리우고 있다.

rider (말·자전거·오토바이를) 타는(탄) 사람　roll up ~을 올리다　ramp 경사로　resurface (도로 등을) 재포장하다　cast a shadow 그림자를 드리우다

6
영M
(A) Some workers are trimming grass along a path.
(B) They are mowing a lawn in front of the house.
(C) A man is watering some trees.
(D) A man is securing the base of a ladder.

(A) 몇몇 인부들이 길을 따라 잔디를 깎고 있다.
(B) 사람들이 집 앞에서 잔디를 깎고 있다.
(C) 남자가 나무에 물을 주고 있다.
(D) 남자가 사다리의 아랫부분을 고정시키고 있다.

trim 자르다; 깎다　path 길　mow a lawn 잔디를 깎다　water 물을 주다　secure (단단히) 고정시키다　base (사물의) 맨 아랫부분　ladder 사다리

Part 2

7
미M 미W
Have you met the management consultant?
(A) Yes, she seemed friendly.
(B) Not yet, I don't have them.
(C) Online consultation is the best.

경영 상담사를 만나 보셨나요?
(A) 네, 그녀는 친절해 보였어요.
(B) 아직요, 저는 그것들을 갖고 있지 않아요.
(C) 온라인 상담이가 제일 좋습니다.

management 경영, 경영진　consultant 상담가, 자문 위한, 컨설턴트　consultation 상담

8
미W 영M
Who's been assigned to do the editing of this feature?
(A) Magda is going to do it.
(B) Use the business credit card.
(C) She had another appointment.

누가 이 특집의 편집에 배정되었나요?
(A) 마그다가 할 거예요.
(B) 법인 카드를 사용하세요.
(C) 그녀는 또 다른 약속이 있어요.

assign 배정하다　edit 편집하다　feature 특집　business credit card 법인 카드　appointment 약속

9
미W 미M
Do you have a room booked at our hotel?
(A) She told me her address.
(B) Yes, I just did it an hour ago.
(C) Three first-class tickets.

우리 호텔에 예약하신 객실이 있나요?
(A) 그녀가 제게 그녀의 주소를 알려 주었어요.
(B) 네, 바로 한 시간 전에 했어요.
(C) 1등석 3장입니다.

first-class (기차·비행기·선박의) 1등석

10
영M 미W
The best place to purchase recycled computers is Bytesize.
(A) No, I won't, thanks.
(B) A special discount.
(C) Yes, they have a great range.

중고 컴퓨터를 구매하기 가장 좋은 곳은 바이트사이즈입니다.
(A) 아니요, 하지 않을 거예요. 감사합니다.
(B) 특별 할인이요.
(C) 네, 그곳은 아주 다양한 상품을 구매하고 있어요.

special discount 특별 할인　range 범주. 범위

11
미W 미M
Isn't Ali's office upstairs?
(A) No, he moved this week.
(B) Yes, in the basement.
(C) We've met before.

알리의 사무실은 위층 아닌가요?
(A) 아니요, 그는 이번 주에 이사했습니다.
(B) 네, 지하에요.
(C) 우리는 전에 만난 적이 있습니다.

upstairs 위층　basement 지하

12 Which vehicle is yours?
[호M] (A) Thanks for your proposal.
[미W] (B) The blue one parked in the car park.
(C) Yes, I just leased it.

어느 자동차가 당신 것인가요?
(A) 제안에 감사드립니다.
(B) **자동차 주차장에 주차된 파란색 차요.**
(C) 네, 제가 방금 대여했습니다.

vehicle 차량, 운송 수단 proposal 제안 lease (특히 부동산·장비를)
임대(임차, 대여)하다

13 Do you want to bring the glass or the plastic samples?
[미W] (A) It costs three hundred dollars.
[미M] (B) That's our main priority.
(C) The glass is hard to transport.

유리로 된 견본을 갖고 오길 원하세요, 플라스틱으로 된 견본을 갖고
오길 원하세요?
(A) 값은 300달러입니다.
(B) **그것이 우리의 주요 우선순위입니다.**
(C) **유리는 운송하기 힘들어요.**

main priority 주요 우선순위 transport 이동하다, 운송하다

14 How much longer will you be using the photocopier?
[미M] (A) At the end of each month.
[미W] (B) I'm almost finished.
(C) We used to be employed here.

복사기를 얼마나 더 사용할 건가요?
(A) 매월 말입니다.
(B) **거의 끝났어요.**
(C) 우리는 여기에 고용된 적이 있어요.

hired 고용된 photographer 사진작가, 사진사 employ 고용하다

15 It's quite hot here in Orlando, don't you think?
[미W] (A) A stunning building.
[호M] (B) No, the flight left earlier.
(C) Yes, do you want to borrow a fan?

이곳 올랜도는 꽤 덥네요, 그렇게 생각하지 않아요?
(A) 매우 아름다운 건물입니다.
(B) 아니요, 비행기는 더 일찍 떠났어요.
(C) **네, 부채를 빌려 드릴까요?**

stunning 매우 아름다운; 멋진 fan 부채; 선풍기

16 Shall we take a lunch break before we reconvene?
[호M] (A) It only took an hour.
[미M] (B) No, let's just keep going.
(C) Yes, it's faulty.

다시 모이기 전에 점심시간을 가질까요?
(A) 한 시간만 걸렸어요.
(B) **아니요, 그냥 계속합시다.**
(C) 네, 그것은 결함이 있습니다.

lunch break 점심시간 reconvene 다시 모이다, 소집하다 faulty
결함이 있는, 고장 난

17 Why is the store already closed?
[미W] (A) You can travel there from here.
[미M] (B) The display units are being changed.
(C) In the hardware department.

왜 그 가게는 벌써 문이 닫혔나요?
(A) 당신은 여기에서 그곳으로 갈 수 있어요.
(B) **디스플레이 장치가 교체되고 있어요.**
(C) 하드웨어 부서에요.

travel 여행하다; 가다 display unit 디스플레이 장치, 영상 표시 장치
hardware 철물; (컴퓨터의) 하드웨어

18 Can you call someone to fix this problem?
[미M] (A) Actually, I think I can solve it.
[미W] (B) Who was at the door?
(C) Save it for lunch then.

이 문제를 해결해 줄 누군가를 불러줄 수 있어요?
(A) 사실, 제가 해결할 수 있을 것 같아요.
(B) 누가 입구에 있었나요?
(C) 그럼 점심을 위해 이거 두세요.

fix 수리하다, 고치다; 해결하다 solve 해결하다

19 I'm leaving for Hawaii tomorrow.
[미W] (A) I prefer flying, too.
[미M] (B) Have a good journey.
(C) At the hotel in the suburbs.

저는 내일 하와이로 떠나요.
(A) 저도 비행기 여행을 선호해요.
(B) **좋은 여행 다녀오세요.**
(C) 근교의 호텔에요.

flying 비행기 여행 journey 여행 suburb 교외, 근교

20 Who's leading the training session next month?
[호M] (A) Two consultants from Austria.

21 Did Andrea end up buying a property or is she going
to carry on leasing?
[미W] (A) It's an unfriendly environment.
[미M] (B) That price sounds practical.
(C) She's renting for now.

안드레아가 부동산을 매입했나요, 아니면 계속해서 임대하기로 했나
요?
(A) 악영향을 끼치는 환경입니다.
(B) 그 가격은 합당한 것처럼 들리네요.
(C) **현재로서 그녀는 임대를 할 것입니다.**

end up 결국 (어떤 처지에) 처하게 되다 buy a property 소유물을 사
다 carry on ~을 계속하다 lease 임대하다 unfriendly 비우호적인
practical 실용적인; 합리적인

22 Aren't you bringing your wife to the banquet?
[호M] (A) Let's leave it in the lobby.
[미M] (B) I'm considering it.
(C) A three-course meal.

당신은 연회에 아내를 데리고 오지 않을 건가요?
(A) 복도에 놓아 둡시다.
(B) **고려 중입니다.**
(C) 3회 코스 식사요.

banquet 연회 lobby 로비 복도 a three-course meal 세 번 접시가 나
오는 식사

23 Why did we order these lasers?
[미W] (A) When we have extra funding.
[호M] (B) They're more durable.
(C) Good, I'll set up the trial.

우리는 왜 이 레이저들을 주문했죠?
(A) 우리가 추가 재정 지원을 받을 때요.
(B) **그것들이 더 오래 내구성이 있거든요.**
(C) 좋아요, 시험을 준비하겠어요.

laser 레이저 funding 자금; 지금 제공, 재정 지원 durable 내구성이
있는, 오래가는 trial 시험(실험)

(B) Sustainable energy.
(C) Opening hours are nine to five.

누가 다음 달의 교육을 진행하나요?
(A) **오스트리아에서 온 자문 위원 두 명이요.**
(B) 지속 가능한 에너지요.
(C) 영업시간은 9시부터 5시입니다.

lead 진행하다, 이끌다 training session 교육
sustainable 지속
가능한 opening hours 영업시간; 개점 시간

Part 3

Questions 32-34 refer to the following conversation. 미M 미W

M Hello, my name is Liam Kavanagh. My department sent an order to this restaurant over an hour ago. Can you tell me if my order is ready?

W Let me check for you. Oh... ㉜ the order has only just been accepted. I apologize, but I have a number of other orders ahead of you. ㉝ So yours won't be available for at least a quarter of an hour.

M I see. Well, ㉞ I was planning to pick up some office supplies during lunch. I'll do that and pick up the order in 15 minutes.

남 안녕하세요. 제 이름은 리암 카버너입니다. 저희 부서가 이 레스토랑에 한 시간도 더 전에 주문을 했었습니다. 제 주문이 가져갈 수 있도록 준비되었는지 알려주실 수 있으세요?

여 제가 확인해 볼게요. 아, 그 주문은 지금 막 수락되었네요. 죄송합니다, 하지만 손님 앞으로 두 주문이 여러 개 있어요. 그래서 이 주문은 적어도 15분 동안은 나오지 않을 것 같아요.

남 그렇군요. 음 저는 점심시간 동안에 사무실 용품을 사러 가려고 했거든요. 그럼, 15분 후에 제 주문된 음식을 찾으러 오겠습니다.

department 부서 | apologize 사과하다 | ahead of ~앞에 | quarter 4분의 1; 15분 | pick up 가져다 가다 | office supplies 사무실 용품

32 Who most likely is the woman?
(A) A supplier
(B) A restaurant worker
(C) A chef
(D) An office employee

여자는 누구일 것 같은가?
(A) 공급업체
(B) 레스토랑 직원
(C) 주방장
(D) 사무실 직원

33 Why does the woman apologize?
(A) She provided the wrong meal.
(B) There is a mistake in the order.
(C) A business is closing late.
(D) An order was not completed on time.

여자는 왜 사과하는가?
(A) 잘못된 음식을
(B) 주문에
(C) 사업체가
(D) 주문이

---

24 Let's take the midday train into the financial center.
미M (A) Yes, I think there is.
미W (B) I'd prefer to drive.
(C) The shopping center.

금융가로 가는 정오 기차를 탑시다.
(A) 네, 있는 것 같네요.
(B) 저는 운전하는 것을 더 좋아해요.
(C) 쇼핑센터요.

midday 정오, 한낮 | financial center 금융가, 금융 중심지

25 What is the procedure for submitting an application?
미W (A) Is it in your home?
영M (B) A lot of practice.
(C) You can post it.

지원서 제출 절차는 어떻게 되나요?
(A) 그건 당신의 집에 있나요?
(B) 많은 연습이요.
(C) 당신은 우편으로 보낼 수 있어요.

procedure 절차 | application 지원서, 신청서 | post 우편으로 보내다

26 This financial application form is not user-friendly, is it?
미M (A) I haven't used it yet.
미W (B) An accounting clerk.
(C) The software was not installed.

이 재정 신청 양식은 사용하기가 설치 되지 않았요, 그렇죠?
(A) 저는 아직 이용해 보지 않았어요.
(B) 회계 직원이요.
(C) 그 소프트웨어는 설치되지 않았어요.

financial application 재정 신청서 | user-friendly 사용하기 쉬운 | accounting clerk 회계 직원 | 정리

27 I heard the senior nursing officers are getting a pay increase.
영W (A) How large will it be?
(B) Four new openings have appeared.
(C) He's not in the main hospital.

수간호사들의 임금이 인상된다고 들었어요.
(A) 얼마나 오르나요?
(B) 4개의 공석이 나왔어요.
(C) 그는 중앙 병동에 있지 않아요.

senior nursing officer 수간호사 | pay increase 임금 인상 | opening 공석

---

28 When should the parcel be delivered?
미M (A) Once you confirm the details.
미W (B) 33 contemporary paintings.
(C) I'll pack an overnight bag.

그 소포는 언제 배달되어야 하나요?
(A) 당신이 세부 사항을 확실히 해 주시면요.
(B) 33점의 현대 미술 작품이요.
(C) 제가 1박용 여행 가방을 쌀게요.

parcel 소포, 꾸러미 | confirm 확실히 하다, 확인하다 | contemporary 동시대의, 현대의 | pack 싸다, 꾸리다 | overnight bag 직은 여행가방, 1박용 여행 가방

29 I'm going to need the addresses of your clients.
미M (A) No more than twice a week.
미W (B) I'll email them to you by tomorrow.
(C) Yes, I'm hoping to leave immediately.

저는 당신의 고객들의 주소가 필요한데요.
(A) 일주일에 2번 이상은 아니에요.
(B) 내일까지 당신에게 이메일을 보내겠습니다.
(C) 네, 즉시 떠날 수 있길 바랍니다.

client 고객

30 Do you think I should take an umbrella on my trip next week?
영M (A) It's forecast to be sunny.
미W (B) You're right, I should do that.
(C) Is it quicker by plane?

제가 다음 주 여행에 우산을 갖고 가야 한다고 생각하세요?
(A) 일기 예보에서는 화창할 거라고 했어요.
(B) 당신 말이 맞아요, 제가 그렇게 해야겠어요.
(C) 비행기가 더 빠른가요?

forecast 예보하다

31 The blueprints for our designs have been scanned, haven't they?
미W (A) A signed invoice.
미M (B) In a blue tone.
(C) They have, every last one.

우리의 디자인들을 위한 청사진들이 스캔 되었죠, 그렇지 않나요?
(A) 서명된 송장이요.
(B) 파란색으로요.
(C) 맞아요, 마지막 한 개까지요.

blueprint (설계용) 청사진 | scan (스캐너로) 스캔하다 | invoice 송장 | every last 마지막 ~까지

여자가 사과하는 이유는?
(A) 그녀가 식사를 잘못 내왔다.
(B) 주문에 실수가 있었다.
(C) 업체가 늦게 문을 닫는다
(D) 주문이 제시간에 완료되지 않았다.

34 What will the man do next?
(A) Go to a neighbor
(B) Pay for an order
(C) Send an e-mail
(D) Do some shopping
남자는 다음에 무엇을 할 것인가?
(A) 이웃에게 가기
(B) 주문에 대해 지불하기
(C) 이메일 보내기
(D) 쇼핑하기

Questions 35-37 refer to the following conversation. 미W 미M

W ㉟ I had to work overtime for a fortnight to meet the demands on the Blundell account. I'm certainly looking forward to enjoying my weeklong vacation.
M I know. You've been putting in a lot of extra hours. So, do you have anything exciting to do during the week?
W Well, ㊱ I'm traveling with family on Monday on a ski trip to Gradia Mountain. We like to go up there when the weather's favorable.
M Oh, did you know ㊲ there will be a snow board gala on Gradia Mountain on Tuesday? You should check it out during your ski trip.

여 저는 블런델 계정의 수요를 맞추기 위해 2주 동안 잔업을 해야 했어요. 일주일간의 휴가를 즐기는 것을 정말 기대하고 있어요.
남 알아요. 당신은 늦게까지 야근을 많이 했죠. 그럼 그 주 동안에 신나게 할 일이 있나요?
여 음, 저는 월요일에 가족들과 그라디아 산으로 스키 여행을 갈 거예요. 우리는 날씨가 좋을 때 그곳에 가기를 좋아해요.
남 오, 화요일에 그라디아 산에서 스노보드 대회가 있을 거라는 걸 알고 있나요? 스키 여행하면서 한번 구경해 보세요.

work overtime 야근하다, 잔업을 하다 fortnight 2주일 meet the demand 수요를 충족시키다 account 계정, 계좌 weeklong 일주일에 걸친, 일주일간의 favorable 호의적인; 유리한 gala 경축 행사, 운동 경기 take a look (~을) 한번 보다 negotiate 협상하다

35 What did the woman have to do this week?
(A) Go on a vacation
(B) Cancel her account
(C) Join a different department
(D) Work extra hours
여자가 이번 주에 해야 했던 것은?
(A) 휴가 가기
(B) 그녀의 계정 취소하기
(C) 다른 부서에 합류하기
(D) 야근하기

36 Where will the woman go on Monday?
(A) To a mountainous area
(B) To a station
(C) To a park
(D) To a concert
여자는 월요일에 어디를 갈 것인가?
(A) 산악 지역
(B) 역
(C) 공원
(D) 콘서트

37 What does the man suggest the woman do?
(A) Work from home
(B) Negotiate a pay raise
(C) Ride in a cable car
(D) Go to watch a sports event
남자는 여자에게 무엇을 하라고 제안하는가?
(A) 집에서 근무하기
(B) 임금 인상 협상하기
(C) 케이블카 타기
(D) 스포츠 행사 가 보기

Questions 38-40 refer to the following conversation. 영M 미W

M Camila, ㊳ I just received a message from a customer asking if we stock the Arnis brand's cameras. We don't sell them here, do we?
W Actually, we generally do have Arnis cameras on display, but we're currently out of stock.
M Do you know when we'll receive a new supply? ㊴ I'd like to call the customer back and get him to reserve one.
W Let me place a request to the order department. ㊵ It looks like we'll get them in two weeks.

남 카밀라, 제가 방금 손님에게서 우리가 아르니스 브랜드의 카메라의 재고가 있는지를 묻는 메시지를 받았어요. 우리는 그것들을 팔지 않아요, 그렇죠?
여 사실은, 우리가 보통은 아르니스 카메라를 전시하고 있지만, 현재는 재고가 없는 상태죠.
남 우리가 언제 새 상품을 받을지 아나요? 손님에게 다시 전화해서 그가 예약을 하도록 하고 싶어요.
여 주문 부서에 요청해 볼게요. 2주 후에 받을 것 같네요.

stock 재고를 갖추다 generally 일반적으로, 보통 on display 전시된 obviously 확실히, 명백히 out of stock 재고가 없는 place a request 요청하다 agenda 안건 write up 작성하다 obsolete 더 이상 쓸모가 없는, 구식의 release 공개하다, 발표하다 in stock 재고가 있는

38 What are the speakers mainly discussing?
(A) A computer system
(B) A delivery charge
(C) A work agenda
(D) A piece of item
화자들은 주로 무엇에 관해 이야기하는가?
(A) 컴퓨터 시스템
(B) 배송비
(C) 직무 안건
(D) 물건

39 What does the man plan to do?
(A) Talk to a customer
(B) Write up an order
(C) Make an appointment
(D) Send an invoice

남자는 무엇을 할 계획인가?
(A) 고객과 이야기하기
(B) 주문서 작성하기
(C) 약속 잡기
(D) 청구서 보내기

40 According to the woman, what will happen in two weeks?
(A) An order will be cancelled.
(B) A catalog will be released.
(C) Some products will be back in stock.
(D) A computer brand will become obsolete.
여자에 따르면, 2주 후에 무슨 일이 일어날 것인가?
(A) 주문이 취소될 것이다.
(B) 카탈로그가 공개될 것이다.
(C) 제품이 다시 재고로 들어올 것이다.
(D) 컴퓨터 브랜드 하나가 쓸모 없어질 것이다.

Questions 41-43 refer to the following conversation. 미W 영M

W Hello, my name is Dai Davies. I'm calling because I was looking at the employment opportunities offered on your Web site. ㊶ I noticed there was a position as an architectural technician. Is that job still open?
M Yes, it is. Do you have any experience in an architectural practice?
W Yes, I do. ㊷ I was employed as an architectural technician at Jones and Fabria in Wales for two years before relocating back to England with my family.
M Oh, yes. I'm aware of that firm. ㊸ Why don't you send me your résumé? Once we have a look at it, I'll be back in touch.

여 안녕하세요, 제 이름은 다이 데이비스입니다. 저는 귀사의 웹 사이트에 제공된 구직 기회들을 보고 전화했습니다. 건축 기사직이 있다는 것을 알게 되었습니다. 그 자리는 아직 공석인가요?
남 네, 그렇습니다. 당신은 건축 실무 경험이 있나요?
여 네. 저는 가족과 영국으로 이사하기 전에 웨일스의 존스 앤 파브리아에서 2년 동안 건축 기사로 일했습니다.
남 오, 그렇군요. 저는 그 회사를 알고 있습니다. 이력서를 보내 주시겠어요? 우리가 한번 검토하고 나서 다시 연락드리겠습니다.

employment opportunity 고용 기회 architectural 건축학[술]의 technician 기사 practice 실행, 연습, 업무 relocate 이전하다, 이사하다 architect 건축가 legal 법률과 관련된 further 추가의

41 What type of position has been advertised?
(A) Architect
(B) Designer
(C) Legal clerk
(D) Lab Technician
어떤 유형의 일자리가 광고되었는가?
(A) 건축 기사
(B) 디자이너
(C) 법무원
(D) 실험실 기술자

42 Where did the woman work most recently?
(A) In Ireland
(B) In Scotland
(C) In England
(D) In Wales
여자는 가장 최근에 어디에서 근무했는가?
(A) 아일랜드
(B) 스코틀랜드
(C) 잉글랜드
(D) 웨일스

43 What does the man ask the woman to do?
(A) Send in further information
(B) Fill out an online form
(C) Check for more details
(D) Submit a portfolio
남자는 여자에게 무엇을 해 달라고 요청하는가?
(A) 추가 정보 보내기
(B) 온라인 양식 작성하기
(C) 더 많은 세부 사항 확인하기
(D) 포트폴리오 제출하기

Questions 44-46 refer to the following conversation. 미M 미W

M Hi, I saw your ad online for an office unit for rent on Main Street. ㊹ I'm contacting you to find out when it is vacant.
W We're looking for a tenant who can take up occupation on September 21. It's an excellent location. ㊺ In fact, it's the only unit in the complex that faces the river. It's really stunning. Would you like to come and see it?
M Yes, I would. I'm available on Thursday all day.
W ㊻ Why don't you come to see the complex on Thursday at 11 A.M.? I'll meet you in the reception area.

남 안녕하세요, 저는 메인 가에 있는 임대용 사무실 공간에 대한 당신의 온라인 광고를 보았습니다. 저는 그곳이 언제 비는지 알아보려고 연락했습니다.
여 저희는 9월 21일에 입주할 수 있는 세입자를 찾고 있습니다. 그곳은 매우 좋은 곳입니다. 실은, 단지 내에서 유일하게 강을 마주보는 곳입니다. 그곳은 굉장히 아름답죠. 오셔서 보길 원하세요?
남 네, 그러겠습니다. 저는 목요일 하루 종일 시간이 가능합니다.
여 목요일 아침 11시에 단지를 보러 오시는 건 어때요? 안내 데스크가 있는 곳에서 뵙도록 하죠.

unit 공동 주택의 한 가구 rent 임대 vacant 비어 있는 tenant 세입자 take up occupation 입주하다 complex 단지 face 마주보다, 바라보다 stunning 매우 아름다운 scenic 경치가 좋은 historic site 유적지

44 What does the man ask about the office?
(A) Where it is located
(B) When it is available
(C) How many other businesses are there
(D) How much is the rent
남자는 사무실에 대해 무엇을 묻는가?
(A) 어디에 위치하는지
(B) 언제 이용 가능한지
(C) 다른 사업체들이 얼마나 있는지
(D) 임대료가 얼마인지

45 What is unique about the unit?

(A) Its scenic view
(B) Its storage space
(C) Its historic site
(D) Its reduced price

사무실 상품에 관해 특별한 것은?

(A) 아름다운 경관
(B) 저장 면적
(C) 유적지
(D) 할인된 가격

46 When will the woman meet the man?

(A) At 10:00 A.M.
(B) At 11:00 A.M.
(C) At 1:00 P.M.
(D) At 11:00 P.M.

여자는 언제 남자를 만날 것인가?

(A) 오전 10시
(B) 오전 11시
(C) 오후 1시
(D) 오후 11시

Questions 47-49 refer to the following conversation. 영M 미W

M Ailey, I have to leave the office now. **47** I'm going to meet a client downtown.

W I see, Mr. Campbell. **47** Are you coming back this afternoon?

M **47** No, it's going to be a long discussion, so I won't be back today.

W **48** I wonder if you remember your 3 o'clock meeting with the marketing team today.

M Oh, I completely forgot about it. Can you call the team manager and reschedule it for some time next week?

W No problem. I'll contact him and let you know the rescheduled date.

M Wait a minute. <u>Come to think of it, I'd better do it myself.</u> **49** I need to discuss some issues with him anyway.

남 에일리, 제가 지금 사무실에서 나가야 해요. 제가 시내에서 고객을 만나려고 합니다.

여 알겠어요, 캠벨 씨. 오후에 다시 들어 오시나요?

남 아니요, 긴 토론이 될 거예요. 그래서 오늘 들어오지 않습니다.

여 오늘 마케팅팀과 3시에 미팅이 있는데 기억하고 있나요?

남 오, 제가 완전히 잊고 있었네요. 팀 매니저에게 전화해서 다음 중 으로 미팅을 다시 잡아 달라고 말해 줄래요?

여 네, 그럴게요. 제가 그에게 연락하고 재조정된 날짜를 알려 드리겠습니다.

남 잠시만요, 생각해 보니, 제가 직접 하는 편이 나을 것 같아요. 어쨌든 제가 마케팅팀 매니저와 몇 가지 문제를 논의해야 하거든요.

issue 문제, 쟁점, 사안

47 What will the man probably do this afternoon?

(A) Have a meeting with coworkers
(B) Attend an appointment with a client
(C) Pick up a friend
(D) Go to a show downtown

남자는 오후에 아마도 무엇을 하겠는가?

(A) 동료들과 미팅을 한다.
(B) 고객과의 약속에 간다.
(C) 친구를 태우러 간다.
(D) 시내에 있는 공연을 보러 간다.

48 What was the man supposed to do at 3:00 P.M.?

(A) Attend a workshop
(B) Visit a branch office
(C) Meet with new employees
(D) Discuss issues with the marketing team

남자는 오후 3시에 무엇을 하기로 되어 있었는가?

(A) 워크숍에 참여한다.
(B) 지점을 방문한다.
(C) 새로운 직원들을 만난다.
(D) 마케팅팀과 논의를 한다.

49 What does the man mean when he says, "Come to think of it, I'd better do it myself"?

(A) He will cancel a reservation.
(B) He will contact a coworker.
(C) He will attend a meeting.
(D) He will email some reports.

남자는 "생각해 보니, 제가 직접 하는 편이 나을 것 같아요"라고 이야기 했을 때 무엇을 의미했는가?

(A) 예약을 취소할 것이다.
(B) 동료에게 연락할 것이다.
(C) 미팅에 참여할 것이다.
(D) 보고서를 이메일로 보낼 것이다.

Questions 50-52 refer to the following conversation. (미W) (미M)

W Rick, I need to go early this evening but there's an extra party of 20 people arriving at 8 P.M. and ⑩ I've been put down to prepare meals for them. Is there any chance you can help me with the preparations?

M Sure, but I understood you were scheduled to work up till midnight tonight. ⑪ If you are planning to leave early, we might not be able to cope. It's one of our busiest nights.

W Oh, I thought the owner told you. I changed shifts with Alex so there'll be plenty of kitchen staff available. Now, ⑫ the 8 o'clock customers want the fish menu as they are all vegetarians. So let's prepare some salmon to be marinated.

여 릭, 저는 오늘 저녁에 일찍 가야 하는데, 오후 8시에 추가 20명의 인원이 도착할 것이고 제가 그들을 위한 식사를 준비하라고 적혀 있어요, 준비하는 것을 도와줄 수 있나요?

남 그럼요, 하지만 저는 당신이 오늘 자정까지 일하도록 일정이 잡혀 있는 것으로 알고 있었어요. 만약 일찍 나갈 계획이시면, 우리는 대처할 수 없을지도 몰라요. 오늘은 가장 바쁜 날 중 하나거든요.

여 오, 저는 주인이 말했다고 생각했어요. 저는 부엌 직원들이 충분히 시간이 가능하도록 저와 알렉스의 교대 근무를 바꿨어요. 자, 8시 손님들은 모두 채식주의자들이기 때문에 생선 요리를 원합니다. 그러니 연어가 양념이 되도록 준비합시다.

extra party 추가 인원 put down 적다 Is there any chance ~? ~할 수 있나요? cope 대처하다 shift 교대 근무 plenty of 충분한 salmon 연어 marinate 양념하다, 양념장에 재우다 short staffed 직원이 부족한

50 What does the woman ask the man to help her with?
여자가 남자에게 무엇을 도와달라고 요청하는가?
(A) Serving drinks
(B) Moving some tables
(C) Preparing meals
(D) Changing his shifts
(A) 음료 서빙
(B) 몇몇 테이블 이동
(C) 식사 준비
(D) 그의 교대조 교체

51 Why is the man concerned?
남자가 걱정하는 이유는?
(A) They might be short staffed.
(B) The party might get out of hand.
(C) The kitchen will not be open.
(D) The ingredients may not be available.
(A) 직원이 부족할 수 있다.
(B) 파티가 감당이 안 될 수 있다.
(C) 부엌이 문을 열지 않을 것이다.
(D) 재료가 이용 가능하지 않을 수 있다.

52 What did some customers request?
일부 손님들이 요청한 것은?
(A) More floor space
(B) A vegetarian menu
(C) A beachfront view
(D) An event calendar
(A) 추가 바닥 면적
(B) 채식주의자 메뉴
(C) 해변의 경관
(D) 행사 달력

Questions 53-55 refer to the following conversation with three speakers. (미M) (호M) (미W)

M1 ⑬ Who do you think the new sales manager is going to be — Ms. Park or Mr. Tatum?

M2 I think both are outstanding candidates for the position.

W Neither of them. I heard the board of directors is looking for someone from outside the company.

M1 Why does the board want to do that? They are talented sales representatives, and they have worked here for over 15 years.

M2 ⑭ And internal promotions happen much faster than recruiting externally.

W I couldn't agree more. ⑮ But the board members want someone who will be able to deliver a dramatic increase in sales.

남1 누가 새로운 영업부 매니저가 될 것이라고 생각하세요, 박 씨예요, 테이텀 씨예요?

남2 제가 생각하기에는 둘 다 두 그 직책에 훌륭한 후보라고 생각해요.

여 둘 다 아녜요. 제가 듣기로는 이사회에서 회사 밖에서 누군가를 영입한다고 하던데요.

남1 이사회가 왜 그 방식을 원하는 거죠? 그 둘 모두 재능 있는 영업사원들이고, 그리고 여기서 15년이 넘게 일해 왔잖아요.

남2 게다가 내부에서 승진시키는 것이 외부에서 영입하는 것보다 훨씬 빨라가고요.

여 전적으로 동의합니다. 그러나 이사회가 보다 회기적으로 판매량을 증가시킬 수 있는 사람을 원하고 있습니다.

outstanding 뛰어난, 훌륭한 representative 직원 internal 내부의, 내부적인 externally 외부에서 deliver (결과를) 내다 dramatic 극적인 restructure 구조를 조정하다

53 What is the conversation mainly about?
대화는 무엇에 관한 것인가?
(A) A sales result
(B) A retiring employee
(C) Candidates for a position
(D) A company's anniversary
(A) 판매 결과
(B) 은퇴하는 직원
(C) 직책에 대한 후보자들
(D) 회사 기념일

54 What does the woman mean when she says, "I couldn't agree more"?

(A) Now is the time for recruiting.
(B) 10 years' working experience is a requirement.
(C) An internal promotion is a fast way to fill a position.
(D) The company needs to contact a staffing agency.

여자가 "전적으로 동의합니다"라고 말했을 때 무엇을 의미했는가?

(A) 구인을 위한 때가 되었다.
(B) 10년 경력이 지격 요건이다.
(C) 내부에서 승진시키는 방법이 직책을 채우는 보다 빠른 방식이다.
(D) 회사는 직원 채용 회사에 연락할 필요가 있다.

55 According to the woman, what do the board members want?

(A) Increased sales
(B) Relocation of one of their branches
(C) Adding new delivery locations
(D) Restructuring of the sales team

여자에 따르면, 이사회는 무엇을 원하는가?

(A) 판매량 증진
(B) 그들의 지점 중 하나를 이전하는 것
(C) 새로운 배송지를 추가하는 것
(D) 영업팀을 다시 구성하는 것

Questions 56-58 refer to the following conversation. (미W) (영M)

W Mr. Bloomberg just called to tell me that he wants quarry flooring for his office instead of carpeting. Oh, he's such a demanding client. He keeps changing his mind. Is he allowing us to push back the deadline?

W No, he wants the remodeling to be completed by August 10th as scheduled.

M Hmm, we need another week to meet his request.

W I think we should hire at least two more skilled workers to keep up with such a tight schedule. That is what I was going to propose, actually.

M I will contact Mr. Ferrell. He probably knows some contractors.

여 블룸버그 씨가 방금 전화를 하셔서 제게 카페트 대신에 암석으로 사무실 바닥을 하고 싶다고 얘기했어요.

남 오, 정말 까다로운 고객이네요. 그가 계속 마음을 바꾸고 있어요. 그가 우리에게 마감일을 늦출 수 있도록 해 줄까요?

여 아니요, 그는 우리가 리모델링을 예정된 8월 10일까지 끝내기를 원합니다.

남 음. 우리가 그의 요청을 수용하려면 한 주가 더 필요합니다. 제 생각에는 우리가 적어도 2명의 숙련된 인부를 더 고용해야 이 빠듯한 일정을 맞출 수 있을 것 같습니다.

여 그게 제가 바로 제안하려던 바입니다.

남 페렐 씨에게 연락하겠습니다. 그가 아마도 시공업자들을 좀 알고 있을 거예요.

quarry 채석장 demanding 요구가 많은, 까다로운 tight 빠듯한 unpredictable 예측할 수 없는 floor plan 평면도 contractor 시공업자, 계약자

56 According to the woman, why did Mr. Bloomberg call her?

(A) To inquire about the status of the project
(B) To discuss costs
(C) To reschedule a deadline
(D) To change a flooring material

여자에 따르면, 왜 블룸버그 씨는 여자에게 전화했는가?

(A) 프로젝트의 진행 상황에 관해 물어보기 위해서
(B) 비용에 관한 논의를 하기 위해서
(C) 마감 기한을 다시 정하기 위해서
(D) 바닥재를 변경하기 위해서

57 What does the man mention about Mr. Bloomberg?

(A) He doesn't like changing plans.
(B) He asked for an additional discount.
(C) He is unpredictable.
(D) He is a frequent client.

남자는 블룸버그 씨에 관해 무엇을 언급했는가?

(A) 그는 계획 변경을 좋아하지 않는다.
(B) 그는 추가적인 할인을 요청했다.
(C) 그는 예측이 불가능하다.
(D) 그는 우량 고객이다.

58 What does the woman mean when she says, "That is what I was going to propose, actually"?

(A) A new floor plan is needed for the client.
(B) Mr. Bloomberg is a demanding client.
(C) Hiring workers will help meet the deadline.
(D) Mr. Ferrell is a popular contractor.

여자는 "그게 제가 바로 제안하려던 바입니다"라고 말했을 때, 무엇을 의미했는가?

(A) 새로운 평면도가 고객을 위해서 필요하다.
(B) 블룸버그 씨는 까다로운 고객이다.
(C) 인부들을 고용하는 것이 마감 일자를 맞추는 데 도움이 될 것이다.
(D) 페렐 씨는 인기 많은 시공업자이다.

Questions 59-61 refer to the following conversation. 미M 미W

M Hi, my wife informed me that ⑤ ⑥ your branch is offering a special deal on Trion car accessories. Can you give me more information?

W Sure, for one month, if you purchase a Trion handheld car vacuum, you'll get 30% off the Trion Car Jet Wash, too. It's an excellent deal if you consider the savings you make on buying both products.

M It certainly is. Do you deliver free of charge?

W Yes, we'll ship the products at no extra cost. If you wish to place an order, ⑪ you'll need the special code. Enter it when you're directed to the checkout page and you'll get 30% off.

남 안녕하세요, 당신의 지사에서 트리온 자동차 부속품에 특별 할인을 제공한다고 아내가 제게 알려 주었어요. 더 많은 정보를 알려 주실 수 있나요?

여 물론입니다, 트리온의 초소형 자동차용 진공청소기를 구매하신다면 당신 한 달 간 트리온 차량 제트 워시의 30퍼센트 할인도 받게 됩니다. 두 가지 제품을 구매하면서 절약되는 것을 고려한다면 훌륭한 거래입니다.

남 확실히 그러네요. 배송은 무료로 해 주시나요?

여 네, 저희는 추가 비용 없이 상품을 배송해 드립니다. 만약 주문을 하고 싶다면, 특별 코드 번호가 필요합니다. 결제 페이지로 안내되면 코드를 입력하면 30퍼센트 할인을 받으세요.

branch 지사　handheld 손바닥 크기의　vacuum 진공　savings 예금　checkout 계산대　at no extra cost 추가 비용 없이

59　Why is the man calling?
(A) To ask about a special deal
(B) To reply to a consumer survey
(C) To track a delivery
(D) To inquire about his savings

남자가 전화하고 있는 이유는?
(A) 특가 상품에 관해 문의하기 위해
(B) 소비자 설문조사에 답변하기 위해
(C) 배송을 추적하기 위해
(D) 그의 예금에 관해 문의하기 위해

60　What products are the speakers discussing?
(A) Electronic products
(B) Gardening equipment
(C) Cooking appliances
(D) Vehicle accessories

화자들이 이야기하고 있는 제품은?
(A) 전자 제품
(B) 원예 장비
(C) 요리 기구
(D) 자동차 부속품

61　What information is the woman told to submit on the Web site?
(A) A delivery schedule
(B) A shipping number
(C) A promotional code
(D) A credit card billing address

여자가 웹 사이트에 제출하라고 말한 정보는?
(A) 배송 일정
(B) 배송 번호
(C) 홍보용 할인 번호
(D) 신용 카드 대금 청구지

Questions 62-64 refer to the following conversation. 미W 미M

W Hello, my name is Mary Blake and ⑫ I'm a marketing agent from 'Blooms Right – All Exotic Flowers.' I'm visiting all shops in the region that we supply to and giving them the option to use our sales material and displays.

M Well, I do think having displays and marketing material is very helpful. I'm certain it would boost the sales of the Blooms Right products. But ⑬ it'll be time-consuming to have my workers set it all up and have to monitor any detailed display.

W Oh, actually Blooms Right would provide someone to do all that. So there's no extra work involved for you. ⑭ This brochure has all the details about the point of sales service including a list of days we are in your area.

여 안녕하세요, 저는 메리 블레이크이고 '블룸스 라이트 – 모든 이국적인 꽃'의 마케팅 대리인입니다. 저는 저희가 공급하는 이 지역의 모든 매장을 방문하고 있고, 저희 판매 자료와 전시물을 사용할 선택권을 드리고 있습니다.

남 음, 저도 전시물과 마케팅 자료를 갖는 것이 매우 도움이 된다고 생각 합니다. 그것이 블룸스 라이트 제품의 판매를 신장시킬 것이라고 확 신합니다. 하지만 제 직원들이 그 모든 것을 다 설치하는 모든 세부적 인 전시를 감독하는 데 시간이 많이 걸릴 것입니다.

여 아, 사실은 블룸스 라이트가 그 모든 것을 할 수 있는 분을 보내 드릴 것입니다. 그러니 추가로 하실 일은 없습니다. 이 책자에 저희가 고객 님의 지역에 있는 날짜를 포함하는 판매 서비스의 요점에 대한 세 부 사항이 모두 있습니다.

marketing agent 시장 대리인, 마케팅 대리인　exotic 이국적인　sales material 판매 자료　display 전시물, 전시품　boost 신장시키다　time consuming 시간을 많이 소모하는　set up 설치하다　monitor 감독하다 representative 대표자　timespan 기간　timetable 시간표

62　Who is the woman?
(A) A florist
(B) A shop owner
(C) A customer
(D) A sales representative

여자는 누구인가?
(A) 꽃집 주인
(B) 매장 주인
(C) 손님
(D) 영업 사원

63　What concern does the man mention about the display?
(A) The cost involved in the process
(B) The time consumption for his employees
(C) The amount of space required
(D) The timespan of delivery

남자가 전시에 관해 언급하는 우려 사항은?
(A) 절차에 관련된 비용
(B) 그의 직원들의 시간 소모
(C) 필요한 공간의 규모
(D) 배송 기간

64　What information does the brochure contain?
(A) A timetable
(B) Cost information
(C) A list of other stores

chamber 방 stuffy 갑갑한

(D) A flower sample
해석에 포함되는 정보는?
(A) 시간표
(B) 가격 정보
(C) 다른 매장 리스트
(D) 꽃 샘플

65 Look at the graphic. Where did the man stay last night?
(A) Room 301
(B) Room 302
(C) Room 303
(D) Room 304

시각 자료를 보시오. 남자는 어젯밤에 어디서 머물렀는가?
(A) 301호실
(B) 302호실
(C) **303호실**
(D) 304호실

Questions 65-67 refer to the following conversation and floor directory. 미W 영M

Hubert Research Center - 3rd Floor	
Laboratory	Room 301
Incubation Room	Room 302
65 Low-Pressure Chamber	Room 303
High-Pressure Chamber	Room 304

W Gerald, why do you look so tired? Are you okay?
M You're not going to believe it. **65 66** I was locked inside the low-pressure chamber last night. I didn't know that all the chamber doors lock automatically at midnight. **67** I barely slept because it was so stuffy.
W Why didn't you call someone else?
M I tried to call the facility manager, but for some reason the phone didn't ring at the time. And it was already too late, so I decided to wait until someone opened the chamber this morning.

허버트 연구소 - 3층	
실험실	301호
배양실	302호
저압실	303호
고압실	304호

여 제럴드, 왜 그리 피곤해 보이나요? 괜찮으세요?
남 아마 믿지 못하실 거예요. 제가 어젯밤에 저압실에 갇혀 있었어요. 모든 저압실 문이 밤 12시에 자동으로 잠긴다는 사실을 모르고 있었거든요. 너무 갑갑해서 밤새 거의 한잠도 못잤습니다.
여 왜 누구한테라도 전화를 하지 않았어요?
남 시설 관리자에게 전화를 걸려고 시도를 했는데, 무슨 이유인지 그 당시에는 전화기 벨이 울리지를 않더라고요. 그리고 이미 너무 늦은 때라 그냥 오늘 아침에 누군가 문을 열어 줄 때까지 기다려야겠다고 생각했어요.

66 What happened to the man?
(A) He lost a garage key.
(B) He left his house door open.
(C) He was locked inside a space.
(D) He was under pressure with his task.

남자에게 무슨 일이 일어났는가?
(A) 남자가 차고 열쇠를 잃어버렸다.
(B) 남자가 그의 집 문을 열어 놨다.
(C) **남자가 어떤 장소에 갇혀 있었다.**
(D) 남자는 업무 때문에 스트레스를 받고 있었다.

67 According to the man, why didn't he sleep well?
(A) The space was cold.
(B) The space was scary.
(C) The space was stuffy.
(D) The space was too noisy.

남자에 따르면, 왜 남자는 잠을 제대로 자지 못했는가?
(A) 장소가 너무 추웠다.
(B) 장소가 너무 무서웠다.
(C) **장소가 너무 갑갑했다.**
(D) 장소가 너무 시끄러웠다.

Questions 68-70 refer to the following conversation and schedule. 미M 미W

Mr. Brooks' schedule	
Tuesday	Urban Kitchen
Wednesday	Polly's Restaurant
Thursday	Top Cloud (in Hotel Dublin)
70 Friday	New York Diner

M I think we're a bit behind schedule. **68** We haven't even started preparing properly for the employee appreciation banquet. I think we need to hurry up. Have you reserved the venue at least, Linda?
W Yes, Mr. Brooks. **69** I paid the deposit to the Oriental Hotel last night. The ballroom I reserved is the largest one in the hotel.
M That's wonderful. Did you find a catering service as well?
W Yes, I did. The company promised to provide high-quality food, drinks, and services to our guests. We have been offered some sample meals to help us decide on the menu items.
M I see. **70** Could you make an appointment to visit the company on Friday?
W Certainly.

부룩스 씨 일정	
화요일	어반 키친
수요일	폴리 식당
목요일	탑 클라우드(호텔 더블린)
금요일	뉴욕 다이너

남 저희가 일정이 좀 뒤처진 것 같아요. 저희가 직원 감사 연회 준비를 아직 제대로 시작조차 하지 나갔습니다. 제 생각에 저희가 조금 서두를 필요가 있을 것 같아요. 린다, 적어도 행사 장소 예약은 했지요?
여 네, 브룩스 씨. 제가 어젯밤에 예약금을 오리엔탈 호텔에 지불했어요. 제가 호텔에서 가장 큰 행사장을 예약했습니다.
남 잘 됐네요. 출장 요리 서비스도 찾아보셨나요?
여 네, 찾아봤습니다. 그 업체가 아주 좋은 품질의 음식, 음료, 서비스를 우리의 손님들에게 제공하기로 약속했습니다. 우리가 메뉴 선정을 위한 음식 샘플들을 제공받았어요.
남 알겠습니다. 금요일에 업체를 방문할 수 있게 약속을 위한 잡아 주시겠습니까?
여 그럼요.

문제 P.197

Part 4

Questions 71-73 refer to the following advertisement. 미M

Looking for something appetizing and refreshing to gratify your craving? ⑦ Plusto-brand vegetable juice has it all. It's filling yet 100% nutritious. You get nothing but pure vegetables, straight from the ground. ⑫ If you visit our Web site www.plusto.com, you will find a selection of money-off vouchers. ⑬ And beginning next month, we'll be launching our latest flavor Tasty Potato. Look for it at a store near you.

식욕을 돋우고 신선해서 당신의 욕구를 만족시키는 것을 찾고 계신가요? 플러스토 채소 주스가 모든 것을 갖추고 있습니다. 포만감을 주면서 100 퍼센트 영양이 풍부합니다. 당신은 오직 땅에서 직접 뽑은 순수 채소만 맛보게 됩니다. 저희 웹 사이트 www.plusto.com을 방문하시면 당신은 할인 쿠폰들을 볼 수 있습니다. 그리고 다음 달부터 우리는 최근에 새로 나온 맛인 테이스티 포테이토를 출시할 것입니다. 가까운 매장에서 찾으세요.

appetizing 식욕이 돋게 만드는　refreshing 신선한　gratify 기쁘게 하다 craving 열망　filling 포만감을 주는　nutritious 영양가 있는　a selection of ~의 모음　money-off voucher 요금할인 쿠폰　launch 출시하다 flavor 맛

71 What is being advertised?
(A) A beverage
(B) A store
(C) A food bar
(D) A dessert

무엇이 광고되고 있는가?
(A) 음료
(B) 가게
(C) 푸드 바
(D) 디저트

72 According to the speaker, what can be found at the Plusto Web site?
(A) Details of ingredients
(B) A list of vegetable growers
(C) A map of store locations
(D) Discount coupons

화자에 따르면, 플러스토 웹 사이트에서 찾을 수 있는 것은 무엇인가?
(A) 재료의 세부 사항
(B) 채소 재배자 명단
(C) 가게 위치의 지도
(D) 할인 쿠폰

73 What will happen next month?
(A) A new flavor will be launched.
(B) Different-colored packaging will be offered.
(C) Prices will be reduced.
(D) A company name will change.

다음 달에 무슨 일이 있을 것인가?
(A) 새로운 맛이 출시될 것이다.
(B) 다른 색의 포장이 제공될 것이다.
(C) 가격이 인하될 것이다.
(D) 회사명이 바뀔 것이다.

Questions 74-76 refer to the following recorded message. 영W

You have reached ⑭ the Coverall Parcel tracking service. ⑮ Starting tomorrow, you can track the transit of all items sent through Coverall on the Internet. Just visit our Web site at www.coverall.com. And enter your tracking number where prompted by the online instructions. This facility will pinpoint exactly where your package is on its route. If you would like to hear this message again, please press the hash key. ⑯ To return to the main menu, please press star.

커버럴 배송 추적 서비스입니다. 내일부터 당신은 커버럴을 통해 보낸 모든 물건의 수송을 인터넷으로 추적할 수 있습니다. 저희 웹 사이트 www. coverall.com을 방문해 주세요. 그리고 온라인 설명서가 유도하는 곳에 당신의 주문 추적 번호를 입력해 주세요. 이 기능은 당신의 택배가 배송 경로 중 어느 지점에 있는지 정확히 찾아 줄 것입니다. 이 메시지를 다시 듣고 싶으면 우물 정자를 눌러 주세요. 메인 메뉴로 돌아가고 싶다면 별 표를 눌러 주세요.

parcel 소포, 꾸러미　tracking service 추적 서비스　transit 수송 prompt 유도하다　instruction 설명, 안내　facility 기능, 특징　pinpoint (위치·시간을) 정확히 찾아내다　hash 우물 정자　alert 경계경보　operator 전화 교환원

(두 번째 열 · 왼쪽)

a bit 다소, 약간　behind schedule 일정보다 늦은　properly 적절하게, 알맞게　deposit 보증금　ballroom 행사장　catering 출장 요리

68 What are the speakers preparing for?
(A) An appreciation event
(B) A retirement party
(C) A grand opening
(D) An employee workshop

화자들은 무엇을 준비하고 있는가?
(A) 감사 행사
(B) 은퇴 파티
(C) 개장 행사
(D) 직원 워크숍

69 What does the woman say she did last night?
(A) Searched for a location
(B) Sampled some food
(C) Paid a deposit
(D) Picked up supplies

여자는 지난밤에 무엇을 했다고 이야기하는가?
(A) 장소를 검색했다.
(B) 음식을 시식했다.
(C) 보증금을 지불했다.
(D) 비품들을 가져 왔다.

70 Look at the graphic. What is the name of the catering service that the woman contacted?
(A) Urban Kitchen
(B) Polly's Restaurant
(C) Top Cloud
(D) New York Diner

시각 자료를 보시오. 여자가 연락한 출장 요리 서비스의 업체명은 무엇인가?
(A) 어반 키친
(B) 폴리 식당
(C) 탑 클라우드
(D) 뉴욕 다이너

74 What type of business created the message?

(A) A delivery service
(B) A bus company
(C) A telephone exchange
(D) A travel agency

어떤 종류의 회사가 메시지를 만들었는가?

(A) 배송 서비스
(B) 버스 회사
(C) 전화 교환국
(D) 여행사

75 What new service does the business offer?

(A) A web-based payment option
(B) Mobile message alerts
(C) Priority delivery options
(D) An online tracking system

회사는 어떤 새로운 서비스를 제공하는가?

(A) 웹 기반 지불 선택권
(B) 휴대폰 경보
(C) 우선 배달 선택권
(D) 온라인 추적 시스템

76 Why would a listener press star?

(A) To speak to an operator
(B) To return to the main menu
(C) To have this message repeated
(D) To hear the message again

청자는 왜 별표를 누르겠는가?

(A) 교환원과 통화하기 위해
(B) 메인 메뉴로 돌아가기 위해
(C) 이 메시지를 반복 청취하기 위해
(D) 메시지를 다시 듣기 위해

77 Who most likely is the speaker?

(A) A fitness trainer
(B) An army doctor
(C) A sports journalist
(D) A medical expert

화자는 누구일 것 같은가?

(A) 신체 단련 트레이너
(B) 군의관
(C) 스포츠 기자
(D) 의료 전문가

78 What are the listeners preparing to do in two months?

(A) Run a race
(B) Take part in an endurance test
(C) Travel overseas
(D) Participate in a fitness program

Questions 77-79 refer to the following talk. 영M

Welcome to Birmingham Armed Forces Training Ground. My name is Stephen and ⑰ I will be in charge of today's endurance test. Our aim is to get you ⑱ prepared for the overseas tour of Kosovo in two months' time. And I want every one of you to increase your stamina levels. Today, we'll be undergoing extensive body fitness training for four hours and will increase this time by 30 minutes every day. Before we begin training, please let the medical staff check your body mass. ⑲ They will check you at every session to record your progress.

버밍엄 군대 훈련장에 오신 것을 환영합니다. 제 이름은 스티븐이고, 저는 오늘의 지구력 테스트를 담당할 것입니다. 우리의 목표는 두 달의 시간 동안 여러분에게 코소보로 해외 순방을 준비시키는 것입니다. 그리고 저는 여러분 모두가 각자의 체력을 증가시키기를 원합니다. 오늘, 우리는 4시간 동안 폭넓은 신체 단련을 거칠 것이고, 이 시간을 매일 30분씩 늘려나 갈 것입니다. 훈련을 시작하기 전에, 의료진들이 여러분의 체질량을 측정하도록 해 주세요. 그들은 매 훈련마다 여러분의 성과를 기록하기 위해 점검할 것입니다.

armed forces 군대 training ground 훈련장 be in charge of ~을 담당하다 endurance test 내구성 시험, 지구력 테스트 overseas 해외의 tour 관광; 순회; 순방 stamina 체력, 스테미나 undergo 겪다 extensive 포괄적인, 폭넓은 body fitness 신체 단련 medical staff 의료진, 전문 progress 성과, 진전 take part in ~에 참여하다 log 일지, 기록

화자는 두 달 동안 무엇을 위한 준비를 하는가?

(A) 달리기 경주하기
(B) 지구력 테스트 참여하기
(C) 해외 여행하기
(D) 신체 단련 프로그램 참여하기

79 What does the speaker encourage the listeners to do?

(A) Take weekly breaks
(B) Purchase appropriate weapons
(C) Consult a medical professional daily
(D) Keep a personal log

화자는 청자들에게 무엇을 하도록 권장하는가?

(A) 주간 휴식 취하기
(B) 적절한 무기 구입하기
(C) 의료 전문가들과 매일 상의하기
(D) 개인 일지 작성하기

Questions 80-82 refer to the following talk. 미W

Welcome to Gringo's Gourmet, the home of Andalusia's favorite frozen meals. In half an hour, we'll commence the tour. ⑳ You'll be taken through all the stages of manufacture of frozen desserts and savouries. We have only one request. Please do not approach any of the factory machinery. This is both for your own protection and the wellbeing of Gringo's operatives. When we finish the tour, ㉑ we'll offer you the chance to make your own frozen snack. Now, ㉒ before we depart from the reception, please take a look at this image of the original factory from 1967. As you can see, our contemporary factory looks very different. The modernization will be explained in the informational booklet I'll hand out.

안달루시아에서 가장 사랑받는 냉동 요리 전문점 그링고스 고어메이에 오신 것을 환영합니다. 30분 후에 우리는 투어를 시작할 것입니다. 여러분은 냉동된 디저트와 짭짤한 음식의 제조 모든 단계를 모두 거치게 될 것입니다. 저희는 단 한 가지 요청 사항이 있습니다. 공장의 기기는 그 어떤 것도 만지지 않아 주세요. 이것은 여러분 자신을 보호하고 그링고스의 직공의 안전을 위함입니다. 투어를 끝내면, 여러분에게 직접 냉동 간식을 만들어 볼 수 있는 기회를 드립니다. 이제, 접수처에서 출발하기 전에, 1967년 최초 공장의 그림을 봐 주세요. 보시다시피, 우리의 현재 공장과는 매우 달라 보입니다. 제가 나눠 주는 정보 책자에 그 근대화 과정이 설명되어 있을 것입니다.

gourmet 미식가, 식도락가 frozen 냉동의 commence 개시하다, 시작하다 take A through B A가 B를 익히도록 하다 manufacture (기계를 이용한 상품의 대량) 제조, 생산 frozen dessert 냉동 디저트 savoury 짭짤한 음식(들이 파티 등에서 아주 작은 양으로 나옴) machinery 기기 wellbeing 안보, 복지 operative 직공 depart 출발하다 contemporary 현대의; 동시대의 modernization 근대화; 현대화 informational 정보의; 정보를 제공하는 booklet 소책자 hand out 나눠주다; 발부하다

80 Where does the talk most likely take place?
(A) At a factory
(B) At a restaurant
(C) At a photographic studio
(D) At a museum

담화는 어디에서 일어날 것 같은가?
(A) 공장
(B) 레스토랑
(C) 사진 스튜디오
(D) 박물관

81 What does the speaker say listeners will receive?
(A) Food samples
(B) A choice of desserts
(C) A photograph
(D) A cookery opportunity

화자는 청자들이 무엇을 받을 것이라고 말하는가?
(A) 음식 샘플
(B) 디저트 선택
(C) 사진
(D) 요리 기회

82 What does the speaker ask the listeners to do in the reception?
(A) Check out a picture
(B) Leave their possessions
(C) Form a line
(D) Listen to an audio message

화자는 청자들이 접수처에서 무엇을 해 달라고 요청하는가?
(A) 그림 확인하기
(B) 그들의 소지품 놓고 가기
(C) 줄 서기
(D) 오디오 메시지 청취

Questions 83-85 refer to the following news report. 호M

And now for the Jinny Ring Fitness Community latest news. This Saturday will be an opportunity for you to join in ⑱ our first annual sports day. Come along to Runnings Park to sign up for a number of events from wrestling competition, 5-a-side soccer games to athletics for athletes of all ages. ⑭ There is a possibility of storms for the afternoon but the afternoon should be clear. Whichever event you want to participate in, ⑮ I advise you to wear suitable sports clothing. Sports equipment is free to borrow, but we cannot provide clothing or running shoes.

fitness 신체 단련 join in 같이 하다, 함께하다 come along 도착하다 sign up 신청하다 wrestling competition 씨름 대회 5-a-side soccer games 5인 축구 athlete 육상 경기 athletics 육상 경기 participate in 참여하다 sports equipment 운동 기구 running shoes 운동화 municipal 지방 자치제의, 시의 fair 박람회

83 What is the main topic of the report?
(A) A concert opening
(B) A community
(C) A sports competition
(D) A municipal fair

보도의 주요 화제는?
(A) 콘서트 개막식
(B) 지역 사회
(C) 스포츠 경연대회
(D) 지역 박람회

84 What problem does the speaker mention?
(A) Bad weather is forecast.
(B) Traffic is expected to be heavy.
(C) Parking is limited.
(D) Some events have been cancelled.

화자가 언급하는 문제점은?
(A) 악천후가 예보된다.
(B) 교통 정체가 예상된다.
(C) 주차가 한정되어 있다.
(D) 일부 행사가 취소되었다.

85 What does the speaker suggest listeners do?
(A) Bring a packed lunch
(B) Use public transport
(C) Run in the park
(D) Wear suitable clothing

화자는 청자들에게 무엇을 하라고 제안하는가?
(A) 점심 싸오기
(B) 대중교통 이용하기
(C) 공원에서 달리기
(D) 적절한 의류 착용하기

Questions 86-88 refer to the following announcement. 영W

⑱ Attention, library users. ⑰ In 30 minutes, we will start a painting class. Professional painter Jay Colman will teach you how to simply draw paintings with your limited painting supplies at home. You can learn some practical tips and techniques. We'd like to invite everyone, whether you are a brand-new painter or have been practicing for years. If you're interested, please come to the community room on the second floor of the library. ⑱ Once the class starts, there will be no further admittance. This is to avoid interruptions. Thank you.

도서관 이용자 여러분. 30분 후에 저희가 그림 수업을 시작하겠습니다. 전문 화가인 제이 콜만이 어떻게 집에서 제한된 그림 재료들을 가지고 간단히 그림을 그릴 수 있는지에 대해 여러분들에게 알려 드릴 것입니다. 여 러분들은 몇 가지의 실용적인 팁과 기술에 관해 배우게 될 것입니다. 저희 는 여러분들이 처음 그림을 시작하시는 분이시든지 혹은 수년 동안 그림 을 그려 오셨던 분이시든지 상관없이 모두를 초대합니다. 관심이 있으시 다면, 도서관 2층에 있는 커뮤니티 공간으로 방문해 주세요. 일단 수업이 시작되고 난 이후에는 입장하실 수 없습니다. 이는 수업에 방해가 되는 것 을 피하기 위함입니다. 감사합니다.

draw 그리다 practical 실용적인 admittance 입장 interruption 중단, 방해 punctual 시간을 지키는

86 Who most likely are the listeners?
(A) Library users
(B) Librarians
(C) Shoppers
(D) Seminar participants

청자들은 누구인 것 같은가?
(A) 도서관 이용자들
(B) 도서관 사서들
(C) 쇼핑객들
(D) 세미나 참가자들

87 What is being announced?
(A) An art exhibition
(B) A community fair
(C) An art class
(D) A painting action

무엇이 공지되고 있는가?
(A) 예술품 전시
(B) 지역 행사
(C) 미술 수업
(D) 액션 페인팅(물감 뿌리기)

88 What does the speaker imply when she says, "This is to avoid interruptions"?
(A) The listeners should register for the event.
(B) The listeners should be punctual for the event.
(C) The listeners should wait in a line.
(D) The listeners should hold their questions for a while.

화자는 "이는 수업에 방해가 되는 것을 피하기 위함입니다"라고 말했을 때, 무엇을 의미했는가?
(A) 청자들은 행사에 등록해야 한다.
(B) 청자들은 행사에 시간에 맞춰서 가야 한다.
(C) 청자들은 줄을 서서 기다려야 한다.
(D) 청자들은 한동안 질문을 하지 말아야 한다.

Questions 89-91 refer to the following advertisement. 호M

⑧⑨ Fresh Groceries is having a big sale on all products for a week from today. ⑨⓪ Buy a 20-pound bag of tomatoes for $2. The regular price is $3. Save one dollar on every pound of carrots, onions, and ginger that you purchase. You can also buy fresh blueberries for only 50 cents per pound, which is 50 cents off the regular price. ⑨① Fresh Groceries' produce is grown locally. That means they travel very little from the farm to your table. So, all our fruits and vegetables are super fresh. That's our trick of the trade. Come and try some samples. You'll realize why Fresh Groceries produce is the best.

프레시 그로서리는 오늘부터 한 주간 모든 제품에 대해 세일을 시작합니다. 20파운드의 토마토가 든 자루를 2달러에 구매하세요. 정상가는 3달러입니다. 당근, 양파, 그리고 생강을 구매하실 때 1파운드마다 1달러를 절약해 보세요. 또한 여러분들은 신선한 블루베리를 정상 가격에서 50센트 할인되는, 파운드당 50센트에 구매하실 수 있습니다. 프레시 그로서리의 농산물들은 현지에서 재배됩니다. 그것은 농장에서 여러분들의 테이블까지 지역 이동이 짧다는 것을 의미합니다. 그러므로 저희 모든 과일과 채소는 매우 신선합니다. 이것이 우리 사업의 비법입니다. 방문하셔서 시식해 보시기 바랍니다. 프레시 그로서리의 농산물이 왜 최고인지 알게 되실 겁니다.

produce 농산물 trick 요령, 방법, 비법 trade 무역, 거래, 사업 publicize 홍보하다 organic 유기농의

89 What is the purpose of the advertisement?
(A) To publicize a grand opening
(B) To advertise job openings
(C) To inform the customers of the origin of the produce
(D) To promote a sale

광고의 목적은 무엇인가?
(A) 오픈 행사를 알리기 위해
(B) 공석을 알리기 위해
(C) 고객들에게 농산물의 산지를 알리기 위해
(D) 할인을 알리기 위해

90 What is Fresh Groceries mainly selling?
(A) Meat
(B) Dairy products
(C) Bakery
(D) Fruits and vegetables

프레시 그로서리는 주로 무엇을 파는가?
(A) 고기
(B) 유제품
(C) 빵류
(D) 과일과 채소

91 What does the speaker mean when he says, "That's our trick of the trade"?
(A) Their products are cheap.
(B) Their products are grown locally.
(C) They import products.
(D) The products are all organic.

남자가 "이것이 우리 사업의 비법입니다"라고 말했을 때 무엇을 의미했는가?
(A) 그들의 제품이 싸다.
(B) 그들의 제품이 현지에서 재배된다.
(C) 그들은 제품을 수입한다.
(D) 제품이 모두 유기농이다.

Questions 95-97 refer to the following talk and map. [영W]

Tom & Stephany is reopening after two months of renovations. We are now proud to serve you in a gorgeously remodeled space. Come and check out our updated store and jewelry selection. To celebrate the reopening, ⑤ all visitors can enter a drawing to win a gift card valued at $200. You will find the finest rings, watches, necklaces, and earrings in our renovated showroom. ⑥ Our jewelry is all of the finest quality and made by top designers. If you are thinking of buying a magical gift for one of your loved ones, visit Tom & Stephany today. ⑦ We are located on the corner of Lincoln Boulevard and 12th Street.

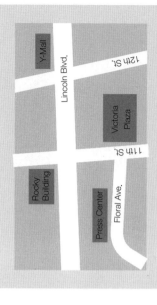

톰 & 스테파니는 2달 동안의 보수 작업을 끝내고 재개장합니다. 우리는 이제 화려하게 리모델링된 공간에서 여러분들께 서비스를 제공하게 되어 기쁩니다. 우리의 새로운 매장에 방문하셔서 보석들을 감상해 보세요, 저희의 재개장을 축하하기 위해서 모든 방문객들은 200달러 상당의 상품권을 받을 수 있는 추첨에 참여하실 수 있습니다. 여러분들께서는 최고급 반지, 시계, 목걸이, 그리고 귀걸이를 새롭게 단장한 전시관에서 만나보실 수 있습니다. 저희의 보석은 모두 최고급이며 최고의 디자이너들에 의해 제작됩니다. 만약 당신이 사랑하는 사람들 중 한 명을 위한 마법 같은 선물을 구매할 생각이라면, 오늘 톰 & 스테파니를 방문해 주세요. 저희는 링컨 대로와 12번가의 모퉁이에 위치하고 있습니다.

Questions 92-94 refer to the following talk and receiving log. [미M]

Received	Vendor	Item	Quantity
12/14	Ralph	Blazer	25
12/15	Dash	Sweater	30
12/16	Custom	⑨③ Trousers	40
12/17	Hiller	Accessory	120

⑨② ⑨③ Okay, everyone, we just received the shipment of pants we were expecting. What I need you to do is to bring the boxes to the front area of the store. When you remove the pants from the boxes, be careful not to remove the price tags that are attached to them. After unpacking, you will have to fold the pants and arrange them in the displays that I have set up between the shirts and the sweaters. They need to be organized by size and color. Large go on the right, medium in the middle, and small on the left. ⑨③ I'll be in my office adding the new shipment to the inventory. ⑨④ When I come back, I'll check the displays. Alright?

수령	판매자	제품	수량
12/14	랄프	블레이저	25
12/15	대쉬	스웨터	30
12/16	커스텀	바지	40
12/17	힐러	액세서리	120

여러분, 저희가 방금 기다리고 있던 바지의 배송을 받았습니다. 제가 여러분께 바라는 것은 매장 앞으로 박스들을 옮기는 것입니다. 박스에서 바지를 꺼낼 때, 가격표가 떨어지지 않도록 조심해 주세요. 박스를 풀고 나서 바지를 접어서 셔츠와 스웨터 사이에 제가 설치해 둔 진열대에 정리해 주세요. 바지는 사이즈와 색깔별로 정리가 되어야 합니다. 큰 사이즈는 오른쪽으로, 중간 사이즈는 중간으로, 작은 사이즈는 왼쪽으로 정리해 주세요. 저는 사무실에서 새로운 물건들을 재고 목록에 추가할 것입니다. 제가 돌아오면 전시된 물건들을 확인하도록 하겠습니다. 아시겠죠?

shipment 배송품   arrange 준비하다, 배치하다   inventory 재고 목록   alter 수선하다

---

92 What most likely is the speaker's job?
(A) Clothing designer
(B) Store manager
(C) Delivery person
(D) Inspector
화자의 직업은 무엇인 것 같은가?
(A) 옷 디자이너
(B) 매장 관리인
(C) 배송사 직원
(D) 검사관

93 Look at the graphic. What quantity will the speaker add to the inventory?
(A) 25
(B) 30
(C) 40
(D) 120
시각 자료를 보시오. 화자는 어느 수량을 재고 목록에 추가하겠는가?
(A) 25
(B) 30
(C) 40
(D) 120

94 What does the speaker say he will do when he returns?
(A) Change the price tags
(B) Send back arrivals
(C) Inspect the displays
(D) Alter some pants
화자는 돌아왔을 때 무엇을 할 것이라고 이야기하는가?
(A) 가격표를 바꾼다.
(B) 도착한 물건들을 돌려 보낸다.
(C) 전시물을 확인한다.
(D) 바지를 수선한다.

수 있습니다. 우리 보석은 최고급 품질이며 최고 수준의 디자이너들에 의해서 제작되었습니다. 만약 여러분들께서 매뉴 같은 선물을 여러분들이 아끼시는 누군가에게 선물하려 하신다면, 오늘 톰 & 스테파니에 방문하시기 바랍니다. 저희는 임건 대로의 12번가에 위치해 있습니다.

gorgeously 화려하게   selection 선정, 선택, 제품군   drawing 추첨
value 평가하다   fine 훌륭한 좋은   complimentary 무료의   voucher 쿠폰

95 What will visitors receive?
(A) A complimentary gift
(B) A voucher for a meal
(C) A discount coupon
(D) A gift certificate
방문객들은 무엇을 받을 것인가?
(A) 무료 선물
(B) 식권
(C) 할인 쿠폰
(D) 상품권

96 What does the speaker mention about Tom & Stephany's products?
(A) They are shipped at no charge.
(B) They are custom made.
(C) They are popular.
(D) They are made by top designers.
화자는 톰 & 스테파니의 제품에 대해 무엇을 언급하는가?
(A) 무료로 배송된다.
(B) 주문 제작 방식이다.
(C) 인기가 많다.
(D) 최고 수준의 디자이너가 만든다.

97 Look at the graphic. Where is Tom & Stephany most likely located?
(A) At the Press Center
(B) At Y-Mall
(C) At Victoria Plaza
(D) At the Rocky Building
시각 자료를 보시오. 톰 & 스테파니는 어디에 위치해 있을 것 같은가?
(A) 프레스 센터
(B) Y몰
(C) 빅토리아 플라자
(D) 로키 빌딩

Questions 98-100 refer to the following report and table. 호M

Winner	Trumpet Shell Weight (Pound)
Brian	5
Jim	4.5
John	3
Jason	4

98 To mark the opening of trumpet shell season, many divers participate in the trumpet shell contest. This annual contest was founded in 1970. This year, about 400 divers competed. Surprisingly enough, a 5-pound trumpet shell was caught. Brian was the diver who caught the giant trumpet shell. Jim placed second with a 4.5 pounder. **99** A 13-year-old boy caught a 3 pounder and won a special prize. What happened to these massive trumpet shells? They were served as the main course at the divers' family dinners. **100** I'll be back with more local news after this commercial break.

98 According to the speaker, what is the purpose of the event?
(A) To raise trumpet shells
(B) To revitalize local business
(C) To honor a person
(D) To celebrate the opening of a season
화자에 따르면, 이 행사의 목적은 무엇인가?
(A) 소라고둥 양식하기
(B) 지역 사업 살리기
(C) 인물 표창하기
(D) 시즌 시작 축하하기

99 Look at the graphic. Who won the special prize?
(A) Brian
(B) Jim
(C) John
(D) Jason
시각 자료를 보시오. 누가 특별상을 수상했는가?
(A) 브라이언
(B) 짐
(C) 존
(D) 제이슨

100 What will listeners probably hear next?
(A) Music
(B) Local news
(C) Advertisements
(D) A traffic report
청자들은 다음에 무엇을 듣게 될 것인가?
(A) 음악
(B) 지역 뉴스
(C) 광고
(D) 교통 방송

소라고둥 시즌의 시작을 알리기 위해 많은 다이버들이 소라고둥 대회에 참여하고 있습니다. 이 연례 대회는 1970년에 시작되었습니다. 올해, 대략 400명의 다이버들이 경쟁을 했습니다. 정말 놀랍게도, 5파운드의 소라고둥이 잡혔습니다. 브라이언이 초대형 소라고둥을 잡은 다이버입니다. 짐은 4.5파운드로서 2위를 했습니다. 13세의 소년이 3파운드로서 특별상을 수상했습니다. 이 거대한 소라고둥에 무슨 일이 벌어졌을까요? 그 소라고둥은 다이버들의 가족을 위한 저녁 메인 요리로 준비되었습니다. 저는 이 광고 이후에 보다 많은 지역 뉴스로 다시 돌아오겠습니다.

우승자	소라고둥 무게(파운드)
브라이언	5
짐	4.5
존	3
제이슨	4

mark 알리다, 기념하다   trumpet shell 소라고둥   contest 대회, 경쟁
found 설립하다   pounder (무게가) ~파운드인 것   revitalize 재활성화시키다

Part 5

문제 P200

101 해설 빈칸 뒤에 목적어가 없으므로 빈칸에는 자동사가 들어가야 한다. 따라서 정답은 자동사인 (A) convene(모이다)이다. implement(실행하다), nominate(지명하다), initiate(착수하다)는 모두 타동사이므로 오답이다.

위원회 회원들은 주주 총회를 위해 하드 레인홀에 모일 것이다.
committee 위원회 shareholder 주주

102 해설 명사 앞은 대명사의 소유격 자리이므로 (B)가 정답이다. theirs는 소유 대명사로 명사 앞에 쓸 수 없으며, them은 목적어 자리에, they는 주어 자리에 쓴다. 참고로 〈be동사 +p.p.〉 다음에 to부정사가 오는 5동사 구조 주요 동사들은 be requested, be required, be advised, be reminded, be encouraged, be told, be urged, be forced, be intended 등이 있다.

직원들은 그들의 시간을 갱신하도록 요구받았다.
update 갱신하다

103 해설 하나로 묶어는 동사구가(was explained) 사이에 빈칸이 있으므로 부사가 들어갈 자리이다. 따라서 정답은 (B) briefly이다.

회사의 격월 예산 보고서는 팜 아이슬리 씨에 의해서 간략하게 설명되었다.
bi-monthly 격월의

104 해설 이미 문장에 본동사 are kept가 있으므로 빈칸에는 동사가 들어갈 수 없다. (B), (D)는 오답이다. 빈칸은 앞에 있는 명사 (items)를 수식을 하므로 형용사구 자리이다. 선택지에서 분사 (A), (C)가 형용사 역할을 하므로 정답이 되는데, 뒤에 목적어가 없으므로 정답은 (A) left이다.

라운지에 두고 간 모든 개인 물건들은 폐기되기 전에 30일 동안 보관된다.
discard 폐기하다

105 해설 빈칸은 전치사 in의 목적어가 들어갈 자리이므로 정답은 명사인 (A) response이다. 참고로 in response to(~에 응하여/ 답하여)라는 숙어를 외워 두면 편하다.

조이스 가전은 결함 있는 부품들에 대한 보고에 응하여 올해의 전자제 인지 라인 제품들을 회수했다.
recall 회수하다 component 부품

106 해설 주어는 All workers, 동사는 must wear이고, who ~ equipment는 앞 명사 workers를 수식하는 관계절이므로 빈칸이 들어가야 한다. 따라서 정답은 (A)이다. 빈칸 뒤에 목적어(electrical equipment)가 있고 문맥상 '전기 장치를 착동하는 직원들'이 적절하므로 능동형 (D)가 정답이다.

전기 장치를 착동시키는 모든 직원들은 안전모를 착용해야 한다.
electrical equipment 전기장치 hard hat 안전모

107 해설 동사 어휘 문제로 문맥상 '건강하게 설명한다'에서 가장 적합하므로 (D)가 정답이다.

설명 경영 컨설턴트에서 저희는 최대한 건강하게 저희의 의견을 고객들에게 설명합니다.
management consultant 경영 컨설턴트 concisely 간결하게

108 해설 but 앞의 절에 동사가 하나 꼭 필요한 자리이다. 선택지에서 동사가 아닌 preserving부터 소거한다. 동사 선택지 중 '~ 타 시제'에 맞는 동사를 선택하는 문제이다. 뒤에 목적어가 없는 것으로 보아 수동태 동사가 들어가야 하므로 정답은 (D) has been preserved이다.

그 건물의 구조는 보존되었지만, 내부는 완전히 리모델링되었다.
structure 구조

109 해설 관사 the 앞에는 형용사가 들어갈 수 없으므로 little과 few는 오답이다. A few가 뒤에는 가산복수명사가 와야 하므로 오답이다. 뒤에 불가산명사(information)를 돌을수 있는 것으로서 정답은 (D) little of이다.

처음에는 그 보고서에 약간의 정보가 빠진 것처럼 보였지만, 그것은 빠르게 확인되었다.

110 해설 to부정사(to manufacture) 사이에서 동사연항을 수식할 자리이므로 부사가 답이 된다. 따라서 정답은 (D)이다. 참고로 more 뒤에는 명사/형용사/부사 모두 들어갈 수 있으므로 more에 의존에서 품지 않도록 주의하자.
explore 분석하다, 모색하다

111 해설 An increasing number of(점점 더 많은 ~)를 세트 표 현으로 외워 두면 편하다. 따라서 정답은 A(n) (increasing) number of 뒤에는 항상 가산 복수명사가 온다는 것도 알아 두자.

점점 더 많은 주택 보유자들이 더 낮은 금리를 활용하기 위해서 그들의 담보대출을 차환하고 있다.
refinance 차환하다 mortgage 담보 대출 interest rates 금리

112 해설 dispose(버리다/처리하다)와 reconcile(화해시키다)은 목적어 씨야 한다. contain(포함하다)과 reconcile(화해시키다)은 목적어(sound file)와 어울리지 않으므로 오답이다. 정답은 의미상 가장 어울리는 '수용하다'는 뜻인 (D) accommodate이다.

큐드라 소프트웨어는 어떤 유형의 음원 파일이라도 수용할 수 있는 음악 플레이어를 발표했다.
unveil 발표하다

113 해설 빈칸은 부사절 접속사가 들어갈 자리이므로 부사인 (D) Even도 오답이다. Whereas(반면에), If(만약 ~라면), Unless(만약 ~가 아니라면) 중에서 '결로에 도달하지 못하면 연기될 것이다'는 뜻이 적절하므로 정답은 (C) Unless이다.

만약 이사회가 오늘 결론에 도달하지 못한다면, 투표는 다음 달 회의까지 연기되어야 할 것이다.
postpone 연기하다

114 해설 알맞은 전치사를 고르는 문제로 받기 뒤에 기간(three years)과 함께 쓰이는 기간 전치사는 (D)이다. 참고로 기간 앞에 오는 전치사에는 for, during, over, through, within, in, throughout이 있다.

예측가들은 다음 3년 동안 렌스터운의 공공 지출이 증가가 있을 것으로 예상한다.
forecaster 예측가 anticipate 예상하다 public spending 공공 지출

115 해설 명사 어휘 문제로 '방문자들의 증가를 예측한다'기 가장 자연스러우므로 정답은 (C)이다. 증가, 감소를 나타내는 명사, 즉 increase, decrease, rise, fall, drop 등은 전치사 in과 함께 사용되므로 받긴 뒤에 in을 단서로 정답을 찾을 수 있다.

동물원의 관리자들은 보기 드문 백호 새끼의 출생에 이은 방문자들의 증가를 예측하고 있다.
cub (곰·사자·여우 등의) 새끼 insert 두입 array 집합체, 무리

Actual Test 05 134 • 135

116 해설 빈칸부터 magazines까지는 앞의 명사를 수식하는 관계절이므로 빈칸은 주어가 될 수 있는 관계대명사 주어이다. 빈칸 뒤에 명사(advertisement)와 결합하여 관계절에서의 주어가 될 수 있는 것은 소유격 관계대명사 (A)이다. who는 주격 관계대명사로 뒤에 동사로 시작하는 절이 와야 하고, which는 주격 혹은 목적격 관계대명사로 주어가 없거나 목적어가 없는 절이 온다.
질문을 받은 소비자들은 중 고급 잡지에 광고를 싣는 그랜빌 화장품에서 제조된 제품군에 익숙한 사람은 많지 않았다.
be familiar with ~에 친숙하다 product line 제품군 manufacture 제조하다 cosmetic 화장품 glossy magazine (유광 종이에 인쇄된) 고급 잡지

117 해설 동사 어휘 문제로 문맥상 '화사의 연례 보고서를 편찬하는 동안에'가 가장 적절하므로 정답은 (A)이다.
프라이스 금융 서비스의 리오 씨는 회사의 연례 보고서를 편찬하는 동 안 대화의상을 사용할 것이다.
financial service 금융 서비스 annual report 연례 보고서 compile 엮다, 편찬하다 respond 응답하다 proceed 진행하다

118 해설 관사(an) 뒤에 명사 자리로 빈칸 뒤에 명사가 없으므로 빈칸은 명사 (C)가 정답이다. 참고로 feature가 명사로 '특징', 동사로 '~을 특징으로 하다'라는 의미를 갖는 것을 알아 둔다.
〈피트니스 포 라이프〉 홍보용 DVD는 상체 운동에 중점을 두어 건강한 신체를 위한 다양한 운동을 특징으로 할 것이다.
feature 특징으로 하다 upper body 상체 strength 힘 기운

119 해설 명사 어휘 문제로 빈칸 뒤의 내용이 해러스 슈퍼마켓의 '목 적'에 해당하므로 문맥상 가장 적절한 선택지는 (C)이다.
해러스 슈퍼마켓의 목적은 더 나은 고객 서비스를 고집함으로써, 더 많은 사람들이 그 매장에서 소핑하도록 하는 것이다.
inquiry 문의 objective 목적 transfer 이전

120 해설 The town ~ evacuated는 문장의 필수 성분을 모두 갖춘 완전한 문장이므로 빈칸부터 towards Netherman Falls 까지는 수식 역할을 한다. 빈칸 뒤에 명사(a bush fire)가 있으므로 명사와 함께 쓰여 수식 역할을 하는 전치사가 와야 하는 자리 이다. 전치사 owing to(때문에)와 instead of(대신에) 중에서 문 맥상 이유를 나타내는 전치사가 더 적절하므로 (B)가 정답이다. provided that(만약 ~라면)과 even if(비록 ~일지라도)는 부사 절 접속사로 뒤에 절이 와야 하므로 오답이다. 참고로 이유를 나 타내는 전치사 because of, due to, owing to, on account of, thanks to를 알아 둔다.
산토스 마을은 네더맨 폭포를 향해 번지고 있는 산불 때문에 대피되었다.
evacuate 대피하다 bush fire 산불, 들불, 들불 head ~로 향하다

121 해설 뒤에 명사구를 이끄는 수식어구 자리이므로 전치사가 들어 갈 자리이다. 선택지에서 전치사이면서 것은 Aside from(~을 제외하 고) 과 Compared to(~와 비교하여)이므로 둘 중에 의미상 어울 리는 것을 고르는 문제이다. 약간의 감소를 제외하고는 전체적으 로 증가했다는 뜻이 적절하므로 정답은 (A) Aside from이다. 참 고로 Although는 부사절 접속사이고, For instance는 부사이다.
주방 제품 매출에서의 약간의 감소를 제외하고는, 불도원 전자는 모든 산업 분야에 걸쳐 급증을 경험했다.
minor 작은 surge 급증

122 해설 permitted는 목적격보어로 to부정사를 취하는 동사이므로 오답이다. included는 의미상 맞지 않고, compiled(준수하다는 전치사 with를 이끄는 자동사이므로 오답이다. 따라서 정답은 (C) consented(동의했다)이다.
노동 조합과의 토론이 시작된 후에, 목스톤 산업은 전 직원들에 대해 급 여를 올리고 근무 시간을 줄이기로 동의했다.
labor union 노동 조합

123 해설 be encouraged to부정사(~할 것을 권장받다/정려 받다)를 세트 표현으로 외워 두자. circulated(순회되는)과 conducted(수행되는)은 주어가 사람(Customers)인 이 문장에 들어가면 의미상 어울리지 않는다. considered(간주되는)는 5형 식 동사로 쓰였을 때 수동태가 되면 뒤에 명사가 형용사가 남아야 하므로 오답이다. 따라서 정답은 (B) encouraged이다.
글로리아 커피 메이커의 세 번째 버전을 구매했던 고객들은 고객 설문 카드를 작성하고 제품을 고정할 것을 권장받는다.
edition 버전, 판

124 해설 형용사 어휘 문제로 문맥상 '5일 연속의 맑은 날을 예상했 다'가 가장 자연스러우므로 정답은 (D)이다.
기상 예보관들은 5일 연속의 맑은 날을 예상했었고, 이는 최근 전례 없는 묵우부터 환영받는 유예의 시간이다.
weather forecaster 일기예보자, 기상예보자 reprieve 유예 unprecedented 전례 없는 refreshed 상쾌 한 atmospheric 대기의, 분위기 있는 rainfall 강우, 폭우 deliberate 고의의, 의도된 consecutive 연속의

125 해설 have와 to부정사 함께 '아직 ~하지 않았다'라는 표현으 로 쓰이는 것은 yet이다. '아직 ~하지 않았다'라는 표현인 have yet to do를 꼭 알아 둔다. 정답은 (A)이다.
연례 글라스턴버리 축제의 시작을 2주 앞두고, 주최자들이 어떤 공연이 메인이 될 것인지 결정을 아직 못했다.
organizer 기획자, 주최자 act (여러 파트로 구성된 쇼의 한) 파트; (연극 등의) 막 headline (콘서트나 쇼의) 주 공연자로 나오다

126 해설 빈칸에는 타동사 start의 목적어로 명사가 와야 하므로 명사 producing을 정답이다. products는 '제품'이라는 의미의 가산 명사로 단독으로 쓰일 수 없으며, 시작하는 대상이 되어야 하므로 '생산력(productivity)'보다는 '생산(production)'이라는 의미가 적절하므로 (A)가 정답이다.
한지 석유 회사인 페트로스 라인의 석유 제품 생산을 시작할 계획입니다.
corporation 회사, 기업 plan to ~을 계획하다

127 해설 동사 어휘 문제로 문맥상 '이점들의 선두적인 제약회사들 중의 하나로 확고히 할 것이다'가 가장 자연스러우므로 정답은 (D)이다.
러스 하이스쿨을 최고 경영자로 임명할 것은 미쉘 사의 입지를 이점트 의 선두적인 제약회사 중 하나로 확고히 할 것이다.
appointment 임명 leading 선두적인 pharmaceutical 제약의 institution 기관 administer 관리하다, 운영하다 incline 마음이 기울다 accomplish 성취하다 solidify 군하다, 확고히 하다

128 해설 접속사 That이며 Because는 뒤에 절(S+V)을 이끌어야 하므로 오답이다. For는 전치사로서 뒤에 동명사를 이끌 수 있 지만, '~을 위해서'라는 의미가 어울리지 않으므로 오답이다. 따 라서 분사구문(adopting ~)을 이끌 수 있는 부사절 접속사인 (D) Since가 정답이다. 참고로 주절에 현재완료 시제(has experienced)가 있을 때 가장 어울리는 접속사는 Since(~ 이 래로)라는 점도 알아 두자.

autopay 자동 납부   balance 잔액   thoroughly 철저하게

129

기업 생산 방법을 채택한 이래로 컨트루스 사는 제품 결함의 감소를 경험했다.

해설 전치사 into의 목적어가 필요한 자리이므로 명사가 들어가야 한다. 따라서 정답은 (A) effect이다. 참고로 go into effect는 '시행되다, 효력이 발생되다'라는 의미로 쓰이다.

adopt 채택하다   defect 결함
be exempt from ~에서 면제되다

130

해설 주어가 Ucham Construction이고 동사가 builds와 requires가 and로 연결되는 완전한 문장 구조이다. 따라서 빈칸은 두 부사 자리로 (A)를 제외한 선택지 모두 정답 후보이다. 문맥상 빈칸 앞의 내용이 뒤의 내용의 근거이므로 (B)가 알맞다.

우량 건설은 에너지 효율적인 주거 건물들을 전 세계에 짓고 있으므로 숙련되고 경험 있는 파트너가 필요하다.

energy efficient 에너지 효율적인   residential 주거의   structure 건물, 구조물   worldwide 세계적으로

131

해설 선택지가 모두 소유격이므로 명사를 수식할 수 있다. 앞 문장에 있는 인털링 크레딧 유니온과 로열원 크레딧 유니온 두 회사를 대신 받는 자리이므로 '그들이 계획이라고 받는 것이 어울린다. 따라서 정답은 (C) their이다.

132

해설 빈칸은 명사를 수식할 형용사 자리이므로, 선택지에서 형용사인 것은 financed(자금을 조달받은)와 financial(금융의)이다. 이 새로 생긴 기업이 자금을 조달받았다는 근거는 없으므로 정답은 (C) financial이다.

133

(A) 세부 사항들은 어제 처음으로 대중들에게 발표되었다.
(B) 공식적인 기록에는 그 기업이 모든 연방 규정을 준수하고 있다고 나와 있다.
(C) 금융권은 가장 빠르게 급부상하는 선물 중 하나이다.
(D) 회원 기업은 특정 단체의 시험들에게 이용 가능하다.

해설 두 기업의 합병에 대한 내용으로 빈칸 앞에서 익명으로 투표했다는 내용이 나오므로 '세부 사항은 어제 처음으로 발표되었다'는 (A)가 정답이다.

134

해설 문맥에 맞는 명사 어휘를 고르는 문제이다. 새로운 합동 법인이 생겨나는 상황이므로 '형성, 구성'이라는 의미의 (D) formation이 정답이다. (A) 구별 / (B) 평가 / (C) 전략, 추정치

135

해설 아래 문단을 보면 이 고객이 아직 돈을 지불하지 않았다는 것을 알 수 있으므로, 앞으로 '내야 할(due)' 총 금액을 알려주는 것이 적절하다. 따라서 정답은 (B)이다.

136

해설 앞머 문맥을 적절히 이어 줄 접속부사를 고르는 문제이다. 앞 문장에서 자동 납부 부분 온셋에 등록되었다고 했고, 뒤 문장에서 신용 카드로 돈이 빠져나갈 거라고 했으므로 인과 관계로 볼 수 있다. 따라서 정답은 (C) Hence(따라서, 그러므로)이다. (A) 사실은 / (B) 그렇지 않으면, 달리 / (D) 그러나

137

해설 주절을 수식할 부사 역할 자리이다. 선택지에서 문서나문의 to부동사가 부사 역할로 쓰일 수 있는데, '~하기 위해서'의 뜻을 가진 to부정사가 의미상 더 적절하므로 정답은 (B)이다.

138

(A) 이 이메일에 동봉된 것은 단골 고객을 위한 특별 쿠폰입니다.
(B) 저희 OSN 텔레콤과 거래해 주셔서 감사합니다.
(C) 고객님의 계정에 관한 중요한 변경 사항들이 청구서에 포함될 수 있습니다.
(D) 늦은 납부 때문에 추가 요금을 청구받게 될 것입니다.

해설 빈칸 뒤에 청구서를 철저히 검토하라는 내용이 나오므로 '중요 변경 사항이 청구서에 포함될 것'임을 나타내는 (C)가 정답이다.

Part 6
문제 P203

[131-134]

5월 1일 - 인털링 크레딧 유니온과 로열원 크레딧 유니온은 오늘 [131]그들의 합병 계획을 공표했다. 이 새로운 기업은 빅토리 크레딧 유니온이라는 이름으로 불리게 될 것이다. 이는 50억달러 이상의 자산과 총 120,000명의 회원을 보유한 이 지역에 본사를 둔 기업 중 가장 큰 [132]금융업체가 될 것이다.

두 신용조합의 이사회는 합병을 고려하기 위해서 몇 개월 전에 모였다. 지난주에 그들은 합병을 위해 익명으로 투표했다. [133]세부 사항들은 어제 처음으로 합병을 공표한 뒤 약 한 주 정도 걸릴 것으로 보인다. 그동안 회원들은 각자의 기관에서 계속 서비스를 이용하면 된다. 그러나 또한 그들의 새로운 파트너 기관의 서비스에도 접근할 수 있을 것이다.

unveil 발표하다, 공개하다   merge 합병하다   entity 단체, 기업   convene 소집하다   credit union 신용조합   unanimously 만장일치로   joint entity 합동 법인   respective 각자의   be compliant with ~을 준수하다   federal 연방 정부의

[135-138]

수신: sanrao@kignet.com
발신: accounts@osn.com
날짜: 11월 15일
제목: 전화 요금 청구서

라오 씨에게,

고객님의 문자리 5110인 OSN 전화의 요금 청구서는 [135]내야 할 총 금액 25달러 80센트입니다.

이때 어떤 다른 조치는 필요하지 않습니다. 고객님은 자동 납부 온셋에 등록되어 있습니다. [136]따라서, 11월 25일에 고객님의 신용 카드로 현재 잔액만큼 청구될 것입니다.

청구서를 [137]확인해 보시려면, www.osntelecom.net로 들어오셔서 고객님의 계정으로 로그인해 보세요. 또한 [138]현재 현재 청구서와 지난 청구서를 다 온로드하거나 인쇄하실 수도 있으실 겁니다.

개정 서비스

[139-142]

수신: harvey@koln.com
발신: kyra@koln.com
제목: 면접
날짜: 9월 2일
첨부 문서: 계약자_목록

하비 씨에게,

제가 맡아는 채용 위원회가 향후 몇 주간 채용 후보자들을 면접할 계획이라는 것을 이미 기억하실 겁니다. 각 [139]지원자들에게 연락해서 개인 면접 일정을 잡아 주세요. 그들의 이름과 연락처가 들어 있는 문서를 첨부했습니다. 그 문서에는 또한 그들의 면접 선호 날짜와 시간이 [140]나와 있습니다. 일단 면접 일정을 잡고 나서, 저에게 즉시 보고해 주세요. [141]이 중요한 새 임원을 처리해 주셔서 감사합니다. 만약 추가 문의가 있으면 알려주세요, 그렇지 않으면 [142]것이지만, 이메일과 먼저 메시지도 확인하겠습니다.

기라

Part 7

candidate 후보자 following 다음의 preferred 선호되는 patronage 후원 애용
objective 목표 identify 확인하다 potential 잠재적인 cost-cutting 비용 절감 evaluate 평가하다 ineffectiveness 비효율성 familiarize 숙지시키다 forward 보내다 allocate 할당하다 cutting-edge 최첨단의

139
해설 첫 문장에서 채용 후보자들을 면접 볼 계획이라고 했으므로, 그 지원자들에게 연락해 달라고 부탁하는 것이 이 문맥적으로 어울린다. 따라서 정답은 (C) applicants이다. (A) 직원들 / (B) 지인들 / (D) 주민들

140
해설 알맞은 동사의 시제를 고르는 문제이다. 문제에 나와 있는 내용을 나타낼 때는 단순 현재시제를 쓴다. 따라서 정답은 (A) lists이다. 참고로 (would have p.p.)는 ~했을 텐데라는 뜻으로 가정법 과거완료에 쓰는 시제이다.

141
(A) 우리는 세부 사항들을 논의하기 위해서 내일 만날 수 있습니다.
(B) 연금 고객으로서 당신의 애용에 감사 드립니다.
(C) 당신이 해야 할 일은 일은 신상사원들을 훈련시키는 것뿐입니다.
(D) 이 중요한 사안을 처리해 주셔서 감사합니다.
해설 연락 일정을 잡아 달라는 내용이 나왔으므로 이 중요한 사안을 처리해 줘서 감사하다는 (D)가 정답이다.

142
해설 선택지 모두 접속사이므로 의미상 어울리는 것을 고르되, 내 일 회사에 접속되는 시점과 이메일과 문제를 확인할 것이라는 사실을 연결하기에 가장 어울리는 접속사는 (C) but이다.

[143-146]
받는: 젠 그레디
수신: 포장 부서
날짜: 12월 2일

부서의 기획들을 위한 우리의 목표 중 하나는 내후에 비용을 143 줄이는 것이었습니다. 우리는 잠재적인 비용 절감을 위한 세 개의 분야를 확인했고 그것은 노동, 자재, 절차입니다. 144 이미 직원 근무 시간은 효율적으로 할당하고 있습니다. 따라서 우리는 다른 두 분야에 집중하기로 결정했습니다. 두 번째 분야에 관해서는 다른 자재로 새로운 더 싼 박스들을 사용하기 시작할 것입니다. 이 새로운 포장재들과 다른 포장재들에 145 관한 세부 사항들은 곧 결정될 것입니다. 세 번째 분야에 관해서는 잠재적인 비효율성을 확인하기 위해서 현재 포장 절차들을 면밀히 평가하고 있습니다. 우리는 이 새로운 절차들이 밝혀지자마자 146 조정이 가해질 것입니다. 그것들이 밝혀질 때 숙지시켜에 대해서 질문이 있으면 당신의 관리자와 상의하세요.

143
해설 다음 문장에서 잠재적인 비용 절감을 위한 분야를 확인했다고 했으므로, 우리의 목표는 비용을 '줄이는 것'이었다고 볼 수 있다. 따라서 정답은 (C)이다. (A) 평가하다 / (D) 개선하다 보하다, 정리하다, 승진시키다

144
(A) 신입 사원들은 교육 시간에 참석할 것을 권장받습니다.
(B) 이미 직원 근무 시간은 효율적으로 할당하고 있습니다.
(C) 다가오는 주에 최신 장비가 설치될 것입니다.
(D) 우리의 성공은 당신의 기여 덕분입니다.
해설 빈칸 앞에서 비용 절감을 위한 분야인 노동, 자재, 절차를 언 급했는데 빈칸 뒤로 자재, 절차에 대한 내용이 나오므로 노동에 대한 내용인 (B)가 정답이다.

145
해설 빈칸은 명사를 이끌며 수식어구를 이루는 전차사 자리이다. 선택지에서 전차사인 것은 (C) regarding(~에 관한)이다. 참고로 같은 의미의 전차사로 concerning, pertaining to, about, as to, as for도 있음을 알아 두자.

146
해설 이 글의 전반적인 내용이 부서의 비용 절감을 위한 '변화'에 관한 내용이므로, 비효율성이 밝혀지자마자 '조정(adjustments)' 을 가할 거라고 예상할 수 있다. 따라서 정답은 (D)이다. (A) 승진 홍보, 정리 / (B) 거래 / (C) 부분, 분할

[147-148]

칼란즈 씨푸드

오션 드라이브 235

오션 드라이브 235: 오전 8시~오후 7시
일요일: 오전 10시~오후 5시
339-555-4481

신선한 해물 요리를 위한 최고의 지역 최고의 도매업체로 다음과 같은 제품을 취급합니다.

오징어, 신선한 어류 및 조개류

대구와 해덕
넙치와 장어

주간 특가: 굴, 홍합, 게살 가재를 25퍼센트 싸게 가져가세요. 2월 2일 한정 종료.

wholesaler 도매업체 squid 오징어 shellfish 조개류 cod 대구 haddock 해덕 halibut 넙치 eel 장어 oyster 굴 mussel 홍합 crab 게 lobster 가재 frozen 냉동한 overseas 해외 specialize in 전문으로 하다 exotic 외국산의

147 칼란즈 씨푸드에 관해 언급된 것은?
(A) 냉동 요리를 판매한다.
(B) 일요일 내내 영업한다.
(C) 해외 주문을 받는다.
(D) 외국산 생선을 전문으로 한다.

148 광고에 따르면 무엇이 할인되는가?
(A) 흰 살 생선
(B) 부드 장비
(C) 심해어
(D) 조개류

[149-150]

루이지스 차 정비소
월요일부터 토요일까지 영업
오전 8시 30분부터 오후 5시까지

고객: 알렉스 장
주문 번호: 20201187
149 10월 8일 수요일 오전 8시 37분

품목	서비스	찾는 날짜/ 시간	비용
승합차	휠얼라인먼트	149 10월 8일 수요일/ 오후 4시	8달러
해치백	차내 청소	10월 10일 금요일/ 오후 6시	20달러
오토바이	서비스	10월 13일 월요일/ 오전 10시	30달러
스쿠터	서비스	10월 13일 월요일/ 오전 10시	30달러

150 총 비용: 88달러
150 입금액: 88달러
잔액: 0달러

루이지스를 선택해 주셔서 감사합니다.
월요일에 있는 차내 청소에 대해 문의하세요.

wheel alignment 휠얼라인먼트, 바퀴 정렬 hatchback 해치백, 치체 뒤쪽에 위로 올려 열 수 있는 문이 있는 차 balance due 잔여 금액 same-day service 당일 서비스 invoice 송장 bill 청구하다

149 장 씨가 당일 서비스를 받은 탈것은?
(A) 오토바이
(B) 해치백
(C) 스쿠터
(D) 승합차

150 영수증에서 장 씨의 서비스에 대해 알 수 있는 것은?
(A) 송장이 보내질 것이다.
(B) 10월 10일에 청구되었다.
(C) 전액 지불되었다.
(D) 승합차 여러 대가 포함되었다.

[151-153]

http://www.appliancereviewer.com

151 200달러 미만 전자레인지

모델	세부 사항	평가자 의견
액세스 T-L	무게 3킬로그램 굽기 기능: 유 제안 소매가: 199달러	스테인리스 스틸로만 구매 가능 152 초고속 해동
비스타4	무게 3킬로그램 굽기 기능: 무 제안 소매가: 49달러	간단하고 쉬운 조작 교체 부품이 매우 비쌈
캐터햄 스페셜	무게 5킬로그램 굽기 기능: 무 153 제안 소매가: 99달러	모터 10년 보증 강력한 굽기 기능
플라스마 700	무게 6킬로그램 굽기 기능: 유 153 제안 소매가: 99달러	매우 무겁고 큼 에너지 효율 등급 높음

microwave 전자레인지 appliance 가전제품 weight 무게 retail price 소매가 defrost 해동 easy-to-use 사용하기 쉬운 replacement 대체 part 부품 guarantee 보증 roast 굽다 facility 기능, 시설 cumbersome 무겁고 큰 energy-efficiency 에너지 효율 rating 등급 component 부품 warranty 품질 보증 capacity 능력

151 누군가 이 도표를 참고할 이유는?
(A) 특정 가격 범위의 전자레인지에 관해 알기 위해
(B) 각 전자레인지의 부품을 찾기 위해
(C) 매주 가게에서 판매하는 전자레인지의 수를 알기 위해
(D) 전자레인지들의 에너지 효율을 비교하기 위해

152 액세스 T-L의 장점으로 언급된 것은?
(A) 여러 색상으로 구매가 가능하다.
(B) 음식을 빨리 해동시킨다.
(C) 10년을 보증해 준다.
(D) 에너지를 효율적으로 쓴다.

153 캐터햄 스페셜과 플라스마 700의 유사점은?
(A) 가격이 같다.
(B) 둘 다 굽기 기능이 있다.
(C) 무게가 같다.
(D) 둘 다 부정적인 평을 받았다.

[154-155]

프레드 맨데일 [오후 1:14]	흥이, 10월에 있을 로봇 컨퍼런스에 우리를 등록했나요?
흥이 응우옌 [오후 1:15]	온라인 양식을 제출하긴 했는데, 답신메일을 못 받은 것 같아요. 답신메일 확인을 하셨습니까
프레드 맨데일 [오후 1:17]	확인해 줄 수 있으세요?
흥이 응우옌 [오후 1:18]	물론이죠.
흥이 응우옌 [오후 1:25]	방금 전화해 봤는데, 저희가 명단에 없었다고 해요. 그쪽 서버에 문제가 있었어요. 지금 저희가 등록되었다고 합니다.
프레드 맨데일 [오후 1:26]	다행이에요! 154 이제 저희가 보스턴에 있는 동안 실험실 직원들을 관리할 사람을 구해야 돼요.
흥이 응우옌 [오후 1:27]	154 마이클이 적절할 것 같은데요.
프레드 맨데일 [오후 1:28]	그분도 컨퍼런스에 가는 거 아닌가요?
흥이 응우옌 [오후 1:29]	155 그러려고 했었는데, 마감이 넘어서 제안서를 못 내라고 했거든요.
프레드 맨데일 [오후 1:30]	알겠어요. 그럼 그분한테 부탁할게요.

confirmation 확인 proposal 제안서 embarrass 당황하게 하다

154 마이클에 대해서 암시된 것은?
(A) 그는 실험실을 감독할 수 없다.
(B) 그는 신입사원이다.
(C) 그는 컨퍼런스에 참석할 것이다.
(D) 그도 보스턴에 가게 될 것이다.

155 오후 1시 15분에 응우옌 씨가 "답신을 하시나니까 믿인데"라고 썼을 때 그 의미는 무엇인가?
(A) 그녀는 등록을 확인하는 것을 잊어버렸다.
(B) 그녀는 세부 사항에 대해서 잊어버리면 안 되겠다고 깨달았다.
(C) 그녀는 맨데일 씨가 말한 것 때문에 무언가를 방금 깨달았다.
(D) 그녀는 맨데일 씨가 등록을 제출할 것이라고 생각했다.

에미론, 시장 점유가 떨어지다

쥬나이드 카심

홍콩. 4월 11일 - 고객 편의가 관한 최근의 시장 조사에 따르면 에미론 에미론은 고객 편의가 좋은 에너지 공급 업체 중 10위를 차지했고, 60퍼센트의 시용자들이 만족하고 있다. -[1]-. 조사는 지난달에 에너를 연구 기관에 의해 시행되었으며, 비록 에미론이 주요 경쟁사인 티블 파워보다는 순위가 높아졌지만, 4위를 했던 지난해보다 급격히 떨어진 것이다. -[2]-.

"다른 경쟁사들보다 순위가 낮지만, 저희의 목적은 고객에 필요에 집중하는 것입니다"라고 에미론의 대변인인 아담 다울링 씨는 말한다. -[3]-. "저의 서비스를 개선을 위한 변화가 이룸 예정입니다. 예를 들어, 내년에는 고객 서비스 개선을 위한 기술 직원들을 한 건물에 통합할 것입니다. 이 일로 다음 해 3월에 완료될 것입니다." -[4]-.

market share 시장 점유율 following ~ 후에; (특정 결과에 따라) rank 순위를 차지하다 customer-friendly 고객 편의가 좋은 supplier 공급업체 claim 차지하다 conduct 수행하다 reveal 공개하다; 밝히다 main 주요한 dramatically 급격히 fall behind ~에 뒤떨어지다 competitor 경쟁사 aim 목표 concentrate on ~에 집중하다 spokesperson 대변인 put ~ in place ~을 시행하다 consolidate 통합하다 short-staffed 직원이 부족한 inconsistent 일관성이 없는 merge 합병하다 carry out 수행하다

156 에미론에 관해 고객이 답한 것으로 가장 가능성이 높은 것은?

(A) 에너지 공급이 너무 느리다.
(B) 가격이 너무 높다.
(C) 콜센터에 직원들이 부족하다.
(D) 기술 서비스가 일관성이 없다.

157 에미론이 내년에 할 일은?

(A) 새 기술을 사용할 것이다.
(B) 다른 경쟁사들과 합병할 것이다.
(C) 모든 기술 직원들을 한 장소에 배치할 것이다.
(D) 더 많은 시장 조사를 할 것이다.

158 [1], [2], [3], [4]로 표시된 위치 중 다음 문장이 들어가기 적절한 것은?

"이러한 변화로 인해 고객들의 의견에 있어 에미론이 인기가 올라갈 것으로 기대된다."

(A) [1]
(B) [2]
(C) [3]
(D) [4]

수신: cbowden@washngo.com
발신: rmansell@plumbbase.com
날짜: 6월 30일
제목: 엘리트 세탁 건조기

바우덴 씨께,

귀사에서 제조하는 세탁 건조기 중 하나인 엘리트 세탁 건조기와 관련하여 연락을 드립니다. 이 제품을 쓰던 엘리트 세탁 건조기이 누락된 니은 하나로 인해 내부의 액체 용기가 느슨하다고 합의하였습니다. 운이 좋게 상하나로 인해 내부에 누출이 재고가 있어서, 고객들에게 공급할 수 있었습니다.

저희 가게에 재고 손실이 없도록 고객들에게 드릴 나사를 돌려주시면 감사하겠습니다.

기개이 이런 경험에 대한 우려로 저하는 그 문제가 수정될 때까지 귀사에 세탁 건조기의 추가 주문을 보류하기로 결정했습니다. 이것이 해결되는 혹선이 생기면 기개이 주문을 재개할 것입니다.

이 문제에 관해 검토해 주셔서 감사합니다.

레이 맨셀
플럼베이스 매니저

washer drier 세탁 건조기 manufacture 제조하다 significant 상당한 internal 내부의 liquid 액체 holder 용기 loose 느슨한 missing 누락된; 없는 in stock 재고 supply 공급하다 grateful 감사하는 profit 이익 fault 결함 delay 연기하다 additional 추가적인 matter 문제 rectify 바로잡다 assurance 확신 resolve 해결하다 resume 재개하다 address (문제를) 다루다 postpone 연기하다 particular 특정한 charge 청구하다 unsatisfactory 불만족스러운 merchandise 상품

159 맨셀 씨가 이메일을 쓴 이유는?

(A) 송장을 문의하려고
(B) 가전제품을 추천하려고
(C) 문제를 해결하려고
(D) 고객에게 답변하려고

160 맨셀 씨가 바우덴 씨에게 요청하는 것은?

(A) 기기 사용법 설명하기
(B) 세탁 건조기 홍보 돕기
(C) 몇 개 물건 돌려주기
(D) 주문에 속도 내기

161 플럼베이스는 어떤 결정을 내렸는가?

(A) 특정 상품에 대해 주문을 보류할 것이다.
(B) 다양한 세탁기를 판매할 것이다.
(C) 손님들에게 나사비에 대해 청구할 것이다.
(D) 불만족스러운 상품 일부를 반품할 것이다.

주간 출장 요리점 소식

금요일에 상로마스 나이트클럽이 세 개의 자매 카지노를 인수하는 조항에 동의했다. 카지노 중 한 곳은 갤런드 인트림에 위치하고, 다른 두 곳은 벨 페스트에 있다. -[1]-.

상표 변경 사항이 발표되지 않았기 때문에 그 카지노들은 갤런트 상표명으로 운영될 것이다. -[2]-. 가지 회견에서 상로마의 최고경영자인 안사 귀다 씨는 "저는 이 카지노를 상로마 브랜드로 인수하게 되어 기쁩니다. 저희는 인트림과 벨페스트에서 유행업계의 선두 주자가 되는 것을 목표로 하고 있습니다. 장기 전략은 이 지역에 저렴하고 신나는 레저 오락 위기에 차려지지 않을 것이라고 강조했다. -[3]-.

상로마스 나이트클럽은 100년도 더 전에 오마에에게 첫 술집을 연 귀 씨의 증조부가 생각내서 나왔다. 귀다 씨는 7년 전 이바지가 돌아가시고 소유권을 인계받았다. 지금은 이잉랜드의 마을과 도시 곳곳에 실로마의 술집이 존재한다. -[4]-.

terms (계약의) 조건 foreseeable future 가까운 장래 venue 장소 press release 가지 회견 incorporate 포함하다 leading 선두적인 앞서는 affordable 저렴한 leisure 여가의 be under long-term 장기적인 brainchild 생각; 발명품 century 100년 take threat 위기에 차려다 over ownership 소유권을 인수하다 acquisition 인수, 매입 recruit 모집하다 relocation 이전 headquarters 본사 entry 입장 retain 유지하다 performance-based bonus 성과급

162 매입을 발표하기 위해?

(A) 게임 시장에 관해 보고하기 위해
(B) 새로운 손실 직원들 모집하기 위해
(C) 새로운 송실 직원들 모집하기 위해
(D) 회사의 이전을 언급하기 위해

163 귀다 씨가 인트림과 벨페스트 지점의 고용에 관해 말한 것은?

(A) 새로운 직원 관행업을 실행하려고 원한다.
(B) 지역 사회의 지지를 기대한다.
(C) 현재의 직원을 유지를 의향이다.
(D) 성과급을 제공할 계획이다.

164 상로마스 나이트클럽에 관해 언급된 것은?

(A) 가족 경영의 사업체이다.
(B) 국제적이 클럽을 갖고 있다.
(C) 곧 스코틀랜드로 확장할 것이다.
(D) 무료 게임을 제공한다.

165 [1], [2], [3], [4]로 표시된 위치 중 다음 문장이 들어가기 적절한 것은?

"매매 가격은 아직 발표되지 않았다."

(A) [1]
(B) [2]
(C) [3]
(D) [4]

(A) [1]
(B) [2]
(C) [3]
(D) [4]

[166-168]

일마 베가	오전 10:08

좋은 아침이에요. 방금 막 저희 지난 분기에 대한 판매 보고서를 준비했습니다. 매출이 지난해 같은 시기와 비교했을 때 20퍼센트 떨어졌습니다. 반전이 필요합니다.

론 퀼와	오전 10:09

사람들을 가게로 끌기 위해서 큰 판촉 행사를 해보는 게 어때요? 하나 사면 하나 공짜로 주는 행사 같은 거요.

일마 베가	오전 10:10

그건 조금 미뤄 둘래요. 일단 저희가 어떤 옵션들을 생각해 낼 수 있을지 보고 싶어요.

캐서린 베이커	오전 10:11

광고를 늘려보면 어떨까요? 아마 사람들이 새로운 쇼핑몰이 오픈한 이래로 저희를 잊어버렸는지도 몰라요.

론 퀼와	오전 10:12

맞아요, 그런데 광고도 비싸요.

캐서린 베이커	오전 10:13

라디오 광고 말고요. 168 추가로 돈을 쓰지 않고도 할 수 있어요.

일마 베가	오전 10:14

좋아요, 계속 말씀해 보세요

캐서린 베이커	오전 10:15

한 번 들어보세요. 지금 현재 저희는 지역 신문에 광고를 운영하는 데 한 달 단에 1,500달러를 쓰고 있어요. 같은 가격이면 매일 3~4개의 억에 광고할 수 있어요.

일마 베가	오전 10:16

괜찮은 많은 광고네요

론 퀼와	오전 10:17

좋아요. 젊은 사람들을 타겟으로 하는 게 더 쉬워질 것 같아요. 169 그들이 최신 유행하는 신발 스타일을 좋아하는 사람들이잖아요

일마 베가	오전 10:18

한번 해 봅시다. 캐서린 씨, 몇몇 역에 전화해서 비용이 얼마나 들지에 대해서 견적서 좀 받아 주실래요?

캐서린 베이커	오전 10:19

물론이죠

일마 베가	오전 10:20

론 광고 리뷰를 위한 몇몇 아이디어를 작성해 주셨으면 좋겠어요. 166 우리는 쇼핑몰에 있는 것과 독립된 신발을 팔건데, 소비자들이 우리 가격이 더 싸다는 걸 알게 해야 해요

론 퀼와	오전 10:20

알겠어요

reverse 전환하다, 반전시키다 hold off 미루다 come up with 생각해 내다 estimate 견적서 jot down 적다 generate 만들어 내다 skeptical 회의적인

166 대화 참여자들은 어디에서 일하는 것 같은가?
(A) 라디오 방송국
(B) 웃가게
(C) 쇼핑몰
(D) 신발 가게

167 론 퀼와는 무엇을 하겠다고 동의하는가?
(A) 광고 아이디어를 내는 것
(B) 몇몇 경쟁업체들의 가격을 확인하는 것
(C) 판촉 행사를 고안해 내는 것
(D) 쇼핑몰 고객들과 이야기하는 것

168 오전 10시 14분에 베가 씨가 "좋아요, 계속 말씀해 보세요"라고 했을 때 그 의미는 무엇인가?
(A) 그녀는 떠나기 위해서 토론을 끝내고 싶어 한다.
(B) 그녀는 퀼와 씨가 제안한 아이디어를 다시 고려 중이다.
(C) 그녀는 베이커 씨가 그녀의 아이디어의 세부 사항을 설명하기를 원한다.
(D) 그녀는 라디오 광고가 효과가 있을 것이라는 사실에 대해 회의적이다.

[169-171]

수신	brinkov@nomak.com
발신	winble@stein.com
날짜	8월 1일
제목	브링크 씨께

브링크 씨께,

오늘 제가 검토한 귀하의 이메일 문의에 감사드립니다. 웹 사이트를 다시 디자인함으로서 노아 프로드 시가 이용자 수를 늘리도록 저희가 어떻게 도울 수 있는지 말씀을 드리겠습니다.

스타인 디자인은 5년 전에 설립되었습니다. 170 저희는 대부분 해외에 있는 많은 대기업의 인터넷 지문가로 일하고 있습니다. 저희의 주요 고객으로는 몸바사의 KKS 으로, 뉴욕의 시그네 디자인, 필라스 주시의 홍이의 방문자 시가 있습니다. 저희의 컨설팅의 결과로 이 기업들은 웹 사이트의 방문객을 급격히 늘렸고, 방문객의 다수가 관심 있는 고객이 되었습니다.

169 저희와 함께 일하신다면, 최고 수준의 작업을 171 보장할 수 있습니다. 스타인 디자인은 기간 내에 예산에 맞춰 프로젝트를 완수하는 인상적인 기록을 갖고 있습니다. 저희는 귀사가 수익의 증가를 보게 될 것이라 확신합니다.

169 귀사의 요구 사항을 더 분석하는 회의를 위해 원하시면 언제든지 901-555-1232로 전화 주십시오. 연락을 기다리고 있겠습니다.

데나 윔블
선임 판매 부장
스타인 디자인

traffic 방문 수 establish 설립하다 appoint 임명하다 as a result of ~의 결과로 dramatic 극적인, 엄청난 assure 보장하다, 장담하다 on time 정시에, 제시간에 profitability 수익성 analyze 분석하다 pursue 추구하다 secure 획득하다 convince 설득하다

169 윔블 씨가 이메일을 보내는 이유는?
(A) 노아 프로드 사에서 온 이을 회의를 확인하기 위해
(B) 기업에 함께 거래하도록 장려하기 위해
(C) 디자인 포럼에 관한 정보를 주기 위해
(D) 새 웹 페이지를 설치하는 방법 설명하기 위해

170 스타인 디자인 사에 관해 언급된 것은?
(A) 해외에서도 사업을 한다.
(B) 다른 자문가들보다 비용이 낮다.
(C) 최근 여러 디자이너들을 고용했다.
(D) 본사가 몸바사에 있다.

171 3번째 문단, 1번째 줄의 단어 '보장하다'와 가장 비슷한 의미를 가진 단어는?

(A) 약속하다
(B) 알리다
(C) 설득하다
(D) 홍보하다

[172-175]

시애틀(3월 3일) — 시애틀에 본점을 두고 있는 말린스 화장품은 최근에 또 다른 연구 개발 시설 건설 계획을 공개했다. 현재 말린스 화장품의 유일한 연구 개발 시설은 본사로부터 200킬로미터 이상 떨어진 메인에 위치해 있다. **이 움직임은 유럽 시장으로의 확장을 위한 새로운 계획의 일환이다.**

경영진인 독일 베를린으로의 이 대담한 움직임이 유럽 화장품 산업의 주요 기업으로서 명성을 신장시킬 것으로 기대한다고 한다. 프로젝트기 끝나면 두 연구 개발 시설은 미국과 유럽 시장의 요구 사항을 쉽게 찾고 수용할 수 있을 것이다. "중요한 이점은 이전에 우리가 공급업체를 찾고 수용해야 했던 유럽의 제품과 재료에 이제 접근할 수 있다는 것입니다. 이 일은 시간이 걸렸고, 비용 마진을 추가했습니다."라고 스티브 베이커 화장이 말했다.

베이커 화장이 이사지인 데이비드 베이커 씨는 캘리포니아에서 대학을 졸업한 후, 1981년에 말린스 화장품을 창업했다. 그가 시애틀에 들어왔을 때 지역의 학생들에게 수입 화장품을 판매하는 시간제 일을 시작했다. 6개월 내에 그의 시간제 일은 큰 수익을 거두었고, 다음 해 그가 정규직으로 일하게 되면서 수익은 더 증가했다. 오늘날 말린스 화장품은 세계적으로 20개국 이상에 전문 매장을 둔 그룹직 제조업체로 국제적으로 알려져 있다. 그러나 최근에 베이커 씨의 지원하에 새 개발팀이 공격적으로 새로운 시도를 하고 있지만 시장은 매출을 떨어졌다.

연구 개발 감독인 안나 보르돈 씨에 의하면 말린스 화장품의 기존 제품 라인은 모두 이번 해 말까지 대다수의 유럽 국가에서 구매가 가능할 것이다. 보르돈 씨는 기존 제품 라인에 보충할 목적으로 노년층을 대상으로 한 최초의 노화 방지 크림을 소개할 것이라는 비전을 갖고 있다. "우리의 목표는 그것이 인정할 새로운 제품을 성장시키고 개발하는 것입니다."라고 그녀는 말했다.

172 말린스 화장품이 새 시설을 짓는 이유는?
(A) 생산 부서가 본사에서 너무 멀어서
(B) 현재 위치에서 운영비가 증가해서
(C) 현대화된 장비를 도입해야 해서
(D) 경영진이 새 지역에서 제품을 판매하려 해서

173 새 시설은 어디에 위치하게 될 것인가?
(A) 시애틀
(B) 메인
(C) 베를린
(D) 캘리포니아

174 말린스 화장품에 관해 언급된 것은?
(A) 최근 제품의 매출 성장을 염려한다.
(B) 더 많은 제품을 해외로 판매한다.
(C) 현재 고객들은 시애틀에서만 제품을 구매할 수 있다.
(D) 간부 몇 명을 해고할 계획이다.

175 말린스 화장품이 개발을 계획 중인 새로운 제품 유형은?
(A) 립스틱
(B) 로션
(C) 크림
(D) 파우더

[176-180]

수신: 안드레아 골딩 (agolding@coverart.com)
발신: 토야 라본 (tlabon@sequencepress.com)
제목: 일금톤
날짜: 6월 14일 오후 2시 44분
첨부: 테니스 삽화.zip

안녕하세요, 안드레아!

오늘 오전에 저는 라스 일금톤 씨에게서 현대의 스포츠 영상에 관한 세 번째 시리즈가 될 그의 최신간 〈세기의 테니스 선수들〉의 표지에 관해 전화를 받았습니다. 그는 우리가 사용하려던 중간색 세조의 그림들에 전성하지 않고, 이 표지가 그의 이전 책들 (아메리카의 축구)의 디자인과 비슷하기를 바랍니다. **176** 그러나 최배는 빨리 일금톤 씨의 승인을 위해 보낼 수 있도록 당신이 초기 디자인을 만들어 주실 수 있나요? 당신이 참고할 수 있도록 테니스 삽화를 첨부했습니다.

제가 일금톤 씨와 대화했을 때 그는 이것 외에 다른 디자인 관련 문제들을 언급했기 때문에 프로젝트에 관해하는 디자인 부서 모두가 그와 이야기하는 것이 매우 도움이 될 것으로 생각합니다. **177** 그래서 저는 고가 오스트리아의 앞쪽에 있는 지방에서 회의을 보낼 것입니다. 질문이 있으시면 제게 알려 주세요.

토야

표지 예술
www.theaustrianreview.com/book-review
8월 11일 화요일

오스트리안 리뷰는 1년에 한 번씩 저명한 예술가들에게 좋아하는 책 표지의 디자인에 투표를 하도록 요청한다. 이번 주에는 받기에에 업트레드 더하여 미술 디자인 감독이 일리아나 드로빅이 그가 가장 좋아하는 작품을 공개한다.

일리아나 드로빅: 저는 내용 자체에 대한 많은 암시를 보여 주고 책에 언급된 일부 인물들을 알아보는 재미가 있는 책 표지를 좋아합니다. 그래서 **180** 안드레아 골딩이 디자인한 〈세기의 테니스 선수들〉 표지를 우연히 발견했을 때, 저는 굉장히 감명을 받았습니다. 이 책은 오스트리아의 라스 일금톤이 저자이며 시몬스 프레스에서 출판되었습니다. 표지 자체에 제목이나 작가가 나타나 있지 않고, 과거와 현재의 테니스 스타들을 만화로 **178** 보여 줍니다. 대신에, 그 표지는 빨간 배경에 흑백의 3부작의 첫 책이기인과 노라를 믿음 흉사합니다. **179** 첫 번째 책의 표지 또한 빨간 그림에 단만 배경입니다. 골딩 씨는 앞부분 선화에 전문가이며, 저는 그녀의 디자인인 작업에 박수를 보냅니다.

based 근거지를 둔 be situated in ~에 위치하다 forefront 맨 앞, 선두 initiative 계획 executive 경영 간부 bold 대담한 boost 신장시키다 reputation 명성 previously 이전에 accommodate 수용하다 access to ~에 접근 source 얻다, 공급업체 found 설립하다 manage (어떻게든) ~하다 margin 차이 quality 양질의 outlet 전문 매장 fall off (양・수가) 줄다 range 범위, 폭 existing 기존의 aggressively 공격적으로 angle 각도, 관점 majority 대다수 anti-aging 노화 방지의 complement 보충하다 appreciate 인정하다 operation 운영 oblige 의무적으로 ~하게 하다 fire 해고하다

attachment 첨부 illustration 삽화 three-volume 3권으로 된 approve of ~을 승인[찬성]하다 neutral 중립의 previous 이전의 rely on ~에 의지하다 come up with ~을 제시하다 initial 초기의 reference 참조 raise 제기하다 beneficial 이로운 conference call 전화 회의 midday 정오, 한낮 recipient 수령인 prominent 유명한 vote for ~에 투표하다 reveal 공개하다, 밝히다 a myriad of ~의 무수한 come across 우연히 마주치다 trilogy 3부작 remarkably 놀랍도록 remarkably 놀랍도록 applaud 박수를 보내다 obviously 명백히 line drawing 선화 adjustment 수정, 조정

수익성의 좋은 adopt 채택하다 lead to ~을 초래하다 revered 존경받는 esteemed 존경받는 unprecedented 전례 없는 purpose-built 특별히 지어진 quest 탐색, 추구 relay 중계하다 consistent 한결 같은 transition 이행 work ethic 직업윤리 shipping division 배송 부서 exemplary 모범적인 in celebration of ~을 축하하여 gourmet 고급 요리 dedication 헌신 rapidly 급속도로 conclusion (조약의) 체결 mark 기념하다

기자 회견   9월 13일

루이지 사는 9월 13일 토요일에 있을 182 팜파와 크르도바의 신규 공장의 개막식을 발표하게 되어 기쁩니다. 덧붙여, 182 투르만의 중심부에 위치한 리소조 제조사와의 합병이 이번 주에 마침내 승인되었음을 밝힙니다. 루이지 사의 회장인 이만테 레소에 따르면 이러한 거래는 아르헨티나에서 기업의 존재감을 증가시키고자 하는 기업의 의지를 강화시킵니다.

발신: 이만테 레소크 [AmandeResok@Luizi.com]
수신: 팀 잔케 [TimJanke@Luizi.com]
날짜: 9월 21일
제목: 좋은 소식

[181-185]

176 이메일의 한 가지 목적은?
(A) 동료에게 그가가 빌린 책을 반납하도록 요청하기 위해
(B) 직원에게 수정이 되어야 한다는 것을 알리기 위해
(C) 프로젝트에 있을 추가 작업의 마감일을 정하기 위해
(D) 작가의 최신 도서의 출판일을 발표하기 위해

177 토아 라인에 관해 알 수 있는 것은?
(A) 세 가지 색상만 사용한다.
(B) 구조 공학의 전문가이다.
(C) 다음 주에 오스트리아의 입프스를 방문할 것이다.
(D) 다섯 권의 책에 저자이다.

178 (아메리카의 축구가의 표지에 관해 언급된 것은? (연계 지문 문제)
(A) 라소 잉금문이 회의에 참여하도록 초청했다.
(B) 일리아나 드로빅이 디자인했다.
(C) 라소 잉금문은 그것에 불만족스러워 했다.
(D) 사진들로 덮여 있다.

179 온라인 기사에 2번째 문단, 5번째 줄의 '보여 줍니다'와 가장 비슷한 의미를 가진 단어는?
(A) 수용하다
(B) 요하다
(C) 보여 주다
(D) 맞다

180 안드레아 골딩에 대해 알 수 없는 것은?
(A) 시원스 프레스에서 출판된 책에 그녀의 작업이 있다.
(B) 3부작 책 중 한 권을 그녀가 디자인했다.
(C) 그녀의 작품은 독보한 색상을 활용한다.
(D) 미술 평론가가 그녀의 작품을 가장 좋아하는 책 표지로 지명했다.

181 기자 회견에 따르면 루이지 사가 성공한 이유는?
(A) 급속히 해외 시장으로 진출했다.
(B) 경쟁사들보다 더 낮은 가격을 제공했다.
(C) 널리 사용되는 도매상 체계를 설치했다.
(D) 볼세로와 제품을 맺었다.

182 루이지 사가 관련된 활동으로 언급되지 않은 것은?
(A) 회사와의 개정
(B) 새 사무실의 개방
(C) 엄그레이드되는 시스템 도입
(D) 훈련의 기회 제공

183 펠란 사는 볼라로 신업에서 얼마나 있었는가?
(A) 2년
(B) 5년
(C) 10년
(D) 15년

184 루이지 사가 연휴를 개최하는 이유는?
(A) 사업 계약이 체결을 축하하기 위해
(B) 이르헨티나에서 더 많은 사업의 기회를 유지하기 위해
(C) 일부 직원들의 공헌을 인정하기 위해
(D) 회사의 설립 기념일을 축하하기 위해

185 9월 25일에 전체 씨가 있을 곳은? (연계 지문 문제)
(A) 투루만
(B) 팜파
(C) 파르나
(D) 크르도바

루이지 사는 조야섬 팜패의 5년 전에 볼래로 신업에서 정리 해고된 후에 설립되었습니다. 10년간 그것에서 일했기 때문에 183 그는 고용이 파르네로 돌아갈 준비가 되었고, 그것에서 그의 가족과 친구들과 협력하여 과립 씨의 개방을 시작했습니다. 멀티 씨의 개방은 지역 공급 네트워크를 이용해 국내 농산물에 집중하는 것이었습니다. 그 전략으로 매우 수익성이 높았고, 펠란 씨의 아이디어는 곧 전국의 유사 도매상들에 의해 채택 되었습니다. 이로 인해 회사는 동종업계에서 가장 존경받는 회사가 되었습니다. 184 시장에서의 전체 없는 성장에도 불구하고 185 5년 전에 특별히 지어진 회사의 사무실은 여전히 회사의 본사로 사용되고, 사업은 혁신을 계속 추구하고 있습니다. 182 최근 저항은 이전 모델들보다 거의 두 배나 더 빨리 주문을 배송하는 선발 시스템을 소개합니다.

인사부에서 당신을 올해의 장기 근속자 수상자로 결정했다는 것을 알리게 되어 기쁩니다. 이 상은 당신이 루이지 사에 합류한 후로 회사에 대한 한신과 기여를 기반으로 해왔습니다. 그때부터 당신은 루이지 사가 지역 사업체에서 남아메리카가 도매 사업의 선두 업체로 변화하는 데 한결같이 도움을 줬습니다. 추가로, 특히 배송부의 책임자로서 당신이 보여 준 작업윤리는 모범적이었습니다. 184 185 올해의 수상을 기념하기 위해 본사에서 9월 25일 화요일 오후 5시에 고급 저녁 만찬이 있을 예정이고, 그 후 상을 수여할 것입니다. 당신의 노고와 한신에 다시 한 번 감사를 드리며, 그곳에서 뵙겠습니다.

이만테 레소
최고경영자

unveiling 제막식 merger 합병 transaction 거래 consolidate 강화하다 determination 의지, 투지 presence 존재(감) make ... redundant ~을 정리 해고하다 in partnership with ...와 제휴[협력]하여 domestic 국내의 produce 농산물 massively 매우 lucrative

오피스 익스프레스
가게 #840 - 신 페드로
555-8203

위클리 스페셜 (3월 2일 - 3월 9일)

세즘 준비 소프트웨어 25달러

모든 휴대용 컴퓨터 10퍼센트 할인 - 단돈 300달러부터 시작(평균: 330달러)

모든 덱스트라 브랜드의 프린터기 20퍼센트 할인 - 단돈 100달러부터 시작 (평균: 120달러)

사무용품 5패센트에서 50퍼센트 할인

75달러 이상 구매하시고 무료 USB 드라이브를 받아 가세요(5달러 짜리)

저희의 리워드 카드에 등록하시고 매장 구매로 www.officeexpress.com에서의 구매 포인트를 쌓으세요. 지출하는 모든 비용에 대해서 포인트를 얻을 수 있습니다. 일부 구매에 대해서는 보너스 포인트도 얻을 수 있습니다. 할인 상품에 대해서는 포인트를 얻을 수 없습니다.

덱스트라 T950 프린터기를 구매해 주셔서 감사합니다. 귀하의 프린터기에는 3색 카트리지 하나와 검정 잉크 카트리지 하나가 포함되어 있습니다. 카트리지를 프린터기에 설명하실 때는 이 카드 뒷면에 있는 설명을 따르세요. 카트리지를 사용하기 전에는 일단 시범 인쇄를 해 보시기를 권장합니다. 이것은 프린트 헤드기 제대로 정렬되어 있는지 확인하는 데 도움이 될 것입니다.

교체 카트리지는 많은 가게에서 구매 가능합니다. 게다가, www.dextra.com의 저희 온라인 가게에서도 구매하실 수 있습니다. 저희 웹 사이트에 주문하신 카트리지는 주문 후 요금 없이 48시간 이내에 배송될 것입니다.

귀하의 첫 주문에서 10퍼센트 추가 할인을 받기 위해서 쿠폰 코드 DT2000을 사용하세요. 이 할인은 저희 웹 사이트에서 이루어진 구매에 대해서만 가능합니다.

만약 귀하의 새로운 프린터기에 대한 질문이 있으시면 연중무휴 연락하실 수 있는 저희에게 자유롭게 연락주세요.

고객 지원: 1-800-555-1818 / customersupport@dextra.com
기술 지원: 1-800-555-0909 / techsupport@dextra.com

발신: 댄 파머 <dfarm@jetmail.net>
수신: 덱스트라 주식회사 <customersupport@dextra.com>
제목: 주문번호 #8945
날짜: 3월 25일

관계자에게:

3월 2일에 저는 산 페드로에 있는 친구를 방문하는 동안 오피스 익스프레스에서 T950 프린터기를 구매했습니다. 그 프린터기는 훌륭하더군요. 제 업무를 위한 고품질 전단지들을 출력하는 데 딱 필요한 것이었어요. 너무 많이 사용해서 거의 잉크가 다 떨어졌어요. 제가 사는 곳에는 오피스 익스프레스 매장이 없어서 귀사의 웹 사이트에서 교체 카트리지를 주문했어요(주문번호 #8945). 안타깝게도, 저한테 배송된 것들이 잘못된 사이즈였어요. 맞는 것으로 교환하고 싶습니다. 어떻게 해야 하는지 알려 주세요.

댄 파머 드림

office supply 사무용품 complimentary 무료의 awesome 훌륭한 redeem 바꾸다, 교환하다

186. 광고에 따르면, 리워드 카드 포인트에 대해서 옳은 것은?
(A) 온라인 구매에 대해서 획득될 수 있다.
(B) 할인되는 데 사용할 수 있다.
(C) 할인된 물건에 대해서 포인트를 얻을 수 있다.
(D) 단골 고객들에게만 이용 가능하다.

187. 파머 씨에 대해서 암시된 것은? (연계 지문 문제)
(A) 그는 가게 #8400에서 정기적으로 쇼핑한다.
(B) 그는 무료 USB 드라이브를 받았다.
(C) 그는 리워드 카드를 신청했다.
(D) 그는 프린터기에 대해서 100달러 미만을 지불했다.

188. 주문 번호 #8945에 대해서 옳은 것은? (연계 지문 문제)
(A) 도착하는 데 4일이 걸렸다.
(B) 배송비가 있었다.
(C) 10퍼센트 할인이 포함되었다.
(D) 부정확한 주소로 왔다.

189. 정보글의 1번째 문단, 5번째 줄에 있는 '확인하는'에 대와 가장 비슷한 의미의 단어는?
(A) 조정하는 데
(B) 전송하는 데
(C) 충전하는 데
(D) 확인하는 데

190. 덱스트라 고객 지원부서에 대해서 암시된 것은?
(A) 주말에도 전화 연결이 가능하다.
(B) 덱스트라 웹 사이트에서 이뤄진 주문을 처리한다.
(C) 직원들은 이메일으로 연락받는 것을 선호한다.
(D) 설치 문제에 대해서 도움을 줄 수 있다.

닥터 시몬 윌슨 사무실
몬타나 61520 빌링스, 마스탱 도로 27
(894) 555-0128
office@doctorwilson.com

마샤 세인즈버리 씨,

귀하의 건강은 저희에게 중요합니다. 그래서 귀하께서 다음의 날짜에 예약되어 있다는 것을 알려드리고 싶습니다.

191 10월 5일 화요일 오전 8시 30분

191 만약 신규 환자라면, 환자 정보 양식과 결제 승인 양식을 작성하기 위해서 예약 10분 전에 도착하세요.

191 만약 어떤 이유로라도 예약을 취소하거나 변경하고자 하신다면 꼭 취소 수수료를 내지 않기 위해 최소한 24시간 전에 연락주세요. 귀하를 받기를 기다리겠습니다.

마샤 세인즈버리

발신: ms2002@netmail.com
수신: office@doctorwilson.com
날짜: 10월 3일 오후 3시 45분

저에게 상기시켜주는 글을 보내주셔서 감사합니다. 예약에 대해서 거의 잊어버리고 있었어요. 직장에서 지난 몇 주간 굉장히 바빴거든요. 그래도, 연간 신체검사를 받는 것이 얼마나 중요한지를 알고 있습니다.

혹시 제가 예약을 10월 8일 금요일로 바꿀 수 있을까요? 시간은 다 괜찮습니다. **193** 서류를 작성하기 위해 꼭 10분 일찍 갈게요.

192 덧붙이자면, 직장 사람들이 저한테 독감 예방주사를 받는 게 좋은 생각인 것 같다고 계속 이야기합니다. 그거이 정말 효과적일지 모르겠네요. 주사 맞는 것에 동의하기 전에 얼슨 선생님과 이것을 논의하고 싶습니다. **194**

감사합니다.

마샤 세인즈버리

환자 대금 청구서

마사 세인즈버리	닥터 사론 월손
1898 제스퍼 캐년 Ln	27 머스탕 도로
몬타나 61520 빌링스	몬타나 61520 빌링스

서비스 개요

신체 검사	125달러
독감 주사	25달러

계정 요약
개설: #8093-034
194 서비스 날짜: 10월 8일
청구된 금액: 150달러   제공업체: 월소원
지불 방법: 보험

메모: 보험 업체에 청구된 모든 요금은 제공업체에 의해서 반드시 승인되어야 합니다. 만약 제공업체가 청구요금을 거절하면, 환자는 전액 지불이 책임이 있어야 합니다. 194 인가하기 전에 보험 범위와 확인하십시오.

191 문자에 언급되지 않은 것은?
(A) 예약 시간
(B) 예약 장소
(C) 예약 이유
(D) 예약 취소 마감 기한

192 세인즈버리 씨에 대해서 암시된 것은? (연계 지문 문제)
(A) 그녀는 최근 건강 문제가 있었다.
(B) 그녀는 닥터 윌슨의 신규 환자이다.
(C) 그녀는 직장에서 자주 아프다.
(D) 그녀는 취소 수수료를 내야 했다.

193 세인즈버리 씨는 왜 이메일을 썼는가?
(A) 추가 정보를 요청하려고
(B) 예약을 하려고
(C) 서류를 제출하려고
(D) 예약을 변경하려고

194 세인즈버리 씨의 예약 방문에 대해서 가장 맞는 것은?
(A) 아침에 이뤄졌다.
(B) 그녀는 예정보다 늦게 도착했다.
(C) 그녀가 선호하는 날짜였다.
(D) 그녀는 독감 예방주사 맞지 않기로 결정했다.

195 청구서의 4번째 문단, 3번째 줄에 있는 '인가하기'와 가장 비슷한 의미의 단어는?
(A) 허락하기
(B) 고려하기
(C) 거절하기
(D) 지불하기

[196-200]

발신: 맥스 오웬스 (mowens@speedys.com)
수신: 톰 카터리지 (tkitteridge@speedy.com)
날짜: 9월 8일
제목: 제안들

톰,

당신과 아이디어를 논의하고 싶었어요. 제 가게 근처에 새로운 아파트가 지어진 이후로, 많은 대학생들이 저희 서비스를 이용하는 것을 알게 됐어요. 그들은 복사를 하고 소포를 붙이기 위해서 정기적으로 옵니다. 199 제 생각에는 대학교 근처에 다른 지점을 고려해야 할 것 같아요. 장사가 잘 될 것 같아요. 197 저렴히 진행하기 전에 테만 리서치를 다시 채용해서 시장 분석을 해볼 수 있어요. 제가 현재 운영 중인 지점을 열기 위한 결정을 내릴 때 그 회사의 데이터가 매우 유용했어요. 198 어떻게 생각하세요?

맥스 드림

발링턴 - (5월 8일) 전국에 체인점으로 둔 인쇄복사업체인 스피디스는 다음달 대학교 캠퍼스 바로 남쪽 동네에 새 지점을 열겠다고 발표했다.
우편 업무도 제공하는 이 회사는 학생들에게 도서관에서 복사본이 되지 않도록 더 빠르고 더 저렴한 대안을 제공하고 싶다고 한다. 197 "우리의 시장 데이터는 도시의 이 구역에서 저희 서비스에 대한 큰 수요가 있다는 것을 보여줍니다"라고 지역 매니저인 톰 카터리지 씨가 설명했다.
지바 맥스 커피숍 옆 홀리가에 위치할 새 지점은 하루 24시간 문을 열 예정이다.
다른 발링턴 지점들과는 달리, 이 지점은 학생들에게 선불 계정을 열수 있게 해줄 것이다. 200 학생들은 미리 지불하는 학생 편의증을 부여 받는다. 이 시스템은 현금이나 신용 카드를 가지고 다녀야 하는 번거로움 없이 준다. 학생들은 가까에 계정 잔액을 쉽게 확인하고 추가하고 사용할 수도 있다.

200 셀프 서비스 프린터기/복사기

설명서
1. 199 신용/직불 카드를 삽입하거나 200 학생 편의증을 입력하세요.
2. 서비스 유형을 선택하세요: 인쇄/복사
   a. 199 인쇄하려면 USB 드라이브를 꽂고 이 저장 장치에 있는 파일을 인쇄하기 위해서는 화면에 있는 해당 메시지를 따르세요.
   b. 복사하면, 복사 종류나 사이즈를 선택하세요.
3. 필요한 페이지 수를 선택하세요.
4. 시작을 누르세요.
5. 직업이 끝나면, 종이 영수증을 받을지 전자 영수증을 받을지 물어볼 겁니다. 만약 신용/직불 카드를 사용한 경우라면, 전자 영수증을 받으려면 이메일 주소가 반드시 제공되어야 합니다.
도움이 필요하세요? 199 프론트 데스크에 있는 친절한 직원에게 물어보세요.

196 이메일의 목적은 무엇인가?
(A) 매출에 대해서 보고하려고
(B) 불만을 제기하려고
(C) 제안을 하려고
(D) 데이터를 요청하려고

197 카트리지 씨에 대해서 맞는 것은? (연계 지문 문제)
(A) 그는 새로운 스피디스 관리점을 낼 것이다.
(B) 그는 오웬스의 직원들 중 한 명이다.
(C) 그는 밸링턴 주민이다.
(D) 그는 마케팅 리서치 회사를 다시 채용했다.

198 가사의 5번째 문단, 4번째 줄에 있는 '변경물'과 가장 비슷한 의미의 단어는?
(A) 불편함
(B) 상호작용
(C) 비용
(D) 모습

199 셀명글에서 언급되지 않은 것은?
(A) 자것들은 신용 카드로 이뤄질 수 있다.
(B) 인쇄는 USB 드라이버로부터 이뤄질 수 있다.
(C) 없으면 도움을 받을 수 있다.
(D) 학생들은 모두 셀프로 인쇄할 수 있다.

200 셀프 서비스 복사기에 대해서 암시된 것은? (연계 지문 문제)
(A) 그것들은 대학교 지점에서만 이용 가능하다.
(B) 그것들은 후대폰에서 복사기로 파일을 보낼 수 있다.
(C) 선불 계정을 가진 학생들이 그것들을 이용할 수 있다.
(D) 그것들은 도서관에서 사용하는 종류와 동일하다.

Actual Test

06

🎧 Listening Comprehension

PART 1

1 (D)	2 (A)	3 (B)	4 (C)	5 (B)	6 (C)			

PART 2

7 (A)	8 (A)	9 (A)	10 (C)	11 (B)	12 (C)	13 (A)	14 (C)	15 (C)	16 (B)
17 (A)	18 (A)	19 (B)	20 (C)	21 (B)	22 (B)	23 (C)	24 (A)	25 (C)	26 (B)
27 (B)	28 (B)	29 (C)	30 (A)	31 (B)					

PART 3

32 (B)	33 (A)	34 (D)	35 (A)	36 (D)	37 (A)	38 (B)	39 (D)	40 (A)	41 (D)
42 (A)	43 (A)	44 (D)	45 (A)	46 (A)	47 (D)	48 (C)	49 (A)	50 (A)	51 (D)
52 (D)	53 (C)	54 (C)	55 (A)	56 (D)	57 (C)	58 (A)	59 (B)	60 (C)	61 (A)
62 (B)	63 (D)	64 (A)	65 (A)	66 (D)	67 (D)	68 (B)	69 (B)	70 (C)	

PART 4

71 (A)	72 (C)	73 (B)	74 (D)	75 (A)	76 (B)	77 (D)	78 (A)	79 (C)	80 (D)
81 (C)	82 (C)	83 (D)	84 (B)	85 (A)	86 (B)	87 (A)	88 (C)	89 (D)	90 (B)
91 (C)	92 (A)	93 (C)	94 (D)	95 (B)	96 (B)	97 (B)	98 (B)	99 (B)	100 (C)

📖 Reading Comprehension

PART 5

101 (B)	102 (A)	103 (B)	104 (D)	105 (B)	106 (A)	107 (B)	108 (A)	109 (A)	110 (A)
111 (A)	112 (C)	113 (A)	114 (A)	115 (B)	116 (B)	117 (B)	118 (B)	119 (C)	120 (C)
121 (B)	122 (D)	123 (C)	124 (A)	125 (D)	126 (A)	127 (C)	128 (B)	129 (B)	130 (A)

PART 6

131 (C)	132 (C)	133 (B)	134 (A)	135 (C)	136 (B)	137 (D)	138 (D)	139 (C)	140 (D)
141 (B)	142 (C)	143 (C)	144 (A)	145 (C)	146 (A)				

PART 7

147 (A)	148 (B)	149 (C)	150 (A)	151 (A)	152 (B)	153 (D)	154 (B)	155 (C)	156 (C)
157 (A)	158 (A)	159 (A)	160 (D)	161 (D)	162 (A)	163 (D)	164 (A)	165 (B)	166 (C)
167 (A)	168 (B)	169 (A)	170 (D)	171 (C)	172 (A)	173 (B)	174 (D)	175 (B)	176 (D)
177 (A)	178 (D)	179 (A)	180 (C)	181 (B)	182 (A)	183 (A)	184 (A)	185 (C)	186 (B)
187 (D)	188 (A)	189 (A)	190 (D)	191 (A)	192 (D)	193 (D)	194 (B)	195 (C)	196 (D)
197 (C)	198 (B)	199 (A)	200 (D)						

Part 1

문제 P231

1 영M
(A) Meals have been brought to a table.
(B) The women are greeting each other.
(C) One woman is carrying some bottles.
(D) One woman is handing the other an item.

(A) 식사가 테이블로 옮겨졌다.
(B) 여자들이 서로 인사를 나누고 있다.
(C) 한 여자가 병들을 나르고 있다.
(D) 한 여자가 다른 사람에게 물건을 건네주고 있다.
greet 반기다, 인사하다 hand 건네다

2 미W
(A) Some clothes are hanging outside.
(B) Some ropes are being tied up.
(C) Some flags are fastened to the poles.
(D) The windows of a building are being polished.

(A) 몇몇 옷들이 밖에 걸려 있다.
(B) 몇몇 줄이 묶이고 있다.
(C) 몇몇 깃발이 깃대에 묶여 있다.
(D) 건물의 창문이 닦이고 있다.
tie up 묶다 fasten 묶다, 고정시키다 pole 깃대 polish 닦다

3 미M
(A) Baskets have been filled with food.
(B) Baked goods are being removed from an oven.
(C) A chef is scrubbing a tray.
(D) A diner is sampling some dessert.

(A) 바구니들이 음식으로 가득 차 있다.
(B) 제과류가 오븐에서 옮겨지고 있다.
(C) 요리사가 쟁반을 문지르고 닦고 있다.
(D) 손님이 디저트를 맛보고 있다.
baked 오븐에 구운 scrub 문지르다 닦다 tray 쟁반 diner 식사는 사람(손님) sample 맛보다, 시식하다

4 미W
(A) Some people are loading some cargo.
(B) Luggage has been stored in the corner.
(C) Passengers are approaching a plane.
(D) Travelers are waiting inside the terminal.

(A) 몇몇 사람들이 화물을 몇 개 싣고 있다.
(B) 짐이 구석에 저장되어 있다.
(C) 승객들이 비행기에 다가가고 있다.
(D) 여행객들이 터미널 안에서 대기하고 있다.
load 싣다, 적재하다 cargo 화물 store 저장하다

5 호M
(A) The man is leaving a construction site.
(B) The man is bending over to draw a line.
(C) Pipes are laid in the trench.
(D) Earth is being shoveled into bags.

(A) 남자가 공사장을 떠나고 있다.
(B) 남자가 선을 그리기 위해 몸을 굽히고 있다.
(C) 파이프들이 도랑 위에 놓여 있다.
(D) 흙이 포대에 삽으로 담기고 있다.
construction site 공사장 bend over 몸을 굽히다 draw a line 선을 긋다 trench 도랑 earth 흙 shovel 삽으로 퍼담다

6 영M
(A) A man is writing on a chart.
(B) A man is pointing at something on the board.
(C) They are reviewing the content of a book.
(D) They are concentrating on their own game.

(A) 남자가 표에 글씨를 쓰고 있다.
(B) 남자가 칠판 위해 무엇을 가리키고 있다.
(C) 사람들이 책의 내용을 검토하고 있다.
(D) 사람들이 자신들만의 게임에 집중하고 있다.
chart 표 point 손가락으로 가리키다 content 내용

Part 2

문제 P234

7 미M
Who ordered the steak?
(A) No one did yet.
(B) Yes, I am.
(C) It's almost complete.

누가 스테이크를 주문했나요?
(A) 아직 아무도 안 했어요.
(B) 네, 제가요.
(C) 거의 끝났습니다.
complete 끝난, 완전한

8 미W
Where do you need my signature?
(A) At the end of this page.
(B) At ROTA Hotel.
(C) Sit over here.

어디에 제 서명이 필요한가요?
(A) 이 페이지 끝에요.
(B) 로타 호텔에서요.
(C) 여기 앉으세요.
signature 서명

9 미W
Do you have the number for the deli?
(A) No, but I can hunt it out for you.
(B) A liter of milk, please.
(C) It's working well.

델리의 전화번호를 갖고 있나요?
(A) 아니요, 하지만 당신을 위해 찾아볼 수 있어요.
(B) 우유 1리터 주세요.
(C) 잘 작동해요.
deli(=delicatessen) 델리카트슨(조리된 육류나 치즈, 흔히는 잘 알려지지 않은 수입 식품 등을 파는 가게) hunt out 찾아내다

10 미W
Are you attending any of the sporting events?
(A) Soccer field 4.
(B) No, I am an assistant coach.
(C) Yes, the one in which Alan's playing.

당신은 참석하는 스포츠 행사가 있나요?
(A) 4번 축구장이요.
(B) 아니요, 저는 보조 코치입니다.
(C) 네, 앨런이 참가하는 경기요.
soccer field 축구장 assistant 조수, 보조원

11 미W 영M
You wrote these articles, didn't you?
(A) Oh, that's very good news.
(B) Paloma worked on them.
(C) Yes, we're hiring three reporters.

당신이 이 기사들을 썼어요, 그렇지 않나요?
(A) 오, 그건 굉장히 좋은 소식이에요.
(B) 팔로마가 그것들을 작업했어요.
(C) 네, 우리는 세 명의 기자를 채용할 거에요.
article 기사 reporter 기자

12 미W 미M
Why don't you inform the landlord that we won't be taking the lease?
(A) A month's notice.
(B) The booking agent.
(C) Sure, I will tell him.

집주인에게 우리가 임대하지 않을 거라고 알리는 건 어때요?
(A) 한 달 전의 통고입니다.
(B) 예약 담당자요.
(C) 그래요, 제가 그에게 말하겠습니다.
landlord 집주인 lease 임대 a month's notice 한 달 전의 통고 booking agent 예약 담당자

Actual Test 06 146 • 147

13 Where is the nearest restroom facility?
영M (A) On the adjacent road.
미M (B) They're behind schedule.
(C) Just one room, please.

가장 가까운 화장실이 어디에 있나요?
(A) 근처 도로에요.
(B) 그들은 예정보다 늦습니다.
(C) 방 하나만요.

adjacent 인접한 가까운   behind schedule 예정보다 늦게

14 Would you prefer I book by phone or via the Web site?
미W (A) Yes, I have them.
영M (B) No, he will do it himself.
(C) Via the Internet is better.

제가 전화로 예약할까요 아님 웹 사이트를 통해 예약할까요?
(A) 네, 저는 그것들을 갖고 있어요.
(B) 아니요, 그가 직접 할 것입니다.
(C) 인터넷을 통해 하는 게 더 좋습니다.

book 예약하다   via ~을 통해

15 You went to the doctor's yesterday, didn't you?
미M (A) Isn't it time?
미W (B) Let's take the elevator.
(C) No, I'm going on Friday.

당신은 어제 병원에 갔어요, 그렇지 않나요?
(A) 그럴 시간이 되지 않았나요?
(B) 엘리베이터를 이용합시다.
(C) 아니요, 저는 금요일에 갈 거예요.

go to the doctor's 병원에 가다

16 Who is in charge of the sales drive?
미W (A) We're going to visit her.
미M (B) Mr. Alverez is overseeing that.
(C) I think he is too busy to do that.

판매 활동을 담당하는 사람은 누구인가요?
(A) 우리가 그녀를 방문할 거예요.
(B) Alverez 씨가 감독하고 있어요.
(C) 그가 그걸 하기에 너무 바쁠 것 같네요.

in charge of ~을 담당하는, ~을 책임지는   oversee 감독하다
section 부문, 부분, 구획, 부서   sales drive 판매 활동

17 What type of wallcovering did you select for your office?
영M (A) I'm still deliberating.
미W (B) It's a beautiful texture.
(C) The fourth office on the left.

당신의 사무실을 위해 어떤 종류의 벽지를 골랐나요?
(A) 아직 생각 중이에요.
(B) 매우 아름다운 질감이에요.
(C) 왼쪽에서 네 번째 사무실입니다.

wallcovering 벽지   deliberate 숙고하다, 신중히 생각하다   texture 감촉, 질감

18 Why did Jules move to the Alexandria area?
미M (A) To be nearer to his office.
미W (B) From the top to the bottom floor.
(C) Because it's still working.

줄스는 왜 알렉산드리아 지역으로 이사했나요?
(A) 그의 사무실에 가까워지기 위해서요.
(B) 꼭대기에서 1층으로요.
(C) 그게 아직도 작동해서요.

nearer to ~에 더 가깝게   bottom floor 1층

19 The inauguration ball will be held next week.
미M (A) It improved steadily.
영M (B) Where will it be?
(C) A group of seven.

취임식 파티는 다음 주에 개최될 거예요.
(A) 꾸준히 향상됐습니다.
(B) 어디에서 하게 되나요?
(C) 7명이요.

inauguration 취임식   ball 무도회, 댄스파티   hold 개최하다
steadily 꾸준히

20 How do I find out if we've been awarded the payrise?
미W (A) Two or three pages.
영M (B) The launch was very successful.
(C) Try asking Ms. Piemont.

우리가 임금 인상을 받았는지 어떻게 알 수 있나요?
(A) 2~3페이지입니다.
(B) 출시는 매우 성공적이었어요.
(C) Piemont 씨에게 물어보세요.

find out 알아내다   award 수여하다   payrise 임금 인상   launch 출시하다

21 Why do you need training to control that machinery?
영M (A) I haven't noticed her.
미M (B) Because it's hazardous.
(C) The instruction manual.

그 기기를 조종하는 데 왜 교육이 필요한가요?
(A) 저는 그녀를 알아보지 못했어요.
(B) 위험하기 때문입니다.
(C) 취급 설명서입니다.

machinery 기계류   hazardous 해로운   instruction manual 취급 설명서

22 Isn't the highway still being repaired?
영M (A) Some overdue programs.
미M (B) Yes, for a long time now.
(C) Over five hundred vehicles.

고속도로가 아직 수리 중이지 않나요?
(A) 기한이 지난 몇몇 프로그램이요.
(B) 네, 지금까지 오랫동안이요.
(C) 500대 이상의 자동차요.

highway 고속도로   overdue 기한이 지난

23 How was your first week lecturing here?
미W (A) I'm coming out soon.
미M (B) Yes, behind the office.
(C) The students were very interactive.

이곳에서의 첫 주 강의는 어땠나요?
(A) 곧 나갈 거예요.
(B) 네, 사무실 뒤에요.
(C) 학생들이 높은 참여도를 보였어요.

lecturing 강의   interactive 상호적인, 상호 작용을 하는

24 Is the buffet being delivered or do we have to collect?
미M (A) It's supposed to be here in an hour.
미W (B) No, I don't like that taste.
(C) Over by the dining room.

뷔페는 배달될 건가요, 아니면 우리가 가지러 가야 하나요?
(A) 한 시간 후 여기로 배달 올 거예요.
(B) 아니요, 저는 그 맛을 좋아하지 않아요.
(C) 식당 근처에요.

collect ~을 가지러 가다   dining room 식당

25 I will print out a picture of our latest clothing range for you.
미W 미M

미M (A) Yes, I will purchase this printer.
(B) It doesn't fit at all.
(C) Thanks for your assistance.

당신을 위해 우리의 신상 의류 사진을 인쇄할게요.
(A) 네, 제가 그 인쇄기를 구매할게요.
(B) 전혀 맞질 않아요.
(C) 도움에 감사드립니다.

print out 인쇄하다 clothing 의류 assistance 도움
take a stroll 산책하다 run out of time 시간이 다 되다

26 Isn't Peter Varlet on the judging panel?
미M 미W

미M (A) He didn't know she was.
(B) I think he is.
(C) It's bigger than usual.

피터 발렛이 재판부에 속해 있지 않나요?
(A) 그녀였다는 걸 그는 몰랐어요.
(B) 그럴 거예요.
(C) 평상시보다 크네요.

judging panel 재판부 judgmental 재멘이

27 You included the attachment with the e-mail, didn't you?
미W 영M

영M (A) Mail is much quicker.
(B) Yes, I sent it yesterday.
(C) An extra amount.

당신은 첨부 파일을 이메일에 포함시켰죠, 그렇지 않았나요?
(A) 우편이 훨씬 더 빨라요.
(B) 네, 어제 보냈어요.
(C) 여분의 액수요.

attachment 첨부 파일 amount 양; 액수

28 Who'd be the head of marketing?
미M 미W

미M (A) The headlines are condemning.
(B) Haven't they already selected someone?
(C) Chris agreed to attend.

누가 마케팅 부장이 될까요?
(A) 표제들이 비판적이네요.
(B) 그들이 벌써 누군가를 뽑지 않았나요?
(C) 크리스가 참석하기로 동의했어요.

headline 표제 condemn 비난하다 select 뽑다; 선발하다

29 Why don't we take a stroll by the lake this afternoon?
미W 미M

미M (A) Because I ran out of time.
(B) No, I don't have any.
(C) Let's meet after work.

우리 오늘 오후 호숫가에서 산책하는 건 어때요?
(A) 왜냐하면 전 시간이 없어서요.
(B) 아니요, 저는 아무것도 없어요.
(C) 퇴근 후 만납시다.

30 Which hall can we practice in?
미M 미W

미M (A) Is the gymnasium large enough?
(B) Yes, you should.
(C) I have a plan of my own.

어느 홀에서 연습할 수 있나요?
(A) 체육관은 충분히 크가요?
(B) 네, 당신은 그래야 합니다.
(C) 저는 제 계획이 있어요.

practice 연습 gymnasium 체육관

31 Would you like to book a translator for the conference in Korea?
미W 미M

미M (A) Because I went there last month.
(B) I don't think we need one.
(C) No, I haven't heard about that facility.

한국에서의 회의를 위해 통역사를 예약해 드릴까요?
(A) 왜냐하면 저는 지난달에 갔거든요.
(B) 필요할 것 같지 않아요.
(C) 아니요, 저는 그 시설에 대해 듣지 못했습니다.

translator 통역사

Part 3

Questions 32-34 refer to the following conversation. 미W 미M

W Hi, this is Rica Dante. ㉜ I ordered a coffee maker from your store more than three days ago, but it still hasn't been delivered. Do you know how much longer I will have to wait?

M Sorry for the inconvenience, Ms. Dante. ㉝ One of our conveyor belt lines has broken down, so we're delivering behind the planned schedules. If you are prepared to wait, it should be there within 48 hours.

W On second thought, ㉞ why don't I drive over to the store to collect the coffee maker myself? I only live three blocks away.

여 안녕하세요, 리카 단테입니다. 제가 3일보다 더 이전에 당신의 가게에서 커피 메이커를 주문했는데, 이직 배달이 되지 않았어요. 제가 얼마나 더 오래 기다려야 할지 아시나요?

남 불편에 대해 사과드립니다. 단테 씨, 저희 컨베이어 벨트 라인 중 하나가 고장 나서 예정된 일정보다 늦게 배달이 되고 있습니다. 기다리실 준비가 되셨다면, 48시간 이내로 도착할 겁니다.

여 다시 생각해 보니, 제가 가게까지 운전해서 커피 메이커를 직접 가지고 가는 건 어때요? 저는 세 블록 떨어진 거리에 살아요.

break down 고장 나다 behind the schedule 예정보다 늦게 on second thought 다시 생각해 보니 drive over to ~까지 차로 가다 collect 수거하다 appliance 가전제품 distribution 분배, 유통 alternative 대체 가능한

32 Where does the man work?
(A) At a café
(B) At an appliance store
(C) At a repair shop
(D) At a distribution center

남자는 어디에서 일하는가?
(A) 카페
(B) 가전제품 매장
(C) 수리점
(D) 유통업체

33 Why is the woman's order delayed?
(A) A fault has occurred in the factory.
(B) A delivery van has broken down.

여자의 주문이 왜 지연되었는가?
(A) 공장에 결함이 발생했다.
(B) 화물 운송 트럭이 고장이 났다.
(C) 지불이 거절되었다.
(D) 그녀의 가전제품이 재고가 없다.

34 What does the woman say she will do?
(A) Select an alternative appliance
(B) Cancel the order
(C) Use a different credit card
(D) Collect her own order

여자는 무엇을 하겠다고 말하는가?
(A) 대체 제품 선택하기
(B) 주문 취소하기
(C) 다른 신용 카드 사용하기
(D) 그녀의 주문품 가지러 가기

Questions 35-37 refer to the following conversation. 미W 영M

W Hello, ㉟ I'm calling to inquire about the theater's new winter schedule. I understand that you'll be closing early some days.

M Yes, from November until the end of February we'll be open only until 5 every Tuesday afternoon. But ㊱ we will be open on Sundays for special children's shows.

W That sounds good. Does it cost extra to see these new shows?

M No, the cost is included in the 5 dollar admission fee. We expect the theater will be busy though. So ㊲ we advise that you buy tickets online. Then you will be able to steer clear of the long ticket line.

여 안녕하세요. 저는 극장의 새 겨울 일정에 관해 문의하려고 전화했습니다. 제가 알기로 어떤 날에는 일찍 문을 닫을 것이라고 해서요.

남 네. 저희는 11월부터 2월 말까지 매주 화요일은 오후 5시까지만 문을 열어요. 하지만 일요일에는 특별 어린이 공연을 위해 문을 엽니다.

여 그거 좋네요. 그 새로운 공연들을 보기 위해 비용이 드나요?

남 아니요. 비용은 입장료 5달러에 포함되어 있습니다. 하지만 극장이 매우 붐빌 것으로 예상합니다. 그래서 온라인으로 표를 구매하실 것을 권합니다. 그러면 티켓 구매의 긴 대기 줄을 피하실 수 있으실 겁니다.

---

admission fee 입장료 steer clear of ~에 가까이 가지 않다, ~을 비키다 sign up for ~을 신청하다 admission 가입, 입장

35 Why is the woman calling?
(A) To ask about a theater schedule
(B) To find out the cost for children
(C) To sign up for membership
(D) To arrange a show

여자가 전화하고 있는 이유는?
(A) 극장의 일정을 문의하기 위해
(B) 어린이의 비용을 알아보기 위해
(C) 회원권을 신청하기 위해
(D) 공연을 준비하기 위해

36 What is the theater going to offer during the winter?
(A) Membership packages
(B) Discounted tickets
(C) Free admission
(D) Special shows

극장은 겨울 동안에 무엇을 제공할 것인가?
(A) 회원 패키지
(B) 할인권
(C) 공짜 입장
(D) 특별 공연

37 What does the man recommend?
(A) Purchasing from the Web site
(B) Checking the times of the shows
(C) Arriving early for tickets
(D) Signing up for discounts

남자는 무엇을 추천하는가?
(A) 웹 사이트에서 구매
(B) 공연 시간 확인
(C) 표를 위해 미리 도착
(D) 할인 신청하기

Questions 38-40 refer to the following conversation. 미W 미M

W ㊳ Is this where I can borrow a security pass for laboratory equipment? I'm a worker here.

M You've come to the right department. Only, we don't give out temporary cards. You can renew your security card for £150. ㊴ I just have to check your employee badge and passport.

W But I can't find any of my identification because I left my wallet in a taxi. Is there anyone who can lend me a security card?

M ㊵ You can always try asking human resources on the third floor. It won't take as long.

여 이곳에서 실험실 장비의 보안용 출입증을 빌릴 수 있나요? 저는 이곳의 직원입니다.

남 해당 부서에 잘 찾아오셨습니다. 다만, 저희는 임시 카드를 내어 드리지 않습니다. 150파운드로 당신의 보안용 출입증을 갱신할 수 있습니다. 저는 당신의 직원 배지와 여권만 확인하면 됩니다.

여 하지만 저는 택시에 지갑을 두고 내려서 제 신분증을 단 하나도 찾을 수 없어요. 혹시 제게 보안 카드를 빌려줄 수 있는 사람이 있을까요?

남 3층의 인사부에 언제든지 요청해 볼 수 있습니다. 그리 오래 걸리지 않을 거예요.

---

security pass 보안용 출입증 laboratory 실험실 give out 내어 주다 temporary 임시의 renew 갱신하다 identification 신분증 human resources 인사부 alternative 대체 가능한, 대체의 entrance (출)입구 certificate 증서, 증명서

38 What does the woman request?
(A) A lab coat
(B) A temporary security pass
(C) An alternative entrance
(D) Directions to a department

여자는 무엇을 요청하는가?
(A) 실험복
(B) 임시 보안용 출입증
(C) 대체 출입구
(D) 어떤 부서로의 길 안내

39 What does the man ask to see?
(A) A registration form
(B) A driver's license
(C) A safety certificate

(D) A form of identification

남자는 무엇을 보길 요청하는가?
(A) 신청서
(B) 운전면허증
(C) 안전 증서
(D) 신분증의 한 형태

40 What does the man suggest?
(A) Contacting a different department
(B) Paying with cash
(C) Changing her ID details
(D) Searching for her wallet

남자는 무엇을 제안하는가?
(A) 다른 부서에 연락
(B) 현금으로 지불
(C) 그녀의 신분 정보 변경
(D) 그녀의 지갑 찾기

Questions 41-43 refer to the following conversation. 미M 미W

M Excuse me, I sent off my application to register for the free seminar on archeology but ❶ I can't see my name tag on the table. There was a small fee for the practical sessions, so I just want to make sure I am on the list.

W Oh, there was a problem with the registration process at the head office and some names were left out of the system. ❷ Can you give me your letter of confirmation?

M Yes, but it's back in my office. I can fetch it.

W That'll be helpful. And when you return, ❸ I'll make sure you get a free pass to our local archeology exhibition. The event coordinators are giving them to people whose registrations were left out. I apologize for the inconvenience.

남 실례합니다, 제가 고고학에 관한 무료 세미나에 등록하기 위한 신청서를 보냈는데, 테이블 위에서 제 명찰을 찾을 수가 없어요. 실습 활동을 위한 소정의 회비가 있었기 때문에, 제가 명단에 있는지 확실히 확인하고 싶습니다.

여 오, 본사에서 등록 절차에 문제가 생겨서 몇몇 이름들이 시스템에서 누락되었어요. 제게 확인서를 보내 주실 수 있으요?

남 네, 하지만 제 사무실에 있습니다. 제가 가지고 올 수 있어요.

여 그게 도움이 될 거예요. 그리고 당신이 돌아오면, 지원 지역 고고학 전시회의 무료 출입증을 확실히 받으실 수 있도록 할게요. 행사 진행 자가 등록이 누락된 사람들에게 주고 있습니다. 불편에 대해 사과드립니다.

41 What is the man's problem?
(A) He left his confirmation at home.
(B) He cannot attend the exhibition.
(C) He forgot to register.
(D) His name is missing from a list.

남자의 문제는 무엇인가?
(A) 그의 확인증을 집에 두고 왔다.
(B) 전시회에 참석할 수 없다.
(C) 등록하는 것을 잊었다.
(D) 그의 이름이 명단에서 누락되었다.

42 What does the woman ask to see?
(A) A letter of confirmation
(B) A payment receipt
(C) A form of identification
(D) A coordinators badge

여자는 무엇을 보길 요구하는가?
(A) 확인서
(B) 구매 영수증
(C) 신분증 양식
(D) 진행자의 배지

43 What is being offered to some conference participants?
(A) Free entry to an exhibition
(B) A voucher for a meal
(C) Access to a conference
(D) A gift shop coupon

몇몇 회의 참여자들에게 제공되는 것은 무엇인가?
(A) 전시회 무료입장
(B) 식사 쿠폰
(C) 회의 출입
(D) 선물가게 쿠폰

send off ~을 발송하다, 보내다 archeology 고고학 name tag 명찰 practical 실습 registration 등록 head office 본사 be left out ~에서 누락되다 letter of confirmation 확인서 fetch 가지고 오다 event coordinator 행사 진행자 entry 입장 voucher 상품권, 쿠폰

Questions 44-46 refer to the following conversation. 미W 미M

W Novak, ㊹ I requested the food for the charity event tonight. But I can't find the meat.

M Oh, ㊺ our delivery was delayed this morning so we don't have any in the freezer.

W Well, ㊹ they asked for chicken and beef and I really wanted to begin preparing the meals now.

M Don't worry. ㊻ I'll call the butchers in Birmingham and see if they can supply us with the meat we need.

여 노박, 제가 오늘 자선 행사 때문에 식재료를 요청했어요. 하지만 고기를 찾을 수가 없어요.

남 오, 저희 배달이 오늘 아침에 지연이 되어서 냉동고에 하나도 없어요.

여 음, 고기들이 닭고기와 소고기를 요구했고 저는 식사 준비를 지금 정말 시작하고 싶어거든요.

남 걱정 마세요. 제가 버밍엄의 정육점 주인에게 전화해 그들이 우리가 필요한 고기를 공급해 줄수 있는지 확인해 볼게요.

charity event 자선 행사 freezer 냉동고 beef 소고기 butcher 정육점 주인 freezer 냉동고 alternative 대체 가능한

44 Where most likely do the speakers work?
(A) At an office
(B) At a jewelry shop
(C) At a supermarket
(D) At a catering business

화자들은 어디에서 일할 것 같은가?
(A) 사무실
(B) 보석 상점
(C) 슈퍼마켓
(D) 요리 조달업체

45 What problem does the man mention?
(A) A delivery did not arrive.
(B) A colleague was late.
(C) A dinner was postponed.
(D) A freezer was faulty.

남자가 언급하는 문제점은 무엇인가?
(A) 배달물이 도착하지 않았다.
(B) 동료가 늦었다.
(C) 저녁 식사가 미뤄졌다.
(D) 냉동고에 결함이 있었다.

46 Why will the man make a telephone call?
(A) To find an alternative supplier
(B) To ask for more time
(C) To confirm the status of an order
(D) To check on a client's booking

남자가 전화를 하려는 이유는 무엇인가?
(A) 대체 공급업체 찾기 위해
(B) 시간을 더 요청하기 위해
(C) 주문 상태를 확인하기 위해
(D) 고객의 예약을 확인하기 위해

Questions 47-49 refer to the following conversation. 미W 영M

W Martin, ㊼ I saw the living room set you designed in this season's catalog! I loved it so much that I got the entire set, including the shelves and the table.

M Really? Thank you so much! I spent a lot of time thinking about the design.

W Actually, I'm setting up four model office spaces for my work this week. I'd like it very much if you would join the team.

M You know I really want to be a part of it, but I'm in the middle of several other projects. I'll have to talk to my supervisor about this.

W I completely understand. ㊽ Why don't I stop by later today and ask if I can borrow you for this project?

M That would be better. Thank you.

여 마틴, 제가 이번 시즌 카탈로그에 들어 있는 당신이 디자인한 거실 가구 세트를 봤어요. 그 세트가 너무 마음에 들어서 선반과 테이블을 포함해서 전체 세트를 하나 구매했어요.

남 정말요? 너무 감사합니다. 제가 그 디자인을 고민하는 데 이주 많은 시간을 썼어요.

여 사실, 제가 이번 주에 업무상 사용하게 될 네 개의 모델용 사무공간을 설치하게 될 거예요. 만약 당신이 팀에 참여해 주신다면 너무 좋을 것 같습니다.

남 팀에 정말 참여하고 싶은데 제가 지금 다른 여러 개의 프로젝트를 진행하는 중이에요. 제 상사에게 이 사항에 관해서 물어봐야 할 것 같습니다.

여 전적으로 이해합니다. 제가 오늘 나중에 그쪽 부서를 방문해서 당신을 이 프로젝트에 잠깐 빌려 와도 되는지 물어보는 건 어때요?

남 그게 좋을 것 같습니다. 감사합니다.

entire 전체의 completely 완전히 stop by 들르다 permission 허가. 허락

47 Where do the speakers most likely work?
(A) At a printing company
(B) At a financial institute
(C) At a construction firm
(D) At an office furniture design firm

화자들은 어디에서 일을 하는 것 같은가?
(A) 인쇄업체
(B) 금융기관
(C) 건설회사
(D) 사무 가구 디자인 회사

48 What does the man mean when he says, "You know I really want to be a part of it"?
(A) He needs some part for repairs.
(B) His supervisor didn't give him permission.
(C) He is interested in joining the team.
(D) He will go on a business trip soon.

남자는 "제가 팀에 정말 참여하고 싶은데"라고 말했을 때 무엇을 의미했는가?
(A) 그는 수리를 위해 부품을 필요로 한다.
(B) 그의 상사가 허가해 주지 않았다.
(C) 그는 팀에 참여하고 싶어 한다.
(D) 그는 곧 출장을 갈 것이다.

49 What does the woman suggest?
(A) Talking to a supervisor
(B) Checking schedules
(C) Postponing a deadline
(D) Borrowing some equipment

여자는 무엇을 제안하는가?
(A) 상사와 이야기하는 것
(B) 일정을 확인하는 것
(C) 마감일을 늦추는 것
(D) 장비를 빌리는 것

Questions 50-52 refer to the following conversation. (영M) (미W)

M Hello, Sarah. This is Rafael Figaro calling from Market Force Lawyers. ⑤ I really want to express thanks for hosting the seminar at the convention center last week, detailing the benefits of online marketing.

W I was happy to do so. The subject's quite complex but your team are very good listeners.

M I'm glad to hear that. They commented that the information was very useful. However, some of our employees couldn't make it due to a client visit. I was hoping you could come to our headquarters soon and ⑤ repeat the lecture for those who missed it the first time.

W Well, I'd be delighted to visit you but ⑥ I am on vacation for two weeks. Let's fix a date when I return.

남 안녕하세요, 사라. 저는 마켓 포스 로이어스의 라파엘 피가로입니다. 저는 지난주 컨벤션 센터에서 온라인 마케팅의 장점을 상세히 다룬 세미나를 개최한 것에 대해 깊이 감사를 드리고 싶습니다.

여 그렇게 할 수 있어서 매우 기뻤습니다. 주제는 꽤 복잡하지만 당신의 팀은 매우 귀 기울여주셨습니다.

남 그 말을 들으니 기쁩니다. 그들은 그 정보가 매우 유용하다고 평했습니다. 그러나 저희 몇몇 직원들은 고객 방문으로 인해 참석할 수 없었습니다. 저는 당신이 조만간 저희 본사를 방문해 처음에 강좌를 듣지 못한 사람들을 위해 다시 강의해 주시길 바라고 싶었습니다.

여 음, 기쁜 마음으로 방문하겠지만, 2주 동안 제가 휴가를 갑니다. 돌아 와서 날짜를 정하도록 하죠.

host 개최하다 complex 복잡한 comment 평하다, 견해를 밝히다 make it (모임 등에) 가다, 참석하다; (어떤 곳에 간신히) 시간 맞춰 가다 press 언론 headquarters 본사 be delighted to ~하게 되어 기쁘다, 기꺼이 ~하길 것이다 inspect 점검하다, 사찰하다 superior 선배, 상사 fortnight 2주일

50 What did the woman do last week?
여자는 지난주에 무엇을 했는가?
(A) She spoke at a seminar. (A) 세미나에서 연설을 했다.
(B) She inspected a college. (B) 대학을 점검했다.
(C) She went on a vacation. (C) 휴가를 갔다.
(D) She visited a headquarters. (D) 본사를 방문했다.

51 What does the man ask the woman to do?
남자는 여자에게 무엇을 해 달라고 요청하는가?
(A) Talk to a superior (A) 상사와 대화하기
(B) Go on a vacation (B) 휴가 가기
(C) Attend a workshop (C) 워크숍 참석하기
(D) Repeat a seminar (D) 세미나 재연하기

52 What problem does the woman mention?
여자는 어떤 문제점을 언급하는가?
(A) She cannot travel to the office. (A) 사무실로 갈 수 없다.
(B) She has forgotten her notes. (B) 노트를 잊어버렸다.
(C) She has not received her fee. (C) 그녀의 회비를 아직 받지 못했다.
(D) She is away for a fortnight. (D) 2주간 부재일 것이다.

Questions 53-55 refer to the following conversation with three speakers. (미W) (미M) (영W)

W1 Hi, Mark and Jessica. ⑤ You worked here in the marketing division for several months before your first performance review, right?

M Yes, that's right.

W2 It was four months before I had my first evaluation. Why?

W1 I've already been with the company for four months, ⑤ but nobody's said anything to me about a performance review yet. ⑤ I wonder if I should bring it up.

M Well, we don't have any specific procedure for this.

W2 That's right. It's possible that your supervisor forgot. You know she's been away on business for the last month. ⑤ She's meeting with some new clients in Thailand.

W1 Well, as soon as she gets back, I'll ask her about it.

여1 안녕하세요, 마크, 제시카: 이곳 마케팅부에서 몇 개월 근무한 후에 인사고과를 받으신 것 맞죠?

남 네, 맞아요.

여2 저는 4개월이 되고 나서 첫 평가를 받았어요. 왜 그러시죠?

여1 제가 입사한 지 벌써 4개월이 됐는데, 아무도 인사고과에 관해 이 야기하지 않아요. 제가 먼저 검을 꺼내야 하는 건지 모르겠어요.

남 글쎄요, 이것에 관해서 특별한 회사 절차는 없어요.

여2 맞아요, 당신의 상사가 잊어버렸을지도 몰라요. 알다시피 그녀가 지 난달에 출장으로 자리를 비웠잖아요. 태국에서 새로운 고객들을 만 나고 있어요.

여1 음, 그녀가 돌아오는 대로 물어봐야겠어요.

performance review 인사고과 evaluation 평가 procedure 절차 put off 연기하다 clarify 명확히 하다

53 What are the speakers mainly discussing?
화자들은 주로 무엇에 관해 논의하고 있는가?
(A) A new contract (A) 새로운 계약
(B) A marketing report (B) 마케팅 보고서
(C) An employee evaluation
(D) A travel itinerary

(A) 신분증
(B) 신청서
(C) 물건에 대한 설명
(D) 그녀의 차

Questions 59-61 refer to the following conversation. 미W 미M

W Oh, look at those cakes! They look delicious!
M Yes, I was thinking of buying something like this for my cousin for his birthday.
W Really? What's special about that package?
M The fruits are hand-dipped in a dark chocolate infused with espresso. Since they're made by hand, they all look slightly different. 59 The problem is that they're only available for a few days, so I don't know if I can order them in time.
W I wish I could buy them for my parents' anniversary that's coming up soon, but I'm actually short of cash now.
M That's fine. 61 I can order for both of us, and you can pay me back later.

여 오, 저 케이크 좀 봐요 아주 맛있어 보이네요!
남 네, 이런 종류의 케이크를 제 사촌의 생일을 위해 구매하려고 생각하고 있었어요.
여 그래요? 이 패키지는 무엇이 특별한가요?
남 에스프레소가 주입된 다크 초콜릿에 과일이 수작업으로 담가져 있어요. 수작업으로 만들어지기 때문에 조금씩 모양이 달라요. 문제가 있다면 며칠 동안에만 구매가 가능하기에 제때 주문을 할 수 있을지 모르겠어요.
여 다가오는 부모님의 기념일을 위해 주문을 할 수 있었으면 좋겠지만 제가 지금 현금이 부족하네요.
남 걱정하실 것 없어요. 우리 두 명 분량을 주문하고, 나중에 제게 돈을 주시면 됩니다.

infuse 불어넣다　slightly 약간, 조금　anniversary 기념일

59 What is mentioned about the products?
(A) They are all the same design.
(B) They can be ordered for a limited time.
(C) They are only available online.
(D) They will not be delivered on time.

여 연장하세요, 제 이름은 니타샤 락입니다. 제가 어제 당신의 택시를 탔었습니다. 목적지에 도착했을 때, 이자에 제 서류 가방을 놓고 내렸을지도 몰라서요. 혹시 누군가 인계했었나요?
남 네, 저희가 갖고 있습니다, 락 씨. 분실물 취급소에 보관되어 있습니다. 지금은 모두 닫혔는데, 한 시간 이내에 문을 열 것입니다.
여 다행이군요! 감사해요! 제가 한 시간 정도 이내에 가져갈게요.
남 그렇게 하세요. 여권이나 주민등록증 같은 신분증을 지참해야 하는 것을 기억해 주세요. 물품을 건네 드리기 전에 그것을 확인해야 합니다.

briefcase 서류 가방　destination 목적지　hand in (분실물 등을) 인계하다; 제출하다　secure 안전하게 두다; 확보하다　lost and found 분실물 취급소　relief 안도, 안심　identification 신분 증명, 신원 확인(이 되는 것)　hand over 넘겨주다; 건네다　arrangement 준비　description 서술, 기술

56 Why is the woman calling?
(A) To discuss travel arrangements
(B) To complain about a service
(C) To request a taxi
(D) To inquire about a missing item

여자가 전화를 하고 있는 이유는 무엇인가?
(A) 여행 준비를 의논하기 위해
(B) 서비스에 대해 불평을 하기 위해
(C) 택시를 요청하기 위해
(D) 분실물에 관해 문의하기 위해

57 Where will the woman most likely go in an hour?
(A) To a client's office
(B) To a restaurant
(C) To a taxi firm
(D) To a department store

여자는 한 시간 후에 어디를 갈 것 같은가?
(A) 고객의 사무실
(B) 레스토랑
(C) 택시 회사
(D) 백화점

58 What does the man tell the woman to bring?
(A) A form of identification
(B) An application form
(C) A description of the item
(D) Her car

(C) 직원 평가
(D) 여행 일정

54 Why does the man say, "we don't have any specific procedure for this"?
(A) To put off an announcement
(B) To give the woman an approval
(C) To clarify an issue
(D) To suggest a policy change

남자가 "이것에 관해서 특별한 회사 절차는 없어요"라고 말한 이유는 무엇인가?
(A) 발표를 연기하려고
(B) 여자에게 허가를 내주려고
(C) 한 문제에 대한 설명을 하려고
(D) 정책 변경을 제안하려고

55 Why is the supervisor unavailable?
(A) She is meeting some clients.
(B) She is training new employees.
(C) She is finalizing a contract.
(D) She is speaking at a convention.

상사를 만날 수 없는 이유는 무엇인가?
(A) 그녀가 몇몇 고객을 만나고 있다.
(B) 그녀가 신입 사원을 교육하고 있다.
(C) 그녀가 계약을 마무리하고 있다.
(D) 그녀가 회의에서 강연하고 있다.

Questions 56-58 refer to the following conversation. 미W 영M

W Hi, my name is Nitasha Lark. I took one of your taxis yesterday. I believe 56 I may have left my briefcase on the seat when I arrived at my destination. Has anyone handed it in?
M Yes, we have it, Ms. Lark. It's secured in the lost-and-found section. We are closed for now but we'll be open in an hour.
W What a relief! Thank you! 57 I'll drop by and collect it in an hour or so.
M You're welcome. Please remember to 58 bring identification with you such as a passport or ID card. We have to check that before we can hand over the item.

제품에 대해서 무엇이 언급되었는가?
(A) 디자인이 모두 동일하다.
(B) 제한된 시간에만 주문할 수 있다.
(C) 온라인에서만 구매가 가능하다.
(D) 제시간에 배송될 수 없다.

60 What does the woman imply when she says, "'I'm actually short of cash now"?
(A) She only has credit cards.
(B) She left some money in her car.
(C) She does not have enough money.
(D) She can lend some cash to the man.

여자는 "제가 지금 현금이 부족해서요"라고 말했을 때, 무엇을 의미했는가?
(A) 그녀는 신용 카드만 가지고 있다.
(B) 그녀는 돈을 차에 두고 왔다.
(C) 그녀는 돈을 충분히 가지고 있지 않다.
(D) 그녀는 현금을 남자에게 빌려줄 수 있다.

61 What will the man probably do next?
(A) Place an order
(B) Borrow some money from the woman
(C) Give the woman a lift
(D) Show the woman around the facility

남자는 다음에 무엇을 할 것인가?
(A) 주문을 한다.
(B) 여자에게 돈을 빌린다.
(C) 여자를 태워준다.
(D) 여자에게 시설을 안내한다.

Questions 62-64 refer to the following conversation. 영M 미W

M Susan, I've been checking the outcome of the research group we arranged to get reaction to 62 our new toddler seat and we might have a problem. Most of the feedback reported that the seat is too large and complicated to fit.

W Oh! I see. Well, perhaps, 63 we should focus more on the ergonomics to ensure the seat is less complicated.

M Um maybe, but we've already allocated the majority of our design funding. We will really require more money 64 if we are proposing to redesign the seat to alter the complexity. At tomorrow's meeting, 64 I can inquire about increasing the funds.

남 수잔, 우리가 새로운 유아용 의자에 대한 반응을 얻기 위해 마련했던 연구 그룹의 결과를 확인해 왔는데, 어쩌면 문제가 있을 수도 있어요. 대부분의 피드백은 의자가 너무 크고, 맞추려면 너무 복잡하다고 보고했습니다.

여 오! 그렇군요. 어쩌면 우리는 의자가 덜 복잡하도록 하기 위해 인체공학에 더 집중해야 할지도 모르겠어요.

남 음... 어쩌면요. 하지만 이미 우리는 디자인 자금의 대부분을 할당했어요. 만약 복잡함을 고치기 위해 의자를 재디자인하는 것을 제안한다면, 정말 더 많은 돈이 필요할 거예요. 내일 회의에서 자금을 늘리는 것에 대해 물어보면 되겠어요.

outcome 결과　research group 연구 그룹　get reaction 반응을 얻다　toddler 걸음마를 배우는 아이　complicated 복잡한　focus on ~에 집중하다　ergonomics 인체공학　allocate 할당하다　majority of 다수의　funding 자금　redesign 다시 디자인하다　alter 변경하다　complexity 복잡함　inquire 문의하다

62 What item are the speakers discussing?
(A) A mobile phone
(B) A child seat
(C) A television
(D) A watch

화자들이 이야기하고 있는 제품은?
(A) 휴대폰
(B) 유아용 의자
(C) 텔레비전
(D) 손목시계

---

63 What does the woman suggest?
(A) Reviewing an advertising strategy
(B) Canceling production
(C) Delaying a consumer survey
(D) Altering a product design

여자는 무엇을 제안하는가?
(A) 광고 전략 검토
(B) 생산 취소
(C) 고객 설문조사 지연
(D) 제품 디자인 변경

64 What topic does the man say he will bring up at the meeting?
(A) A request for funding
(B) More time for research
(C) A changed schedule
(D) An alternative product

남자는 회의에서 어떤 화제를 말할 것이라고 하는가?
(A) 자금 요청
(B) 연구를 위한 더 많은 시간
(C) 바뀐 일정
(D) 대체 상품

Questions 65-67 refer to the following conversation and chart.
[미M] [미W]

Vacation Packages	Price (per person)
Single ticket	$700
Couple ticket	$500
Family member	$450
65 Group of 6 or more	$400

M 65 Melanie, there's going to be a company trip to Poland. A couple of us from the office are planning to go together. Do you want to join us?

W Oh, I don't know if I have enough money for an overseas vacation.

M It's not that expensive! 66 There are different travel packages, and if we form a group of six or more, we can get a group discount.

W Sure, why not? What should I do?

M Here's a brochure with all of the packages explained. 67 You should also call Karl from accounting and tell him that you want to be part of our group.

W That sounds good! When do we leave?

M Our flight leaves early on Friday morning!

남 멜라니, 폴란드로의 우리 회사 여행이 예정되어 있습니다. 우리 사무실에서 몇 명이 같이 가기로 했어요. 같이 가실래요?

여 오, 제가 해외로 휴가를 갈 충분한 돈이 있는지 잘 모르겠어요.

남 그렇게 비싸지 않아요! 여러 가지 여행 패키지가 있는데요, 우리가 6명 혹은 더 많은 인원으로 단체를 만들면, 단체 할인을 받을수 있어요.

여 그럼 가지 않을 이유가 없죠. 제가 어떻게 하면 되나요?

남 여기 모든 패키지에 관한 설명이 되어 있는 안내서가 있습니다. 회계부서에 있는 칼에게 전화를 하셔서 그룹에 함께하고 싶다고 이야기해야 해요.

여 좋은데요, 언제 출발하게 되나요?

남 우리 비행기는 금요일 오전 일찍 떠나요.

overseas 해외의, 해외로   accounting 회계부서

---

65 What are the speakers talking about?

(A) A vacation
(B) An overseas business trip
(C) A package delivery
(D) An accounting staff

화자들은 무엇에 관한 이야기를 하고 있는가?

(A) 휴가
(B) 해외 출장
(C) 소포 배송
(D) 회계 직원

---

66 Look at the graphic. What ticket price will the speakers most likely pay?

(A) $700
(B) $500
(C) $450
(D) $400

시각 자료를 보시오. 화자들은 어느 티켓 가격을 지불하게 될 것 같은가?

(A) 700달러
(B) 500달러
(C) 450달러
(D) 400달러

---

67 What does the man suggest the woman do?

(A) Go to an accounting office
(B) Buy tickets as soon as possible
(C) Work overtime
(D) Call a colleague

남자는 여자가 무엇을 하는 것을 제안하는가?

(A) 회계 사무소에 간다.
(B) 가능한 한 빨리 티켓을 구매한다.
(C) 초과 근무를 한다.
(D) 동료에게 전화한다.

Questions 68-70 refer to the following conversation and schedule.
[영M] [미W]

Conference Room A	
Accounting	11:00 A.M.
68 Marketing	2:00 P.M.
Sales	3:00 P.M.
Advertising	4:00 P.M.

M Mrs. Park, have you reserved Conference Room A?

W 68 We need to make a sales presentation about our new probiotic pill. And it is the only room where we can make conference calls.

M 69 Ron's team specifically asked for Conference Room A for two o'clock to train the new staff. Audrey is in charge of arranging a meeting room, but she is on vacation.

M I don't think that they need the conference call option. 70 Could you call and ask them if they can use Conference Room B? Be sure to mention that it's a newly renovated room.

W 70 Understood. I'll get right on it.

컨퍼런스룸 A	
회계부	오전 11시
마케팅부	오후 2시
영업부	오후 3시
광고부	오후 4시

남 박 씨, 컨퍼런스룸 A를 예약하셨어요? 우리가 프로바이오틱 알약에 관한 영업 발표를 해야 합니다. 그리고 그 장소가 전화 회의를 진행할 수 있는 유일한 곳이에요.

여 론의 팀이 신입 직원들을 교육하기 위해서 2시에 컨퍼런스룸 A를 명확히 요청했어요. 오드리가 회의장 예약을 담당하는데, 지금 휴가 중입니다.

남 제가 생각하기에는 그들이 전화 회의를 필요로 하지는 않을 것 같아요. 전화해서 혹시 그들이 컨퍼런스룸 B를 써도 안 되는지를 물어봐 주시겠어요? 최근에 업그레이드 작업이 있었던 방이라는 사실을 꼭 언급해 주세요.

여 네, 바로 하겠습니다.

probiotic 프로바이오틱의 pill 알약 specifically 특별히, 정확하게 in charge of 책임을 지는 arrange 준비하다, 배열하다 pharmaceutical 제약의

Part 4

68 Where do the speakers most likely work?
(A) At a shipping company
(B) At a pharmaceutical company
(C) At a real estate agency
(D) At a software manufacturer
화자들은 어디에서 일하는 것 같은가?
(A) 배송 업체
(B) 제약회사
(C) 부동산 중개업소
(D) 소프트웨어 제조업체

69 Look at the graphic. In which department does Ron most likely work?
(A) Accounting
(B) Marketing
(C) Sales
(D) Advertising
시각 자료를 보시오. 론은 어느 부서에서 일할 것 같은가?
(A) 회계
(B) 마케팅
(C) 영업
(D) 광고

70 What will the woman probably do next?
(A) Bring some presentation materials
(B) Conduct an online survey
(C) Ask a coworker to change rooms
(D) Reschedule a meeting
여자는 다음에 무엇을 할 것인가?
(A) 발표 자료들을 가져온다.
(B) 온라인 설문조사에 참여한다.
(C) 동료에게 방을 변경해 달라고 요청한다.
(D) 회의 일정을 변경한다.

본책 P239

Questions 71-73 refer to the following advertisement. 미M

Are you searching for a substitute to television and books? Then come to **71** Ziggy's, the area's largest retailer of computer games and apps. Our customers keep returning because we stock the most extensive selection of games available, including award winning fantasy, war, sport and adventure games. **72** We also have a children's games arena for them to try out games under adult supervision. So you can look around while we look after them. And if you are unable to visit the store, you can order any of our games straight from our warehouse. **73** We assure overnight delivery. You'll receive your order the next day.

텔레비전과 책을 대체할 것을 찾고 계신가요? 그렇다면 지역 최대 규모의 컴퓨터 게임과 어플리케이션 전문 소매점인 지기스로 오세요. 상을 받은 판타지물, 전쟁, 스포츠와 어드벤처 게임을 포함해, 저희는 시중에 나와 있는 게임이 가장 폭넓은 상품군을 구비하고 있으므로, 고객님은 계속해서 저희 가게를 찾으십니다. 저희는 또한 어른들이 감독 하에 게임을 해볼 수 있는 어린이용 게임 경기장이 있습니다. 그래서 어른분은 저희가 이들을 돌보는 동안에 게임 경기장이 있습니다. 그리고 만약 매장을 방문할 수 없다면, 저희 창고에서 어떤 게임이든 바로 주문을 받을 수 있습니다. 저희는 익일 배송을 보장합니다. 당신은 바로 다음날 주문품을 받게 될 것입니다.

substitute 대체물 retailer 소매업자 stock (판매할 상품을 갖춰 두고) 있다 extensive 광범위한, 폭넓은 selection 선발, 선정, 선택 award winning 수상한, 상을 받은 arena 경기장 under supervision 감독 하에 look around 구경하다 look after 돌보다 straight 똑바로, 곧장; 곧바로 warehouse 창고 assure 장담하다, 보장하다 overnight delivery 익일 배송 parental 부모의, 아버지의

71 What kind of business is Ziggy's?
(A) A gaming store
(B) A bookstore
(C) A video store
(D) A music store
지기스는 어떤 종류의 사업인가?
(A) 게임 매장
(B) 서점

(C) 비디오 매장
(D) 음반 매장

72 What does Ziggy's offer for families with children?
(A) Free drinks in the evenings
(B) A parental list of safe games
(C) A supervised gaming area
(D) A monthly free workshop
지기스는 어린이들이 있는 가족들에게 무엇을 제공하는가?
(A) 저녁의 무료 음료
(B) 부모를 위한 안전한 게임 목록
(C) 감독 보호 하의 게임 구역
(D) 월간 무료 워크숍

73 What does the advertisement say about online orders?
(A) They are shipped at a small cost.
(B) They are delivered overnight.
(C) They will come with special discounts.
(D) They can be gift wrapped.
광고에서 온라인 주문에 관해 무엇을 말하고 있는가?
(A) 낮은 비용으로 배송된다.
(B) 익일 배송된다.
(C) 특별 할인이 된다.
(D) 선물 포장이 가능하다.

Questions 74-76 refer to the following announcement. 미W

74 Attention, all Vanquis Bank customers. We'll be **75** closing the Rianta branch earlier than normal. We apologize for any inconvenience this may cause you. Customers who are paying a bill due today, please make your way to the front desk where you will be dealt with immediately. Please note that **76** any money paid in today will be immediately transmitted without delay. Again, we apologize for the inconvenience at Vanquis Bank.

주목해 주세요, 모든 뱅퀴스 은행 고객 여러분. 저희는 리엔타 지점을 평상시보다 더 일찍 닫겠습니다. 이로 인해 끼치는 불편에 대해 사과드립니다. 오늘이 마감인 청구서를 지불하는 손님들은 바로 처리될 안내 데스크로 가 주시기 바랍니다. 오늘 입금된 돈들은 모두 지체 없이 곧바로 송금이 될 것임을 기억해 주세요. 다시 한 번, 뱅퀴스 은행에서 불편을 드린 점 사과드립니다.

normal 평상시 pay a bill 청구서를 지불하다, 어음을 지급하다 due 마감인
make one's way to ~로 나아가다 deal with 처리하다 note 기억하다
pay in 입금하다 account 계좌, 계좌

74 Where most likely is the announcement being made?
(A) On a tour bus
(B) On an airplane
(C) In a hotel
(D) In a bank

발표는 어디에서 일어나고 있을 것 같은가?
(A) 관광버스
(B) 비행기
(C) 호텔
(D) 은행

75 What does the speaker apologize for?
(A) Early closure
(B) A cancelled service
(C) Delayed payments
(D) A bomb alert

화자는 무엇에 대해 사과하는가?
(A) 일찍 문을 닫는 것
(B) 취소된 서비스
(C) 지불 연체
(D) 폭탄 경보

76 What are customers paying bills assured of?
(A) Their payments will not be accepted.
(B) Their bills will be paid at once.
(C) Another option will be offered.
(D) Refunds will be issued.

청구서를 지불하는 손님들은 무엇을 확답받는가?
(A) 그들의 지불은 받아들여지지 않을 것이다.
(B) 그들의 청구서가 즉시 처리될 것이다.
(C) 다른 옵션이 제안될 것이다.
(D) 환불금이 지급될 것이다.

Questions 77-79 refer to the following excerpt from a speech. 호M

And the next matter to discuss, the closing date for submissions for the Picoult Awards is July 23rd. You know these are the most influential awards in dance and performance arts. 77 For the last two years, we came second overall in the contemporary dance category. And our management trustees would like to better that this year. So they've requested that we select the best performances from the past twelve months 77 to put forward for the competition. 78 Does anyone have any memorable performances we should choose from?

그리고 다음 이야기할 사항은 Picoult 상을 위한 제출 마감일이 7월 23일이라는 것입니다. 여러분들도 알다시피 이들은 무용과 공연 예술에서 가장 영향력 있는 상들입니다. 지난 2년간 우리는 현대 무용 부문에서 종합 2위를 차지했습니다. 그리고 우리 경영 이사들은 이것이 올해 더 나아졌으면 합니다. 그래서 대회에 내보내기 위해 지난 1년 동안의 공연 중 가장 좋은 공연을 엄선하도록 그들이 요청했습니다. 우리가 선택을 만한 것으로 기억에 남는 공연이 있는 것 있으신가요?

closing date 마감일 influential 영향력 있는 performance arts 공연 예술 contemporary 동시대의, 현대의 trustee 신탁 관리자; 이사 put forward (대회 등에) 내보내다 competition 경연 대회 memorable 기억에 남는 appoint 임명하다 routine 루틴(연이 정해져 있는 일련의 동작; 동작 등)

77 What is the speaker discussing?
(A) A television program
(B) A theater production
(C) An advertising campaign
(D) A performance competition

화자는 무엇에 관해 이야기하고 있는가?
(A) 텔레비전 프로그램
(B) 극장 제작물
(C) 광고 캠페인
(D) 공연 경연 대회

78 What does the speaker say happened two years ago?
(A) The company won an award.
(B) A new director was appointed.
(C) The company changed its dance routine.
(D) An alternative schedule was introduced.

화자는 2년 전에 무슨 일이 있었다고 말하는가?
(A) 회사가 상을 탔다.
(B) 새로운 이사가 임명되었다.
(C) 무용이 그들의 동작을 바꾸었다.
(D) 대체 일정이 소개되었다.

79 What are listeners asked to do?
(A) Appoint a trustee
(B) Contact an audience
(C) Make recommendations
(D) Plan a new routine

청자들은 무엇을 하도록 요구받는가?
(A) 이사 임명하기
(B) 청중에게 연락하기
(C) 추천하기
(D) 새로운 동작 짜기

Questions 80-82 refer to the following telephone message. 미W

Hello, this message is for Okambe Kwan. My name is Rosalind Laker and 80 I'm ringing from the Holiday Club Tour on Lister Street. Last month, you entered a photographic competition and I'm delighted to inform you that you have won the first prize of a weekend city break for two worth £300. 81 We have your prize waiting for you in the store. Please 82 remember to bring your passport when you come in to claim your prize. Thank you for entering the Holiday Club Tour competition and we look forward to meeting you soon.

안녕하세요, 오캄베 콴에게 전하는 메시지입니다. 제 이름은 로절린드 레이커이고, 리스터 가에 있는 홀리데이 클럽 투어에서 전화드립니다. 지난달 당신은 사진 경연 대회에 출전했고, 저는 당신이 300파운드에 상당하는 2인용 주말 도시 여행이 1등상을 받게 된 것을 알리게 되어 기쁩니다. 우리는 당신의 상을 매장에 준비시켜 놓았습니다. 상을 받으러 오실 때, 여권을 지참하는 것을 기억해 주세요. 홀리데이 클럽 투어 경연 대회에 출전해 주신 것에 감사드리고 곧 만나뵙길 기대하겠습니다.

photographic competition 사진 경연 city break 도시 여행 claim 주장하다, 요구하다 retrieve 되찾아오다 identification 신분증

Questions 83-85 refer to the following telephone message. (호M)

Hello, this message is for Mr. Desi Landau. **83** I'm calling from the Frenhill Surgery to confirm your attendance for a mandatory eye examination at 10:30 this Friday morning. As the test requires you to see at long and short distances, please ensure that you **84** bring any glasses or contact lenses with you. If not, it may affect the outcome of the test. Could you give me a call when you receive this voicemail? Also **85** I need the address of your workplace. We'll see you on Friday.

안녕하세요, 이 메시지는 데시 랜다우 씨를 위한 메시지입니다. 이번 주 금요일 아침 10시 30분에 있을 당신의 의무 시력 검사 참석을 확인하기 위해 프렌힐 병원에서 전화드렸습니다. 검사가 장거리와 단거리에서의 시력을 필요로 하므로, 안경이나 콘택트렌즈를 확실히 지참해 주세요. 그렇지 않을 경우, 검사 결과에 영향을 끼칠 수 있습니다. 이 음성 메시지를 받으면 제게 전화 주시겠어요? 또한, 당신의 직장 주소가 필요합니다. 금요일에 뵙겠습니다.

surgery 병원; 수술, 수술실　attendance 참석　mandatory 의무의　eye examination 시력 검사　long and short distance 장거리와 단거리　ensure 확실히 하다　outcome 결과　voicemail 음성 메시지　workplace 직장　referral 보내기, 소개

83 What is the purpose of the message?
(A) To provide a referral
(B) To change a date
(C) To provide a driving test
(D) To confirm an appointment

메시지의 목적은?
(A) 소개하기 위해
(B) 날짜를 변경하기 위해
(C) 운전면허 시험을 제공하기 위해
(D) 예약을 확인하기 위해

84 What does the speaker remind Mr. Landau to do on Friday morning?
(A) Submit an insurance claim
(B) Bring eye glasses if necessary
(C) Call back for examination results
(D) Arrive half an hour early

화자가 랜다우 씨가 금요일 아침에 무엇을 하라고 상기시키는가?
(A) 보험금 청구서 제출하기
(B) 필요할 경우 안경 지참하기
(C) 시험 결과를 위해 전화 회신하기
(D) 30분 더 일찍 도착하기

85 What information does the speaker need from Mr. Laundau?
(A) The address of his workplace
(B) An alternative contact number
(C) An identification number
(D) A date for a repeat visit

화자가 랜다우 씨에게 필요한 정보는 무엇인가?
(A) 그의 직장 주소
(B) 대체 전화번호
(C) 식별 번호
(D) 재방문 날짜

Questions 86-88 refer to the following telephone message. (영W)

Hi, Jim. It's Lisa, your next-door neighbor. I was supposed to come back from a business trip early this evening, but the subway's currently shut down, and buses are really slow because of all the heavy rain. **86** I've been trying to get a taxi, but it isn't easy thus far. I have a huge favor to ask of you. **87** Could you possibly go to my apartment and feed my cat? She tends to get cranky and scratches the furniture when she is hungry. There's a bag of cat food on the counter that you can open and put into her bowl. Thanks.

안녕하세요, 집 자는 옆집에 사는 이웃인 리사예요. 제가 오늘 저녁 일찍 출장에서 돌아오기로 예정되어 있었는데요, 전철이 현재 가동을 하지 않고 있고 버스도 폭우로 인해 아주 느리게 움직이고 있어요. 택시를 잡으려고 해봤지만, 지금까지도 여의치가 않네요. 제가 한 가지만 부탁드려도 될까요? 가능하시다면 제 아파트로 가셔서 제 고양이에게 먹이를 좀 주실 수 있으신가요? 제 고양이는 배가 고프면 짜증내고 가구들을 긁어 놓거든요. 조리대 위에 고양이 먹이 가방이 있는데 그것을 그릇에 좀 넣어 주실 수 있으신가요? 감사합니다.

shut down 멈추다　thus far 여태까지　tend to ~하는 경향이 있다　cranky 짜증을 내는

---

80 Where most likely does the speaker work?
(A) At a photographic store
(B) At a supermarket
(C) At an art gallery
(D) At a travel agency

화자는 어디에서 일할 것 같은가?
(A) 사진관
(B) 슈퍼마켓
(C) 미술관
(D) 여행사

81 Why does the speaker ask the listener to come to the business?
(A) To refund a holiday
(B) To enter a competition
(C) To pick up a prize
(D) To retrieve a lost item

화자가 청자에게 회사에 오라고 하는 이유는?
(A) 휴가를 반납하기 위해
(B) 경연 대회 출전을 위해
(C) 상을 찾아오기 위해
(D) 분실물을 되찾아오기 위해

82 What does the speaker ask the listener to bring?
(A) An invoice
(B) Holiday brochures
(C) Passport identification
(D) Account details

화자는 청자에게 무엇을 지참하라고 요구하는가?
(A) 송장
(B) 휴가 안내 책자
(C) 여권 신분증
(D) 계좌 정보

86 Where is the speaker most likely calling from?
(A) An airport
(B) A taxi stand
(C) A bus stop
(D) A pet shop

화자는 어디서 전화를 하고 있는 것 같은가?!
(A) 공항
(B) 택시 정류장
(C) 버스 정류장
(D) 애완동물 가게

87 What does the speaker imply when she says, "but it isn't easy thus far"?
(A) She cannot get a taxi.
(B) She is stuck in traffic.
(C) She doesn't know where the taxi stand is.
(D) She thinks the destination is too far away.

화자는 "지금까지도 여의치가 않네요"라고 말했을 때 무엇을 의미했는가?!
(A) 그녀는 택시를 잡을 수 없다.
(B) 그녀는 교통 체증에 갇혀 있다.
(C) 그녀는 택시 정류장이 어디에 있는지 모른다.
(D) 그녀는 목적지가 너무 멀다고 생각한다.

88 What does the speaker ask the listener to do?
(A) Call back
(B) Walk the pet
(C) Feed her pet
(D) Close the bedroom door

화자는 청자가 무엇을 하기를 원하는가?!
(A) 전화하기
(B) 애완동물 산책시키기
(C) 애완동물에게 먹이주기
(D) 침실 문 닫기

Questions 89-91 refer to the following announcement. 미W

Hello, and 89 welcome to the annual conference on building harmony in the office. This conference was originally scheduled to end at 3:30 P.M., but I'm going to need you for a little more time 90 as we have a lot of material to cover and many activities to do. 91 What we are handing out right now are questionnaires that we would like for you to fill out as a show of participation and also evidence that you attended this conference. Once you complete the questionnaire, please drop it in the white plastic box right by the door at the end of the day.

안녕하세요, 사무실 내에서의 조화 증진에 대한 연례 컨퍼런스에 오신 것을 환영합니다. 이 컨퍼런스는 원래 3시 30분에 끝나기로 예정이 되어 있으나 다룰 자료가 많고 해야 할 활동들도 많기 때문에 여러분들께 좀 더 긴 시간을 요청해야겠습니다. 저희가 지금 나누어 드리는 것은 설문지인데요, 이는 행사에 참석했다는 표시 뿐만 아니라 이 컨퍼런스를 수료했다는 증명서가 되기에 작성해 주세요. 설문을 작성하시고 나면, 컨퍼런스가 종료될 때, 문 옆에 있는 하얀색 플라스틱 박스에 넣어 주세요.

harmony 조화, 화합   cover 다루다   questionnaire 설문지   evidence 증거   goer 자주 가는 사람

89 Who most likely are the listeners?
(A) Competition participants
(B) Festival goers
(C) Security guards
(D) Conference attendees

청자들은 누구인 것 같은가?!
(A) 경쟁 참가자
(B) 축제 참가자
(C) 보안 요원
(D) 컨퍼런스 참가자

90 What does the speaker imply when she says, "I'm going to need you for a little more time"?
(A) The listeners are in a hurry to leave.
(B) The event will go longer than expected.
(C) The speaker is busy with other projects.
(D) The audience wants the event to end soon.

화자는 "여러분들께 좀 더 긴 시간을 요청해야겠습니다"라고 말했을 때 무엇을 암시했는가?
(A) 청자들이 서둘러 나가야 한다.
(B) 행사가 예정보다 길어질 것이다.
(C) 화자가 다른 프로젝트로 인해 바쁘다.
(D) 청자들은 행사가 곧 끝나기를 원한다.

91 What is the speaker distributing to the listeners?
(A) Brochures
(B) Greeting cards
(C) Survey forms
(D) Vouchers

화자는 청자들에게 무엇을 나누어 주는가?
(A) 안내서
(B) 연하장
(C) 설문 조사 양식
(D) 쿠폰

Questions 95-97 refer to the following announcement and chart. 호M

Survey Results	
Waste treatment system	35%
⑨⑤ Enlarging Parking Lot	30%
Fitness Facility	25%
Repainting work	10%

I'd like to share the results of the residents' survey taken the last month to start this meeting. As you can see on the screen, ⑨⑤ the question we focused on from the survey was "Which of the following improvements would you like to see in your residence?" The top four results are on the next slide. Although the most popular answer was waste treatment system, I'm afraid to say that this is not a possible option for now considering we have to get it approved by the city, which may take more than 6 months. ⑨⑥ The second most popular option would be best to address first. ⑨⑦ By the end of this meeting, I want an outline of possible layouts and a calculation of the costs of two new parking lots for the complex.

조사 결과	
쓰레기 처리 시스템	35%
주차 시설 확장	30%
헬스클럽	25%
페인트 다시 칠하기	10%

지난달에 실시된 주민 설문조사의 결과를 공유하면서 이 회의를 시작하 겠습니다. 이 화면에서 보실 수 있듯이, 저희가 초점을 맞추었던 설문은 "다음 중 당신의 주거 공간에서 어떠한 개선 사항을 보고 싶나요?"였습니다. 상위 네 개의 결과는 다음 슬라이드에 있습니다. 가장 많이 나온 답변 은 쓰레기 처리 시스템이었으나, 시에서 승인을 받아야 하는데 이는 6개월 이상 걸리기 때문에 지금으로서는 가능한 옵션이 아님을 여러분께 알려드립니다. 두 번째로 많이 나온 옵션이 우선적으로 처리되기에 가장 좋아 보입니다. 이 미팅이 끝날 때까지, 저는 단지를 위한 두 개의 새로운 주차장이 가능한 설계 개요와 가격 견적을 원합니다.

---

92 Who most likely is the speaker?
(A) A business owner
(B) A retiring employee
(C) A technician
(D) A professor in a college

화자는 누구인 것 같은가?
(A) 업체 사장
(B) 은퇴하는 직원
(C) 기술자
(D) 대학 교수

93 What is the main purpose of the meeting?
(A) To recruit more employees
(B) To open a new branch
(C) To improve the service
(D) To analyze a rival company

회의의 주요 목적은 무엇인가?
(A) 직원들을 더 고용하기 위해
(B) 새로운 지점을 열기 위해
(C) 서비스를 개선하기 위해
(D) 경쟁업체를 분석하기 위해

94 Look at the graphic. What will the speaker most likely discuss next?
(A) Additional charge for international shipping
(B) Arrival notification service
(C) Package pickup
(D) Breakage insurance

시각 자료를 보시오. 화자는 다음에 무엇을 논의할 것 같은가?
(A) 해외 배송을 위한 추가 금액
(B) 도착 알림 서비스
(C) 소포 픽업
(D) 파손 보험

Questions 92-94 refer to the following excerpt from a meeting and table. 경M

Types of services	Fastshipping	BSS
Additional charge for an international shipping	O	O
Arrival notification service	O	O
Package pickup	O	
⑨④ Breakage insurance		O

⑨② Before we get started, we should congratulate ourselves on how much Fastshipping, our online business, has grown in the last ten months. When we first started, we were in the red because we were getting maybe a couple of orders a month. Because the number of orders is rising rapidly, ⑨③ we need to improve our services. The table you see on the screen compares our company with our competitor, BSS. ⑨④ I'd like to discuss how we can improve our service to keep up with BSS.

서비스 종류	패스트쉬핑	BSS
해외 배송을 위한 추가 금액	O	O
도착 알림 서비스	O	O
소포 픽업	O	
파손 보험		O

시작하기 전에, 지난 10개월간 얼마나 많이 우리 온라인 사업인 패스트 쉬핑이 성장해 왔는지에 대해 우리 모두를 축하해 줍시다. 우리가 처음 시 작했을 때, 한 달에 한두 건 정도의 주문만 들어와서 적자를 면치 못했습니다. 주문이 아주 빠르게 늘어나고 있기 때문에 우리는 서비스를 개선해야 할 상황이 되었습니다. 화면에 보이는 표는 우리 회사와 우리의 경쟁업체인 BSS를 비교해 주고 있습니다. 저는 BSS와 경쟁하기 위해 우리 서 비스에 관해 무엇을 개선할 수 있을지 논의하고 싶습니다.

in the red 적자 상태인 rapidly 빠르게, 급격하게 compare 비교하다 keep up with 뒤지지 않게 따라가다 notification 통지, 알림 breakage insurance 파손 보험

문제 P242

resident 거주자, 주민 improvement 개선, 향상 residence 거주지, 주거 공간 treatment 처리, 치료, 처치 considering ~을 감안하면 address 처리하다 outline 개요 layout 배치, 설계 enlarge 확장하다 tentative 잠정적인 floor plan 평면도

95 What is the focus on the meeting?
(A) Improving the community center
(B) Meeting residents' requests
(C) Raising money
(D) Remodeling commercial facilities

미팅의 중점은 무엇인가?
(A) 주민센터 개선
(B) 주민 요청 처리
(C) 모금
(D) 상업용 시설 리모델링

96 Look at the graphic. What does the speaker want to focus on?
(A) Waste treatment system
(B) Enlarging parking lot
(C) Fitness facility
(D) Repainting work

시각 자료를 보시오. 화자는 무엇에 초점을 두고자 하는가?
(A) 쓰레기 처리 시스템
(B) 주차 시설 확장
(C) 운동 시설
(D) 페인트 다시 칠하기

97 What does the speaker want from the listeners?
(A) A decision on whether to increase rent
(B) A suggestion for a new parking lot
(C) A tentative contract
(D) A new floor plan

화자는 청자들로부터 무엇을 원하는가?
(A) 임대료를 인상할 것인지 아닌지에 관한 결정
(B) 새로운 주차장에 대한 의견
(C) 잠정적인 계약
(D) 새로운 평면도

Questions 98-100 refer to the following announcement and timetable. (09W)

Departing Flight	Destination	Departure Time
742	London	2:00 P.M.
707	⑨ Seattle	3:15 P.M.
747	Los Angeles	3:30 P.M.
778	Hawaii	5:30 P.M.

Attention, ⑨ all passengers waiting for the flight bound for Seattle. ⑨ As announced earlier, the flight has been grounded for the time being due to several mechanical issues of the aircraft. I am more than glad to announce that repairs are now successfully underway. Since the flight will not take off until these concerns are fully addressed, ⑩ please follow the airport staff members to the lounge to enjoy some refreshments. ⑨ The updated departure time has been posted on the screen. We apologize for any inconveniences and thank you for your patience.

출발 비행기	목적지	출발 시간
742	런던	오후 2:00
707	시애틀	오후 3:15
747	로스엔젤레스	오후 3:30
778	하와이	오후 5:30

시애틀로 가는 비행기를 기다리고 계시는 승객 여러분 주목해 주시기 바랍니다. 앞서 공지드린대로 이 비행기는 몇 가지 기계적인 결함으로 한동안 출발이 지연되고 있었습니다. 지금 이 비행기에 대한 수리가 잘 진행되고 있어 여러분들께 말씀드리게 되어 정말 기쁩니다. 모든 문제가 완전히 해결될 때까지 이 비행기는 출발할 수 없기 때문에 공항 직원을 따라 라운지로 이동하셔서 간단한 음식을 드시길 바랍니다. 새로운 출발 시간은 화면에 게시되어 있습니다. 불편을 드린 점 사과드리며, 여러분의 이해에 감사드립니다.

98 What is the cause of the delay?
(A) Inclement weather
(B) A mechanical flaw
(C) A human error
(D) A routine maintenance

지연의 원인은 무엇인가?
(A) 좋지 않은 날씨
(B) 기계적인 결함
(C) 사람의 실수
(D) 일상적인 점검

99 Look at the graphic. What is the updated time for the flight?
(A) 2:00 P.M.
(B) 3:15 P.M.
(C) 3:30 P.M.
(D) 5:30 P.M.

시각 자료를 보시오. 이 비행기의 새로운 출발 시간은 언제인가?
(A) 오후 2:00
(B) 오후 3:15
(C) 오후 3:30
(D) 오후 5:30

100 What are the listeners asked to do?
(A) Board the airplane in advance
(B) Wait for the announcement
(C) Follow the staff members
(D) Buy some food

청자들은 무엇을 하라고 요청받는가?
(A) 비행기에 미리 탑승한다.
(B) 공지를 기다린다.
(C) 직원들을 따라간다.
(D) 음식을 산다.

bound for ~ 행의, ~로 가는 ground 이륙하지 못하게 하다 underway 진행 중인 take off 출발하다, 뜨다, 떠나다 refreshments 다과류 inconvenience 불편함 patience 인내 inclement 날씨가 안 좋은 flaw 결함 routine 일상적인

Part 5

101 **해설** has와 p.p. 사이는 동사를 수식하는 부사 자리로 (B)가 정답이다. successs는 명사, successfully은 형용사로 동사를 수식할 수 없다.
샌마크는 새 부엌 기기를 시장에 성공적으로 도입했다.
introduce 도입하다 appliance 기기, 전자제품

102

해설 상관 접속사 문제로 빈칸 뒤 or과 어울리는 것은 either A or B(A와 B 둘 중 하나)이므로 (A)가 정답이다. neither A nor B, both A and B, not only A but (also) B 등이 상관 접속사도 알아 둔다.

광대역 접속이 마느테 커뮤니케이션즈 또는 서비스 제공업체에 의해 중단될 수 있다.

broadband 광대역 access 접근 cut off 자르다, 잘라내다 service provider 서비스 제공업체

103

해설 관사(a)와 형용사(well-known) 다음 빈칸은 명사 자리로 environmentalist와 environments가 명사인데 앞에 주어가 사람이고 이와 동격을 이루어야 하므로 사람 명사인 (B)가 정답이다.

유명한 환경 운동가인 가브리엘 신체코는 복구금을 살리라는 그녀의 캠페인으로 찬사를 받았다.

well-known 잘 알려진, 유명한 praise 찬사 environmentalist 환경운동가 environmentally 환경보호적으로

positive 긍정적인 response 반응, 대답 promotion 홍보 production 생산, 생산물

104

해설 빈칸은 동사 plan의 목적어 자리로 to부정사를 취하는 동사이므로 (D)가 정답이다. to부정사를 취하는 동사 need, wish, hope, desire, expect, plan, aim, decide, propose, offer, ask, promise, agree, refuse, fail, serve, pretend, afford, manage, prefer 등을 알아 둔다.

일라시 유기농 식품 홍보에 대한 아주 긍정적인 반응으로, 마케팅 팀은 앞으로 6개월 안에 생산량을 40퍼센트까지 증가시키려는 계획을 잡고 있다.

partnership 동업자 관계 lead to ~으로 이어지다 excel 뛰어나다, 특출나다

105

해설 빈칸 뒤에 명사가 있으므로 빈칸은 명사를 수식하는 형용사 자리로 (B)가 정답이다. excellently는 부사, excel은 동사, excellence는 명사로 빈칸에 들어갈 수 없다. 참고로 how트 뒤에 형용사나 부사가 바로 올 수 있다.

홍보 운동에 대한 우리의 동안자 관계는 탐파크가 얼마나 효율적으로 훌륭한 결과로 이어질 수 있는지 보여 주는 사례이다.

publicity 언론의 관심: 홍보(업) drive (조직적인) 운동

106

해설 동사 어휘 문제로 문맥상 '특별히 고안되었다'가 가장 자연스러우므로 정답은 (A)이다.

맥브라이드 씨는 최근 생산이 가동되는 동안 직원들의 한신에 대해 박수를 보냈다.

applaud 박수를 치다 dedication 헌신 run 운영

107

해설 be동사 뒤에서 보어 역할을 하면서 문맥상 서류 뭉치가 그 너의 것이라고 일렀다가 적절하므로 (B)가 정답이다.

이틀 전, 헤이스 씨는 사람들에게 구석에 있는 서류 뭉치가 그녀의 것이라고 일렀다.

pile 더미, 뭉치 paperwork 서류

108

해설 부사 어휘 문제로 문맥상 '원래 2월 11일에 완공될 예정이었다가 가장 적절하므로 (A)가 정답이다.

파이프라인의 재건은 원래 2월 11일에 완공될 계획이었다.

reconstruction 복원, 재건 pipeline 파이프라인(석유 · 가스 등이 장거리 수송을 위하여, 보통 지하에 매설하는 관로) originally 원래, 처음에 highly 매우

monitor 감독하다 away from ~에서 떠나서 appoint 임명하다 accomplish 성취하다

109

해설 명사 자리 문제로 빈칸은 앞 명사 employee와 함께 전치사 뒤 목적어 역할을 하면서 의미상 복합명사가 되어야 하므로 (A)가 정답이다. suggested는 과거분사로 단독으로 쓸 수 있지만 employee는 가산 명사로 단독으로 쓸 수 없기 때문에 정답이 될 수 없다.

직원 의견들에 대한 반응으로, 사무실은 이음에 한 번 더 일찍 문을 열 것이다.

response 응답

110

해설 전치사 문제로 문맥상 '직원 환영 시간 동안에'가 가장 적절하므로 정답은 (A)이다. 참고로 about과 의미가 유사한 on, over, as to[for], regarding, concerning, pertaining to, in reference to, with[in] respect to, in[with] regard to, when it comes to 등을 알아 둔다.

청량음료를 비롯하여, 다양한 카나페가 직원 환영 시간 동안에 제공될 것이다.

soft drink 청량음료 a selection of 다양한

111

해설 전치사(for)와 명사(dedication) 사이 빈칸으로 명사 앞 대명사의 소유격 자리이므로 (A)가 정답이다.

리벤즈 소프트웨어는 사무실 밖에 있을 때 직원들을 감독하고 싶어 하는 기관들을 위해 특별히 고안되었다.

112

해설 명사 어휘 문제로 문맥상 '고객 서비스에 대해 긍정적인 피드백을 받았다'가 가장 자연스러우므로 정답은 (C)이다.

레이먼즈 DVD 매장은 일반 회원들에게서 고객 서비스에 대해 긍정적인 피드백을 받았다.

impact (강력한) 영향, 충격

113

해설 before 뒤에 올 수 있는 것은 announcing과 announcement, announcer이다. 빈칸 뒤에 명사(the winners)가 있으므로 목적어를 가질 수 있는 동사 (A)가 정답이다.

수상자를 발표하기 전에, 그들이 모두 메인 식당에 참석했는지 확인해 주세요.

in attendance 참석한 dining hall 식당

114

해설 of 뒤에 which는 efforts를 선행사로 취하는 관계대명사이다. 빈칸은 관계절의 주어 자리인데 문맥상 그중 아무것도 해결하지 못했다가 적절하므로 (A)가 정답이다.

주요 고속도로의 교통 문제를 경감하기 위해 여러 처리 노력했으나, 그 중 어떤 문제도 해결하지 못했다.

ease 덜다, 경감하다 main highway 주요 고속도로

115

해설 빈칸 뒤에 목적어가 없기 때문에 수동태 동사가 들어갈 자리이다. 정답은 (B)이다.

댐블 가운데 역사 박물관은 그 지역의 역사 연구 협회에 의해서 유지되고 있다.

maintain 유지하다

116

해설 빈칸 뒤에 명사구를 이끌며 수식어구를 이루는 자리이므로 전치사가 들어갈 수 있다. as a result(그 결과로)에는 부사, now that(~이므로)과 because(때문에)는 접속사이므로 빈칸 전치사인 (B) owing to(때문에)가 정답이다. 참고로 이유를 나타내는 전치사는 due to와 on account of도 있으니 알아 두자.

아메리즈 가운데는 낮은 세금과 풍부한 노동력 때문에 많은 새로운 사업체를 끌어들였다.

bountiful 풍부한 workforce 인력

117

해설 notify A of B(A에게 B에 대해서 알리다) 숙어로 읽어 두자. 따라서 정답은 (B)이다. 참고로 notify(알리다)는 바로 뒤에 알릴 '대상'을 목적어로 놓고, 그 뒤에 알릴 내용을 놓으므로 동사는, 4형식 구조로(notify A that ~)로도 활용할 수 있는 동사이니 정확한 쓰임을 위해 두자.

최근 궂은 날씨로 인해 써니사이드 아일랜드의 관광 선업이 감소할 것을 걱정하여 몇몇 지역 호텔 운영자들은 특가 판매를 발표했다.
inclement (날씨가) 궂은

118

우리는 당신에게 11월 1일 또는 그 이후에 우리의 채용 결정에 대해서 알려줄 것이다.

119

해설 반길은 소유주(a company's)과 형용사(overall)의 수식을 동시에 받는 자리이므로 명사가 들어가야 한다. 따라서 정답은 (B) profitability(수익성)이다.
최신 정부의 구매가 회사의 전반적인 수익성에 상당한 영향력을 미칠 수 있다.
acquisition 취득, 획득, 구매

120

해설 previously(이전에)는 과거시제의 동사와 함께 써야 하므로 오답이며, accordingly(그에 따라서)는 의미상 맞지 않고 extremely(매우)는 동사를 수식할 수 없는 부사이므로 오답이다. 따라서 정답은 (C) periodically이다. 참고로 frequently, usually, periodically, often과 같은 빈도부사들은 단순현재시제의 동사와 함께 자주 쓰이다는 것을 알아 두자.
전 직원들이 고객들과 직접적으로 업무를 기회를 가지는 것을 확실시 하기 위해서 우리의 직원 업무는 주기적으로 조정된다.
adjust 조정하다

121

해설 빈칸부터 콤마까지는 문장 전체를 수식하는 부사 역할을 하는 자리이다. 선택지에서 분사구문과 부사절이 부사 역할을 할 수 있는데, be동사 자체는 자동사라서 p.p.로 축약이 불가능하므로 (C) Been concerned는 오답으로 소거한다(Being concerned는 가능). 남은 선택지 중 능동/수동을 구별해서 쓰는 데, concern(영향을 미치다/걱정시키다)이라는 동사는 뒤에 대상 목적어(보통 사람)를 놓는 동사이므로 이렇게 바로 뒤에 그 대상이 남아 있을 때는 목적어가 없는 것으로 보아 한다. 따라서 선택지에 서 수동태로 쓰일 수 있는 (B) concerned가 정답이다.

122

해설 뒤의 명사구를 이끄는 수식어구 자리이므로 전치사가 들어갈 자리이다. 선택지에서 As well as는 양 옆에 같은 품사를 놓고 별렬시키는 등위접속사이므로 오답이다. Instead off(대신에), On behalf of(대신하여/대표하여), In accordance with (~에 따라서) 중에서 의미상 어울리는 전치사로서 정답은 (D) In accordance with이다.
회사 정책에 따라서, 영업 사원들은 회사 장비를 개인적으로 사용하기 전에 반드시 상관으로부터 허가를 받아야 한다.
associate 직원

123

해설 형용사 어휘 문제로 문맥상 '여유로운 산책을 즐길 수 있다' 가 가장 적절하므로 정답은 (C)이다.
버킨 국립공원에서 당신은 기운을 북돋아주는 산책로와 트레킹과 숲 속 근처의 여유로운 산책을 즐길 수 있다.
trek 트레킹 mountainside 산비탈 persistent 끈기있는 conclusive 결정적인 leisurely 여유로운 tolerant 관대한, 이량 있는

124

해설 빈칸 뒤의 절(S+V)을 이끄는 자리이므로 접속사가 들어갈 자리이다. 선택지에서 접속사로 쓰일 수 있는 것은 However(아무리 ~하더라도)와 Although(비록 ~이지만)이 둘 중에 의미상 어울리는 (C) Although가 정답이다. Despite(~에도 불구하고)는 전치사이고, Nevertheless(그럼에도 불구하고)는 부사이므로 오답으로 소거할 수 있다. 참고로 However는 형용사나 부사로 쓰일 때는 '아무리 ~하더라도'로 해석되고, 부사로 쓰일 때는 '그래나'로 해석을 알아 두자.
비록 호텔의 접수 데스크는 24시간 내내 열려 있지만, 공항으로 일부와 는 무료 셔틀 서비스는 아침 6시에서 저녁 10시까지만이 이용 가능하다.
around the clock 24시간 내내 to and from ~를 오가는

125

해설 빈칸에 들어가 적절한 형장사를 고르는 문제이다. 문맥상 금 장문에서 '어떠한 ~이라도 쉽게 이용로 쓰이는 (D)가 정답이다.
다른 사람에게 회사 기밀 정보를 유출하는 웨슬리 서 직원은 누구든지 해고될 것이다.
reveal 드러내다, 밝히다 confidential 기밀의 terminate 끝내다, 종료되다

126

해설 명사 어휘 문제로 문맥상 '현재 협상하느라 바쁘다'가 가장 자연스러우므로 정답은 (A)이다.
스타크랜드 공무원들과 스토닝 건설의 기사들은 현재 도시의 새 순환 도로 건설 제안에 대해 협상하느라 바쁘다.

official 공무원 currently 현재 be engaged in ~으로 바쁘다 proposal 제안, 제안서 ring road (도시의) 순환 도로 negotiation 협상

127

해설 주어가 initiative이고 동사는 involved이다. 주어와 동사 사이가 '~ that ~ highways는 initiative를 수식하는 관계절이다. 빈 칸은 관계절 안의 동사 자리로 동사가 들어가야 하므로 highways 뒤에는 implementing과 수 일자가 되지 않는 implement는 정답에서 제외된다. 현재 시제와 과거 시제 중에서 문맥상 적절한 것은 과거 시제 (C)이다.
톰린슨 시장이 고속도로를 개선하기 위해 시행한 마지막 계획은 22번 도로의 일부를 대중교통이 다닐 수 있도록 분함을 것이다.
initiative 계획 mayor 시장 section off ~을 분할하다 public transport 대중교통 implement 시행하다

128

해설 형용사 어휘 문제로 문맥상 '연금 정책에 자격을 가지기 위 해서가 가장 적절하므로 정답은 (B)이다. compatible은 전 치사 with과 함께 쓰이며 '~와 호환 가능한'이라는 뜻이다. responsive는 전치사 to와 함께 쓰이며 '~에 반응하는'이라는 뜻이다.
직원들이 회사의 연금 정책에 대한 자격을 가지려면 최소 1년간 고용되 있어야 한다.
employ 고용하다 pension scheme 연금 정책 compatible 호환이 되는, 양립 가능한 be eligible for 자격이 되는

129

해설 빈칸 앞뒤로 완수 성분을 모두 갖춘 완전한 문장이 있으 므로 빈칸에는 부사절 접속사 혹은 등위 접속사가 올 수 있다. somewhere는 부사, himself는 대명사로 정답에서 제외되고 whether와 whenever 중에서 문맥상 '그의 기업이 미래 전망에 도움이 될 때면 언제든지'가 적절하므로 (B)가 정답이다. whether 가 부사절 접속사로 쓰이면 '~이든 아니든 상관없이'라는 의미이다.
킬라드 씨는 그의 기업의 전망에 도움이 될 때면 언제든지 해외여행을 가까이 갈 것이라고 밝혔다.
indicate 나타내다, 보여 주다 abroad 해외로 prospect 전망, 기망

130

해설 justification(정당한 이유), condolence(애도), translation (번역), diagnosis(진단) 중에서 '정당한 이유 중 하나이다'는 뜻이 적절하므로 정답은 (A) justification이 정답이다.
운영비의 절감은 직원에서 새로운 기술에 투자하는 것에 대한 정당한 이유 중 하나다.
reduction 절감

Part 6

문제 P245

[131-134]

공연 예술가들에게 알립니다!

자체 극장 무대에서 공연할 수 있는 독창적인 기회에 관심이 있으신가요? [131] 만약 그렇다면 6월 23일에 있을 요크 공개 페스티벌에서 공연하기 위해 신청하세요.

참가 신청서는 www.yorkopen.org에 들어가 온라인으로 작성해야 합니다. 귀하의 공연은 자체 극장 지역 주민에게 올려질 행사들에 참가한 여러 공연들에 의해 심사될 것입니다. 작성한 참가 신청서와 함께, 귀하의 전문 분야의 [132]세부 사항을 업로드해 주세요. [133] 이는 심사위원들이 귀하를 올바른 범주에 넣는 데 도움이 될 것입니다.

신청 마감일은 5월 1일이고 심사위원들의 결정은 그걸 이루어질 것입니다. [134]초대받은 지원자들은 무료 시설을 사용할 수 있고, 행사 기간 동안 계속 재료들의 할 것입니다.

performing artist 공연 예술가 / perform 공연하다 exclusive 독점적인 / display 보이다 / sign up 등록하다 / judge 심사하다; 심사위원 / talent 재능 / entry form 참가 신청서 / specialist area 전문 분야 / application 등록, 신청 / duration 지속 기간

131
해설 앞 문장과 뒤 문장을 해석해 보고 어울리는 접속부사를 찾아야 한다. 문제상 If you interested in it을 축약한 형태인 (C) If so (만약 그렇다면)이 적절하다. (A) 대신에 / (B) 그럼에도 불구하고 / (D) 그 이후에

132
해설 행사에 참가하길 원하는 공연 예술가들이 참가 신청서와 함께 무엇을 업로드해야 할지를 묻는 문제이다. 빈칸 뒤의 of your specialist area가 단서이다. 즉, 귀하의 전문 분야 상세히 기독한 것이므로 (C)가 적절하다. (A) 발견 / (B) 지시 / (D) 요건

133
(A) 저희는 이미 모든 참가 양식들의 검토를 끝냈습니다.
(B) 이는 심사위원들이 귀하를 올바른 범주에 넣는 데 도움이 될 것입니다.
(C) 당신은 접수 데스크에서 필요한 양식을 얻어야 합니다.
(D) 무대에서 공연하는 것은 용기와 순발력을 요구합니다.
해설 빈칸 앞에서 세부 사항을 업로드해 달라는 내용이 나왔으므로 이를 통해 올바른 범주에 넣는 데 도움이 된다는 것을 알 수 있다. 따라서 (B)가 정답이다.

134
해설 빈칸은 명사 applicants(지원자들)를 수식하는 형용사가 올 자리이므로 (A)는 일단 제외한다. 지원자들은 누군가를 초대하는 것이 아니라 초대를 받은 것이므로 과거분사 형용사인 (A)가 적절하다.

[135-138]

몬타나 (3월 15일) - 유명한 국내 주유소 체인 중 하나인 맥스 가스가 곧 몬타나에 처음으로 두 개의 주유소를 오픈합니다. [135] 앞 문장에서 이 주유소의 특징이 등장했고, 뒤 문장에서 주유소가 유명한 이유인 이곳을 설명하고 있으므로 [136] 그들은 또한 안전하고 깨끗한 편의시설에 대해서 자랑스럽게 여깁니다.

몬타나 지역의 첫 번째 맥스 가스는 로이드 가와 10번가 사이의 코너에 지어질 것입니다. 키스코 가와 20번가에 지어질 [137] 두 번째 것은 작은 부식 시설을 갖춘 특별한 맥스 가스 주유소가 될 것입니다. 다른 특별 주유소들처럼, 이곳도 고객들이 앉아서 [138] 먹을 수 있는 테이블과 의자들이 있을 것입니다.

gas stations 주유소 / feature 특징으로 하다 / necessity 필수품 / well known for 유명한 / friendly 친절한 / patron 고객 / amenity 편의시설 / consumer goods 소비재

135
해설 앞뒤 문장을 자연스럽게 연결할 접속부사를 고르는 문제이다. 앞 문장에서 이 주유소의 특징이 등장했고, 뒤 문장에서 주유소가 유명한 이유를 설명하고 있으므로 (A) 그럼에도 불구하고 / (B) 결국에는 / (D) 즉, 다시 말해

136
(A) 고속도로의 향상은 정부의 노력 덕분입니다.
(B) 그들은 또한 안전하고 깨끗한 편의시설에 대해서 자랑스럽게 여깁니다.
(C) 기솔린 거래가 오르고 있기 때문에 통근자들의 지갑은 점점 줄어들고 있습니다.
(D) 소비재의 이용 가능성은 가까운 미래에 증가될 것입니다.
해설 빈칸 앞에서 맥스 가스 주유소의 특징이 언급되고 있으므로 이를 자연스럽게 연결하는 다음 (B)가 정답이다.

137
해설 첫 문장에서 새로운 주유소 두 개가 오픈한다고 했으므로, 첫 번째 주유소에 대해서 설명한 다음 '두 번째' 주유소에 대해서 설명을 이어가는 것이 가장 자연스럽다. 따라서 정답은 (D)이다. (A) 우사한 (B) 이전의 (C) 경쟁의

138
해설 뒤에 절을 이끌고 있으므로 접속사가 필요한 자리이다. there는 부사이므로 오답으로 소거한다. 넘은 선택지는 모두 앞에 있는 명사(선행사)를 수식하는 형용사절을 이끌 수 있는 접속사들이다. 선행사인 tables and chairs는 고객들이 앉아서 먹을 수 있는 '장소로서의 역할을 하므로 정답은 (D) where이다.

[139-142]

수신: dcarlton@jetmail.net
발신: jdelphi@houndban.com
날짜: 4월 5일
제목: 귀하의 면접

길트 씨에게,

저는 하운드반 기업의 채용팀을 대표해서 이 편지를 씁니다. 저희 팀은 목요일에 있었던 귀하의 면접에 깊은 경험을 받으셨습니다. [139] 사실, 귀하께서는 가장 유망한 후보자들 중 한 명이었으므로 [140] 안타깝게도, 저희는 이번에는 귀하에게 일자리를 제공할 수 없을 것 같습니다. 대신 저희의 파트너 지사로 이력서를 보내 볼 것을 권장합니다. 그곳은 현재 선임 회계사를 찾고 있습니다. 귀하의 경력과 지식을 만약 파인으로 이동하는 것을 고려할 의향이 있으시다면, 저희가 그곳의 [142] 문의에 귀하를 기꺼이 추천하겠습니다.

진심을 담아,
조안 델피

on behalf of ~을 대신/대표하여 / promising 유망한 / be willing to 기꺼이 ~하다 / recommend 추천하다 / reference letter 추천서

139
해설 앞뒤 문장의 의미를 자연스럽게 이어 줄 접속부사를 고르는 문제이다. 앞 문장에서 면접이 매우 인상 깊었다고 했고, 뒤 문장에서 가장 유망한 후보자들 중 한 명이었으므로 내용을 구체화하는 의미로서 사실이란이라는 접속부사가 가장 적절하다. 정답은 (C)이다. (A) 그렇지 않으면 / (B) 그동안에 / (D) 항상 그렇듯

140
(A) 저희는 귀하의 추천서를 받은 적이 없습니다.
(B) 저희는 귀하의 경력이 충분하지 않다고 생각합니다.
(C) 저희는 귀하께서 저희 회사의 인턴이 되기를 바랍니다.
(D) 안타깝게도, 저희는 이번에는 귀하에게 일자리를 제공할 수 없을 것 같습니다.
해설 빈칸 앞에서 면접이 인상 깊었다고 했지만 뒤에서는 다른 일 자리를 제안하고 있으므로 이번에는 일자리를 제공하기 어렵다는 (D)가 정답이다.

Actual Test 06   164 • 165

141

해설 빈칸은 명사구를 이끄는 전치사 자리이다. Now that(~이 므로)은 접속사이고 Also(또한)는 부사이므로 오답이다. Given(~을 고려하면)과 Unlike(~와 달리) 중에서 의미상 어울리는 것으로 정답은 (B) Given이다. 참고로 Given은 접속사와 전치사의 역할 을 둘 다 할 수 있다.

142

해설 채용팀에서 지원자에게 쓰는 글이라는 것을 고려해 보며 그 지사의 공석에 지원자를 추천해 주겠다고 말하는 것이 가장 적절 하다. 정답은 (C)이다. 정답은 (A) 프로그램 / (B) 숙박시설 / (D) 훈련

[143-146]

새로운 도서관 개관

9월 10일 - 빅토리 센터에 있는 도서관이 이틀 전 운영을 시작했다. 그 개관 행사에 시의 새로운 지점이 이틀 전 단체 회원들과 하생들도 그 행사에 몇몇 지역 참여했다.

이 새로 생긴 1,200 평방 미터의 도서관은 환경을 고려하여 디자인되었 다. **143** 그것은 완전히 태양열에 의해서만 난방이 된다. 건물 전기 의 60%가 지붕에 있는 태양열 전지판에서 생산된다.

이 도서관의 목표 중 하나는 사용자들을 최신 **144** 기술로 연결시켜 주는 것이다. 그것에는 많은 컴퓨터 단말기가 있지만, 많은 컴퓨터 단말기도 있 다. 사용자들은 또한 본인의 장비를 가져와서 도서관의 무료 초고속 인터 넷을 사용할 수도 있다.

solar panel 태양열 전지판 cutting-edge 최신의 reference material 참고 문헌 computer terminal 컴퓨터 단말기

143

해설 be동사 뒤에 보어가 들어갈 자리이므로 일반 형용사, 현재 분사, 과거분사가 정답이 될 수 있다. 현재분사는 뒤에 목적어가 있어야 하므로 오답이다. 정답은 일반 형용사인 (C) present(참석 한)이다.

144

해설 동사의 시제를 묻는 문제이다. 첫 문장에서 이틀전에 도 서관 운영이 시작되었다고 했고, 그 다음 문장에서도 시점이 참 석했었다(was present)는 과거시제가 쓰였으므로 정답은 (A) participated이다.

145

(A) 그곳에는 다섯 개의 큰 에어컨이 있다.
(B) 유명한 건축가가 그곳을 디자인했다.
(C) 그곳은 완전히 태양열에 의해서만 난방이 된다.
(D) 그곳은 지하철 역에서 가깝다.

해설 빈칸 바로 뒤에 태양열 전자판에 대한 내용이 나오므로 (C) 가 정답이다.

146

해설 위 문장을 보면 많은 컴퓨터 단말기가 있고, 사용자들이 초 고속 인터넷도 사용할 수 있다고 했으므로 최신 기술을 제공하는 도서관이라고 볼 수 있다. 따라서 정답은 (A) technology이다.
(B) 차량 / (C) 교육 / (D) 가전제품

문제편 P249

Part 7

[147-148]

누헤이븐 실버타운

누헤이븐 실버타운이 1거재 임대를 합니다!

• 한 개 또는 두 개의 침실이 딸린 아파트

• 누헤이븐의 중심에 위치한 48개 가구의 주거용 타운으로 은퇴하신 분들을 위한 것입니다.

• 두 개의 공용 휴게실, 수영장과 헬스클럽, 충분한 주차장 등의 생활 편 의 시설이 있고, 모두 걸기 대에로에 포함됩니다.

• 실버타운은 워터다운 교를 내려다보고, 상가와 공공 편의 시설에 가까 워, 완벽히 위치합니다.

148 전시용 아파트를 방문하셔서 이용할 수 있는 아파트를 확인하세요
임대 중개인은 예상 입주자분들께 실버타운을 보여 드릴 준비가 되어 있 습니다.

누헤이븐 실버타운
트리를 로드 32
누헤이븐
857-555-4125
www.newhavenretirementvillage.com

retirement village 실버타운 lease 임대하다; 임대 unit 단위 residential 주거용 cater to ~을 충족시키다 on-site 현장의, 현지의 amenities 편의 시설 communal 공용의 ample 충분한 rental charge 임대료 overlook 내려다보다 showroom 전시실 on hand 구할 수 있는 prospective 장래의, 유망한 tenant 입주자 deposit payment 보증금 지불

문제편 P249

147 광고가 설명하는 것은?

(A) 임대 양로원
(B) 기업 이전 서비스
(C) 지역 방문객을 위한 명소
(D) 별장 매매

148 독자들은 무엇을 하도록 권장되는가?

(A) 회원권 구매하기
(B) 둘러보기
(C) 함수에 서명하기
(D) 보증금 보내기

[149-150]

수신: 켈머 제조사 직원들
발신: 셜리 이튼드 (arsally@kelmer.com)
날짜: 2월 12일
제목: 회사 정보

최근 모든 직원들에게 별도로 당신 양수와 함께 새로운 직원 안내서의 사 본을 보내셨습니다.

149 안내서는 켈머 제조사의 방침과 절차에 관한 전체 정보를 포함하고 있습니다. 또한 업무 내용과 직원의 복리 후생 제도에 관한 세부 정보를 포함하고 있습니다. 설명서를 자세히 읽고, 안내서에 기술된 규칙과 절차 를 이해했으며 회사와 규칙을 준수한다는 것을 확인하는 것을 동봉된 답신 양 식에 서명하세요.

150 서명한 양식은 인사부의 존 페디스에게 보내세요.
협조에 감사드립니다.
셜리 이튼드
인사부 상무 이사

employee manual 직원 수칙 separate 별도의 acknowledgement 인정 manual 안내서 regarding ~을 관련하여 procedure 절차 job descriptions 직무 기술 employee benefits 복리 후생 제도 enclosed 동봉된 undertake 약속하다 cooperation 협조 publication 출간(물)

149 이튼드 씨가 이메일에서 논의하고 있는 것은?

(A) 훈련 강좌
(B) 취업 기회
(C) 회사 출간물
(D) 고용 절차의 변화

150 이튼드 씨가 직원들에게 요구하는 것은?

(A) 양식에 서명하여 보내기
(B) 직무 해택 검토하기
(C) 회의 참석하기
(D) 책 반납하기

[151-153]

🟦151 미션 B-452 노트북 컴퓨터를 구매해 주셔서 감사합니다. 이 제품은 무료 바이러스 방지용 소프트웨어가 포함되어 있습니다. 이것은 출시 기념용 버전이므로, 기존 정품을 구매하도록 하세요. www.missioncomputers.com에서 온라인으로 정품을 직접 주문하실 수 있습니다. 즉시 다운로드 받으실 수 있으며, 🟦152 소프트웨어 패키지는 영업일 5일 내로 배달됩니다. 그 기간 내에 받지 못하시면 전체 돌려받으실 수 있습니다. 🟦153 소중한 고객으로서, 첫 소프트웨어 구매에 15퍼센트 할인을 받게 됩니다. 주문하실 때 41230을 입력하시면 됩니다. 매장을 통해 소프트웨어를 구매하면 원하시면 저희 패키지는 모든 컴퓨터 가게에서 찾으실 수 있습니다. 그러나 대다수의 소매상들은 질문 또는 피드백을 받습니다.

24시간 내내 이용 가능한 800-555-3412로 전화하셔서 기술 지원을 받으실 수 있고, 월요일부터 금요일, 오전 8시부터 오후 9시까지 800-555-3412로 구매품에 대한 질문 또는 피드백을 받습니다.

anti-virus 바이러스 퇴치용인 introductory 소개용의, 출시 기념용의 guarantee 보장하다 type in ~을 입력하다 place an order 주문하다 retail outlet 소매점 stock 재고를 갖추다 aware 알고 있는 query 문의 promptly 지체 없이 leading 선두 하는 24/7 하루 24시간 1주 7일 동안, 연중무휴인 voucher 할인권

151 공지는 누구를 위한 것인가?
(A) 새 노트북 컴퓨터 주인
(B) 영업 고문
(C) 기술 지원 전문가
(D) 소프트웨어 개발자

152 소프트웨어를 주문할 때 약속되는 것은?
(A) 출시 기념용 소프트웨어에는 3개월간 지속된다.
(B) 배달이 늦을 경우, 구매자는 소프트웨어를 무료로 받는다.
(C) 기술부 문의에 신속하게 답변할 것이다.
(D) 고객 서비스는 일주일에 7일간, 24시간 내내 운영된다.

153 구매자들이 할인을 받을 수 있는 방법은?
(A) 컴퓨터 매장에서 물건을 구매해서
(B) 할인권을 우편으로 보내서
(C) 고객 지원부에 전화해서
(D) 온라인 주문 시 번호를 입력해서

[154-155]

벤 차일즈 [오전 9:19]	네이트, 나 지금 가게에 있는데 내가 가져다 달라고 한 프로젝터 전구를 못 찾았어. 다른 모델은 있는데 우리가 필요한 건 아닌 것 같아.
네이트 라이트 [오전 9:20]	고객 서비스 데스크로 가 봤어? 🟦154 매니저가 나한테 재고가 있다고 우리를 위해서 보관하고 있었다고 했거든.
벤 차일즈 [오전 9:21]	아, 알겠어! 🟦155 그 사람한테 바로 확인해 볼게.
벤 차일즈 [오전 9:22]	됐다. 찾았어. 모델 번호를 두 번이나 확인했어. 이게 우리한테 필요한 거야.
벤 차일즈 [오전 9:25]	좋아. 서울러서 사무실로 들어와 줄래? 한 시간 후에 회의가 시작돼. 전구를 설치하고 사전에 프로젝터를 테스트해 봐야 해.
네이트 라이트 [오전 9:26]	알겠어.
벤 차일즈 [오전 9:27]	가는 길이야.

beforehand 사전에

154 라이트 씨에 대해서 옳은 것은?
(A) 그는 차일즈 씨에게 잘못된 모델 번호를 알려줬다.
(B) 그는 프로젝터 전구에 대해서 가게에 연락했었다.
(C) 그는 바로 사무실로 돌아갈 계획이다.
(D) 그는 발표를 할 것이다.

155 오전 9시 22분에 차일즈 씨가 "아, 알겠어"라고 했을 때 그 의미는 무엇인가?
(A) 그는 마지막 프로젝터 전구를 찾았다.
(B) 그는 여전히 가게를 둘러보고 있다.
(C) 그는 이제 상황을 이해했다.
(D) 그는 고객 서비스 데스크를 볼 수 있다.

[156-158]

편집자 쪽지

이번 (타일랜드 퀴진) 9월 호는 잡지사의 2주년 기념일과 겹칩니다. 첫 호를 출간한지 2년이 되었으며, 그 이후로 저희는 이 지역에서 민속 요리에 관한 가장 인기 있는 잡지 중 하나가 되었습니다. 🟦157 판매 부수가 최근 22,000부를 돌파했고, 계속해서 증가하고 있습니다.

현지 미식가들이 저희의 출판에 찬사를 보냈고, 🟦158 지난날 세계 음식 축제에서 베스트 뉴 푸드 매거진을 수상했습니다. 🟦156 편집 차장으로서, 지희의 성공에 크게 기여한 직원들과 작가들, 광고주들 증가하고 있는 지역 사회의 독자들에게 감사를 표하고 싶습니다.

스텔라 모린

cuisine 요리(법) coincide 동시에 발생하다 ethnic 민족의 circulation (책의) 판매 부수 accolade 포상, 청찬 dedicated 헌신적인 advertiser 광고주 contribute 기여하다 contribution 기여 distribute 배포하다 contributor 기고자

156 모린 씨의 메모의 목적은?
(A) 이용 가능한 제안을 하기 위해
(B) 기부금을 요청하기 위해
(C) 감사를 표현하기 위해
(D) 작가를 소개하기 위해

157 (타일랜드 퀴진)에 관해 언급된 것은?
(A) 점점 더 인기가 높아지고 있다.
(B) 광고비를 인상했다.
(C) 분 세계적으로 유통될 것이다.
(D) 추가 기고자를 모집 중이다.

158 모린 씨는 왜 세계 음식 축제를 언급하는가?
(A) 잡지가 그 행사에서 상을 받았기 때문에
(B) 출판사들이 그 행사를 후원했기 때문에
(C) 그녀가 그곳의 추가 자원봉사자들을 모집했기 때문에
(D) 그녀가 요리 시연을 열었기 때문에

샘 젠킨스	오전 10:15

자리가 차기 회계 연도를 위한 예산을 준비 중이라서 영업부가 쓰고 있는 휴대용 컴퓨터들을 교체하는 것에 대해서 논의해야 해요. 그들은 한동안 컴퓨터 때문에 불만이 있었어요.

| 루이스 파커 | 오전 10:17 |

무슨 문제가 있나요? 165 그들에게 새 휴대용 컴퓨터를 줄 걸로 알고 있는데요.

| 애미 스완슨 | 오전 10:22 |

165 벌써 5년이 지났어요. 166 점점 느려지고 있는데, 더 큰 문제는 자회의 다음 소프트웨어 업그레이드를 처리하지 못한다는 거예요. 그럴 만한 능력이 안 돼요.

| 제프 롱 | 오전 10:25 |

자회는 몇 개월 후에 새로운 재고 조사 데이터베이스를 설치할 예정이에요. 그래서 결정을 내릴 시간이 많지 않아요.

| 애미 스완슨 | 오전 10:28 |

맞아요, 167 그리고 이번에는 손상을 좀 더 잘 이겨낼 수 있는 걸 구입하기를 제안합니다.

| 제프 롱 | 오전 10:29 |

167 그럼 저는 킹스턴을 추천해요. 그 회사가 막 XM 라인의 새 모델을 출시했는데 평이 좋더라고요.

| 루이스 파커 | 오전 10:30 |

가격 면에서는 어떻게 이야기가 되고 있는 거죠?

| 제프 롱 | 오전 10:31 |

각 1,000달러에서 시작해요. 22명의 직원들에게 제공하는 것은 가격이 만만치는 않아요.

| 루이스 파커 | 오전 10:32 |

만약이 않죠. 그래도 만약 장기적으로 비용을 절감시켜 준다면, 가치가 있다고 봐요.

| 샘 젠킨스 | 오전 10:33 |

168 결정하기 전에 최소 3개에서 4개의 옵션을 비교해 봐야 한다고 생각해요.

| 제프 롱 | 오전 10:36 |

좋아요, 그럼 168 결정하기 전에 최소 3개에서 4개의 옵션을 비교해 봐야 한다고 생각해요.

재고 조사해 볼게요

[159-161]

삼 라 호텔

메리노 스트리트 50

카이로, 이집트

164 8월 7일

관심 있는 모든 지원자들께

162 삼 라 호텔에 교육 기회와 관련해 문의해 주셔서 감사합니다. 저희는 휴양 및 휴일 산업에서 경력을 쌓고자 하는 자격을 갖춘 지원자들에게 소수의 여름 교육을 제공합니다. 교육 계획에 참여하도록 선택된 지원자들은 전형적인 업무 환경에서 직접 채용하는 경험을 할 수 있으며, 개인의 성장적으로 일체 일었습니다. 그 결과 매출을 지속적으로 상당히 높아, 발표 또는 현재 아시아에서 인정받은 회사가 되었습니다.

159 해인즈 씨는 지난 2년간 상가포르 지사의 온라인 마케팅 부서 설립에 는 세부적인 내용을 다룰 것이며, 이후 질의응답 시간이 있겠습니다. 161 참석자들은 회의 후에 필기할 것을 권장합니다.

모든 직원들이 참석해야 하지만 일정이 겹칠 경우, 워커 씨나 사무실 관리자에게 연락하도록 하세요.

곧 뵙겠습니다.

빌포드 마케팅

managing director 상무 이사   analyst 분석가   transfer 옮기다   set up 설립하다   sales figures 매출   significantly 상당히, 많이   established 인정받는, 확실히 자리를 잡은   in the case of ~에 관하여   말하면   scheduling conflict 일정 중복

159 메모에서는 무엇을 알려 주는가?

(A) 곧 있을 사업 발표
(B) 회사의 5주년 기념식
(C) 상가포르 지사에서의 취업 기회
(D) 새로운 회사 이사 임명

160 해인즈 씨에 관해 언급된 것은?

(A) 최근에 빌포드 씨에 의해 고용되었다.
(B) 빌포드 마케팅에 그녀를 추천했다.
(C) 워싱턴 지사를 관리할 것이다.
(D) 온라인 마케팅 개발의 경험이 있다.

161 메모에 따르면 참가자들이 회의에 지원해야 하는 것은?

(A) 준비된 질문 용지
(B) 마케팅 주제 목록
(C) 이력서 사본
(D) 필기도구

삼 라 호텔

162 편지의 수령인에 대해 알 수 있는 것은?

(A) 삼 라 호텔에 이미 연락했었다.
(B) 셀마 뱅크스 씨에 의해 면접을 받을 것이다.
(C) 휴가를 계획하고 있다.
(D) 여행사에서 일한다.

163 편지의 수령인이 검토해야 하는 것은?

(A) 호텔을 설명하는 브로슈어
(B) 회사의 재무 절차
(C) 프로그램의 변경 사항
(D) 훈련 프로그램에 관한 정보

164 지원서를 제출해야 하는 날은?

(A) 8월 31일
(B) 9월 4일
(C) 2월 1일
(D) 3월 10일

traineeship 훈련   qualified 자격 있는   tutor 개인 교사   aspiration 열망, 야망   enclosed 동봉된   scheme 계획   hands-on 직접 해 보는   shortly 곧   thoroughly 철저히   조만간; 곧

---

budget 예산   fiscal year 회계 연도   inventory 재고 조사   withstand 견뎌 내다   wear and tear 손상   in the long run 장기적으로, 결국에는   obsolete 더 이상 쓸모가 없는

[169-171]

브라질의 통합형 관개와 채소 생산(IIVPB)
54 루아 3
그라바타, 브라질
www.vpb.br

공석

10년 동안 IIVPB는 유기농 재배법의 활용에 있어서 소작농들을 교육해 왔습니다. -[1]-. 관계 방식에 대한 최신의 연구를 활용하여 유기농 재배법의 고품질을 유지하면서 생산량을 늘리는 것이 목표입니다. -[2]-. 저희는 상세료로에 본사를 두고 독립적으로 지금이 제공되는 기관으로, 파라이바, 바히아, 페르남부쿠, 리오 그란데 두 노르테와 같은 브라질의 주에 추가로 지원을 두고 있습니다.

-[3]-. 합격자는 연구를 이끌고, -[170]- 연구팀과 소규모 농지 소유주들 사이의 연락 담당자로서 활동할 것입니다. 합격자는 기금적 봉의 되어에 탄탄한 관리 경력이 있어야 하고, -[170]- 최소 4년의 전문적인 관리 경력이 있어야 합니다.

자기소개서와 이력서를 포함한 지원서를 직접 또는 이메일이나 보통 우편 저희 웹 사이트 www.iivpb.br/careers를 통해 11월 10일까지 제출해 주세요. -[170]- 합격자는 12월 10일에 업무를 시작하게 됩니다. -[4]-.

integrate 통합하다 irrigation 관개 vacant 공석 smallholder 소규모 liaison 연락 담당자 successful candidate 합격자 smallholding 소규모 농지 solid 탄탄한 managerial 관리의 preferably 가급적이면 agricultural 농업의 accompanied by ~을 동반한 cover letter 자기소개서 revise 수정하다

169 IIVPB에 관해 언급된 것은?
(A) 현대적 관개 절차를 이용하는 데 전념하고 있다.
(B) 기업 경영을 수정하고 있다.
(C) 관개 설비를 판매한다.
(D) 정부로부터 재정 지원을 받는다.

170 직책에 대해 알 수 없는 것은?
(A) 올해가 가기 전에 채용될 것이다.
(B) 관계자들 간 연락하는 일을 수반한다.
(C) 프로젝트 관리 경력을 필요로 한다.
(D) 브라질 국민으로만 제한되어 있다.

171 [1], [2], [3], [4]로 표시된 위치 중 다음 문장이 들어가기 적절한 곳은?
"저희는 파라이바 지역의 프로젝트 관리자를 모집하고 있습니다."
(A) [1]
(B) [2]
(C) [3]
(D) [4]

[172-175]

화제된 직업: 스테이시 메이

3월에 상금 보험사에서 오랫동안 물러날 계획인 계획이 씨는 트라포드 보험사에서 25년간 많은 역할을 해 왔다. 보험사 회장인 제로리 막스 씨는 "트라포드 보험사에서 스테이시가 지닌 경력의 범위를 보유한 사람을 찾기란 힘듭니다."라고 말했다. -[1]-.

메이 씨는 할무어에 있는 쉽슨 보험 중개소으로 보험 업계에서의 경력을 시작했다. -176- 그녀는 업무를 매우 만족스러워했고, 계약이 급여나 정규직을 찾기 시작했다. -172-. 18개월 동안 전화를 받고 입상적인 행정 업무를 한 후, 메이 시는 트라포드 보험사의 에이전트 지식에서 보험사 훈련생으로 고용되었고, 6개월도 채 안되었을 때 하급 보험사로 승진이 되었다. -[3]-.

그러나 메이 씨는 자력 상승을 멈추지 않았다. "저는 보험 정책에 대해 배우는 것을 좋았고, 상급 보험사가 되기를 연원했습니다. 에이전트 지시에서 저희 그 씨의 경우로 자는 크가 5년 전에 그랬던 것처럼 엔드에 있는 버티를 대화에 보험사 과정에 지원하기로 결정했습니다. 하거금 대출로 하반을 마련했고, 계속해서 시간제로 하급 보험사 일을 했습니다. 저가 거의 하위를 완료하기까지 6년이 결렸습니다."라고 그녀는 설명했다. -[4]-.

버티 대화을 졸업하자마자, 메이 씨는 트라포드 보험사 본사의 보험 부서에 입사했다. 2년 후, 상급 보험사 호프 베싱 씨의 보조원으로 임명되었다.

-174- 베싱 씨가 거의 청구 부서로 이전되었을 때 메이 씨가 그의 자리를 대신하게 되었다. "생각해 보세요." 메이 씨가 말했다. "저는 파일 정리 일부터 시작해서 결국 본사의 상급 보험사가 되었습니다."

step down 물러나다 underwriter 보험사 range 범위 temporary 임시의 administrative 행정의 insurance broker 보험 중개사(중개업체) permanent position 정규직 routine 일상적인 trainee 훈련생 climb 상승 upwards 위로 rank 지위 finance 자금을 대다 appoint 임명하다 take one's place ~의 자리를 대신하다 filing 서류 정리 varied 여러 가지의

172 기사의 목적은 무엇인가?
(A) 훈련 강좌 신청에 관한 정보를 주기 위해
(B) 보험 회사에 있는 모든 공석을 설명하기 위해
(C) 한 직원의 다양한 직무를 보고하기 위해
(D) 오랫동안 재직한 후 은퇴하는 한 직원을 소개하기 위해

173 링 씨에 대해 언급된 것은?
(A) 기사를 위해 인터뷰되었다.
(B) 보험을 공부했다.
(C) 가르치는 경력이 있다.
(D) 보험 회사의 시간제 보험사이다.

---

165 영업부에 대해서 암시된 것은?
(A) 그들은 최근에 재고 조사 소프트웨어를 업데이트했다.
(B) 그들은 몇 년 동안 똑같은 장비를 사용해 왔다.
(C) 그들은 최근에 휴대용 컴퓨터를 위한 예산 요청서를 제출했다.
(D) 그들은 판매 주문들을 처리하는 데 어려움을 겪고 있다.

166 현재의 휴대용 컴퓨터에 대해서 암시된 것은?
(A) 1,000달러 이상이다.
(B) 전략 공급에 문제가 발생했다.
(C) 곧 더 이상 쓸모가 없어질 것이다.
(D) 할인되 가격으로 구매되었다.

167 칩소트에 대해서 암시된 것은?
(A) 그 회사의 휴대용 컴퓨터는 내구성이 좋다.
(B) 회사는 그것들을 지털들을 할인이 안 된다.
(C) 하나의 모델을 만든다.
(D) 가장 인기 있는 브랜드이다.

168 오전 10시 36분에 롱 씨가 "제가 조사해 볼게요"라고 했을 때 그 의미는 무엇인가?
(A) 그는 얼마의 돈이 절약될 수 있는지 알아낼 것이다.
(B) 그는 다른 모델들에 대한 정보를 모을 것이다.
(C) 그는 직원들에게 어떤 휴대용 컴퓨터를 선호하는지 물어볼 것이다.
(D) 그는 칩소트의 가격을 확인할 것이다.

174 트라포드 보험사에 관해 알 수 있는 것은?
(A) 직원들에게 대한 등록금 할인을 제공한다.
(B) 최근에 심은 보험 중개소와 합병했다.
(C) 본사가 에딘튼에 있다.
(D) 거액 청구 부서가 있다.

175 [1], [2], [3], [4]로 표시된 위치 중 다음 문장이 들어가기 적절한 곳은?

"그녀는 트라포드 보험사의 앤더튼 지사에서 정규직 행정원 자리를 찾고 있다."

(A) [1]
(B) [2]
(C) [3]
(D) [4]

---

prominent 유명한; 중요한 refreshments 다과 craft 공예(품) admission 입장(료) open air theater 야외극장 Peruvian 페루의 choir 성가대 memorial 기념관 ethnic 민속의 theater company 극단 playwright 극작가 pre-booking 사전 예매 heavily 아주 많이 indoors 실내에서 ovation (열렬한) 박수 privilege 특권 duration 기간

제10회 맨스필드 예술과 드라마 축제
10월 10~12일

맨스필드 문화 협회의 후원을 받는 맨스필드 예술 드라마 드라마 축제는 모든 사람들이 즐길 수 있습니다. 행사는 3일간 지속되고, 유명한 예술가의 전시회와 현지 음악가와 배우들의 오락 시간이 있을 예정입니다. 다과와 공연 품을 구매하실 수 있고, 아이들을 위한 다양한 활동들도 있을 것입니다.

일부 행사는 아래와 같습니다.

10월 10일 금요일 오후 4시, 피카소 미술관
엘레나 마틴이 (우리 가족의 초상화)의 개관 전시회는 11월 17일까지 운영합니다. 월요일부터 금요일까지는 오전 10시 30분부터 오후 8시까지, 토요일에 입장은 정오부터 오후 6시까지입니다. 입장 무료

10월 11-12일 토요일과 일요일, 오전 11시~오후 7시, 성 메리 RC 교회
어린이들의 미술 및 공예 품을 구매. 입장 무료

10월 11일 토요일 오후 3시, 라이즈데일 야외극장
(온천 시 이동 장소: 월베리 극장) 맨스 청소년 성가대의 음악회(대중의 요구에 의함). 입구에서 표 구입 가능

10월 11-12일 토요일과 일요일, 오후 1시~오후 7시, 매들레인 기념관
민속 요리와 공예 축제

10월 12일 일요일 오후 6시~오후 8시, 페니모어 극장
스토브리지 극단의 극작가 스텔 그레이의 (농장에서의 여름)을 선보입니다. 사전 예매는 10월 1일부터 가능. 입구에서 표 구입 가능
사전 예매는 www.madf.org를 방문해 주세요.

176 일요일 오후 6시에 예정되어 있지 않은 행사는?
(A) 공예 프로그램
(B) 미술 전시회
(C) 민속 요리 시장
(D) 발레 공연

177 축제에 대해 언급된 것은?
(A) 온라인으로 광고되고 있다.
(B) 매일 아침 오전 11시에 시작한다.
(C) 1년에 3번 개최된다.
(D) 현재 진행 중이다.

178 연극은 언제 공연될 예정인가?
(A) 10월 1일
(B) 10월 9일
(C) 10월 10일
(D) 10월 12일

179 로사도 씨가 멀라니 씨에게 이메일을 보낸 이유는?
(A) 감사를 표현하기 위해
(B) 공연 표를 요구하기 위해
(C) 이메일을 취소하기 위해
(D) 공연을 취소하기 위해

수신: 노아 멀라니 (nmullany@madf.org)
발신: 마리아 로사도 (mrcsado@peruvianyouth.com)
제목: 정보
날짜: 10월 15일
멀라니 씨께,

저희 매주 음악을 맨스필드 예술 드라마 축제에서 공연하도록 초청해 주신 것에 대해 다시 한 번 감사드립니다. 안타깝게도 비가 너무 많이 와서 실내에서 공연할 수밖에 없었고, 그로 인해 관객이 많지 않았습니다. 그러나 관객들로부터 받은 열렬한 박수에 기뻤습니다. 많은 사람들이 저희 CD를 구매했고, 유명 음악 웹 사이트에서 다운로드받을 수 있는지 물어보셨습니다.

다음 번 축제에 참여할 수 있는 기회가 있길 바랍니다.

마리아 로사도
페루 청소년 성가대 행사 관리자

180 매주 청소년 성가대에 관해 알 수 있는 것은? (연계 지문 문제)
(A) 웹 사이트에 접속하는 사람들이 더 많아졌다.
(B) 현재 남미를 순회 중이다.
(C) 월베리 극장에서 공연했다.
(D) 그 축제에 처음으로 참여했다.

유마크 2 이층 오븐 가스레인지
EM-3189 모델

특징:
- 특대 이층 오븐은 표준 레인지보다 더 넓은 요리 공간을 제공한다.
- 열처리강 외면으로 녹이 슬지 않고 청소가 쉽다.
- 자동 타이머가 내장되어 있어 언제 음식이 요리되는지 알려 준다.
- 조림 등이 최적의 요리 온도를 보여 준다.
- 새로운 유마크 제어 기술이 대부분의 다른 모델보다 가스를 덜 사용하는 다양한 온도 조절 기능을 제공한다.
- 소형, 중형, 대형 요리 냄비를 위한 다양한 요리판
- 3층 선반형 디자인은 굽기, 익히기, 대류는 것을 동시에 할 수 있어, 식사를 조화롭게 해 준다.

평가	제품	계약 조건	위치

www.eumark.com

"돈 들일 가치가 충분하다."

게시자: 애비게일 데이비스
게시일: 9월 14일
위치: 버크시, 영국

전에 쓰던 레인지는 다른 회사에서 제조되었으나, 겨우 3년이 되었습니다. 유마크가 매우 고급이지만 저렴한 이 모델을 제작했을 때 저는 매우 기뻤습니다. 전에 사용했던 가스제품만큼 경제적일 것이라고 생각하지 않았는데, 실제 놀랐습니다. 이 제품도 모든 유형의 음식을 완벽하게 요리합니다. 내부적으로 층이 3개가 있으므로(굽기, 익히기, 대우기), 다양한 크기의 냄비에 맞추기 위한 4개의 다른 요리판(소형, 중형, 대형 두 개)이 있습니다. 또한 신경 쓰지 않고 외출할 수 있도록, 요리가 다 되었을 때 저절로 까지는 것에 감명을 받았습니다. 무엇보다 좋은 점은 유마크가 오래 사용할 수 있는 제품을 만들었다는 것입니다. 기능이 너무 많아 그것들을 이해하기가 오랜 시간이 걸렸다는 점이 유일한 불만입니다. 모든 지시 사용을 따르기 위해 설명서를 자세히 읽어야 했습니다.

gas cooker 가스레인지 extra-large 특대 heat-treated steel 열처리강 exterior 외면 rust 녹 integral 내장된 optimum 최적의 cooking pan 냄비 roast 익히다 coordinate 조화시키다 terms and

conditions (계약 등의) 조건 advanced 발달한; 고급의 inexpensive 저렴한 economical 경제적인 appliance 가전제품 tier 계단 조석 internally 내부적으로 suit 맞추다 long lasting 오래 지속되는 study 자세히 보다 durability 내구성

181 특성 목록에 표기된 것은 무엇인가?
(A) 조리법을 위한 지시 사항
(B) 제품의 긍정적인 특징
(C) 다양한 종류의 오븐 가스레인지에 관한 정보
(D) 유제품 2 0 이층 오븐 가스레인지로 조리될 수 있는 모든 음식의 종류

182 특성 목록에 따르면 유미크 제어 기술의 이점은?
(A) 에너지를 덜 소모한다.
(B) 고객의 시간을 절약한다.
(C) 가전제품의 내구성을 늘린다.
(D) 제품 청소를 더 쉽게 만든다.

183 웹 사이트에서 1번째 문단, 5번째 줄의 '맞추다'와 의미상 가장 가까운 단어는?
(A) 맞추다
(B) 갖춰 입다
(C) 지격을 갖추다
(D) 호소하다

184 데이비스 씨는 제품에 관해 어떤 비판을 하는가?
(A) 복잡하다.
(B) 무겁다.
(C) 시끄럽다.
(D) 비싸다.

185 제품 설명서에 언급되지 않은 특징 중 데이비스 씨가 마음에 들어 한 것은? (연계 지문 문제)
(A) 요리판의 개수
(B) 큰 오븐 크기
(C) 외관의 다양성
(D) 조리 설명

[186-190]

뉴 테크놀로지 캠퍼스에서 당신의 컴퓨터 능력을 향상시키세요
가을 학기 1개월 (1학기)

데이터베이스 활용하기(기초 과정)   975달러
8회 수업 (오전 9시 30분 – 오전 11시 45분)
시작: 9월 3일

워드 프로세싱 훈련(중급 과정)   825달러
6회 수업 (오전 8시 30분 – 오전 11시 30분)
시작: 9월 10일

프레젠테이션 소프트웨어 완성하기(상급 과정)   775달러
5회 수업 (오후 1시 – 오후 5시 30분)
시작: 9월 17일

스프레드시트 비법(중급 과정)   450달러
4회 수업 (오전 9시 – 오후 12시 15분)
시작: 9월 24일

모든 수업은 도움입에 있습니다.

로우맨 컨티뉴잉 에듀케이션 빌딩
바트 라이트룻 애비뉴 8904
(818) 555-9303

www.newtechnologycampus.com에서 등록하세요
환불 불가능한 예치금(수업료의 10퍼센트)을 등록하실 때 내셔야 합니다.

발신: 톰 바튼 <tbarton@nevis.com>
수신: 브레디 레인 <blane@newtechnologycampus.com>
날짜: 8월 20일
제목: 가을 교육 과정

레인 씨에게,

온라인 등록을 제출하는 데 어려움이 있어서 이 글을 씁니다. 지불이 다음 달 제공되는 초보자들을 위한 수업에 등록하고 싶습니다. 지불을 어떻게 처리해야 하는지 알려 주세요. 저는 선불로 수업료 전액을 지불할 준비가 되어 있는데, 제 회사에 환급을 요청할 거예요. 따라서 저는 영수증이 필요해요.

톰 바튼

바튼 씨에게,

귀하의 수업은 다음 주에 시작됩니다. 강의실이 이주 배정되지 않았음을 알려드립니다. 따라서, 수업 시작 예정 시간 15분 전에 와 주시기를 요청드립니다. 도착하시면, 건물 동쪽 입구에 있는 보안 데스크에 체크인해 주세요. 임시 주차 허가증과 ID 배지를 받으실 겁니다. 또한, 그때 귀하의 강의실로 안내받게 될 겁니다.

만약 수업료의 전액을 지불하지 않으셨다면, 시작 날짜에는 지불하셔야 합니다. 임차 사무소의 직원이 로비에 있을 겁니다.

질문이 있으시면, (818) 555-8787로 자유롭게 연락주세요.

nonfundable 환불 불가능한 deposit 예치금 tuition 수업료 up front 선불로 reimbursement 상환 balance 잔액 in-person 직접의

186 뉴 테크놀로지 캠퍼스 교육 과정에 대해서 암시된 것은?
(A) 현장 등록을 해야한다.
(B) 사전 납부를 요구한다.
(C) 수업이 이침에만 제공된다.
(D) 참가자들의 수를 제한한다.

187 바튼 씨가 듣고 싶어 하는 수업에 대해서 옳은 것은? (연계 지문 문제)
(A) 총 6번 만날 것이다.
(B) 오후에 열린다.
(C) 그의 회사에게 450달러를 쓰게 할 것이다.
(D) 한 번에 3시간 미만으로 만날 것이다.

188 이메일의 1번째 문단, 3번째 줄에 있는 '잔액'과 가장 비슷한 의미의 단어는?
(A) 전체의
(B) 추가
(C) 중요한
(D) 기인이 지난

189 염서에 따르면, 바튼 씨는 무엇을 해야 하는가?
(A) 첫 수업에 일찍 도착해야 한다.
(B) 신분증을 가져와야 한다.
(C) 특별 구역에 추가해야 한다.
(D) 주차 허가증을 발급해야 한다.

190 염서에 대해서 암시된 것은? (연계 지문 문제)
(A) 바트 씨의 직장으로 보내졌다.
(B) 레인 씨에 의해서 쓰여졌다.
(C) 바트 씨의 담장을 요구한다.
(D) 9월 3일 전에 보내졌다.

[191-195]

www.fabulousfoods.com

소개	제품	지점	온라인 판매	연락처

회사 스토리

패뷸러스 푸드는 1920년도 뉴욕 서부의 작은 마을에서 패뷸러스 베이커리로 시작했습니다. 오이아자 창립자인 데이빗 헤드 씨는 가족의 비법 레시피를 사용해서 빵과 스낵을 만들기 시작했습니다. 회사는 1950년대에 감자칩을 비롯한 다른 스낵들을 만들기 시작했습니다. 헤드 씨는 1958년도에 투자자들에게 회사를 팔기로 결정했으나 그들은 패뷸러스 푸드로 이름을 다시 지었습니다. 새 오너들은 베이커리, 우수 **191** 운영법과 팔고 감자칩, 옥수수칩, 팝콘과 건강에 신경 쓰는 소바자들에게 인기 있는 저지방 라인을 포함한 다른 맛있는 스낵류를 개발하고 생산하는 것에만 집중했습니다. 오늘날, 패뷸러스 푸드는 미국의 50개 전체 주와 주요 캐나다, 멕시코에 있는 소매점들에게 제품을 납품하고 있습니다.

192 버몬로 (7월 16일) – 7월 21일 일요일, 건강 교육을 위한 모금하기 위해서 사이의 1번째 벌링트 파크에서 경주가 개최된다. **194** 레이스 포 유어 헬스는 15킬로미터, 10킬로미터, 5킬로미터의 경주를 특색으로 하고, 가장 빨리 시작하는 것은 이점 7시 30분에 시작된다. **193** 참가자들은 나이와 성별에 따라 6개의 다른 카테고리에서 경쟁할 수 있다. **183** 각 카테고리에서 우승자 3위까지는 상을 받게 된다. 또한 모든 연령대가 참여할 수 있는 경쟁 없는 2킬로미터의 재미삼아 하는 산책도 있다. **192** 세인트 제임스 병원만 아니라, 벌링트 스포츠 드링크와 패뷸러스 푸드를 포함한 몇몇 지역 업체들이 이 행사를 후원한다. 등록하려면, www.racehealth.org를 방문하면 된다. 제미삼아 하는 산책은 25달러이고 경주는 45달러이다. **195** 참가자들은 후원 업체들로부터 티셔츠와 무료 음료, 판촉물을 받게 된다.

founder 창립자 **exclusively** 오로지 **health-conscious** 건강을 의식하는 ~을 특징으로 하다 **sponsor** 후원하다 **nonetheless** 그럼에도 **feature** 불구하고 **put together** 준비하다

191 웹 사이트는 1번째 문단, 5번째 줄에 있는 '운영'과 가장 비슷한 의미의 단어는?
(A) 사업
(B) 장비
(C) 절차
(D) 수술

192 패뷸러스 푸드에 대해서 암시된 것은?
(A) 정기적으로 행사들을 후원한다.
(B) 학교에 도움 기부한다.
(C) 캐나다에 공장이 있다.
(D) 버몬로에 위치해 있다.

193 가서에서 행사에 대해 언급되지 않은 것은?
(A) 아이들은 참가할 자격이 있다.
(B) 등록을 위해서 자물이 요구된다.
(C) 18개의 상이 수요될 것이다.
(D) 모든 경주는 장외에 끝날 것이다.

194 스탠트 씨는 누구인가? (연계 지문 문제)
(A) 15킬로미터의 경주의 승자
(B) 레이스 포 유어 헬스의 기획자
(C) 세인트 제임스 병원의 보건소 직원
(D) 토바이스 씨의 회사 동료

195 토바이스 씨에 대해서 암시된 것은? (연계 지문 문제)
(A) 10킬로미터의 행사에서 달렸다.
(B) 참가하기 위해 25달러를 냈다.
(C) **무료 음식을 받았다.**
(D) 상을 받았다.

[196-200]

이메일 메시지

194 수신: 켄 스탠트
195 발신: 론 토바이스
날짜: 7월 22일

스탠트 씨에게,

새로운 경주에 대해서 저에게 알려주셔서 정말 감사해요. **195** 몇몇 동료들과 저는 아래 가장 긴 경주에 참가하겠다고, 저희 중 누구도 우승을 뽐한 사람은 없었지만, 그래도 재미있는 시간을 보냈어요. **194** 내친에도 이 행사를 마련해 주셨으면 좋겠습니다. 제가 다른 직장 동료들에게 말했더니, 모두 노고에 감사에 신경 쓰는 소바자들에게 관심이 있었어요.

모든 노고에 다시 한 번 감사드립니다.

론 토바이스 드림

빅 짐스 여름 세일

이번 담아: 진행
8월 1일 일요일 시작을 함께하십시오
아이들을 위한 통선 재품

특정 액세서리 20퍼센트 할인 모든 매직 헤드조각 블랙엘 카메라 케이스 포함	**196** 소형 가전 15퍼센트 할인 G5, 리뱅스토, 워드 사 재품
199 198 대형 가전 10퍼센트 할인 티렉스, 리뱅스토, 워드 사 재품	모든 TV, 스테레오, LCD 프로젝터 5퍼센트 할인

196 단골 고객 클럽에 가입하시고 모든 구매에 대해서 포인트를 얻으세요. 포인트는 사은품이나 할인으로 돌려받을 수 있습니다. 더 많은 세부 사항을 보시려면 www.bigjims.com으로 방문해 주세요. **199** 이 재안은 다음의 빅 짐스 지점들에서 유효합니다.

88 리스 로드 미스턴 555–0340
7816 0급 로드 림커 555–2149
908 제스제 가 윈스터 555–3873

일부 재품들은 무료 배송 가능합니다. 지점 매니저에게 확인하세요.

수신: 셀 롱 (slong@bigjims.com)
발신: 도나 킹슬리 (dkingsley@netnet.com)
제목: 배송
날짜: 9월 2일 오전 8시 29분
롱 씨에게,

198 지난주 귀하의 지점에서 워드 브랜드의 스키 세척기를 구매했을 때, 저는 원래 3일에 배송해 달라고 요청했었어요. **197** 그러나, 일이 좀 생겨서 그 날짜는 제 일정과 맞지 않게 되었어요. **200** 6일 오후 4시나 7일 오전 10시에 배송 가능할까요? 이 날짜와 시간이 괜찮으면 알려주세요. 저 스키 가 지점이 저희 집에서 멀지 않기 때문에 해당 해줄 수 있으리라 생각할게요. 이 사안에 대해서 도 빨리 연락하지 못해서 죄송합니다.

감사합니다.

도나 킹슬리

수신: 도나 킹슬리 〈dkingsley@netnet.com〉
발신: 셈 롱 〈slong@bigjims.com〉
제목: 회신: 배송
날짜: 9월 2일 오전 9시 9분

킹슬리 씨에게,

귀하께서 제안하신 **200** 이른 시간 배송에 대한 요청을 저희가 **199** 수용할 함 수 있게 되어서 기쁩니다. 저희 배송원 중 한 명이 귀하의 주소와 배송 시간을 확인하기 위해 연락드릴 겁니다. 그동안에 만약 질문이나 우려가 생기시면 언제든 연락주세요.

저희와 거래하시기로 결정해 주셔서 감사합니다.

셈 롱

kickoff 시작   redeem 교환하다   accommodate 수용하다   multiple 다수의   carry 취급하다

196 박 점소에 대해서 암시되지 않은 것은?
(A) 다수의 지점이 있다.
(B) 전자 장비를 취급한다.
(C) 단골 고객들에게 혜택을 제공한다.
(D) 온라인에서 제품을 판다.

197 킹슬리 씨는 왜 롱 씨에게 연락했는가?
(A) 최근의 주문을 확인하기 위해서
(B) 할인에 대해서 문의하기 위해서
(C) 약속을 변경하기 위해서
(D) 배송 주소를 알려주기 위해서

198 킹슬리 씨에 대해서 옳은 것은? (연계 지문 문제)
(A) 그녀는 배송비를 지불했다.
(B) 그녀는 10퍼센트 할인을 받았다.
(C) 그녀는 링컨에 산다.
(D) 그녀는 포인트를 얻었다.

199 두번째 이메일의 1번째 문단, 1번째 줄에 있는 '수용할'과 가장 비슷한 의미의 단어는?
(A) 수용할
(B) 조정할
(C) 검토할
(D) 보호할

200 킹슬리 씨는 언제 구매한 물건을 받을 것인가? (연계 지문 문제)
(A) 9월 2일
(B) 9월 3일
(C) 9월 6일
(D) 9월 7일

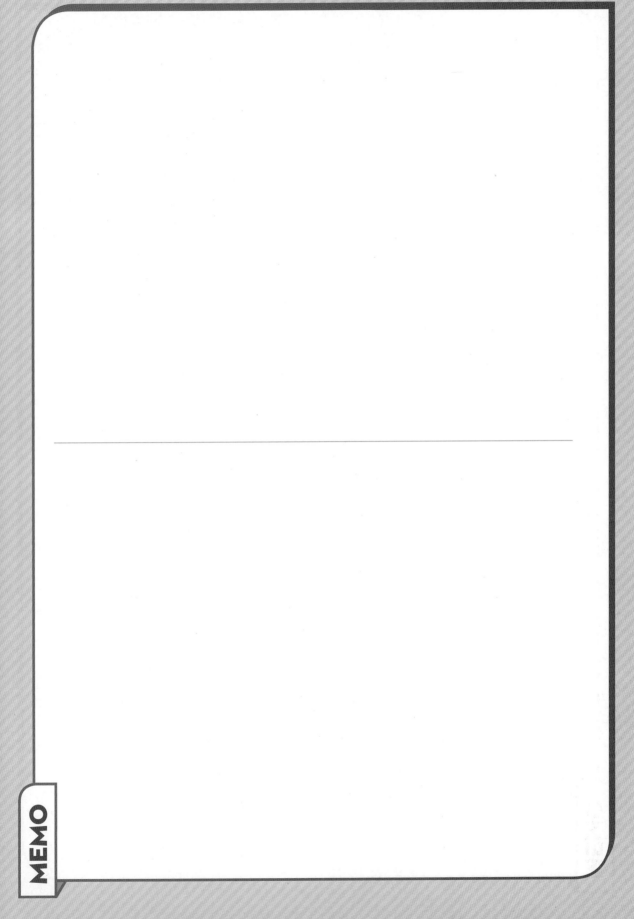

MEMO

MEMO

나혼자 끝내는 新 토익
기출모의
1200 제

+ 최신 출제 경향을 완벽 반영한 실전 모의고사 6회분 수록
+ 문제집과 해설집이 한 권으로 구성된 LC+RC 합본 실전서
+ 문제의 키워드를 단숨에 파악하는 핵심 강의 해설집 수록
+ 전문 성우의 발음을 통한 미국식, 영국식, 호주식 발음 완벽 대비
+ 실전용·복습용·고사장 버전의 3종 MP3 무료 다운로드
+ 청취력 향상 및 핵심 구문을 복습하는 받아쓰기 테스트 제공 } QR코드 & 홈페이지
+ 정답만 입력하면 점수를 바로 확인할 수 있는 자동 채점 시스템 제공
+ 신토익 빈출 어휘 리스트 & 테스트지 제공 ▶ www.nexusbook.com